CLAIMS HANDLING LAW AND PRACTICE

A Practitioners' Guide

WITHERBYS
INSURANCE

British Library Cataloguing in Publication Data
A catalogue record for this book is available from the British Library.

[80026]

CLAIMS HANDLING LAW AND PRACTICE

A Practitioners' Guide

Richard West • Andrew Caplan
Kieron West • Janet Sayers
Danny McShee • Fred Heath •
Gibbs, Wyatt, Stone

WITHERBYS
INSURANCE

First Edition 2008

WITHERBYS
INSURANCE

ISBN 10: 1 85609 333 9
ISBN 13: 978 1 85609 339 2

Printed & bound in Great Britain by Bell & Bain Ltd. Glasgow

Published by
Witherby Insurance
4 Dunlop Square, Deans Estate
Livingston, EH54 8SB
United Kingdom

Tel No: +44(0)1506 463 227
Fax No: +44(0)1506 468 999
Email: info@emailws.com
www.witherbyseamanship.com

Foreword

Too often Lawyers are guilty of clouding issues whilst attempting to provide explanations. That is something that we try not to do at Kennedys and in many ways I feel this book exemplifies our approach to providing legal services to our clients.

I am sure that all involved in claims have from time to time wished for access to a simple guide to the areas of law with which we most commonly deal, to ideally refer to one book only and not have to trek to a law library or open a number of tomes to find the answer. The practitioners' guide, written by a number of my partners at Kennedys, seeks to deliver such a book covering a wide variety of disciplines within one pair of covers.

This user-friendly guide covers fields as diverse as clinical negligence, health and safety, occupiers' liability, child abuse, manual handling, the Road Traffic Act, disease and highways law. In addition, reflecting the trend of insurers to turn to external cost providers to advise on the issue of third party costs, there are two chapers on funding.

The book's aim is to assist claims handlers with those areas of law with which they have to deal on a day-to-day basis. It is an "aide memoire" for the experienced but also sets out the basics for the novice. Our clients have told us that it is a helpful core text for in-house training.

The authors of this book are all leaders in their own fields but they and I would welcome any and all suggestions that you may have as to how the book may be improved for the Second edition.

Nick Thomas
Senior Partner
Kennedys

September 2008

Preface

At the end of 2000, the prototype for this book appeared for another publisher. It met with rather more success than we had imagined and we have found over the last five years or so that it is far more widely used than we had anticipated.

We hope that the title of this edition "Claims Handling – Law and Practice – A Practitioner's Guide" explains the purpose of this book. The first book was aimed at the general liability and motor claims handler and that is still true with this edition. However, we have expanded the book so that claims handlers in the fields of clinical negligence, health and safety, occupational disease, abuse and housing disrepair will now all find assistance within these pages. A chapter on funding has also been written by an external costs draftsman and we hope that too will prove to be of great assistance to claims handlers.

The authors have continued to keep the manual as simple as possible whilst addressing the areas to which claims handlers most often need to refer in everyday practice. By definition, the guide is intended to be relevant but not complex and suggestions of further reading are included where appropriate.

We do hope that it tackles most of the legal questions that claims handlers need answered on a day-to-day basis.

The law is stated on the basis of cases reported and legislation published on or before 1 September 2008.

Richard West
Partner
Kennedys

The Authors

	Chapters
Richard West Kennedys – Partner r.west@kennedys-law.com	What is the law? Negligence, Nuisance, Rylands and Fletcher, Occupiers' Liability, Employers' Liability, Quantum, Fatal Claims, Calculating Future Losses, Compensation Recovery Unit, Civil Procedure Rules 1998, Subsidence
Andrew Caplan Kennedys – Partner a.caplan@kennedys-law.com	Child abuse, Housing Disrepair, Subsidence
Kieron West Kennedys – Partner k.west@kennedys-law.com	Occupational Disease and Work Related Illness Claims
Janet Sayers Kennedys – Partner j.sayers@kennedys-law.com	Clinical Negligence
Danny McShee Kennedys – Partner d.mcshee@kennedys-law.com	Health and Safety
Fred Heath Kennedys – Litigation Manager FCII a.heath@kennedys-law.com	Manual Handling, Highways Claims, Road Traffic Act 1988, Third Party Liabilities.
Gibbs, Wyatt, Stone Costs Draftsmen	Funding Methods, fixed recoverable costs in RTAs

Contents

Table of Acts

Table of Cases

1 WHAT IS THE LAW?

1 WHAT IS THE LAW?

Contents

The law is a system of rules, enactments and decisions that set out rights and obligations within society.

The law is made up of the following:

1. *Acts of Parliament (also known as Legislation or Statute)*
2. *Previously decided Case Law (also known as Common Law or Precedent)*
3. *European Community Law*

1.1 Acts of Parliament

Parliament through the House of Commons and House of Lords creates laws by enacting Legislation.

Examples of Legislation that will be known to Claims Handlers are as follows:

i) The Road Traffic Act 1988

ii) The Occupiers' Liability Acts 1957 and 1984

iii) Health and Safety at Work Act 1974

When enacting Legislation, Parliament sets out in some detail the Laws that it wishes to bring into force.

Often explanatory notes are provided with an Act. However they are not legally binding.

Therefore, a Judge who is faced with a new piece of Legislation is tasked with interpreting that Legislation and will give his or her judgment based upon that interpretation.

The judicial interpretation of Acts of Parliament is an important part of the law making process.

Judicial decisions are known as Common Law or precedent.

As an Act of Parliament becomes older there will be more decisions by Judges interpreting that Legislation. The amount of precedent relating to that Act will therefore increase.

1.2 Previously Decided Case Law

Previous decisions of the Courts are known as Precedents. Sometimes they have to be followed (Binding Precedent) and sometimes they can simply be taken into account by a Judge when deciding a case (Persuasive Precedent).

Whether a previous decision binds a court or not will depend upon the level of the Court that reached that previous decision.

The European Court of Justice

Decisions from the European Court of Justice on points of European Law bind all English and Welsh Courts. However, the European Court of Justice is not bound by its own previous decisions.

The House of Lords

The House of Lords is the superior Court of England and Wales. All decisions made by the House of Lords are binding on inferior Courts. The House of Lords however is not bound by its own previous decisions.

Court of Appeal

The Court of Appeal is bound to follow previous decisions of the House of Lords. It is also generally bound by its own previous decisions. Courts that are inferior to the Court of Appeal are bound by the Court of Appeal's decisions.

High Court (Queens Bench Division)

The High Court's decisions do not bind lower Courts but are often considered to be highly persuasive.

The High Court is not bound by its own previous decisions although the Court of Appeal and House of Lords' decisions are binding on it. However, the High Court and in particular the Queens Bench Division will consider carefully any decisions that it has made previously.

County Court

The County Court Judiciary must follow the previous decisions of the House of Lords and Court of Appeal. They may find previous High Court decisions strongly persuasive and can often also be persuaded by other County Court decisions.

It must be remembered that a persuasive precedent is an important part of the legal process. Courts will often follow previous decisions even if they do not bind them, if doing so ensures a common sense and consistent approach across the Courts.

Distinguishing Cases

It is possible for Judges to "distinguish" earlier cases. Judges can avoid a binding precedent by pointing out differences between past decisions and the case before them. They can argue for example that the case that they have to deal with is not "on all fours" or precisely the same as an earlier decision that would otherwise be binding

1.3 European Community Legislation

Regulations, Directives and Decisions from the European Community constitute European Community Legislation. They are all important.

Regulations are directly applicable and binding upon English Courts.

A Regulation made in Europe is binding in English Courts and does not need to be enacted within separate Legislation by the UK Government.

Regulations, once made, become part of English Law.

Directives must be implemented by Parliament into English Law within a specified period of time.

Generally, they only bind English Courts once they have been enacted by Parliament. As with Acts of Parliament, Regulations will be subject to Judicial Interpretation and may therefore generate a bank of precedent of their own.

2 NEGLIGENCE

2 NEGLIGENCE

Contents

2.1 Introduction

A negligent act or omission is a Tort or a Civil Wrong. It is based mainly in Common Law.

The usual remedy to correct a Civil Wrong is to seek a sum of money by way of damages. That is done through the Courts.

Negligence is a Tort which Claims Handlers will have to deal with almost everyday.

A negligent act is an act (or omission) by one party which is inexcusable and which causes damage to another.

There are three components of negligence. Each component must be proved before a claim in negligence can succeed.

1. *The Defendant must have owed the Claimant a duty of care.*
2. *The Defendant must have failed in or breached that duty of care.*
3. *The Claimant must have suffered damage as a result.*

2.2 The Defendant must owe the Claimant a duty of care

Broadly, this is a matter of common sense. For example:

i) *doctors owe their patients a duty of care.*

ii) *employers owe their employees a duty of care.*

iii) *motorists owe other road users and pedestrians a duty of care.*

Whether a duty of care is owed will generally depend on whether a Defendant could have reasonably foreseen that the Claimant would have been affected by his negligent act or omission.

Lord Atkin gave the leading explanation of when such a duty of care exists in the case of ***Donoghue v Stevenson (1932)***. He said:

> **"the rule that you are to love your neighbour becomes in law, you must not injure your neighbour; and the lawyers question, "who is my neighbour?" receives a restricted reply. You must take reasonable care to avoid acts or omissions that you can reasonably foresee would be likely to injure your neighbour. Who, then, in law, is my neighbour? The answer seems to be – persons who are so closely and directly effected by my act that I ought reasonably to have them in contemplation as being so effected when I was directing my mind to the acts or omissions that are called into question"**

2.3 There must have been a breach of that duty of care by the Defendant.

The issue here is whether the Defendant has done something that he should not have done or has not done something that he should have done.

A party can breach their duty of care to another therefore either by an act or by an omission.

The Courts will apply an objective test.

Broadly that test will be "has the Defendant acted reasonably" or, "would the Reasonable Man have done more"?

Whether a party has acted reasonably will depend upon the particular facts of each case.

For example, a person driving a car at 75 miles per hour on a motorway keeping up well with the traffic may be driving at a reasonable speed albeit that he is driving in excess of the speed limit. However, the driving of a car at the same speed (75 miles per hour) in a built-up area within a speed limit of 30 miles per hour will almost certainly be found to be unreasonable.

Similarly, an employer may act reasonably in asking an appropriately experienced, trained and muscular employee to carry coal sacks without assistance. However the same employer will probably act unreasonably in asking an inexperienced employee to do the same task.

What is reasonable will therefore depend on each set of facts. The Courts will tend to look at the following:

a) *The nature of the act or omission in question (for example could the act or omission be easily avoided?);*

b) *The risks attached (for example how serious is the risk and how much damage could be caused?);*

c) *Who the Defendant is (for example is the Defendant in a position of responsibility – such as an employer, a doctor or a local authority)?;*

d) *Who the Claimant is (for example is the Claimant in a class of persons who are particularly vulnerable – such as employees or patients)?;*

e) *How easy it would be to protect the Claimant from the breach of duty (for example how much would it cost, what procedures would need to be put in place, etc)?*

2.4 The Claimant must have suffered damage as a result

2.4.1 The Damage must not be too remote

The test here is whether the damage is of the kind that could reasonably have been foreseen.

It is clearly foreseeable that driving a car at speed into the rear of another vehicle will cause damage to that car and injury to its occupants.

However, oil spilt from a ship into a harbour, which then ignites, causing the destruction of a wharf by fire, has been found not to be foreseeable damage.

In the ***Wagonmound 1961 (Australia)*** the Court found that fire caused by sparks from welding equipment that ignited the oil in the harbour, was too remote a consequence of the oil spillage, which had arisen as a result of a breach of duty.

It can therefore be seen that even though damage may arise directly from a breach of duty, if that damage could not have been reasonably foreseen, a Court will find it to be too remote and would therefore find that the damage had not arisen as a result.

2.4.2 The Defendant must take the Claimant as he finds him

This is the so-called "eggshell skull" rule. This principle generally arises in personal injury actions.

For example, if a minor blow causes an unexpected but nevertheless a genuinely severe reaction because of the Claimant's physiology, the Defendant cannot say, "that is not reasonably foreseeable" or, "how was I to know that that would happen?"

The Defendant, it has been decided by the Courts, must take his victim as he finds him.

Bourhill v Young [1943] A.C.92, 109-110

Lord Wright stated,

> **"It has long ago been stated and often restated that if the wrong is established the wrong doer must take the victim as he finds him...on the condition that the wrong has been established or admitted"**

Lord Justice Mackinnon in ***Owens v Liverpool Corporation [1939] 1K.B.394, 400-401*** stated that,

> **"One who is guilty of negligence to another must put up with idiosyncrasies of his victim that increase the likelihood or the extent of the damage to him; there is no answer to a claim for a fractured skull if its owner had an unusually fragile one"**

This situation often arises in claims involving psychiatric injury.

There may have been a minor road traffic accident causing little physical injury. A Claimant may claim however that he can no longer work, having been so traumatised by the accident that he can no longer cope with employment.

A Defendant in such circumstances might obtain access to such a Claimant's medical records. These may show that the Claimant has had a pronounced psychiatric history for many years prior to the accident. What if such records show that the Claimant was, before the accident, taking large periods of time off from work and had considerable difficulties domestically, socially and professionally because of his pre-accident personality?

The Defendant in that situation could argue that the accident has not caused the Claimant's problems but that they were pre-existing.

If the Court accepted that the accident had caused a psychiatric injury, the Court would have to reach one of two conclusions. Either that:

i) the accident had caused an increase in the pre-accident problems that the Claimant was suffering from, and that the Claimant had returned to his pre-accident state. In other words, that the accident had temporarily exacerbated or worsened the pre-existing psychiatric condition or,

ii) the accident, minor though it was had, when combined with the Claimant's pre-existing frailties, created a new and more serious condition that prevented the Claimant from working.

In the case of i), the Defendant would pay compensation for the period during which his negligence has caused the Claimant's condition to be temporarily worsened.

In the case of ii), the Defendant cannot argue that the injury was not foreseeable even though it may appear disproportionate. He must take his victim, frailties and all, as he finds him. He must pay the Claimant compensation for the new and more serious condition that his negligence has caused.

Claims Handlers will see therefore the importance in ensuring that their own experts are asked to deal with this particular issue carefully.

(See also "Causation" below)

2.4.3 Causation

It must be the breach of duty that causes the damage.

Therefore, if the Court find, in the psychiatric example above, that the accident has caused a temporary increase in the pre-existing condition but that the ongoing problems are not accident related, the Judge will make a finding that the Claimant has not proved a causal link between the accident and the **ongoing** problems.

Consider also an example of an employer who has failed to carry out appropriate Manual Handling assessments for his employees.

One of those employees visits a customer's premises for a delivery, and has to deliver a large, awkward and heavy item to a customer. In carrying the item from his van, he slips on some oil in the customer's car park, falling to the ground and injuring his back. That oil had been recently deposited in a usually clean car park by an unknown vehicle.

If the employer can show that the slip was unconnected with his breach of duty (his failure to carry out proper manual handling assessments) that employer would escape liability. The employer would have breached the duty of care to his employee (by failing to carry out Manual Handling assessments and possibly by failing to train his staff properly) but may be able to argue that the slip was not caused by that breach. There would therefore be a denial of causation.

2.5 Contributory Negligence

As all Claims Handlers will be aware, a Court can find that one party or the other is entirely to blame or indeed that both parties are to blame.

The law is now set out in Section 1 *Law Reform (Contributory Negligence) Act 1945*, which states,

> **"Where any person suffers damage as the result partly of his own fault and partly of the fault of any other person or persons, a claim in respect of that damage shall not be defeated by reason of the fault of the person suffering the damage, but the damages recoverable in respect thereof shall be reduced to such an extent as the court thinks just and equitable having regard to the Claimant's share in the responsibility of the damage."**

Lord Denning explained the concept of contributory negligence in 2 of his Judgments.

In ***Jones v Livox Quarries Ltd (1952)*** he stated:

> **"Contributory negligence does not depend on the existence of a duty. Although contributory negligence does not depend on a duty of care, it does depend on foreseeablity. Just as actionable negligence requires the foreseeablity of harm to others, so contributory negligence requires the forseeability of harm to oneself. A person is guilty of contributory negligence if he ought reasonably to have foreseen that, if he did not act as a reasonable prudent man, he might be hurt himself; and in his reckonings he must take into account the possibility of others being careless"**

In ***Froom v Butcher (1975)*** he stated:

> **"...negligence depends on a breach of duty, whereas contributory negligence does not. Negligence is a man's carelessness in breach of duty to others. Contributory negligence is a man's carelessness in looking after his own safety"**

If a Court finds that both parties are to blame, then liability will generally be apportioned between the parties on a percentage basis.

A Defendant can therefore argue that the Claimant has contributed towards his own damage by his own acts or omissions.

For example, a speeding motorist may suggest that the pedestrian who he has run over, and who walked out into his path giving him no chance to stop, was contributory negligent and therefore partly responsible for the accident.

An employer may argue that his injured employee failed to use appropriate lifting equipment that he had been trained to use and told to use many times before. The employer, if unable to defend the matter entirely, would therefore argue that his employee had been contributory negligent.

Therefore, if a Claimant has partially caused his own damage he will receive less in damages from a Defendant than he would have done had he not contributed to his own injury.

For example, a Claimant found to be 50% contributory negligent will have the damages that he would have received, had he been blameless, reduced by one half.

2.5.1 100% Contributory Negligence?

A Defendant's liability to a Claimant cannot be entirely extinguished by that Claimant's contributory negligence.

In ***William Percy Anderson v Newham College of Further Education (2002)***, the Court of Appeal decided that whether a claim was in negligence or for breach of statutory duty, there could be no finding of 100% contributory negligence. The court held that either the Claimant was wholly to blame for his injuries and there was no liability on the Defendant, or the Defendant was to blame subject to a degree of contributory negligence on behalf of the Claimant.

2.6 Negligence of Joint Tortfeasors

As well as finding a Claimant and a Defendant equally or partly to blame, the court can find that more than one third party has contributed to the Claimant's loss and damage.

For example a speeding motorist may swerve to avoid a vehicle that has pulled out into his path without warning. The speeding vehicle may then collide with an oncoming vehicle causing injury and loss to the occupant of that vehicle. In such a situation a court may find that the speeding motorist (for driving too fast), and the emerging motorist (for pulling out when it was unsafe to do so) are both to blame for the accident.

The court would apportion blame for the accident, on a percentage basis, between the two negligent motorists.

2.7 Vicarious Liability

It can often be the case that an employee of a large enterprise or company acting in the course of his employment, personally commits a breach of duty.

For example, the driver of a van in the course of his employment who collides with the rear of a stationary motor vehicle causing injury to its driver. It is the driver of the van and not his employers who has been negligent.

However, as such a driver was driving in the course of his employment, the Claimant can also sue the employers for the negligent act of their employee.

Similarly, the Local Authority whose Highway Inspector fails to spot a defect in need of urgent repair, could be held vicariously liable for their highway Inspector's omission.

Employers therefore will be held vicariously liable for the torts of their employees, when such torts are committed in the course of the employees' employment. Such liability is imposed without the necessity for a primary breach of duty on the employer's part.

2.8 Independent Contractors

A person who hires an independent contractor will generally not be liable for the negligent acts or omissions of that independent contractor.

There are circumstances in which the acts of an independent contractor can cause an employer to be primarily liable. In brief, this will depend upon whether or not the employer at the time that the independent contractor was working, was also in breach of a duty of care to a Claimant.

Such liability can arise where the independent contractor has not been supervised properly or indeed, where there is a strict duty on the part of the "employer", to ensure that no duty is breached. That will be a question of law and outside the remit of this guide.

However, where there is potential liability for an independent contractor's acts or omissions, an employer can only be held liable if the negligent act in question falls within the contract for which the independent contractor was hired. Any negligent acts falling outside the scope of the contract (collateral negligence) will not impose a liability upon the "employer".

If an independent contractor's acts or omissions result in the person who hired him being liable, that person should be able to seek a contractual indemnity from the independent contractor (or his insurers) for any third party claims intimated.

2.9 Suggested Further Reading

The Law of Tort – Butterworth's Common Law Series

3 NUISANCE

YES!
IN MOST CASES
PROBABLY
MAYBE
WELL...
IT MIGHT...
COULD BE
PERHAPS
UP TO YOU
MAYBE
MAYBE
PERHAPS
THAT DEPENDS
perhaps
IN SOME CASES
Maybe?
sometimes
IT MIGHT
PERHAPS
WELL...
Could be
LET ME THINK
HOW? INTERESTING
maybe?

3 NUISANCE

Contents

3.1 Introduction

Nuisance, like negligence, is a Tort or a Civil Wrong.

Public nuisances and statutory nuisances are not dealt with within this text.

Claims handlers will however need to deal with private nuisances.

3.2 Definition

Professor Winfield has defined a Private Nuisance as:

> **"Unlawful interference with a person's use or enjoyment of land or some right over or in connection with it"**

The Courts have tended to find that an unlawful interference must be continuous.

A noisy barbecue party in a neighbour's garden 2 or 3 times a year; a birthday party or a smokey bonfire which causes smoke in the autumn are all unlikely to constitute acts of private nuisance. They are not sufficiently continuous in nature.

However, continuous noise, smells or vibration, which interfere with private use of land, can all constitute a nuisance.

Butler v Standard Telephone & Cables Limited (1940) held that tree roots growing from one property under its boundary line and into another property causing damage could constitute a private nuisance.

Household insurers often therefore seek recovery of monies paid to remedy damage caused to a policyholder's property by the roots of vegetation emanating from a neighbouring property. In such circumstances they could seek, among other things, damages for nuisance. *(See also chapter on "Subsidence")*

3.3 Remedies

There are three particular remedies that can be sought for private nuisance. These are as follows:

i) damages

ii) an injunction

iii) abatement

Therefore, a house owner whose property is subsiding because a neighbouring tree's roots are extracting moisture from the soil under his home's foundations could seek one or more of the above remedies.

3.3.1 Damages

Damages that could be sought include reimbursement of the costs of repairs and underpinning, additional accommodation costs and compensation for inconvenience caused by the encroaching roots.

3.3.2 Injunctions

An injunction could be obtained to compel a neighbour to maintain or remove the vegetation that constitutes the nuisance. The effect of the vegetation's roots would then be removed or diminished.

Damages and injunctions are remedies that must be sought through the courts.

3.3.3 Abatement

Abatement may also be an option. The victim can seek to abate the nuisance. The victim could have the roots cut back. This would be acceptable as long as the roots are trimmed and only then trimmed on the victim's land. There must be no trespass onto the neighbour's land. The roots that are trimmed and removed must be offered back to the neighbour.

Abatement is a self-help remedy that does not need court approval. Abatement is therefore a remedy potentially fraught with difficulties. A neighbour whose tree has been pruned by his neighbour may claim that a criminal damage has been committed to his property. If the tree dies the owner may sue for damages.

The courts dislike abatement because it is a self-help remedy. Judges have cautioned that abatement should only be adopted as a remedy of last resort; and then only employed when notice has been given of an intention to carry out the abatement.

3.4 Suggested Further Reading

The Law of Tort – Butterworths common law series.

4 THE RULE IN *RYLANDS V FLETCHER*

4 THE RULE IN *RYLANDS V FLETCHER*

Contents

Street on tort defines the rule in ***Rylands v Fletcher*** as follows:

> **"A person who, in the course of non-natural use of land, is held to be responsible for the accumulation on it of anything likely to do harm if it escapes, is liable for the interference with the use of land of another which results of the escape of the thing from his land"**

4.1 The Rule

The House of Lords decided the case of ***Rylands v Fletcher*** in 1866. It has been refined since the initial Judgment. There are now five conditions that must be satisfied in order for a claim to succeed under this common law rule.

a) The matter that has escaped must have initially been brought on to the land.

   The reason for bringing the item on to the land and keeping it must amount to a **"non-natural use of the land"**.

   The Courts now tend to interpret "non-natural use" narrowly.

   It has been held that the storing of water, gas and electricity in bulk in mains and the like, and indeed the storage if ignitable material in a barn can constitute a non-natural use of land.

However, water pipe installations in buildings and the lighting of a fire in a fireplace of a house have been defined as "natural use".

b) The matter that has escaped must be likely to do harm having escaped.

The House of Lords in ***Rylands v Fletcher*** spoke of, "anything likely to do mischief if it escapes".

c) There must be an escape from the land.

d) There must then be an interference with the use of the land of the Claimant.

For example, does the property have to be repaired, or does remedial action have to be taken because of the escape? If so, then the Court is likely to find that there has been an interference with the Claimant's land.

e) Finally, there must be damage caused.

Please note that there is an overlap here with "interference of the use of land" above.

4.2 *Rylands v Fletcher*, Negligence or Nuisance?

Claimants now use the rule in ***Rylands v Fletcher (1866)*** much less frequently as it is now generally easier to pursue actions under the torts of Negligence or Nuisance.

Consider the following example:

Mr. X is a domestic homeowner. He has on his land a domestic central heating oil tank. The tank rests adjacent to Mrs Y's property.

Unbeknown to Mr. X, the oil tank is leaking steadily and constantly. Over a period of time, the oil leaks under the boundary line of Mr. X's property and underneath the property of Mrs Y. The oil seeps into her home causing damage to its foundations and brickwork. As a result, significant remedial works are required.

It may well be that Mrs Y has a right to claim under the tort of negligence. Mr. X will owe her a duty of care to ensure that the oil does not escape. Mrs Y may be able to argue that if the tank is old that it should have been replaced sooner or should have been inspected on a regular basis. To succeed she would need to show that had the inspection been carried out on a regular basis, the leak would have been spotted. Mr. X may be able to argue that even if he had inspected the tank that he would not have spotted the leak and therefore that he has a defence to a claim of Negligence.

Mrs Y may be able to claim under the tort of Private Nuisance. She would need to prove that there has been an interference with her property and that the interference with her land was reasonably foreseeable in the circumstances. Again, Mr. X may be able to argue that it was not foreseeable to him that the damage would occur, as he was unaware of the oil leak and would not have been aware of it if he had inspected the tank.

Mrs Y may therefore be left to pursue the matter in the tort of ***Rylands v Fletcher***.

Applying the rule in the case, we can see the following.

1. That the oil was brought on to the land by the Defendant. It was delivered to his property and stored there for the purposes of central heating.
2. If the oil escaped it was likely to do harm.
3. It did escape and did harm.
4. It has interfered with the use of Mrs Y's land because she has had to have her property repaired.
5. The final question is whether or not the use of the oil amounts to a "non-natural" use of land?

It is suggested that in this situation, a Court would not find that the storing of domestic heating oil amounted to a "non-natural use of land". That is because is it now common for domestic central heating to be run on oil and for the oil to be stored in tanks on domestic properties.

However, if a large number of fireworks had been stored in Mr. X's shed in the middle of a town and they had exploded (and therefore escaped) causing damage to Mrs Y's house, that damage we would suggest, would have arisen out of a non-natural use of land. A claim made under the rule in ***Rylands-v-Fletcher*** would succeed in those circumstances because the storing of a large quantity of fireworks in a domestic shed is likely to amount to a non-natural use of land. Such a claim would not rely upon any negligent act or omission by Mr. X, or upon a continuous interference with the use of Mrs.Y's land, as would be the case if the claim were pursued in negligence or nuisance.

The rule in ***Rylands v Fletcher*** is mentioned in this guide to show claims handlers that negligence and nuisance are far more likely to be used as causes of action than this tort which is now more difficult to succeed under than it has been in years gone by.

Claims handlers should be alive to arguments in relation to "non-natural use of land" and resist claims where appropriate.

4.3 Recent Developments

The rule in ***Rylands v Fletcher*** was considered by the House of Lords in the case of ***Transco v Stockport MBC 2003***.

The court, finding for the Defendant on appeal ruled that the test was whether the local authority had done something on its land which it (1) recognised, or ought reasonably to have recognised judged by the standards appropriate to the place and time, as giving rise to an exceptionally high risk of danger or mischief if there should be an escape, and (2) recognised or ought to have recognised, as being quite out of the ordinary for the place and time.

In 2005 the High Court again considered this tort in the case of ***LMS International Ltd and ors v Styrene Packaging & Insulation LTD and ors (2005)***.

This case arose out of a fire that had spread from a factory. The fire had started while an employee of the Defendant was cutting expanded polystyrene blocks with a hot wire-cutting machine.

The court held that the cause of the fire was probably an arc or spark caused by the breaking of a wire that ignited the block that was being cut. The Defendant had brought onto their premises things that were likely to cause and/or catch fire. The polystyrene was kept in such a way that if it ignited the fire was likely to spread to The Claimant's premises. The polystyrene and the hot wire-cutting machine represented a recognisable risk to the Claimant; and the use of the land was a non-natural user.

4.4 Suggested Further Reading

Street on Torts

The Law of Tort – Butterworths Common Law Series

5 OCCUPIERS' LIABILITY

5 OCCUPIERS' LIABILITY

Contents

The Occupiers' Liability Acts 1957 and 1984.

Prior to the 1957 Act, a person who was injured on another person's land had to rely upon the Tort of Negligence.

Since the Acts have been passed, occupiers can be rendered liable by statute for injuries suffered by those visiting or trespassing on their property.

Therefore, if a Claimant is injured in a shop, in a factory or school or on some other premises they will often sue under these Acts.

Section 2(1) of the 1957 Act states:

> **"an occupier of premises owes the same duty, the "common duty of care", to all his visitors, except in so far as he is free to and does extend, restrict, modify or exclude his duty to any visitor or visitors by agreement or otherwise".**

Section 2(2) of the Act states that the common duty of care is:

> **"a duty to take such care as in all the circumstances of the case is reasonable to see that the visitor will be reasonably safe in using the premises for the purposes for which he is invited or permitted to be there".**

This test then, is very similar to the duty of care that exists in the Tort of Negligence *(see chapter on Negligence).*

5.1 An Occupier?

An occupier is more than just a person who owns or is in occupation of land. The definition of occupier extends to a person who exercises his control over the land (for example somebody who permits or denies access to it).

5.2 Premises?

A "premise" is defined by Section 1(3) and includes **"any fixed or moveable structure, including any vessel, vehicle or aircraft"**. Therefore, for example, a bus can be classed as "premises" and fall within the Acts.

Examples of incidents which can give rise to claims under the *Occupiers' Liability Acts* include the customer who has slipped in a grocery shop on some produce that has fallen from one of the shelves; a member of staff in a restaurant who has slipped on a liquid spillage; and a teacher in a school who has slipped on a recently polished floor. In each case, the Defendants would need to show that they had not breached their common duty of care to the Claimant under the two Acts.

The occupier of the shop would need to show that he had adequate procedures in place to clear up any produce that fell from shelves. If the produce had been on the floor for some time when the customer fell, it is unlikely that that the Defendant would be able to persuade the Court that he had such adequate procedures in place.

The occupier of the restaurant would need to show that he too had adequate procedures in place to clear up spills. Again, the length of time that the spill had been left 'in situ' would be important.

The Defendant school would need to show that when cleaning the floor, they too had adequate procedures in place for ensuring the safety of staff, pupils and visitors. For example, did they have warning signs up, was the floor unusually slippery, and had the cleaning process been carried out properly?

Signs on the garden gates of domestic or other premises stating, for example, "no salesmen" or "no free newspapers" or "no tradesmen" are still fairly common. If such a party then goes through that gate and on to the home owner's property, the home owner has a lesser duty to them under the 1957 Act as that person would be classed as a trespasser.

The 1957 Act imposes a duty of care upon occupiers of premises to people with permission to be on the premises.

However, the 1984 Act imposes a duty of care upon occupiers of premises to people who are on the premises without permission or who are therefore trespassers or unlawful visitors.

5.3 The 1957 Act

It must be remembered by Claims Handlers that a strict liability will not arise simply because a Claimant has been injured on premises occupied by the insured. The common duty of care that one would consider in negligence (please see above) would need to be considered under the 1957 *Occupiers' Liability Act*.

Although in general the common duty of care would apply as in negligence, there is specific guidance given within the *Occupiers' Liability Act* for certain types of visitor.

Children

Section 2(3)(a):

> **"An occupier must be prepared for children to be less careful than adults. If the occupier allows a child to enter the premises then the premises must be reasonably safe for a child of that age"**

The Courts have had little sympathy for Defendants who are faced with very young unsupervised children that have been injured. For example, it is worth considering the ***Phipps v Rochester Corporation***

(1955). Although this case pre-dates the 1957 Act the Courts are likely to approach matters in the same way still.

In **Phipps**, the Defendant building company were aware that children were coming on to their land without their permission but did nothing to stop it. The Court found that those children were lawful visitors and that therefore, the building company owed them a duty of care.

More recently in 1972 the House of Lords in ***British Railways Board v Herrington (1972)*** altered the law.

The Claimant was a 6-year-old boy. He was badly injured and had been playing on a railway track.

The Defendant knew that children had been seen playing on a track and further knew that the fence next to the track where the children were gaining access was damaged. It had been damaged for some weeks before the Claimant was injured but the Defendants did nothing about it.

The House of Lords held that the Defendants knew that there was a danger and yet did nothing to stop trespassers from coming onto the premises. They therefore owed such trespassers a duty of care. Having breached that duty of care when the trespasser was injured, they would be liable.

In 1984, legislation was passed to take the above into account.

5.4 The 1984 Act

The 1984 Act imposed a duty of care on occupiers to "non-visitors" or trespassers.

Trespassers can be said to be people who have no reason to be on the premises and whose presence the occupier of the premises would not tolerate if that presence were known of.

A trespasser can therefore be as sinister as a burglar, or as innocent as a rambler in the country who strays unwittingly on to a private piece of land.

The 1984 Act places a duty of care upon an occupier to trespassers in three particular situations.

i) if the occupier is aware of the danger on his premises or has reasonable grounds to believe that it exists; and

ii) the occupier knows or should reasonably have grounds to believe that there are trespassers in the vicinity of that danger or that trespassers may come into the vicinity; and

iii) that the risk in question is one which in all of the circumstances the occupier may reasonably be expected to offer the trespassers some protection.

If a trespasser is injured, liability will rest with an occupier only where the above criteria are fulfilled.

The common duty of care imposed by the 1957 Act does not apply with the 1984 Act.

The Court of Appeal applied the 1984 Act in 1999, in the case of ***White v St. Albans City (1990)***.

The Defendant owned some land adjacent to a car park. The Claimant decided to take a short cut across that land to get to the car park. The land was fenced and was obviously private.

There was no evidence that the Defendants were aware that the land was being used as a short cut.

In using the short cut, the Claimant fell into a trench that had been excavated, and was injured.

The Court of Appeal held, because the Defendant had no knowledge that the land was being used as a short cut and because it was clearly private, that the Claimant was a trespasser.

The Defendant, being unaware of the presence of trespassers did not have a duty of care placed on it under the 1984 Act. The Claimant failed to satisfy limb ii) of the above test.

It can therefore be seen that there is a distinction drawn by the two Acts between lawful visitors and trespassers.

5.5 Exclusion Clauses

Occupiers may place signs on their premises stating, "the owners accept no responsibility whatsoever for any death, personal injury or loss arising on these premises howsoever arising"; or words to that effect.

They may seek to rely upon such a notice as a defence to claims made under the *Occupiers' Liability Acts.*

Such exclusion clauses are different to notices that occupiers may post to warn visitors to premises of potential hazards in an effort to make visitors reasonably safe. Examples of this latter type of notice may include notices warning of a dangerous dog in a domestic property, or of deep water in a boating lake.

The *Unfair Contract Terms Act 1977* states at Section 2:

> **"(1) A person cannot by reference to any contract term or to a notice exclude or restrict his liability for death or personal injury resulting from negligence;**
>
> **(2) In the case of other loss or damage, a person cannot so exclude or restrict his liability for negligence accept in so far as the term or notice satisfies the requirement of reasonableness."**

The prohibition of seeking to avoid liability under the *Unfair Contract Terms Act 1977* for personal injury and death only applies to occupiers whose occupation of the premises is **in the course of a business**.

1. Restricting Liability for death or personal injury.

The "notice" referred to in Section 2(1) includes signs at the entry to premises, signs in car parks etc.

"Negligence" is specifically said by the Act to include breaches of the common duty of care imposed by the 1957 *Occupiers' Liability Act*.

Therefore, notwithstanding the presence of a sign which purports to exclude injury of death on premises, if the injury or death has arisen as a result of the negligence/or breach of duty of the occupier, the occupier cannot rely upon the notice to avoid a finding of liability against him for that injury or death.

2. Other loss or damage.

The occupier can rely upon a notice to exclude liability for negligence or loss or damage but only if the contractual term or notice is reasonable.

The sign must be in a prominent place, must be large enough to be noticed and some steps must have been taken to draw the attention of visitors to the premises to it before the occupier can rely upon it.

5.6 Recent Developments

Since 2001 Claimants who bring claims for injuries caused by their own behaviour have had less success before the courts than had previously been the case.

The scene was set by a decision of the Court of Appeal in the case of ***Diane Darby v National Trust (2001)***.

In ***Darby*** the Claimant and her family had visited a park owned by the Defendant. In the park was a pond which visitors regularly used for paddling. The pond was shallow at the edges but deepened towards the middle at which point it became too deep to stand in. The Claimant's husband swam towards the middle of the pond but disappeared under water. He had to be dragged from the pond but, sadly, later died. The Claimant sued the Defendant under S2 of the 1957 Act.

At first instance the judge had accepted the Claimant's expert's evidence that the death had been caused by cold water shock, cramp or sudden unexplained drowning of swimmers' syndrome. The judge held that the Defendant had failed to install sufficient notices prohibiting swimming, failed to provide prevention wardens and had failed to take any proper steps to enforce a no-swimming policy.

On appeal, the Court found among other things, that the deceased was a competent swimmer and the risks of swimming in the pond were perfectly obvious. It was also held that one or more warning notices would only have told the deceased what he already knew. There could be no duty imposed on occupiers to warn visitors of the risks of swimming in open water and the same had to apply to occupiers of land on which were lakes or ponds. The court concluded that there was no duty on the Defendant to warn competent swimmers of the dangers of swimming in open ponds because the dangers were obvious.

In 2003 the Court of Appeal considered another water based set of facts in the case of ***John Simon Donoghue v Folkestone Properties Ltd (2003)***

The Defendants owned and occupied Folkestone harbour. Just after midnight on the 27th December 1997 the Claimant decided to go for a swim in the harbour. He jumped from the slipway, struck his head on an underwater obstruction and broke his neck. He had no right to be there at the time. He was considered to be a trespasser as he had been in the harbour without permission.

On appeal, the court held when the Claimant has sustained his injury, the Defendant had no reason to believe that anyone would be swimming from the slipway. The test to be applied when considering whether a duty of care arose under the 1984 Act had to be determined having regard to the circumstances prevailing at the time that it was alleged that the breach of duty had resulted in injury. In the circumstances the Claim was dismissed.

The House of Lords considered another similar set of facts, in the case of ***Tomlinson v Congleton BC (2003)*** only 5 months after the Court of Appeal's decision in ***Donoghue***.

The Defendant was the owner and occupier of Brereton Heath Country Park within which was a lake that had formed in a derelict sand quarry. The Claimant walked into the lake intending to swim there. When the water had reached just above his knees, and while he could not see the bottom of the lake, he dived in. Tragically he struck his head on the bottom and broke his neck rendering him tetraplegic.

He accepted in court that he knew that he should not have dived in shallow water and that he knew that there were notices in the park prohibiting swimming.

The Defendant had also distributed leaflets warning of the dangers of swimming in the lake.

It was accepted that when he had entered the water, the Claimant had become a trespasser by virtue of the prohibition on swimming. His claim was therefore pursued under the 1984 Act.

At first instance the court found for the Claimant on the basis that the notices displayed had been ignored by people and that they were therefore obviously ineffectual.

On appeal it was held that the lake did not present risks due to the state of the premises or anything done or omitted to be done on the premises as required by s1 (1)(a) of the 1984 Act. Further it was held that even if swimming had not been prohibited, and the Defendant had owed a duty under s2(2) of the 1957 Act, there would have been no requirement to take steps to prevent the Claimant from diving or to warn him against dangers that were obvious.

The Court of Appeal once again considered the 1984 Act in the case of ***Higgs v WH Foster (T/A Avalon Coaches) (2004)***.

The Claimant was a policeman. He entered the Defendant's premises in order to take up a surveillance position overlooking a neighbouring property. The Defendant's premises were on open land on which the Defendant had parked coaches. The Claimant searched around the coaches in case a suspect was hiding amongst them. The Claimant had a torch with him but did not use it. In carrying out his search the Claimant fell into an uncovered inspection pit at the rear of the Defendant's premises.

The Claimant was a trespasser and so his claim was brought under the 1984 Act.

The Court of Appeal found for the Defendant. It was held that even if the Defendant could be shown to have had reasonable grounds to believe that trespassers may enter their premises at night, there was no evidence to disclose reasonable grounds for believing that they might come into contact with the uncovered pit.

In 2005 the Court of Appeal decided the case of ***Lorraine Ann Clare v Roderick Perry (T/A Widemouth Manor Hotel) (2005)***

The Claimant was a visitor to the Defendant's coastal hotel.

The Claimant attempted to leave the property with her partner by climbing down a retaining wall to the road. The route chosen was not a designated exit. There was a designated exit nearby. The Claimant jumped from the wall while it was dark and was seriously injured. The Claimant agued that the Defendant had not taken sufficient precautions to prevent an accidental fall from the site and that the site should have been fenced off.

The Court of Appeal found that deliberately choosing to jump from the wall was wholly different to an accidental fall and the Claimant's actions could not have been foreseen or guarded against by the Defendant. Further, it was found that the Claimant had been foolish.

The actions of an 11-year-old child trespasser were considered by the Court of Appeal in ***Keown v Coventry Health Care Trust (2006)***.

In this case an 11 year old boy who had climbed the outside of a fire escape was held to have put himself at risk through his own choice to indulge in a dangerous activity. The child was aware that what he was doing was dangerous. His fall from the fire escape was not caused by a defect in the state of the premises. His claim was dismissed. He was a trespasser and his claim failed also because it was held that although the Defendants knew that the fire escape was unfenced (s.1 (3)(a) 1984 Act), and knew that children played in the vicinity (s.1 (3)(b) 1984 Act); it was not reasonable to expect the Trust to offer protection from such a risk (s.1 (3)(b) 1984 Act).

Finally, the Court of Appeal found for the Defendant in the much publicised case of ***Cole v Davis – Gilbert & Others*** in March 2007.

The Claimant stepped into an exposed hole on a village green and broke her leg. The hole had been dug so that a maypole could be erected for a village fete. It was found that the organisation responsible for digging the hole had neither been negligent nor breached a duty of care as it had previously sealed the hole and it was the unexplained removal of the infill, not the infill itself, that was the primary causative factor in the accident.

5.7 Occupiers' Liability Check-list

1. Was the Claimant a lawful visitor?
2. If the Claimant was a lawful visitor, consider whether the occupier has fulfilled the common duty of care under Section 2(2) of the 1957 Act. For example, are any warning signs displayed?
3. If the Claimant was a trespasser, consider the 1984 Act.
    a) Was the occupier aware of the danger; or did the occupier have reasonable grounds to believe that the danger existed? If yes then: -
    b) Did the occupier know or should the occupier have reasonably believed that there were trespassers in the vicinity of the danger? If yes then: -
    c) Is the danger one that in all of the circumstances the occupier may reasonably to be expected to offer the

trespassers some protection? If yes then the occupier is primarily liable.

4. Do not forget that visitors and trespassers can be contributory negligent.

5. Consider the effect and/or validity of any exclusion clauses or signs displayed.

5.8 Suggested Further Reading

Street on Torts

6 EMPLOYERS' LIABILITY

6 EMPLOYERS' LIABILITY

Contents

There is a great deal of overlap between this chapter and others in this guide. Please also see the chapters on Negligence (Vicarious Liability and Contributory Negligence), and Manual Handling.

Employers owe their employees particular duties.

These duties are imposed upon the employer both by common law and by statute.

The first issue to consider therefore is "who is an employee?"

6.1 An Employee?

This needs to be considered because not all individuals who are paid to work can be described as employees.

They may, for example, be independent contractors, agency workers or indeed may actually be employees but be described as "self-employed".

The Courts therefore employ a number of tests to decide whether an individual is an employee or not. These tests are as follows:

The manner in which the parties describe themselves

This is a starting point for the Courts. Simply because a person wishes to be paid on a gross basis and refers to himself as "self-employed", does not mean that such a person is not an employee.

Does the individual have to provide personal service?

If the worker in question does not have to provide personal service but can send along a substitute worker, then there is some evidence that the person in question is an independent contractor.

A worker providing personal service is central to a finding that that person is an employee.

However, this test also must be considered in the light of the others as set out above and below.

The Control Test

Does the employer control how much work the worker carries out and where and when that work is done? More importantly, does the employer decide how that work is to be carried out? If the employer controls the manner in which the work is done and provides that work, then it is likely that the worker is an employee.

The Business Integration Test

Does the worker actually form part of the organisation at which the work is being carried out? Do they work within the organisation or do they simply do work for it? If the former, they are likely to be an employee. If the latter, they may be an independent contractor.

Is the worker actually running a business of his own?

In other words, is the worker an independent contractor who attends and does work for a particular organisation, but who prepares their own tax assessment forms, keeps receipt books, and pays VAT etc? In that situation there is economic evidence that the worker is an independent contractor as opposed to an employee.

Conversely, if the worker is paid their salary net, on a PAYE basis, that is good evidence that the worker is an employee.

What obligations do the employer and worker have to one another?

If the worker is obliged to turn up to work at a particular time every day and the employer is obliged to provide work to that employee, that is evidence that the worker is an employee. An independent contractor could arrange for a substitute worker to attend in his stead to carry out the contract. An employee however may be obliged personally to attend work to perform the duties given to him by an employer.

What about "agency" workers?

There is a growing trend for certain types of worker to be contracted to an agency. Construction workers, nurses, secretaries and the like may sign up with an agency and agree to be placed at various types of business in order to supply labour. The agency will charge the business for supplying the labour. The business will provide the work. The agency will pay the worker for the hours worked at an agreed rate.

Is the agency worker an employee? If so who employs them? Is the agency paying the employer for the worker and sending them to work for another business? Alternatively, is the business the employer because it provides the actual work, instructs how it is done and controls the worker's day-to-day movements?

The Courts have recently tended to revert to a test laid down in the 1968 case of ***Ready Mixed Concrete (South East) Ltd v Minister of Pensions and National Insurance (1967)***.

It was held in this case that an employment contract exists if the three following conditions are satisfied.

i) the worker agrees that in return for his pay he will provide his own work and skill in the performance of his work to his master;

ii) the worker agrees (expressly or impliedly), that in the course of his work he will be controlled as if he was subject to a master;

iii) the other conditions of the contract are consistent with it being an employment contract.

The Court of Appeal followed the above test in the 2001 case of ***Montgomery v Johnson Underwood Ltd (2001).***

The Claimant approached the Defendant's employment agency and through the agency was offered work with a local company. Her hours were agreed and the Defendant sent the Claimant a letter confirming her appointment. The Claimant worked for the local company for 2 years. She was paid by the Defendant on the basis of time sheets prepared at and approved by the local company.

The local company sought to terminate the Claimant's appointment following a dispute. She took the Defendant and the local company to an employment tribunal arguing that one or the other employed her.

The Court of Appeal found that neither employed her. There was an insufficient degree of control by the Defendant and by the local company to have created a contract of employment.

The court went on to say that there could be circumstances in which an offer of work by an employment agency, even at another's workplace, could satisfy the requirements of control and "mutual obligation".

It is suggested that if an agency worker can show that the agency exercised control to a degree sufficient to convey the status of "master" upon the agency; and if the worker can also demonstrate that he and the agency owe each other obligations ("mutuality of obligation"); that the worker will be able to satisfy a court that he is an employee of the agency.

Each case will therefore turn on it's own facts. If it is not certain that a policyholder is the employer of a Claimant making a claim; the claims handler should obtain a detailed statement from the policyholder as to the role, obligations, methods of remuneration, and working practices of the parties. Once that information has been gathered a decision can be made as to whether or not the Claimant is an employee of the policyholder.

6.2 The Employer's Liability

An employer owes his employees duties both in common law and statute.

6.2.1 Common Law duties

In ***Wilsons & Clyde Coal Company Limited v English (1938)*** Lord Wright found that the employer's duty to his employees included:

> **"... the provision of a competent staff of men, adequate material and a proper system and effective supervision".**

Wilson v Tyneside Window Cleaning Company (1958) extended the employer's duty of care to also provide a safe place of work:

> **"if [the employer's premises] are dangerously in need of repair he can and must rectify the fault at once if he is to escape a censure of negligence".**

It can be seen therefore that the employer's common law duty to his employees overlaps considerably with his duty of care to avoid negligently injuring his staff.

i) provision of competent staff

The employer must make sure that the staff that he employs are suitably qualified and experienced for the particular job. If they are to be trained, they must be given adequate training and supervision until they become sufficiently competent.

If the employer takes on an employee who is not appropriately competent or who is then not trained properly and that member of staff negligently injures a co-worker, then the employer may be liable.

An employer will also be vicariously liable for the negligent acts or omissions of an employee who injures a co-worker in the course of employment.

However, there are situations where an injured party cannot claim that his employers are vicariously liable.

Hudson v Ridge Manufacturing Co Limited (1957).

In this case an employee who was known to play practical jokes on co-workers, injured a co-worker in the course of one practical joke.

The injured person could not sue his employers under the principle of vicarious liability because the practical joke fell outside the scope of the course of the joker's employment.

The victim successfully sued the employer, however, for failing to provide a competent co-worker.

It was successfully argued that because the employer knew of the perpetrator's pre-disposition to play practical jokes, that the joker should have been disciplined and prevented from conducting any further such jokes. The employer's failure to discipline the joker rendered him liable in common law.

ii) provision of adequate material.

This includes the provision of adequate equipment.

Employers have a duty to take reasonable steps to provide their employees with adequate equipment. That includes protective clothing, appropriate tools, appropriate working materials etc. This duty can also extend to obliging employers to train particular employees how to use particular equipment.

Paris v Stepney Borough Council (1951) emphasises this point.

The Claimant at the time worked in a garage. He carried out general mechanical duties. The Claimant was blind in one eye.

During the course of his work he was striking some metal when a metal splinter flew into his good eye. He was blinded in that eye.

It was not, at the time, usual practice to supply goggles to mechanics.

The Claimant claimed that his employer had breached his duty of care to him by allowing him to carry out the work without wearing goggles.

The Claimant argued that his employer knew that he was blind in one eye and that he was therefore at more of a risk to this particular injury than his co-workers.

The Claimant succeeded.

The Court decided that the employer's duty of care to employees could be a personal duty to each particular employee taking into account each particular employee's circumstances. **Lord Simmons** stated:

> **"I will say at once that I do not dissent from the view that the employer owes a particular duty of care to his employees. His liability in tort arises from his failure to take reasonable care in regard to the particular employee and that it is clear that, if so, all of the circumstances relevant to the employee must be taken into consideration."**

Therefore, employers who take on employees with particular frailties may, depending upon the type of work that they are carrying out, need to make special provision for them. A failure to do so could result in the employer being found liable if the employee is injured as a result of the employer's failure to take reasonable steps to protect that employee.

Equipment

Please note the **Employer's Liability (Defective Equipment) Act 1969 Section 1(1)**.

If equipment which is defective injures an employee, in common law. an employer may be able to argue that he had no way of knowing that the equipment was defective (i.e. the defence of latent defect), and that therefore he has not breached his duty of care to the employee and should not be found negligent. In such circumstances, the employee would have to sue the manufacturer of the product. That may be expensive and difficult to do.

The 1969 Act places a strict liability upon the employer and allows the employee to sue the employer and/or the manufacturer. In such circumstances, it would then be for the employer to seek an indemnity from the manufacturer. Please see also the statutory obligations of employers covered below.

iii) provision of a proper system and effective supervision (There is some overlap here in the above areas)

If an employer fails to properly supervise employees and as a result an employee is injured, the employer can be found liable.

Similarly, if an employee is asked to carry out work in a manner which is dangerous and which causes injury, then the employer can be found negligent for breaching his duty of care to that employee.

Employers are also obliged to ensure, if equipment is provided, that their employees use it appropriately and consistently.

Pape v Cumbria County Council (1992).

The Claimant had to carry out cleaning duties and developed a skin disorder as a result of coming into contact with various solvents and cleaning products.

The Defendants had provided their employees, with protective gloves. They had not told their staff to wear the gloves at all times. They did not tell their staff that if they did not wear them they might be injured.

In view of those omissions, the Claimant succeeded in recovering damages for personal injury.

The Court found that the employers should have had procedures in place to ensure that their employees did wear the equipment provided.

iv) a safe place of work

This has been particularly highlighted by the case of ***Andrews v Initial Cleaning Services (Court of Appeal 1999).***

As a general principle, the employer must ensure that the place at which his employees are working is safe and does not pose a risk to their health.

Therefore, a working environment which is too noisy and which has damaged hearing; a mine which causes lung disease to miners working there, and a factory with an unsafe floor that causes an employee to trip and fall and be injured; are all examples of premises which are unsafe. Again, liability will arise because the employer has breached the duty of care to his employees. He has acted negligently.

The employer may also be in breach of the Occupiers' Liability Acts *(see Occupiers' Liability Chapter).*

One particular difficulty highlighted in the above case of ***Andrews*** arises when an employer sends his staff to work at premises occupied by another party.

The Court of Appeal in ***Andrews*** found that the primary responsibility for an employee's safety rested with his employer.

In ***Andrews***, the employer was not the occupier of the building in which the Claimant was injured. However the employer had sent the Claimant there to work. Having done so:

a) The employer was aware of a defect at the premises and was aware that it was an actual and potential danger. The building owner/occupier was not aware of the defect.

b) The building owner was not performing a site management role.

c) The danger did not arise from the activities of the building owner.

d) The employer had taken no steps to remove the potential danger or to remedy the defect.

As a result, the employer was found responsible even though the injury occurred in premises that were neither owned, nor occupied by that employer.

See also chapter dealing with The Occupiers' Liability Acts.

6.2.2 Employers' Statutory Obligations

This section of this chapter should be read in conjunction with the chapter on "Health and Safety". This part of this guide deals with matters other than those dealt with within that chapter.

Statutory obligations have now been put in place by the implementation of a set of Regulations that have been enacted into domestic law by parliament following European Directives. There are six main regulations that are relevant in this area. They are known as "The Six Pack". Others may apply, such as the Construction (Health, Safety and Welfare) Regulations 1996, but are not considered by this guide.

The main regulations are as follows:

i) the Management of Health and Safety at Work Regulations 1999 (as amended)

Since 27th October 2003 a breach of these regulations has conferred a civil right of action on employees but not non-employees, bringing these regulations in line with the rest of the six-pack.

The "highlights" are:

a) Risk Assessments – Regulation 3

b) Health surveillance – Regulation 6.

c) Procedures for serious and imminent danger and for danger areas – Regulation 8

d) Information for Employees – Regulation 10.

e) Capabilities and Training – Regulation 13.

ii) the Work Place (Health, Safety and Welfare) Regulations 1992 (as amended)

These regulations cover particular aspects of the work place such as safety glass, doors, floors, stairs, ramps, falling objects.

a) The workplace is to be maintained in an efficient state, in efficient working order and in good repair – Regulation 5.1

b) The workplace should have suitable and efficient lighting – Regulation 8.

c) Workstations shall be suitable for any person likely to work there and for the work to be done there – Regulation 11.

d) Seats must be suitable for persons for whom they are provided as well as for operations to be performed and a suitable footstool must be provided where necessary – Regulation 11.

e) Suitability and repair and obstructions – Regulation 12.

f) Traffic routes – Regulation 17.

g) Falls or falling objects – Regulation 13 (now repealed by The Work at Height Regulations 2005).

h) Windows and transparent or translucent doors, gates and walls – Regulation 14.

iii) the Provision and Use of Work Equipment Regulations 1998 (as amended)

These cover detailed examples such as leased equipment, defective or poorly maintained equipment, training and instruction etc.

a) Work equipment means "any machinery, appliance, apparatus tool or installation for use at work.

b) Work equipment must be suitable for the purpose it is being used for in any respect in which it is reasonably foreseeable that it will affect the health and safety of any person – Regulations 4.1 and 4.4.

c) The employer must consider the working conditions under which the equipment is to be used and ensure that it is only used under conditions and for operations for which it is suitable – Regulation 4.3.

d) Every employer shall ensure that work equipment is maintained in an efficient state, in efficient working order and good repair – Regulation 5

e) When the use of equipment involves specific risks, there is a restriction as to who is to use and who is to maintain the work equipment.

f) Adequate training in the use of work equipment for health and safety purposes must be provided to users and supervisors – Regulation 9 (also see Regulation 11. Effective measures must be taken to prevent access to any dangerous part of machinery and to stop the movement of any dangerous part of the machinery before any part of a person enters a danger zone.

iv) the Manual Handling Operations Regulations 1992(as amended)

Please see chapter on Manual Handling.

v) the Health and Safety (Display Screen) Equipment Regulations 1992

a) The employer must carry out an analysis of workstations in order to assess the health and safety risks to those using them

b) The employer must reduce any risks identified to the lowest level that is reasonably practicable.

c) Schedule 1 sets out the minimum requirement s regarding the screen, keyboard, work surface, chair, the space available, lighting and reflection.

d) Activities must be planned so that there are periodic interruptions of work from the display screen.

e) The employer must provide eyesight tests for users and special corrective appliances if needed.

f) The employer must provide adequate health and safety training.

vi the Personal Protective Equipment at Work Regulations 1992

a) Employers have a duty to provide suitable personal protective equipment to employees who may be exposed to a risk to their health and safety except where the risk can be as effectively controlled by other means – Regulation 4.

b) The equipment must be appropriate both for the risk and the individual user.

c) Employers must assess the suitability of equipment before providing it – Regulation 6.

d) Employers shall ensure that equipment is maintained (which includes the effective replacement and repair) in an efficient state and working order and repair – Regulation 7.

e) Employers must provide information, instruction and training on risks, purpose, use and maintenance of equipment – Regulation 9.

f) Employers must take all reasonable steps to ensure that the equipment is used – Regulation 10.

g) Employees must use equipment in accordance with training and instruction given.

h) Employees must immediately report to their employer any loss or obvious defect in equipment – Regulation 11.

6.2.3 The Regulations and Strict Liability?

It does appear to be the case that if there is a breach of these Regulations that it may not be necessary for a Claimant to establish that the employer has also been negligent.

The Courts will often interpret a breach of Regulation strictly and find the employer responsible whatever the circumstances surrounding the breach.

On the 2nd March 2000 the Court of Appeal gave Judgment in the case of ***Stark v The Post Office (2000)***.

This case concerned Regulation 6(1) of the Provision and Use of Work Equipment Regulations 1992. The Regulations provided:

> **"every employer shall ensure that work equipment is maintained in an efficient state, in an efficient working order and in a good repair"**

The Court of Appeal found that the Regulation imposed an absolute duty upon the Post Office to ensure that the bicycle provided to the Claimant for use in the course of his employment, was in a state in which it worked efficiently at all times.

Part of the bicycle had broken injuring the Claimant. The Court of Appeal found that the Claimant could therefore recover compensation as the Post Office was in breach of its statutory duty and that breach had caused the Claimant's injuries.

The Post Office was not permitted to succeed in it's argument that it could not have known that there was a defect with the bicycle.

Whilst there may be strict liability for a breach of some of the regulations, it is important to understand that in order to succeed in his claim, the Claimant must still show that his injuries were caused by that breach.

6.3 Employers' Liability Checklist

1. Is the Claimant an employee?

2. What breach does the Claimant allege?
   a Is it a common law breach?
   b) Is it a statutory breach? (If so, which Regulation?)

3. If a common law breach is alleged – consider whether duty of care has been breached. Remember:
   Wilsons v Clyde Coal Company Limited v English (1938)
   Wilson v Tyneside Window Cleaning Company (1958)

4. If a statutory breach is alleged – consider the appropriate Regulation. Is there strict liability?

5. Contributory Negligence?

6.4 Suggested Further Reading

Monkman on Employer's Liability

Redgrave's Health and Safety

6.5 1992, 1998 and 1999 Regulations

See following pages.

UK Parliament SIs 1990-1999/1992/2751-2800/Health and Safety (Display Screen Equipment) Regulations 1992 (SI 1992/2792)

1992 No 2792

Health and Safety (Display Screen Equipment) Regulations 1992

Made - - - 5th November 1992

The Secretary of State, in exercise of the powers conferred on her by sections 15(1), (2), (5)(b) and (9) and 82(3)(a) of, and paragraphs 1(1)(a) and (c) and (2), 7, 8(1), 9 and 14 of Schedule 3 to, the Health and Safety at Work etc Act 1974 and of all other powers enabling her in that behalf and for the purpose of giving effect without modifications to proposals submitted to her by the Health and Safety Commission under section 11(2)(d) of the said Act after the carrying out by the said Commission of consultations in accordance with section 50(3) of that Act, hereby makes the following Regulations

UK Parliament SIs 1990-1999/1992/2751-2800/Health and Safety (Display Screen Equipment) Regulations 1992 (SI 1992/2792)/1 Citation, commencement, interpretation and application

1 Citation, commencement, interpretation and application

(1) These Regulations may be cited as the Health and Safety (Display Screen Equipment) Regulations 1992 and shall come into force on 1st January 1993.

(2) In these Regulations--

(a) "display screen equipment" means any alphanumeric or graphic display screen, regardless of the display process involved;

(b) "operator" means a self-employed person who habitually uses display screen equipment as a significant part of his normal work;

(c) "use" means use for or in connection with work;

(d) "user" means an employee who habitually uses display screen equipment as a significant part of his normal work; and

(e) "workstation" means an assembly comprising--

(i) display screen equipment (whether provided with software determining the interface between the equipment and its operator or user, a keyboard or any other input device),

(ii) any optional accessories to the display screen equipment,

(iii) any disk drive, telephone, modem, printer, document holder, work chair, work desk, work surface or other item peripheral to the display screen equipment, and

(iv) the immediate work environment around the display screen equipment.

(3) Any reference in these Regulations to--

(a) a numbered regulation is a reference to the regulation in these Regulations so numbered; or

(b) a numbered paragraph is a reference to the paragraph so numbered in the regulation in which the reference appears.

(4) Nothing in these Regulations shall apply to or in relation to--

(a) drivers' cabs or control cabs for vehicles or machinery;

(b) display screen equipment on board a means of transport;

(c) display screen equipment mainly intended for public operation;

(d) portable systems not in prolonged use;

(e) calculators, cash registers or any equipment having a small data or measurement display required for direct use of the equipment; or

(f) window typewriters.

UK Parliament SIs 1990-1999/1992/2751-2800/Health and Safety (Display Screen Equipment) Regulations 1992 (SI 1992/2792)/2 Analysis of workstations

2 Analysis of workstations

(1) Every employer shall perform a suitable and sufficient analysis of those work-stations which--

(a) (regardless of who has provided them) are used for the purposes of his undertaking by users; or

(b) have been provided by him and are used for the purposes of his undertaking by operators,

for the purpose of assessing the health and safety risks to which those persons are exposed in consequence of that use.

(2) Any assessment made by an employer in pursuance of paragraph (1) shall be reviewed by him if--

(a) there is reason to suspect that it is no longer valid; or

(b) there has been a significant change in the matters to which it relates;

and where as a result of any such review changes to an assessment are required, the employer concerned shall make them.

(3) The employer shall reduce the risks identified in consequence of an assessment to the lowest extent reasonably practicable.

(4) The reference in paragraph (3) to "an assessment" is a reference to an assessment made by the employer concerned in pursuance of paragraph (1) and changed by him where necessary in pursuance of paragraph (2).

UK Parliament SIs 1990-1999/1992/2751-2800/Health and Safety (Display Screen Equipment) Regulations 1992 (SI 1992/2792)/[3 Requirements for workstations]

[3 Requirements for workstations]

[Every employer shall ensure that any workstation which may be used for the purposes of his undertaking meets the requirements laid down in the Schedule to these Regulations, to the extent specified in paragraph 1 thereof.]

NOTES

Amendment

Substituted by SI 2002/2174, reg 3(a).

Date in force: 17 September 2002: see SI 2002/2174, reg 1.

UK Parliament SIs 1990-1999/1992/2751-2800/Health and Safety (Display Screen Equipment) Regulations 1992 (SI 1992/2792)/4 Daily work routine of users

4 Daily work routine of users

Every employer shall so plan the activities of users at work in his undertaking that their daily work on display screen equipment is periodically interrupted by such breaks or changes of activity as reduce their workload at that equipment.

UK Parliament SIs 1990-1999/1992/2751-2800/Health and Safety (Display Screen Equipment) Regulations 1992 (SI 1992/2792)/5 Eyes and eyesight

5 Eyes and eyesight

[(1) Where a person--

(a) is a user in the undertaking in which he is employed; or

(b) is to become a user in the undertaking in which he is, or is to become, employed,

the employer who carries on the undertaking shall, if requested by that person, ensure that an appropriate eye and eyesight test is carried out on him by a competent person within the time specified in paragraph (2).

(2) The time referred to in paragraph (1) is--

(a) in the case of a person mentioned in paragraph (1)(a), as soon as practicable after the request; and

(b) in the case of a person mentioned in paragraph (1)(b), before he becomes a user.]

(3) At regular intervals after an employee has been provided [(whether before or after becoming an employee)] with an eye and eyesight test in accordance with paragraphs (1) and (2), his employer shall, subject to paragraph (6), ensure that he is provided with a further eye and eyesight test of an appropriate nature, any such test to be carried out by a competent person.

(4) Where a user experiences visual difficulties which may reasonably be considered to be caused by work on display screen equipment, his employer shall ensure that he is provided at his request with an appropriate eye and eyesight test, any such test to be carried out by a competent person as soon as practicable after being requested as aforesaid.

(5) Every employer shall ensure that each user employed by him is provided with special corrective appliances appropriate for the work being done by the user concerned where--

(a) normal corrective appliances cannot be used; and

(b) the result of any eye and eyesight test which the user has been given in accordance with this regulation shows such provision to be necessary.

(6) Nothing in paragraph (3) shall require an employer to provide any employee with an eye and eyesight test against that employee's will.

NOTES

Amendment

Paras (1), (2): substituted by SI 2002/2174, reg 3(b).

Date in force: 17 September 2002: see SI 2002/2174, reg 1.

Para (3): words "(whether before or after becoming an employee)" in square brackets inserted by SI 2002/2174, reg 3(c).

Date in force: 17 September 2002: see SI 2002/2174, reg 1.

UK Parliament SIs 1990-1999/1992/2751-2800/Health and Safety (Display Screen Equipment) Regulations 1992 (SI 1992/2792)/6 Provision of training

6 Provision of training

[(1) Where a person--

(a) is a user in the undertaking in which he is employed; or

(b) is to become a user in the undertaking in which he is, or is to become, employed,

the employer who carries on the undertaking shall ensure that he is provided with adequate health and safety training in the use of any workstation upon which he may be required to work.

(1A) In the case of a person mentioned in sub-paragraph (b) of paragraph (1) the training shall be provided before he becomes a user.]

(2) Every employer shall ensure that each user at work in his undertaking is provided with adequate health and safety training whenever the organisation of any workstation in that undertaking upon which he may be required to work is substantially modified.

NOTES

Amendment

Paras (1), (1A): substituted, for para (1) as originally enacted, by SI 2002/2174, reg 3(d).

Date in force: 17 September 2002: see SI 2002/2174, reg 1.

UK Parliament SIs 1990-1999/1992/2751-2800/Health and Safety (Display Screen Equipment) Regulations

1992 (SI 1992/2792)/7 Provision of information

7 Provision of information

(1) Every employer shall ensure that operators and users at work in his undertaking are provided with adequate information about--

(a) all aspects of health and safety relating to their workstations; and

(b) such measures taken by him in compliance with his duties under regulations 2 and 3 as relate to them and their work.

(2) Every employer shall ensure that users at work in his undertaking are provided with adequate information about such measures taken by him in compliance with his duties under regulations 4 and 6(2) as relate to them and their work.

(3) Every employer shall ensure that users employed by him are provided with adequate information about such measures taken by him in compliance with his duties under regulations 5 and 6(1) as relate to them and their work.

UK Parliament SIs 1990-1999/1992/2751-2800/Health and Safety (Display Screen Equipment) Regulations 1992 (SI 1992/2792)/8 Exemption certificates

8 Exemption certificates

(1) The Secretary of State for Defence may, in the interests of national security, exempt any of the home forces, any visiting force or any headquarters from any of the requirements imposed by these Regulations.

(2) Any exemption such as is specified in paragraph (1) may be granted subject to conditions and to a limit of time and may be revoked by the Secretary of State for Defence by a further certificate in writing at any time.

(3) In this regulation--

(a) "the home forces" has the same meaning as in section 12(1) of the Visiting Forces Act 1952;

(b) "headquarters" has the same meaning as in article 3(2) of the Visiting Forces and International Headquarters (Application of Law) Order 1965; and

(c) "visiting force" has the same meaning as it does for the purposes of any provision of Part I of the Visiting Forces Act 1952.

UK Parliament SIs 1990-1999/1992/2751-2800/Health and Safety (Display Screen Equipment) Regulations 1992 (SI 1992/2792)/9 Extension outside Great Britain

9 Extension outside Great Britain

These Regulations shall, subject to regulation 1(4), apply to and in relation to the premises and activities outside Great Britain to which sections 1 to 59 and 80 to 82 of the Health and Safety at Work etc Act 1974 apply by virtue of the Health and Safety at Work etc Act 1974 (Application Outside Great Britain) Order 1989 as they apply within Great Britain.

UK Parliament SIs 1990-1999/1992/2751-2800/Health and Safety (Display Screen Equipment) Regulations 1992 (SI 1992/2792)/SCHEDULE (Which Sets Out the Minimum Requirements for Workstations Which Are Contained in the Annex to Council Directive 90/270/EEC on the Minimum Safety and Health Requirements for Work With Display Screen Equipment)

SCHEDULE

(WHICH SETS OUT THE MINIMUM REQUIREMENTS FOR WORKSTATIONS WHICH ARE CONTAINED IN THE ANNEX TO COUNCIL DIRECTIVE 90/270/EEC ON THE MINIMUM SAFETY AND HEALTH REQUIREMENTS FOR WORK WITH DISPLAY SCREEN EQUIPMENT)

Regulation 3

1 Extent to which employers must ensure that workstations meet the requirements laid down in this schedules

An employer shall ensure that a workstation meets the requirements laid down in this Schedule to the extent that--

(a) those requirements relate to a component which is present in the workstation concerned;

(b) those requirements have effect with a view to securing the health, safety and welfare of persons at work; and

(c) the inherent characteristics of a given task make compliance with those requirements appropriate as respects the workstation concerned.

2 Equipment

(a) General comment

The use as such of the equipment must not be a source of risk for operators or users.

(b) Display screen

The characters on the screen shall be well-defined and clearly formed, of adequate size and with adequate spacing between the characters and lines.

The image on the screen should be stable, with no flickering or other forms of instability.

The brightness and the contrast between the characters and the background shall be easily adjustable by the operator or user, and also be easily adjustable to ambient conditions.

The screen must swivel and tilt easily and freely to suit the needs of the operator or user.

It shall be possible to use a separate base for the screen or an adjustable table.

The screen shall be free of reflective glare and reflections liable to cause discomfort to the operator or user.

(c) Keyboard

The keyboard shall be tiltable and separate from the screen so as to allow the operator or user to find a comfortable working position avoiding fatigue in the arms or hands.

The space in front of the keyboard shall be sufficient to provide support for the hands and arms of the operator or user.

Page 7

The keyboard shall have a matt surface to avoid reflective glare.

The arrangement of the keyboard and the characteristics of the keys shall be such as to facilitate the use of the keyboard.

The symbols on the keys shall be adequately contrasted and legible from the design working position.

(d) Work desk or work surface

The work desk or work surface shall have a sufficiently large, low-reflectance surface and allow a flexible arrangement of the screen, keyboard, documents and related equipment.

The document holder shall be stable and adjustable and shall be positioned so as to minimise the need for uncomfortable head and eye movements.

There shall be adequate space for operators or users to find a comfortable position.

(e) Work chair

The work chair shall be stable and allow the operator or user easy freedom of movement and a comfortable position.

The seat shall be adjustable in height.

The seat back shall be adjustable in both height and tilt.

A footrest shall be made available to any operator or user who wishes one.

3 Environment

(a) Space requirements

The workstation shall be dimensioned and designed so as to provide sufficient space for the operator or user to change position and vary movements.

(b) Lighting

Any room lighting or task lighting provided shall ensure satisfactory lighting conditions and an appropriate contrast between the screen and the background environment, taking into account the type of work and the vision requirements of the operator or user.

Possible disturbing glare and reflections on the screen or other equipment shall be prevented by co-ordinating workplace and workstation layout with the positioning and technical characteristics of the artificial light sources.

(c) Reflections and glare

Workstations shall be so designed that sources of light, such as windows and other openings, transparent or translucid walls, and brightly coloured fixtures or walls cause no direct glare and no distracting reflections on the screen.

Windows shall be fitted with a suitable system of adjustable covering to attenuate the daylight that falls on the workstation.

(d) Noise

Noise emitted by equipment belonging to any workstation shall be taken into account when a workstation is being equipped, with a view in particular to ensuring that attention is not distracted and speech is not disturbed.

(e) Heat

Equipment belonging to any workstation shall not produce excess heat which could cause discomfort to operators or users.

(f) Radiation

All radiation with the exception of the visible part of the electromagnetic spectrum shall be reduced to negligible levels from the point of view of the protection of operators' or users' health and safety.

(g) Humidity

An adequate level of humidity shall be established and maintained.

4 Interface between computer and operator/user

In designing, selecting, commissioning and modifying software, and in designing tasks using display screen equipment, the employer shall take into account the following principles:

(a) software must be suitable for the task;

(b) software must be easy to use and, where appropriate, adaptable to the level of knowledge or experience of the operator or user; no quantitative or qualitative checking facility may be used without the knowledge of the operators or users;

(c) systems must provide feedback to operators or users on the performance of those systems;

(d) systems must display information in a format and at a pace which are adapted to operators or users;

(e) the principles of software ergonomics must be applied, in particular to human data processing.

UK Parliament SIs 1990-1999/1992/2751-2800/Manual Handling Operations Regulations 1992 (SI 1992/2793)

1992 No 2793

Manual Handling Operations Regulations 1992

Made - - - 5th November 1992

The Secretary of State, in exercise of the powers conferred on her by sections 15(1), (2), (3)(a), (5)(a) and (9) and 80(1), (2)(a) and (4) of, and paragraphs 1(1)(a) and (c) and 8 of Schedule 3 to, the Health and Safety at Work etc. Act 1974 ("the 1974 Act") and of all other powers enabling her in that behalf and--

(a) for the purpose of giving effect without modifications to proposals submitted to her by the Health and Safety Commission under section 11(2)(d) of the 1974 Act after the carrying out by the said Commission of consultations in accordance with section 50(3) of that Act; and

(b) it appearing to her that the repeal of section 18(1)(f) of the Children and Young Persons Act 1933 and section 28(1)(f) of the Children and Young Persons (Scotland) Act 1937 except insofar as those provisions apply to such employment as is permitted under section 1(2) of the Employment of Women, Young Persons, and Children Act 1920 is expedient in consequence of the Regulations referred to below after the carrying out by her of consultations in accordance with section 80(4) of the 1974 Act,

hereby makes the following Regulations

UK Parliament SIs 1990-1999/1992/2751-2800/Manual Handling Operations Regulations 1992 (SI 1992/2793)/1 Citation and commencement

1 Citation and commencement

These Regulations may be cited as the Manual Handling Operations Regulations 1992 and shall come into force on 1st January 1993.

UK Parliament SIs 1990-1999/1992/2751-2800/Manual Handling Operations Regulations 1992 (SI 1992/2793)/2 Interpretation

2 Interpretation

(1) In these Regulations, unless the context otherwise requires--

"injury" does not include injury caused by any toxic or corrosive substance which--

(a) has leaked or spilled from a load;

(b) is present on the surface of a load but has not leaked or spilled from it; or

(c) is a constituent part of a load;

and "injured" shall be construed accordingly;

"load" includes any person and any animal;

"manual handling operations" means any transporting or supporting of a load (including the lifting, putting down, pushing, pulling, carrying or moving thereof) by hand or by bodily force.

(2) Any duty imposed by these Regulations on an employer in respect of his employees shall also be imposed on a self-employed person in respect of himself.

UK Parliament SIs 1990-1999/1992/2751-2800/Manual Handling Operations Regulations 1992 (SI 1992/2793)/3 Disapplication of Regulations

3 Disapplication of Regulations

These Regulations shall not apply to or in relation to the master or crew of a sea-going ship or to the employer of such persons in respect of the normal ship-board activities of a ship's crew under the direction of the master.

UK Parliament SIs 1990-1999/1992/2751-2800/Manual Handling Operations Regulations 1992 (SI 1992/2793)/4 Duties of employers

4 Duties of employers

(1) Each employer shall--

(a) so far as is reasonably practicable, avoid the need for his employees to undertake any manual handling operations at work which involve a risk of their being injured; or

(b) where it is not reasonably practicable to avoid the need for his employees to undertake any manual handling operations at work which involve a risk of their being injured--

(i) make a suitable and sufficient assessment of all such manual handling operations to be undertaken by them, having regard to the factors which are specified in column 1 of Schedule 1 to these Regulations and considering the questions which are specified in the corresponding entry in column 2 of that Schedule,

(ii) take appropriate steps to reduce the risk of injury to those employees arising out of their undertaking any such manual handling operations to the lowest level reasonably practicable, and

(iii) take appropriate steps to provide any of those employees who are undertaking any such manual handling operations with general indications and, where it is reasonably practicable to do so, precise information on--

(aa) the weight of each load, and

(bb) the heaviest side of any load whose centre of gravity is not positioned centrally.

(2) Any assessment such as is referred to in paragraph (1)(b)(i) of this regulation shall be reviewed by the employer who made it if--

(a) there is reason to suspect that it is no longer valid; or

(b) there has been a significant change in the manual handling operations to which it relates;

and where as a result of any such review changes to an assessment are required, the relevant employer shall make them.

[(3) In determining for the purposes of this regulation whether manual handling operations at work involve a risk of injury and in determining the appropriate steps to reduce that risk regard shall be had in particular to--

(a) the physical suitability of the employee to carry out the operations;

(b) the clothing, footwear or other personal effects he is wearing;

(c) his knowledge and training;

(d) the results of any relevant risk assessment carried out pursuant to regulation 3 of the Management of Health and Safety at Work Regulations 1999;

(e) whether the employee is within a group of employees identified by that assessment as being especially at risk; and

(f) the results of any health surveillance provided pursuant to regulation 6 of the Management of Health and Safety Regulations 1999.]

NOTES

Amendment

Para (3): inserted by SI 2002/2174, reg 4.

Date in force: 17 September 2002: see SI 2002/2174, reg 1.

UK Parliament SIs 1990-1999/1992/2751-2800/Manual Handling Operations Regulations 1992 (SI 1992/2793)/5 Duty of employees

5 Duty of employees

Each employee while at work shall make full and proper use of any system of work provided for his use by his employer in compliance with regulation 4(1)(b)(ii) of these Regulations.

UK Parliament SIs 1990-1999/1992/2751-2800/Manual Handling Operations Regulations 1992 (SI 1992/2793)/6 Exemption certificates

6 Exemption certificates

(1) The Secretary of State for Defence may, in the interests of national security, by a certificate in writing exempt--

(a) any of the home forces, any visiting force or any headquarters from any requirement imposed by regulation 4 of these Regulations; or

(b) any member of the home forces, any member of a visiting force or any member of a headquarters from the requirement imposed by regulation 5 of these Regulations;

and any exemption such as is specified in sub-paragraph (a) or (b) of this paragraph may be granted subject to conditions and to a limit of time and may be revoked by the said Secretary of State by a further certificate in writing at any time.

(2) In this regulation--

(a) "the home forces" has the same meaning as in section 12(1) of the Visiting Forces Act 1952;

(b) "headquarters" has the same meaning as in article 3(2) of the Visiting Forces and International Headquarters (Application of Law) Order 1965;

(c) "member of a headquarters" has the same meaning as in paragraph 1(1) of the Schedule to the International Headquarters and Defence Organisations Act 1964; and

(d) "visiting force" has the same meaning as it does for the purposes of any provision of Part I of the Visiting Forces Act 1952.

UK Parliament SIs 1990-1999/1992/2751-2800/Manual Handling Operations Regulations 1992 (SI 1992/2793)/7 Extension outside Great Britain

7 Extension outside Great Britain

These Regulations shall, subject to regulation 3 hereof, apply to and in relation to the premises and activities outside Great Britain to which sections 1 to 59 and 80 to 82 of the Health and Safety at Work etc. Act 1974 apply by virtue of the Health and Safety at Work etc. Act 1974 (Application Outside Great Britain) Order 1989 as they apply within Great Britain.

UK Parliament SIs 1990-1999/1992/2751-2800/Manual Handling Operations Regulations 1992 (SI 1992/2793)/8 Repeals and revocations

8 Repeals and revocations

(1) The enactments mentioned in column 1 of Part I of Schedule 2 to these Regulations are repealed to the extent specified in the corresponding entry in column 3 of that part.

(2) The Regulations mentioned in column 1 of Part II of Schedule 2 to these Regulations are revoked to the extent specified in the corresponding entry in column 3 of that part.

UK Parliament SIs 1990-1999/1992/2751-2800/Manual Handling Operations Regulations 1992 (SI 1992/2793)/SCHEDULE 1 Factors to Which the Employer Must Have Regard and Questions he Must Consider When Making an Assessment of Manual Handling Operations

SCHEDULE 1

FACTORS TO WHICH THE EMPLOYER MUST HAVE REGARD AND QUESTIONS HE MUST CONSIDER WHEN MAKING AN ASSESSMENT OF MANUAL HANDLING OPERATIONS

Regulation 4(1)(b)(i)

Column 1 *Factors*	Column 2 *Questions*
1 The tasks	**Do they involve:** --holding or manipulating loads at distance from trunk?

		--unsatisfactory bodily movement or posture, especially: --twisting the trunk? --stooping? --reaching upwards? --excessive movement of loads, especially: --excessive lifting or lowering distances? --excessive carrying distances? --excessive pushing or pulling of loads? --risk of sudden movement of loads? --frequent or prolonged physical effort? --insufficient rest or recovery periods? --a rate of work imposed by a process?
2	The loads	**Are they:** --heavy? --bulky or unwieldy? --difficult to grasp? --unstable, or with contents likely to shift? --sharp, hot or otherwise potentially damaging?
3	The working environment	**Are there:** --space constraints preventing good posture? --uneven, slippery or unstable floors? --variations in level of floors or work surfaces? --extremes of temperature or humidity? --conditions causing ventilation problems or gusts of wind? --poor lighting conditions?
4	Individual capability	**Does the job:** --require unusual strength, height, etc? --create a hazard to those who might reasonably be considered to be pregnant or to have a health problem? --require special information or training for its safe performance?
5	Other factors	**Is movement or posture hindered by personal protective equipment or by clothing?**

UK Parliament SIs 1990-1999/1992/2751-2800/Manual Handling Operations Regulations 1992 (SI 1992/2793)/SCHEDULE 2 Repeals and Revocations

SCHEDULE 2

REPEALS AND REVOCATIONS

Regulation 8

UK Parliament SIs 1990-1999/1992/2751-2800/Manual Handling Operations Regulations 1992 (SI 1992/2793)/SCHEDULE 2 Repeals and Revocations/Part I Repeals

Part I

Repeals

Column 1 *Short title of enactment*	Column 2 *Reference*	Column 3 *Extent of repeal*
The Children and Young Persons Act 1933.	1933 c.12.	Section 18(1)(f) except insofar as that paragraph applies to such employment as is permitted under section 1(2) of the Employment of Women, Young Persons, and Children Act 1920 (1920 c.65).
The Children and Young Persons (Scotland) Act 1937.	1937 c.37.	Section 28(1)(f) except insofar as that paragraph applies to such employment as is permitted under section 1(2) of the Employment of Women, Young Persons, and Children Act 1920.
The Mines and Quarries Act 1954.	1954 c.70.	Section 93; in section 115 the word "ninety-three".
The Agriculture (Safety, Health and Welfare Provisions) Act 1956.	1956 c.49.	Section 2.
The Factories Act 1961.	1961 c.34.	Section 72.
The Offices, Shops and Railway Premises Act 1963.	1963 c.41.	Section 23 except insofar as the prohibition contained in that section applies to any person specified in section 90(4) of the same Act. In section 83(1) the number "23".

UK Parliament SIs 1990-1999/1992/2751-2800/Manual Handling Operations Regulations 1992 (SI 1992/2793)/SCHEDULE 2 Repeals and Revocations/Part II Revocations

Part II

Revocations

Column 1 *Title of instrument*	Column 2 *Reference*	Column 3 *Extent of revocation*
The Agriculture (Lifting of Heavy Weights) Regulations 1959.	S.I. 1959/2120.	The whole Regulations.
The Construction (General Provisions) Regulations 1961.	S.I. 1961/1580.	In regulation 3(1)(a) the phrase "and 55"; regulation 55.

UK Parliament SIs 1990-1999/1992/2951-3000/Personal Protective Equipment at Work Regulations 1992 (SI 1992/2966)

1992 No 2966

Personal Protective Equipment at Work Regulations 1992

Made - - - 25th November 1992

The Secretary of State, in exercise of the powers conferred upon her by sections 15(1), (2), (3)(a) and (b), (5)(b) and (9) of, and paragraphs 11 and 14 of Schedule 3 to the Health and Safety at Work etc. Act 1974, and of all other powers enabling her in that behalf and for the purpose of giving effect without modifications to proposals submitted to her by the Health and Safety Commission under section 11(2)(d) of the said Act after the carrying out by the said Commission of consultations in accordance with section 50(3) of that Act, hereby makes the following Regulations:

UK Parliament SIs 1990-1999/1992/2951-3000/Personal Protective Equipment at Work Regulations 1992 (SI 1992/2966)/1 Citation and commencement

1 Citation and commencement

These Regulations may be cited as the Personal Protective Equipment at Work Regulations 1992 and shall come into force on 1st January 1993.

UK Parliament SIs 1990-1999/1992/2951-3000/Personal Protective Equipment at Work Regulations 1992 (SI 1992/2966)/2 Interpretation

2 Interpretation

(1) In these Regulations, unless the context otherwise requires, "personal protective equipment" means all equipment (including clothing affording protection against the weather) which is intended to be worn or held by a person at work and which protects him against one or more risks to his health or safety, and any addition or accessory designed to meet that objective.

(2) Any reference in these Regulations to--

(a) a numbered regulation or Schedule is a reference to the regulation or Schedule in these Regulations so numbered; and

(b) a numbered paragraph is a reference to the paragraph so numbered in the regulation in which the reference appears.

UK Parliament SIs 1990-1999/1992/2951-3000/Personal Protective Equipment at Work Regulations 1992 (SI 1992/2966)/3 Disapplication of these Regulations

3 Disapplication of these Regulations

(1) These Regulations shall not apply to or in relation to the master or crew of a sea-going ship or to the employer of such persons in respect of the normal ship-board activities of a ship's crew under the direction of the master.

(2) Regulations 4 to 12 shall not apply in respect of personal protective equipment which is--

(a) ordinary working clothes and uniforms which do not specifically protect the health and safety of the wearer;

(b) an offensive weapon within the meaning of section 1(4) of the Prevention of Crime Act 1953 used as self-defence or as deterrent equipment;

(c) portable devices for detecting and signalling risks and nuisances;

(d) personal protective equipment used for protection while travelling on a road within the meaning (in England and Wales) of section 192(1) of the Road Traffic Act 1988, and (in Scotland) of section 151 of the Roads (Scotland) Act 1984;

(e) equipment used during the playing of competitive sports.

(3) Regulations 4 and 6 to 12 shall not apply where any of the following Regulations apply and in respect of any risk to a person's health or safety for which any of them require the provision or use of personal protective equipment, namely--

(a) the Control of Lead at Work Regulations 1980;

(b) [the Ionising Radiations Regulations 1999 [SI 1999/3232]];

(c) [the Control of Asbestos Regulations 2006];

(d) the Control of Substances Hazardous to Health Regulations 1988;

(e) *the Noise at Work Regulations 1989* [the Control of Noise at Work Regulations 2005];

(f) the Construction (Head Protection) Regulations 1989.

NOTES

Amendment

Para (3): in sub-para (b) words "the Ionising Radiations Regulations 1999 [SI 1999/3232]" in square brackets substituted by SI 1999/3232, reg 41(1), Sch 9, para 3.

Date in force: 1 January 2000: see SI 1999/3232, reg 1(a).

Para (3): in sub-para (c) words "the Control of Asbestos Regulations 2006" in square brackets substituted by SI 2006/2739, reg 36(2), Sch 5.

Date in force: 13 November 2006: see SI 2006/2739, reg 1.

Para (3): in sub-para (e) words "the Noise at Work Regulations 1989" in italics revoked and subsequent words in square brackets substituted by virtue of SI 2005/1643, reg 15(1)(a).

Date in force (for certain purposes): 6 April 2006: see SI 2005/1643, reg 1.
Date in force (for remaining purposes): 6 April 2008: see SI 2005/1643, regs 1(a), 15(3).

1992/2966)/4 Provision of personal protective equipment

4 Provision of personal protective equipment

(1) [Subject to paragraph (1A),] every employer shall ensure that suitable personal protective equipment is provided to his employees who may be exposed to a risk to their health or safety while at work except where and to the extent that such risk has been adequately controlled by other means which are equally or more effective.

[(1A) Where the characteristics of any policing activity are such that compliance by the relevant officer with the requirement in paragraph (1) would lead to an inevitable conflict with the exercise of police powers or performance of police duties, that requirement shall be complied with so far as is reasonably practicable.]

(2) Every self-employed person shall ensure that he is provided with suitable personal protective equipment where he may be exposed to a risk to his health or safety while at work except where and to the extent that such risk has been adequately controlled by other means which are equally or more effective.

(3) Without prejudice to the generality of paragraphs (1) and (2), personal protective equipment shall not be suitable unless--

[(a) it is appropriate for the risk or risks involved, the conditions at the place where exposure to the risk may occur, and the period for which it is worn;

(b) it takes account of ergonomic requirements and the state of health of the person or persons who may wear it, and of the characteristics of the workstation of each such person;]

(c) it is capable of fitting the wearer correctly, if necessary, after adjustments within the range for which it is designed;

(d) so far as is practicable, it is effective to prevent or adequately control the risk or risks involved without increasing overall risk;

(e) it complies with any enactment (whether in an Act or instrument) which implements in Great Britain any provision on design or manufacture with respect to health or safety in any relevant Community directive listed in Schedule 1 which is applicable to that item of personal protective equipment.

[(4) Where it is necessary to ensure that personal protective equipment is hygienic and otherwise free of risk to health, every employer and every self-employed person shall ensure that personal protective equipment provided under this regulation is provided to a person for use only by him.]

NOTES

Amendment

Para (1): words "Subject to paragraph (1A)," in square brackets inserted by SI 1999/860, reg 4(1), (2).

Date in force: 14 April 1999: see SI 1999/860, reg 1.

Para (1A): inserted by SI 1999/860, reg 4(1), (3).

Date in force: 14 April 1999: see SI 1999/860, reg 1.

Para (3): sub-paras (a), (b) substituted by SI 2002/2174, reg 5(a).

Date in force: 17 September 2002: see SI 2002/2174, reg 1.

Para (4): inserted by SI 2002/2174, reg 5(b).

Date in force: 17 September 2002: see SI 2002/2174, reg 1.

UK Parliament SIs 1990-1999/1992/2951-3000/Personal Protective Equipment at Work Regulations 1992 (SI 1992/2966)/5 Compatibility of personal protective equipment

5 Compatibility of personal protective equipment

(1) Every employer shall ensure that where the presence of more than one risk to health or safety makes it necessary for his employee to wear or use simultaneously more than one item of personal protective equipment, such equipment is compatible and continues to be effective against the risk or risks in question.

(2) Every self-employed person shall ensure that where the presence of more than one risk to health or safety makes it necessary for him to wear or use simultaneously more than one item of personal protective equipment, such equipment is compatible and continues to be effective against the risk or risks in question.

UK Parliament SIs 1990-1999/1992/2951-3000/Personal Protective Equipment at Work Regulations 1992 (SI 1992/2966)/6 Assessment of personal protective equipment

6 Assessment of personal protective equipment

(1) Before choosing any personal protective equipment which by virtue of regulation 4 he is required to ensure is provided, an employer or self-employed person shall ensure that an assessment is made to determine whether the personal protective equipment he intends will be provided is suitable.

(2) The assessment required by paragraph (1) shall include--

(a) an assessment of any risk or risks to health or safety which have not been avoided by other means;

(b) the definition of the characteristics which personal protective equipment must have in order to be effective against the risks referred to in sub-paragraph (a) of this paragraph, taking into account any risks which the equipment itself may create;

(c) comparison of the characteristics of the personal protective equipment available with the characteristics referred to in sub-paragraph (b) of this paragraph;

[(d) an assessment as to whether the personal protective equipment is compatible with other personal protective equipment which is in use and which an employee would be required to wear simultaneously].

(3) Every employer or self-employed person who is required by paragraph (1) to ensure that any assessment is made shall ensure that any such assessment is reviewed if--

(a) there is reason to suspect that it is no longer valid; or

(b) there has been a significant change in the matters to which it relates, and where as a result of any such review changes in the assessment are required, the relevant employer or self-employed person shall ensure that they are made.

NOTES

Amendment

Para (2): sub-para (d) inserted by SI 2002/2174, reg 5(c).

Date in force: 17 September 2002: see SI 2002/2174, reg 1.

UK Parliament SIs 1990-1999/1992/2951-3000/Personal Protective Equipment at Work Regulations 1992 (SI 1992/2966)/7 Maintenance and replacement of personal protective equipment

7 Maintenance and replacement of personal protective equipment

(1) Every employer shall ensure that any personal protective equipment provided to his employees is maintained (including replaced or cleaned as appropriate) in an efficient state, in efficient working order and in good repair.

(2) Every self-employed person shall ensure that any personal protective equipment provided to him is maintained (including replaced or cleaned as appropriate) in an efficient state, in efficient working order and in good repair.

UK Parliament SIs 1990-1999/1992/2951-3000/Personal Protective Equipment at Work Regulations 1992 (SI 1992/2966)/8 Accommodation for personal protective equipment

8 Accommodation for personal protective equipment

Where an employer or self-employed person is required, by virtue of regulation 4, to ensure personal protective equipment is provided, he shall also ensure that appropriate accommodation is provided for that personal protective equipment when it is not being used.

UK Parliament SIs 1990-1999/1992/2951-3000/Personal Protective Equipment at Work Regulations 1992 (SI 1992/2966)/9 Information, instruction and training

9 Information, instruction and training

(1) Where an employer is required to ensure that personal protective equipment is provided to an employee, the employer shall also ensure that the employee is provided with such information, instruction and training as is adequate and appropriate to enable the employee to know--

(a) the risk or risks which the personal protective equipment will avoid or limit;

(b) the purpose for which and the manner in which personal protective equipment is to be used; and

(c) any action to be taken by the employee to ensure that the personal protective equipment remains in an efficient state, in efficient working order and in good repair as required by regulation 7(1),

[and shall ensure that such information is kept available to employees].

(2) Without prejudice to the generality of paragraph (1), the information and instruction provided by virtue of that paragraph shall not be adequate and appropriate unless it is comprehensible to the persons to whom it is provided.

[(3) Without prejudice to the generality of paragraph (1) the employer shall, where appropriate, and at suitable intervals, organise demonstrations in the wearing of personal protective equipment.]

NOTES

Amendment

Para (1): words "and shall ensure that such information is kept available to employees" in square brackets inserted by SI 2002/2174, reg 5(d).

Date in force: 17 September 2002: see SI 2002/2174, reg 1.

Para (3): inserted by SI 2002/2174, reg 5(e).

Date in force: 17 September 2002: see SI 2002/2174, reg 1.

UK Parliament SIs 1990-1999/1992/2951-3000/Personal Protective Equipment at Work Regulations 1992 (SI 1992/2966)/10 Use of personal protective equipment

10 Use of personal protective equipment

(1) Every employer shall take all reasonable steps to ensure that any personal protective equipment provided to his employees by virtue of regulation 4(1) is properly used.

(2) Every employee shall use any personal protective equipment provided to him by virtue of these Regulations in accordance both with any training in the use of the personal protective equipment concerned which has been received by him and the instructions respecting that use which have been provided to him by virtue of regulation 9.

(3) Every self-employed person shall make full and proper use of any personal protective equipment provided to him by virtue of regulation 4(2).

(4) Every employee and self-employed person who has been provided with personal protective equipment by virtue of regulation 4 shall take all reasonable steps to ensure that it is returned to the accommodation provided for it after use.

UK Parliament SIs 1990-1999/1992/2951-3000/Personal Protective Equipment at Work Regulations 1992 (SI 1992/2966)/11 Reporting loss or defect

11 Reporting loss or defect

Every employee who has been provided with personal protective equipment by virtue of regulation 4(1) shall forthwith report to his employer any loss of or obvious defect in that personal protective equipment.

UK Parliament SIs 1990-1999/1992/2951-3000/Personal Protective Equipment at Work Regulations 1992 (SI 1992/2966)/12 Exemption certificates

12 Exemption certificates

(1) The Secretary of State for Defence may, in the interests of national security, by a certificate in writing exempt--

(a) any of the home forces, any visiting force or any headquarters from those requirements of these Regulations which impose obligations on employers; or

(b) any member of the home forces, any member of a visiting force or any member of a headquarters from the requirements imposed by regulation 10 or 11;

and any exemption such as is specified in sub-paragraph (a) or (b) of this paragraph may be granted subject to conditions and to a limit of time and may be revoked by the said Secretary of State by a further certificate in writing at any time.

(2) In this regulation--

(a) "the home forces" has the same meaning as in section 12(1) of the Visiting Forces Act 1952;

(b) "headquarters" has the same meaning as in article 3(2) of the Visiting Forces and International Headquarters (Application of Law) Order 1965;

(c) "member of a headquarters" has the same meaning as in paragraph 1(1) of the Schedule to the International Headquarters and Defence Organisations Act 1964; and

(d) "visiting force" has the same meaning as it does for the purposes of any provision of Part I of the Visiting Forces Act 1952.

UK Parliament SIs 1990-1999/1992/2951-3000/Personal Protective Equipment at Work Regulations 1992 (SI 1992/2966)/13 Extension outside Great Britain

13 Extension outside Great Britain

These Regulations shall apply to and in relation to the premises and activities outside Great Britain to which sections 1 to 59 and 80 to 82 of the Health and Safety at Work etc. Act 1974 apply by virtue of the Health and Safety at Work etc. Act 1974 (Application Outside Great Britain) Order 1989 as they apply within Great Britain.

UK Parliament SIs 1990-1999/1992/2951-3000/Personal Protective Equipment at Work Regulations 1992 (SI 1992/2966)/14 Modifications, repeal and revocations

14 Modifications, repeal and revocations

(1) The Act and Regulations specified in Schedule 2 shall be modified to the extent specified in the corresponding Part of that Schedule.

(2) . . .

(3) The instruments specified in column 1 of Schedule 3 are revoked to the extent specified in column 3 of that Schedule.

NOTES

Amendment

Para (2): repeals the Factories Act 1961, s 65.

UK Parliament SIs 1990-1999/1992/2951-3000/Personal Protective Equipment at Work Regulations 1992 (SI 1992/2966)/[SCHEDULE 1 Relevant Community Directive]

[SCHEDULE 1

RELEVANT COMMUNITY DIRECTIVE]

Regulation 4(3)(e)

[1

Council Directive 89/686/EEC on the approximation of the laws of the member States relating to personal protective equipment (OJ No L399, 30.12.89, p 18).

2

Council Directive 93/42/EEC concerning medical devices (OJ No L169, 12.7.93, p.1).]

NOTES

Amendment

Substituted by SI 1994/3017, reg 25.

UK Parliament SIs 1990-1999/1992/2951-3000/Personal Protective Equipment at Work Regulations 1992 (SI 1992/2966)/SCHEDULE 2 Modifications

SCHEDULE 2

MODIFICATIONS

Regulation 14(1)

UK Parliament SIs 1990-1999/1992/2951-3000/Personal Protective Equipment at Work Regulations 1992 (SI 1992/2966)/SCHEDULE 2 Modifications/Part I The Factories Act 1961

Part I

TheFactories Act 1961

. . .

NOTES

Amendment

This Part amends the Factories Act 1961, s 30(6).

UK Parliament SIs 1990-1999/1992/2951-3000/Personal Protective Equipment at Work Regulations 1992 (SI

1992/2966)/SCHEDULE 2 Modifications/Part II The Coal and Other Mines (Fire and Rescue) Order 1956

Part II

The Coal and Other Mines (Fire and Rescue) Order 1956

. . .

NOTES

Amendment

This Part amends SI 1956/1768, Sch 1, regs 23(a), (b), 24(a).

UK Parliament SIs 1990-1999/1992/2951-3000/Personal Protective Equipment at Work Regulations 1992 (SI 1992/2966)/SCHEDULE 2 Modifications/Part III The Shipbuilding and Ship-Repairing Regulations 1960

Part III

The Shipbuilding and Ship-Repairing Regulations 1960

. . .

NOTES

Amendment

This Part amends SI 1960/1932, regs 50, 51(1), 60(1).

UK Parliament SIs 1990-1999/1992/2951-3000/Personal Protective Equipment at Work Regulations 1992 (SI 1992/2966)/SCHEDULE 2 Modifications/Part IV . . .

Part IV

. . .

NOTES

Amendment

Revoked by SI 2007/1894, reg 14(3).

Date in force: 1 October 2007: see SI 2007/1894, reg 1.

. . .

NOTES

Amendment

Revoked by SI 2007/1894, reg 14(3).

Date in force: 1 October 2007: see SI 2007/1894, reg 1.

UK Parliament SIs 1990-1999/1992/2951-3000/Personal Protective Equipment at Work Regulations 1992 (SI 1992/2966)/SCHEDULE 2 Modifications/Part V The Control of Lead at Work Regulations 1980

Part V

The Control of Lead at Work Regulations 1980

. . .

NOTES

Amendment

This Part amends SI 1980/1248, regs 7, 8, 9, 18 and inserts regs 8A, 8B, 13(3).

UK Parliament SIs 1990-1999/1992/2951-3000/Personal Protective Equipment at Work Regulations 1992 (SI 1992/2966)/SCHEDULE 2 Modifications/Part VI . . .

Part VI

. . .

NOTES

Amendment

Revoked by SI 1999/3232, reg 41(2)(c).

Date in force: 1 January 2000: see SI 1999/3232, reg 1(a).

. . .

NOTES

Amendment

Revoked by SI 1999/3232, reg 41(2)(c).

Date in force: 1 January 2000: see SI 1999/3232, reg 1(a).

UK Parliament SIs 1990-1999/1992/2951-3000/Personal Protective Equipment at Work Regulations 1992 (SI 1992/2966)/SCHEDULE 2 Modifications/Part VII . . .

Part VII

. . .

NOTES

Amendment

Revoked by SI 2006/2739, reg 36(1), Sch 4.

Date in force: 13 November 2006: see SI 2006/2739, reg 1; for savings see reg 36(3) thereof.

. . .

NOTES

Amendment

Revoked by SI 2006/2739, reg 36(1), Sch 4.

Date in force: 13 November 2006: see SI 2006/2739, reg 1; for savings see reg 36(3) thereof.

UK Parliament SIs 1990-1999/1992/2951-3000/Personal Protective Equipment at Work Regulations 1992 (SI 1992/2966)/SCHEDULE 2 Modifications/Part VIII . . .

Part VIII

. . .

. . .

NOTES

Amendment

Revoked by SI 1994/3246.

UK Parliament SIs 1990-1999/1992/2951-3000/Personal Protective Equipment at Work Regulations 1992 (SI 1992/2966)/SCHEDULE 2 Modifications/Part IX The Noise at Work Regulations 1989

***Part* IX**

The Noise at Work Regulations 1989

NOTES

Amendment

Revoked by SI 2005/1643, reg 15(2), Sch 3.

Date in force (for certain purposes): 6 April 2006: see SI 2005/1643, reg 1.
Date in force (for remaining purposes): 6 April 2008: see SI 2005/1643, regs 1(a), 15(3).

. . .

NOTES

Amendment

Revoked by SI 2005/1643, reg 15(2), Sch 3.

Date in force (for certain purposes): 6 April 2006: see SI 2005/1643, reg 1.
Date in force (for remaining purposes): 6 April 2008: see SI 2005/1643, regs 1(a), 15(3).

This Part inserts SI 1989/1790, reg 8(3).

UK Parliament SIs 1990-1999/1992/2951-3000/Personal Protective Equipment at Work Regulations 1992 (SI 1992/2966)/SCHEDULE 2 Modifications/Part X The Construction (Head Protection) Regulations 1989

Part X

The Construction (Head Protection) Regulations 1989

. . .

NOTES

Amendment

This Part amends SI 1989/2209, regs 3, 6, 9.

UK Parliament SIs 1990-1999/1992/2951-3000/Personal Protective Equipment at Work Regulations 1992 (SI 1992/2966)/SCHEDULE 3 Revocations

SCHEDULE 3

REVOCATIONS

Regulation 14(3)

(1) *Title*	(2) *Reference*	(3) *Extent of Revocation*
Regulations dated 26th February 1906 in respect of the processes of spinning and weaving of flax and tow and the processes incidental thereto (the Flax and Tow-Spinning and Weaving Regulations 1906).	SR & O 1906/177, amended by SI 1988/1657.	In regulation 9, the words "unless waterproof skirts, and bibs of suitable material, are provided by the occupier and worn by the workers". Regulation 13.
Order dated 5th October 1917 (the Tin or Terne Plates Manufacture Welfare Order 1917).	SR & O 1917/1035.	Paragraph 1.
Order dated 15th August 1919 (the Fruit Preserving Welfare Order 1919).	SR & O 1919/1136, amended by SI 1988/1657.	Paragraph 1.
Order dated 23rd April 1920 (the Laundries Welfare Order 1920).	SR & O 1920/654.	Paragraph 1.
Order dated 28th July 1920 (the Gut-Scrapping, Tripe Dressing, etc Welfare Order 1920).	SR & O 1920/1437.	Paragraph 1.
Order dated 3rd March 1921 (the Glass Bevelling Welfare Order 1921).	SR & O 1921/288.	Paragraph 1.
The Aerated Water Regulations 1921.	SR & O 1921/1932; amended by SI 1981/686.	The whole Regulations.
The Sacks (Cleaning and Re-	SR & O 1927/860.	Paragraph 1.

pairing) Welfare Order 1927.		
The Oil Cake Welfare Order 1929.	SR & O 1929/534.	Paragraph 1.
The Cement Works Welfare Order 1930.	SR & O 1930/94.	Paragraph 1.
The Tanning Welfare Order 1930.	SR & O 1930/312.	Paragraph 1 and the Schedule.
The Magnesium (Grinding of Castings and Other Articles) Special Regulations 1946.	SR & O 1946/2107.	Regulation 12.
The Clay Works (Welfare) Special Regulations 1948.	SI 1948/1547.	Regulation 5.
The Iron and Steel Foundries Regulations 1953.	SI 1953/1464, amended by SI 1974/1681 and SI 1981/1332.	Regulation 8.
The Shipbuilding and Ship-Repairing Regulations 1960.	SI 1960/1932; amended by SI 1974/1681.	Regulations 73 and 74.
The Non-Ferrous Metals (Melting and Founding) Regulations 1962.	SI 1962/1667; amended by SI 1974/1681.	Regulation 13.
The Abstract of Special Regulations (Aerated Water) Order 1963.	SI 1963/2058.	The whole Order.
The Construction (Health and Welfare) Regulations 1966.	SI 1966/95; to which there are amendments not relevant to these regulations.	Regulation 15.
The Foundries (Protective Footwear and Gaiters) Regulations 1971.	SI 1971/476.	The whole Regulations.
The Protection of Eyes Regulations 1974.	SI 1974/1681; amended by SI 1975/303.	The whole Regulations.
The Aerated Water Regulations (Metrication) Regulations 1981.	SI 1981/686.	The whole Regulations.

UK Parliament SIs 1990-1999/1992/3001-3050/Workplace (Health, Safety and Welfare) Regulations 1992 (SI 1992/3004)

1992 No 3004

Workplace (Health, Safety and Welfare) Regulations 1992

Made - - - 1st December 1992

The Secretary of State, in exercise of the powers conferred on her by sections 15(1), (2), (3)(a) and (5)(b), and 82(3)(a) of, and paragraphs 1(2), 9 and 10 of Schedule 3 to, the Health and Safety at Work etc Act 1974("the 1974 Act") and of all other powers enabling her in that behalf and for the purpose of giving effect without modifications to proposals submitted to her by the Health and Safety Commission under section 11(2)(d) of the 1974 Act after the carrying out by the said Commission of consultations in accordance with section 50(3) of that Act, hereby makes the following Regulations:--

UK Parliament SIs 1990-1999/1992/3001-3050/Workplace (Health, Safety and Welfare) Regulations 1992 (SI 1992/3004)/1 Citation and commencement

1 Citation and commencement

(1) These Regulations may be cited as the Workplace (Health, Safety and Welfare) Regulations 1992.

(2) Subject to paragraph (3), these Regulations shall come into force on 1st January 1993.

(3) Regulations 5 to 27 and the Schedules shall come into force on 1st January 1996 with respect to any workplace or part of a workplace which is not

(a) a new workplace; or

(b) a modification, an extension or a conversion.

UK Parliament SIs 1990-1999/1992/3001-3050/Workplace (Health, Safety and Welfare) Regulations 1992 (SI 1992/3004)/2 Interpretation

2 Interpretation

(1) In these Regulations, unless the context otherwise requires--

["disabled person" has the meaning given by section 1 of the Disability Discrimination Act 1995;]

["mine" means a mine within the meaning of the Mines and Quarries Act 1954;]

"new workplace" means a workplace used for the first time as a workplace after 31st December 1992;

"public road" means (in England and Wales) a highway maintainable at public expense within the meaning of section 329 of the Highways Act 1980 and (in Scotland) a public road within the meaning assigned to that term by section 151 of the Roads (Scotland) Act 1984;

["quarry" means a quarry within the meaning of the Quarries Regulations 1999;]

"traffic route" means a route for pedestrian traffic, vehicles or both and includes any stairs, staircase, fixed ladder, doorway, gateway, loading bay or ramp;

"workplace" means, subject to paragraph (2), any premises or part of premises which are not domestic premises and are made available to any person as a place of work, and includes--

(a) any place within the premises to which such person has access while at work; and

(b) any room, lobby, corridor, staircase, road or other place used as a means of access to or egress from that place of work or where facilities are provided for use in connection with the place of work other than a public road;

. . ..

(2) Any reference in these Regulations, except in paragraph (1), to a modification, an extension or a conversion is a reference, as the case may be, to a modification, an extension or a conversion of a workplace started after 31st December 1992.

(3) Any requirement that anything done or provided in pursuance of these Regulations shall be suitable shall be construed to include a requirement that it is suitable for any person in respect of whom such thing is so done or provided.

(4) Any reference in these Regulations to--

(a) a numbered regulation or Schedule is a reference to the regulation in or Schedule to these Regulations so numbered; and

(b) a numbered paragraph is a reference to the paragraph so numbered in the regulation in which the reference appears.

NOTES

Amendment

Para (1): definition "disabled person" inserted by SI 2002/2174, reg 6(a).

Date in force: 17 September 2002: see SI 2002/2174, reg 1.

Para (1): definition "mine" inserted by SI 1995/2036, reg 11, Sch 3.

Date in force: 26 July 1998: see SI 1995/2036, reg 1(2).

Para (1): definition "quarry" substituted by SI 1999/2024, reg 48(2), Sch 5, Pt II.

Date in force: 1 January 2000: see SI 1999/2024, reg 1(1).

Para (1): in definition "workplace" words omitted revoked by SI 2002/2174, reg 6(b).

Date in force: 17 September 2002: see SI 2002/2174, reg 1.

UK Parliament SIs 1990-1999/1992/3001-3050/Workplace (Health, Safety and Welfare) Regulations 1992 (SI 1992/3004)/3 Application of these Regulations

3 Application of these Regulations

(1) These Regulations apply to every workplace but shall not apply to--

(a) a workplace which is or is in or on a ship within the meaning assigned to that word by regulation 2(1) of the Docks Regulations 1988;

[(b) a workplace which is a construction site within the meaning of the Construction (Design and Management) Regulations 2007, and in which the only activity being undertaken is construction work within the meaning of those regulations, save that--

(i) regulations 18 and 25A apply to such a workplace; and

(ii) regulations 7(1A), 12, 14, 15, 16, 18, 19 and 26(1) apply to such a workplace which is indoors] [or

(c) a workplace located below ground at a mine]

(d) . . .

(2) In their application to temporary work sites, any requirement to ensure a workplace complies with any of regulations 20 to 25 shall have effect as a requirement to so ensure so far as is reasonably practicable.

(3) As respects any workplace which is or is in or on an aircraft, locomotive or rolling stock, trailer or semi-trailer used as a means of transport or a vehicle for which a licence is in force under the Vehicles (Excise) Act 1971 or a vehicle exempted from duty under that Act--

(a) regulations 5 to 12 and 14 to 25 shall not apply to any such workplace; and

(b) regulation 13 shall apply to any such workplace only when the aircraft, locomotive or rolling stock, trailer or semi-trailer or vehicle is stationary inside a workplace and, in the case of a vehicle for which a licence is in force under the Vehicles (Excise) Act 1971, is not on a public road.

(4) As respects any workplace which is in fields, woods or other land forming part of an agricultural or forestry undertaking but which is not inside a building and is situated away from the undertaking's main buildings--

(a) regulations 5 to 19 and 23 to 25 shall not apply to any such workplace; and

(b) any requirement to ensure that any such workplace complies with any of regulations 20 to 22 shall have effect as a requirement to so ensure so far as is reasonably practicable.

[(5) As respects any workplace which is at a quarry or above ground at a mine regulation 12 shall only apply to a floor or traffic route which is located inside a building.]

NOTES

Amendment

Para (1): sub-para (b) substituted by virtue of SI 2007/320, reg 48(2), Sch 5.

Date in force: 6 April 2007: see SI 2007/320, reg 1.

Para (1): sub-para (c) substituted by SI 1995/2036, reg 11, Sch 3.

Date in force: 26 July 1998: see SI 1995/2036, reg 1(2).

Para (1): sub-para (d) revoked by SI 1995/2036, reg 11, Sch 3.

Date in force: 26 July 1998: see SI 1995/2036, reg 1(2).

Para (5): inserted by SI 1995/2036, reg 11, Sch 3.

Date in force: 26 July 1998: see SI 1995/2036, reg 1(2).

UK Parliament SIs 1990-1999/1992/3001-3050/Workplace (Health, Safety and Welfare) Regulations 1992 (SI 1992/3004)/4 Requirements under these Regulations

4 Requirements under these Regulations

(1) Every employer shall ensure that every workplace, modification, extension or conversion which is under his control and where any of his employees works complies with any requirement of these Regulations which--

(a) applies to that workplace or, as the case may be, to the workplace which contains that modification, extension or conversion; and

(b) is in force in respect of the workplace, modification, extension or conversion.

(2) Subject to paragraph (4), every person who has, to any extent, control of a workplace, modification, extension or conversion shall ensure that such workplace, modification, extension or conversion complies with any requirement of these Regulations which--

(a) applies to that workplace or, as the case may be, to the workplace which contains that modification, extension or conversion;

(b) is in force in respect of the workplace, modification, extension, or conversion; and

(c) relates to matters within that person's control.

(3) Any reference in this regulation to a person having control of any workplace, modification, extension or conversion is a reference to a person having control of the workplace, modification, extension or conversion in connection with the carrying on by him of a trade, business or other undertaking (whether for profit or not).

(4) Paragraph (2) shall not impose any requirement upon a self-employed person in respect of his own work or the work of any partner of his in the undertaking.

(5) Every person who is deemed to be the occupier of a factory by virtue of section 175(5) of the Factories Act 1961 shall ensure that the premises which are so deemed to be a factory comply with these Regulations.

UK Parliament SIs 1990-1999/1992/3001-3050/Workplace (Health, Safety and Welfare) Regulations 1992 (SI 1992/3004)/[4A Stability and solidity]

[4A Stability and solidity]

[Where a workplace is in a building, the building shall have a stability and solidity appropriate to the nature of the use of the workplace.]

NOTES

Amendment

Inserted by SI 2002/2174, reg 6(c).

Date in force: 17 September 2002: see SI 2002/2174, reg 1.

UK Parliament SIs 1990-1999/1992/3001-3050/Workplace (Health, Safety and Welfare) Regulations 1992 (SI 1992/3004)/5 Maintenance of workplace, and of equipment, devices and systems

5 Maintenance of workplace, and of equipment, devices and systems

(1) The workplace and the equipment, devices and systems to which this regulation applies shall be maintained (including cleaned as appropriate) in an efficient state, in efficient working order and in good repair.

(2) Where appropriate, the equipment, devices and systems to which this regulation applies shall be subject to a suitable system of maintenance.

(3) The equipment, devices and systems to which this regulation applies are--

(a) equipment and devices a fault in which is liable to result in a failure to comply with any of these Regulations; . . .

(b) mechanical ventilation systems provided pursuant to regulation 6 (whether or not they include equipment or devices within sub-paragraph (a) of this paragraph); [and]

[(c) equipment and devices intended to prevent or reduce hazards].

NOTES

Amendment

Para (3): in sub-para (a) word omitted revoked by SI 2002/2174, reg 6(d)(i).

Date in force: 17 September 2002: see SI 2002/2174, reg 1.

Para (3): in sub-para (b) word "and" in square brackets inserted by SI 2002/2174, reg 6(d)(ii).

Date in force: 17 September 2002: see SI 2002/2174, reg 1.

Para (3): sub-para (c) inserted by SI 2002/2174, reg 6(d)(iii).

Date in force: 17 September 2002: see SI 2002/2174, reg 1.

UK Parliament SIs 1990-1999/1992/3001-3050/Workplace (Health, Safety and Welfare) Regulations 1992 (SI 1992/3004)/6 Ventilation

6 Ventilation

(1) Effective and suitable provision shall be made to ensure that every enclosed workplace is ventilated by a sufficient quantity of fresh or purified air.

(2) Any plant used for the purpose of complying with paragraph (1) shall include an effective device to

give visible or audible warning of any failure of the plant where necessary for reasons of health or safety.

(3) . . .

NOTES

Amendment

Para (3): revoked by SI 2002/2174, reg 6(e).

Date in force: 17 September 2002: see SI 2002/2174, reg 1.

UK Parliament SIs 1990-1999/1992/3001-3050/Workplace (Health, Safety and Welfare) Regulations 1992 (SI 1992/3004)/7 Temperature in indoor workplaces

7 Temperature in indoor workplaces

(1) During working hours, the temperature in all workplaces inside buildings shall be reasonable.

[(1A) Without prejudice to the generality of paragraph (1)--

(a) a workplace shall be adequately thermally insulated where it is necessary, having regard to the type of work carried out and the physical activity of the persons carrying out the work; and

(b) excessive effects of sunlight on temperature shall be avoided.]

(2) A method of heating or cooling shall not be used which results in the escape into a workplace of fumes, gas or vapour of such character and to such extent that they are likely to be injurious or offensive to any person.

(3) A sufficient number of thermometers shall be provided to enable persons at work to determine the temperature in any workplace inside a building.

NOTES

Amendment

Para (1A): inserted by SI 2002/2174, reg 6(f).

Date in force: 17 September 2002: see SI 2002/2174, reg 1.

UK Parliament SIs 1990-1999/1992/3001-3050/Workplace (Health, Safety and Welfare) Regulations 1992 (SI 1992/3004)/8 Lighting

8 Lighting

(1) Every workplace shall have suitable and sufficient lighting.

(2) The lighting mentioned in paragraph (1) shall, so far as is reasonably practicable, be by natural light.

(3) Without prejudice to the generality of paragraph (1), suitable and sufficient emergency lighting shall be provided in any room in circumstances in which persons at work are specially exposed to danger in the event of failure of artificial lighting.

UK Parliament SIs 1990-1999/1992/3001-3050/Workplace (Health, Safety and Welfare) Regulations 1992 (SI 1992/3004)/9 Cleanliness and waste materials

9 Cleanliness and waste materials

(1) Every workplace and the furniture, furnishings and fittings therein shall be kept sufficiently clean.

(2) The surfaces of the floors, walls and ceilings of all workplaces inside buildings shall be capable of being kept sufficiently clean.

(3) So far as is reasonably practicable, waste materials shall not be allowed to accumulate in a workplace except in suitable receptacles.

UK Parliament SIs 1990-1999/1992/3001-3050/Workplace (Health, Safety and Welfare) Regulations 1992 (SI 1992/3004)/10 Room dimensions and space

10 Room dimensions and space

(1) Every room where persons work shall have sufficient floor area, height and unoccupied space for purposes of health, safety and welfare.

(2) It shall be sufficient compliance with this regulation in a workplace which is not a new workplace, a modification, an extension or a conversion and which, immediately before this regulation came into force in respect of it, was subject to the provisions of the Factories Act 1961, if the workplace does not contravene the provisions of Part I of Schedule 1.

UK Parliament SIs 1990-1999/1992/3001-3050/Workplace (Health, Safety and Welfare) Regulations 1992 (SI 1992/3004)/11 Workstations and seating

11 Workstations and seating

(1) Every workstation shall be so arranged that it is suitable both for any person at work in the workplace who is likely to work at that workstation and for any work of the undertaking which is likely to be done there.

(2) Without prejudice to the generality of paragraph (1), every workstation outdoors shall be so arranged that--

(a) so far as is reasonably practicable, it provides protection from adverse weather;

(b) it enables any person at the workstation to leave it swiftly or, as appropriate, to be assisted in the event of an emergency; and

(c) it ensures that any person at the workstation is not likely to slip or fall.

(3) A suitable seat shall be provided for each person at work in the workplace whose work includes operations of a kind that the work (or a substantial part of it) can or must be done sitting.

(4) A seat shall not be suitable for the purpose of paragraph (3) unless--

(a) it is suitable for the person for whom it is provided as well as for the operations to be performed; and

(b) a suitable footrest is also provided where necessary.

UK Parliament SIs 1990-1999/1992/3001-3050/Workplace (Health, Safety and Welfare) Regulations 1992 (SI 1992/3004)/12 Condition of floors and traffic routes

12 Condition of floors and traffic routes

(1) Every floor in a workplace and the surface of every traffic route in a workplace shall be of a construction such that the floor or surface of the traffic route is suitable for the purpose for which it is used.

(2) Without prejudice to the generality of paragraph (1), the requirements in that paragraph shall include requirements that--

(a) the floor, or surface of the traffic route, shall have no hole or slope, or be uneven or slippery so as, in each case, to expose any person to a risk to his health or safety; and

(b) every such floor shall have effective means of drainage where necessary.

(3) So far as is reasonably practicable, every floor in a workplace and the surface of every traffic route in a workplace shall be kept free from obstructions and from any article or substance which may cause a person to slip, trip or fall.

(4) In considering whether for the purposes of paragraph (2)(a) a hole or slope exposes any person to a risk to his health or safety--

(a) no account shall be taken of a hole where adequate measures have been taken to prevent a person falling; and

(b) account shall be taken of any handrail provided in connection with any slope.

(5) Suitable and sufficient handrails and, if appropriate, guards shall be provided on all traffic routes which are staircases except in circumstances in which a handrail can not be provided without obstructing the traffic route.

UK Parliament SIs 1990-1999/1992/3001-3050/Workplace (Health, Safety and Welfare) Regulations 1992 (SI 1992/3004)/13 Falls or failing objects

13 Falls or failing objects

(1) . . .

(2) . . .

(3) . . .

(4) . . .

(5) So far as is practicable, every tank, pit or structure where there is a risk of a person in the workplace falling into a dangerous substance in the tank, pit or structure, shall be securely covered or fenced.

(6) Every traffic route over, across or in an uncovered tank, pit or structure such as is mentioned in paragraph (5) shall be securely fenced.

(7) In this regulation, "dangerous substance" means--

(a) any substance likely to scald or burn;

(b) any poisonous substance;

(c) any corrosive substance;

(d) any fume, gas or vapour likely to overcome a person; or

(e) any granular or free-flowing solid substance, or any viscous substance which, in any case, is of a nature or quantity which is likely to cause danger to any person.

NOTES

Amendment

Paras (1)-(4): revoked by SI 2005/735, reg 19, Sch 8.

Date in force: 6 April 2005: see SI 2005/735, reg 1.

UK Parliament SIs 1990-1999/1992/3001-3050/Workplace (Health, Safety and Welfare) Regulations 1992 (SI 1992/3004)/14 Windows, and transparent or translucent doors, gates and walls

14 Windows, and transparent or translucent doors, gates and walls

(1) Every window or other transparent or translucent surface in a wall or partition and every transparent or translucent surface in a door or gate shall, where necessary for reasons of health or safety--

(a) be of safety material or be protected against breakage of the transparent or translucent material; and

(b) be appropriately marked or incorporate features so as, in either case, to make it apparent.

UK Parliament SIs 1990-1999/1992/3001-3050/Workplace (Health, Safety and Welfare) Regulations 1992 (SI 1992/3004)/15 Windows, skylights and ventilators

15 Windows, skylights and ventilators

(1) No window, skylight or ventilator which is capable of being opened shall be likely to be opened, closed or adjusted in a manner which exposes any person performing such operation to a risk to his health or safety.

(2) No window, skylight or ventilator shall be in a position when open which is likely to expose any person in the workplace to a risk to his health or safety.

UK Parliament SIs 1990-1999/1992/3001-3050/Workplace (Health, Safety and Welfare) Regulations 1992 (SI 1992/3004)/16 Ability to clean windows etc safely

16 Ability to clean windows etc safely

(1) All windows and skylights in a workplace shall be of a design or be so constructed that they may be cleaned safely.

(2) In considering whether a window or skylight is of a design or so constructed as to comply with paragraph (1), account may be taken of equipment used in conjunction with the window or skylight or of devices fitted to the building.

UK Parliament SIs 1990-1999/1992/3001-3050/Workplace (Health, Safety and Welfare) Regulations 1992 (SI 1992/3004)/17 Organisation etc of traffic routes

17 Organisation etc of traffic routes

(1) Every workplace shall be organised in such a way that pedestrians and vehicles can circulate in a safe manner.

(2) Traffic routes in a workplace shall be suitable for the persons or vehicles using them, sufficient in number, in suitable positions and of sufficient size.

(3) Without prejudice to the generality of paragraph (2), traffic routes shall not satisfy the requirements of that paragraph unless suitable measures are taken to ensure that--

(a) pedestrians or, as the case may be, vehicles may use a traffic route without causing danger to the health or safety of persons at work near it;

(b) there is sufficient separation of any traffic route for vehicles from doors or gates or from traffic routes for pedestrians which lead onto it; and

(c) where vehicles and pedestrians use the same traffic route, there is sufficient separation between them.

(4) All traffic routes shall be suitably indicated where necessary for reasons of health or safety.

(5) Paragraph (2) shall apply so far as is reasonably practicable, to a workplace which is not a new workplace, a modification, an extension or a conversion.

UK Parliament SIs 1990-1999/1992/3001-3050/Workplace (Health, Safety and Welfare) Regulations 1992 (SI 1992/3004)/18 Doors and gates

18 Doors and gates

(1) Doors and gates shall be suitably constructed (including being fitted with any necessary safety devices).

(2) Without prejudice to the generality of paragraph (1), doors and gates shall not comply with that paragraph unless--

(a) any sliding door or gate has a device to prevent it coming off its track during use;

(b) any upward opening door or gate has a device to prevent it falling back;

(c) any powered door or gate has suitable and effective features to prevent it causing injury by trapping any person;

(d) where necessary for reasons of health or safety, any powered door or gate can be operated manually unless it opens automatically if the power fails; and

(e) any door or gate which is capable of opening by being pushed from either side is of such a construction as to provide, when closed, a clear view of the space close to both sides.

UK Parliament SIs 1990-1999/1992/3001-3050/Workplace (Health, Safety and Welfare) Regulations 1992 (SI 1992/3004)/19 Escalators and moving walkways

19 Escalators and moving walkways

Escalators and moving walkways shall:--

(a) function safely;

(b) be equipped with any necessary safety devices;

(c) be fitted with one or more emergency stop controls which are easily identifiable and readily accessible.

UK Parliament SIs 1990-1999/1992/3001-3050/Workplace (Health, Safety and Welfare) Regulations 1992 (SI 1992/3004)/20 Sanitary conveniences

20 Sanitary conveniences

(1) Suitable and sufficient sanitary conveniences shall be provided at readily accessible places.

(2) Without prejudice to the generality of paragraph (1), sanitary conveniences shall not be suitable unless--

(a) the rooms containing them are adequately ventilated and lit;

(b) they and the rooms containing them are kept in a clean and orderly condition; and

(c) separate rooms containing conveniences are provided for men and women except where and so far as each convenience is in a separate room the door of which is capable of being secured from inside.

(3) It shall be sufficient compliance with the requirement in paragraph (1) to provide sufficient sanitary conveniences in a workplace which is not a new workplace, a modification, an extension or a conversion and which, immediately before this regulation came into force in respect of it, was subject to the provisions of the Factories Act 1961, if sanitary conveniences are provided in accordance with the provisions of Part II of Schedule 1.

UK Parliament SIs 1990-1999/1992/3001-3050/Workplace (Health, Safety and Welfare) Regulations 1992 (SI 1992/3004)/21 Washing facilities

21 Washing facilities

(1) Suitable and sufficient washing facilities, including showers if required by the nature of the work or for health reasons, shall be provided at readily accessible places.

(2) Without prejudice to the generality of paragraph (1), washing facilities shall not be suitable unless--

(a) they are provided in the immediate vicinity of every sanitary convenience, whether or not provided elsewhere as well;

(b) they are provided in the vicinity of any changing rooms required by these Regulations, whether or not provided elsewhere as well;

(c) they include a supply of clean hot and cold, or warm, water (which shall be running water so far as is practicable);

(d) they include soap or other suitable means of cleaning;

(e) they include towels or other suitable means of drying;

(f) the rooms containing them are sufficiently ventilated and lit:

(g) they and the rooms containing them are kept in a clean and orderly condition; and

(h) separate facilities are provided for men and women, except where and so far as they are provided in a room the door of which is capable of being secured from inside and the facilities in each such room are intended to be used by only one person at a time.

(3) Paragraph (2)(h) shall not apply to facilities which are provided for washing hands, forearms and face only.

UK Parliament SIs 1990-1999/1992/3001-3050/Workplace (Health, Safety and Welfare) Regulations 1992 (SI 1992/3004)/22 Drinking water

22 Drinking water

(1) An adequate supply of wholesome drinking water shall be provided for all persons at work in the workplace.

(2) Every supply of drinking water required by paragraph (1) shall--

(a) be readily accessible at suitable places; and

(b) be conspicuously marked by an appropriate sign where necessary for reasons of health or safety.

(3) Where a supply of drinking water is required by paragraph (1), there shall also be provided a sufficient number of suitable cups or other drinking vessels unless the supply of drinking water is in a jet from which persons can drink easily.

UK Parliament SIs 1990-1999/1992/3001-3050/Workplace (Health, Safety and Welfare) Regulations 1992 (SI 1992/3004)/23 Accommodation for clothing

23 Accommodation for clothing

(1) Suitable and sufficient accommodation shall be provided--

(a) for the clothing of any person at work which is not worn during working hours; and

(b) for special clothing which is worn by any person at work but which is not taken home.

(2) Without prejudice to the generality of paragraph (1), the accommodation mentioned in that paragraph shall not be suitable unless--

(a) where facilities to change clothing are required by regulation 24, it provides suitable security for the clothing mentioned in paragraph (1)(a);

(b) where necessary to avoid risks to health or damage to the clothing, it includes separate accommodation for clothing worn at work and for other clothing;

(c) so far as is reasonably practicable, it allows or includes facilities for drying clothing; and

(d) it is in a suitable location.

UK Parliament SIs 1990-1999/1992/3001-3050/Workplace (Health, Safety and Welfare) Regulations 1992 (SI 1992/3004)/24 Facilities for changing clothing

24 Facilities for changing clothing

(1) Suitable and sufficient facilities shall be provided for any person at work in the workplace to change clothing in all cases where--

(a) the person has to wear special clothing for the purpose of work; and

(b) the person can not, for reasons of health or propriety, be expected to change in another room.

(2) Without prejudice to the generality of paragraph (1), the facilities mentioned in that paragraph shall not be suitable unless they include separate facilities for, or separate use of facilities by, men and women where necessary for reasons of propriety [and the facilities are easily accessible, of sufficient capacity and provided with seating].

NOTES

Amendment

Para (2): words "and the facilities are easily accessible, of sufficient capacity and provided with seating" in square brackets inserted by SI 2002/2174, reg 6(g).

Date in force: 17 September 2002: see SI 2002/2174, reg 1.

UK Parliament SIs 1990-1999/1992/3001-3050/Workplace (Health, Safety and Welfare) Regulations 1992 (SI 1992/3004)/25 Facilities for rest and to eat meals

25 Facilities for rest and to eat meals

(1) Suitable and sufficient rest facilities shall be provided at readily accessible places.

(2) Rest facilities provided by virtue of paragraph (1) shall--

(a) where necessary for reasons of health or safety include, in the case of a new workplace an extension or a conversion, rest facilities provided in one or more rest rooms, or, in other cases, in rest rooms or rest areas;

UK Parliament SIs 1990-1999/1998/2301-2350/Provision and Use of Work Equipment Regulations 1998 (SI 1998/2306)

1998 No 2306

HEALTH AND SAFETY

Provision and Use of Work Equipment Regulations 1998

Made 15th September 1998

Laid before Parliament 25th September 1998

Coming into force 5th December 1998

The Secretary of State, in the exercise of the powers conferred on him by sections 15(1), (2), (3)(a), (5) and (6)(a), 49 and 82(3)(a) of, and paragraphs 1(1), (2) and (3), 9, 14, 15(1) and 16 of Schedule 3 to, the Health and Safety at Work etc Act 1974 ("the 1974 Act") and of all other powers enabling him in that behalf and for the purpose of giving effect without modifications to proposals submitted to him by the Health and Safety Commission under section 11(2)(d) of the 1974 Act, after the carrying out by the said Commission of consultations in accordance with section 50(3) of that Act, hereby makes the following Regulations:

UK Parliament SIs 1990-1999/1998/2301-2350/Provision and Use of Work Equipment Regulations 1998 (SI 1998/2306)/Part I Introduction/1 Citation and commencement

Part I

Introduotion

1 Citation and commencement

These Regulations may be cited as the Provision and Use of Work Equipment Regulations 1998 and shall como into force on 5th December 1998.

NOTES

Initial Commencement

Specified date

Specified date: 5 December 1998: see above.

UK Parliament SIs 1990-1999/1998/2301-2350/Provision and Use of Work Equipment Regulations 1998 (SI 1998/2306)/Part I Introduction/2 Interpretation

2 Interpretation

(1) In these Regulations, unless the context otherwise requires--

"the 1974 Act" means the Health and Safety at Work etc Act 1974;

"employer" except in regulation 3(2) and (3) includes a person to whom the requirements imposed by these Regulations apply by virtue of regulation 3(3)(a) and (b);

"essential requirements" means requirements described in regulation 10(1);

"the Executive" means the Health and Safety Executive;

"inspection" in relation to an inspection under paragraph (1) or (2) of regulation 6--

(a) means such visual or more rigorous inspection by a competent person as is appropriate for the purpose described in the paragraph;

(b) where it is appropriate to carry out testing for the purpose, includes testing the nature and extent of which are appropriate for the purpose;

"power press" means a press or press brake for the working of metal by means of tools, or for die proving, which is power driven and which embodies a flywheel and clutch;

"thorough examination" in relation to a thorough examination under paragraph (1), (2), (3) or (4) of regulation 32--

(a) means a thorough examination by a competent person;

(b) includes testing the nature and extent of which are appropriate for the purpose described in the paragraph;

"use" in relation to work equipment means any activity involving work equipment and includes starting, stopping, programming, setting, transporting, repairing, modifying, maintaining, servicing and cleaning;

"work equipment" means any machinery, appliance, apparatus, tool or installation for use at work (whether exclusively or not);

and related expressions shall be construed accordingly.

(2) Any reference in regulations 32 to 34 or Schedule 3 to a guard or protection device is a reference to a guard or protection device provided for the tools of a power press.

(3) Any reference in regulation 32 or 33 to a guard or protection device being on a power press shall, in the case of a guard or protection device designed to operate while adjacent to a power press, be construed as a reference to its being adjacent to it.

(4) Any reference in these Regulations to--

(a) a numbered regulation or Schedule is a reference to the regulation or Schedule in these Regulations so numbered; and

(b) a numbered paragraph is a reference to the paragraph so numbered in the regulation in which the reference appears.

NOTES

Initial Commencement

Specified date

Specified date: 5 December 1998: see reg 1.

UK Parliament SIs 1990-1999/1998/2301-2350/Provision and Use of Work Equipment Regulations 1998 (SI 1998/2306)/Part I Introduction/3 Application

3 Application

(1) These Regulations shall apply--

(a) in Great Britain; and

(b) outside Great Britain as sections 1 to 59 and 80 to 82 of the 1974 Act apply by virtue of the Health and Safety at Work etc Act 1974 (Application outside Great Britain) Order 1995 ("the 1995 Order")

(2) The requirements imposed by these Regulations on an employer in respect of work equipment shall apply to such equipment provided for use or used by an employee of his at work.

(3) The requirements imposed by these Regulations on an employer shall also apply--

(a) to a self-employed person, in respect of work equipment he uses at work;

(b) subject to paragraph (5), to a person who has control to any extent of--

(i) work equipment;

(ii) a person at work who uses or supervises or manages the use of work equipment; or

(iii) the way in which work equipment is used at work,

and to the extent of his control.

(4) Any reference in paragraph (3)(b) to a person having control is a reference to a person having control in connection with the carrying on by him of a trade, business or other undertaking (whether for profit or not).

(5) The requirements imposed by these Regulations shall not apply to a person in respect of work equipment supplied by him by way of sale, agreement for sale or hire-purchase agreement.

(6) Subject to paragraphs (7) to (10), these Regulations shall not impose any obligation in relation to a ship's work equipment (whether that equipment is used on or off the ship)

(7) Where merchant shipping requirements are applicable to a ship's work equipment, paragraph (6) shall relieve the shore employer of his obligations under these Regulations in respect of that equipment only where he has taken all reasonable steps to satisfy himself that the merchant shipping requirements are being complied with in respect of that equipment.

(8) In a case where the merchant shipping requirements are not applicable to the ship's work equipment by reason only that for the time being there is no master, crew or watchman on the ship, those requirements shall nevertheless be treated for the purpose of paragraph (7) as if they were applicable.

(9) Where the ship's work equipment is used in a specified operation paragraph (6) shall not apply to regulations 7 to 9, 11 to 13, 20 to 22 and 30 (each as applied by regulation 3).

(10) Paragraph (6) does not apply to a ship's work equipment provided for use or used in an activity (whether carried on in or outside Great Britain) specified in the 1995 Order save that it does apply to--

(a) the loading, unloading, fuelling or provisioning of the ship; or

(b) the construction, reconstruction, finishing, refitting, repair, maintenance, cleaning or breaking up of the ship.

(11) In this regulation--

"master" has the meaning assigned to it by section 313(1) of the Merchant Shipping Act 1995;

"merchant shipping requirements" means the requirements of regulations 3 and 4 of the Merchant Shipping (Guarding of Machinery and Safety of Electrical Equipment) Regulations 1988 and regulations 5 to 10 of the Merchant Shipping (Hatches and Lifting Plant) Regulations 1988;

"ship" has the meaning assigned to it by section 313(1) of the Merchant Shipping Act 1995 save that it does not include an offshore installation;

"shore employer" means an employer of persons (other than the master and crew of any ship) who are engaged in a specified operation;

"specified operation" means an operation in which the ship's work equipment is used--

(a) by persons other than the master and crew; or

(b) where persons other than the master and crew are liable to be exposed to a risk to their health or safety from its use.

NOTES

Initial Commencement

Specified date

Specified date: 5 December 1998: see reg 1.

UK Parliament SIs 1990-1999/1998/2301-2350/Provision and Use of Work Equipment Regulations 1998 (SI 1998/2306)/Part II General/4 Suitability of work equipment

Part II

General

4 Suitability of work equipment

(1) Every employer shall ensure that work equipment is so constructed or adapted as to be suitable for the purpose for which it is used or provided.

(2) In selecting work equipment, every employer shall have regard to the working conditions and to the risks to the health and safety of persons which exist in the premises or undertaking in which that work equipment is to be used and any additional risk posed by the use of that work equipment.

(3) Every employer shall ensure that work equipment is used only for operations for which, and under conditions for which, it is suitable.

[(4) In this regulation "suitable"--

(a) subject to sub-paragraph (b), means suitable in any respect which it is reasonably foreseeable will affect the health or safety of any person;

(b) in relation to--

(i) an offensive weapon within the meaning of section 1(4) of the Prevention of Crime Act 1953 provided for use as self-defence or as deterrent equipment; and

(ii) work equipment provided for use for arrest or restraint,

by a person who holds the office of constable or an appointment as police cadet, means suitable in any respect which it is reasonably foreseeable will affect the health or safety of such person.]

NOTES

Initial Commencement

Specified date

Specified date: 5 December 1998: see reg 1.

Amendment

Para (4): substituted by SI 1999/860, reg 5(1).

Date in force: 14 April 1999: see SI 1999/860, reg 1.

UK Parliament SIs 1990-1999/1998/2301-2350/Provision and Use of Work Equipment Regulations 1998 (SI 1998/2306)/Part II General/5 Maintenance

5 Maintenance

(1) Every employer shall ensure that work equipment is maintained in an efficient state, in efficient working order and in good repair.

(2) Every employer shall ensure that where any machinery has a maintenance log, the log is kept up to date.

NOTES

Initial Commencement

Specified date

Specified date: 5 December 1998: see reg 1.

UK Parliament SIs 1990-1999/1998/2301-2350/Provision and Use of Work Equipment Regulations 1998 (SI 1998/2306)/Part II General/6 Inspection

6 Inspection

(1) Every employer shall ensure that, where the safety of work equipment depends on the installation conditions, it is inspected--

(a) after installation and before being put into service for the first time; or

(b) after assembly at a new site or in a new location,

to ensure that it has been installed correctly and is safe to operate.

(2) Every employer shall ensure that work equipment exposed to conditions causing deterioration which is liable to result in dangerous situations is inspected--

(a) at suitable intervals; and

(b) each time that exceptional circumstances which are liable to jeopardise the safety of the work equipment have occurred,

to ensure that health and safety conditions are maintained and that any deterioration can be detected and remedied in good time.

(3) Every employer shall ensure that the result of an inspection made under this regulation is recorded and kept until the next inspection under this regulation is recorded.

(4) Every employer shall ensure that no work equipment--

(a) leaves his undertaking; or

(b) if obtained from the undertaking of another person, is used in his undertaking,

unless it is accompanied by physical evidence that the last inspection required to be carried out under this regulation has been carried out.

(5) This regulation does not apply to--

(a) a power press to which regulations 32 to 35 apply;

(b) a guard or protection device for the tools of such power press;

(c) work equipment for lifting loads including persons;

(d) winding apparatus to which the Mines (Shafts and Winding) Regulations 1993 apply;

(e) work equipment required to be inspected by [regulations 31(4) or 32(2) of the Construction (Design and Management) Regulations 2007];

[(f) work equipment to which regulation 12 of the Work at Height Regulations 2005 applies].

NOTES

Initial Commencement

Specified date

Specified date: 5 December 1998: see reg 1.

Amendment

Para (5): in sub-para (e) words "regulations 31(4) or 32(2) of the Construction (Design and Management) Regulations 2007" in square brackets substituted by SI 2007/320, reg 48(2), Sch 5.

Date in force: 6 April 2007: see SI 2007/320, reg 1.

Para (5): sub-para (f) inserted by SI 2005/735, reg 17.

Date in force: 6 April 2005: see SI 2005/735, reg 1.

UK Parliament SIs 1990-1999/1998/2301-2350/Provision and Use of Work Equipment Regulations 1998 (SI 1998/2306)/Part II General/7 Specific risks

7 Specific risks

(1) Where the use of work equipment is likely to involve a specific risk to health or safety, every employer shall ensure that--

(a) the use of that work equipment is restricted to those persons given the task of using it; and

(b) repairs, modifications, maintenance or servicing of that work equipment is restricted to those persons who have been specifically designated to perform operations of that description (whether or not also authorised to perform other operations).

(2) The employer shall ensure that the persons designated for the purposes of sub-paragraph (b) of paragraph (1) have received adequate training related to any operations in respect of which they have been so designated.

NOTES

Initial Commencement

Specified date

Specified date: 5 December 1998: see reg 1.

UK Parliament SIs 1990-1999/1998/2301-2350/Provision and Use of Work Equipment Regulations 1998 (SI 1998/2306)/Part II General/8 Information and instructions

8 Information and instructions

(1) Every employer shall ensure that all persons who use work equipment have available to them adequate health and safety information and, where appropriate, written instructions pertaining to the use of the work equipment.

(2) Every employer shall ensure that any of his employees who supervises or manages the use of work equipment has available to him adequate health and safety information and, where appropriate, written instructions pertaining to the use of the work equipment.

(3) Without prejudice to the generality of paragraphs (1) or (2), the information and instructions required by either of those paragraphs shall include information and, where appropriate, written instructions on--

(a) the conditions in which and the methods by which the work equipment may be used;

(b) foreseeable abnormal situations and the action to be taken if such a situation were to occur; and

(c) any conclusions to be drawn from experience in using the work equipment.

(4) Information and instructions required by this regulation shall be readily comprehensible to those concerned.

NOTES

Initial Commencement

Specified date

Specified date: 5 December 1998: see reg 1.

UK Parliament SIs 1990-1999/1998/2301-2350/Provision and Use of Work Equipment Regulations 1998 (SI 1998/2306)/Part II General/9 Training

9 Training

(1) Every employer shall ensure that all persons who use work equipment have received adequate training for purposes of health and safety, including training in the methods which may be adopted when using the work equipment, any risks which such use may entail and precautions to be taken.

(2) Every employer shall ensure that any of his employees who supervises or manages the use of work equipment has received adequate training for purposes of health and safety, including training in the methods which may be adopted when using the work equipment, any risks which such use may entail and precautions to be taken.

NOTES

Initial Commencement

Specified date

Specified date: 5 December 1998: see reg 1.

UK Parliament SIs 1990-1999/1998/2301-2350/Provision and Use of Work Equipment Regulations 1998 (SI 1998/2306)/Part II General/10 Conformity with Community requirements

10 Conformity with Community requirements

[(1) Every employer shall ensure that an item of work equipment conforms at all times with any essential requirements, other than requirements which, at the time of its being first supplied or put into service in any place in which these Regulations apply, did not apply to work equipment of its type.

(2) In this regulation "essential requirements", in relation to an item of work equipment, means requirements relating to the design and construction of work equipment of its type in any of the instruments listed in Schedule 1 (being instruments which give effect to Community directives concerning the safety of products).]

(3) This regulation applies to items of work equipment provided for use in the premises or undertaking of the employer for the first time after 31st December 1992.

NOTES

Initial Commencement

Specified date

Specified date: 5 December 1998: see reg 1.

Amendment

Paras (1), (2): substituted by SI 2002/2174, reg 7(a).

Date in force: 17 September 2002: see SI 2002/2174, reg 1.

UK Parliament SIs 1990-1999/1998/2301-2350/Provision and Use of Work Equipment Regulations 1998 (SI 1998/2306)/Part II General/11 Dangerous parts of machinery

11 Dangerous parts of machinery

(1) Every employer shall ensure that measures are taken in accordance with paragraph (2) which are effective--

(a) to prevent access to any dangerous part of machinery or to any rotating stock-bar; or

(b) to stop the movement of any dangerous part of machinery or rotating stock-bar before any part of a person enters a danger zone.

[(2) The measures required by paragraph (1) shall consist of--

(a) the provision of fixed guards enclosing every dangerous part or rotating stock-bar where and to the extent that it is practicable to do so, but where or to the extent that it is not, then

(b) the provision of other guards or protection devices where and to the extent that it is practicable to do so, but where or to the extent that it is not, then

(c) the provision of jigs, holders, push-sticks or similar protection appliances used in conjunction with the machinery where and to the extent that it is practicable to do so,

and the provision of such information, instruction, training and supervision as is necessary.]

(3) All guards and protection devices provided under sub-paragraphs (a) or (b) of paragraph (2) shall--

(a) be suitable for the purpose for which they are provided;

(b) be of good construction, sound material and adequate strength;

(c) be maintained in an efficient state, in efficient working order and in good repair;

(d) not give rise to any increased risk to health or safety;

(e) not be easily bypassed or disabled;

(f) be situated at sufficient distance from the danger zone;

(g) not unduly restrict the view of the operating cycle of the machinery, where such a view is necessary;

(h) be so constructed or adapted that they allow operations necessary to fit or replace parts and for maintenance work, restricting access so that it is allowed only to the area where the work is to be carried out and, if possible, without having to dismantle the guard or protection device.

(4) All protection appliances provided under sub-paragraph (c) of paragraph (2) shall comply with sub-paragraphs (a) to (d) and (g) of paragraph (3).

(5) In this regulation--

"danger zone" means any zone in or around machinery in which a person is exposed to a risk to health or safety from contact with a dangerous part of machinery or a rotating stock-bar;

"stock-bar" means any part of a stock-bar which projects beyond the head-stock of a lathe.

NOTES

Initial Commencement

Specified date

Specified date: 5 December 1998: see reg 1.

Amendment

Para (2): substituted by SI 2002/2174, reg 7(b).

Date in force: 17 September 2002: see SI 2002/2174, reg 1.

UK Parliament SIs 1990-1999/1998/2301-2350/Provision and Use of Work Equipment Regulations 1998 (SI 1998/2306)/Part II General/12 Protection against specified hazards

12 Protection against specified hazards

(1) Every employer shall take measures to ensure that the exposure of a person using work equipment to any risk to his health or safety from any hazard specified in paragraph (3) is either prevented, or, where that is not reasonably practicable, adequately controlled.

(2) The measures required by paragraph (1) shall--

(a) be measures other than the provision of personal protective equipment or of information, instruction, training and supervision, so far as is reasonably practicable; and

(b) include, where appropriate, measures to minimise the effects of the hazard as well as to reduce the likelihood of the hazard occurring.

(3) The hazards referred to in paragraph (1) are--

(a) any article or substance falling or being ejected from work equipment;

(b) rupture or disintegration of parts of work equipment;

(c) work equipment catching fire or overheating;

(d) the unintended or premature discharge of any article or of any gas, dust, liquid, vapour or other substance which, in each case, is produced, used or stored in the work equipment;

(e) the unintended or premature explosion of the work equipment or any article or substance produced, used or stored in it.

(4) For the purposes of this regulation "adequately" means adequately having regard only to the nature of the hazard and the nature and degree of exposure to the risk.

(5) This regulation shall not apply where any of the following Regulations apply in respect of any risk to a person's health or safety for which such Regulations require measures to be taken to prevent or control such risk, namely--

(a) the Ionising Radiations Regulations 1985;

(b) [the Control of Asbestos Regulations 2006];

(c) the Control of Substances Hazardous to Health Regulations 1994;

(d) *the Noise at Work Regulations 1989* [the Control of Noise at Work Regulations 2005];

(e) the Construction (Head Protection) Regulations 1989;

(f) the Control of Lead at Work Regulations 1998;

[(g) the Control of Vibration at Work Regulations 2005].

NOTES

Initial Commencement

Specified date

Specified date: 5 December 1998: see reg 1.

Amendment

Para (5): in sub-para (b) words "the Control of Asbestos Regulations 2006" in square brackets substituted by SI 2006/2739, reg 36(2), Sch 5.

Date in force: 13 November 2006: see SI 2006/2739, reg 1.

Para (5): in sub-para (d) words "the Noise at Work Regulations 1989" in italics revoked and subsequent words in square brackets substituted by virtue of SI 2005/1643, reg 15(1)(b).

Date in force (for certain purposes): 6 April 2006: see SI 2005/1643, reg 1.
Date in force (for remaining purposes): 6 April 2008: see SI 2005/1643, regs 1(a), 15(3).

Para (5): sub-para (g) inserted by SI 2005/1093, reg 13(2).

Date in force: 6 July 2005: see SI 2005/1093, reg 1.

UK Parliament SIs 1990-1999/1998/2301-2350/Provision and Use of Work Equipment Regulations 1998 (SI 1998/2306)/Part II General/13 High or very low temperature

13 High or very low temperature

Every employer shall ensure that work equipment, parts of work equipment and any article or substance produced, used or stored in work equipment which, in each case, is at a high or very low temperature shall have protection where appropriate so as to prevent injury to any person by burn, scald or sear.

NOTES

Initial Commencement

Specified date

Specified date: 5 December 1998: see reg 1.

UK Parliament SIs 1990-1999/1998/2301-2350/Provision and Use of Work Equipment Regulations 1998 (SI

1998/2306)/Part II General/14 Controls for starting or making a significant change in operating conditions

14 Controls for starting or making a significant change in operating conditions

(1) Every employer shall ensure that, where appropriate, work equipment is provided with one or more controls for the purposes of--

(a) starting the work equipment (including re-starting after a stoppage for any reason); or

(b) controlling any change in the speed, pressure or other operating conditions of the work equipment where such conditions after the change result in risk to health and safety which is greater than or of a different nature from such risks before the change.

(2) Subject to paragraph (3), every employer shall ensure that, where a control is required by paragraph (1), it shall not be possible to perform any operation mentioned in sub-paragraph (a) or (b) of that paragraph except by a deliberate action on such control.

(3) Paragraph (1) shall not apply to re-starting or changing operating conditions as a result of the normal operating cycle of an automatic device.

NOTES

Initial Commencement

Specified date

Specified date: 5 December 1998: see reg 1.

UK Parliament SIs 1990-1999/1998/2301-2350/Provision and Use of Work Equipment Regulations 1998 (SI 1998/2306)/Part II General/15 Stop controls

15 Stop controls

(1) Every employer shall ensure that, where appropriate, work equipment is provided with one or more readily accessible controls the operation of which will bring the work equipment to a safe condition in a safe manner.

(2) Any control required by paragraph (1) shall bring the work equipment to a complete stop where necessary for reasons of health and safety.

(3) Any control required by paragraph (1) shall, if necessary for reasons of health and safety, switch off all sources of energy after stopping the functioning of the work equipment.

(4) Any control required by paragraph (1) shall operate in priority to any control which starts or changes the operating conditions of the work equipment.

NOTES

Initial Commencement

Specified date

Specified date: 5 December 1998: see reg 1.

UK Parliament SIs 1990-1999/1998/2301-2350/Provision and Use of Work Equipment Regulations 1998 (SI 1998/2306)/Part II General/16 Emergency stop controls

16 Emergency stop controls

(1) Every employer shall ensure that, where appropriate, work equipment is provided with one or more readily accessible emergency stop controls unless it is not necessary by reason of the nature of the hazards and the time taken for the work equipment to come to a complete stop as a result of the action of any control provided by virtue of regulation 15(1).

(2) Any control required by paragraph (1) shall operate in priority to any control required by regulation 15(1).

NOTES

Initial Commencement

Specified date

Specified date: 5 December 1998: see reg 1.

UK Parliament SIs 1990-1999/1998/2301-2350/Provision and Use of Work Equipment Regulations 1998 (SI 1998/2306)/Part II General/17 Controls

17 Controls

(1) Every employer shall ensure that all controls for work equipment are clearly visible and identifiable, including by appropriate marking where necessary.

(2) Except where necessary, the employer shall ensure that no control for work equipment is in a position where any person operating the control is exposed to a risk to his health or safety

(3) Every employer shall ensure where appropriate--

(a) that, so far as is reasonably practicable, the operator of any control is able to ensure from the position of that control that no person is in a place where he would be exposed to any risk to his health or safety as a result of the operation of that control, but where or to the extent that it is not reasonably practicable;

(b) that, so far as is reasonably practicable, systems of work are effective to ensure that, when work equipment is about to start, no person is in a place where he would be exposed to a risk to his health or safety as a result of the work equipment starting, but where neither of these is reasonably practicable;

(c) that an audible, visible or other suitable warning is given by virtue of regulation 24 whenever work equipment is about to start.

(4) Every employer shall take appropriate measures to ensure that any person who is in a place where he would be exposed to a risk to his health or safety as a result of the starting or stopping of work equipment has sufficient time and suitable means to avoid that risk.

NOTES

Initial Commencement

Specified date

Specified date: 5 December 1998: see reg 1.

UK Parliament SIs 1990-1999/1998/2301-2350/Provision and Use of Work Equipment Regulations 1998 (SI 1998/2306)/Part II General/18 Control systems

18 Control systems

[(1) Every employer shall ensure, so far as is reasonably practicable, that all control systems of work equipment--

(a) are safe; and

(b) are chosen making due allowance for the failures, faults and constraints to be expected in the planned circumstances of use.]

(2) Without prejudice to the generality of paragraph (1), a control system shall not be safe unless--

(a) its operation does not create any increased risk to health or safety;

(b) it ensures, so far as is reasonably practicable, that any fault in or damage to any part of the control system or the loss of supply of any source of energy used by the work equipment cannot result in additional or increased risk to health or safety;

(c) it does not impede the operation of any control required by regulation 15 or 16.

NOTES

Initial Commencement

Specified date

Specified date: 5 December 1998: see reg 1.

Amendment

Para (1): substituted by SI 2002/2174, reg 7(c).

Date in force: 17 September 2002: see SI 2002/2174, reg 1.

UK Parliament SIs 1990-1999/1998/2301-2350/Provision and Use of Work Equipment Regulations 1998 (SI 1998/2306)/Part II General/19 Isolation from sources of energy

19 Isolation from sources of energy

(1) Every employer shall ensure that where appropriate work equipment is provided with suitable means to isolate it from all its sources of energy.

(2) Without prejudice to the generality of paragraph (1), the means mentioned in that paragraph shall not be suitable unless they are clearly identifiable and readily accessible.

(3) Every employer shall take appropriate measures to ensure that re-connection of any energy source to work equipment does not expose any person using the work equipment to any risk to his health or safety.

NOTES

Initial Commencement

Specified date

Specified date: 5 December 1998: **see reg 1**.

UK **Parliament SIs 1990-1999/1998**/2301-2350/**Provision and** Use **of** Work **Equipment** Regulations **1998** (**SI 1998**/2306)/**Part II** General/**20 Stability**

20 Stability

Every employer shall ensure that work equipment or any part of work equipment is stabilised by clamping or otherwise where necessary for purposes of health or safety.

NOTES

Initial Commencement

Specified date

Specified date: 5 December 1998: **see reg 1**.

UK **Parliament SIs 1990-1999/1998**/2301-2350/**Provision and** Use **of** Work **Equipment** Regulations **1998** (**SI 1998**/2306)/**Part II** General/21 **Lighting**

21 Lighting

Every employer shall ensure that suitable and sufficient lighting, which takes account of the operations to be carried out, is provided at any place where a person uses work equipment.

NOTES

Initial Commencement

Specified date

Specified date: 5 December 1998: **see reg 1**.

UK **Parliament SIs 1990-1999/1998**/2301-2350/**Provision and** Use **of** Work **Equipment** Regulations **1998** (**SI 1998**/2306)/**Part II** General/22 **Maintenance operations**

22 Maintenance operations

Every employer shall take appropriate measures to ensure that work equipment is so constructed or adapted that, so far as is reasonably practicable, maintenance operations which involve a risk to health or safety can be carried out while the work equipment is shut down, or in other cases--

(a) **maintenance operations can be carried out without exposing the person carrying them out to a risk to his health or safety; or**

(b) appropriate measures can be taken for the protection of any person carrying out maintenance operations which involve a risk to his health or safety.

NOTES

Initial Commencement

Specified date

Specified date: 5 December 1998: see reg 1.

UK Parliament SIs 1990-1999/1998/2301-2350/Provision and Use of Work Equipment Regulations 1998 (SI 1998/2306)/Part II General/23 Markings

23 Markings

Every employer shall ensure that work equipment is marked in a clearly visible manner with any marking appropriate for reasons of health and safety.

NOTES

Initial Commencement

Specified date

Specified date: 5 December 1998: see reg 1.

UK Parliament SIs 1990-1999/1998/2301-2350/Provision and Use of Work Equipment Regulations 1998 (SI 1998/2306)/Part II General/24 Warnings

24 Warnings

(1) Every employer shall ensure that work equipment incorporates any warnings or warning devices which are appropriate for reasons of health and safety.

(2) Without prejudice to the generality of paragraph (1), warnings given by warning devices on work equipment shall not be appropriate unless they are unambiguous, easily perceived and easily understood.

NOTES

Initial Commencement

Specified date

Specified date: 5 December 1998: see reg 1.

UK Parliament SIs 1990-1999/1998/2301-2350/Provision and Use of Work Equipment Regulations 1998 (SI 1998/2306)/Part III Mobile Work Equipment/25 Employees carried on mobile work equipment

Part III

Mobile Work Equipment

25 Employees carried on mobile work equipment

Every employer shall ensure that no employee is carried by mobile work equipment unless--

(a) it is suitable for carrying persons; and

(b) it incorporates features for reducing to as low as is reasonably practicable risks to their safety, including risks from wheels or tracks.

NOTES

Initial Commencement

Specified date

Specified date: 5 December 1998: see reg 1.

UK Parliament SIs 1990-1999/1998/2301-2350/Provision and Use of Work Equipment Regulations 1998 (SI 1998/2306)/Part III Mobile Work Equipment/26 Rolling over of mobile work equipment

26 Rolling over of mobile work equipment

(1) Every employer shall ensure that where there is a risk to an employee riding on mobile work equipment from its rolling over, it is minimised by--

(a) stabilising the work equipment;

(b) a structure which ensures that the work equipment does no more than fall on its side;

(c) a structure giving sufficient clearance to anyone being carried if it overturns further than that; or

(d) a device giving comparable protection.

(2) Where there is a risk of anyone being carried by mobile work equipment being crushed by its rolling over, the employer shall ensure that it has a suitable restraining system for him.

(3) This regulation shall not apply to a fork-lift truck having a structure described in sub-paragraph (b) or (c) of paragraph (1).

(4) Compliance with this regulation is not required where--

(a) it would increase the overall risk to safety;

(b) it would not be reasonably practicable to operate the mobile work equipment in consequence; or

(c) in relation to an item of work equipment provided for use in the undertaking or establishment before 5th December 1998 it would not be reasonably practicable.

NOTES

Initial Commencement

Specified date

Specified date: 5 December 1998: see reg 1.

UK Parliament SIs 1990-1999/1998/2301-2350/Provision and Use of Work Equipment Regulations 1998 (SI 1998/2306)/Part III Mobile Work Equipment/27 Overturning of fork-lift trucks

27 Overturning of fork-lift trucks

Every employer shall ensure that a fork-lift truck to which regulation 26(3) refers and which carries an employee is adapted or equipped to reduce to as low as is reasonably practicable the risk to safety from its overturning.

NOTES

Initial Commencement

Specified date

Specified date: 5 December 1998: see reg 1.

UK Parliament SIs 1990-1999/1998/2301-2350/Provision and Use of Work Equipment Regulations 1998 (SI 1998/2306)/Part III Mobile Work Equipment/28 Self-propelled work equipment

28 Self-propelled work equipment

Every employer shall ensure that, where self-propelled work equipment may, while in motion, involve risk to the safety of persons--

(a) it has facilities for preventing its being started by an unauthorised person;

(b) it has appropriate facilities for minimising the consequences of a collision where there is more than one item of rail-mounted work equipment in motion at the same time;

(c) it has a device for braking and stopping;

(d) where safety constraints so require, emergency facilities operated by readily accessible controls or automatic systems are available for braking and stopping the work equipment in the event of failure of the main facility;

(e) where the driver's direct field of vision is inadequate to ensure safety, there are adequate devices for improving his vision so far as is reasonably practicable;

(f) if provided for use at night or in dark places--

(i) it is equipped with lighting appropriate to the work to be carried out; and

(ii) is otherwise sufficiently safe for such use;

(g) if it, or anything carried or towed by it, constitutes a fire hazard and is liable to endanger employees, it carries appropriate fire-fighting equipment, unless such equipment is kept sufficiently close to it.

NOTES

Initial Commencement

Specified date

Specified date: 5 December 1998: see reg 1.

UK Parliament SIs 1990-1999/1998/2301-2350/Provision and Use of Work Equipment Regulations 1998 (SI 1998/2306)/Part III Mobile Work Equipment/29 Remote-controlled self-propelled work equipment

29 Remote-controlled self-propelled work equipment

Every employer shall ensure that where remote-controlled self-propelled work equipment involves a risk to safety while in motion--

(a) it stops automatically once it leaves its control range; and

(b) where the risk is of crushing or impact it incorporates features to guard against such risk unless other appropriate devices are able to do so.

NOTES

Initial Commencement

Specified date

Specified date: 5 December 1998: see reg 1.

UK Parliament SIs 1990-1999/1998/2301-2350/Provision and Use of Work Equipment Regulations 1998 (SI 1998/2306)/Part III Mobile Work Equipment/30 Drive shafts

30 Drive shafts

(1) Where the seizure of the drive shaft between mobile work equipment and its accessories or anything towed is likely to involve a risk to safety every employer shall--

(a) ensure that the work equipment has a means of preventing such seizure; or

(b) where such seizure cannot be avoided, take every possible measure to avoid an adverse effect on the safety of an employee.

(2) Every employer shall ensure that--

(a) where mobile work equipment has a shaft for the transmission of energy between it and other mobile work equipment; and

(b) the shaft could become soiled or damaged by contact with the ground while uncoupled,

the work equipment has a system for safeguarding the shaft.

NOTES

Initial Commencement

Specified date

Specified date: 5 December 1998: see reg 1.

UK Parliament SIs 1990-1999/1998/2301-2350/Provision and Use of Work Equipment Regulations 1998 (SI 1998/2306)/Part IV Power Presses/31 Power presses to which Part IV does not apply

Part IV

Power Presses

31 Power presses to which Part IV does not apply

Regulations 32 to 35 shall not apply to a power press of a kind which is described in Schedule 2.

NOTES

Initial Commencement

Specified date

Specified date: 5 December 1998: see reg 1.

UK Parliament SIs 1990-1999/1998/2301-2350/Provision and Use of Work Equipment Regulations 1998 (SI 1998/2306)/Part IV Power Presses/32 Thorough examination of power presses, guards and protection devices

32 Thorough examination of power presses, guards and protection devices

(1) Every employer shall ensure that a power press is not put into service for the first time after installation, or after assembly at a new site or in a new location unless--

(a) it has been thoroughly examined to ensure that it--

(i) has been installed correctly; and

(ii) would be safe to operate; and

(b) any defect has been remedied.

(2) Every employer shall ensure that a guard, other than one to which paragraph (3) relates, or protection device is not put into service for the first time on a power press unless--

(a) it has been thoroughly examined when in position on that power press to ensure that it is effective for its purpose; and

(b) any defect has been remedied.

(3) Every employer shall ensure that that part of a closed tool which acts as a fixed guard is not used on a power press unless--

(a) it has been thoroughly examined when in position on any power press in the premises to ensure that it is effective for its purpose; and

(b) any defect has been remedied.

(4) For the purpose of ensuring that health and safety conditions are maintained, and that any deterioration can be detected and remedied in good time, every employer shall ensure that--

(a) every power press is thoroughly examined, and its guards and protection devices are thoroughly examined when in position on that power press--

(i) at least every 12 months, where it has fixed guards only; or

(ii) at least every 6 months, in other cases; and

(iii) each time that exceptional circumstances have occurred which are liable to jeopardise the safety of the power press or its guards or protection devices; and

(b) any defect is remedied before the power press is used again.

(5) Where a power press, guard or protection device was before the coming into force of these Regulations required to be thoroughly examined by regulation 5(2) of the Power Presses Regulations 1965 the first thorough examination under paragraph (4) shall be made before the date by which a thorough examination would have been required by regulation 5(2) had it remained in force.

(6) Paragraph (4) shall not apply to that part of a closed tool which acts as a fixed guard.

(7) In this regulation "defect" means a defect notified under regulation 34 other than a defect which has not yet become a danger to persons.

NOTES

Initial Commencement

Specified date

Specified date: 5 December 1998: see reg 1.

UK Parliament SIs 1990-1999/1998/2301-2350/Provision and Use of Work Equipment Regulations 1998 (SI 1998/2306)/Part IV Power Presses/33 Inspection of guards and protection devices

33 Inspection of guards and protection devices

(1) Every employer shall ensure that a power press is not used after the setting, re-setting or adjustment of its tools, save in trying out its tools or save in die proving, unless--

(a) its every guard and protection device has been inspected and tested while in position on the power press by a person appointed in writing by the employer who is--

(i) competent; or

(ii) undergoing training for that purpose and acting under the immediate supervision of a competent person,

and who has signed a certificate which complies with paragraph (3); or

(b) the guards and protection devices have not been altered or disturbed in the course of the adjustment of its tools.

(2) Every employer shall ensure that a power press is not used after the expiration of the fourth hour of a working period unless its every guard and protection device has been inspected and tested while in position on the power press by a person appointed in writing by the employer who is--

(a) competent; or

(b) undergoing training for that purpose and acting under the immediate supervision of a competent person,

and who has signed a certificate which complies with paragraph (3).

(3) A certificate referred to in this regulation shall--

(a) contain sufficient particulars to identify every guard and protection device inspected and tested and the power press on which it was positioned at the time of the inspection and test;

(b) state the date and time of the inspection and test; and

(c) state that every guard and protection device on the power press is in position and effective for its purpose.

(4) In this regulation "working period", in relation to a power press, means--

(a) the period in which the day's or night's work is done; or

(b) in premises where a shift system is in operation, a shift.

NOTES

Initial Commencement

Specified date

Specified date: 5 December 1998: see reg 1.

UK Parliament SIs 1990-1999/1998/2301-2350/Provision and Use of Work Equipment Regulations 1998 (SI 1998/2306)/Part IV Power Presses/34 Reports

34 Reports

(1) A person making a thorough examination for an employer under regulation 32 shall--

(a) notify the employer forthwith of any defect in a power press or its guard or protection device which in his opinion is or could become a danger to persons;

(b) as soon as is practicable make a report of the thorough examination to the employer in writing authenticated by him or on his behalf by signature or equally secure means and containing the information specified in Schedule 3; and

(c) where there is in his opinion a defect in a power press or its guard or protection device which is or could become a danger to persons, send a copy of the report as soon as is practicable to the enforcing authority for the premises in which the power press is situated.

(2) A person making an inspection and test for an employer under regulation 33 shall forthwith notify the employer of any defect in a guard or protection device which in his opinion is or could become a danger to persons and the reason for his opinion.

NOTES

Initial Commencement

Specified date

Specified date: 5 December 1998: see reg 1.

UK Parliament SIs 1990-1999/1998/2301-2350/Provision and Use of Work Equipment Regulations 1998 (SI 1998/2306)/Part IV Power Presses/35 Keeping of information

35 Keeping of information

(1) Every employer shall ensure that the information in every report made pursuant to regulation 34(1) is kept available for inspection for 2 years after it is made.

(2) Every employer shall ensure that a certificate under regulation [33] is kept available for inspection--

(a) at or near the power press to which it relates until superseded by a later certificate; and

(b) after that, until 6 months have passed since it was signed.

NOTES

Initial Commencement

Specified date

Specified date: 5 December 1998: see reg 1.

Amendment

Para (2): reference to "33" in square brackets substituted by SI 2002/2174, reg 7(d).

Date in force: 17 September 2002: see SI 2002/2174, reg 1.

UK Parliament SIs 1990-1999/1998/2301-2350/Provision and Use of Work Equipment Regulations 1998 (SI 1998/2306)/Part V Miscellaneous/36 Exemption for the armed forces

Part V

Miscellaneous

36 Exemption for the armed forces

(1) The Secretary of State for Defence may, in the interests of national security, by a certificate in writing exempt any of the home forces, any visiting force or any headquarters from any requirement or prohibition imposed by these Regulations and any such exemption may be granted subject to conditions and to a limit of time and may be revoked by the said Secretary of State by a certificate in writing at any time.

(2) In this regulation--

(a) "the home forces" has the same meaning as in section 12(1) of the Visiting Forces Act 1952;

(b) "headquarters" has the same meaning as in article 3(2) of the Visiting Forces and International Headquarters (Application of Law) Order 1965;

(c) "visiting force" has the same meaning as it does for the purposes of any provision of Part I of the Visiting Forces Act 1952.

NOTES

Initial Commencement

Specified date

Specified date: 5 December 1998: see reg 1.

UK Parliament SIs 1990-1999/1998/2301-2350/Provision and Use of Work Equipment Regulations 1998 (SI 1998/2306)/Part V Miscellaneous/37 Transitional provision

37 Transitional provision

The requirements in regulations 25 to 30 shall not apply to work equipment provided for use in the undertaking or establishment before 5th December 1998 until 5th December 2002.

NOTES

Initial Commencement

Specified date

Specified date: 5 December 1998: see reg 1.

UK Parliament SIs 1990-1999/1998/2301-2350/Provision and Use of Work Equipment Regulations 1998 (SI 1998/2306)/Part V Miscellaneous/38 Repeal of enactment

38 Repeal of enactment

Section 19 of the Offices, Shops and Railway Premises Act 1963 is repealed.

NOTES

Initial Commencement

Specified date

Specified date: 5 December 1998: see reg 1.

UK Parliament SIs 1990-1999/1998/2301-2350/Provision and Use of Work Equipment Regulations 1998 (SI 1998/2306)/Part V Miscellaneous/39 Revocation of instruments

39 Revocation of instruments

The instruments specified in column 1 of Schedule 4 are revoked to the extent specified in column 3 of that Schedule.

NOTES

Initial Commencement

Specified date

Specified date: 5 December 1998: see reg 1.

UK Parliament SIs 1990-1999/1998/2301-2350/Provision and Use of Work Equipment Regulations 1998 (SI 1998/2306)/Signature(s)

Signed by authority of the Secretary of State

Alan Meale

Parliamentary Under Secretary of State,

Department of the Environment, Transport and the Regions

15th September 1998

UK Parliament SIs 1990-1999/1998/2301-2350/Provision and Use of Work Equipment Regulations 1998 (SI 1998/2306)/SCHEDULE 1 Instruments which give Effect to Community Directives Concerning the Safety of Products

SCHEDULE 1

INSTRUMENTS WHICH GIVE EFFECT TO COMMUNITY DIRECTIVES CONCERNING THE SAFETY OF PRODUCTS

Regulation 10

(1)	(2)
Title	Reference
The Construction Plant and Equipment (Harmonisation of Noise Emission Standards) Regulations 1985	SI 1985/1968, amended by SI 1989/1127
The Construction Plant and Equipment (Harmonisation of Noise Emission Standards) Regulations 1988	SI 1988/361, amended by SI 1992/488, 1995/2357
The Electro-medical Equipment (EEC Requirements) Regulations 1988	SI 1988/1586, amended by SI 1994/3017
The Low Voltage Electrical Equipment (Safety) Regulations 1989	SI 1989/728, amended by SI 1994/3260
The Construction Products Regulations 1991	SI 1991/1620, amended by SI 1994/3051
The Simple Pressure Vessels (Safety) Regulations 1991	SI 1991/2749, amended by SI 1994/3098
The Lawnmowers (Harmonisation of Noise Emission Standards) Regulations 1992	SI 1992/168
The Gas Appliances (Safety) Regulations 1992	SI 1992/711
The Electromagnetic Compatibility Regulations 1992	SI 1992/2372, amended by SI 1994/3080
The Supply of Machinery (Safety) Regulations 1992	SI 1992/3073, amended by SI 1994/2063[, 2005/831]
The Personal Protective Equipment (EC Directive) Regulations 1992	SI 1992/3139, amended by SI 1993/3074, 1994/2326, 1996/3039
The Active Implantable Medical Devices Regulations 1992	SI 1992/3146, amended by SI 1995/1671
The Medical Devices Regulations 1994	SI 1994/3017
The Electrical Equipment (Safety) Regulations 1994	SI 1994/3260
The Gas Appliances (Safety) Regulations 1995	SI 1995/1629
The Equipment and Protective Systems Intended for	[SI 1996/192, amended by SI

Use in Potentially Explosive Atmospheres Regulations 1996	1998/81, 2001/3766, 2005/830]
The Lifts Regulations 1997	SI 1997/831[, amended by SI 2005/831]
[The Pressure Equipment Regulations 1999	SI 1999/2001]
[The Noise Emission in the Environment by Equipment for use Outdoors Regulations 2001	SI 2001/1701]
[The Cableway Installations Regulations 2004	SI 2004/129]

NOTES

Initial Commencement

Specified date

Specified date: 5 December 1998: see reg 1.

Amendment

In entry relating to "The Supply of Machinery (Safety) Regulations 1992" in column (2) reference to ", 2005/831" in square brackets inserted by SI 2005/831, reg 4(a).

Date in force: 1 May 2005: see SI 2005/831, reg 1.

In entry relating to "the Equipment and Protective Systems Intended for Use in Potentially Explosive Atmospheres Regulations 1996" in column 2 words "SI 1996/192, amended by SI 1998/81, 2001/3766, 2005/830" in square brackets substituted by SI 2005/830, reg 3.

Date in force: 1 May 2005: see SI 2005/830, reg 1.

In entry relating to "The Lifts Regulations 1997" in column (2) words ", amended by SI 2005/831" in square brackets inserted by SI 2005/831, reg 4(b).

Date in force: 1 May 2005: see SI 2005/831, reg 1.

Entry relating to "The Pressure Equipment Regulations 1999" inserted by SI 1999/2001, reg 29(1).

Date in force: 29 November 1999: see SI 1999/2001, reg 1(3).

Entry relating to "The Noise Emission in the Environment by Equipment for use Outdoors Regulations 2001" inserted by SI 2001/1701, reg 22(1).

Date in force: 3 July 2001: see SI 2001/1701, reg 1(3).

Entry relating to "The Cableway Installations Regulations 2004" inserted by SI 2004/129, reg 32(1).

Date in force: 3 May 2004: see SI 2004/129, reg 1.

UK Parliament SIs 1990-1999/1998/2301-2350/Provision and Use of Work Equipment Regulations 1998 (SI 1998/2306)/SCHEDULE 2 Power Presses to which Regulations 32 to 35 do Not Apply

SCHEDULE 2

POWER PRESSES TO WHICH REGULATIONS 32 TO 35 DO NOT APPLY

Regulation 31

Page 27

1

A power press for the working of hot metal.

2

A power press not capable of a stroke greater than 6 millimetres.

3

A guillotine.

4

A combination punching and shearing machine, turret punch press or similar machine for punching, shearing or cropping.

5

A machine, other than a press brake, for bending steel sections.

6

A straightening machine.

7

An upsetting machine.

8

A heading machine.

9

A riveting machine.

10

An eyeletting machine.

11

A press-stud attaching machine.

12

A zip fastener bottom stop attaching machine.

13

A stapling machine.

14

A wire stitching machine.

15

A power press for the compacting of metal powders.

NOTES

Initial Commencement

Specified date

Specified date: 5 December 1998: see reg 1.

UK Parliament SIs 1990-1999/1998/2301-2350/Provision and Use of Work Equipment Regulations 1998 (SI 1998/2306)/SCHEDULE 3 Information to be Contained in a Report of a Thorough Examination of a Power Press, Guard or Protection Device

SCHEDULE 3

INFORMATION TO BE CONTAINED IN A REPORT OF A THOROUGH EXAMINATION OF A POWER PRESS, GUARD OR PROTECTION DEVICE

Regulation 34(1)(b)

1

The name of the employer for whom the thorough examination was made.

2

The address of the premises at which the thorough examination was made.

3

In relation to each item examined--

(a) that it is a power press, interlocking guard, fixed guard or other type of guard or protection device;

(b) where known its make, type and year of manufacture;

(c) the identifying mark of--

(i) the manufacture,

(ii) the employer.

4

In relation to the first thorough examination of a power press after installation or after assembly at a new site or in a new location--

(a) that it is such thorough examination;

(b) either that it has been installed correctly and would be safe to operate or the respects in which it has not been installed correctly or would not be safe to operate;

(c) identification of any part found to have a defect, and a description of the defect.

5

In relation to a thorough examination of a power press other than one to which paragraph 4 relates--

(a) that it is such other thorough examination;

(b) either that the power press would be safe to operate or the respects in which it would not be safe to operate;

(c) identification of any part found to have a defect which is or could become a danger to persons, and a description of the defect.

6

In relation to a thorough examination of a guard or protection device--

(a) either that it is effective for its purpose or the respects in which it is not effective for its purpose;

(b) identification of any part found to have a defect which is or could become a danger to persons, and a description of the defect.

7

Any repair, renewal or alteration required to remedy a defect found to be a danger to persons.

8

In the case of a defect which is not yet but could become a danger to persons--

(a) the time by which it could become such danger;

(b) any repair, renewal or alteration required to remedy it.

9

Any other defect which requires remedy.

10

Any repair, renewal or alteration referred to in paragraph 7 which has already been effected.

11

The date on which any defect referred to in paragraph 8 was notified to the employer under regulation 34(1)(a).

12

The qualification and address of the person making the report; that he is self-employed or if employed, the name and address of his employer.

13

The date of the thorough examination.

14

The date of the report.

15

The name of the person making the report and where different the name of the person signing or otherwise authenticating it.

NOTES

Initial Commencement

Specified date

Specified date: 5 December 1998: see reg 1.

UK Parliament SIs 1990-1999/1998/2301-2350/Provision and Use of Work Equipment Regulations 1998 (SI 1998/2306)/SCHEDULE 4 Revocation of Instruments

SCHEDULE 4

REVOCATION OF INSTRUMENTS

Regulation 39

(1) Title	(2) Reference	(3) Extent of revocation
The Operations at Unfenced Machinery (Amended Schedule) Regulations 1946	SR & O 1946/156	The whole Regulations
The Agriculture (Circular Saws) Regulations 1959	SI 1959/427	The whole Regulations
The Prescribed Dangerous Machines Order 1964	SI 1964/971	The whole order
The Power Presses Regulations 1965	SI 1965/1441	The whole Regulations
The Abrasive Wheels Regulations 1970	SI 1970/535	The whole Regulations
The Power Presses (Amendment) Regulations 1972	SI 1972/1512	The whole Regulations
The Woodworking Machines Regulations 1974	SI 1974/903	The whole Regulations
The Operations at Unfenced Machinery (Amendment) Regulations 1976	SI 1976/955	The whole Regulations
The Factories (Standards of Lighting) (Revocation) Regulations 1978	SI 1978/1126	The whole Regulations
The Offshore Installations (Application of Statutory Instruments) Regulations 1984	SI 1984/419	The whole Regulations
The Offshore Installations (Operational Safety, Health and Welfare and Life-Saving Appliances) (Revocations) Regulations 1989	SI 1989/1672	The whole Regulations
The Provision and Use of Work Equipment Regulations 1992	SI 1992/2932	The whole Regulations
. . .		

NOTES

Initial Commencement

Specified date

Specified date: 5 December 1998: see reg 1.

Amendment

Entry relating to "The Construction (Health, Safety and Welfare) Regulations 1996" (omitted) revoked by SI 2007/320, reg 48(1), Sch 4.

Date in force: 6 April 2007: see SI 2007/320, reg 1.

UK Parliament SIs 1990-1999/1998/2301-2350/Provision and Use of Work Equipment Regulations 1998 (SI 1998/2306)/EXPLANATORY NOTE

EXPLANATORY NOTE

(This note is not part of the Regulations)

1

These Regulations impose health and safety requirements with respect to the provision and use of work equipment, which is defined in regulation 2(1).

2

The Regulations revoke and re-enact the Provision and Use of Work Equipment Regulations 1992 ("the 1992 Regulations"), which gave effect as respects Great Britain, except in relation to certain matters, to Council Directive 89/655/EEC (OJ No L393, 30.12.89, p 13) on the minimum health and safety requirements for the use of work equipment by workers at work ("the Directive").

3

In addition to minor and drafting changes these Regulations contain new provision giving effect as respects Great Britain to the provisions of the Directive identified below and inserted in it by the amending Council Directive 95/63/EC (OJ No L335, 30.12.95, p 28).

4

Save in the case of regulation 34 (reports) these Regulations, as the 1992 Regulations, place duties on employers. They also place those duties (not required by the Directive) on others, who now include (regulation 3(3) to (5)) certain persons having control of work equipment, of persons at work who use or supervise or manage its use or of the way it is used, to the extent of their control.

5

These Regulations, as the 1992 Regulations, have limited application to ships. The way in which they so apply is revised (regulation 3(6) to (11)).

6

The Regulations (giving effect to the replaced last paragraph of point 2.1 of Annex I to the Directive) require that control systems of work equipment are chosen making due allowance for the failures, faults and constraints to be expected in the planned circumstances of use (regulation 19(1)(b)).

7

The Regulations, in giving effect to Article 4a of the Directive, require--

(a) the inspection of work equipment in specified circumstances by a competent person (regulation 6(1) and (2));

(b) the recording and keeping of the result (regulation 6(3)); and

(c) that evidence of the last inspection accompany work equipment used outside the undertaking (regulation 6(4)). Work equipment subject to equivalent provision is excepted (regulation 6(5)) "Inspection" is defined in regulation 2(1).

8

The Regulations give effect to point 3.1 of Annex I to the Directive in making provision in relation to mobile work equipment for--

(a) its suitability for carrying persons and its safety features (regulation 25);

(b) means to minimise the risk to safety from its rolling over (regulation 26);

(c) means to reduce the risk to safety from the rolling over of a fork-lift truck (regulation 27);

(d) the safety of self-propelled work equipment (regulation 28) and remote-controlled self propelled work equipment (regulation 29); and

(e) the drive shafts of mobile work equipment (regulation 30),

and as permitted by Article 4.1(c) of the Directive give relief until 5th December 2002 for existing mobile work equipment.

9

Regulations 32 to 36 and Schedules 2 and 3 re-enact with modifications the Power Presses Regulations 1965/1441 ("the 1965 Regulations"). In so doing they include provision giving effect, as regards power presses, to Article 4a of the Directive. Certain power presses, excluded by the 1965 Regulations or exempted under them, are excluded (regulation 31 and Schedule 2). The Regulations provide for--

(a) the thorough examination (defined in regulation 2(1)) of power presses and their guards and protection devices (regulation 32);

(b) their inspection after setting, re-setting or adjustment of their tools, and every working period (regulation 33); and

(c) the making (regulation 34 and Schedule 3) and keeping (regulation 35) of reports.

10

The Regulations repeal section 19 of the Offices, Shops and Railway Premises Act 1963 (regulation 38) and revoke provisions of instruments (regulation 39 and Schedule 4).

11

Copies of the cost benefit assessment prepared in respect of these Regulations other than regulations 31 to 35 (power presses), of that prepared in respect of regulations 3 to 35, and of that prepared in respect of woodworking machines, may be obtained from the Economic Adviser's Unit, the Health and Safety Executive, Rose Court, 2 Southwark Bridge, London SE1 9HS.

UK Parliament SIs 1990-1999/1999/3201-3250/Management of Health and Safety at Work Regulations 1999 (SI 1999/3242)

1999 No 3242

HEALTH AND SAFETY

Management of Health and Safety at Work Regulations 1999

Made 3rd December 1999

Laid before Parliament 8th December 1999

Coming into force 29th December 1999

The Secretary of State, being a Minister designated for the purposes of section 2(2) of the European Communities Act 1972 in relation to measures relating to employers' obligations in respect of the health and safety of workers and in relation to measures relating to the minimum health and safety requirements for the workplace that relate to fire safety and in exercise of the powers conferred on him by the said section 2 and by sections 15(1), (2), (3)(a), (5), and (9), 47(2), 52(2), and (3), 80(1) and 82(3)(a) of and paragraphs 6(1), 7, 8(1), 10, 14, 15, and 16 of Schedule 3 to, the Health and Safety at Work etc Act 1974 ("the 1974 Act") and of all other powers enabling him in that behalf--

(a) for the purpose of giving effect without modifications to proposals submitted to him by the Health and Safety Commission under section 11(2)(d) of the 1974 Act after the carrying out by the Commission of consultations in accordance with section 50(3) of that Act; and

(b) it appearing to him that the modifications to the Regulations marked with an asterisk in Schedule 2 are expedient and that it also appearing to him not to be appropriate to consult bodies in respect of such modifications in accordance with section 80(4) of the 1974 Act,

hereby makes the following Regulations:

UK Parliament SIs 1990-1999/1999/3201-3250/Management of Health and Safety at Work Regulations 1999 (SI 1999/3242)/1 Citation, commencement and interpretation

1 Citation, commencement and interpretation

(1) These Regulations may be cited as the Management of Health and Safety at Work Regulations 1999 and shall come into force on 29th December 1999.

(2) In these Regulations--

"the 1996 Act" means the Employment Rights Act 1996;

"the assessment" means, in the case of an employer or self-employed person, the assessment made or changed by him in accordance with regulation 3;

"child"--

(a) as respects England and Wales, means a person who is not over compulsory school age, construed in accordance with section 8 of the Education Act 1996; and

(b) as respects Scotland, means a person who is not over school age, construed in accordance with section 31 of the Education (Scotland) Act 1980;

"employment business" means a business (whether or not carried on with a view to profit and whether or not carried on in conjunction with any other business) which supplies persons (other than seafarers) who are employed in it to work for and under the control of other persons in any capacity;

"fixed-term contract of employment" means a contract of employment for a specific term which is fixed in advance or which can be ascertained in advance by reference to some relevant circumstance;

"given birth" means delivered a living child or, after twenty-four weeks of pregnancy, a stillborn child;

"new or expectant mother" means an employee who is pregnant; who has given birth within the previous six months; or who is breastfeeding;

"the preventive and protective measures" means the measures which have been identified by the employer or by the self-employed person in consequence of the assessment as the measures he needs to take to comply with the requirements and prohibitions imposed upon him by or under the relevant statutory provisions . . .;

"young person" means any person who has not attained the age of eighteen.

(3) Any reference in these Regulations to--

(a) a numbered regulation or Schedule is a reference to the regulation or Schedule in these Regulations so numbered; or

(b) a numbered paragraph is a reference to the paragraph so numbered in the regulation in which the reference appears.

NOTES

Initial Commencement

Specified date

Specified date: 29 December 1999: see para (1) above.

Amendment

Para (2): in definition "the preventive and protective measures" words omitted revoked in relation to England and Wales by SI 2005/1541, art 53(2), Sch 5 and in relation to Scotland by SSI 2006/457, art 2(2), Sch 2.

Date in force (in relation to England and Wales): 1 October 2006: see SI 2005/1541, art 1(3) (as amended by SI 2006/484, art 2).
Date in force (in relation to Scotland): 1 October 2006: see SSI 2006/457, art 1.

UK Parliament SIs 1990-1999/1999/3201-3250/Management of Health and Safety at Work Regulations 1999 (SI 1999/3242)/[2 Disapplication of these Regulations]

[2 Disapplication of these Regulations]

[(1) These Regulations shall not apply to or in relation to the master or crew of a ship, or to the employer of such persons, in respect of the normal ship-board activities of a ship's crew which are carried out solely by the crew under the direction of the master.

(2) Regulations 3(4), (5), 10(2) and 19 shall not apply to occasional work or short-term work involving work regarded as not being harmful, damaging or dangerous to young people in a family undertaking.

(3) In this regulation--

"normal ship-board activities" include--

(a) the construction, reconstruction or conversion of a ship outside, but not inside, Great Britain; and

(b) the repair of a ship save repair when carried out in dry dock;

"ship" includes every description of vessel used in navigation, other than a ship belonging to Her Majesty which forms part of Her Majesty's Navy.]

NOTES

Amendment

Substituted by SI 2003/2457, regs 2, 3.

Date in force: 27 October 2003: see SI 2003/2457, reg 1.

UK Parliament SIs 1990-1999/1999/3201-3250/Management of Health and Safety at Work Regulations 1999 (SI 1999/3242)/3 Risk assessment

3 Risk assessment

(1) Every employer shall make a suitable and sufficient assessment of

(a) the risks to the health and safety of his employees to which they are exposed whilst they are at work; and

(b) the risks to the health and safety of persons not in his employment arising out of or in connection with the conduct by him of his undertaking,

for the purpose of identifying the measures he needs to take to comply with the requirements and prohibitions imposed upon him by or under the relevant statutory provisions . . ..

(2) Every self-employed person shall make a suitable and sufficient assessment of--

(a) the risks to his own health and safety to which he is exposed whilst he is at work; and

(b) the risks to the health and safety of persons not in his employment arising out of or in connection with the conduct by him of his undertaking,

for the purpose of identifying the measures he needs to take to comply with the requirements and prohibitions imposed upon him by or under the relevant statutory provisions.

(3) Any assessment such as is referred to in paragraph (1) or (2) shall be reviewed by the employer or self-employed person who made it if--

(a) there is reason to suspect that it is no longer valid; or

(b) there has been a significant change in the matters to which it relates;

and where as a result of any such review changes to an assessment are required, the employer or self-employed person concerned shall make them.

(4) An employer shall not employ a young person unless he has, in relation to risks to the health and safety of young persons, made or reviewed an assessment in accordance with paragraphs (1) and (5).

(5) In making or reviewing the assessment, an employer who employs or is to employ a young person shall take particular account of--

(a) the inexperience, lack of awareness of risks and immaturity of young persons;

(b) the fitting-out and layout of the workplace and the workstation;

(c) the nature, degree and duration of exposure to physical, biological and chemical agents;

(d) the form, range, and use of work equipment and the way in which it is handled;

(e) the organisation of processes and activities;

(f) the extent of the health and safety training provided or to be provided to young persons; and

(g) risks from agents, processes and work listed in the Annex to Council Directive 94/33/EC on the protection of young people at work.

(6) Where the employer employs five or more employees, he shall record--

(a) the significant findings of the assessment; and

(b) any group of his employees identified by it as being especially at risk.

NOTES

Initial Commencement

Specified date

Specified date: 29 December 1999: see reg 1(1).

Amendment

Para (1): words omitted revoked in relation to England and Wales by SI 2005/1541, art 53(2), Sch 5 and in relation to Scotland by SSI 2006/457, art 2(2), Sch 2.

Date in force (in relation to England and Wales): 1 October 2006: see SI 2005/1541, art 1(3) (as amended by SI 2006/484, art 2).
Date in force (in relation to Scotland): 1 October 2006: see SSI 2006/457, art 1.

Miscellaneous

Para (3): words from "and where as" to "shall make them" (originally part of sub-para (b)) reformatted by virtue of SI 2003/2457, regs 2, 4.

UK Parliament SIs 1990-1999/1999/3201-3250/Management of Health and Safety at Work Regulations 1999 (SI 1999/3242)/4 Principles of prevention to be applied

4 Principles of prevention to be applied

Where an employer implements any preventive and protective measures he shall do so on the basis of the principles specified in Schedule 1 to these Regulations.

NOTES

Initial Commencement

Specified date

Specified date: 29 December 1999: see reg 1(1).

UK Parliament SIs 1990-1999/1999/3201-3250/Management of Health and Safety at Work Regulations 1999 (SI 1999/3242)/5 Health and safety arrangements

5 Health and safety arrangements

(1) Every employer shall make and give effect to such arrangements as are appropriate, having regard to the nature of his activities and the size of his undertaking, for the effective planning, organisation, control, monitoring and review of the preventive and protective measures.

(2) Where the employer employs five or more employees, he shall record the arrangements referred to in paragraph (1).

NOTES

Initial Commencement

Specified date

Specified date: 29 December 1999: see reg 1(1).

UK Parliament SIs 1990-1999/1999/3201-3250/Management of Health and Safety at Work Regulations 1999 (SI 1999/3242)/6 Health surveillance

6 Health surveillance

Every employer shall ensure that his employees are provided with such health surveillance as is appropriate having regard to the risks to their health and safety which are identified by the assessment.

NOTES

Initial Commencement

Specified date

Specified date: 29 December 1999: see reg 1(1).

UK Parliament SIs 1990-1999/1999/3201-3250/Management of Health and Safety at Work Regulations 1999 (SI 1999/3242)/7 Health and safety assistance

Page 6

7 Health and safety assistance

(1) Every employer shall, subject to paragraphs (6) and (7), appoint one or more competent persons to assist him in undertaking the measures he needs to take to comply with the requirements and prohibitions imposed upon him by or under the relevant statutory provisions . . ..

(2) Where an employer appoints persons in accordance with paragraph (1), he shall make arrangements for ensuring adequate co-operation between them.

(3) The employer shall ensure that the number of persons appointed under paragraph (1), the time available for them to fulfil their functions and the means at their disposal are adequate having regard to the size of his undertaking, the risks to which his employees are exposed and the distribution of those risks throughout the undertaking.

(4) The employer shall ensure that--

(a) any person appointed by him in accordance with paragraph (1) who is not in his employment--

(i) is informed of the factors known by him to affect, or suspected by him of affecting, the health and safety of any other person who may be affected by the conduct of his undertaking, and

(ii) has access to the information referred to in regulation 10; and

(b) any person appointed by him in accordance with paragraph (1) is given such information about any person working in his undertaking who is--

(i) employed by him under a fixed-term contract of employment, or

(ii) employed in an employment business,

as is necessary to enable that person properly to carry out the function specified in that paragraph.

(5) A person shall be regarded as competent for the purposes of paragraphs (1) and (8) where he has sufficient training and experience or knowledge and other qualities to enable him properly to assist in undertaking the measures referred to in paragraph (1).

(6) Paragraph (1) shall not apply to a self-employed employer who is not in partnership with any other person where he has sufficient training and experience or knowledge and other qualities properly to undertake the measures referred to in that paragraph himself.

(7) Paragraph (1) shall not apply to individuals who are employers and who are together carrying on business in partnership where at least one of the individuals concerned has sufficient training and experience or knowledge and other qualities--

(a) properly to undertake the measures he needs to take to comply with the requirements and prohibitions imposed upon him by or under the relevant statutory provisions; and

(b) properly to assist his fellow partners in undertaking the measures they need to take to comply with the requirements and prohibitions imposed upon them by or under the relevant statutory provisions.

(8) Where there is a competent person in the employer's employment, that person shall be appointed for the purposes of paragraph (1) in preference to a competent person not in his employment.

NOTES

Initial Commencement

Specified date

Specified date: 29 December 1999: see reg 1(1).

Amendment

Para (1): words omitted revoked in relation to England and Wales by SI 2005/1541, art 53(2), Sch 5 and in relation to Scotland by SSI 2006/457, art 2(2), Sch 2.

Date in force (in relation to England and Wales): 1 October 2006: see SI 2005/1541, art 1(3) (as amended by SI 2006/484, art 2).
Date in force (in relation to Scotland): 1 October 2006: see SSI 2006/457, art 1.

UK Parliament SIs 1990-1999/1999/3201-3250/Management of Health and Safety at Work Regulations 1999 (SI 1999/3242)/8 Procedures for serious and imminent danger and for danger areas

8 Procedures for serious and imminent danger and for danger areas

(1) Every employer shall--

(a) establish and where necessary give effect to appropriate procedures to be followed in the event of serious and imminent danger to persons at work in his undertaking;

(b) nominate a sufficient number of competent persons to implement those procedures in so far as they relate to the evacuation from premises of persons at work in his undertaking; and

(c) ensure that none of his employees has access to any area occupied by him to which it is necessary to restrict access on grounds of health and safety unless the employee concerned has received adequate health and safety instruction.

(2) Without prejudice to the generality of paragraph (1)(a), the procedures referred to in that sub-paragraph shall--

(a) so far as is practicable, require any persons at work who are exposed to serious and imminent danger to be informed of the nature of the hazard and of the steps taken or to be taken to protect them from it;

(b) enable the persons concerned (if necessary by taking appropriate steps in the absence of guidance or instruction and in the light of their knowledge and the technical means at their disposal) to stop work and immediately proceed to a place of safety in the event of their being exposed to serious, imminent and unavoidable danger; and

(c) save in exceptional cases for reasons duly substantiated (which cases and reasons shall be specified in those procedures), require the persons concerned to be prevented from resuming work in any situation where there is still a serious and imminent danger.

(3) A person shall be regarded as competent for the purposes of paragraph (1)(b) where he has sufficient training and experience or knowledge and other qualities to enable him properly to implement the evacuation procedures referred to in that sub-paragraph.

NOTES

Initial Commencement

Specified date

Specified date: 29 December 1999: see reg 1(1).

UK Parliament SIs 1990-1999/1999/3201-3250/Management of Health and Safety at Work Regulations 1999 (SI 1999/3242)/9 Contacts with external services

9 Contacts with external services

Every employer shall ensure that any necessary contacts with external services are arranged, particularly as regards first-aid, emergency medical care and rescue work.

NOTES

Initial Commencement

Specified date

Specified date: 29 December 1999: see reg 1(1).

UK Parliament SIs 1990-1999/1999/3201-3250/Management of Health and Safety at Work Regulations 1999 (SI 1999/3242)/10 Information for employees

10 Information for employees

(1) Every employer shall provide his employees with comprehensible and relevant information on--

(a) the risks to their health and safety identified by the assessment;

(b) the preventive and protective measures;

(c) the procedures referred to in regulation 8(1)(a) . . .;

(d) the identity of those persons nominated by him in accordance with regulation 8(1)(b) . . .; and

(e) the risks notified to him in accordance with regulation 11(1)(c).

(2) Every employer shall, before employing a child, provide a parent of the child with comprehensible and relevant information on--

(a) the risks to his health and safety identified by the assessment;

(b) the preventive and protective measures; and

(c) the risks notified to him in accordance with regulation 11(1)(c).

(3) The reference in paragraph (2) to a parent of the child includes--

(a) in England and Wales, a person who has parental responsibility, within the meaning of section 3 of the Children Act 1989, for him; and

(b) in Scotland, a person who has parental rights, within the meaning of section 8 of the Law Reform (Parent and Child) (Scotland) Act 1986 for him.

NOTES

Initial Commencement

Specified date

Specified date: 29 December 1999: see reg 1(1).

Amendment

Para (1): in sub-para (c) words omitted revoked in relation to England and Wales by SI 2005/1541, art 53(2), Sch 5 and in relation to Scotland by SSI 2006/457, art 2(2), Sch 2.

Date in force (in relation to England and Wales): 1 October 2006: see SI 2005/1541, art 1(3) (as amended by SI 2006/484, art 2).
Date in force (in relation to Scotland): 1 October 2006: see SSI 2006/457, art 1.

Para (1): in sub-para (d) words omitted revoked in relation to England and Wales by SI 2005/1541, art 53(2), Sch 5 and in relation to Scotland by SSI 2006/457, art 2(2), Sch 2.

Date in force (in relation to England and Wales): 1 October 2006: see SI 2005/1541, art 1(3) (as amended by SI 2006/484, art 2).
Date in force (in relation to Scotland): 1 October 2006: see SSI 2006/457, art 1.

UK Parliament SIs 1990-1999/1999/3201-3250/Management of Health and Safety at Work Regulations 1999 (SI 1999/3242)/11 Co-operation and co-ordination

11 Co-operation and co-ordination

(1) Where two or more employers share a workplace (whether on a temporary or a permanent basis) each such employer shall--

(a) co-operate with the other employers concerned so far as is necessary to enable them to comply with the requirements and prohibitions imposed upon them by or under the relevant statutory provisions . . .;

(b) (taking into account the nature of his activities) take all reasonable steps to co-ordinate the measures he takes to comply with the requirements and prohibitions imposed upon him by or under the relevant statutory provisions . . . with the measures the other employers concerned are taking to comply with the requirements and prohibitions imposed upon them by that legislation; and

(c) take all reasonable steps to inform the other employers concerned of the risks to their employees' health and safety arising out of or in connection with the conduct by him of his undertaking.

(2) Paragraph (1) . . . shall apply to employers sharing a workplace with self-employed persons and to self-employed persons sharing a workplace with other self-employed persons as it applies to employers sharing a workplace with other employers; and the references in that paragraph to employers and the reference in the said paragraph to their employees shall be construed accordingly.

NOTES

Initial Commencement

Specified date

Specified date: 29 December 1999: see reg 1(1).

Amendment

Para (1): in sub-paras (a), (b) words omitted revoked in relation to England and Wales by SI 2005/1541, art 53(2), Sch 5 and in relation to Scotland by SSI 2006/457, art 2(2), Sch 2.

Date in force (in relation to England and Wales): 1 October 2006: see SI 2005/1541, art 1(3) (as amended by SI 2006/484, art 2).
Date in force (in relation to Scotland): 1 October 2006: see SSI 2006/457, art 1.

Para (2): words omitted revoked in relation to England and Wales by SI 2005/1541, art 53(2), Sch 5 and in relation to Scotland by SSI 2006/457, art 2(2), Sch 2.

Date in force (in relation to England and Wales): 1 October 2006: see SI 2005/1541, art 1(3) (as amended by SI 2006/484, art 2).
Date in force (in relation to Scotland): 1 October 2006: see SSI 2006/457, art 1.

UK Parliament SIs 1990-1999/1999/3201-3250/Management of Health and Safety at Work Regulations 1999 (SI 1999/3242)/12 Persons working in host employers' or self-employed persons' undertakings

12 Persons working in host employers' or self-employed persons' undertakings

(1) Every employer and every self-employed person shall ensure that the employer of any employees from an outside undertaking who are working in his undertaking is provided with comprehensible information on--

(a) the risks to those employees' health and safety arising out of or in connection with the conduct by that first-mentioned employer or by that self-employed person of his undertaking; and

(b) the measures taken by that first-mentioned employer or by that self-employed person in compliance with the requirements and prohibitions imposed upon him by or under the relevant statutory provisions . . . in so far as the said requirements and prohibitions relate to those employees.

(2) Paragraph (1) . . . shall apply to a self-employed person who is working in the undertaking of an employer or a self-employed person as it applies to employees from an outside undertaking who are working therein; and the reference in that paragraph to the employer of any employees from an outside undertaking who are working in the undertaking of an employer or a self-employed person and the references in the said paragraph to employees from an outside undertaking who are working in the undertaking of an employer or a self-employed person shall be construed accordingly.

(3) Every employer shall ensure that any person working in his undertaking who is not his employee and every self-employed person (not being an employer) shall ensure that any person working in his undertaking is provided with appropriate instructions and comprehensible information regarding any risks to that person's health and safety which arise out of the conduct by that employer or self-employed person of his undertaking.

(4) Every employer shall--

(a) ensure that the employer of any employees from an outside undertaking who are working in his undertaking is provided with sufficient information to enable that second-mentioned employer to identify any person nominated by that first mentioned employer in accordance with regulation 8(1)(b) to implement evacuation procedures as far as those employees are concerned; and

(b) take all reasonable steps to ensure that any employees from an outside undertaking who are working in his undertaking receive sufficient information to enable them to identify any person nominated by him in accordance with regulation 8(1)(b) to implement evacuation procedures as far as they are concerned.

(5) Paragraph (4) shall apply to a self-employed person who is working in an employer's undertaking as it applies to employees from an outside undertaking who are working therein; and the reference in that paragraph to the employer of any employees from an outside undertaking who are working in an employer's undertaking and the references in the said paragraph to employees from an outside undertaking who are working in an employer's undertaking shall be construed accordingly.

NOTES

Initial Commencement

Specified date

Specified date: 29 December 1999: see reg 1(1).

Amendment

Para (1): in sub-para (b) words omitted revoked in relation to England and Wales by SI 2005/1541, art 53(2), Sch 5 and in relation to Scotland by SSI 2006/457, art 2(2), Sch 2.

Date in force (in relation to England and Wales): 1 October 2006: see SI 2005/1541, art 1(3) (as amended by SI 2006/484, art 2).
Date in force (in relation to Scotland): 1 October 2006: see SSI 2006/457, art 1.

Para (2): words omitted revoked in relation to England and Wales by SI 2005/1541, art 53(2), Sch 5 and in relation to Scotland by SSI 2006/457, art 2(2), Sch 2.

Date in force (in relation to England and Wales): 1 October 2006: see SI 2005/1541, art 1(3) (as amended by SI 2006/484, art 2).
Date in force (in relation to Scotland): 1 October 2006: see SSI 2006/457, art 1.

UK Parliament SIs 1990-1999/1999/3201-3250/Management of Health and Safety at Work Regulations 1999 (SI 1999/3242)/13 Capabilities and training

13 Capabilities and training

(1) Every employer shall, in entrusting tasks to his employees, take into account their capabilities as regards health and safety.

(2) Every employer shall ensure that his employees are provided with adequate health and safety training--

(a) on their being recruited into the employer's undertaking; and

(b) on their being exposed to new or increased risks because of--

(i) their being transferred or given a change of responsibilities within the employer's undertaking,

(ii) the introduction of new work equipment into or a change respecting work equipment already in use within the employer's undertaking,

(iii) the introduction of new technology into the employer's undertaking, or

(iv) the introduction of a new system of work into or a change respecting a system of work already in use within the employer's undertaking.

(3) The training referred to in paragraph (2) shall--

(a) be repeated periodically where appropriate;

(b) be adapted to take account of any new or changed risks to the health and safety of the employees concerned; and

(c) take place during working hours.

NOTES

Initial Commencement

Specified date

Specified date: 29 December 1999: see reg 1(1).

UK Parliament SIs 1990-1999/1999/3201-3250/Management of Health and Safety at Work Regulations 1999 (SI 1999/3242)/14 Employees' duties

14 Employees' duties

(1) Every employee shall use any machinery, equipment, dangerous substance, transport equipment, means of production or safety device provided to him by his employer in accordance both with any training in the use of the equipment concerned which has been received by him and the instructions respecting that use which have been provided to him by the said employer in compliance with the requirements and prohibitions imposed upon that employer by or under the relevant statutory provisions.

(2) Every employee shall inform his employer or any other employee of that employer with specific responsibility for the health and safety of his fellow employees--

(a) of any work situation which a person with the first-mentioned employee's training and instruction would reasonably consider represented a serious and immediate danger to health and safety; and

(b) of any matter which a person with the first-mentioned employee's training and instruction would reasonably consider represented a shortcoming in the employer's protection arrangements for health and safety,

in so far as that situation or matter either affects the health and safety of that first mentioned employee or arises out of or in connection with his own activities at work, and has not previously been reported to his employer or to any other employee of that employer in accordance with this paragraph.

NOTES

Initial Commencement

Specified date

Specified date: 29 December 1999: see reg 1(1).

UK Parliament SIs 1990-1999/1999/3201-3250/Management of Health and Safety at Work Regulations 1999 (SI 1999/3242)/15 Temporary workers

15 Temporary workers

(1) Every employer shall provide any person whom he has employed under a fixed-term contract of employment with comprehensible information on--

(a) any special occupational qualifications or skills required to be held by that employee if he is to carry out his work safely; and

(b) any health surveillance required to be provided to that employee by or under any of the relevant statutory provisions,

and shall provide the said information before the employee concerned commences his duties.

(2) Every employer and every self-employed person shall provide any person employed in an employment business who is to carry out work in his undertaking with comprehensible information on--

(a) any special occupational qualifications or skills required to be held by that employee if he is to carry out his work safely; and

(b) health surveillance required to be provided to that employee by or under any of the relevant statutory provisions.

(3) Every employer and every self-employed person shall ensure that every person carrying on an employment business whose employees are to carry out work in his undertaking is provided with comprehensible information on--

(a) any special occupational qualifications or skills required to be held by those employees if they are to carry out their work safely; and

(b) the specific features of the jobs to be filled by those employees (in so far as those features are likely to affect their health and safety);

and the person carrying on the employment business concerned shall ensure that the information so provided is given to the said employees.

NOTES

Initial Commencement

Specified date

Specified date: 29 December 1999: see reg 1(1).

UK Parliament SIs 1990-1999/1999/3201-3250/Management of Health and Safety at Work Regulations 1999 (SI 1999/3242)/16 Risk assessment in respect of new or expectant mothers

16 Risk assessment in respect of new or expectant mothers

(1) Where--

(a) the persons working in an undertaking include women of child-bearing age; and

(b) the work is of a kind which could involve risk, by reason of her condition, to the health and safety of a new or expectant mother, or to that of her baby, from any processes or working conditions, or physical, biological or chemical agents, including those specified in Annexes I and II of Council Directive 92/85/EEC on the introduction of measures to encourage improvements in the safety and health at work of pregnant workers and workers who have recently given birth or are breastfeeding, the assessment required by regulation 3(1) shall also include an assessment of such risk.

(2) Where, in the case of an individual employee, the taking of any other action the employer is required to take under the relevant statutory provisions would not avoid the risk referred to in paragraph (1) the employer shall, if it is reasonable to do so, and would avoid such risks, alter her working conditions or hours of work.

(3) If it is not reasonable to alter the working conditions or hours of work, or if it would not avoid such risk, the employer shall, subject to section 67 of the 1996 Act suspend the employee from work for so long as is necessary to avoid such risk.

(4) In paragraphs (1) to (3) references to risk, in relation to risk from any infectious or contagious disease, are references to a level of risk at work which is in addition to the level to which a new or expectant mother may be expected to be exposed outside the workplace.

NOTES

Initial Commencement

Specified date

Specified date: 29 December 1999: see reg 1(1).

UK Parliament SIs 1990-1999/1999/3201-3250/Management of Health and Safety at Work Regulations 1999 (SI 1999/3242)/17 Certificate from registered medical practitioner in respect of new or expectant mothers

17 Certificate from registered medical practitioner in respect of new or expectant mothers

Where--

(a) a new or expectant mother works at night; and

(b) a certificate from a registered medical practitioner or a registered midwife shows that it is necessary for her health or safety that she should not be at work for any period of such work identified in the certificate,

the employer shall, subject to section 67 of the 1996 Act, suspend her from work for so long as is necessary for her health or safety.

NOTES

Initial Commencement

Specified date

Specified date: 29 December 1999: see reg 1(1).

UK Parliament SIs 1990-1999/1999/3201-3250/Management of Health and Safety at Work Regulations 1999 (SI 1999/3242)/18 Notification by new or expectant mothers

18 Notification by new or expectant mothers

(1) Nothing in paragraph (2) or (3) of regulation 16 shall require the employer to take any action in relation to an employee until she has notified the employer in writing that she is pregnant, has given birth

within the previous six months, or is breastfeeding.

(2) Nothing in paragraph (2) or (3) of regulation 16 or in regulation 17 shall require the employer to maintain action taken in relation to an employee--

(a) in a case--

(i) to which regulation 16(2) or (3) relates; and

(ii) where the employee has notified her employer that she is pregnant, where she has failed, within a reasonable time of being requested to do so in writing by her employer, to produce for the employer's inspection a certificate from a registered medical practitioner or a registered midwife showing that she is pregnant;

(b) once the employer knows that she is no longer a new or expectant mother; or

(c) if the employer cannot establish whether she remains a new or expectant mother.

NOTES

Initial Commencement

Specified date

Specified date: 29 December 1999: see reg 1(1).

UK Parliament SIs 1990-1999/1999/3201-3250/Management of Health and Safety at Work Regulations 1999 (SI 1999/3242)/19 Protection of young persons

19 Protection of young persons

(1) Every employer shall ensure that young persons employed by him are protected at work from any risks to their health or safety which are a consequence of their lack of experience, or absence of awareness of existing or potential risks or the fact that young persons have not yet fully matured.

(2) Subject to paragraph (3), no employer shall employ a young person for work--

(a) which is beyond his physical or psychological capacity;

(b) involving harmful exposure to agents which are toxic or carcinogenic, cause heritable genetic damage or harm to the unborn child or which in any other way chronically affect human health;

(c) involving harmful exposure to radiation;

(d) involving the risk of accidents which it may reasonably be assumed cannot be recognised or avoided by young persons owing to their insufficient attention to safety or lack of experience or training; or

(e) in which there is a risk to health from--

(i) extreme cold or heat;

(ii) noise; or

(iii) vibration,

and in determining whether work will involve harm or risks for the purposes of this paragraph, regard shall be had to the results of the assessment.

(3) Nothing in paragraph (2) shall prevent the employment of a young person who is no longer a child for work--

(a) where it is necessary for his training;

(b) where the young person will be supervised by a competent person; and

(c) where any risk will be reduced to the lowest level that is reasonably practicable.

(4) . . .

NOTES

Initial Commencement

Specified date

Specified date: 29 December 1999: see reg 1(1).

Amendment

Para (4): revoked by SI 2003/2457, regs 2, 5.

Date in force: 27 October 2003: see SI 2003/2457, reg 1.

UK Parliament SIs 1990-1999/1999/3201-3250/Management of Health and Safety at Work Regulations 1999 (SI 1999/3242)/20 Exemption certificates

20 Exemption certificates

(1) The Secretary of State for Defence may, in the interests of national security, by a certificate in writing exempt--

(a) any of the home forces, any visiting force or any headquarters from those requirements of these Regulations which impose obligations other than those in regulations 16-18 on employers; or

(b) any member of the home forces, any member of a visiting force or any member of a headquarters from the requirements imposed by regulation 14;

and any exemption such as is specified in sub-paragraph (a) or (b) of this paragraph may be granted subject to conditions and to a limit of time and may be revoked by the said Secretary of State by a further certificate in writing at any time.

(2) In this regulation--

(a) "the home forces" has the same meaning as in section 12(1) of the Visiting Forces Act 1952;

(b) "headquarters" means a headquarters for the time being specified in Schedule 2 to the Visiting Forces and International Headquarters (Application of Law) Order 1999;

(c) "member of a headquarters" has the same meaning as in paragraph 1(1) of the Schedule to the International Headquarters and Defence Organisations Act 1964; and

(d) "visiting force" has the same meaning as it does for the purposes of any provision of Part I of the Visiting Forces Act 1952.

NOTES

Initial Commencement

Specified date

Specified date: 29 December 1999: see reg 1(1).

UK Parliament SIs 1990-1999/1999/3201-3250/Management of Health and Safety at Work Regulations 1999 (SI 1999/3242)/21 Provisions as to liability

21 Provisions as to liability

Nothing in the relevant statutory provisions shall operate so as to afford an employer a defence in any criminal proceedings for a contravention of those provisions by reason of any act or default of--

(a) an employee of his, or

(b) a person appointed by him under regulation 7.

NOTES

Initial Commencement

Specified date

Specified date: 29 December 1999: see reg 1(1).

UK Parliament SIs 1990-1999/1999/3201-3250/Management of Health and Safety at Work Regulations 1999 (SI 1999/3242)/[22 Restriction of civil liability for breach of statutory duty]

[22 Restriction of civil liability for breach of statutory duty]

[(1) Breach of a duty imposed on an employer by these Regulations shall not confer a right of action in any civil proceedings insofar as that duty applies for the protection of a third party.

(2) Breach of a duty imposed on an employee by regulation 14 shall not confer a right of action in any civil proceedings insofar as that duty applies for the protection of a third party.

(3) In this regulation, "third party", in relation to the undertaking, means any person who may be affected by that undertaking other than the employer whose undertaking it is and persons in his employment.]

NOTES

Amendment

Substituted by SI 2006/438, reg 2.

Date in force: 6 April 2006: see SI 2006/438, reg 1.

UK Parliament SIs 1990-1999/1999/3201-3250/Management of Health and Safety at Work Regulations 1999 (SI 1999/3242)/23 Extension outside Great Britain

23 Extension outside Great Britain

(1) These Regulations shall, subject to regulation 2, apply to and in relation to the premises and activities outside Great Britain to which sections 1 to 59 and 80 to 82 of the Health and Safety at Work etc Act 1974 apply by virtue of the Health and Safety at Work etc Act 1974 (Application Outside Great Britain) Order 1995 as they apply within Great Britain.

(2) For the purposes of Part I of the 1974 Act, the meaning of "at work" shall be extended so that an employee or a self-employed person shall be treated as being at work throughout the time that he is present at the premises to and in relation to which these Regulations apply by virtue of paragraph (1); and, in that connection, these Regulations shall have effect subject to the extension effected by this paragraph.

NOTES

Initial Commencement

Specified date

Specified date: 29 December 1999: see reg 1(1).

UK Parliament SIs 1990-1999/1999/3201-3250/Management of Health and Safety at Work Regulations 1999 (SI 1999/3242)/24 Amendment of the Health and Safety (First-Aid) Regulations 1981

24 Amendment of the Health and Safety (First-Aid) Regulations 1981

Regulation 6 of the Health and Safety (First-Aid) Regulations 1981 is hereby revoked.

NOTES

Initial Commencement

Specified date

Specified date: 29 December 1999: see reg 1(1).

UK Parliament SIs 1990-1999/1999/3201-3250/Management of Health and Safety at Work Regulations 1999 (SI 1999/3242)/25 Amendment of the Offshore Installations and Pipeline Works (First-Aid) Regulations 1989

25 Amendment of the Offshore Installations and Pipeline Works (First-Aid) Regulations 1989

(1) The Offshore Installations and Pipeline Works (First-Aid) Regulations 1989 shall be amended in accordance with the following provisions of this regulation.

(2) In regulation 7(1) for the words "from all or any of the requirements of these Regulations", there shall be substituted the words "from regulation 5(1)(b) and (c) and (2)(a) of these Regulations".

(3) After regulation 7(2) the following paragraph shall be added--

"(3) An exemption granted under paragraph (1) above from the requirements in regulation 5(2)(a) of these Regulations shall be subject to the condition that a person provided under regulation 5(1)(a) of these Regulations shall have undergone adequate training.".

NOTES

Initial Commencement

Specified date

Specified date: 29 December 1999: see reg 1(1).

UK Parliament SIs 1990-1999/1999/3201-3250/Management of Health and Safety at Work Regulations 1999 (SI 1999/3242)/26 Amendment of the Mines Miscellaneous Health and Safety Provisions Regulations 1995

26 Amendment of the Mines Miscellaneous Health and Safety Provisions Regulations 1995

(1) The Mines Miscellaneous Health and Safety Provisions Regulations 1995 shall be amended in accordance with the following provisions of this regulation.

(2) Paragraph (2)(b) of regulation 4 shall be deleted.

(3) After paragraph (4) of regulation 4 there shall be added the following paragraph--

"(5) In relation to fire, the health and safety document prepared pursuant to paragraph (1) shall--

(a) include a fire protection plan detailing the likely sources of fire, and the precautions to be taken to protect against, to detect and combat the outbreak and spread of fire; and

(b) in respect of every part of the mine other than any building on the surface of that mine--

(i) include the designation of persons to implement the plan, ensuring that the number of such persons, their training and the equipment available to them is adequate, taking into account the size of, and the specific hazards involved in the mine concerned; and

(ii) include the arrangements for any necessary contacts with external emergency services, particularly as regards rescue work and fire-fighting; and

(iii) be adapted to the nature of the activities carried on at that mine, the size of the mine and take account of the persons other than employees who may be present.".

NOTES

Initial Commencement

Specified date

Specified date: 29 December 1999: see reg 1(1).

UK Parliament SIs 1990-1999/1999/3201-3250/Management of Health and Safety at Work Regulations 1999 (SI 1999/3242)/27

27 ...

. . .

NOTES

Amendment

Revoked by SI 2007/320, reg 48(1), Sch 4.

Date in force: 6 April 2007: see SI 2007/320, reg 1.

UK Parliament SIs 1990-1999/1999/3201-3250/Management of Health and Safety at Work Regulations 1999 (SI 1999/3242)/28 . . .

28 ...

. . .

NOTES

Amendment

Revoked in relation to England and Wales by SI 2005/1541, art 53(2), Sch 5 and in relation to Scotland by SSI 2006/457, art 2(2), Sch 2.

Date in force (in relation to England and Wales): 1 October 2006: see SI 2005/1541, art 1(3) (as amended by SI 2006/484, art 2).
Date in force (in relation to Scotland): 1 October 2006: see SSI 2006/457, art 1.

UK Parliament SIs 1990-1999/1999/3201-3250/Management of Health and Safety at Work Regulations 1999 (SI 1999/3242)/29 Revocations and consequential amendments

29 Revocations and consequential amendments

(1) The Management of Health and Safety at Work Regulations 1992, the Management of Health and Safety at Work (Amendment) Regulations 1994, the Health and Safety (Young Persons) Regulations 1997 and Part III of the Fire Precautions (Workplace) Regulations 1997 are hereby revoked.

(2) The instruments specified in column 1 of Schedule 2 shall be amended in accordance with the corresponding provisions in column 3 of that Schedule.

NOTES

Initial Commencement

Specified date

Specified date: 29 December 1999: see reg 1(1).

UK Parliament SIs 1990-1999/1999/3201-3250/Management of Health and Safety at Work Regulations 1999 (SI 1999/3242)/30 Transitional provision

30 Transitional provision

The substitution of provisions in these Regulations for provisions of the Management of Health and Safety at Work Regulations 1992 shall not affect the continuity of the law; and accordingly anything done under or for the purposes of such provision of the 1992 Regulations shall have effect as if done under or for the purposes of any corresponding provision of these Regulations.

NOTES

Initial Commencement

Specified date

Specified date: 29 December 1999: see reg 1(1).

UK Parliament SIs 1990-1999/1999/3201-3250/Management of Health and Safety at Work Regulations 1999 (SI 1999/3242)/Signature(s)

Signed by authority of the Secretary of State

Whitty,

Parliamentary Under Secretary of State,

Department of the Environment, Transport and the Regions

3rd December 1999

UK Parliament SIs 1990-1999/1999/3201-3250/Management of Health and Safety at Work Regulations 1999 (SI 1999/3242)/SCHEDULE 1 General Principles of Prevention

SCHEDULE 1

GENERAL PRINCIPLES OF PREVENTION

Regulation 4

(This Schedule specifies the general principles of prevention set out in Article 6(2) of Council Directive 89/391/EEC)

(a) avoiding risks;

(b) evaluating the risks which cannot be avoided;

(c) combating the risks at source;

(d) adapting the work to the individual, especially as regards the design of workplaces, the choice of work equipment and the choice of working and production methods, with a view, in particular, to alleviating monotonous work and work at a predetermined work-rate and to reducing their effect on health;

(e) adapting to technical progress;

(f) replacing the dangerous by the non-dangerous or the less dangerous;

(g) developing a coherent overall prevention policy which covers technology, organisation of work, working conditions, social relationships and the influence of factors relating to the working environment;

(h) giving collective protective measures priority over individual protective measures; and

(i) giving appropriate instructions to employees.

NOTES

Initial Commencement

Specified date

Specified date: 29 December 1999: see reg 1(1).

UK Parliament SIs 1990-1999/1999/3201-3250/Management of Health and Safety at Work Regulations 1999 (SI 1999/3242)/SCHEDULE 2 Consequential Amendments

SCHEDULE 2

CONSEQUENTIAL AMENDMENTS

Regulation 29

Column 1 *Description of Instrument*	*Column 2* *References*	*Column 3* *Extent of Modification*
The Safety Representatives and Safety Committees Regulations 1977	SI 1977/500; amended by SI 1992/2051; SI 1996/1513; SI 1997/1840; SI 1999/860 and by section 1(1) and (2) of the Employment Rights (Dispute Resolution) Act 1998.	In regulation 4A(1)(b) for "regulations 6(1) and 7(1)(b) of the Management of Health and Safety at Work Regulations 1992", there shall be substituted "regulations 7(1) and 8(1)(b) of the Management of Health and Safety at Work Regulations 1999;".
The Offshore Installations (Safety Representatives and Safety Committees) Regulations 1989	SI 1989/971; amended by SI 1992/2885; SI 1993/1823; SI 1995/738; SI 1995/743; and SI 1995/3163.	In regulation 23(4) for "regulation 6(1) of the Management of Health and Safety at Work Regulations 1992", there shall be substituted "regulation 7(1) of the Management of Health and Safety at Work Regulations 1999".
The Railways (Safety Case) Regulations 1994	SI 1994/237; amended by SI 1996/1592.	In paragraph 6 of Schedule 1 for "regulation 3 of the Management of Health and Safety at Work Regulations 1992 and particulars of the arrangements he has made pursuant to regulation 4(1) thereof.", there shall be substituted "regulation 3 of the Management of Health and Safety at Work Regulations 1999 and particulars of the arrangements he has made in accordance with regulation 5(1) thereof.".
The Suspension from Work	SI 1994/2930.	In article 1(2)(b) for ""the 1992

(on Maternity Grounds) Order 1994*		Regulations" means the Management of Health and Safety at Work Regulations 1992", there shall be substituted, ""the 1999 Regulations" means the Management of Health and Safety at Work Regulations 1999"; and In article 2(b) for "regulation 13B of the 1992 regulations", there shall be substituted "regulation 17 of the 1999 Regulations".
. . .	. . .	. . .
The Escape and Rescue from Mines Regulations 1995	SI 1995/2870.	In regulation 2(1) for ""the 1992 Regulations" means the Management of Health and Safety at Work Regulations 1992", there shall be substituted ""the 1999 Regulations" means the Management of Health and Safety at Work Regulations 1999"; and In regulation 4(2) for "regulation 3 of the 1992 Regulations," there shall be substituted "regulation 3 of the 1999 Regulations.".
The Mines Miscellaneous Health and Safety Provisions Regulations 1995	SI 1995/2005.	In regulation 2(1) for ""the 1992 regulations" means the Management of Health and Safety at Work Regulations 1992;", there shall be substituted ""the 1999 Regulations" means the Management of Health and Safety at Work Regulations 1999;"; and In regulation 4(1)(a) for "regulation 3 of the 1992 Regulations;", there shall be substituted "regulation 3 of the 1999 Regulations;".
The Quarries Miscellaneous Health and Safety Provisions Regulations 1995	SI 1995/2036.	In regulation 2(1) for ""the 1992 Regulations" means the Management of Health and Safety at Work Regulations 1992;", there shall be substituted ""the 1999 Regulations" means the Management of Health and Safety at Work Regulations 1999;" and In regulation 4(1)(a) for "regulation 3 of the 1992 Regulations;", there shall be substituted "regulation 3 of the 1999 Regulations;".
The Borehole Sites and Operations Regulations 1995	SI 1995/2038.	In regulation 7(5) for ""the Management Regulations" means the Management of Health and Safety at Work Regulations

		1992", there shall be substituted ""the Management Regulations" means the Management of Health and Safety at Work Regulations 1999.".
The Gas Safety (Management) Regulations 1996	SI 1996/551.	In paragraph 5 of Schedule 1 for "regulation 3 of the Management of Health and Safety at Work Regulations 1992, and particulars of the arrangements he has made in accordance with regulation 4(1) thereof.", there shall be substituted "regulation 3 of the Management of Health and Safety at Work Regulations 1999, and particulars of the arrangements he has made in accordance with regulation 5(1) thereof.".
The Health and Safety (Safety Signs and Signals) Regulations 1996	SI 1996/341.	In regulation 4(1) for "paragraph (1) of regulation 3 of the Management of Health and Safety at Work Regulations 1992", there shall be substituted "paragraph (1) of regulation 3 of the Management of Health and Safety at Work Regulations 1999".
The Health and Safety (Consultation with Employees) Regulations 1996	SI 1996/1513.	In regulation 3(b) for "regulations 6(1) and 7(1)(b) of the Management of Health and Safety at Work Regulations 1992", there shall be substituted "regulations 7(1) and 8(1)(b) of the Management of Health and Safety at Work Regulations 1999".
The Fire Precautions (Workplace) Regulations 1997	SI 1997/1840; amended by SI 1999/1877.	In regulation 2(1) for ""the 1992 Management Regulations" means the Management of Health and Safety at Work Regulations 1992", there shall be substituted ""the 1999 Management Regulations" means the Management of Health and Safety at Work Regulations 1999"; In regulation 2(1) in the definitions of "employee" and "employer" for "1992" substitute "1999"; and In regulation 9(2)(b) for the words "regulations 1 to 4, 6 to 10 and 11(2) and (3) of the 1992 Management Regulations (as amended by Part III of these

		Regulations)", there shall be substituted "regulations 1 to 5, 7 to 12 and 13(2) and (3) of the 1999 Management Regulations".
The Control of Lead at Work Regulations 1998	SI 1998/543.	In regulation 5 for "regulation 3 of the Management of Health and Safety at Work Regulations 1992", there shall be substituted "regulation 3 of the Management of Health and Safety at Work Regulations 1999".
The Working Time Regulations 1998*	SI 1998/1833.	In regulation 6(8)(b) for "regulation 3 of the Management of Health and Safety at Work Regulations 1992", there shall be substituted "regulation 3 of the Management of Health and Safety at Work Regulations 1999".
The Quarries Regulations 1999	SI 1999/2024.	In regulation 2(1) for ""the 1992 Regulations means the Management of Health and Safety at Work Regulations 1992;", there shall be substituted ""the 1999 Regulations" means the Management of Health and Safety at Work Regulations 1999;". In regulation 7(1)(a) for "paragraphs (1) to (3c) of regulation 3 of the 1992 Regulations;" there shall be substituted "regulation 3 of the Management of Health and Safety at Work Regulations 1999". In regulation 43 for "regulation 5 of the 1992 regulations" there shall be substituted "regulation 6 of the 1999 Regulations".

Note

The Regulations marked with an asterisk are referred to in the Preamble to these Regulations.

NOTES

Initial Commencement

Specified date

Specified date: 29 December 1999: see reg 1(1).

Amendment

Entry relating to "The Construction (Design and Management) Regulations 1994" (omitted) revoked by SI 2007/320, reg 48(1), Sch 4.

Date in force: 6 April 2007: see SI 2007/320, reg 1.

UK Parliament SIs 1990-1999/1999/3201-3250/Management of Health and Safety at Work Regulations 1999 (SI 1999/3242)/EXPLANATORY NOTE

EXPLANATORY NOTE

(This note is not part of the Regulations)

1 These Regulations re-enact the Management of Health and Safety at Work Regulations 1992, with the following modifications--

2 A new regulation 4 requires an employer to implement preventive and protective measures on the basis of general principles of prevention set out in Article 6(2)(a)-(i) of Council Directive 89/391/EEC (OJ No L 183, 29.6.89, p 1) and specified in Schedule 1 to the Regulations.

3 A new regulation 7(8) requires that a competent person in the employer's employment shall be appointed for the purpose of paragraph (1) of regulation 7 in preference to a competent person who is not in such employment. Minor consequential amendments are made to regulation 7(5) of these Regulations.

4 A new regulation 9 requires every employer to arrange any necessary contacts with external services, especially as regards first-aid, emergency medical care and rescue work.

5 A new regulation 21 provides that an employer is not to be afforded a defence for contravention of the relevant statutory provisions as defined in section 53 of the Health and Safety at Work etc Act 1974 by reason of any act or default caused by his employee or by a person appointed by the employer under regulation 7 of these Regulations.

6 The Regulations revoke regulation 6 of the Health and Safety (First-Aid) Regulations 1981 which confers power on the Health and Safety Executive to grant exemptions from those Regulations (regulation 24). The Regulations also amend the Offshore Installations and Pipeline Works (First-Aid) Regulations 1989 to limit the scope of the exemptions that may be granted by the Health and Safety Executive to those specified in regulation 5(1)(b)(c) and (2)(a) of those Regulations, and to impose a condition that where an exemption is granted the person provided under regulation 5(1)(a) shall have undergone adequate training (regulation 25).

7 These Regulations amend the Mines Miscellaneous Health and Safety Provisions Regulations 1995 so as to give full effect to Articles 8(1) and 8(2) of Council Directive 89/391/EEC. A new paragraph (5) in regulation 4 requires that a fire protection plan be included in all cases in the health and safety document prepared under the Regulations. In respect of all parts of a mine other than buildings on the surface, the provision requires every mine owner to designate in the document the persons who are to implement the plan and to include in the document the arrangements for the necessary contacts with external services especially as regards rescue work and fire-fighting (regulation 26).

8 These Regulations amend the Construction (Health, Safety and Welfare) Regulations 1996 so as to give full effect to Article 8(1) and 8(2) of the Directive. Regulation 20 is amended so that arrangements for dealing with foreseeable emergencies on construction sites include the designation of persons to implement the arrangements and the inclusion of necessary contacts with external services, especially as regards rescue work and fire-fighting (regulation 27).

9 The Regulations provide that, subject to the exceptions specified in regulation 9 of the Fire Precautions (Workplace) Regulations 1997, they have effect as health and safety regulations within the meaning of the Health and Safety at Work etc Act 1974 (regulation 28).

7 MANUAL HANDLING

7 MANUAL HANDLING

Contents

7.1 Introduction

More than 1 in 4 of all reportable injuries sustained at work arise out of manual handling operations, that is the transporting, supporting, lifting, putting down, pushing, pulling carrying or moving a load by hand or bodily force. Since the 1st January 1993 these operations have been governed by the Manual Handling Operations Regulations 1992 which were introduced under Section 15 of the Health and Safety at Work Act 1974 and are intended to implement the EC Directive of the 29th May 1990 (90/269/EEC).

7.2 Manual Handling Operation Regulations 1992

7.2.1 On whom is the duty laid?

Regulation 5 places a duty on an employee to make full and proper use of any system of work provided for his use by his employer. The regulations are however principally concerned with the duties of employers to their employees. A self-employed person owes the duties set down under the regulations to himself. One of the first matters therefore to determine when considering any claim being made under the Manual Handling Operations and Directives is whether the injured person is truly an employee or whether he is an independent contractor.

The regulations do not cover the crew of a seagoing ship but they would apply to an offshore gas or oil installation and to work being carried out on ships and the loading and unloading of ships in port.

The regulations apply to servants of the Crown but the Secretary of State for Defence may in the interest of national security exempt any of the home forces, visiting force or headquarters from the requirements of Regulation 4 and 5.

In respect of agency staff the duty lies with the agency, which employs them, not with the firm to which the agency hires them out, although that firm could still have common law and other statutory duties to them.

7.2.2 What are manual handling operations?

These are defined in Regulation 2 as:

> **"any transporting or supporting of a load including the lifting, putting down, pushing, pulling, carrying or moving thereof by hand or by bodily force."**

A load includes any person and any animal. The regulations therefore have considerable importance for nursing and social service professions as well as for the more obvious types of manual handling such as bin emptying or furniture removal. They do not however apply to every use of the hand. The task must include the moving or supporting of a load, so for example they do not apply to typing or operating the controls of a machine even though these tasks may involve a risk of injury.

7.3 Duties of Employers

There are essentially just two duties under the Regulations.

The first duty is, in so far as is **reasonably practicable**, to **avoid** the need for his employees to undertake **any** manual handling operations at work which **involve a risk of their being injured**.

It really cannot be stressed too strongly that this duty has seriously to be considered and dealt with in meeting any claim made for a manual handling injury. The employer can only acquit himself by showing that he has reduced the risk of injury to the lowest practicable level if he has already shown that it is not reasonably practicable to avoid doing the task manually in the first place.

The second duty is, if the need to carry out a manual handling operation, which involves the risk of injury, cannot be avoided, then the risk of injury must be reduced to the lowest level reasonably practicable.

7.3.1 Avoiding the need for manual handling

Points that need to be considered in relation to this duty are:

i) is it a manual handling operation?

ii) is this an employee who has been required to carry it out?

iii) is there a risk of their being injured?

iv) what do we mean by injury?

v) is it reasonably practicable to avoid this operation?

vi) is it a manual handling operation?

The claims handler will inevitably be presented with claims under these regulations where the task clearly does not fall within the definition. These regulations are essentially concerned with the movement of loads, if you think of "supporting" as an aid to or of prevention of movement that may assist in determining whether a task is a manual handling operation. The regulations do not apply to manually working on an object, which is static and secured by non-manual means; the example of typing has already been given.

On the other hand do not overlook the fact that a task whose main component does not fall within the regulations nonetheless has components, which do. For example the employee who slipped while carrying out gritting was able to show this was a manual handling operation because he was moving the grit in a barrow.

ii) an Employee?

The definition of employee is dealt with in the Employers Liability chapter, but do bear in mind the duty in respect of Agency employees lies with the Agency, which employs them.

iii) and iv). risk of injury?

Injury, it should be noted, is any form of injury excluding injury caused by any toxic or corrosive substance that has either leaked or spilled from the load or is present on the surface of the load or is a constituent part of the load. It is not restricted to back injury although the manual handling directive refers to avoiding or reducing the risk "particularly of back injury to workers".

The regulations are relevant if the injury sustained is caused by the employee falling perhaps because he could not see where he was going because of the load; we have already given the example of the man slipping on ice while pushing a barrow. Another example would be an employee cutting himself on part of the load or indeed on something adjacent whilst moving the load.

The question of whether the operations involve "a risk" of an employee being injured is likely to be contentious.

In ***Anderson v Lothian Health Board (1996)*** it was held that "for there to be a risk of injury, injury need be no more than a foreseeable possibility; it need not be a probability.

In ***Hawkes v London Borough of Southwark (1998)*** a "slight" risk of falling was nonetheless held to be "a real risk".

On the other hand in ***Hillhouse v South Ayrshire Council (2000)*** the task of carrying tables about 86 yards was found not to involve a risk of injury, and in ***Koonjul v Thameslink Healthcare Services (2000)*** the Court of Appeal were similarly unimpressed by the risks of bed-making.

There is unfortunately no alternative to looking at each task on its own merits. Even the HSE guidelines, which attempt to establish "an approximate boundary within which the load is unlikely to create a risk of injury sufficient to warrant a detailed assessment", go on to say: "There is no threshold below which Manual Handling operations may be regarded as "safe". Even operations lying within the boundary mapped out by the guidelines should be avoided or made less demanding."

v). reasonably practicable to avoid the operation?

As already stated if the task does involve a risk of injury it is absolutely essential to show that it is not reasonably practicable to avoid Manual Handling or your Defence falls at the first hurdle. ***King v RCO Support Services Ltd (2001), Hall v Edinburgh City Council (1999).***

The Courts do accept that it is not reasonably practicable to avoid the risk of injury in some tasks. For example in nursing e.g. ***Brown v East and Midlothian NHS Trust (2000).***

In considering whether it is reasonably practicable to avoid a manual handling operation, which involves the risk of injury, it is probably helpful to see the standard as being the counsel of perfection. If mechanical means could be used to move the load then they should be. If for example a load can be placed in a lorry using a forklift truck rather than being lifted manually then it should be. If a non-weight bearing patient can be transferred from bed to toilet using a hoist then the patient should be so moved.

7.3.2 Reducing the Risk of Injury to the Lowest Level Reasonably Practicable

A. Making an Assessment

If an employee is going to have to manually handle a load and if there is a risk of him being injured in doing so, an employer must make an assessment. What is required to be dealt with in the assessment is covered in Schedule One of the Regulations and is reproduced below.

The employer is also required to give employees carrying out manual handling operations general or if possible precise indications as to the weight of each load and the heaviest side of any load whose centre of gravity is not positioned centrally.

The employer is also required to carry out a fresh assessment if there is reason to suspect that the original assessment is no longer valid or if there has been a significant change in the manual handling operations to which it relates.

The Courts do however take the view that the making of an Assessment is in itself not always reasonably practicable. For example it may not be practicable to do so in an emergency. Indeed it was held, in ***Fraser v Greater Glasgow Health Board (1996)***, that Regulation 4 did not apply to an emergency lift performed by a nurse and that Regulation 4.1(b) was only applicable to manual handling operations, which were regularly undertaken.

At the other end of the scale there is the case of ***Koonjul v Thames Link Health Care Services NHS Trust (2000).*** This involved a health care assistant having to pull a low bed away from the wall and bend low whilst making it. The Court of Appeal held that there had to be an element of realism. That it was unrealistic where a number of every day tasks were undertaken that the level of risk involved should be met by a precise evaluation of each task with a warning as to how each task was to be performed.

It has also been held that an Assessment need not be formal ***Rowe v Swansea City and County Council (1999).***

It has also been held that training can satisfy the need for an Assessment. ***Brown v East and Midlothian NHS Trust (2000).***

UK Parliament SIs 1990-1999/1992/2751-2800/Manual Handling Operations Regulations 1992 (SI 1992/2793)/SCHEDULE 1 Factors to Which the Employer Must Have Regard and Questions he Must Consider When Making an Assessment of Manual Handling Operations

SCHEDULE 1

FACTORS TO WHICH THE EMPLOYER MUST HAVE REGARD AND QUESTIONS HE MUST CONSIDER WHEN MAKING AN ASSESSMENT OF MANUAL HANDLING OPERATIONS

Regulation 4(1)(b)(i)

Column 1 *Factors*	Column 2 *Questions*
1 The tasks	**Do they involve:** --holding or manipulating loads at distance from trunk? --unsatisfactory bodily movement or posture, especially: --twisting the trunk? --stooping? --reaching upwards? --excessive movement of loads, especially: --excessive lifting or lowering distances? --excessive carrying distances? --excessive pushing or pulling of loads? --risk of sudden movement of loads? --frequent or prolonged physical effort? --insufficient rest or recovery periods? --a rate of work imposed by a process?
2 The loads	**Are they:** --heavy? --bulky or unwieldy? --difficult to grasp? --unstable, or with contents likely to shift? --sharp, hot or otherwise potentially damaging?
3 The working environment	**Are there:** --space constraints preventing good posture? --uneven, slippery or unstable floors? --variations in level of floors or work surfaces? --extremes of temperature or humidity? --conditions causing ventilation problems or gusts of wind? --poor lighting conditions?
4 Individual capability	**Does the job:** --require unusual strength, height, etc? --create a hazard to those who might reasonably be considered to be pregnant or to have a health problem? --require special information or training for its safe performance?
5 Other factors	**Is movement or posture hindered by personal protective equipment or by clothing?**

B. Taking appropriate steps to reduce the risk of injury to the lowest level reasonably practicable

There are a number of steps, which the employer can take when he is presented with a risky form of manual handling.

1. Systems of Work

One obvious solution where there is a particularly heavy load is to stipulate that two, three or more employees, as appropriate, should carry out the lift. It is essential where this is done that everyone understands the manoeuvre they are undertaking and that someone makes sure their efforts are co-ordinated. If a gang of four is carrying a heavy object and three leave go things will not go well for the fourth.

The employer could consider such matters as breaking down loads or containing them in such as way to make them more straightforward to handle.

2. Equipment

Another obvious solution would be to use some form of mechanical aid. For example in caring for the sick and elderly it has become common to use hoists. These unfortunately can introduce new dangers such as the patient falling out of the sling, and may cause employers to overlook that there can still be a manual handling risk from getting the patient in and out of the hoist and moving the hoist. These new risks have to be assessed and dealt with. And appropriate information, instruction and training given.

It must be borne in mind also that this equipment will be work equipment and fall under the Provision and Use of Work Equipment Regulations 1998.

3. Working Environment

Where the problems relate to the working environment clearly the employer should be able to improve things such as uneven or slippery floors, and deal with poor lighting or ventilation problems. Where the employer takes such steps he must make sure that his employees are provided with proper instructions and proper supervision in order to make sure that they understand and carry out the steps necessary to reduce the risk.

It may be more difficult where the work is being carried on away from the employer's premises. A good example is Home Care Workers working in private homes full of furniture and not designed to accommodate large pieces of equipment like hoists and with flooring which wheeled equipment will not traverse easily.

Remember in such cases that the duty is to reduce the risk to the lowest level reasonably practicable. The employer must maximise space as much as possible and ensure that the Care Assistants have proper instruction and systems of work to make the best of the space available, but the employer is not required to eliminate all risk.

4. Training

Strangely the Manual Handling Operations Regulations contain no requirement for training in manual handling operations. This is odd because the ECC directive on manual handling at Article 6 requires that employers must ensure that workers receive proper training and information on how to handle loads correctly and the risk that they may be open to particularly if those tasks are not performed correctly.

Despite this apparent serious omission, an employer would not be able to argue successfully that he had taken appropriate steps to reduce the risk of injury to the lowest level reasonably practicable, if he had undertaken no training or inadequate training of the employees who were to carry out the work.

The Courts in fact find training to be an essential element in reducing the risk of injury e.g. ***Peck v Chief Constable of Avon and Somerset (1999)***; and as stated above good training can on occasion replace the need for a risk assessment.

The level of training necessary would obviously vary according to the variety and complexity of tasks that an employee would be required to carry out.

If there is a risk of injury in a manual handling operation, and the employer has decided on the safest way of carrying out the operation to reduce that risk to the minimum; then clearly he must show the employee how to carry out that operation and he must warn him against incorrect ways of carrying out that operation and point out the dangers to him of doing it in that incorrect manner.

The employer must ensure that the training is done in such a way that it is understandable by the employee. Further training must be reinforced by proper supervision and it will not help the employer if he has given adequate training but subsequently his supervisors have then tolerated bad practice.

7.4 Individual Capability

The checklist for manual handling assessment, contained in schedule one of the regulations, requires the employer to consider the individual capability of the employee in the following terms:

1. Does the job require unusual strength, height, etc.
2. Create a hazard to those who might be considered to be pregnant or have a health problem.
3. Require special training for it's safe performance

It is interesting that the regulations do not consider the position of the unusually short or weak employee. One wonders whether the courts would consider shortness a health problem! The Directive in Annex 2 puts the question more broadly and requires the employer to consider whether the employee is physically unsuited to carry out the task in question. One suspects that in this respect the Regulations would be interpreted in line with the Directive. ***Wells v West Hertfordshire Health Authority 2000 and Wiles v Bedfordshire County Council (2001)*** are examples of workers with particular health problems succeeding with cases where others might have failed.

Note on the other hand that special training can be a reasonable answer to a particularly hazardous task, that might well be particularly true in respect of the emergency services.

7.5 The Impact of the EC Directive

As has been pointed out there are a number of respects in which the Manual Handling Regulations do not fully implement the EC Directive on manual handling. The regulations do not appear to apply to temporary agency workers. Reference to reasonable practicability in Regulation 4(1) is not contained in Article 3 of the manual handling directive and the consideration of the personal limitations of the employee is more restricted in the Regulations than in the Directive.

Where regulations are intended to implement a European Directive, as clearly is the case here, they must be construed "purposively". That is, they must be interpreted in such a way that they will bring about the results envisaged by the directive.

The Judgement of the European Court of Justice in ***Marleasing SA v La Commercial Internacional de Alimentacion SA (1990)*** stated that:

> **"in applying the National Law whether the provisions in question were adopted after the Directive the national Court called upon to interpret it is required to do so as far as possible in the light of the wording and the purpose of the Directive in order to achieve the result pursued by the latter and thereby comply with Article 189 of the Treaty".**

If however the regulations cannot be interpreted in order to achieve the purpose of the Directive, a Directive will apply directly where the employer is an emanation of the state. This would include Central Government and Local Government bodies, Health Authorities, Police Authorities and even privatised utilities.

It does not follow however that the Court would find that the duty imposed by the Directive is greater than that by the Regulations.

It should be borne in mind that whilst Regulation 4(1) requires the employer to avoid the need for his employees to undertake any manual handling operations at work which involve a risk of their being injured "so far as is reasonably practicable", Article 3.1 certainly envisages that it will not always be possible to avoid manual handling which involves the risk of injury. Whilst Regulation 4B(2) requires the employer to reduce the risk of injury to the lowest level reasonably practicable Article 3(2) requires the employer to reduce the risk of manual handling of such loads, not to eliminate it.

7.6 Some Practical Guidance

The Health and Safety Executive has produced some numerical guidelines. These deal with weights of loads being:

a) Lifted and lowered

b) Pushed and pulled

c) Handled while seated.

They take into account such factors as handling the load away from the body, twisting and frequency of effort. The aim of the guidelines is to establish an initial filter. If the load exceeds what the guidelines suggest the Health and Safety Executive does not say that that operation is dangerous but that it merits a detailed assessment. The Health and Safety Executive's own words are:

> "the guidelines set out an approximate boundary within which operations are unlikely to create a risk of injury sufficient to warrant a more detailed assessment".

Please bear in mind however what is said above about what the Courts consider to be a real risk of injury. In particular we refer again to the Judgement in *Anderson v Lothian Health Board (1996)*:

> "for there to be a risk of injury, injury need be no more than a foreseeable possibility".

We believe these guidelines are useful to the claims handler however in considering the approximate parameters of risk involved in a manual handling task. We would say that if a task fell beyond the guidelines and there had been no assessment the probabilities of a successful Defence would be very low. We reproduce the guidelines below but stress that they should be used with caution.

HSE

Health and Safety
Executive

General risk assessment guidelines

There is no such thing as a completely 'safe' manual handling operation. But working within the following guidelines will cut the risk and reduce the need for a more detailed assessment.

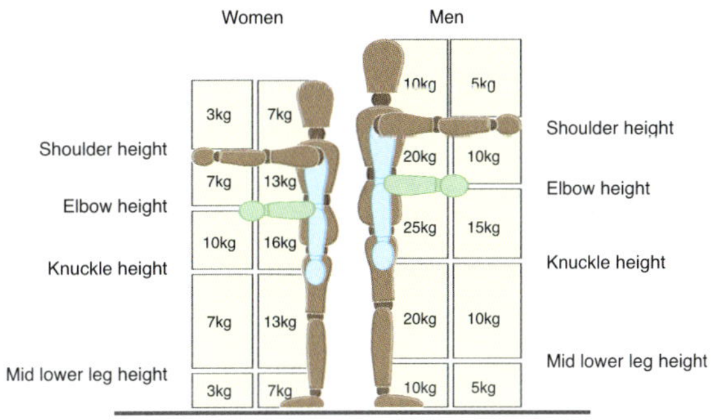

Figure 2 Lifting and lowering

- Use Figure 2 to make a quick and easy assessment. Each box contains a guideline weight for lifting and lowering in that zone. (As you can see, the guideline weights are reduced if handling is done with arms extended, or at high or low levels, as that is where injuries are most likely to occur.)
- Observe the work activity you are assessing and compare it to the diagram. First, decide which box or boxes the lifter's hands pass through when moving the load. Then, assess the maximum weight being handled. If it is less than the figure given in the box, the operation is within the guidelines.
- If the lifter's hands enter more than one box during the operation, use the smallest weight. Use an in-between weight if the hands are close to a boundary between boxes.
- The guideline weights assume that the load is readily grasped with both hands and that the operation takes place in reasonable working conditions, with the lifter in a stable body position.

Twisting

Reduce the guideline weights if the handler twists to the side during the operation. As a rough guide, reduce them by 10% if the handler twists beyond 45°, and by 20% if the handler twists beyond 90°.

Frequent lifting and lowering

The guideline weights are for infrequent operations - up to about 30 operations per hour - where the pace of work is not forced, adequate pauses to rest or use different muscles are possible, and the load is not supported by the handler for any length of time. Reduce the weights if the operation is repeated more often. As a rough guide, reduce the weights by 30% if the operation is repeated once or twice per minute, by 50% if the operation is repeated five to eight times a minute, and by 80% where the operation is repeated more than 12 times a minute.

HSE

Health and Safety Executive

Manual handling injuries can occur wherever people are at work - on farms and building sites, in factories, offices, warehouses, hospitals, banks, laboratories, and while making deliveries. Heavy manual labour, awkward postures, manual materials handling, and previous or existing injury are all risk factors implicated in the development of MSDs. More information and advice on MSDs is available on the HSE website, including advice on managing back pain at work (see 'Further reading').

Prevention and control of MSDs, such as manual handling injuries, has been identified as a priority by the Health and Safety Commission. Taking the action described in this booklet will help prevent these injuries and is likely to be cost-effective. However you cannot prevent all MSDs, so it is still essential to encourage early reporting of symptoms and make arrangements for the proper treatment and rehabilitation of anybody who does get injured.

What should I do about it?

Consider the risks from manual handling to the health and safety of your employees - the rest of this booklet will help you to do this. If there are risks, the Regulations apply.

Consult and involve the workforce. Your employees and their representatives know first-hand what the risks in the workplace are. They can probably offer practical solutions to controlling them.

What are my duties?

The Regulations require employers to:

- **avoid** the need for hazardous manual handling, so far as is reasonably practicable;
- **assess** the risk of injury from any hazardous manual handling that can't be avoided; and
- **reduce** the risk of injury from hazardous manual handling, so far as is reasonably practicable.

These points are explained in detail under 'Avoiding manual handling' and 'Assessing and reducing the risk of injury'.

Employees have duties too. They should:

- follow appropriate systems of work laid down for their safety;
- make proper use of equipment provided for their safety;
- co-operate with their employer on health and safety matters;
- inform the employer if they identify hazardous handling activities;
- take care to ensure that their activities do not put others at risk.

7.7 Check-list

The following check list should help to consider a manual handling claim in a structured way:

1. Is the Claimant an employee making a claim against his employer? If not then the regulations do not apply.
2. Was there a manual handling operation to be carried out?
3. Was the manual handling of a type that would carry a foreseeable risk of injury?
4. If it was, has an assessment been carried out?
5. If an assessment has been carried out is the assessment adequate? Consider here the requirements of Schedule 1 of the Regulations.
6. Could the need for manual handling be avoided by the use of mechanical means entirely?
7. If it could not what steps have been taken in terms of equipment, system of work and training?
8. Do the equipment system and training reduce the risk to the lowest possible level? Some might consider them adequate, but if it is reasonably practicable to reduce the risk even further, then they do not comply with the regulations.

8 OCCUPATIONAL DISEASE AND WORK RELATED ILLNESS CLAIMS

8 OCCUPATIONAL DISEASE AND WORK RELATED ILLNESS CLAIMS

Contents

8.1 General Introduction

It is a sad indictment of our industrial development that work related diseases have blighted and, in some cases, taken the lives of workers in countless occupations. Moreover, despite statutory regulation and improved industrial hygiene, newer work related illnesses and medical conditions have occurred in environments not previously considered to be hazardous such as offices, shops and hospitals.

It is not possible to deal with each and every occupational disease or work related illness in a single chapter. This chapter is heavily biased towards asbestos induced disease claims because of a plethora of recent case law. Nevertheless, much of what is said relative to investigating and defending an asbestos attributable disease claim, should be useful to a claims handler who finds himself dealing with a claim for say occupational deafness, vibration white finger or a repetitive strain injury. For simplicity and brevity, I shall for the remainder of this chapter refer to disease and occupational illness claims under the generic term "disease claims".

8.2 The Nature of Disease Claims

Disease claims arise as a result of a Claimant's culpable exposure by a Defendant to a toxic or dangerous substance or to an activity which induces injury.

Commonly, disease claims are employers' liability claims in that the culpable exposure to the toxic or dangerous substance occurred during the course of the Claimant's employment.

Disease claims may, however, be public liability claims, for example where a Claimant's exposure stems, not from the negligence or breach of statutory duty on the part of his own employer, but from the activities of other trades he worked alongside. A further example of a public liability disease claim is where a factory or installation allows a toxic or dangerous disease causing substance to escape from its premises thus exposing local inhabitants.

A public liability disease claim may also arise where the owner or occupier of premises used for manufacturing or storing toxic or dangerous substances, fails to take any or adequate steps to prevent visitors to those premises from being exposed to those substances.

Disease claims can also fall into the category of product liability claims where for example a Claimant claims compensation from a manufacturer or supplier of a product containing a toxic or dangerous substance with no warning as to the product's toxicity/danger, and where exposure caused the Claimant to contract a disease (e.g. moulded building materials containing asbestos).

8.3 The Unusual Characteristics of a Disease Claim

Most employers' liability and public liability personal injury claims result from an accident which occurred on a specific date. Commonly, there are witnesses to the accident and there is usually little doubt that the Claimant's injury was sustained in the index event.

Many occupational diseases are latent and arise long after the culpable exposure to a toxic or dangerous substance has ceased. Industrial diseases may be attributable to short, prolonged or intermittent exposure by one or several sources. By the time the Claimant has developed the first symptoms of his disease, there may be no independent witness evidence available to corroborate or controvert his alleged employment (in the case of an employers' liability claim) or his culpable exposure by the Defendant. In an asbestos induced mesothelioma claim, the disease may not manifest itself until 30 years or more after the Claimant was first exposed to the toxic or dangerous agent (asbestos dust and fibres) and, by the time of those first symptoms arise, the Claimant may have a life expectancy of only a few months.

The issue of medical causation comes into play more frequently in a disease claim because the symptoms of some industrial diseases (e.g. impaired lung function) may be caused or contributed to by some other unrelated medical condition.

In a typical accident at work claim, the Defendant will usually (a) be aware that the accident occurred and (b) will know something of the circumstances. Further, the Defendant will usually receive an intimation of any claim relatively soon after the incident occurred. A Defendant in a disease claim however has no specific incident upon which he can focus. There will be no entry in the accident report book. The culpable exposure may have occurred many years ago at a time when the Defendant company had different owners. The liabilities (realised or otherwise) as well as the assets of a Defendant company may have passed to the current proprietors upon the purchase of the company. Further, the new proprietors may never have utilised the toxic or dangerous substance which caused the Claimant's disease during the period of their proprietorship and yet they may still be liable since they may have acquired the company's liabilities as well as its assets.

When defending a disease claim, the Defendant frequently finds himself in the position of having to prove a negative. The Claimant may intimate a claim that he was culpably exposed to a toxic or dangerous substance during the course of his employment by the Defendant many years earlier. The Defendant may not have have their old employment records. They are very unlikely to have kept records which show whether or not they were using the toxic or dangerous substances at the time of the Claimant's alleged exposure. The Defendant may not have kept records from which he may establish who his insurers were at the time of the alleged culpable exposure. The Claimant may (in the absence of any documentary evidence) establish that he was once employed by the Defendants simply by giving oral evidence. There is little a Defendant can do in the absence of contemporaneous records to contradict the Claimant's evidence of employment. If the Claimant appears to be a truthful witness and a reasonable historian, then his evidence is likely to be accepted.

Defending a disease claim can feel akin to boxing with one arm tied behind one's back. Once a claim is intimated, a Defendant has a lot of ground to make up. The Claimant's solicitor will already have carried out his investigation and will be chomping at the bit to prosecute his client's claim as quickly as possible. In the case of a serious and life threatening industrial disease, the Claimant's solicitor will be unable to grant a Defendant much indulgence and it is not uncommon for such a case to be the subject of an Order for a speedy trial. Speedy directions in mesothelioma claims where the life expectancy of the victim is very short have resulted in trials only six weeks or so after the letters intimating those claims were written!

8.4 The History of Disease Claims

Historically, disease claims have resulted from poor levels of industrial hygiene, ignorance and even exploitation.

Until the latter third of the 20th Century, the attitude of employers and employees alike to health and safety in the work place was at best indifferent and at worst reckless. Up until the 1960s it was not uncommon for machinery to be operated without guards or other safety features. Airborne dust of many types was common in the work place and the provision of effective respirators and/or dust extracting systems was inadequate or non existent. Likewise, the provision of proper training and the enforcement of safe working practices did not feature in the workplace.

Legislation going back to the beginning of the last century imposed duties on owners and operators of factories to use all practicable steps to suppress and where possible, to remove from working areas, "gases, vapours, dust or other impurities... that may be injurious to health" (*Factory and Workshop Act*, 1901 s.1(1)(d)

As a result of the latent effect of many industrial diseases, and because of the law on limitation, most industrial disease claims were, until the 1960's, confined to claims for Workmen's Compensation under the Acts of 1897 and 1925. These Acts enabled a victim of an injury resulting from a breach of the Factories Acts or any similar legislation (e.g. The Asbestos Industry Regulations 1931) to obtain compensation without having to prove negligence on the part of his employer. An employer was able to insure against Workmen's Compensation Act liability (although there was no obligation to do so). Workmen's Compensation was confined to lost earnings up to specific limits. There was no compensation for pain, suffering and loss of amenity. Although a victim of an industrial disease could bring a common law claim for damages against his employer prior to the 1960's, there were difficulties. Many manual workers were poorly educated and were unaware of their rights. Prior to the introduction of Legal Aid, many manual workers, particularly those who were not members of a trade union, would not have had the means to sue their employers nor did they have the comfort of the employment protection laws that exist today. Of all the difficulties which beset a Claimant with an industrial disease, it was probably the law on limitation which caused the biggest problem.

Under the Limitation Act 1939, a Claimant in an action founded in tort could not bring an action after the expiration of six years from the date the cause of action accrued. The cause of action was deemed to have accrued once the damage had occurred. Therefore, in the case of an asbestotic, he may have sustained a significant injury to his lungs more than six years before he was diagnosed as having asbestosis. In such a case, the 1939 Act would have prevented him from bringing a civil action.

Matters were subsequently made worse for Claimants. Under the Limitation Act 1954 the limitation period in personal injury claims was reduced to 3 years from the date that damage occurred.

This obvious injustice was only temporary and under the Limitation Act 1963 the primary 3 year period for bringing a personal injury claim could be extended by the Court provided the Claimant was able to show that certain material facts remained outside his knowledge (actual or constructive) until after the expiration of the primary 3 year period.

It was the 1963 Act coupled with Legal Aid which lead to an increase in civil claims and a reduction in workmen's compensation claims. The Limitation Acts 1975 and 1980 (particularly the latter with its discretionary provisions) have further assisted Claimants in disease claims.

8.5 Types of Industrial Disease

As previously stated, it is not possible to deal with the many types of industrial disease in a single chapter. The following list of occupational diseases comprises a small selection:

8.5.1 Chest Diseases

a) Pneumoconiosis

Pneumoconiosis is a generic term for a group of diseases which result in the fibrosing (scarring) of the lung tissue following the inhalation of harmful dusts. The most common of these diseases are:

i) Asbestosis – from the inhalation of asbestos dust and fibres.

ii) Silicosis – from the inhalation of silica (rock dust).

iii) Berylliosis – from the inhalation of beryllium.

iv) Byssinosis – from the inhalation of cotton fibre or hemp dust.

v) Farmers' lung – from the inhalation of fungal spores from rotting hay or straw.

b) Allergic Chest Conditions

Allergic Chest conditions include occupationally induced:

i) Asthma – an allergic reaction to numerous substances found in the workplace such as dust and fumes which cause symptoms such as wheezing, coughing and breathlessness.

ii) Hard Metal Disease – an allergic condition contracted by workers engaged in the manufacture of certain metals and in particular cobalt and tungston carbide. Minor symptoms include asthma-like symptoms. The more serious cases can result in permanent pulmonary disease.

(iii) Welders Lung – a generic term commonly used to describe respiratory conditions caused by exposure to the fumes given off in welding. Symptoms include breathlessness, chronic bronchitis, emphysema and lung inflammation with reduced lung function.

8.5.2 Skin Conditions

These include:

a) Dermatitis – inflammation of the skin caused by exposure to numerous substances but commonly cement, detergents, solvents, hairdressing materials and bitumen. Dermatitis can be either irritant contact dermatitis or allergic contact dermatitis. The former is by far the most common.

b) Skin Cancer – caused by exposure to radiation, certain mineral oils, tar, pitch and arsenic.

c) Inflammation and Ulceration of the Skin – caused by exposure to electro magnetic radiations and ionising particles.

8.5.3 Industrial Deafness

Industrial deafness claims arise as a result of being exposed to excessive noise in the workplace. Prolonged exposure to noise was first identified as the cause of hearing loss as long ago as 1830 when Dr John Fosbroke published a paper in the Lancet.

A Claimant in an industrial deafness claim must establish (a) that he has sustained a hearing loss (b) that such loss of hearing was caused by him being exposed to excessive noise in his workplace and (c) that the level of noise to which he was exposed constituted a breach of duty on the part of his employer.

It is perhaps surprising that there was no statutory regulation which dealt expressly with noise in the workplace until the introduction of the control of noise regulations 1975. Prior to these regulations, a Claimant would have to establish negligence or a breach of Section 29 (i) of the Factories Act 1961 which imposed a general duty to make and keep a workplace safe. In 1963, the HSE published a pamphlet entitled "Noise and the Worker". Indeed, the date of "guilty" knowledge by which employers are judged to be fixed with liability appears to be 1963 (see ***Thomson v Smiths Ship Repairers Limited 1984*** AII ER 881)

In 1972 the Industrial Health Advisory Committee published its Code of Practice for Reducing Exposure of Employed Persons to Noise. This provided that continuous sound levels in the workplace would not exceed 90d(B)A.

In January 1990 the Noise at Work Regulations 1989 came into force. These regulations reduced the permissible noise threshold to 85d(B)A.

Several attempts have been made by Claimants to reduce the pre-1990 actionable noise threshold to 85d(B)A. One of these cases is worthy of a mention, namely ***Harris v BRB (Residuary) Limited (2005)*** EWCA Civ900. The Claimant alleged a hearing loss as a result of his exposure to noise from different types of locomotives he drove between 1974 and 1999. The Claimant's hearing loss had been established. At first instance the Judge held that the daily noise level to which the Claimant had been subjected (85d(B)A to 90d(B)A) imposed a common law duty on the Defendants; that the Claimant had been exposed to noise levels above 85dB(A); that the Defendant was not liable in negligence because it had consciously considered what precautions could have been taken but had reasonably rejected them; and that the Defendants were not in breach of their statutory duty because the proposed precautions were "not practicable".

On appeal it was found that the Judge had erred in not finding that the Defendant was in breach of its duty at least insofar as providing ear protection for the Claimant when he drove the noisiest types of train. Further, once it accepted that the 85dB(A) threshold involves a real risk of damage to an employee's hearing, it follows that this gives rise to a duty of care. Whilst each case must be considered on its individual facts, there should be a general applicable standard to apply to the facts of a particular case. A good working approach is that the 90dB(A) gives rise to a presumption that if noise exceeds this level the onus of proof passes to the employer to show why he was not negligent. If the noise is below that level, then it is for the Claimant to establish why a duty should be imposed at all.

Since Harris, the Noise at Work Regulations 2005 have been introduced. These new regulations came into effect on 6 April 2006 and replaced the 1989 regulations. Under the new regulations, the level at which employers must provide hearing protection is 85dB(A) (daily or weekly average) and the level at which employers now need to assess the risk to workers' health and provide them with information and training is 80dB(A).

Regulation 9 of the 2005 Regulations introduces a requirement for health surveillance of employees who are considered to be at risk as a result of exposure to noise.

There are unlikely to be any claims concerning a breach of the 2005 Regulations in the foreseeable future.

In February 2007, several industrial deafness claims were decided upon by HH Judge Inglis in a group action by employees of companies within the Courtaulds Group (2007) EWHC B1 (QB). In his judgment Judge Inglis found for the Defendant saying that 90dB(A) was the official limit for the great majority of employers to work to and that there was no duty as far as exposure to noise below that level unless it was prior to the Noise at Work Regulations 1989. Further, in the case of six of the seven Claimants the Judge could not be convinced that they had been deafened by noise generated by machines within the factory at which they worked. The decision, unless successfully appealed, means that there are likely to be causation problems for Claimants who bring claims under the 2005 Regulations. Further, in the case of a

Claimant seeking compensation for noise induced hearing loss within the range 80dB(A) to 85dB(A), such loss can just as readily be attributed to the natural ageing process or to some other idiopathy.

8.5.4 Vibration White Finger

This condition occurs in workers whose hands are regularly exposed to high vibration by the use of vibratory tools and machinery. VWF is a prescribed disease where symptoms are episodic and there is finger blanching of at least two distal phalanges of three or more fingers of one hand occurring throughout the year. Since April 1986, VWF has been a reportable disease.

Many months (even years) exposure may be required before first symptoms occur. Initial symptoms are tingling and numbness. Episodic blanching are commonly precipitated by cold weather. Early symptoms of tingling and numbness may develop and result in a loss of dexterity. There is no effective treatment.

In 1970, the Industrial Injuries Advisory Council produced an interim report on the subject of vibration syndrome. The report concluded that further research should be undertaken.

In 1974, a study by Taylor et al entitled 'Vibration White Finger in Industry' was published.

In 1975 the Industrial Injuries Advisory Council produced its further report. In the same year, the British Standards Institution published its Guide to the Evaluation of Exposure of the Human Hand – Arm System to Vibration. The Guide recommended maximum vibration levels beyond which vibration was considered to have an adverse effect on the hand – arm.

In 1987, British Standard BS6842 entitled 'British Standard Guide to Measurement and Evaluation of Human Exposure to Vibration Transmitted to the Hand' was published. This set out recommended preventative measures where exposure to vibration regularly exceeded a certain level.

In 1994 the Health & Safety Executive published a Guidance Booklet which provided a standard which was considered reasonable for a prudent employer to employ when considering the appropriate level of permissible exposure.

The date of "Guilty Knowledge" when an employer is fixed with liability is considered to be 1975.

In order to establish a breach of duty it is necessary for the Claimant to prove that his employer exposed him to excessive vibration and that his employer failed to take appropriate precautionary measures to limit the risk of injury. The 1994 Guidance document sets out tables for determining the safety or otherwise of vibration levels.

8.5.5 Work Related Upper Limb Disorder

This is a generic term which describes pain, swelling and other discomfort occurring in the soft tissues of the fingers, hand, wrist, arm and shoulder. These symptoms are caused by prolonged repetitive work and are exacerbated by poor posture. The condition is commonly found in assembly line workers, supermarket cashiers and secretaries and other persons using computer equipment.

A successful Claimant in a claim against his employer must establish that his employer ought reasonably to have foreseen the risk of injury from the activity the Claimant was required to carry out. He must also establish that there were steps the employer could and should have taken and that the employer failed to take adequate steps to avoid the risk.

In November 1972, the Department of Employment published a Guidance Note which dealt specifically with tenosynovitis which was said to occur in certain industries as a result of repetitive activities.

In 1983 the Health & Safety Executive published a guide 'Visual Display Units' which made recommendations in relation to employees using computer keyboards and VDUs. This guide was followed in 1986 by another HSE publication 'Working with VDUs'.

In 1990 a further Guidance Note was published entitled 'Work Related Upper Limb Disorders – A Guide to Prevention'. As its title suggests, the guide contained guidance on the measures to be adopted by employers to prevent their employees contracting upper limb disorders. These measures included carrying out risk assessments of work equipment, postural changes and appropriate training.

In 1992, the HSE produced a further guidance booklet relative to the Health & Safety (Display Screen Equipment) Regulations 1992. This set out in unequivocal terms the risks associated with the use of visual display units.

In a claim by a computer operator complaining of an upper limb disorder, the date of an employers "knowledge" is likely to be 1986.

For a Claimant to succeed in an action concerning an upper limb disorder, he/she will need to establish that the injury was reasonably foreseeable; that his or her employers were in breach of duty by failing to take the appropriate measures to minimise the risk of injury; and that it was the employers' breach which caused the injury.

In ***Fifield v Denton Hall Legal Services (2006)*** EWEA Civ 169 a secretary with an upper limb disorder brought proceedings against her employers alleging negligence and breaches of the Health & Safety Display Screen Equipment Regulations 1992. The Claimant alleged that there was a casual link between a significant increase in her workload and the onset of symptoms. The Defendants denied that the Claimant's symptoms were work related and in the alternative contended that even if they were, they were not caused by any negligence or breach of duty on their part. The Judge at first instance rejected the Defendant's defence. The Defendants appealed. In the Court of Appeal the decision of the Court below was upheld. The Court of Appeal considered the evidence which established that the Claimant's symptoms were work related to have been overwhelming. It also held that it was for the employer to intervene and alter work practices if changes were necessary. An employer could not rely on an employee who may not (in the absence of proper training) appreciate the importance of taking breaks and varying working routines.

8.6 Prescribed Diseases and the Obligation to Report

Schedule 1 Part 1 to the Social Security (Industrial Injuries) (Prescribed Disease) Regulations 1985 (SI1 985/967) as amended provides a comprehensive list of occupational diseases and medical conditions; the attributable occupations; and the symptoms caused.

Likewise, the Reporting of Injuries Disease and Dangerous Occurrences Regulations 1995 (SI 1995/3163) as amended provides a list of medical conditions contracted by employees which employers are required to report. The list specifies the type of medical condition, and its cause.

8.7 Defending a Disease Claim

The first intimation a Defendant will receive of a disease claim is likely to be a letter from the Claimant's solicitors containing minimal information alleging negligence on the part of the Defendant and seeking an early admission of liability.

Until relatively recently, disease claims had not been the subject of any pre-action protocol. Some Claimant lawyers did nonetheless use the Personal Injury Pre-action Protocol as a template for intimating and pursuing a claim. Others did not, and so the Defendant had to engage the Claimant's solicitors in a long correspondence to extract information which the Claimant's solicitors should have had to hand (had they properly investigated their client's claim before firing off a letter of claim) and which the Defendant requires in order to form a reasoned view on issues such as liability and causation.

A Pre-Action Protocol for Disease and Illness claims was prepared in 2001 but for reasons outwith the author's knowledge, its introduction was delayed. Happily, the protocol is now in common use.

8.8 Main Features of the Pre-Action Protocol for Disease and Illness Claims

The Protocol applies to all personal injury claims where the injury complained of arises not from an accident or a single event but where it takes the form of an illness or disease. "Disease" covers any illness physical or psychological, any disorder, ailment, affliction, complaint, malady or derangement other than a physical or psychological injury solely caused by an accident or other single event. The Protocol is not limited to diseases occurring in the workplace.

The aim of the Protocol is to try and resolve claims without litigation or where a claim cannot be resolved, to identify the relevant issues which remain in dispute.

Early communication between the parties is encouraged as is the early and voluntary exchange of information and documents.

In an appropriate case, a potential Claimant may request certain documents (e.g. occupational health records) before sending a formal letter of claim. Such records should, except in exceptional circumstances, be supplied by a Defendant (without cost) within 40 days. If a Defendant fails to comply, then a Claimant may seek an order for pre-action disclosure.

Once a Claimant decides to make a claim, he must send to the Defendant a letter of claim in the prescribed form together with an additional copy. The letter should provide a chronology of relevant events (e.g. dates or periods of exposure) and in an occupational disease claim an employment history particularly when the Claimant has been employed by a number of employers and the illness complained of has a long latency period. The letter of claim must identify relevant documents not already in the Defendant's possession (e.g. General Practitioner's medical case notes). In the case of claims under the Law Reform (Miscellaneous Provisions) Act 1934 or the Fatal Accidents Act 1976, the relevant documents will include the Death Certificate, the Post Mortem Report, the Inquest Depositions and any Grant of Administration. The letter of claim should state whether a claim is being made against any other party. Proceedings should not normally be commenced until after three months from the date a Defendant acknowledges the letter of claim.

Under the Protocol, a Defendant should acknowledge a letter of claim within 21 days (identifying his insurers) and, if he fails to acknowledge the letter the Claimant will be permitted to begin proceedings.

The Defendant's formal response to the claim should be written within three months of the date of the acknowledgement letter. The response should indicate whether liability is admitted wholly or in part and where liability is not admitted the response should enclose copies of relevant documents upon which the Defendant's denial is based.

Where it is not practicable for a Defendant to complete his investigations into liability within three months, he should request an extension stating the reasons why an extension is required. A Claimant should agree to an extension where justifiable reasons have been provided. A lapse of time from the circumstances which gave rise to the claim will not by itself constitute reasonable justification for further time.

As in a normal personal injury claim, under the Disease and Illness Pre-action Protocol, a Claimant must serve a Schedule of Loss with supporting documents as soon as practicable. It also encourages joint instruction of experts but recognises the need for flexibility as in many cases it will be necessary for a Claimant to commission a medical report before writing a letter of claim. In such cases, a Defendant will be entitled to instruct his own medical expert.

In a matter where joint instruction of an expert is considered appropriate, the party proposing joint instructions should provide the other party with a list of one or more experts in the required discipline. Within 14 days that other party should indicate his preparedness or otherwise to participate in a joint instruction of one of the experts proposed. If a Claimant proposes joint instruction of an expert in the letter of claim, then the said 14 day period is treated as being in addition to the 21 days for acknowledging the letter of claim. If the party who is invited to agree to the joint instruction of an expert expressly objects to the proposed joint instruction, then the parties will be entitled to instruct experts of their own choice. If the party who is being invited to agree a joint instruction does not expressly object to one of the suggested experts, then he shall not be entitled to rely on his own expert evidence without the other party's agreement or the Court's permission. Either party may send an agreed expert written questions.

Where a Defendant admits liability, in whole or in part before a medical report is obtained under the Protocol, the report should be disclosed once it becomes available. Likewise, where a Defendant admits liability in whole or in part before proceedings are issued, he should disclose any medical report he has obtained under the Protocol and which he intends to rely on.

Part 36 CPR applies to disease claims.

The parties are encouraged to disclose experts' reports relative to liability and causation before proceedings are issued. Indeed, Claimants are encouraged to delay issuing proceedings for 21 days from disclosure of such reports.

Under paragraph 2.5 of the Protocol a Claimant may commence proceedings without complying with the Disease Pre-Action Protocol (a) if by complying with that Protocol his claim would become time-barred under any provision in the Limitation Act 1980 (or any similar legislation) or (b) where the Claimant has a terminal illness and his life expectancy is short. Where a Claimant begins proceedings without complying with the disease Pre-Action Protocol he may apply on notice to the Court for a directions timetable to be set.

A complete copy of the Protocol appears at Appendix A (see post).

8.9 Limitation

The limitation period for bringing any claim is now governed by the Limitation Act 1980.

In a normal personal injury action a Claimant must commence an action within three years. The primary three year period begins to run on the date the cause of action accrued (i.e. the date of the accident); or the date of knowledge (if later) of the person injured.

In a disease claim it can be difficult to establish with precision when damage occurred. Time does not begin to run against a Claimant until some material damage actually occurs.

Under Section 14 of the 1980 Act, the date of knowledge is defined as being the date upon which a person first had knowledge of the following facts:

a) that the injury was significant; and

b) that the injury was attributable in whole or in part to the act or omission which is alleged to constitute negligence, nuisance or breach of duty.

c) of the identity of the Defendant; and

d) if it is alleged that the act or omission was that of a person other than the Defendant, the identity of that person and the additional facts supporting the bringing of an action against the Defendant.

Under Section 14 (2) an injury is significant if the person whose date of knowledge is in question would reasonably have considered it sufficiently serious to justify his instituting proceedings for damages against the Defendant who did not dispute liability and was able to satisfy a Judgment.

A person's knowledge includes knowledge which he might reasonably be expected to acquire:

a) from facts observable or ascertainable by him; or

b) from facts ascertainable by him with the help of medical or other appropriate expert advice which it is reasonable for him to seek.

Under Section 33 of the 1980 Act, the Court has discretionary powers to allow an action to proceed notwithstanding the fact that it was commenced outside the prescribed period should it consider it to be equitable to do so and after taking into account the relative prejudice to the Claimant and the Defendant. Section 33 (3) contains a list of some of the matters the Court must consider when deciding whether or not to exercise its discretionary powers. The list of matters is not exhaustive but include the length and reasons for the delay in bringing proceedings; the extent to which the delay has affected the cogency of the evidence; the conduct of the Defendant; the duration of any disability of the Claimant after the date his cause of action accrued; the extent to which the Claimant acted promptly and reasonably once he became aware that the Defendant's act or omission giving rise to his injury might give rise to a claim for damages; and the steps taken by the Claimant to obtain expert advice and the nature of the advice received.

A claim under the Law Reform (Miscellaneous Provisions Act) 1934, on the part of the disease victim's estate will be statute barred if at the date of the deceased's death he could not for reasons of limitation have maintained a claim in his own right.

If, however, a disease victim dies before the period for him bringing a claim expired, then his cause of action will survive and his estate may bring a claim in respect of the deceased's injuries within three years of (a) the deceased's death or (b) the date of the personal representatives' knowledge (whichever is later).

Under Section 12 of the 1980 Act, a claim for dependency under the Fatal Accidents Act 1976 may be brought within three years from (a) the date of death or (b) the date of knowledge of the person for whose benefit the action is brought (whichever is later). If an action under the Fatal Accidents Act 1976 is barred by reason of the expiry of three years, then the dependants may seek the Court's discretion (under Section 33 of the 1980 Act) to dis apply the 3 year period.

8.10 Investigating a Claim

The first notification of a claim a Defendant is likely to receive is a Protocol letter of claim or, more rarely, a letter seeking pre-action disclosure of documents. The letter may relate to a current or ex-employee of the Defendant or to a person who has never been employed by the Defendant but whose disease is allegedly attributable to the negligent acts and omissions of the Defendant, the commission of which occurred many years ago.

Since companies can have similar names (particularly companies within the same group) and companies can cease to exist by reason of liquidation or acquisition, it is important to establish whether or not the letter of claim is addressed (a) to the correct company and (b) to one which remains in existence. It is also important to establish whether there was any valid liability insurance cover in place at the time of the negligent acts or omissions complained of.

Hopefully, the letter of claim will contain specific allegations of exposure including the exact location where the exposure is alleged to have occurred, the nature of the alleged exposure and the period involved. If this information is not provided in the letter of claim, then the Defendant should request it. In an employers' liability claim, the Defendant should be asked to provide some evidence of his employment by the Defendant (e.g. the letter of appointment; a redundancy notice; an old payslip).

A Defendant may or may not still have employment records going back to the time of the alleged exposure. This should be checked. Whether or not the Defendant's old employment records survive, the Claimant should be asked to obtain and disclose an HM Revenue and Customs Schedule of Employment. Such a schedule will identify all of the Claimant's employers beginning with tax year 1961/1962 to date. It will not, however, provide confirmation of the exact dates upon which any employment began or ceased.

If no employment records survive, the Defendant should consider asking the Claimant to identify his immediate superior and any other work colleagues during the period of his alleged employment. If the Claimant is able to identify former colleagues and if those former work colleagues can be identified in the Defendant's old employment records, then this will be fairly persuasive evidence that the Claimant's alleged employment is *bona fide*.

Besides seeking to verify the Claimant's alleged employment by them, the Defendants also need to establish whether the culpable exposure alleged against them was the Claimant's only material exposure, or whether there was culpable exposure elsewhere. Therefore, the Defendant should press the Claimant for a comprehensive employment history going back to the date he left school, particularly in those cases where the Claimant entered the labour market before tax year 1961/1962. The HM Revenue and Customs Schedule of Employment may provide an insight into whether the Claimant is likely to have had culpable exposure elsewhere, post 1961/1962.

With a view to expediting the Defendant's investigation and decision on liability, the Claimant should be invited to make early disclosure of witness statements on a without prejudice basis.

Once a full employment history is available, this should enable a Defendant to determine whether there is some other potential source of culpable exposure from which indemnity/contribution may be sought, or whether he alone must bear the full burden of any damages and costs the Claimant may ultimately be awarded.

Each disease claim needs to be considered on its merits but it may be that the Defendant has a previous claims history in relation to the disease a Claimant complains of. Insurers may therefore have settled similar claims on behalf of the Defendant. Indeed, the Claimant's solicitors may have been involved in those earlier claims. In a claim against an asbestos manufacturing company who have faced numerous other similar claims, it may be unnecessary to carry out extensive enquiries to determine whether or not they used asbestos during the relevant period or whether conditions inside their factory premises were such that they were negligent or in breach of their statutory duty. In such a case the Defendant will simply wish to verify the Claimant's alleged employment; to determine whether there is another party from whom contribution may be sought; and to consider whether the symptoms the Claimant exhibits are attributable wholly or in part to the industrial disease complained of or to some other non-related medical condition.

Where a disease claim is being made against a Defendant for the first time, it will be necessary to ascertain whether that Defendant used the toxic or dangerous substance complained of during the period of the Claimant's employment. If they did, it will be necessary to determine whether the Defendants knew or ought reasonably to have known of the toxicity or dangers associated with that substance, and if so, what precautionary steps were taken to avoid or reduce exposure and, whether in the light of such knowledge, they took all reasonable steps to protect the Claimant from harm.

A 'knowledge' defence was maintained by the Defendants in the case of ***Margereson and Hancock v J W Roberts Limited (1996).*** These claims concerned two individuals who, as children, had lived and played in close proximity to an asbestos factory and who many years later contracted fatal mesothelioma. It was asserted by the Defendants that no one within the industrialised world was likely to have known during the period 1925 –1965 that residents living in close proximity to an asbestos factory were at risk of injury. In rejecting the defence, the Court held that conditions on a loading bay immediately outside the factory where children (including the Claimants) played effectively replicated the appalling conditions inside the factory. It was, however, suggested in the first instance Judgment of Holland, J. that exposure which occurred further away from the factory may not have been culpable exposure.

In the similar but more recent case of ***Pinder v Cape Plc (2006)*** LTL 25/-1/07, the Defendant's 'knowledge' defence succeeded. During the 1950s, Mr Pinder played as a child on a local rubbish tip where the Defendants disposed of their asbestos waste. The tip was some five miles from the Defendant's factory. It was alleged that the Defendants were under an obligation to dispose of waste asbestos safely and that they had a duty to ensure that they did not replicate the risk of exposure to that which their employees were exposed. Despite finding that the Claimant's material exposure resulted from playing on the waste tip, the Court held that it would not have been until a decade later that there was a foreseeable risk of injury from low and intermittent exposure to asbestos. Further, there was no evidence that the Defendants knew that children played on the waste tip.

There are two other cases where 'knowledge' defences have succeeded. In the unreported case of ***Gunn v Wallsend Slipway and Engineering Company (1988)*** Mrs Gunn had, between 1948 and early 1965, laundered her husband's work clothes which were contaminated by asbestos dust and fibres. Before laundering those work clothes by hand, it was her practice to shake the clothing in the back yard. In doing so, she inhaled asbestos dust and fibres. Towards the end of 1984, Mrs Gunn became ill and about 2 months before her death she was diagnosed as having a malignant mesothelioma. Numerous medical and scientific papers were analysed in an attempt to establish the extent of the knowledge a prudent employer should have had as to the hazards of asbestos exposure during the period of Mrs Gunn's exposure. Waterhouse, J. found on the evidence before him that no one in the industrial world had, before the publication of a paper by Newhouse and Thompson in October 1965, directed his or her mind to the risk of physical injury from domestic exposure to asbestos dust and, in particular, to the risk of injury to anyone coming into contact with asbestos dust on work clothes. Accordingly, Judgment was entered for the Defendant.

In March 2004, the very similar case of Maguire v Harland and Wolff and Another (2005). fell to be determined by Morland, J. Mrs Maguire had laundered her husband's work clothes which had been contaminated by asbestos dust and fibres but the Defendants denied that they owed Mrs Maguire any duty of care because it was unforeseeable that she was at risk having regard to the nature of her exposure and the state of knowledge at the time. Morland, J. refused to follow Waterhouse, J. in the Gunn case. Instead, he held that the Defendants had not needed prophetic vision to foresee that the wives of their workers were exposed to substantial quantities of asbestos dust on their husband's work clothes and that the attendant risks of serious injury to health were well known at the time of Mr Maguire's exposure. Further, he considered the risk to Mrs Maguire's health was not only foreseeable but obvious. The Defendants appealed. By a majority of 2:1 the Court of Appeal, in 2005, held that on the basis of the contemporary literature the date of knowledge of an employer of the potential risk to spouses of employees was late 1965 and that since Mrs Maguire's exposure had ceased by April 1965, her claim must fail. It would therefore appear from this case that the imputed date of knowledge in "household" exposure claims is considered to be much later than in the case of claims concerning direct exposure.

8.11 Breach of Duty

So when will a Defendant be found to be culpable and therefore liable to a Claimant in a disease claim?

In terms of negligence, the same essential components apply to a disease case as those which apply to any other injury claim, that is to say the Claimant must establish:

a) that the Defendant owed him a duty to take care;

b) that the Defendant committed a breach of that duty;

c) that damage resulted which was causally connected with the breach.

In an employers' liability disease claim the Defendant employer will be adjudged to have been under a non-delegable common law and statutory duty not to expose his employee to the risk of harm during the course of his employment. Therefore, if an employer deployed his employee to carry out work at say an asbestos manufacturing factory where he was subjected to airborne asbestos dust and fibres without adequate respiratory protection, then that employer is likely to be found to have been in breach of duty. The employer may have a right of indemnity or contribution against the asbestos manufacturer but that will not affect his primary liability to his employee. If the employee pursued a claim against the asbestos manufacturer, then in order to succeed, he would have to establish that the asbestos manufacturer owed him a duty and that he committed a breach of that duty. It is therefore easier for a Claimant to pursue a claim against his employer than against some other party because the duty on an employer is onerous.

It should be borne in mind that the burden of proving a breach of duty still rests with the Claimant.

In the case of ***Brett v Reading University (2007)*** LTL 14/02/07 the Deceased spent all of his working life within construction and engineering. During the Second World War, the Deceased worked in various power stations. From 1953-1967 he worked for London Electricity Board. Thereafter, he was employed by Surrey University between 1973 and 1982 and by Reading University between 1983 to 1988. A claim arising out of the Deceased's contraction of mesothelioma was brought against Reading University. The Deceased's other employers were not implicated because of a lack of evidence of culpable exposure, although there was insufficient evidence of culpable exposure by them. On appeal, the Court of Appeal upheld the decision below and emphasised the necessity for the Claimant to establish that the Defendants had failed to take all necessary precautions to ensure that they had not exposed the Deceased to respirable asbestos fibres. It did not fall to the Defendants to establish that all precautions had been taken.

In determining whether an employer was in breach of his common law duty in a disease claim, the Claimant may rely on published literature which highlighted the risk associated with the toxic/dangerous substance or activity complained of and which the employer was or ought reasonably to have been aware of. Such literature may consist of medical or other scientific papers, or HSE publications and circulars. A Claimant may also establish liability on the part of the Defendant by demonstrating that the Defendant was in breach of a statutory duty.

Again, it is impossible to identify and discuss in a single chapter all of the statutory regulations a Defendant can fall foul of in relation to a disease claim. However, the following comprise some examples:

Asbestos attributable disease claims

- The Asbestos Industry Regulations 1931
- The Factories Acts 1937, 1948 and 1961
- The Building Safety Health and Welfare Regulations 1948
- The Construction (Working Practices) Regulations 1966
- The Asbestos Regulations 1969
- The Asbestos (Licensing) Regulations 1983
- The Asbestos Products (Safety) Regulations 1985
- The Asbestos (Prohibitions) Regulations 1992
- The Control of Asbestos at Work Regulations 2002

Silicosis

- The Grinding of Metals (Miscellaneous Industries) Regulations 1925
- The Factories' Act 1937
- The Control of Substances Hazardous to Health Regulations 1994
- The Control of Substances Hazardous to Health (Amendment) Regulations 1998

Industrial Deafness Claims

- The Construction Working Places Regulations 1966
- The Control of Noise (Code of Practice For Construction Sites) Regulations 1975
- The Noise at Work Regulations 1989
- The Control of Noise at Work Regulations 2005

Vibration White Finger

- The Factories Act 1961
- The Employers Liability (Defective Equipment) Act 1969
- The Construction (Working Places) Regulations 1992
- The Provision and Use of Work Equipment Regulations 1992
- The Personal Protective Equipment at Work Regulations 1992
- The Manual Handling Operation Regulations 1992
- The Control of Vibration at Work Regulations 2005

Occupational Dermatitis

The Factories Act 1961
The Offices, Shops and Railways Premises Act 1963
The Employers Liability Defective Equipment Act 1969
The Personal Protective Equipment at Work Regulations 1992
The Work Place (Health, Safety and Welfare) Regulations 1992
The Control of Substances Hazardous to Health Regulations 1998-2004

Work Related Upper Limb Disorder

The Manual Handling Operations Regulations 1992
The Workplace, (Health, Safety and Welfare) Regulations 1992
The Provision and Use of Work Equipment Regulations 1998
The Management of Health and Safety at Work Regulations 1999

8.12 Causation

As well as establishing that the Defendant owed him a duty of care and that the Defendant breached that duty, a Claimant must also establish that any injury and loss he suffered was caused by the breach.

Generally speaking, where a Claimant succeeds in establishing that a Defendant owed him a duty of care which was breached, and where he has adduced medical evidence attributing the occupational disease complained of to that breach of duty, the Claimant is home and dry. However, the issue of causation in a mesothelioma case recently required careful analysis by the House of Lords in the case of ***Fairchild v Glenhaven Funeral Services and Others (2002)*** UKHL22.

The brief facts of this case were that the deceased had been employed at different times by two employers who negligently exposed him to asbestos dust and fibres during the course of his employment. As a result the deceased contracted malignant mesothelioma, an invariably fatal asbestos induced cancer of the pleura (lining of the lung) or peritoneum. Mesothelioma is a latent condition and frequently first symptoms of the disease do not appear until 30 years or more after first exposure. Unlike some asbestos attributable conditions, mesothelioma can result from relatively light exposure to asbestos fibres, although the greater the exposure the greater is the risk of contracting the disease. The medical experts were unable to say with any certainty whether the Claimant's mesothelioma was attributable to his exposure by either or both Defendants. As a result, the Claimant's claim failed at first instance because he was unable to establish who his employer was at the date he ingested the fibre or fibres which actually lead to the mutation of his fatal illness. The first instance decision was upheld in the Court of Appeal (2002) 1wlr 1052. The Claimant appealed to the House of Lords.

The House of Lords were concerned by the obvious injustice the conventional approach to the issue of causation had caused the Claimant. There was no doubt that both Defendants had negligently exposed the Claimant to asbestos dust and fibres. Further, that negligent exposure had, on a balance of probabilities, lead to the Claimant ingesting the fibre or fibres which had, many years later, caused the mutation of a cancerous cell within the Claimant's pleural cavity. Justice and commonsense lead the Court to conclude that the Claimant's inability to prove which of the Defendants had exposed the Claimant to the offending fibre or fibres should not defeat his otherwise worthy claim. It was therefore held that if a breach of duty contributed substantially to the increased risk of the Claimant contracting a disease, then there was a causal connection between the breach of duty complained of and the injury sustained. For the Court to have found otherwise would have resulted in the culpable employers avoiding liability and a blameless dependent widow being denied of her legal remedy.

But Fairchild was not the end of the story because it remained unclear whether a Defendant's liability in a mesothelioma case remained joint and several or whether there were limits to the extent of a Defendant's liability.

On 13 May 2006, the House of Lords handed down their judgment in the subsequent mesothelioma case of ***Barker v Corus (UK) Ltd. (2006)*** UKHL20. The issues the House of Lords had to resolve were (a) what were the limits of the exception to causation under Fairchild and (b) the extent of a Defendant's liability in the light of Fairchild.

Unlike Mr Fairchild who was the "innocent victim" of someone else's negligent acts and omissions, Mr Barker had himself been negligent by exposing himself to asbestos dust and fibres during a seven year period when he worked as a self employed plasterer. The Defendants had culpably exposed Mr Barker for about six months and it was their contention that the Fairchild exception should not apply in a case where the Claimant had himself been guilty of negligence. They went on to argue that the law relating to causation had been modified in Fairchild on public policy grounds and to prevent the culpable Defendants from avoiding liability simply because a Claimant could not establish which of more than one source of culpable exposure triggered his illness. It would push the bounds of tortuous liability too far to extend the Fairchild exception to a Claimant who had negligently and significantly exposed himself to asbestos. The Defendants also contended that in the event of them being found liable, then their liability should be apportioned to reflect the period Mr Barker had been culpably exposed elsewhere.

In the Court of Appeal, the first instance decision of Moses, J was upheld. Moses, J had held that the Defendant's liability was joint and several and that the Deceased's status as an innocent victim in Fairchild was not a pre-requisite for establishing causation. He further found that there was no good reason for finding that Mr Barker's negligence should deprive his widow of all compensation. Justice could be met by reducing damages under the Law Reform (Contributory Negligence) Act 1945. Thus he reduced the damages payable by 20%.

In the House of Lords it was held that the Fairchild exception applied even though not all periods of exposure were tortious. The source of the Deceased's other exposure was irrelevant, even if it resulted from his own negligence. However, in relation to apportionment, the House of Lords sought to balance any injustice caused to the Defendants by their earlier decision in Fairchild by finding that a Defendant was only liable to pay a mesothelioma victim damages to the extent that his breach of duty had contributed to the risk of the Claimant contracting the disease.

The Defendants' success in Barker was short lived because the protestations of Claimant lawyers, trade unions and certain politicians lead to the government tagging on to the Compensation Bill (which was passing through parliament at the same time) a new clause designed to negate the House of Lords decision

Section 3 of the Compensation Act 2006 provides that each negligent employer who has contributed towards the mesothelioma victims' illness, shall have joint and several liability and as such shall be liable for all of the damage caused to that person. This statutory provision will not affect the right of a Defendant to seek contribution from a joint tortfeasor but in the event of them being a defunct and uninsured joint tortfeasor, the surviving Defendant will be liable to pay the Claimant all of his damages and costs. However, under Section 3 (3) (b) a Defendant is permitted to seek a reduction of his liability to reflect the Claimant's contributory negligence.

8.13 Other Culpable Exposure

A Claimant may intimate a claim against one or all of the entities who have culpably exposed him to the toxic or dangerous substance complained of.

If he intimates a claim against all of the entities concerned, then it will be important to establish the identity of those other entities and their insurers. It may be that one or more of the other Defendants were insured by more than one insurer during the period of the alleged exposure. It is therefore important to establish which insurers are involved for each Defendant and the period that each insurer was on cover. Having established the insurance position, the next step is to establish what each Defendants' attitude is to the claim. Assuming none of the Defendants are able to assert a positive defence, then it should be ascertained whether each Defendant/insurer is prepared to make a voluntary contribution towards the burden of the Claimant's claim and costs. If a Defendant cannot identify his insurers or if that Defendant is no longer in being, it may be possible to ascertain which insurers were on cover for that particular Defendant during the requisite period by carrying out a search at the Association of British Insurers.

Once all interested Insurers have been identified, it is usual for the Defendant with the largest potential interest to co-ordinate the defence and produce a provisional contribution schedule identifying each Defendant and the period of culpable exposure attributed to them. It will then be possible to express the apportionment in percentage terms, showing the percentage contribution each Defendant should be making.

In a case where one or more of the Defendants were uninsured, during any period that they are alleged to have culpably exposed the Claimant, that Defendant will be personally liable to contribute in respect of the uninsured period.

Where a Defendant is no longer in being, and no valid liability insurance can be traced, then the remaining Defendants will, unless a 'Holtby' situation exists (see post), agree to absorb the burden of the defunct Defendant's liability on the basis of their agreed contributions.

Where a claim is intimated against more than one Defendant and one of those Defendants refuses to contribute voluntarily towards the claim and costs, then the remaining Defendant or Defendants may seek to protect their position by making a joint Part 36 CPR offer of contribution to the Defendant concerned and, if necessary bring Part 20 CPR proceedings against that Defendant.

Where a Claimant does not intimate a claim against all culpable parties, but instead chooses to pursue a claim against only one Defendant, there is no reason why that Defendant should not seek a voluntary contribution from another culpable employer on the basis that if he agrees to do so, it will not be necessary to implicate him in the proceedings or to begin Part 20 proceedings.

8.14 Extent of Defendant's Liability

Where a Claimant sustained injury by reason of his negligent exposure to a toxic or dangerous substance by two or more former employers, is one of those former employers liable for the entirety of the Claimant's loss and damage, or is his liability limited to that part of the loss and damage he actually caused? This is a question which fell to be determined by the House of Lords in ***Fairchild v Glenhaven*** **and in** ***Barker v Corus (UK) Ltd (2002)*** (see ante). It should be borne in mind that both of those cases concerned mesothelioma victims. Likewise it needs to be remembered that mesothelioma is considered to be an 'indivisible' injury i.e. one which cannot be attributed with any certainty to exposure at a particular time.

However, in the earlier case of ***Holtby v Brigham and Cowan (2000)*** 3 ALL ER 421. Which was determined by the Court of Appeal in April 2002, the Claimant had contracted asbestosis as a result of his negligent exposure to asbestos by the Defendants and by other former employees who were not implicated in the action. At first instance the trial Judge had heard medical evidence to the effect that the degree of exposure to asbestos dust determines the extent to which a person will contract and suffer from asbestosis. Cumulative exposure causes and aggravates the condition. The trial Judge went on to find that the Defendants were only liable for that damage which they themselves caused. Since it was impossible to make a mathematical apportionment based purely on the available medical evidence, it was held that the amount of damages the Claimant should recover from the Defendants should be discounted by 25%.

The Claimant appealed to the Court of Appeal. The appeal was dismissed. Since asbestosis was a 'divisible' condition (i.e. one which was made worse by further exposures) it was held that the Defendants were only liable to the extent of the disability they themselves had caused and that the Court should do the best it could to achieve justice between the parties. Had the Claimant suffered a mesothelioma (an 'indivisible' injury) then he would have succeeded in full against the Defendants.

It can be seen that it is important to draw a distinction between divisible and indivisible injury. If the extent of a Claimant's injury can be attributed to the acts and omissions of a particular Defendant, that Defendant's liability should be limited to the extent of the damage he caused. Therefore, in an asbestosis claim or an industrial deafness claim where the injury is divisible, and maybe attributed to exposure by different employers, each employer's liability should be limited to the amount of damage he actually caused.

But what is the extent of a Defendant's liability in a disease claim where the Claimant has, by reason of his own acts and omissions, contributed towards the contraction of the disease complained of?

This issue was considered by Stanley Burton, J. in the recent case of ***Badger v Ministry of Defence (2005)*** LTL 16/12/2005. The deceased was employed by the MOD as a boiler maker between 1954 and 1987. During the course of his employment, he was exposed to asbestos and died of lung cancer at the age of 63. Primary liability was admitted. It was further admitted that the Deceased's exposure to asbestos had made a material contribution to the risk of him contracting lung cancer. It was, however, contended by the Defendant that the deceased's smoking had also made a material contribution to the deceased's contraction of lung cancer and that damages should be reduced to reflect his contributory negligence. In his Judgment, Stanley Burton, J. referred to Section 1(1) of the Law Reform (Contributory Negligence) Act 1945 which provides that where a person sustains damage in part because of his own fault, the damages recoverable will be reduced to reflect the share of his own culpability. The Judge went on to find that since health warnings first appeared on cigarette packets in 1971, it was by the mid 1970s reasonably foreseeable by a reasonably prudent man that if he continued to smoke he was putting his health in jeopardy. Accordingly, the deceased's continued smoking of 20 cigarettes per day post 1975 constituted contributory negligence on his part and the damages payable should be reduced by 20%.

The decision in Badger was followed in the subsequent case of ***Bone v Ministry of Defence (2006)*** LTL PI 22/11/2006 where again the Claimant's damages were reduced by 20% to reflect the contribution the Deceased's smoking habit had made to his contraction of lung cancer.

8.15 Medical Causation

In addition to considering the issues of liability and contribution, it will be necessary for the claim handler to consider the issue of medical causation.

Whereas in a tripping accident there can be little doubt that the victim's broken wrist can be directly attributable to the accident itself, in a disease claim closer analysis of the Claimant's symptoms and medical history will be necessary. Is the Claimant's deafness attributable to him having worked for the Defendants in a noisy workshop, or is it in fact attributable in whole or in part to him being a member of a 'heavy rock' band? Is the Claimant's breathlessness attributable to him having been exposed to airborne dust or fumes whilst in the employ of the Defendants or does he in fact suffer from an unrelated pulmonary or cardiac condition? For a Claimant to recover damages in a disease claim, he must not only establish that the Defendant was negligent or in breach of his statutory duty. He must also establish that the medical symptoms of which he complains are directly attributable in whole or in part to the negligence of each breach of duty complained of. To the extent that the symptoms complained of do not relate to the industrially induced disease or illness, the Claimant's damages should be reduced to reflect other non-related causes.

8.16 Medical Records

The Defendant needs to call for early disclosure of all general practitioner and hospital records. In requesting the hospital records the Defendant should emphasise that he wishes to see not only the Claimant's hospital records attributable to the industrial disease complained of but **all** hospital records. Further, the Defendant should ask to see copies of all pathological and histological reports.

Check with the Defendants whether they are in possession of the Claimant's occupational health and personnel records and if they are, obtain the Claimant's signed authority for their disclosure.

If the Claimant is no longer in the Defendants' employ but is now employed by someone else, it might prove useful to see copies of any occupational health records kept by that employer.

Where the victim of the industrial disease is dead, the Defendant should call for copies of the inquest depositions (including the post mortem report) and any histological reports relative to the post mortem.

Where the Claimant is in receipt of state benefits which are attributable to the industrial disease complained of, the Defendant should request a copy of the Claimant's application for benefits and any correspondence with the medical boarding centre including the MBC's diagnosis and all assessments. These frequently contain use of useful information which is relevant to the issue of limitation. They also frequently contain information about the nature and extent of culpable exposure by other employers.

The various medical records alluded to above should inform a Defendant when the Claimant first began to suffer the symptoms he attributes to his alleged occupationally induced condition and when that condition was first diagnosed. Such information is essential to a Defendant in determining whether the claim is being made within the limitation period. The Defendant's medical records will also reveal whether or not the Claimant has some other medical condition which may be the cause (in whole or in part) of the symptoms complained of. Chronic bronchitis causes severe respiratory disability but it is not an asbestos attributable condition. Therefore, severe breathlessness in a person with the earliest radiological signs of asbestos induced pleural plaques who suffers from bronchitis and who smokes heavily is, on a balance of probabilities, more likely to be caused by his smoking induced bronchitis than his benign asbestos condition.

In some cases it is particularly important to establish when the Claimant's first symptoms occurred. For example, asbestos induced pleural plaques do not become visible on a normal chest x-ray until 15 years or more from first exposure. If a victim of pleural plaques intimates a claim on the basis of occupational exposure which occurred only five years ago, the Defendant can justifiably contend that the Claimant's material exposure must have occurred earlier and elsewhere. Routine chest x-rays invariably point out the presence of asbestos induced pleural plaques even though the chest x-ray was not commissioned for the purpose of diagnosing an asbestos attributable injury. Therefore, all chest x-ray reports are potentially relevant in determining whether all or any of the Claimant's relevant exposure occurred during the period alleged.

It also helps to know something about the clinical presentation of the industrial disease the Claimant is alleged to have contracted. For example, asbestosis is the fibrosing or scarring of the lungs caused by the inhalation of asbestos dust and fibres. The lungs' capacity to expand are restricted and thus the victim becomes breathless. The condition is progressive, incurable and can be fatal. To contract asbestosis the Claimant will have needed to have had very substantial exposure, usually over a long period. Therefore, if the Claimant's alleged exposure was minimal and over a short period, a Defendant should be dubious of any assertion that he has asbestosis. Further, asbestosis is a slow progressive and insidious disease. If a Claimant has gone from being reasonably well to having severe and disabling fibrosis of his lungs within a short period of time, a Defendant should again be dubious of a diagnosis of asbestosis. In such a case any fibrosing of the lungs is likely to be idiopathic fibrosis (formally known as cryptogenic fibrosing alveolitis) which is not asbestos attributable. In a Vibration White Finger case, consideration needs to be given to the history of the Claimant's symptoms; the history of his exposure; his familial history; his past medical history (particularly any vascular problems) and to any medication he may be taking (particularly for hypertension) before accepting a diagnosis of VWF. In a deafness case, consideration of the Claimant's medical records relative to the state of his hearing pre exposure is obviously important. Account should also be taken of the Claimant's age since age has an impact on hearing.

There is also medical literature which shows that excessive smoking may be associated with sensorineural hearing loss (Cruikshanks et al: Cigarette Smoking and Hearing Loss: the epidemiology of hearing loss study; Journal of the American Medical Association 1998; 279; 1715-1719). Therefore, investigate the Claimant's smoking history and require him to submit to objective audiometry testing before accepting a diagnosis of industrial deafness or the apportionment between exposure to noise and constitutional causes. Obviously, a Claimant's smoking history is invariably relevant to any occupational lung condition.

In a pneumoconiosis claim (which includes an asbestos claim) enquire whether the Claimant (or his widow in the case of a fatal injury) has received a lump sum payment under the Pneumoconiosis, etc (Workers Compensation) Act 1979. In ***Ballantine v Newalls Insulation Co Limited (2000)*** PIQR Q327 the Court of Appeal held that compensatory awards under the Act were deductible from the whole of the Claimant's damages, otherwise a Claimant stood to make a double recovery. However, it should be noted that at the time this chapter is being written, there are moves afoot to negate the Court of Appeal's decision in Ballantine in relation to lump sum payments to mesothelioma victims under the Act. Recently the government has announced its intention to introduce legislation under which mesothelioma victims will receive a lump sum payment from the Department of Work & Pensions within six weeks of making a claim, irrespective of their employment history. In order to fund these measures, it is proposed that the cost will be recouped from compensators under the compensation recovery system. Therefore, it will be even more important for a Defendant to set off a mesothelioma victims lump sum payment under the Act against any claim for damages, otherwise the Defendant will end up paying twice, once to the Claimant and again the DWP!

8.17 Medical Experts

Depending on what a Defendant may find in the Claimant's medical notes and the severity of the condition complained of, he may decide to commission medical evidence of his own. Such evidence will establish whether or not the medical condition of which the Claimant complains has been accurately diagnosed and, if so, whether it is the sole or partial cause of the Claimant's symptoms. A medical report will also enable a Defendant to establish the extent of the Claimant's incapacity and ascertain a prognosis. A Defendant will want his expert to consider whether there is anything in the Claimant's medical history which impacts on his present condition or prognosis. If the Claimant has a cardiac condition, is it contributing towards his breathlessness? If so, will that cardiac condition adversely affect the Claimant's working and/or normal life expectancy? Such information is very important where there is a continuing loss claim.

It is also important that a Defendant retains a medical expert in the applicable medical discipline. It is worth taking a bit of time to find an expert who is suitably qualified and who is experienced in preparing legal medical reports and defending them in the witness box.

In a Fatal Accident Act claim, it may be appropriate for a Defendant to have the deceased's pathological and histological examples examined by an independent consultant pathologist. As a result of what is said in the post mortem report, it may be appropriate for a Defendant to seek a medical opinion elsewhere on the question of life expectancy. Although the Claimant may have died from an industrial disease, the post mortem report may suggest that his life expectancy was severely impaired in any event by reason of some other medical condition. If this is so, then the Defendant will be able to contend for a lower multiplier.

8.18 Types of Medical Expert

It is not possible to provide a comprehensive list of the applicable medical experts in every occupational disease claim. However, the following list may prove to be of assistance:

Lung disease – consultant chest physician
Vibration white finger – consultant vascular surgeon
Industrial deafness – consultant ear, nose and throat surgeon
Work related upper limb disorders – consultant hand surgeon
Occupational stress – consultant psychiatrist
Occupational cancers – consultant epidemiologist

8.19 Settlement – Final or Provisional Damages?

As in the case of other personal injury claims, the Claimant in most disease claims will be compensated on a full and final basis. However, where there is a chance that the Claimant may at some future date develop another and perhaps more serious medical condition, he may elect to be compensated on the assumption that the more serious medical condition will not develop. He will then be entitled to seek further damages if, at some future date he succumbs to the other medical condition.

It is best practice for any settlement on a provisional damages basis to be recorded in a Consent Order and registered with the Court. The order should expressly record the fact that the Claimant is being compensated on a provisional damages basis and should state with precision the medical condition or conditions in respect of which the Claimant will be permitted to seek further damages. It is also best practice for a case file containing the Particulars of Claim, medical reports and a copy of the Order for provisional damages to be lodged with the Court.

A good example of where provisional damages were (until the case of Rothwell – see post) considered appropriate were asbestos attributable pleural plaque claims. Although pleural plaques are usually benign and symptonless, they carry a lifetime risk of developing into a malignant mesothelioma and, depending on the extent of exposure, asbestosis, lung cancer and diffuse pleural thickening. Such conditions will (depending on the medical evidence) frequently feature as "comeback" conditions in a judgment for provisional damages. Whenever lung cancer is a 'come back' condition, qualify this by adding the phrase "which is asbestos attributable".

In the case of an elderly Claimant where the risk of future injury or deterioration is small he may elect to be compensated on a full and final rather than on a provisional damages basis. By doing so, he will be entitled to be compensated to reflect the percentage risk of him succumbing to further injury. It should be noted that it is the Claimant's prerogative to decide whether he should be compensated on a full and final or on a provisional damages basis.

Asbestos induced pleural plaque claims have until recently been in a state of flux pending the outcome of an appeal to the House of Lords in the case of ***Rothwell v Chemical and Insulating Limited (2005)*** AC 281. Their Lordships have now provided some clarity.

The Rothwell case (formerly known as ***Grieves and Others v F T Everard and Sons and Others) (2006)*** LTL 16/2/2005 originally came before Holland, J. in February 2005 and consisted of 10 Claimants who had radiological evidence of benign pleural plaques. Each Claimant was totally asymptomatic. The radiological evidence was merely a marker that the Claimants had at some time been exposed to asbestos. The issue in the action was whether pleural plaques should be regarded as a disease and whether a Claimant should be compensated for a condition which caused no physical pain or impairment and which did not impact on bodily function. In his Judgment, Holland, J. defined "damage" or "injury" as:

"The permanent physical penetration of the chest by asbestos fibres to such an extent as to give rise to:

a) the actual development of pleural plaques;

b) the possible future onset of symptoms, even if a terminal condition; and

c) consequent potentially continuing anxiety".

The Judge went on to find that significant permanent physical penetration [of lung tissue] raises a potential for damage, but no more. He also found that although pleural plaques could not be categorised as a "disease" or an "impairment of physical condition" he was nevertheless bound by ***Cartledge v Jopling & Sons Ltd*** (1963) AC 758 and that accordingly anxiety engendered by physical damage did give rise to a cause of action. The Judge went on to find that the appropriate figure for pain and suffering was somewhere between £3,500 and £4,000. For those Claimants seeking damages on a full and final basis where the anticipated risk of further injury was low, the Judge refused to follow the approach adopted in some County Courts (where awards of around £12,500 were common) and indicated that a bracket of £6,000 to £7,000 was more realistic.

The Defendants appealed in eight of the ten cases on liability and on quantum. The Claimants cross – appealed on quantum only.

On 26 January 2006, the Court of Appeal allowed the Defendants appeals by a majority 2:1 LTL 26/1/2006. The majority decision was that the development of pleural plaques, which were only detectable by x-ray, and which caused no respiratory deficit or other physical symptoms, were merely evidence of previous asbestos exposure and as such did not constitute damage significant enough to give rise to a cause of action. Further, on the issue of whether a Claimant should be awarded damages for psychiatric injury caused by the anxiety of succumbing to a more serious condition at a future date, the Court followed the Supreme Court of Ireland's decision in ***Fletcher v The Commissioners of Public Works in Ireland (2003)*** 1IR 465. and on policy grounds refused to treat the anxiety felt by a Claimant with only a remote risk of further injury as a psychiatric injury. The Court of Appeal decision was a majority decision. After delivering her dissenting Judgment, Smith, L J went on to expound the principles upon which she considered damages in a pleural plaque case should be assessed. In doing so, she expressed the view that the damages (suggested by Holland, J) were too low.

Pending the House of Lords decision litigants in pleural plaque cases entered into "standstill" agreements under which the parties agreed that for the purposes of limitation, any unexpired period as at the date the agreement was entered into, will cease to run against the Claimant until 28 days after the House of Lords published their decision.

On 17 October 2007 the House of Lords unanimously upheld the Court of Appeal's decision by finding that benign pleural plaques which do not cause any respiratory or other physical symptoms, cannot constitute damage significant enough to give rise to a claim in tort. Further, their Lordships refused to treat the anxiety felt by a Claimant with only a remote risk of further injury as giving rise to an actionable psychiatric injury.

That would have been the end of the matter, but Lord Scott observed that had the Claimant's claim been founded in contract, then they may have established that their employers were in breach of a parallel duty in their contract of employment not to expose them to harm in their workplace. Proof of damage is not necessary to found a claim in contract.

In reality, had the claims been brought in contract, then even if the Defendants had been found to be in breach, the damages awarded were likely to have been nominal.

The Scottish Parliament is currently considering introducing legislation to negate the effects of the House of Lords decision in Rothwell so as to allow victims with symptomless pleural plaques in Scotland to pursue claims. The UK Government has, however, decided that it would be inappropriate to introduce similar legislation.

8.20 Coverage

There is perhaps one other recent case that should be mentioned. This will be of particular interest to local authorities (and their co-Defendants). The case in question is ***Bolton MDC v Municipal Mutual Insurance and Another (2006)*** Lloyd's Rep IR15.

In this case the Judge was required (inter alia) to interpret in the context of a claim for personal injuries, the insuring clauses in two public liability policies which Bolton had taken out with MMI and with the predecessors in title of Commercial Union.

Bolton's claim for indemnity from its public liability insurers arose as a result of them settling a public liability claim of a mesothelioma victim who died of the disease in November 1991 having earlier been diagnosed with the illness in or about January 1991. All of the medical experts involved were agreed that the deceased's mesothelioma probably began to mutate about 10 years before his first physical symptoms manifested themselves. His first physical symptoms occurred during 1990 and so therefore the injury was deemed to have occurred in 1980.

From 1960–1965, Bolton had public liability cover with the predecessors in title of Commercial Union. Thereafter, and as at the date the deceased's mesothelioma began to mutate up until the date of his death, MMI were on risk for Bolton's public liability claims.

The MMI policy wording provided an indemnity for accidental bodily injury when such injury occurred during the currency of the policy. The Commercial Union PL policy wording provided indemnity in respect of bodily injury to or illness to any person which occurred during the period of indemnity (i.e. during the specific period the insurers agreed to go on risk).

The Judge found that "bodily injury or illness" does not include the inhalation of fibres which, though potentially harmful, may not reach the lungs or cause a mutation of a cancerous cell. That being the case, the Judge exonerated Commercial Union from any liability to indemnify Bolton. The Judge also went on to find that as at the date the MMI PL policy came into existence, MMI would have been aware of the possibility of mesothelioma claims arising long after exposure and could, had they chosen to do so, have worded their PL policy so as to exclude liability arising from circumstances occurring outside the currency of the policy.

In the subsequent appeal by MMI, the Court of Appeal upheld the first instance decision and dismissed MMI's appeal (The Times: 9 February 2006).

The Bolton decision has had a significant impact on all mesothelioma claims in which MMI were on cover or where other insurers provided indemnity in respect of accidental bodily injury occurring during the currency of the policy. Whereas in the past MMI (and other insurers) had been content to indemnify an insured in respect of an injury which is attributable to negligent acts and omissions committed during the period they were on risk, MMI (and some other insurers who had a similar policy wording) are now only granting indemnity where the mutation of the cancerous cell occurred during a period when they were on risk (i.e. 10 years before physical symptoms of a mesothelioma became manifest).

MMI and some other insurers with an 'injury incurring' policy wording have relied on the Bolton decision to avoid employers' liability mesothelioma claims. As a result, more and more local authorities are finding a "black hole" in their insurance cover. Consider the following example:

> C was employed by a local authority from 1965-1985 during which period he was culpably exposed to asbestos. During the period of exposure MMI provided the local authority's' employers' liability cover. In 1992, MMI ceased to write insurance and the local authority sought new cover from ABC Insurance whose policy wording was in conventional terms (i.e. providing indemnity in respect of injury or illness caused as a result of the insured's negligence/breach of duty during the period for which ABC Insurance agreed to go on risk). The Claimant's first physical symptoms of mesothelioma occurred in March 2007. The deemed date of injury (i.e. the mutation of the mesothelial cell) was therefore in March 1997. According to Bolton, on a true construction of MMI's policy, it only responded to an injury or an illness which occurred during the currency of the policy. But at the deemed date of the Claimant's injury (March 1997) MMI had ceased to write insurance. Further, the policy issued by ABC Insurance only provided

> indemnity in respect of an injury or illness which was caused during the period they agreed to go on risk (1992 onwards). The ABC Insurance policy did not respond to an injury which was deemed to have occurred in 1997. Accordingly, there is no valid insurance cover upon which the Local Authority can rely and it will end up paying this claim out of its own pocket.

At the date this Chapter is being written there is pending litigation in which MMI are seeking a declaration from the Court that on a true construction of their policy wording they are entitled to repudiate all employers' liability claims in accordance with the Bolton decision. The ten Local Authority Defendants are counterclaiming and are seeking to distinguish the Bolton case and to restore the status quo which existed before that decision. The local authorities are contending that when they took out employers' liability cover with MMI, both parties had intended that cover should be on a conventional or 'causation' basis. Until the Bolton decision, this was the basis upon which MMI had dealt with claims. The local authorities also assert that a course of dealing had been established within the insurance industry and thus MMI were estopped from dealing with mesothelioma claims on a different basis. The local authorities are also contending that the Court should look at the intention of the parties at the time the insurance was entered into and should not simply look at the policy wording.

Finally, the Local Authorities assert that cover under an employers' liability policy has to be on the basis of a 'causation' policy wording (ie in respect of injury or disease caused by negligent acts or omissions occurring during the period the insurer was on risk), otherwise this would undermine the intention of Parliament when it passed the Employers' Liability (Compulsory Insurance) Act 1969.

It is anticipated that judgment in the litigation between MMI and the ten Local Authorities will be handed down in Autumn 2008.

8.21 Conclusion

It is to be hoped that the narrative in this chapter will provide the reader with a useful guide for defending a disease claim. However, there is no substitute for delving into the major reference books which are commended and listed below.

8.22 Other Reference Material

Hunters Diseases of Occupations (Ninth Edition) – Baxter et al (Oxford University Press) 2000

Occupational Illness Litigation – McDonald Georges (Sweet and Maxwell) 2002

Redgrave's Health and Safety (5th Edition) – Hendy and Ford (Butterworths) 2007

Occupational Lung Diseases (3rd Edition) – Morgan & Seaton (W.B. Saunders Co) 1995

Asbestos Claims, Law Practice and Procedure – The Chambers of John Foy, QC, 9 Gough Square, London

Civil Procedure Rules

PRE-ACTION PROTOCOL FOR DISEASE AND ILLNESS CLAIMS

CONTENTS

1 INTRODUCTION

1.1 Lord Woolf in his final Access to Justice Report of July 1996 recommended the development of protocols: 'To build on and increase the benefits of early but well informed settlement which genuinely satisfy both parties to dispute.'

1.2 The aims of these protocols are:

- more contact between the parties
- better and earlier exchange of information
- better investigation by both sides
- to put the parties in a position where they may be able to settle cases fairly and early without litigation
- to enable proceedings to run to the court's timetable and efficiently, if litigation does become necessary.

1.3 The concept of protocols is relevant to a range of initiatives for good claims practice, especially:

- predictability in the time needed for steps to be taken
- standardisation of relevant information, including documents to be disclosed.

1.4 The Courts will be able to treat the standards set in protocols as the normal reasonable approach. If proceedings are issued, it will be for the court to decide whether non-compliance with a protocol should merit adverse consequences. Guidance on the court's likely approach will be given from time to time in practice directions.

1.5 If the court has to consider the question of compliance after proceedings have begun, it will not be concerned with minor infringements, e.g. failure by a short period to provide relevant information. One minor breach will not exempt the 'innocent' party from following the protocol. The court will look at the effect of non-compliance on the other party when deciding whether to impose sanctions.

2 NOTES OF GUIDANCE

SCOPE OF THE PROTOCOL

2.1 This protocol is intended to apply to all personal injury claims where the injury is not as the result of an accident but takes the form of an illness or disease.

2.2 This protocol covers disease claims which are likely to be complex and frequently not suitable for fast-track procedures even though they may fall within fast track limits. Disease for the purpose of this protocol primarily covers any illness physical or psychological, any disorder, ailment, affliction, complaint, malady, or derangement other than a physical or psychological injury solely caused by an accident or other similar single event.

2.3 This protocol is not limited to diseases occurring in the workplace but will embrace diseases occurring in other situations for example through occupation of premises or the use of products. It is not intended to cover those cases, which are dealt with as a 'group' or 'class' action.

2.4 The 'cards on the table' approach advocated by the personal injury protocol is equally appropriate to disease claims. The spirit of that protocol, and of the clinical negligence protocol is followed here, in accordance with the sense of the civil justice reforms.

2.5 The timetable and the arrangements for disclosing documents and obtaining expert evidence may need to be varied to suit the circumstances of the case. If a party considers the detail of the protocol to be inappropriate they should communicate their reasons to all of the parties at that stage. If proceedings are subsequently issued, the court will expect an explanation as to why the protocol has not been followed, or has been varied. In a terminal disease claim with short life expectancy, for instance for a claimant who has a disease such as mesothelioma, the time scale of the protocol is likely to be too long. In such a claim, the claimant may not be able to follow the protocol and the defendant would be expected to treat the claim with urgency.

2A ALTERNATIVE DISPUTE RESOLUTION

2A.1 The parties should consider whether some form of alternative dispute resolution procedure would be more suitable than litigation, and if so, endeavour to agree which form to adopt. Both the Claimant and Defendant may be required by the Court to provide evidence that alternative means of resolving their dispute were considered. The Courts take the view that litigation should be a last resort, and that claims should not be issued prematurely when a settlement is still actively being explored. Parties are warned that if the protocol is not followed (including this paragraph) then the Court must have regard to such conduct when determining costs.

2A.2 It is not practicable in this protocol to address in detail how the parties might decide which method to adopt to resolve their particular dispute. However, summarised below are some of the options for resolving disputes without litigation:

- Discussion and negotiation.
- Early neutral evaluation by an independent third party (for example, a lawyer experienced in the field of disease or illness, or an individual experienced in the subject matter of the claim).
- Mediation – a form of facilitated negotiation assisted by an independent neutral party.

2A.3 The Legal Services Commission has published a booklet on 'Alternatives to Court', CLS Direct Information Leaflet 23 (www.clsdirect.org.uk/legalhelp/leaflet23.jsp), which lists a number of organisations that provide alternative dispute resolution services.

2A.4 *It is expressly recognised that no party can or should be forced to mediate or enter into any form of ADR.*

3 THE AIMS OF THE PROTOCOL

3.1 The ***general*** aims of the protocol are –

- to resolve as many disputes as possible without litigation;
- where a claim cannot be resolved to identify the relevant issues which remain in dispute.

3.2 The ***specific*** objectives are –

OPENNESS

- to encourage early communication of the perceived problem between the parties or their insurers;
- to encourage employees to voice any concerns or worries about possible work related illness as soon as practicable;
- to encourage employers to develop systems of early reporting and investigation of suspected occupational health problems and to provide full and prompt explanations to concerned employees or former employees;
- to apply such principles to perceived problems outside the employer/employee relationship, for example occupiers of premises or land and producers of products;
- to ensure that sufficient information is disclosed by both parties to enable each to understand the other's perspective and case, and to encourage early resolution;

TIMELINESS

- to provide an early opportunity for employers (past or present) or their insurers to identify cases where an investigation is required and to carry out that

investigation promptly;
- to encourage employers (past or present) or other defendants to involve and identify their insurers at an early stage;
- to ensure that all relevant records including health and personnel records are provided to employees (past or present) or their appointed representatives promptly on request, by any employer (past or present) or their insurers. This should be complied with to a realistic timetable;
- to ensure that relevant records which are in the claimant's possession are made available to the employers or their insurers by claimants or their advisers at an appropriate stage;
- to proceed on a reasonable timetable where a resolution is not achievable to lay the ground to enable litigation to proceed at a reasonable and proportionate cost, and to limit the matters in contention;
- to communicate promptly where any of the requested information is not available or does not exist;
- to discourage the prolonged pursuit of unmeritorious claims and the prolonged defence of meritorious claims.
- To encourage all parties, at the earliest possible stage, to disclose voluntarily any additional documents which will assist in resolving any issue.

4 THE PROTOCOL

This protocol is not a comprehensive code governing all the steps in disease claims. Rather it attempts to set out **a code of good practice** which parties should follow.

OBTAINING OCCUPATIONAL RECORDS INCLUDING HEALTH RECORDS

4.1 In appropriate cases, a **potential claimant** may request Occupational Records including Health Records and Personnel Records before sending a Letter of Claim.

4.2 Any request for records by the **potential claimant** or his adviser should **provide sufficient information** to alert the **potential defendant** or his insurer where a possible disease claim is being investigated; Annex A1 provides a suggested form for this purpose for use in cases arising from employment. Similar forms can be prepared and used in other situations.

4.3 The copy records should be provided **within a maximum of 40 days** of the request at no cost. Although these will primarily be occupational records, it will be good practice for a **potential defendant** to disclose product data documents identified by a **potential claimant** at this stage which may resolve a causation issue.

4.4 In the rare circumstances that the **potential defendant** or his insurer is in difficulty in providing information quickly details should be given of what is being done to resolve it with a reasonable time estimate for doing so.

4.5 If the **potential defendant** or his insurer fails to provide the records including health records within 40 days and fails to comply with paragraph 4.4 above, the **potential claimant** or his adviser may then apply to the court for an **order for pre-action disclosure**. The Civil Procedure Rules make pre-action applications to the court easier. The court also has the power to impose costs sanctions for unreasonable delay in providing records.

5 COMMUNICATION

5.1 If either the **potential claimant** or his adviser considers **additional records are required from a third party**, such as records from previous employers or general practitioner records, in the first instance these should be requested by the **potential claimant** or their advisers. Third party record holders would be expected to co-operate. The Civil Procedure Rules enable parties to apply to the court for pre-action disclosure by third parties.

5.2 As soon as the records have been received and analysed, the **potential claimant** or his adviser should consider whether a claim should be made. General practitioner records will normally be obtained before a decision is reached.

5.3 If a decision is made not to proceed further at this stage against a party identified as a **potential defendant**, the **potential claimant** or his adviser should notify that **potential defendant** as soon as practicable.

6 LETTER OF CLAIM

6.1 Where a decision is made to make a claim, the claimant shall send to the proposed defendant two copies of a letter of claim, as soon as sufficient information is available to substantiate a realistic claim and before issues of quantum are addressed in detail. One copy is for the defendants, the second for passing on to his insurers.

6.2 This letter shall contain a **clear summary of the facts** on which the claim is based, including details of the illness alleged, and the **main allegations of fault**. It shall also give details of present condition and prognosis. The **financial loss** incurred by the claimant should be outlined. Where the case is funded by a conditional fee agreement, notification should be given of the existence of the agreement and where appropriate, that there is a success fee and insurance premium, although not the level of the success fee or premium.

6.3 Solicitors are recommended to use **a standard format** for such a letter – an example is at Annex B: this can be amended to suit the particular case, for example, if the client has rehabilitation needs these can also be detailed in the letter.

6.4 A **chronology** of the relevant events (e.g. dates or periods of exposure) should be provided. In the case of alleged occupational disease an appropriate employment history should also be provided, particularly if the claimant has been employed by a number of different employers and the illness in question has a long latency period.

6.5 The letter of claim should identify any **relevant documents**, including health records not already in the defendant's possession e.g. any relevant general practitioner records. These will need to be disclosed in confidence to the nominated insurance manager or solicitor representing the defendant following receipt of their letter of acknowledgement. Where the action is brought under the Law Reform Act 1934 or the Fatal Accidents Act 1976 then **relevant documents** will normally include copies of the death certificate, the post mortem report, the inquest depositions and if obtained by that date the grant of probate or letters of administration.

6.6 The letter of claim should indicate whether a claim is also being made against any **other potential defendant** and identify any known insurer involved.

6.7

Sufficient information should be given to enable the defendant's insurer/solicitor to commence **investigations** and at least to put a broad valuation on the 'risk'.

6.8 It is not a requirement for the claimant to provide **medical evidence** with the letter of claim, but the claimant may choose to do so in very many cases.

6.9 **Letters of claim and response** are not intended to have the same **status** as a statement of case in proceedings. Matters may come to light as a result of investigation after the letter of claim has been sent, or after the defendant has responded, particularly if disclosure of documents takes place outside the recommended three-month period. These circumstances could mean that the 'pleaded' case of one or both parties is presented slightly differently than in the letter of claim or response. It would not be consistent with the spirit of the protocol for a party to 'take a point' on this in the proceedings, provided that there was no obvious intention by the party who changed their position to mislead the other party.

6.10 **Proceedings should not be issued until after three months from the date of acknowledgement** (see paragraph 7), unless there is a limitation problem and/or the claimant's position needs to be protected by early issue. (See paragraph 2.5)

7 THE RESPONSE

7.1 The defendant should **send an acknowledgement within 21 calendar days** of the date of posting of the letter of claim, identifying the liability insurer (if any) who will be dealing with the matter and, if necessary, identifying specifically any significant omissions from the Letter of Claim. If there has been no acknowledgement by the defendant or insurer within 21 days, the claimant will be entitled to issue proceedings.

7.2 The identity of all relevant insurers, if more than one, should be notified to the claimant by the insurer identified in the acknowledgement letter, within one calendar month of the date of that acknowledgement.

7.3 The defendant or his representative should, **within three months of the date of the acknowledgement letter**, provide a **reasoned answer**: –

- if the **claim is admitted**, they should say so in clear terms;
- if only **part of the claim is admitted** they should make clear which issues of fault and/or causation and/or limitation are admitted and which remain in issue and why;
- if the **claim is not admitted in full**, they should explain why and should, **for example**, include comments on the employment status of the claimant, (including job description(s) and details of the department(s) where the claimant worked), the allegations of fault, causation and of limitation, and if a synopsis or chronology of relevant events has been provided and is disputed, their version of those events;
- if the **claim is not admitted in full**, the defendant should enclose with his letter of reply **documents** in his possession which are **material to the issues** between the parties and which would be likely to be ordered to be disclosed by the court, either on an application for pre-action disclosure, or on disclosure during proceedings. Reference can be made to the documents annexed to the personal injury protocol.
- where more than one defendant receives a letter of claim, the timetable will be activated for each defendant by the date on the letter of claim addressed to them. If any defendant wishes to extend the timetable because the number of defendants will cause complications, they should seek agreement to a different

timetable as soon as possible.

7.4 If the parties reach agreement on liability and/or causation, but time is needed to resolve other issues including the value of the claim, they should aim to agree a reasonable period.

7.5 Where it is not practicable for the defendant to complete his investigations within 3 months, the defendant should indicate the difficulties and outline the further time needed. Any request for an extension of time should be made, with reasons, as soon as the defendant becomes aware that an extension is needed and normally before the 3 month period has expired. Such an extension of time should be agreed in circumstances where reasonable justification has been shown. Lapse of many years since the circumstances giving rise to the claim does not, by itself, constitute reasonable justification for further time.

7.6 Where the relevant negligence occurred outside England and Wales and/or where the defendant is outside the jurisdiction, the time periods of 21 days and three months should normally be extended up to 42 days and six months.

8 SPECIAL DAMAGES

8.1 The claimant will send to the defendant as soon as practicable a Schedule of Special Damages with supporting documents, particularly where the defendant has admitted liability.

9 EXPERTS

9.1 In disease claims expert opinions will usually be needed: -

- on knowledge, fault and causation;
- on condition and prognosis;
- to assist in valuing aspects of the claim.

9.2 The civil justice reforms and the Civil Procedure Rules encourage economy in the use of experts and a less adversarial expert culture. It is recognised that in disease claims, the parties and their advisers will require flexibility in their approach to expert evidence. Decisions on whether experts might be instructed jointly, and on whether reports might be disclosed sequentially or by exchange, should rest with the parties and their advisers. Sharing expert evidence may be appropriate on various issues including those relating to the value of the claim. However, this protocol does not attempt to be prescriptive on issues in relation to expert evidence.

9.3 Obtaining expert evidence will often be an expensive step and may take time, especially in specialised areas where there are limited numbers of suitable experts. Claimants, defendants and their advisers, will therefore need to consider carefully how best to obtain any necessary expert help quickly and cost-effectively.

9.4 The protocol recognises that a flexible approach must be adopted in the obtaining of medical reports in claims of this type. There will be very many occasions where the claimant will need to obtain a medical report before writing the letter of claim. In such cases the defendant will be entitled to obtain their own medical report. In some other instances it may be more appropriate to send the letter of claim before the medical report is obtained. Defendants will usually need to see a medical report before they can reach a view on causation.

9.5 Where the parties agree the nomination of a single expert is appropriate, before any party instructs an expert he should give the other party a list of the **name**(s) of **one or more experts** in the relevant speciality whom he considers are suitable to instruct. The parties are encouraged to agree the instruction of a single expert to deal with discrete areas such as cost of care.

9.6 **Within 14 days** the other party may indicate **an objection** to one or more of the named experts. The first party should then instruct a mutually acceptable expert. If the Claimant nominates an expert in the original letter of claim, the 14 days is in addition to the 21 days in paragraph 7.1.

9.7 If the second party objects to all the listed experts, the parties may then instruct **experts of their own choice**. It would be for the court to decide subsequently, if proceedings are issued, whether either party had acted unreasonably.

9.8 If the **second party does not object to an expert nominated**, he shall not be entitled to rely on his own expert evidence within that particular speciality unless:

(a) the first party agrees,
(b) the court so directs, or
(c) the first party's expert report has been amended and the first party is not prepared to disclose the original report.

9.9 **Either party may send to an agreed expert written questions** on the report, relevant to the issues, via the first party's solicitors. The expert should send answers to the questions separately and directly to each party.

9.10 The cost of a report from an agreed expert will usually be paid by the instructing first party: the costs of the expert replying to questions will usually be borne by the party which asks the questions.

9.11 Where the defendant admits liability in whole or in part, before proceedings are issued, any medical report obtained under this protocol which **the claimant** relies upon, should be disclosed to the other party.

9.12 Where the defendant admits liability in whole or in part before proceedings are issued, any medical report obtained under this protocol which **the defendant** relies upon, should be disclosed to the claimant.

10 RESOLUTION OF ISSUES

10.1 The Civil Procedure Rules Part 36 enable claimants and defendants to make formal offers to settle before proceedings are started. Parties should consider making such an offer, since to do so often leads to settlement. If such an offer is made, the party making the offer must always supply sufficient evidence and/or information to enable the offer to be properly considered.

10.2 Where a claim is not resolved when the protocol has been followed, the parties might wish to carry out a 'stocktake' of the issues in dispute, and the evidence that the court is likely to need to decide those issues, before proceedings are started.

10.3 Prior to proceedings it will be usual for all parties to disclose those expert reports relating to liability and causation upon which they propose to rely.

10.4 The claimant should delay issuing proceedings for 21 days from disclosure of reports to enable the parties to consider whether the claim is capable of settlement.

10.5 Where the defendant is insured and the pre-action steps have been conducted by the insurer, the insurer would normally be expected to nominate solicitors to act in the proceedings and the claimant's solicitor is recommended to invite the insurer to nominate solicitors to act in the proceedings and to do so 7-14 days before the intended issue date.

11 LIMITATION

11.1 If by reason of complying with any part of this protocol a claimant's claim may be time-barred under any provision of the Limitation Act 1980, or any other legislation which imposes a time limit for bringing an action, the claimant may commence proceedings without complying with this protocol. In such circumstances, a claimant who commences proceedings without complying with all, or any part, of this protocol may apply to the court on notice for directions as to the timetable and form of procedure to be adopted, at the same time as he requests the court to issue proceedings. The court will consider whether to order a stay of the whole or part of the proceedings pending compliance with this protocol.

ANNEX A

LETTER REQUESTING OCCUPATIONAL RECORDS INCLUDING HEALTH RECORDS

APPLICATION ON BEHALF OF A POTENTIAL CLAIMANT FOR USE WHERE A DISEASE CLAIM IS BEING INVESTIGATED

ANNEX B

TEMPLATE FOR LETTER OF CLAIM

PDF

LETTER REQUESTING OCCUPATIONAL RECORDS INCLUDING HEALTH RECORDS

Dear Sirs,

We are acting on behalf of the above-named who has developed the following ***(insert disease)***. We are investigating whether this disease may have been caused: -

- ***during the course of his employment with you / name of employer if different***
- ***whilst at your premises at (address)***
- ***as a result of your product (name)***

We are writing this in accordance with the Protocol for Disease and Illness Claims

We seek the following records: -

(Insert details e.g. personnel / occupational health)

Please note your insurers may require you to advise them of this request.

We enclose a request form and expect to receive the records within 40 days.
If you are not able to comply with this request within this time, please advise us of the reason.

Yours faithfully

APPLICATION ON BEHALF OF A POTENTIAL CLAIMANT FOR USE WHERE A DISEASE CLAIM IS BEING INVESTIGATED

This should be completed as fully as possible

Company
Name
And
Address

1 a)	Full name of claimant (including previous surnames)	
b)	Address now	
c)	Address at date of termination of employment, if different	
d)	Date of birth (and death, if applicable)	
e)	National Insurance number, if available	
2	Department(s) where claimant worked	
3.	This application is made because the claimant is considering	
a)	a claim against you as detailed in para 4	YES/NO
b)	Pursuing an action against someone else	YES/NO
4	If the answer to Q3(a) is 'Yes' details of	
	a) the likely nature of the claim, eg dermatitis	
	b) grounds for the claim, eg exposure to chemical	
	c) approximate dates of the events involved	

5	If the answer to Q3(b) is 'Yes' insert	
	a) the names of the proposed defendants	
	b) have legal proceedings been started?	YES/NO
	c) if appropriate, details of the claim and action number	
6	Any other relevant information or documents requested	
	Signature of Solicitor	
	Name	
	Address	
	Ref.	
	Telephone Number	
	Fax number	

I authorise you to disclose all of your records relating to me/the claimant to my solicitor and to your legal and insurance representatives.

Signature of Claimant

Signature of personal representative where claimant has died

TEMPLATE FOR LETTER OF CLAIM

To: - Defendant

Dear Sirs

Re: Claimant's full name
Claimant's full address
Claimant's National Insurance Number
Claimant's Date of Birth
Claimant's Clock or Works Number
Claimant's Employer *(name and address)*

We are instructed by the above named to claim damages in connection with a claim for: -
Specify occupational disease

We are writing this letter in accordance with the pre-action protocol for disease and illness claims.

Please confirm the identity of your insurers. Please note that your insurers will need to see this letter as soon as possible and it may affect your insurance cover if you do not send this to them.

The Claimant was employed by you ***(if the claim arises out of public or occupiers' liability give appropriate details)*** as ***job description*** from ***date*** to ***date***. During the relevant period of his employment he worked: -
description of precisely where the Claimant worked and what he did to include a description of any machines used and details of any exposure to noise or substances

The circumstances leading to the development of this condition are as follows: -
Give chronology of events

The reason why we are alleging fault is: -
Details should be given of contemporary and comparable employees who have suffered from similar problems if known; any protective equipment provided; complaints; the supervisors concerned, if known.

Our client's employment history is attached.

We have also made a claim against: -
Insert details
Their insurers' details are: -
Insert if known

We have the following documents in support of our client's claim and will disclose these in confidence to your nominated insurance manager or solicitor when we receive their acknowledgement letter.
e.g. Occupational health notes; GP notes

We have obtained a medical report from (name) and will disclose this when we receive your acknowledgement of this letter.
(This is optional at this stage)

From the information we presently have: -

(i) the Claimant first became aware of symptoms on ***(insert approximate date)***
(ii) the Claimant first received medical advice about those symptoms on ***(insert date) (give details of advice given if appropriate)***
(iii) the Claimant first believed that those symptoms might be due to exposure leading to this claim on ***(insert approximate date)***

A description of our client's condition is as follows: -
This should be sufficiently detailed to allow the Defendant to put a broad value on the claim

He has the following time off work: -
Insert dates

He is presently employed as a ***job description*** and his average net weekly income is **£**

If you are our client's employers, please provide us with the usual earnings details, which will enable us to calculate his financial loss.

Please note that we have entered into a conditional fee agreement with our client dated in relation to this claim which provides for a success fee within the meaning of section 58(2) of the Courts and Legal Services Act 1990. Our client has taken out an insurance policy dated with (name of insurance company) to which section 29 of the Access to Justice Act 1999 applies in respect of this claim.

A copy of this letter is attached for you to send to your insurers. Finally we expect an acknowledgement of this letter within 21 days by yourselves or your insurers.

Yours faithfully

PRE-ACTION PROTOCOL FOR CONSTRUCTION AND ENGINEERING DISPUTES

CONTENTS

1 INTRODUCTION

1.1 This Pre-Action Protocol applies to all construction and engineering disputes (including professional negligence claims against architects, engineers and quantity surveyors).

EXCEPTIONS

1.2 A claimant shall not be required to comply with this Protocol before commencing proceedings to the extent that the proposed proceedings (i) are for the enforcement of the decision of an adjudicator to whom a dispute has been referred pursuant to section 108 of the Housing Grants, Construction and Regeneration Act 1996 ('the 1996 Act'), (ii) include a claim for interim injunctive relief, (iii) will be the subject of a claim for summary judgment pursuant to Part 24 of the Civil Procedure Rules, or (iv) relate to the same or substantially the same issues as have been the subject of recent adjudication under the 1996 Act, or some other formal alternative dispute resolution procedure.

OBJECTIVES

1.3 The objectives of this Protocol are as set out in the Practice Direction relating to Civil Procedure Pre-Action Protocols, namely:

(i) to encourage the exchange of early and full information about the prospective legal claim;

(ii) to enable parties to avoid litigation by agreeing a settlement of the claim before commencement of proceedings; and

(iii) to support the efficient management of proceedings where litigation cannot be avoided.

COMPLIANCE

1.4 If proceedings are commenced, the court will be able to treat the standards set in this Protocol as the normal reasonable approach to pre-action conduct. If the court has to consider the question of compliance after proceedings have begun, it will be concerned with substantial compliance and not minor departures, e.g. failure by a short period to provide relevant information. Minor departures will not exempt the 'innocent' party from following the Protocol. The court will look at the effect of non-compliance on the other party when deciding whether to impose sanctions. For sanctions generally, see paragraph 2 of the Practice Direction-Protocols 'Compliance with Protocols'.

PROPORTIONALITY

1.5 The overriding objective (CPR rule 1.1) applies to the pre-action period. The Protocol must not be used as a tactical device to secure advantage for one party or to generate unnecessary costs. In lower value claims (such as those likely to proceed in the county court), the letter of claim and the response should be simple and the costs of both sides should be kept to a modest level. In all cases the costs incurred at the Protocol stage should be proportionate to the complexity of the case and the amount of money which is at stake. The Protocol does not impose a requirement on the parties to marshal and disclose all the supporting details and evidence that may ultimately be required if the case proceeds to litigation.

2 OVERVIEW OF THE PROTOCOL

GENERAL AIM

2. The general aim of this Protocol is to ensure that before court proceedings commence:

(i) the claimant and the defendant have provided sufficient information for each party to know the nature of the other's case;

(ii) each party has had an opportunity to consider the other's case, and to accept or reject all or any part of the case made against him at the earliest possible stage;

(iii) there is more pre-action contact between the parties;

(iv) better and earlier exchange of information occurs;

(v)

there is better pre-action investigation by the parties;

(vi) the parties have met formally on at least one occasion with a view to

- defining and agreeing the issues between them; and
- exploring possible ways by which the claim may be resolved;

(vii) the parties are in a position where they may be able to settle cases early and fairly without recourse to litigation; and

(viii) proceedings will be conducted efficiently if litigation does become necessary.

3 THE LETTER OF CLAIM

3. Prior to commencing proceedings, the claimant or his solicitor shall send to each proposed defendant (if appropriate to his registered address) a copy of a letter of claim which shall contain the following information:

(i) the claimant's full name and address;

(ii) the full name and address of each proposed defendant;

(iii) a clear summary of the facts on which each claim is based;

(iv) the basis on which each claim is made, identifying the principal contractual terms and statutory provisions relied on;

(v) the nature of the relief claimed: if damages are claimed, a breakdown showing how the damages have been quantified; if a sum is claimed pursuant to a contract, how it has been calculated; if an extension of time is claimed, the period claimed;

(vi) where a claim has been made previously and rejected by a defendant, and the claimant is able to identify the reason(s) for such rejection, the claimant's grounds of belief as to why the claim was wrongly rejected;

(vii) the names of any experts already instructed by the claimant on whose evidence he intends to rely, identifying the issues to which that evidence will be directed.

4 THE DEFENDANT'S RESPONSE

THE DEFENDANT'S ACKNOWLEDGMENT

4.1 Within 14 calendar days of receipt of the letter of claim, the defendant should acknowledge its receipt in writing and may give the name and address of his insurer (if any). If there has been no acknowledgment by or on behalf of the defendant within 14 days, the claimant will be entitled to commence proceedings without further compliance with this Protocol.

OBJECTIONS TO THE COURT'S JURISDICTION OR THE NAMED DEFENDANT

4.2 Objections to the court's jurisdiction or the named defendant

4.2.1 If the defendant intends to take any objection to all or any part of the claimant's claim on the grounds that (i) the court lacks jurisdiction, (ii) the matter should be referred to arbitration, or (iii) the defendant named in the letter of claim is the wrong defendant, that objection should be raised by the defendant within 28 days after receipt of the letter of claim. The letter of objection shall specify the parts of the claim to which the objection relates, setting out the grounds relied on, and, where appropriate, shall identify the correct defendant (if known). Any failure to take such objection shall not prejudice the defendant's rights to do so in any subsequent proceedings, but the court may take such failure into account when considering the question of costs.

4.2.2 Where such notice of objection is given, the defendant is not required to send a letter of response in accordance with paragraph 4.3.1 in relation to the claim or those parts of it to which the objection relates (as the case may be).

4.2.3 If at any stage before the claimant commences proceedings, the defendant withdraws his objection, then paragraph 4.3 and the remaining part of this Protocol will apply to the claim or those parts of it to which the objection related as if the letter of claim had been received on the date on which notice of withdrawal of the objection had been given.

THE DEFENDANT'S RESPONSE

4.3

4.3.1 Within 28 days from the date of receipt of the letter of claim, or such other period as the parties may reasonably agree (up to a maximum of 3 months), the defendant shall send a letter of response to the claimant which shall contain the following information:

(i) the facts set out in the letter of claim which are agreed or not agreed, and if not agreed, the basis of the disagreement;

(ii) which claims are accepted and which are rejected, and if rejected, the basis of the rejection;

(iii) if a claim is accepted in whole or in part, whether the damages, sums or extensions of time claimed are accepted or rejected, and if rejected, the basis of the rejection;

(iv) if contributory negligence is alleged against the claimant, a summary of the facts relied on;

(v) whether the defendant intends to make a counterclaim, and if so, giving the information which is required to be given in a letter of claim by paragraph 3(iii) to (vi) above;

(vi) the names of any experts already instructed on whose evidence it is intended to rely, identifying the issues to which that evidence will be directed;

4.3.2 If no response is received by the claimant within the period of 28 days (or such other period as has been agreed between the parties), the claimant shall be entitled to commence proceedings without further compliance with this Protocol.

CLAIMANT'S RESPONSE TO COUNTER CLAIM

4.4 The claimant shall provide a response to any counterclaim within the equivalent period allowed to the defendant to respond to the letter of claim under paragraph 4.3.1 above.

5 PRE-ACTION MEETING

5.1 Within 28 days after receipt by the claimant of the defendant's letter of response, or (if the claimant intends to respond to the counterclaim) after receipt by the defendant of the claimant's letter of response to the counterclaim, the parties should normally meet.

5.2 The aim of the meeting is for the parties to agree what are the main issues in the case, to identify the root cause of disagreement in respect of each issue, and to consider (i) whether, and if so how, the issues might be resolved without recourse to litigation, and (ii) if litigation is unavoidable, what steps should be taken to ensure that it is conducted in accordance with the overriding objective as defined in rule 1.1 of the Civil Procedure Rules.

5.3 In some circumstances, it may be necessary to convene more than one meeting. It is not intended by this Protocol to prescribe in detail the manner in which the meetings should be conducted. But the court will normally expect that those attending will include:

(i) where the party is an individual, that individual, and where the party is a corporate body, a representative of that body who has authority to settle or recommend settlement of the dispute;

(ii) a legal representative of each party (if one has been instructed);

(iii) where the involvement of insurers has been disclosed, a representative of the insurer (who may be its legal representative); and

(iv) where a claim is made or defended on behalf of some other party (such as, for example, a claim made by a main contractor pursuant to a contractual obligation to pass on subcontractor claims), the party on whose behalf the claim is made or defended and/or his legal representatives.

5.4 In respect of each agreed issue or the dispute as a whole, the parties should consider whether some form of alternative dispute resolution procedure would be more suitable than litigation, and if so, endeavour to agree which form to adopt. It is expressly recognised that no party can or should be forced to mediate or enter into any form of alternative dispute resolution.

5.5 If the parties are unable to agree on a means of resolving the dispute other than by litigation they should use their best endeavours to agree:

(i) if there is any area where expert evidence is likely to be required, how the relevant issues are to be defined and how expert evidence is to be dealt with

9 HEALTH AND SAFETY ENFORCEMENT – A CHANGING LANDSCAPE

9 HEALTH AND SAFETY ENFORCEMENT – A CHANGING LANDSCAPE

Contents

9.1 Section 1 – New Duties for Directors

Risks for Insureds

Historically the HSE focused on the conduct of a company or organization and only prosecuted individuals in exceptional cases. However, that position is changing.

In 2000 the Government issued its revitalising health and safety strategy. This included an action point that the Health and Safety Commission will develop a Code of Practice on Director's responsibilities for health and safety and also to advise ministers on how the law would need to be changed to make these responsibilities statutory so that directors and responsible persons of similar status are clear about what is expected of them in their management of health and safety. It went on that it was the intention to introduce legislation on those responsibilities.

In 2003 the HSE produced for the first time comprehensive guidance to its inspectors on this issue entitled simply "Prosecuting Individuals".

There are a number of reasons for this drift towards making directors and senior managers personally accountable under health and safety law. These include:

- the ever growing blame culture and associated press pressure
- political pressure for HSE and the police to have a harder and higher profile
- the conclusion that self-regulation, persuasion and education have not brought about enough of a change in safety culture and accident statistics
- the desire to attempt to get at those with the real power to change corporate attitudes to safety
- the failure to get successful corporate manslaughter prosecutions off the ground in respect of large companies
- the failure to get the offence of "corporate killing" onto the statute book

Under the Health and Safety at Work Act, prosecutions against individuals will be in relation to possible breaches of section 7 and section 37. S 7 imposes duties on all employees while at work to take reasonable care for the health and safety of himself and of other persons (including members of the public) who may foreseeably be affected by his acts or omissions at work

A ***Director, Manager or Secretary*** of a Company can also be liable under section 37 of HSWA where an offence under the Act is committed by his company with his consent, connivance or was attributable to any neglect on his part.

Section 37(1) states:

"Where an offence under any of the relevant statutory provisions committed by a body corporate is proved to have been committed with the consent or connivance of, or to have been attributable to any neglect on the part of, any director, manager, secretary or other similar officer of the body corporate or a person who was purporting to act in any such capacity, he as well as the body corporate shall be guilty of an offence and shall be proceeded against and punished accordingly."

"Connivance" is not defined in any of the health and safety legislation but has generally been accepted to mean something akin to "wilful blindness". "Attributable to" has been interpreted in its broadest sense. In ***Wotherspoon v HM Advocate*** "neglect" was said to require some form of duty or obligation on the part of the person so charged which is breached.

In ***R v Boal*** the Court of Appeal suggested by reference to the Fire Precautions Act 1976, that the section was intended "to fix with criminality only those who were in a position of real authority, the decision makers within the company, who had both the power and the responsibility to decide corporate policy and strategy".

There has been a clear head of steam behind the investigation and prosecution of section 37 as evidenced in the Hatfield trial. In that case 12 individuals were initially charged with Section 37 (some of course were also charged with manslaughter). None were convicted.

In 2007, the Criminal Discussion of the Court of Appeal (***R v P** [2007]* AU ER (D) 173) took the opportunity to reconsider the test for neglect. It held that whether a Director has been neglectful – in cases where there was not actual knowledge – would depend on whether the Director should have, by reason of the surrounding circumstances, been put on enquiry. The court stressed that this would depend on the evidence in each case but would require a detailed analysis of the Director's responsibilities.

The penalty for an offence under section 37 is the same as the substantive offences the corporation faces namely a fine. However, in many cases the real sanction will be the stigma attached to a conviction for a criminal offence related (usually) to causing a person's death in a work-related incident. In addition there is a Private Members bill currently before Parliment that would make imprisonment an option for nearly all health and safety offences, which would obviously be a very significant development.

In addition, the Company Directors Disqualification Act 1986 enables a Court to make a disqualification order against a Director convicted of an indictable offence (this includes manslaughter and offences under the HSWA) connected with the promotion, formation, management or liquidation of a company. The conduct at which the legislation is aimed is defined in Section 2 and includes health and safety matters.

The HSC published guidance on Directors' responsibilities in 2001 "designed to raise the profile of health and safety at board level". The guidance is aimed at employing organisations in both the private and public sector. It is not compulsory for the guidance to be followed. However, the HSE has indicated that if Directors follow the note they will "normally be doing enough to comply with the law". The five action points set out in the guidance are:

1 The board needs to accept formally and publicly its collective role in providing health and safety leadership in its organisation.

2 Each member of the board needs to accept their individual role in providing health and safety leadership for their organisation.

3 The board needs to ensure that all board decisions reflect its health and safety intentions, as articulated in the health and safety policy statements.

4 The board needs to recognise its role in engaging in the active participation of workers in improving health and safety. There are already for example legal requirements about consulting your workers, via their trade union representatives if appropriate under the Health and Safety (Consultation with Employees) Regulations 1996 and the Safety Representatives and Safety Committees Regulations 1977.

5 The board needs to ensure that it is kept informed of, and alert to, relevant health and safety risk management issues.

A recent HSE survey found that that since 2001, the percentage that reported health and safety is directed at Board level rose from 58% to 79%. However, despite this increase in figures the guidance has widely been seen as a failure in achieving its central aim of raising health and safety awareness in the Board Room.

In March 2005 the Minister of State for Work and Pensions gave an assurance to the House of Commons that the power of disqualification under the Act has been and will continue to be used.

In the Financial World following widely publicized scandals at Worldcom, Enron and Tyco in the US and Barings in the UK, new guidance was produced by the London Stock Exchange in 2003 explicitly articulating the responsibilities that the Board assumes and those for which management is accountable.

The guidance entitled the Combined Code on Corporate Governance is not compulsory but listed companies are expected to comply with its provisions.

As a result throughout the last few years the HSE has been looking for ways to either build on or replace the current guidance for health and safety with more detailed prescriptive guidance for Directors. This has included a project to survey the use and effectiveness of the Company Directors Disqualification Act as a legal sanction against Directors convicted of health and safety offences.

The new guidance was issued jointly with the Institute of Directors in November 2007. It sets out a series of "core actions" and "good practice" points for Directors to follow to allow them to:

1. Plan for direction of health and safety
2. Deliver health and safety
3. Monitor health and safety
4. Review health and safety

and giving advice on what happens when "leadership falls short".

Risks for Insurers

The inevitable risk to insurers from more action against Directors is an increase of claims for cover under EL/PL and D&O policies. In addition, there is a risk of increased costs per claim even on a guilty plea as Insured's will want to ensure that the most favourable basis is obtained to avoid possible prison sentences or at least hugely damaging reputation risks of a criminal conviction and possibly in some cases large fines. Currently HSE succeed in c90% of prosecutions against companies but the conviction rate against individuals in only 60% meaning that cases involving individuals are more likely to be more contested.

The current policy of investigating more individuals including directors and officers is already very significant. The proposal to introduce specific health and safety duties for directors and amend S37 increases the risk of investigations against individuals and is a very significant development for both those people and insurers who might be asked to foot defence legal costs where there is valid cover.

It may be an opportune time, in conjunction with the introduction of a new offence of corporate manslaughter, for insurers to assess their policies and check wordings, especially for high-risk sectors such as construction and to give careful consideration to their Insured's safety records and risk management practices.

9.2 Section 2 – A Guide to the Corporate Manslaughter and Corporate Homicide Act 2007

Introduction

The passing of the of the Corporate Manslaughter and Corporate Homicide Act 2007 to introduce a statutory offence of "Corporate manslaughter" (called Corporate Homicide in Scotland) follows many years of promises by this and previous Governments to reform the law of corporate manslaughter. The new offence came into force on 6 April 2008. Previously there was a common law offence that, in order for a company to be found guilty of it, required the conviction of an individual person for gross negligence manslaughter and for that person to be so senior within the company that he represented its "directing mind". This requirement was known as the Identification Principle. The common law offence will remain for any management failure resulting in an incident up to 6 April 2008 and will then be abolished.

It is important to emphasise that the Act is an offence creating statute rather than a duty setting one. The Act itself imposes no new health and safety duties.

The New Offence of Corporate Manslaughter

The Act is designed to make it easier to prosecute organisations where their gross negligence leads to death. As outlined above under the old law a corporate body could only be prosecuted based on the identification principle. Whilst attempts were made to prosecute big companies under the old law these attempts were all unsuccessful.

The new Act abolishes the common law offence altogether from 6 April 2008 and replaces it with a statutory offence at section 1 creating a completely new framework for finding an organisation guilty of corporate manslaughter.

The wording of the offence is that an organisation will be guilty of an offence if the way in which its activities are managed or organised:

(a) causes a person's death, and

(b) amounts to a gross breach of a relevant duty of care owed by the organisation to the deceased.

An organisation is only guilty if the way in which its activities are managed or organised by its senior management is a substantial element in the breach.

Organisations

Whereas the common law offence only applied to corporate bodies, the new offence will apply to a much wider group of organisations including corporations, specified government departments, police forces and partnerships.

Senior Management

"Senior Management" is defined in section 1(4) (c) as the persons who play significant roles in:

(i) the making of decisions about how the whole or a substantial part of its activities are to be managed or organised, or

(ii) the actual managing or organising of the whole or a substantial part of those activities.

Clearly there will be some people e.g. members of the Board who will be involved in substantial, arguably the whole of the company's decision-making process and fulfil the test in 1(4) (c) (i) above.

Under the current law those individuals would be identified as representing the directing mind and there does not appear to be any change in respect of people at that level.

However, the definition in s.1(4) (c) (ii) a person "*actually* managing or organising ... a substantial part of those activities" is a major change. The definition includes two strands, the taking of decisions and actually managing those activities.

The term "significant" is intended to capture those whose role in the relevant management activity is decisive or influential, rather than playing a supporting role.

What amounts to a "substantial" part of an organisation's activities will be important in determining the level of management responsibility engaging the new offence. The scale of the organisation's activities overall will be a factor and it is stated that the offence is intended to cover, for example, management at regional level within a national organisation.

In many big companies there will be managers who manage areas or are responsible for a particular discipline. The definition in s1(4)(c) (ii) – "actually managing a substantial part" – would appear to potentially lower the threshold for these managers who might then become "senior management" under the new law but who would not be identified as directing mind under the current common law. As such the definition is bound to catch a layer of management lower in the organisation that would not have been classified as representing the directing mind under the old law. It should also be noted that senior management would cover both those in the direct operational chain of management as well as those in, for example, strategic or regulatory compliance roles.

The other key point about the definition of "senior management" is that the new offence allows the prosecutor to aggregate the failures of a number of senior managers rather than relying on the conduct of one single "directing mind" as previously required by the identification principle.

These two points are the key changes from the old law and will undoubtedly increase the potential for the new offence to be investigated against medium and bigger companies. However, as explained below, there will remain hurdles to overcome particularly as the new legal test requires a significant element of "gross" failure to be at a senior management level.

Meaning of Duty of Care

The new offence only applies in circumstances where an organisation owes a duty of care to the victim. This is no different from the old law. Section 2(1) requires the duty of care to arise out of certain specific functions or activities. The effect is that the offence will only apply where an organisation owes a duty of care:

- to its employees or other persons working for the organisation
- as an occupier of premises
- when the organisation is supplying goods or services

- when constructing or maintaining buildings, infrastructure or vehicles etc or when using plant or vehicles etc
- when carrying out other activities on a commercial basis

Excluded from being a relevant duty of care is the exercise of public policy decision making by a public authority.

Gross Breach

Section 8 of the new Act requires there to have been a gross breach of the duty of care. The requirement for a breach to be gross is a positive one as it provides a jury with a reminder that the offence should be reserved only for the most serious cases. The decision of what is gross is one for the jury.

The definition in the Act requires a jury to do the following:-

It ***must*** consider whether the evidence shows the organisation failed to comply with any health and safety legislation relating to the alleged breach, and if so:

(a) how serious that failure was; and

(b) how much of a risk of death it posed

Section 8(3) goes on that in assessing grossness a jury ***may also*** consider:

(a) the extent to which the evidence shows that there were attitudes, policies, systems or accepted practices within the organisation that were likely to have encouraged any such failure or to have produced tolerance of it.

(b) Have regard to any health and safety guidance relating to the alleged breach

Part (a) of this definition causes concern. It leaves open to the jury a very subjective assessment of "corporate culture" which they may not be in a proper position to judge in context having never been part of the industry concerned.

Causation

The wording of the offence makes it clear that the gross breach must have "caused" a person's death. Although this is not explained further in the Act, the guidance that went with the Bill is likely to mean that the usual principles of causation in criminal law will apply namely that it need not be the sole cause but need only be a cause.

The offence in section 1 specifies that an organisation is only guilty if the way in which its activities are managed or organised by its **senior management** is a substantial element in the breach. Whilst the failure need not be the only cause, the difficulty of proving a causal link between failures by someone classified as senior management and the victim's death will still provide a significant hurdle to the prosecuting authorities similar to the way it does already, albeit to a lesser degree.

Fines

The sanction for a conviction of corporate manslaughter is a potentially unlimited fine in the Crown Court (section 1(6)), although perhaps the worst sanction that can apply is the stigma and reputational impact of being branded a "corporate killer".

The Home Office paper that went with the original Bill stated that the offence would be targeted at the worst cases of management failure causing death. If this is so, it is likely that fines for conviction will be set at a very high level and probably significantly in excess of record fines under HSWA.

Fines for offences under HSWA have generally been increasing particularly for the major disasters. The fines imposed on Transco, Balfour Beatty Rail Maintenance and Network Rail in the last few years for HSWA breaches arising out of major disasters, heralded a new age in health and safety sentencing, at least in cases at the top end of the scale.

In late 2008 the Ministry of justice issued a consultation document suggesting that fines for corporate manslaughter should be set based on the organisations turnover and that this should be somewhere between 5% and 10% of turnover. It is yet to be seen whether this will be introduced, but if it were it could lead to massive fines of many millions of pounds for big organisations.

Remedial Orders

Section 9 of the new Act gives a Court the power to make a remedial order requiring a Defendant to take action to put right health and safety breaches.

The section states that an order can only be made "on an application by the prosecution specifying the terms of the proposed order". Further that any such order must be on such terms (whether those proposed or others) as the court considers appropriate having regard to any representations made and any evidence adduced by the prosecution or the accused.

The power is not a new one. The HSWA (s.42) contains a similar power for the Court to make remedial orders and has done so for 30 years. It is rarely if hardly ever used. The potential sanction is fraught with difficulties. Any such orders would need to be consistent with the strategy of improving safety across a whole industry.

Publicity orders

Section 10 of the Act allows a Court hearing a Corporate Manslaughter offence to make a publicity order requiring the convicted organisation to publicise the fact that it has been convicted, particulars of the offence, the level of fine and any remedial order made.

This is a somewhat odd power to have included since it does not identify in what manner a convicted company should publicise its guilt. Further, given the small number of cases that are expected to be prosecuted, one would expect publicity to be given to the case in any event. This specific penalty is not yet in force.

DPP Consent

Section 17 of the Act requires the consent of the Director of Public Prosecutions before proceedings will be instituted. This is a sensible policy decision to reduce the risk of insufficiently well-founded prosecutions whether brought by the authorities or private individuals, which would ultimately fail but have an unfair, possibly irreparable, effect on organisation's reputation.

Who will investigate?

The notes to the draft Bill made it clear that only the police and CPS would investigate. Although the Act is silent on this it appears that the HSE, although likely to assist in the police investigation, will not be a prosecuting authority for Corporate Manslaughter.

Individual Liability

As stated, the Act imposes no new liability on individuals. The proposals in the earlier drafts to disqualify a manager who had "any influence" on a management failure and to potentially imprison someone who "contributed substantially" were conceptually unsound. They would have lowered the level of possible criminal sanction to an unacceptable and unreasonable level. If an individual's acts or omissions are judged to be sufficiently serious and causative of a death then regardless of the new law, they can still be liable for an offence of gross negligence manslaughter.

It should also be recalled that the enforcing authorities can prosecute senior managers and directors under s.37 of the HSWA where an offence by the organisation is committed with their consent, connivance or neglect. Similarly s.7 creates a duty in the case of employees to take reasonable care for other employees and others affected.

Commencement and Extent

The Act applies to the whole of England, Wales, Scotland and Northern Ireland to incidents from 6 April 2008. Section 27 makes it clear that the legislation is not retrospective.

Conclusion

The new offence creates a completely new framework for the prosecution of Corporate Manslaughter. There is no doubt that the new offence will have an impact on the potential criminal liability of organisations for manslaughter where there have been serious failures since it will no longer be necessary to convict one individual alone. The aggregated failures of a number of senior managers, who form the senior management, will be sufficient.

In addition, the second part of the definition of senior management will catch people lower in the management chain than those who represented the "directing mind" under the old law meaning that a much wider part of the workforce is considered by the prosecuting authorities when looking at whether the offence has been committed.

Having said that, the new offence continues to have a number of safeguards ensuring that the offence is likely to be restricted for the worst cases. In particular, the requirements for senior management involvement and for any breach to be gross, is likely to mean that the floodgates will not open.

The Risks for Insurers

The Association of British Insurers has welcomed the Act because it believes it will drive up standards further by ensuring accountability and responsibility at a senior level within organisations.

From a claims perspective the Act is not as potentially serious to Insurers (and Insured's) as it could have been had new secondary liability for directors and officers been introduced as a specific element of the corporate manslaughter legislation. The Act does not shift the focus of corporate manslaughter to the responsibilities of individual directors but remains fixed on determining the guilt of the corporate entity itself. The offence will still be hard to prove and is unlikely to give massive encouragement to prosecutors to bring charges in every case of death at work, as such the flood gates are unlikely to open.

However, there would appear to be some risk to Insurers of an increased number of claims for legal defence costs for corporate manslaughter investigations.

In summary, it does seem likely that more investigations and prosecutions for corporate manslaughter will result than under the current law, where it is rare. Whilst, there may not be a flood of cases one can envisage that some of the more serious incidents that may once have been subject to investigations only under the HSWA by the HSE will now be subject to police investigation.

In addition, in the cases where corporate manslaughter is investigated and prosecuted there will almost certainly be an increase in the costs per claim as a result of more defended actions. Very few individuals admit to an offence of manslaughter under the current law (particularly as their liberty may be at stake). There is therefore a real risk to Insurers of an increased cost per claim should secondary liability be introduced with the Bill.

Similarly, organisations are unlikely to plead guilty to an offence with the stigma of corporate manslaughter – i.e. the emphatic denunciation that your business has unlawfully killed, by gross negligence, an employee or member of the public. The consequent risk to reputation is enormous and this may in insurance terms be reflected in claims experience and premiums. However, in pure business terms the impact on the insured's business may be immeasurable and not many organisations are going to be willing to accept such a stigma, without a good fight, save for in the worst cases where there is clear evidence of a total reckless disregard for health and safety.

As it may be an opportune time for insurers to assess their policies and check wordings. Indeed from looking at a number of different EL/PL policies it would appear that some will need to be revised. A lot of policies will not explicitly cover corporate manslaughter and many appear to make reference only to HSWA investigations and proceedings. The ABI has indicated that it expects the market to offer similar cover against the risk of being prosecuted for corporate manslaughter as given to HSWA prosecutions.

The ABI does not anticipate that the proposed offence should have a substantial impact on the price of relevant insurance products, such as EL insurance, as the financial impact across the whole economy is likely to be minimal. Having said that, it would still appear to be prudent for Insurers to give careful consideration to their insureds' safety records and risk management practices, especially for high-risk sectors such as construction and to consider whether in light of their record for health and safety under the HSWA they wish to obtain extensions to EL and PL policies for corporate manslaughter.

9.3 Section 3 – Fines in Health and Safety Cases

General Principles

The maximum penalty on indictment for breaches of the Health and Safety at Work Act 1974 (HSWA) is an unlimited fine. For less serious cases dealt with in the Magistrates Court the maximum fine is £20,000 for a breach of a general duty under HSWA or £5,000 for a breach of an H&S Regulation.

The Court of Appeal has provided a statement as to the factors to be applied when sentencing for offences contrary to the ***HSWA in R v Howe & Son (Engineers) Ltd*** [1999] 2 Cr. App. R.(S) 37.

First, the Court pointed to the particularly serious nature of breaches of the general duties under sections 2 and 3 of the Act which were to be regarded as "the foundations for protecting health and safety".

Secondly the Court set out a series of factors that should be considered either aggravating or mitigating features for the majority of health and safety prosecutions.

The potential aggravating features were:

- how far below the standard to be expected the Defendant had fallen;
- death or serious injury resulting from the breach (the penalty should reflect the public disquiet at unnecessary loss of life);
- where a deliberate breach occurred with a view to cutting costs or maximising profits;
- the degree of risk and the extent of the danger created by the offence;
- any failure to heed warnings.

The mitigating features were:

- guilty plea or prompt admission of responsibility;
- previous good safety record;
- steps to remedy deficiencies after they have been brought to the Defendant's attention.

The Court emphasised the public disquiet that had been increasing for a considerable period in respect of offences of this nature and the need for financial penalties that adequately reflected those concerns.

The approach in *Howe* has been reinforced on a number of occasions since 1997 and has led to an increasing trend in fines since. However, at the top end of the scale things have changed beyond all recognition since August 2005 with the Transco decision considered below.

In R v Rollco Screw and Rivet Co Ltd [1999] 2 Cr App R (S) 436, the Court stated that the *Howe* factors *'amount to a very clear and correct statement of the principles that should guide the court in cases of this sort'*.

R v (1) Balfour Beatty Civil Engineering Ltd (2) Geoconsult Ges (1999) the court cited with approval the passage from *Howe* stating that the object for prosecuting health and safety offences in the workplace was to achieve a safe environment for those who work there and members of the public who may be affected. When the Defendant was a company the fine had to be large enough to bring that message home to the managers and also to the shareholders.

R v Thames Trains Ltd (2004) A fine of £2m against a train company for a breach of s.3 HSWA in relation to the Ladbroke Grove train collision. The Court said that the fine should be substantial enough to have a real economic impact and sufficient to be a constant reminder to it and other rail companies of the paramount importance of safety and of prompt attention to any identifiable risk.

Two further additional principles have been enunciated by the Court of Appeal that may have relevance to the present trial.

In ***R v Jarvis Facilities Ltd (2005)*** The Court made clear that in sentencing for breaches of health and safety at work provisions, cases where there was a significant public element, for example, in transport, would often be treated more seriously than those in which the breaches were confined within the private sector, even where the gravity of the breach and the economic strength of the Defendant were otherwise comparable.

The objective of prosecutions for health and safety offences in the work place is to achieve a safe environment for those who work there and for other members of the public who may be affected. A fine needs to be large enough to bring that message home where the Defendant is a company not only to those who manage it but also to its shareholders and the fact that one company is now a "not for dividend" company is immaterial.

Level of Fine

Any fine should reflect not only the gravity of the offence but also the means of the offender, and this applies just as much to corporate Defendants as to any other. (*Howe* and s.128(3) ***Powers of Criminal Courts (Sentencing) Act 2000.)***.

When sentencing a company that is part of a wider group the groups financial standing is of potential relevance when assessing the level of fine – especially where the group will meet the subordinate's liability – see ***R v Keltbray Ltd*** [2001] 1 Cr. App. R (S) 39. The fine must "hurt".

It is impossible to lay down any tariff or to say that the fine should bear any specific relationship to the turnover or net profit of the Defendant.

Each case must be dealt with according to its own particular circumstances (*Howe*).

In ***R v Great Western Trains Co Ltd (1999)*** Great Western Trains pleaded guilty to one offence which arose from a train crash at Southall which killed seven people and injured 150. The company was fined **£1.5 million**. One of the Defendant's trains, travelling between Swansea and Paddington at speeds of up to 125 mph, had passed through a red light it collided with a goods train crossing the up fast. The judge sentenced on the basis that the Defendant's management allowed a high speed train to run with the Automatic Warning System ('AWS') isolated. The prosecution further submitted that the Defendant should have taken other safety measures, such as adding another power car or double manning the cab. The defence argued that it did not reverse the train to place an effective AWS unit at the front because, firstly, was not required by the rules to do so, secondly, such a course of action was never suggested by either Railtrack or the Railway Inspectorate, thirdly, it was not the practice of train operating companies to do so and fourthly, AWS isolation was a category B failure as opposed to a category A and it was therefore permissible for the train to continue on its journey.

R v (1) Balfour Beatty Civil Engineering Ltd etc Balfour Beatty was fined **£1.2m**. BB were the main contractors in the construction of a railway tunnel under the Piccadilly Line beneath the central terminal at Heathrow Airport. Geo-consult was the specialist tunnelling advisers to BB. On 20 to 21 October 1994 the tunnels collapsed causing one of the worst civil engineering disasters in the UK in the last quarter of a century.

The New Austrian Tunnelling Method ('NATM') was used to construct the tunnels. That method involved progressively forming a temporary lining of quick-setting sprayed concrete called 'shortcrete' with steel reinforcement. Under NATM a permanent lining to the tunnels would then be constructed at a later date. Until that time, which could be months later, the lining would move with pressure from the ground. The use of NATM was not criticised by the prosecution as it was possible to construct a tunnel safely by that method. However, monitoring and repairs had to be continuous in the use of the method. The need for a high standard of care was particularly critical in the present case given, inter alia, the location of the tunnel beneath the world's busiest airport and the Piccadilly Line. Experts found that the state of the unrepaired invert (lateral support) was the principal component for explaining the collapse, and that there had been indications since August 1994 that there were faults in the lining.

R v Thames Trains Ltd (2004) A fine of **£2m** against a train company for a breach of HSWA concerning driver training and route knowledge in relation to the Ladbroke Grove train collision should be substantial enough to have a real economic impact and sufficient to be a constant reminder to it and other rail companies of the paramount importance of safety and of prompt attention to any identifiable risk.

R v Transco (August 2005 High Court Scotland) Utility firm Transco was **fined £15m** – the highest ever in the UK – for its failure to maintain a leaking gas main which resulted in a fatal explosion. The case concerned the death of a Lanarkshire family, whose garden lay above a Transco gas main. The iron gas main was corroded and leaking, and by December 1999 the gas that had been escaping into the foundations of their house had built up to form a highly explosive atmosphere. The resulting early morning explosion ripped apart the house of Andrew and Janette Findlay, killing the two of them and their two children. Surrounding properties were also damaged.

Transco was charged with failure to carry out its duties under **Section 3 of the Health and Safety at Work Act 1974**. Following a trial in Edinburgh that lasted six months, the jury returned a unanimous verdict. A fine of £15m was imposed on Transco for its failure to maintain the gas main and to keep accurate records of its maintenance schedule.

The company was convicted after a lengthy trial and in passing sentence the court said that an aspect of its defence had demonstrated that "the corporate mind of Transco has little or no remorse for this tragedy which, they ought at least now to accept was exclusively their own creation".

Whilst the company fine was clearly affected by the fact that it came after a strongly contested trial without corporate expressions of remorse, these should not be seen as the main reasons for the imposition of such a massive penalty.

The court clearly had in its mind also the size of the company which was said to have had a pre-tax profit of over £1bn in 1999 and paid out dividends that year in excess of £300m. The court stressed the need to bring home to shareholders the seriousness with which the courts view flagrant breaches of health and safety legislation.

The question following Transco was whether this was a one-off "rogue" decision and fines would return to the record level previously identified at about £2 million in the Thames Trains case. However, in light of the fines very recently imposed on Network Rail (as successor to Railtrack) and, more notably, Balfour Beatty Rail Maintenance for their part in the Hatfield rail crash, the Transco fine can no longer be seen as a "one off".

On 7 October 2005 at the Old Bailey Mr Justice Mackay fined BBRM £10m for what he described as "the worst example of sustained, industrial negligence in a high-risk industry" he had seen in 30 years of professional experience. He went on to categorise Network Rail's failures as "of a lower order by a clear margin", fining the company whose job it was to oversee BBRM's activities £3.5m. In a nutshell, BBRM were found to have failed to ensure that visual track patrols were carried out effectively, or in certain circumstances at all, or to act appropriately in response to ultrasonic testing reports highlighting the deteriorating condition of the section of track in question. Network Rail's failure was not to do more to detect and put right those failures of BBRM.

9.4 Conclusion

The fines imposed on Transco, BBRM and Network Rail heralded a new age in health and safety sentencing, at least in cases at the top end of the scale.

Some will no doubt say that the fines of c£10m are still small beer when compared to the massive turnover and profits of some of the companies involved in the worst cases. However, the sums are of course substantial to anyone and are a massive increase in previous fines for similar types of cases. In turn larger fines will be more newsworthy and thus generate more publicity and often the stigma of widespread negative publicity can hit home as hard as the direct financial penalty.

Risks for Insurers

For public policy reasons criminal fines are not indemnified by Insurers. As described above the level of fine may be increasing. This has the effect of the organisation not only having to pay a higher financial penalty but also has a knock-on effect on an organisation's reputation. This is because higher fines tend to be more widely reported and if fines do significantly increase this is likely to lead to more publicity for health and safety breaches loss of reputation for those "named and shamed".

This is likely to lead to Insured's fighting to get the most favourable basis of any plea in order to avoid being sentenced to higher fines with increased publicity. Whilst this development is unlikely to increase the number of investigations and prosecutions under the HSWA and consequently unlikely to increase the number of claims for defence costs under the HSWA, it may well increase costs per claim, even on a guilty plea, as Insured's will want to ensure that the most favourable basis is obtained to avoid large fines.

General Issues for Insurers

None of the above is particularly good news for insurers who may find themselves under increased pressure to provide coverage in an increased number of cases prosecuted for corporate manslaughter and directors' liability under the HSWA. As mentioned, on several occasions above, it is an area of the law that when dealing with renewal terms insurers should give careful consideration to their insured's safety records and risk management practices.

Where a successful defence is mounted or charges are otherwise not pursued a Defendant's costs order, entitling the recovery from Central Funds of an assessed proportion of defence costs, is available.

Subject to particular caveats which are unlikely in corporate manslaughter/HSWA proceedings, recovery of legal costs for a successful defence is a general rule. Thus insurers should recover some, if not all, of the outlay on legal costs where either a successful defence is mounted or certain elements of the prosecution are not pursued to a conclusion.

It can often be argued successfully that the majority of defence costs of combined prosecutions against companies and one or more directors that succeed against company but fail against director are recoverable.

It is now therefore more than ever essential for those facing charges to have access to specialist advice. With more contested hearings and the difficulties in proving these offences, the Insurer has the same interest that a specialist should represent the Insured recognising that breaches of health and safety law are criminal offences, thus maximising the potential for (a) less wide-ranging prosecutions, (b) sensibly negotiated bases of plea, or (c) successful defences in full or in part and consequent recovery of costs.

A specialist in this field should also be able to make an early assessment, particularly in proceeding under the HSWA if only in those cases where an early guilty plea is advisable and thus take early steps to minimise costs that are not going to be recoverable. There are in fact few specialist advisers in this field, it is not general crime, nor is it a civil injury claim; Insurers should examine their panel to ensure that it contains specialist advisers.

9.5 Other Reference Material

Redgrave's Health and Safety (4th Edition) – Ford (Butterworths) 2002

Health and Safety Enforcement: Law and Practice – Matthews and Ageros (Buttherworths) 2003

Health and Safety Executive Website – www.hse.gov.uk/index.htm

10 CLINICAL NEGLIGENCE CLAIMS

10 CLINICAL NEGLIGENCE CLAIMS

Contents

Clinical negligence claims are generally claims for damages for personal injury. In that respect clinical negligence claims are dealt with in the same way as any claim for personal injury (be it EL or PL) is dealt with. This chapter deals with clinical negligence claims separately as some areas differ from personal injury cases. It does not discuss quantum as clinical negligence claims are quantified in the same way as other claims for damages for personal injury.

10.1 Defendants: NHS or Private

10.1.1 The National Health Service

Since January 1990 Health Authorities and Trusts have been vicariously liable for the negligent acts and omissions of their employees (doctors, nurses and other clinicians) and so it is usually the NHS Trust or Health Authority that will be named in any proceedings. As with any employers liability claim, there is no need to join an individual as a Defendant to proceedings. It is usual to name his employer.

In 1995 the NHS Litigation Authority was established. It is a Special Health Authority and therefore part of the NHS. It is responsible for handling clinical negligence claims made against NHS bodies in England.

The Existing Liabilities Scheme (ELS) applies to claims occurring up to 1 April 1995. Claims occurring after this date are dealt with by the Clinical Negligence Scheme for Trusts (CNST).

The NHS Litigation Authority manage claims through a panel of solicitors (1 firms of which Kennedys is one) and are responsible for payment of any damages and legal costs.

10.1.2 The Private Healthcare Sector

Private hospitals and clinics are insured by medical malpractice underwriters in the open insurance market. The insurance cover is for employees of the healthcare establishment (it might be a private hospital, private fertility clinic or perhaps a private clinic conducting MRI scans). The policy will only cover employees of the establishment.

Consultants working on a private basis in a private hospital are obliged to make their own funding arrangements. They are independent contractors and not employees.

Most Consultants acting in a private capacity (and also the majority of General Practitioners) will belong to one of the medical defence organisations, either the Medical Defence Union (MDU) or Medical Protection Society (MPS). A small number may obtain insurance on the open market (for example clinicians in alternative medicine).

There are some instances now where Independent Sector Treatment Centres (ISTCs) are indemnified under the CNST Scheme (see paragraph 10.1.1).

10.2 A Claimant's Right of Action: Contract or Tort?

There is probably no contractual relationship between a patient and the NHS although there is no case law on this either way. For this reason a Claimant will bring his claim against the NHS for the civil wrong or tort of negligence.

Where a Claimant is basing his claim on an issue of consent (see paragraph 10.7) he may also consider the tort of battery or assault. In extreme cases criminal law may apply and the police may be asked to investigate an alleged wrongful killing or possibly charges of grievous bodily harm.

In the private healthcare sector a patient may enter into a contract with the private hospital. He will usually bring a claim in both contract and tort.

10.3 Negligence

To prove negligence the patient will have to show the Court that:

a) he was owed a duty of care by the Defendant (hospital/consultant), and

b) the Defendant was in breach of that duty, and

c) the patient has suffered a loss as a result of that breach.

If one of these criteria is not established, then any claim for clinical negligence will fail.

10.4 The Standard of Care

Where doctors and other medical personnel are concerned, the law imposes a duty of care where the standard of care is one of medical, not legal, judgment. So it is the medical profession which determines the standards of proper medical practice. A doctor treating a patient in accordance with approved medical practice, even a practice approved and followed by only a minority of the profession, will not be found negligent.

The standard for "reasonable care" depends upon the nature of the activity undertaken, the risk being created and the seriousness of the consequences if due care is not exercised. The test for negligence was set out in the case of ***Bolam v Friern Hospital Management Committee (1957) 2 All ER 118*** widely viewed as the case setting out the basis for the standard of care in clinical negligence claims.

In ***Sidaway v Governors of Bethlehem Royal Hospital (1985) 1 All ER 643*** Lord Scarman said:

> *"The Bolam principle may be formulated as a rule that a doctor is not negligent if he acts in accordance with a practice accepted at the time as proper by a responsible body of medical opinion even though other doctors adopt a different practice. In short the Court imposes a duty of care; the standard of care is a matter of medical judgment".*

Basically, the doctor must have acted in accordance with "a responsible body of opinion". So, for example, a Consultant Anaesthetist who allegedly treats a patient negligently will be judged by the standard of a responsible body of Consultant Anaesthetists opinion. It suffices if the Consultant Anaesthetist only finds one other expert to support his actions. (Whether as a lawyer/claims handler you would want to rely on one opinion, when everyone else is at complete odds to your expert, is another matter).

A doctor must however always exercise ordinary skill and be ready to accept that a commonly used practice may be considered negligent in some circumstances.

10.5 Causation

A Claimant may be able to prove that a hospital was negligent but to establish liability, it is essential to show that the hospital's negligence caused the Claimant's loss or damage.

The burden of proof is on the Claimant to show that, on the balance of probabilities, the Defendant's negligent act or omission caused his harm or loss. If the Claimant is unable to prove this, his claim will fail.

The test which the Courts consider in relation to causation is the *"but for"* test, i.e. but for the negligence of the Defendant, would the Claimant have suffered his injuries, loss or damage?

If the Claimant would have suffered loss or damage in any event then he is unable to prove the second element of a claim ie the Defendant's negligence is not causative of his loss or damage.

10.6 Loss of Chance

When considering the circumstances of a Claimant who has undergone medical treatment to improve or cure his illness, it is necessary to consider his underlying condition and whether that would have prevented a full recovery in any event.

A loss of chance may be described where the Claimant has lost an opportunity to make a better or full recovery (possibly through a delay in treatment of cancer) or for the condition to improve as might have been expected. The House of Lords decision in ***Gregg v Scott (2005)*** *2A.C.176* is the leading case on this.

10.7 Consent to Treatment

Consent is required for any medical treatment. It is now well established and accepted that all medical practitioners (doctors, midwives and dentists) should seek their patient's consent before embarking on any treatment (except in emergencies) otherwise they may face civil or even criminal proceedings for assault.

The manner in which consent is obtained may vary greatly. It was not so long ago that patients were instructed to roll up their sleeves only to find they were given an injection. One doctor may mumble a generalised formula and then proceed quickly as the patient looks on enquiringly whilst another doctor may deliver a thoughtful and thorough explanation of what is going to be done and ask his patient whether he understands or would like to know more and explains any material risk.

10.7.1 Form of consent

Written consent provides the clearest proof that the patient has consented to a procedure and for that reason is preferred by health service bodies when they may subsequently have to defend legal proceedings. Indeed the NHS Executive has provided a series of model consent forms for Health Authorities and Trusts.

The patient's signature on the consent form makes it difficult for him to allege he did not give his consent. However, if a patient has not in fact consented, any treatment will be unlawful even where he has signed a consent form. **The reality prevails over the writing**.

It is not always necessary for consent to be expressed in writing. Consent may be implied if it is clear from the circumstances that the patient has accepted and consented to the treatment. If a patient has been asked to undress to enable a doctor to perform an examination, the act of undressing indicates the patient's agreement to the examination. When patients roll up their sleeves to receive an injection (having first been informed by the doctor of benefits and risks) this is an indication of their consent to it.

10.7.2 Valid consent

The validity of a patient's consent depends on a number of factors. To be valid, consent must be *"real"* and this means that patients must be competent or able to give their consent. They must know in broad terms what they are consenting to and they must give their consent freely and without being deliberately misled.

The basic rule is that a medical practitioner is entitled to assume that his patient is able to consent to or refuse treatment. The fact that a patient does not appear to the professional to make a wise choice is not itself evidence of incapacity.

The leading case on adult competency is ***F v West Berkshire Health Authority (1989) 2 WLR 1025*** where the Court said a patient should be able to appreciate what will be done to them if they accept treatment, the likely consequences of leaving their condition untreated and understanding the risks and side effects that the health professionals explain to them.

10.7.3 Informed consent

This is a phrase that we hear quite often. Basically how much information should the patient be given? English law does not require consent to be fully informed but if medical practitioners fail to counsel patients in a way recognised by their peers as appropriate then they may be negligent. This important aspect of consent is governed by the test of *"what would a responsible body of opinion have discussed?"*

It was argued in the case of *Sidaway* that patients had a right to decide what happened to them. In that case the House of Lords believed this right was supported by a further right to be given all information that is "material" in deciding whether to accept the treatment advised.

If a "material risk" is not disclosed then the doctor responsible for counselling the patient will be negligent.

In order to decide whether something is a material consideration the Court needs to ask *"whether a reasonable person in the patient's position would have regarded it as being significant"*.

Article 3 of the European Convention on Human Rights 1968 states that no one shall be subjected to torture or inhumane or degrading treatment or punishment. This is an absolute right and treatment given without consent may also fall within the ambit of Article 3.

10.7.4 Legally incompetent patients

Medical practitioners are obliged to treat these patients in accordance with the "best interest" principle.

10.7.5 The mentally incompetent

Generally if a patient is unable to make a decision then his medical practitioner must act in his best interest. Treatment will be lawful in such circumstances providing a responsible body of professional opinion would accept that it was in the patient's best interest. The statutory test of capacity under Part 4 of the Mental Health Act 1983 is that the patient is capable of understanding the nature, purpose and likely effects of the treatment (Sections 57 and 58).

10.7.6 Minors

Parents may consent on behalf of their children until they reach the age of 18. Following the case of ***Gillick v West Norfolk & Wisbeach Area Health Authority (1985) 3 All ER 402*** a child under 18 may be competent to consent if he has sufficient understanding and intelligence to understand fully what is proposed.

10.7.7 Undue influence

Consent or refusal of consent may be as a result of **undue influence**. If that is the case, the consent would not be voluntary and would be invalid. This was considered by the Court of Appeal in *Re T (1992 4 All ER 649*). In that case a young woman told hospital staff when admitted to hospital after a car accident that she did not wish to have a blood transfusion. She made that decision after speaking to her mother who was a Jehovah's Witness. The Court of Appeal decided that while it was to be expected a patient will seek advice before deciding whether to accept treatment, it was possible that their will might be overborne by pressure brought by others or in this case, the patient's mother. The refusal of consent to treatment was therefore invalid.

Article 6 of the Human Rights Act provides the right to a fair trial. It is arguable that hospitals will now have to apply more frequently to the Courts for declarations of incapacity and for approval that a proposed treatment is in the patient's best interest. If a clinician considers a patient incompetent but the patient's relatives disagree then I would advise that an Application to Court now be made.

Hospitals are also now more willing to seek legal advice where a patient lacks the necessary capacity and his relatives are disagreeing with treatment. Indeed this is exactly what happened recently when Portsmouth NHS Trust asked the High Court for a declaration allowing doctors not to ventilate baby Charlotte Wyatt if she subsequently had difficulty in breathing. While this would mean allowing her to die, it was, the Trust argued, in her *"best interests"*.

In that case the Court granted the declaration sought by the Trust (although recently the Claimant has been discharged home).

The Human Rights Act does not alter the position where a patient with capacity refuses treatment as it is clear that their wishes must be respected whatever the consequences.

10.7.8 Withholding or withdrawing treatment

The Human Rights Act has had an effect on these decisions. A number of Articles apply for example, Article 2 the right to life; Article 3 the right to freedom from torture and inhuman or degrading treatment; Article 8 the right to respect for private and family life; and Article 14 a prohibition or discrimination on the grounds of age.

Article 2 is an absolute right to life which clearly conflicts with the existing principle that clinicians need not intervene or may withdraw treatment if they consider it is in the patient's best interests to do so. Some actions have already been brought under the Human Rights Act on this very topic. The Courts have held that patients diagnosed as being in a permanent vegetative state are alive and Article 2 of the Convention protects them. Article 2 also contains an obligation on the State not to take life intentionally. Courts have also held however that it is incorrect to interpret Article 2 as meaning that a decision to cease treatment in the patient's best interests, is an intentional deprivation of life. So where a responsible clinical decision is made to withhold treatment because it is in the patient's best interests and the clinical decision is made in accordance with a responsible body of medical opinion, the State's obligation under Article 2 is discharged.

Hospitals and clinicians can do no better than keep relatives closely advised of any decision and their reasons for doing so. If it is clear that the patient's relatives do not agree with the decision then legal advice must be sought. As always, the clinicians must be able to show that the decision is in the best interests of the patient.

10.7.9 Justifying treatment without consent

Emergencies justify treatment without consent as long as the treatment is in the patient's best interests. Emergencies are in essence an example of implied consent.

10.8 Confidentiality

There is a general duty of confidentiality between a patient and those treating him. Confidentiality is necessary so as to generate trust between a patient and the doctor treating him. There are however exceptional circumstances which may arise which allow this duty to be breached:

- In civil procedures there is a legal duty to disclosure. If a patient makes complaints or brings proceedings, he has impliedly consented to his medical records and details being disclosed to lawyers representing the hospital/healthcare professional.
- Statutory provision is made for doctors to report details of notifiable diseases to the Public Health Authority.

- Sharing information within a team of healthcare workers. For example where they work within a practice, partnership or within a consultant team in hospital.

10.9 Disclosure of Medical Records

When a clinical negligence claim is first investigated the Claimant will be asked to sign a form of authority giving his authority for the disclosure of all relevant medical notes and records to his legal adviser and to those defending the hospital. Any individual can request access to his medical records under the Access to Health Records Act 1990. A request cannot reasonably be refused unless the material contained in the notes is liable to harm the patient. This is a common concern for example when the patient's notes may relate to mental health issues. Disclosure will generally be to a limited number of individuals for example lawyers for both parties and medical experts.

During the course of litigation if a doctor wishes to withhold medical records then they may be released to certain specified named experts to allow the matter to proceed and the allegations to be considered properly.

10.9.1 Continuing duty of disclosure

A claims handler or lawyer investigating a claim will be hampered in the course of his work unless there is unfettered access to the Claimant's records. Under the Civil Procedural Rules the duty of disclosure is an ongoing one throughout the course of proceedings. The Defendant hospital or medical practitioner is entitled to see all the material that the Claimant has seen and vice versa.

10.10 Limitation

The Limitation Act 1980 does not make specific provision for clinical negligence claims although there are specific rules relating to cases of personal injury or death and in practice most clinical negligence claims, as stated before, will be for damages for personal injury or death.

In most cases the patient has three years from the date his course of action arises (usually the date when the accident or incident occurred) or three years from his *"date of knowledge"* in which to issue proceedings. So for example in a case where a Claimant is alleging that she is now permanently paralysed as a result of an epidural not being properly administered during labour, time will begin to run from the date when the anaesthetic was administered or alternatively three years from when the Claimant discovered that the reason for her paralysis can be attributed to the administration of the anaesthetic.

But what if:

- **The patient dies before the limitation period expires?** His Estate has three years from his death or the date of his personal representative's "*knowledge*" in which to commence his claim; or
- **The alleged negligent act proves fatal?** The Deceased's dependents have three years from the date of death to bring an action or three years from their date of knowledge or that of the personal representative of the Deceased;
- **The Claimant is under a disability** (i.e. minors and those of unsound mind)? The limitation period does not begin to run until their disability ceases.

In the case of a minor he ceases to be under a disability when he reaches the age of 18 and time will only begin to run from then, assuming he has the relevant "*knowledge*". If he does not have the necessary "*knowledge*", the period will only begin to run when he acquires that knowledge.

Parents or representatives of a minor or person under a disability can commence an action on the child's behalf before the child attains majority.

If the patient is of unsound mind, by reason of mental disorder within the meaning of Section 1(2) of the Mental Health Act 1983 and is incapable of managing his own affairs, time will not run until he ceases to be under a disability. If the patient's condition is permanent, time will only start to run upon his death.

The limitation period therefore is not necessarily the date of the alleged negligent act or omission and whilst a hospital or medical practitioner may investigate an incident that may lead to a claim, soon after the negligent act or omission has occurred, it could be many years before any claim is made which may not be statute barred, i.e. brought outside the limitation period. Even if the claim is statute barred, the Court has a discretion to disapply the time limits for personal injury and death cases and allow the case to proceed.

It is for these reasons that records belonging to hospitals and medical practitioners must be retained for a number of years. As time does not run in respect of any claim a child may have until they reach their majority, their notes and records should be retained until at least their 21st birthday, i.e. up to the age of majority and three years thereafter.

As regards those of unsound mind, there is no limitation period and for that reason a hospital, particularly a Mental Health Trust, is under an obligation to retain those patient's notes and records for as long as is reasonably practicable.

10.10.1 What knowledge is required?

The extent of knowledge necessary to start running against a patient is defined within the Limitation Act 1980 Section 14. There must be knowledge, not just "*reasonable belief*" or "*suspicion*" of the following:

- That the injury complained of is significant.
- That the injury was attributable in whole or in part to the act or omission which is alleged to constitute negligence or a breach of duty.
- The identity of the Defendant.

10.11 Clinical Negligence Pre-action Protocol

The Civil Procedure Rules make provision for the use of a pre-action protocol for the resolution of clinical disputes. There is also a protocol for obtaining hospital medical records.
(See www.justice.gov.uk/civil/procrules-fin/contents.protocols/prot-rtc.htm).

The protocol requires early disclosure of medical records (within 40 days of a request).

The Letter of Claim must follow a prescribed format and include as much detail as possible on the allegations that will be made, the injuries sustained and details of the claim for damages. All this information will enable the Defendant to assess reserves for the claim and respond accordingly.

The Letter of Response, due three months from the date of receipt of the Letter of Claim, should also be detailed and provide information obtained from the Defendant's investigation and/or independent medical expert evidence. The Letter of Response must specifically state whether a claim or part of it is admitted or denied.

10.12 Proceedings

Clinical negligence claims are generally allotted to the multi-track as evidence is rarely straightforward and the Court will need to hear evidence from witnesses of fact and also independent medical experts.

In the County Court the claim is dealt with by a District Judge through interlocutory stages before the case is sent to a Trial Centre for hearing.

In the High Court two Masters are allotted to clinical negligence claims and oversee the initial interlocutory stages before the matter comes to trial. Trial will be by a Judge sitting on his own without a jury as in other personal injury claims. The Judge does not have to have experience of clinical negligence claims or indeed personal injury claims.

10.12.1 Witnesses of fact

When a claim is first intimated by a patient initial investigations should include identification of the clinicians involved in his care and witness statements taken from them as soon as possible. Sometimes it can be difficult to identify all of the relevant staff from the medical records and they may only be identified once other witnesses are interviewed. It is important to trace and make contact with all witnesses involved, however minor their role.

10.12.2 Expert witnesses

Independent medical experts are crucial to the clinical negligence claim. If proceedings are issued Court Rules provide that the Claimant must serve with his proceedings (amongst other documents) a medical report relating to his condition and prognosis. It follows that the Claimant's medical expert will want to see at an early stage the Claimant's medical notes and records. This will enable the Claimant medical expert to evaluate whether the Claimant has a claim and secondly to prepare a report to serve with proceedings.

By the same token the Defendant will need to instruct an independent medical expert at the early stage so as to enable the Letter of Response that is served to be detailed. It also means that the Defendant knows at a very early stage whether he is likely to be in breach of duty and if in breach of duty whether that breach was causative of the Claimant's present condition.

Often different experts will be required to comment on breach of duty and causation.

It may be the case that the Defendant's witnesses of fact are also eminent experts in their particular field and so their evidence carries more weight. The Court of Appeal held in the case of ***ES Chesterfield and North Derbyshire Royal Hospital NHS Trust (2003) EWCA Civ 1284*** that where the Defendant is relying on witnesses of fact who are also regarded as experts, the Claimant should be allowed to call two experts to every one of the Defendant's experts. ***(Distinguished in Heyward v Plymouth Hospital NHS Trust 2005 EWCA CIV 939.)***

10.13 The Future

All governments are understandably concerned about the rising cost of clinical negligence claims. It was for this reason that the NHS Litigation Authority was established over 13 years ago and the ELS and CNST Schemes created so as to streamline management of these claims and reduce legal costs.

A number of governments have looked into the possibilities of "no fault" compensation schemes for medical accidents but to date this has not been implemented.

11 QUANTUM

11 QUANTUM

Contents

11.1 Introduction

There are three main aspects to any given case that determine that case's value.

1. Liability
2. Quantum
3. Interest

1. Liability

As has been seen previously in this book, a party can be found to be responsible (and therefore liable) if they have committed a tort or have breached some statutory duty. It may be the case that liability will rest solely with one party.

Liability, however, can be apportioned between the parties.

If liability is apportioned between the parties, (e.g. more than one Defendant is found liable or the Claimant is found to have been contributory negligent in some way), that will reduce the amount that one Defendant has to pay and therefore the value of the claim for that Defendant *(see chapter on Negligence).*

2. Quantum

The value of the claim is known as quantum.

The value of the claim will be made up by the Claimant's damages. Examples of damages that can be awarded include compensation for injuries or for damage to property as well as financial losses such as lost earnings, the cost of repairs to motor vehicles and the cost of underpinning homes.

The level of general damages and special damages that could be awarded by a Court to a Claimant will determine the quantum of a case.

In practise, lawyers and the Courts will define general damages as compensation for personal injury, and special damages as compensation for financial losses.

3. Interest

The third aspect of any claim's value is the interest that the Claimant can receive on general and on special damages. The rate of interest will vary depending on the claim that it relates to. This is discussed further below.

11.2 General Damages

As stated above, the main "general" damage that is considered by insurers and lawyers alike is compensation for personal injuries.

The main parts of a general damage claim are:

i) *Compensation for pain, suffering and loss of amenity.*

ii) *Compensation for Handicap on the Labour Market (also known as disadvantage on the labour market or a* ***Smith v Manchester*** *claim)*

A Court will award the Claimant compensation for past and future pain and suffering attributable to the incident in question. Psychiatric injury is also compensated. The severity and type of a Claimant's injuries together with the Claimant's age and sex are factors that must be considered when assessing the level of a general damages award.

Claims handlers will no doubt be familiar with the **Judicial Studies Board Guidelines for the Assessment of General Damages in Personal Injury Cases** that are now in their eighth edition. All members of the Judiciary and most personal injury practitioners have this booklet. It acts as a ready reckoner to the appropriate bracket of compensation for any given injury.

In order to refine the likely level of an award of compensation for any given injury, it is recommended that a claims handler consider past judicial decisions (precedents) that deal with similar injuries.

Publications such as Current Law, and Kemp and Kemp provide precedents that can be useful.

When negotiating with a Claimant's solicitor, it is useful to refer the solicitor in question to the case law that you rely upon in order to support your valuation.

When assessing any general damage claim the following check-list may help:

1. Will the Claimant recover fully from the injuries? If the answer to that question is no, then the Claimant will recover a higher level of damages because a permanent disability has been suffered.

2. What is the age of the Claimant? If the Claimant has suffered a permanent disability, the number of years for which the Claimant will have to suffer from that disability will effect the level of compensation that can be expected.

3. What sex is the Claimant? Certain types of injury will give rise to greater compensation for one sex or another. For example, facial scarring on a young female Claimant will attract a higher compensation award than identical scarring in a similarly aged male Claimant.

4. Did the Claimant have any relevant pre-existing medical conditions? If so, an expert opinion will be needed to determine whether or not the injury in question has permanently worsened that condition, whether it has caused a temporary flare up of that condition or whether it has accelerated that condition by a particular period of time. The effect of the injury on the pre-existing condition will affect the level of compensation that can be expected.

5. What effect does the accident have on the Claimant's everyday life? – If the Claimant has suffered a permanent disability but it is minor and does not effect the Claimant's way of life unduly, then the compensation would be less than, for example, a professional sportsman who has been injured and who can no longer participate in his sport, or an avid hiker who can no longer walk long distances.

(See also sections that follow on outlines of orthopaedic and psychiatric injuries)

11.3 Interest on General Damages

At the date of publication, interest on compensation for general damages runs at 2% per annum from the date of issue of proceedings.

It is important to remember to factor interest into any Part 36 Offer made.

11.4 An Outline of Orthopaedic Injuries

By far the most common personal injury claims made are for orthopaedic injury.

Of claims made for orthopaedic injuries, by far the most common are for whiplash injuries.

In brief, most whiplash injuries occur when a vehicle collides to the rear of another. An occupant of the front vehicle may, in such circumstances, be injured.

Such a "rear shunt" has an effect on the neck of the occupant of the vehicle in front. That occupant will be thrown forward by the impact and then thrown backwards in a very short space of time. That movement can cause a tearing of muscles and ligaments in the neck and back.

Claims handlers often rely heavily upon a client's incident report form, which states that no injury was apparent at the scene of the accident. However it would be wrong in those circumstances to assume that no injury had occurred. Whiplash symptoms can develop a day or so after the accident. This is because torn muscles swell and become painful, often overnight or on the following day.

Most whiplash injuries are treated by a general practitioner, or by the Accident and Emergency department of a local hospital. Treatment is usually limited to the taking of anti-inflammatory tablets or possibly the use of a soft supportive neck collar.

The symptoms usually resolve over a week or so. Usually none, or very little time is lost from work.

However, it can be the case that symptoms will last for a number of months and, in relatively serious cases, symptoms can last for a year or more.

Most whiplash injuries recover completely unless the injured party was particularly susceptible to a neck injury.

A Claimant may be susceptible to a neck injury because he already has a pre-existing orthopaedic condition such as arthritis in the neck (cervical spondylosis) or some pre-existing injury.

It is important to remember that a Claimant who has a pre-existing weakness that is made worse by an accident, can expect compensation for the worsened condition.

This is known as the "egg-shell skull" principle. In brief, a person who is negligent and who causes injury must take his victim as he finds him. It is not a defence to argue that the injury could not have been foreseen or that it is not proportionate to the consequences of the negligence. *(See chapter on Negligence).*

If a Claimant has suffered an orthopaedic injury that appears to be disproportionate to the accident circumstances, our recommendation is that claims handlers obtain a medical report (on a joint or agreed basis if appropriate – *see chapter on Civil Procedure Rules 1998*). The claims handler should ensure that the medical expert appointed has access to all of the Claimant's medical records (and not just those relating to the accident).

11.4.1 Instruction of an Expert

It is important that the expert has access to all of the Claimant's medical records and not just those relating to the accident. In that way, any relevant pre-existing medical conditions can be considered by the expert and commented upon.

Questions that must be asked of the expert are as follows:

a) What are the effects of the accident?

b) Is there a relevant pre-existing condition?

c) What have been the effects of the accident on that relevant pre-existing condition, if any?

d) How long will the Claimant take to recover (if a recovery has not yet taken place)?

e) Is there any treatment that the Claimant can have to speed the recovery? If the answer to this is yes, what is the cost of the treatment and how long will it last? With such treatment, when can the Claimant expect to improve or recover?

f) If the accident has had an effect on a pre-existing condition, has the accident:

i) caused a permanent worsening of the pre-existing condition? or;

ii) caused a temporary flare up of that pre-existing condition which will in due course return to normal? (If yes, when will that recovery take place?) or;

iii) has the accident caused any pre-existing condition to be accelerated in some way? (And if so by how much?)

g) With treatment what is the best recovery that the Claimant can hope to achieve and when will that recovery take place?

h) If the Claimant will not recover fully, what will the effect of the ongoing symptoms be on the Claimant's professional and personal life?

11.4.2 Orthopaedic Check-list

Claims handlers should also consider the following to ensure that the claim is genuine:

1. When did the Claimant first seek medical help for the injury? If it was very soon after the accident, all things being equal, a Court will believe that the Claimant has been injured.

2. If the claim has not been presented for some time and treatment has been ongoing, make sure that you not only obtain Claimant's pre-accident medical records but also all of those relating to the Claimant's treatment. They will need to be seen by your expert who can then consider whether the treatment given is consistent with the alleged injury or some pre-existing condition.

3. Once you have obtained your medical report consider the checklist in the section on General Damages (paragraph 11.2) in order to assess an appropriate valuation for the injuries in question.

4. Consider the Judicial Studies Board Guidelines for the Assessment of Personal Injuries.

5. Consider appropriate precedents.

6. Ensure that the claim is registered with the Compensation Recovery Unit *(see chapter on CRU)*

7. Take into account relevant deductible benefits before making any offer.

8. If you are concerned that the claim is not a genuine one, consider instructing an appropriately experienced investigator to place the Claimant under a period of video surveillance. If this is to be considered bear in mind the following:

   a) The cost of such surveillance – which is likely to exceed £1,000.00.

   b) Do not tell your medical expert that the Claimant is under surveillance until the medical report has been completed. If your expert knows of the surveillance before he completes his report, he may feel professionally compromised. If the matter proceeds to trial he may be cross-examined on this point.

   c) The timing of service of the videotape.

      If you obtain video footage of the Claimant doing something he has said he cannot do, that may suggest that the claim is not genuine.

      However, if the video is served immediately the Claimant will have an opportunity to suggest that he was caught on video on a "good day" or that he has started to recover. It may therefore be preferable to hold the videotape in reserve, until after medical reports and witness statements have been provided and/or exchanged. It may not be possible to assess the value of the surveillance evidence until this point in any event.

      If the Claimant has told the medical experts in the case, for example, that he has not had a "good day" since the accident, and cannot walk more than 500 metres; and you have a video of him walking further without apparent difficulty; the Claimant will have great difficulty in explaining away the video evidence. That will particularly be the case if the Claimant has given similar evidence in his witness statement.

      Therefore correctly timing the service of good video evidence is crucial.

11.5

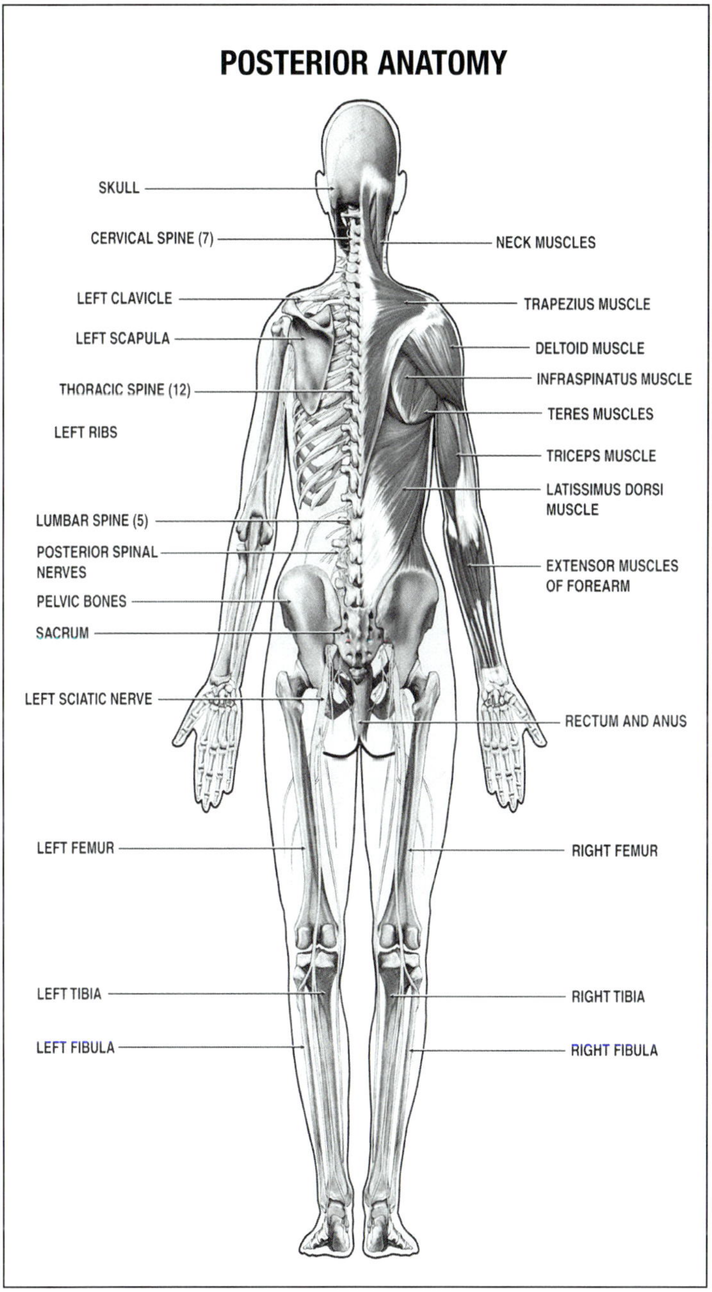
POSTERIOR ANATOMY
SKULL
CERVICAL SPINE (7)
NECK MUSCLES
LEFT CLAVICLE
TRAPEZIUS MUSCLE
LEFT SCAPULA
DELTOID MUSCLE
INFRASPINATUS MUSCLE
THORACIC SPINE (12)
TERES MUSCLES
LEFT RIBS
TRICEPS MUSCLE
LATISSIMUS DORSI MUSCLE
LUMBAR SPINE (5)
POSTERIOR SPINAL NERVES
EXTENSOR MUSCLES OF FOREARM
PELVIC BONES
SACRUM
LEFT SCIATIC NERVE
RECTUM AND ANUS
LEFT FEMUR
RIGHT FEMUR
LEFT TIBIA
RIGHT TIBIA
LEFT FIBULA
RIGHT FIBULA

ANTERIOR ANATOMY

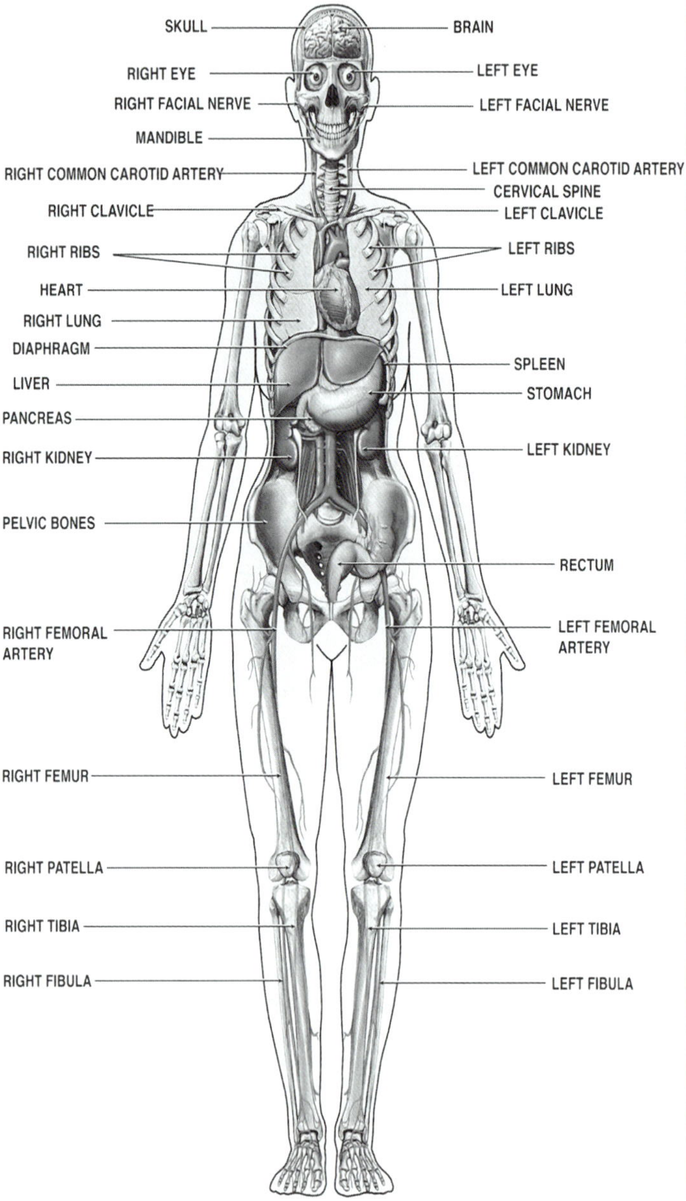

11.6 An Outline of Psychiatric Injuries

As a general rule, compensation will only be payable to a Claimant who has suffered a genuine and recognised psychiatric illness arising out of an accident. It matters not whether an accident has caused PTSD, Reactive Depression, Phobic Anxiety or some other type of psychiatric illness, as all are compensatible. Different levels of compensation will however be awarded for different levels of psychiatric illnesses.

Some can be treated easily while others will require more prolonged treatment. It is therefore important to obtain an accurate diagnosis.

In some cases no psychiatric illness will have developed, notwithstanding the diagnosis made by the Claimant's medical expert.

11.6.1 Psychiatrist v Psychologist?

It is particularly important to note the difference between psychiatric and psychological experts.

A psychiatrist is a medically qualified doctor, who having qualified, has subsequently specialised in the field of psychiatry. Psychiatry can readily be defined as the study and treatment of mental disease.

Psychologists generally have no medical qualification. They have a psychology degree. Those that call themselves doctors are entitled to do so generally by having obtained a Doctorate in psychology. Psychologists, who are not medically qualified, have no authority to make a medical diagnosis of psychiatric conditions

The definition of psychology can readily be defined as the science of the nature, functions and phenomena of the human mind. Psychology deals with the mental characteristics of people.

In medical practise, psychiatrists diagnose psychiatric conditions and will often then refer a patient to a psychologist for treatment.

Therefore, if a Claimant relies upon a psychologist's report, be wary of accepting a diagnosis of a serious mental illness made within that report.

It is worth noting the Introduction of the third edition of the Judicial Studies Board Guidelines for the Assessment of Personal Injury Damages. It commented as follows in relation to PTSD:

> **"a particular trend which seems to have emerged in the last few years has caused the working party some concern. It is the extent to which in recent cases emphasis on the subjective reaction of a Claimant to the physical injuries and the circumstances in which they were sustained has been used as a means of inflating the award for damages. Every injured person suffers a reaction to the situation and its causes and that reaction has always been considered in the assessment of damages for pain and suffering. Such an approach must be separated carefully from the wholly distinct head of damages which is [Psychiatric injury] ...unless that condition exists... it is suggested that the general guidelines are appropriate"**.

11.6.2 When can a Claimant seek compensation for a psychiatric injury?

The position was set out in the case of ***White & Others v Chief Constable of South Yorkshire Police and Other [1999]***.

Whenever investigating a psychiatric injury claim the issues below must be considered first.

The Claimant must show that the injury is a recognised psychiatric disorder or illness. "Shock and shaking" claims following a road traffic accident are not compensatible.

What were the circumstances of the injury?

i) for psychiatric injuries suffered at the same time as a physical injury is suffered, a Claimant can recover compensation for a recognised psychiatric condition.

ii) if no physical injury is suffered at the time that the Claimant suffers a recognised psychiatric condition, the Claimant can still recover compensation if he or she was within the range of a potential physical injury.

iii) if the Claimant is a bystander who witnesses an accident or it's aftermath he or she can claim compensation if he or she develops a recognised psychiatric condition only if:

a) They have a sufficiently close relationship with the victim (husband, wife, parent or child) and,

b) They were close enough to the accident to be affected by it. They must therefore have actually seen the accident or its immediate aftermath. If they saw the highlights of the accident on the television or were affected by having to identify a loved one at the mortuary many hours after an accident, they would not be able to recover compensation.

c) They must actually have witnessed the accident or its aftermath themselves. They can therefore not recover for a psychiatric illness having been told of the accident in gruesome detail by another person.

see:

– Alcock v Chief Constable of South Yorkshire [1992] 1AC310

– Page v Smith (1996) 1AC155

d) The Claimant who is a rescuer and suffers no physical injury but goes on to develop a recognised psychiatric condition can recover only if the Claimant was in actual danger or believed that he was in actual danger.

11.6.3 Psychiatric Claim Check-list

1. Does the Claimant fall into a class that allows him to claim compensation for a psychiatric injury.

2. Does the Claimant have a recognised psychiatric illness? Consider whether you are prepared to accept the Claimant's medical report. Has a diagnosis been provided by an appropriately qualified medical doctor? Does it refer to the Claimant's medical records? The expert should rely on those as well as his examination of the Claimant to support his conclusions. If the expert appears to over rely upon tests that have been given during the examination, consider whether those tests are appropriate or whether the Claimant could have manipulated them.

3. If you are to obtain your own report, instruct a consultant psychiatrist *(see "instruction of an expert" in section on Orthopaedic injuries in this chapter).*

4. Make sure that your expert has sight of the Claimant's previous medical records as the Claimant may have a relevant psychiatric medical history.

5. Make sure that the expert has the Claimant's medical records post-dating the accident. When did the Claimant first report to a doctor that he was suffering from the symptoms that have been diagnosed as a psychiatric condition? The symptoms of any psychiatric condition are likely to be at their worst a short time after the accident. If there is a delay in the onset of the symptoms, can that be explained?

6. Consider obtaining surveillance evidence if you feel the claim is not genuine. For example if the Claimant claims that he cannot drive (because he is so traumatised) can you obtain video evidence of him doing just that. *(see also comments on surveillance evidence in Orthopaedic Check-list).*

7. If the Claimant has been to see his GP complaining of physical symptoms arising from an accident but for some considerable time has failed to report any psychiatric symptoms, the claim should be regarded cautiously. Your own expert can consider whether the Claimant has a legitimate reason for failing promptly to report psychiatric symptoms. Such a history of reporting may be genuine and the Claimant may have legitimate concerns about reporting such symptoms. However, such a history can equally be evidence of a claim that is less than genuine.

11.7 Handicap on the Open Labour Market *(Smith v Manchester Awards)*

Notwithstanding the publication of the sixth edition of the Ogden Tables, such claims will still be made.

A Claimant is entitled to compensation if, as a result of injuries caused, he would be at a disadvantage if he was thrust back on to the Open Labour Market.

Claims under this head can arise even when the Claimant remains in his pre-accident employment and where there is no sign of that employment ending.

Broadly, the Courts have to decide whether the Claimant, if he were to lose his job, would find it more difficult to find another suitable job because of his injuries than he would have done had his injuries not occurred.

The case that confirmed that compensation could be given for a handicap on the open labour market was ***Smith v Manchester Corporation [1974].***

The Court must first consider whether a Claimant would be at a disadvantage because of the injury, if he were thrown back into the job market. The Court must then consider what the risk of that Claimant being thrown back into the job market is. The Court of Appeal, suggested a dual test approach to the issue of when compensation should be paid, in the case of ***Moeliker v Reyrolle & Co. Limited [1976]***. The test is as follows:

1. ***Is the Claimant in work at risk at some time before retirement of losing his job and finding himself on the labour market?***
2. ***If so what is that risk?***

   There has to be a real risk that this will occur.

   It would seem that if there is a real risk, albeit a slight one, that that would suffice.

   The Court will therefore look at the following matters:

   a) The age of the Claimant.
   b) The type of his work.
   c) The Claimant's employer's business.
   d) The nature of the injuries and their effect on his employment and employability.
   e) Any comments made by the Claimant's employers as to future employment prospects

If there is a "substantial" or a "real" risk then the Court will have to place a monetary value on that risk.

There is no "rule of thumb" which can be adopted in assessing how much should be awarded. Assessing an award very much comes down to experience.

The position was set out by Lord Justice Lloyd in the case of ***Foster v Tyne & Wear County Council [1986]1.A11ER567***

> **"...There is no rule of thumb which can be applied. It would be so much easier if there were. But there is not. In each case the trial Judge has to do his best to assess the Claimant's handicap, as an existing disability, by reference to what may happen in the future. As has been said so often, that is necessarily a matter of speculation; it is necessarily a matter of weighing up risks and chances in all of the circumstances of a particular case..."**

He went on to accept that the approach to be adopted was by its very nature "speculative".

11.8 Special Damages

As previously stated, in practise special damages are the financial losses arising out of the claim. These include past and future lost earnings, claims for care, accommodation costs, travel expenses etc.

11.8.1 Loss of Earnings

There is no magic or mystery to examining a loss of earnings claim.

There are two types of loss of earnings claim. These are:

1. ***Past loss of earnings claims*** (i.e. those losses that have been incurred from the date of the injury to the date of the assessment/settlement or trial) and;
2. ***Future loss of earnings claims*** (i.e. those earnings that will be lost as a result of the injury from the date of the assessment, settlement or trial into the future)

Claimants can also broadly be divided into two types.

1. ***Claimants who are employed*** (and pay tax PAYE or through completing a tax assessment form if they are higher tax payers) or;
2. ***Claimants who are self-employed*** (those Claimants who complete tax assessment forms annually if they are paying tax).

It must be remembered that the overriding objective of a Court in awarding compensation is to put a Claimant back into the position that he or she would have been in if the injuries in question has not occurred. Claimants are not entitled to make a profit or to receive a benefit as a result of the accident. However Claimants should not be expected to suffer a loss.

Past Loss of Earnings Claims

a) Employed Claimants

Employed Claimants will generally pay tax directly out of their salary under the PAYE (Pay As You Earn) scheme. They are entitled to claim their lost net pay (i.e. take home pay net of tax and National Insurance). Do not pay them their gross pay. Pay slips must therefore be checked to confirm the following:

a) The salary received prior to the date of the injury,

b) The level of earnings received for three calendar months (13 weeks) prior to the injury.

c) The level of earnings received after the accident (if any).

It is important to check the level of earnings received by a Claimant in the three calendar months prior to the injury. In that way, you can confirm whether there are any seasonal variations in the level of the Claimant's income and the level of any commission paid.

Both of those aspects are important.

For example, a Claimant who is an Estate Agent and who is injured in October would have received relatively high commission for sales through the three months prior to the injury. This is because, traditionally, the housing market is buoyant throughout the summer months. If that Claimant is then kept away from work for the following three months, claims handlers should be alive to the argument that the Claimant's commission would drop over the winter months as the housing market dips.

Claims handlers should therefore be conscious of the type of the Claimant's employment and consider whether that employment is subject to fluctuations in income levels. Of course, the Claimant's solicitors will also be alive to those arguments and may use them to their advantage.

If the Claimant has changed jobs since the accident occurred, then ask for a P45. That is a tax document provided by an employer to individuals upon the termination of their employment. It sets out the total income paid to the employee in the tax year to the date of termination of the employment.

If past tax years need to be considered (perhaps because a claim has not been intimated for some time following an accident date), then ask for copies of P60's. Employers provide these to their employees at the end of each tax year. These confirm the total level of income received by an employee within each tax year.

Employees' contractual obligations to their employers to recover monies

Claims handlers should also investigate whether the Claimant was actually paid by his employers during his period of sickness. It can often be the case that an employer will remunerate a member of staff who is away from work sick for a few weeks or months on a full pay basis.

If the employers have paid the Claimant's salary in full whilst the Claimant has been away from work, then on the face of it, the Claimant has suffered no loss and cannot make a loss of earnings claim.

However, some employers will have ensured within the contract of employment they have with the Claimant, that the Claimant is obliged to recover from the person who has caused the injury (and therefore who has caused the absence from work), any monies paid by the employer.

That is a contractual obligation and can be exercised by a Claimant. In such circumstances, the Claimant can seek repayment of such monies from the Defendant. If it is alleged therefore that a Claimant is making a claim pursuant to that contractual obligation, ask for a copy of the contract of employment. Do not be satisfied with a letter from an employer simply stating that the employee is obliged to recover those monies. Ask for the contract and make sure that the Claimant entered into it before the accident/injury date.

As stated above, the Claimant is only entitled to be put back into the position that he or she would have been in had the accident had not happened. Therefore, if the employer paid the Claimant while he was away from work he or she would not have suffered any loss and therefore cannot claim for a loss of earnings. They can do so however if there is a contractual relationship as set out above.

Therefore, always ask for the Claimant's pay slips for the time that it is alleged that the Claimant has been away from work or in the alternative ask for a letter from the employer confirming the time away from work. The employer can also confirm the level of lost pay.

Commission and Overtime

If lost commission is claimed, ask for details of the commission paid to other employees who are in a similar position to the Claimant. Such comparable figures will show the level of commission that has been paid whilst the Claimant was away from work and will therefore reflect any seasonal variations in commission income.

Be careful in case those employees have received extra commission whilst the Claimant was away from work (by doing his work for him). In such a situation the figures may be distorted in the Claimant's favour as they may suggest a higher level of commission than would have been earned by the Claimant.

The same principle applies for overtime.

Remember that overtime and commission are both taxable.

Again check past payslips to ensure the pre-injury net level of commission received by the Claimant.

Check-list

1. Is the Claimant employed or self employed?
2. What was the level of their pre-injury income (including commission and overtime)?
    a) Ask for pay slips for 13 weeks (3 months) prior to the injury
    b) Ask for copies of self-assessment forms for higher rate taxpayers if the lost earnings arise in past tax years.
    c) Calculate their average net weekly income over those 13 weeks.
    d) Carry out the same calculation for commission and overtime bearing in mind seasonal variations of income.

3. Has the Claimant received any income whilst away from work (e.g. Statutory sick pay, etc)? Ask for copies of all payslips since the accident occurred.

4. Is it the injury that is keeping the Claimant away from work? Check medical evidence.

5. How long was the Claimant away from work? Ask for details from the Claimant's employer.

6. If a Claimant is employed, he is only entitled to be put back into the position that he would have been in had the injury had not occurred. If he has suffered a loss of earnings as a result of an injury, his compensation will be his net lost pay. You are entitled to deduct tax and national insurance from any monies paid.

7. Therefore, make sure that the sums claimed are net of tax and national insurance and not gross.

8. If the Claimant seeks to recover monies on behalf of an employer pursuant to a contractual obligation, ask for a copy of the contract. Ensure that the contract was signed and dated before the date of the accident. Do not accept a contract that post-dates the accident. Do not only accept a letter from an employer that purports to confirm the Claimant's contractual obligations.

b) Self-employed Claimants

Self –employed Claimants, rather than paying taxes on a monthly basis out of their earnings, have to complete a tax self-assessment form once, and occasionally twice, every financial year.

Claims handlers should ask for the following documentation when dealing with a claim for loss of earnings by a self-employed Claimant:

1. A copy of the Claimant's self-assessment form for the full tax year prior to the injury.

2. A copy of the Claimant's self-assessment form covering the year of the injury (if one has been prepared).

3. Copies of Profit and Loss accounts for the year prior to the injury and for the year including the injury. These may need to be obtained from the Claimant's accountant.

4. Copies of any correspondence written between the Claimant/his accountant and the Inland Revenue in relation to the tax position.

The Claimant is only entitled to be put back into the position that he or she would have been in but for the accident.

Self-employed Claimants are not entitled to claim for loss of their turnover. They are however entitled to claim for a loss of their net profit. The loss of their net profit can be described as follows:

Loss of net profit = Monies received by the Business less expenses and overheads.

Claims handlers are entitled to deduct tax and National Insurance from a self-employed Claimant's compensation for lost earnings. Payments should therefore be made net.

Future Loss of Earnings Claims

If a Claimant is prevented by his injuries from working into the future (beyond the date of assessment, settlement or trial) then he will be entitled to claim for the loss of earnings that will arise in the future *(see chapter on "Calculating Future Losses")*.

It may be the case that the Claimant will not be able to return to work at all or will only be able to return to a different form of employment.

It may be that the Claimant's injuries are such that he cannot continue in his pre-injury employment. However, claims handlers should be alive to the possibility that the Claimant may well be able to return to work in an alternative form of employment. In such a situation the Claimant will still have a residual earning capacity.

If the alternative form of employment ensures that the Claimant recovers income at an equivalent level to the income received prior to the injury, then the Claimant has suffered no actual loss and there should be no claim for future lost earnings. There may however still be a claim for "handicap on the labour market" (see section on ***Smith v Manchester*** awards).

However, the Claimant may only be able to return to an alternative employment that pays less well than his or her pre-accident employment. In that situation the Claimant will suffer a continuing loss.

For example, the Claimant may be a man of 40 who intended to work until he was 65. Before he was injured he could earn £20,000.00 per annum net. Following the accident and because of his injuries he has had to give up his previous job and is now re-employed earning £10,000.00 per annum net.

The annual loss is known as a multiplicand.

Therefore his loss of earnings multiplicand is £10,000.00.

As has been stated above, the Claimant is entitled to be put back into the position that he would have been if the accident had not happened. He is however not entitled to make a profit.

The Claimant intended to work until he is 65 and therefore for a further 25 years.

However, it would not be appropriate to pay him £250,000.00 (25 years remaining in his working life multiplied by a multiplicand of £10,000.00).

If the Claimant was paid £250,000.00 he would be able to invest that sum and would through that investment, receive a benefit greater than the total of his future lost income.

This correct approach is explained in detail in the chapter "**Calculating Future Losses**".

11.8.2 Care Claims

If a Claimant has been injured and genuinely requires help with day to day activities as a result of those injuries, the reasonable cost of obtaining that help can be sought by way of compensation. Such compensation is usually calculated on a cost per hour of care basis.

Care claims will fall broadly into 2 types.

i) care provided by family and friends (Gratuitous care).

ii) professional care.

Care provided by family and friends (Gratuitous care)

In a range of cases, family members may give a Claimant care. For example, If a Claimant is bedridden for a week following a car accident, claims for care provided by a spouse or other family members can be made. Similarly a seriously injured Claimant may receive gratuitous care until such time as a formal care package can be arranged privately. This may arise when liability for an accident is in dispute and there are no funds available to pay for privately provided care.

In Cunningham v Harrison (1973) Lord Denning MR stated:

> "It is only right and just that if the wife renders services to [the Defendant] instead of a nurse, he should recover compensation for the value of the services that his wife has rendered"

In ***Mills v British Rail Engineering LTD (1992,)*** Staughton L stated that the care provided should go, "distinctly beyond that which is part of the ordinary regime of family life"

When claims for gratuitous care are made, claims handlers should not pay for such care at a commercial rate. Commercial rates are appropriate for commercial carers where overheads are to be borne and tax and National Insurance to be paid by those carers.

A reduced rate is therefore appropriate if a family member or friend provides the care. It is suggested that a reduction of 25% to 33% from a commercial care rate should be made in order to reflect the non-payment of tax and National Insurance.

A claim for care by a family member is inappropriate if it is that family member who has caused the injury in question (***Hunt v Severs 1994***).

Claims handlers should also be alive to the fact that some care may have been given by a family even if the accident had not happened and that element of the care should be deducted from any care claim presented.

The following check-list may assist:

1. Is care necessary? – Consider medical evidence, type of injury and description of care given.
2. Who has provided the care? is it the person who caused the injury?, could anybody else have reasonably given the care more cheaply?
3. Is the carer , in giving the care, going, "distinctly beyond that which is part of the ordinary regime of family life"?

4. How much care should have been necessary per day, bearing in mind the level of the injury or incapacity? You may need an expert medical opinion on this point.
5. What would be the appropriate hourly rate for that care, if a family member has given the care then a commercial rate would not be appropriate?
6. Multiply the number of hours per day for care that would be appropriate by the hourly rate that would be appropriate. That will give you a figure for the daily cost of care figure.
7. How long did or will the care reasonably go on for?
8. Build into your calculations/offer the fact that the care being given should normally diminish as the Claimant recovers.

Professional Care

In serious injury cases, professional care both past and future may be appropriate. Such care may be necessary indefinitely.

The type and level of care will need to be investigated. This will usually be done by commissioning a Care Consultant's report.

Such a report will assess the injury, the Claimant, and any needs that arise together with the likely level of care that will have to be given in the future. The report will take into account any prognosis provided by medical experts. It will then set out the cost of the care that will be necessary into the future.

Calculating the cost of a future claim for care

Please see chapter on "Calculating Future Losses".

If care will be required for years into the future the annual cost of care can be investigated by the commissioning of a care consultant's report.

Claims handlers must then decide whether the Claimant's life expectancy has been affected by the accident. If it has, that will reduce the future cost of care claim. A medical expert will be able to assist here.

In any event, the appropriate multiplier must then be adopted applying the principles laid out in ***Wells v Wells*** for future financial loss.

The Ogden tables should be considered. *(See chapter on "Calculating Future Losses".)*

Please also bear in mind the effect of The Courts Act 2003 and the possible effect that a Periodical Payments Order can have on the claim and reserve. This is also covered in the chapter "Calculating future losses"

11.8.3 Interest on Special Damages

Interest on past special damages that have ceased to accrue is calculated at 6% per annum from the date of the loss to the date of assessment of the loss.

If a loss is continuing, interest will be calculated at 3% from the date that such a loss started. It is claimed at half the "special account rate" in those circumstances.

Interest on special damages will only begin to run when a loss has been suffered (payment made or sum lost). Therefore, interest will not run on the cost of repairs to a motor vehicle until those repairs are paid for; and may never run on the sum claimed for credit hire.

Interest on special damages must be calculated when making a Part 36 Offer to settle. A failure to calculate interest correctly could result in the offer being beaten by the Claimant.

11.9 Suggested Further Reading

Butterworths Personal Injury Litigation Service

Buchan, Kennedy and Woolf: *Personal Injury*

12 FATAL CLAIMS

12 FATAL CLAIMS

Contents

The Law in this section has been subject to a number of recommendations from The Law Commission. As yet those recommendations have yet to be implemented so are not considered in this guide.

Damages for death are dealt with differently to personal injury damages.

A person who has been killed in an accident caused by another's wrongdoing is unable to sue in his or her own right for damages. The right to do so vests in their estate under the **Law Reform (Miscellaneous) Act 1934**.

If the deceased has left dependants who have suffered a loss as a result of the death, they may bring a claim under the **Fatal Accidents Act 1976**.

As will be seen below there can be duplication of claims between the two Acts. If a claim under the Law Reform (Miscellaneous Provisions) Act 1934 duplicates a claim under the Fatal Accident Act 1976, the second claim cannot be pursued. This avoids double compensation.

12.1 The Law Reform (Miscellaneous Provisions) Act 1934

On death, caused by another's wrongdoing, the deceased's right to sue for compensation vests in his estate. The Personal Representatives (the Executors or Administrators) of the estate can seek compensation.

There are broadly three possible heads of claim under this Act as follows:

1. Pain, suffering and loss of amenity suffered by the deceased between the date of the accident and the date of death. For obvious reasons, if the accident and death occur almost simultaneously, there may be no (or negligible) damages recoverable under this head.

If however the accident caused injuries from which the deceased died some time later, and in the interim the deceased had remained aware of his injuries, then some compensation will be recoverable.

2. The deceased's estate can recover special damages. If the deceased suffered a loss of earnings between the date of the accident and date of death, or suffered any damage to property in the accident, the estate can claim it under this Act.

3. The third possible head of claim under this Act is for funeral expenses. The estate can recover the costs of a reasonable funeral and wake, and the cost of a reasonably priced headstone. Generally, reasonable expenses can be recovered.

12.2 Fatal Accidents Act 1976

(This Act has been amended by the Administration of Justice Act 1982)

A claim can be brought under this Act by dependants of the deceased who have been deprived of the support (financial or otherwise) of the deceased.

The following categories of people are able to claim as dependants:

a) Spouses

b) Former spouses still receiving maintenance/financial assistance or services from the deceased.

c) Children or persons treated as children

d) Parents or persons treated as parents

e) Grandparents

f) Grandchildren

g) Co-habitiees of the opposite sex who have lived with the deceased for more than two years.

In each case, the person claiming must be able to show that they were dependant on the deceased financially or otherwise.

Claims under this Act fall into three heads as follows:

A) Bereavement damages
Bereavement damages are awarded in the sum of £10,000 for causes of action accruing before 1st January 2008 and in the sum of £11,800 for causes of action accruing on or after that date. Such damages are recoverable by people who fall into the following categories:

i) a surviving spouse

ii) parents of a legitimate child under the age of 18 at the time of death.

iii) the mother of an illegitimate child under the age of 18 at the time of death.

If there is more than one person who has been bereaved and who falls into the category set out above, then the bereavement damages sum is shared.

B) Funeral expenses (see above)

C) A claim for the value of the dependency. (Please see list of potential dependants above).

As in personal injury cases, the first step for claims handlers is to assess an appropriate multiplicand for the dependency claim. This is dealt with below.

An appropriate multiplier must then be considered. For assessing multiplicands and multipliers generally please see chapter "Calculating Future Losses".

The Multiplicand

As in other personal injury cases, the multiplicand is the annual value of the loss, in this case the dependency.

Some rules of thumb apply in claims under this Act in relation to income lost as a result of the deceased's death as follows:

1. For a deceased breadwinner leaving a spouse and no children, the multiplicand will generally be two thirds of the deceased's annual income.

2. For a deceased breadwinner leaving a spouse and 2 children, the multiplicand will generally be three quarters of the deceased's annual income.

As is stated above, these are only rules of thumb and can be varied in particular circumstances.

Claimant's lawyers will often adopt another approach. They may deduct the deceased's personal living expenses from the deceased's annual income. That calculation should result in a multiplicand that equates to the financial contribution made by the deceased for his or her family and children.

The loss of dependency however is not limited solely to strict financial loss. The deceased may have provided services in other areas. For example, a deceased may have carried out DIY, car maintenance, gardening, housework, and the taking care of his or her children. The value of such services does need to be valued on a commercial basis. The same principles will apply as in personal injury cases. Please consider chapter on Quantum.

Each head as set out above can then be assessed as a "multiplicand" and an appropriate multiplier must be applied.

Multipliers

Multipliers for the various heads of claim will be as follows:

1. For lost earnings – the multiplier will have to take into account the age of the deceased at the date of death, the anticipated date of retirement and the appropriate Ogden Tables. They are calculated from the date of death *(see chapter on Calculating Future Losses)*.

2. Multipliers for other services will vary. They will be calculated from the date of death and will take into account the Claimant's age. Different services will have different multipliers depending upon when they could reasonably have expected to

cease to have been given by the deceased to his dependants in any event. For example, it may be reasonable for a claims handler to argue that the deceased would not have been able to continue gardening and decorating beyond, say, the age of 75 (perhaps for health reasons that are established during the course of investigation).

Apportionment

If a surviving spouse and infant children bring claims, the awards must be apportioned. Most of the monies will be paid to the surviving spouse to allow for provisions for the future care of the children. The calculation is the responsibility of the Claimants' solicitor.

Approval

The Court will need to be asked to approve any part of the claim relating to childrens' dependency. Without such approval, any settlement will be invalid.

12.3 Suggested Further Reading

Buchan, Kennedy and Woolf: *Personal Injury Practice*

Munkman: *Damages of Personal Injuries and Death*

Fatal Accident Claims – Tim Kevan and Maria Kwiatkowska.

13 CALCULATING FUTURE LOSSES

13 CALCULATING FUTURE LOSSES

Contents

13.1 Introduction

We have seen in previous chapters how to calculate past losses.

If a Claimant has suffered a financial loss as a result of an accident, he is entitled to be put back into the position that he would have been in if the accident had not happened. It is relatively easy to calculate past losses.

However, the same principles cannot be applied in order to calculate future losses.

For example, what of the 40 year old man who will not be able to work again and who has no residual earning capacity? If he intended to retire at 65 he has been denied the opportunity of 25 years' salary. However he cannot expect to receive 25 years' salary as compensation for his future loss of earnings.

13.2 The Starting Point

The actual type of loss must be identified. For example, is it a future loss of earnings claim, a future cost of care claim or a future cost of gardening expenses etc?

It is important that Claims Handlers check all evidence, especially medical records and the employment report (if one has been obtained) to ensure that the future loss claim is warranted.

For example, a Claimant's injuries may prevent that Claimant from returning to his pre-accident employment. However the Claimant may still have some residual earning capacity in that he can still carry out some form of less well paid employment.

The loss suffered in that situation would comprise of the Claimant's pre-accident earnings figure, but less his residual earning capacity. Such a residual earning capacity will therefore reduce a potential future loss of earnings claim.

Such a Claimant must take steps to mitigate his or her losses by taking such employment as is available to him and which he could reasonably be expected to do given his physical condition.

In relation to a care claim, there may be a great deal of care necessary immediately after the accident. In the most serious cases it may be the case that such care will last indefinitely and for the rest of the Claimant's life. However, in most cases the amount of care required generally will decrease or plateau as time goes on and the Claimant's recovery progresses. It is necessary therefore to identify how much care will be required into the future and whether that care arises out of the Defendant's breach of duty. Again, medical evidence can be useful in determining the amount of care that a Claimant will require in the future and the cause of that care.

By considering matters such as above, Claims Handlers should be able to identify the annual net loss or cost to the Claimant.

The annual loss or cost is known as the **multiplicand**.

13.3 The Second Stage

Claims Handlers must then consider the individual Claimant. Are they male or female? How badly injured are they and how old are they? How well educated are they?

In the case of a future loss of earnings claim, if the accident had not happened how much longer would the Claimant have continued to work for? Consider here the usual retirement age in the Claimant's line of work, the Claimant's own wishes and the risk of premature redundancy or retirement in the Claimant's particular profession.

13.4 Calculating the Future Loss Claim

Consider a 40-year-old employed Claimant who earns £20,000.00 per annum net of Tax and National Insurance. But for his injuries he would have worked until the age of 65 and has no residual earning capacity. He has therefore been deprived of 25 years of his salary of £20,000.00 per annum net.

His loss of earnings multiplicand is therefore £20,000.00.

However it would **not** be appropriate to pay him 25 years lost salary of £20,000.00 per annum net, a total of £500,000.00.

13.5 Placing the Claimant Back into the Position that he or she Would have Been in but for the Accident

The Claimant is only entitled to be put back into the position he or she would have been in if the accident had not happened.

Paying the above Claimant the sum of £500,000.00 would in fact over compensate him.

That is because he would be able to invest the sum of £500,000.00 as soon as he had it and, over the subsequent 25 years, he would earn interest on the capital sum. He would therefore do rather better then had he remained at work.

The Courts have avoided this problem of over compensation by reducing the number of years' earnings to be paid to Claimants for future losses. Claimants receive less by way of a lump sum because of the accelerated payment.

The number of years by which the multiplicand is to be multiplied by is known as the **multiplier**.

In the above example, a multiplier of 25 is inappropriate because overcompensation would occur. The Claimant would recover all lost earnings and by receiving them as a lump sum would also have the benefit of interest that he would not have had but for his injuries.

The House of Lords in ***Wells v Wells [1999]*** decided that the multiplier must be based upon the assumption that a Claimant who prudently invests his compensation receives income from the capital investment at a particular percentage rate per annum. This is now assumed to be 2.5%.

The aim of the Court is to ensure that a Claimant who receives compensation for future lost earnings, will have a sum which, when invested, will run out on the date of the previously anticipated retirement.

The House of Lords in ***Wells v Wells*** recognised and encouraged the use of Actuarial Tables, known in practice as the Ogden Tables. These are now in their 6th edition can be found at the end of this chapter.

It is emphasised however that the Ogden Tables are not legislation and therefore are only a starting point; albeit a commonly used one.

13.6 Some Useful Formulae

a) For future loss of earnings claims adopt the following:

Multiplicand = net annual loss, less residual earning capacity (if any).

Multiplier = anticipated retirement date, less age of Claimant (subject to Ogden Tables).

b) Other future losses

Other future losses are treated slightly differently. Non-earnings related future losses, subject to medical evidence etc, often run for the rest of the Claimant's life. Life expectancy is therefore more important than the anticipated date of retirement. Therefore:

Multiplicand = Net annual loss/cost

Multiplier = Life expectancy of Claimant less age/sex of Claimant (Subject to Ogden Tables).

13.7 Working Example

There are now 28 Ogden "tables". These tables all calculate multipliers taking projected mortality rates into account.

Multipliers however can be adjusted to reflect contingencies other than mortality. The Sixth Edition of the Ogden Tables is based on some research carried out in 2004 which demonstrated that people without disabilities spend more time out of employment than earlier research suggested. It was therefore felt by the Ogden working party that is was appropriate to apply a higher discount for contingencies other than mortality than had been felt to be the case in earlier editions of the Ogden tables. The effect of this is that some claims for loss of earnings are likely to come down.

The research also demonstrates that the factors, other than gender, which have the most effect on a person's future employment status are:

i) Whether the person was employed or unemployed at the outset.

ii) whether the person is disabled or not, and

iii) the education attainment of that person (see the introduction to the Sixth edition of the Ogden Tables prepared by Mr Robin DeWilde QC).

Consider the following example taken from those given in the Explanatory Notes to the 6th edition of the Ogden tables.

The Claimant is female, aged 35 at the date of the trial. She has three A levels, but not a degree, and was in employment at the date of the accident at a salary of £25,000 a year net of tax. She was not disabled before the accident. As a result of her injuries, she is now disabled and has lost her job but has found part time employment at a salary of £5,000 a year net of tax.

Her cost of future care is £5,000 per annum.

Step 1

From the above information we know that the Claimant is 35 years old, female and intended to work until the age of 60.

Her multiplicand for earnings is £25,000.00.

Her multiplicand for cost of care is £25,000.00.

Step 2 – Earnings

In relation to earnings Claims Handlers should look at Table 8 in the Ogden Tables.

The table is headed "Multipliers for loss of earnings to pension age 60 (females)".

The Claimant is 35 and the current appropriate rate of return to adopt is 2.5%.

The appropriate multiplier therefore for loss of earnings for this Claimant is 18.39

Before any adjustments are made therefore, the future loss of earnings claim would be calculated as £25,000 net multiplied by 18.39 = £459,750.

Step 3 – Earnings adjustments

Any appropriate adjustments for earnings must then be considered.

Now take account of risks other than mortality.

Allowing for the Claimant being employed but not disabled and having achieved A levels at the date of trial, Table C would require 18.39 to be multiplied by 0.86, resulting in a revised multiplier of 15.82.

The damages for loss of earnings are assessed as £395,500 (15.82 x £25,000).

We then need to allow for mitigation of loss of earnings in respect of post injury earnings. As before, Table H shows that, on the basis of a 2.5% rate of return, the multiplier for a female aged 35 is 18.39.

We therefore take into account risks other than mortality and allowing for the Claimant being employed, disabled and having achieved A levels at the date of trial, Table D would require 18.39 to be multiplied by 0.48 resulting in a revised multiplier of 8.83.

The amount of mitigation for post injury earnings is assessed as £44,150 (8.83 x £5,000).

Therefore the award for loss of earnings after allowing for mitigation is £395,000 – £44,150 = £351,350

Step 4 – Care

Look up Table 2 for the multiplier age 35. At the appropriate rate of return of 2.5% the multiplier at age 35 is 28.71.

No further adjustment is made for risks other than mortality and therefore the future cost of care claim would be calculated as £5,000 net multiplied by 28.71 = £143,550.00

13.8 Can the Real Rate of Return be Varied from 2.5%?

The Lord Chancellor has the power under **Section 1(1) of the Damages Act 1996** to set the rate of return that the Courts must assume can be recovered by a Claimant when investing a lump sum received by way of compensation.

Claims Handlers should be aware that at some point in the future the rate of return will be varied. It was reduced from 3% to 2.5% in June 2001.

If the rate of return is lowered, the cost to those paying compensation will increase and the Claimant will recover more money. This is because the Court will have to award more by way of compensation to ensure that the same rate of return is achieved.

Conversely, if the rate is increased, the amount paid by way of compensation to a Claimant will decrease. That is because the Court will be able to award less by way of compensation for future losses than they had to when the assumed interest rate was 2.5%.

13.9 The Courts Act 2003

This Act, governing periodical payments came into force on 1st April 2005. The Courts are now obliged to consider whether a periodical payments order (PPO) will be appropriate in all cases involving future losses, regardless of the size of the award.

a PPO results in a Claimant receiving a predetermined amount for specific heads of loss every year until the Claimant's pre accident retirement date in the case of future loss of earnings claims; or possibly for life in the case of other future loss claims.

The Courts have the power to impose a PPO irrespective of the parties' wishes.

Much of the finer detail of the Act will become relevant only after the issue of proceedings and will therefore fall to be dealt with by claims handlers' lawyers. However, it is important that claims handlers understand how the Act works in outline and, just as importantly, the impact that a PPO would have upon a reserve.

When deciding whether to make a PPO the Courts will consider Claimants' needs rather than Claimants' wishes.

The operation of a PPO

Before ordering a PPO a Court must be satisfied that the payment provider is secure.

An insurer that wishes to self-fund the periodical payments must be protected by the Financial Services Compensation Scheme ("FSCS"), as set out within the Act.

If an insurer is not protected by the FSCS, or if it chooses not to self-fund the ordered periodical payments, it will be obliged to purchase an annuity in the open financial market. The annuity would then guarantee the payment of the predetermined sum to the Claimant for the relevant period(s).

Currently, there are only limited products available and these tend to be expensive. Our experience has suggested that the purchase of an annuity can currently add as much as 25%-40% to the cost of a claim.

What are the risks of a PPO being made?

However, we suggest that it would be a very unusual case in which a PPO was made against a fully capable Claimant's wishes. Such a Claimant would no doubt feel that he should be able to decide how his compensation is paid. If a Claimant has the capacity to make his own decisions why should the Court impose a PPO upon him? At the date of this edition it is not yet clear how the Courts will react in different circumstances. However we believe that it is possible to classify particular cases as having low, medium or high risks of concluding with a PPO. Each case will of course turn on its own facts but it is hoped that the following general guide will assist.

High-risk cases

These will include the following:

i) cases in which the Claimant lacks capacity to act without the assistance of a litigation friend. A Court will be attracted to making a PPO on the basis that it is probable that such a Claimant would not be able to manage his compensation appropriately if it was to be awarded as a lump sum.

ii) cases involving relatively high value future care claims. The Courts are likely to feel that a Claimant's needs will be better served by ensuring the receipt of regular annual payments into the future, as opposed to the payment of a lump sum for the future cost of care.

iii) high value claims in which the Claimant asks for a PPO and has good grounds for doing so. As the Claimant's needs are paramount, if the Claimant can show a need and a desire for a PPO one is likely to be made.

Medium risk cases

These will include the following:

i) Cases in which there is no indication from the Claimant that he desires a PPO, but in which there is the potential for a high value future loss claim. As the Court must consider the Claimant's needs rather than his wishes, it is possible that a PPO could be imposed.

ii) High value cases in which there is a relatively small finding of contributory negligence (c25%) against the Claimant. The reduction of a future loss claim as a result of the Claimant's contributory negligence may well make it more appropriate for such damages to be paid as a lump sum as opposed to being received under a PPO.

Low risk cases

These will include the following:

(i) low value cases, although please do note that the Court has the power to make a PPO in any case involving a future loss claim regardless of the value.

(ii) cases involving a finding of a relatively high level of contributory negligence against the Claimant (50% or more).

(iii) high value cases but with a low level continuing loss.

Thompstone v NHSLA (2008) Court of Appeal

This case was recently heard in the Court of Appeal with three other cases, which were all concerned with which index should apply to calculate the annual increase of the Claimant's PPO. Section 2(8) of the Courts At 2003 provides that a PPO shall vary by reference to the Retail Price Index (RPI). Section 2(9) allows the Court discretion to order an alternative index.

The Claimants in these cases were seeking to apply the ASHE 6115 index (Annual Survey of Hours and Earnings), which focuses on the earnings of carer assistants and home carers. Despite a range of objections on behalf of the Defendants, the Court held that indexation on the basis of ASHE 6115 was appropriate and that "it will not be appropriate to reopen that issue in any further proceedings unless the Defendant can produce evidence from, and more persuasive than, that which has been deployed in the present cases". This is likely to have a significant impact on the cost of PPOs and claims handlers should have this issue in mind when considering reserving claims that are likely to include a PPO.

Conclusion

It is still relatively early days following the coming into force of The Courts Act and the new regime for potential PPO's. Claims handlers should however be alive to the risks of such orders being made and take appropriate steps to factor such risks and costs into their reserves.

We suggest that claims handlers ask Claimants' solicitors at an early stage for an indication of their clients' wishes as to how they would wish to be compensated for future loss claims. We anticipate that most capable Claimants will prefer to receive such compensation by way of "traditional" lump sum. If it is felt that the claim carries a medium or high risk of a PPO ultimately being made, insurers may wish to seek a quotation from a respected financial advisor for the cost of purchasing an annuity to pay an annual sum for the anticipated future losses. This will only be of use for guidance at an early stage and of course the investment market may well change before the case can be concluded. However, the quotation may help insurers for reserving purposes.

13.10 *Sowden v Lodge* (2004) Court of Appeal – Local Authority Care Provision

This case is important when claims handlers come to consider the cost of future care and accommodation, generally in the most serious injury cases.

The Court of Appeal decided that an award of damages for personal injury could, in principle, be made on the basis that residential care and accommodation provided by the local authority would be topped up by a payment for the provision of further care on the basis that the feasibility of the proposed topping up had to be proved by evidence.

The Claimant had been seriously injured and prior to trial had been a resident in a local authority residential home. The Court decided that the correct test to be applied was what was required to meet the Claimant's reasonable needs.

This decision has been followed in the 2007 case of ***Crofton v NHSLA*** which also held that a local authority was obliged, in determining whether it was necessary for it to meet a Claimant's care needs, to disregard any awards of damages for personal injury.

It is strongly recommended that claims handlers dealing with claims for future care and accommodation read the two judgments in full.

A further example has recently been seen in ***Peters v East Midland Strategic Health Authority* (2008).** In this case the Defendants joined the local authority as Part 20 Defendants and sought a declaration that the local authority was not entitled to charge the Claimant for her care. the local authority asserted that they should be able to recover a contribution from the Claimant's award of damages.

The Court held, applying ***Crofton,*** that an award of damages, or income produced from that award, was not to be taken into acount when assessing a person's assets for the purposes of contribution toward their care costs. Further, in this particular case, the Claimant's disability was so severe that she would never have any assets other than those awarded by way of damages and it was unlikely that the local authority would be able to accommodate the level of care the Claimant had become accustomed to. The Defendant was therefore liable to pay the Claimant's past and future care costs.

On 7 April 2008 the National Assistance (Sums for Personal Requirements and Assessment of Resources) Amendment (England) Regulations 2008 (SI 2008/593) came into force, bringing about a major change in the way local authorities assess a person's entitlement to care provisions. The Regulations provide that where an award of damages for personal injury is placed into a trust, any amount awarded in respect of care will no longer be disregarded by the local authority. This will have the effect of meaning that significantly more Claimants will be deemed self-funders for the purposes of residential and domiciliary care. It should be noted however, that this provision does not apply to funds administered by the Court of Protection, which are still to be disregarded.

13.11 Future Losses Check-list

1. What future losses are being claimed?
2. Does the evidence support the future loss? Consider here medical reports, medical records, personnel records, employment reports, care reports etc.
3. In the case of loss of earnings, does the Claimant have a residual earning capacity? In other words, even if it is accepted that the Claimant cannot return to his pre-accident employment, can he usefully carry out some other form of paid employment? If the answer to this question is yes, that will reduce the loss of earnings multiplicand. Remember that the Claimant is under an obligation to mitigate his losses and cannot simply say, "I have been injured, I need not work at all". If he is capable of some form of paid work, and work is available, he must take steps to accept it.

4. In relation to other future cost or loss claims (such as care, gardening, decorating, car maintenance) what is the actual cost to the Claimant? Is it supported by evidence? Again consider the evidence that you have in order to reach a multiplicand for each head of claim. Ensure that the Claimant has suffered a loss and was not paying for the items claimed for before the accident.

5. Consider the Ogden Tables, taking into account the age, sex, health and education of the Claimant and, in the case of earnings, their anticipated retirement date. Adopt the appropriate rate of return. At the date of this edition, the rate is 2.5%. Make the appropriate adjustments to the multiplier.

6. Remember that some future loss claims should not be allowed for the rest of the Claimant's life. It is unlikely that the Claimant would have decorated his own home for the rest of his life. At some point his age would have prevented him from doing so in any event. Such future claims should be limited therefore and paid up to a reasonable age.

7. Having assessed the future claims, consider the Compensation Recovery Unit's position. You will be able to withhold appropriate benefits from appropriate damages (see chapter on CRU). You should do so before paying the Claimant his or her compensation.

8 Ensure that you pay the appropriate sum to the Compensation Recovery Unit.

9. Consider the operation of The Courts Act 2003 and the possibility of a periodical payments order.

13.12 Suggested Further Reading

Buchan, Kennedy and Woolf: *Personal Injury Practice*

13.13 The Ogden Tables

INTRODUCTION to the 6th Edition of the OGDEN TABLES

"When it comes to the explanatory notes we must make sure that they are readily comprehensible. We must assume the most stupid circuit judge in the country and before him are the two most stupid advocates. All three of them must be able to understand what we are saying."

Sir Michael Ogden QC,
on his explanatory notes to the
First Edition of the Ogden Tables.[1]

1. This is the second edition published since Sir Michael Ogden's death. The new multipliers provided by the Government Actuary's Department use mortality rates from the latest available population projections, which take account of data following the last National Census. In general, such figures have added about 1% for most younger ages to the previous figures. There are, however, other matters here, which are discussed below and described in detail in the Explanatory Notes.

The purpose of the Ogden Tables

2. The Tables are designed to help in the calculation of future pecuniary losses.

3. The number of cases that actually fall into the multitrack, that is are worth more than £15,000, is small, and estimated by some to be only some 5% of the total claims notified. I express it as 'claims notified' for the practice of insurers has changed and now many cases are settled early without the need for the issue of proceedings.

4. When the Tables were first produced, it was on the basis that the appropriate discount rate should be chosen with regard to the yields on Index Linked Government Stock (ILGS). This was the argument presented to the House of Lords in **Wells v. Wells [1999] 1 A.C. 345** and accepted by them in their speeches. When Lord Chancellor Irvine set the discount rate, he elected not to follow that course, but gave his own reasoning for selecting the discount rate that he chose. This was something that he was entitled to do under the powers granted to him in the Damages Act 1996. He is also required under the Act to keep the discount rate he chooses under constant review, which it is said that both Lord Chancellor Irvine and his successor Lord Falconer constantly did and do.

Mortality

5. For the most part, the new multipliers provided by the Government Actuary's Department use mortality rates from the latest available population projections, which take account of data following the last National Census. In general, such figures have had most effect on the multipliers at younger ages for loss of pension; there has been very little change in the multipliers for loss of earnings and increases of between 0% and 4% for multipliers for pecuniary loss for life compared to those in the Fifth Edition.

Contingencies other than Mortality

6. This is the most significant contribution to this edition of the Ogden Tables. It is based on two recent and interesting pieces of research which consider the impact of contingencies other than mortality on working life. This research was carried out, in two separate exercises, by Professor Richard Verrall, Professor Steven Haberman and Mr Zoltan Butt of City University, London and by Dr Victoria Wass of Cardiff University.

7. The findings of these two pieces of research have been combined to produce the tables which are set out in Section B of this edition of the Ogden Tables and which replace the Section B tables which were introduced in the Second Edition.

8. The Ogden Working Party thinks that these tables are likely to prove useful to lawyers when it comes to assessing the appropriate discount to the working life multiplier for contingencies other than mortality.

9. The research demonstrates that people without disabilities spend more time out of employment than earlier research had suggested. It is therefore appropriate to apply a higher discount for contingencies other than mortality than was indicated in the Section B tables introduced in the Second Edition of the Ogden Tables. The effect of this is that some claims for loss of earnings are likely to come down.

10. The research also demonstrates that the factors, other than gender, which have the most effect on a person's future employment status are: (i) whether the person was employed or unemployed at the outset, (ii) whether the person is

[1] Memoirs of Sir Michael Ogden QC, 'Variety is the Spice of Legal Life', p.182; The Book Guild, 2002

disabled or not, and (iii) the educational attainment of the person. Interestingly the research has shown that the effect of factors previously thought important, such as occupation, industrial sector, geographic location and levels of economic activity, are relatively insignificant once educational attainment has been taken into account.

11. Accordingly, the discount to be applied to a working life multiplier (or at least a starting point) can be determined from the tables by looking up the discount factor to be applied to a person of the claimant's gender, age, educational attainment and employment status at the time of injury.

12. The tables now included at Section B may also assist those having to deal with the question of a disabled claimant's residual earnings capacity. Again, unsurprisingly to me, the research has demonstrated that disabled people are more likely to be out of employment than people without disabilities, therefore justifying a higher discount for contingencies other than mortality.

13. Both pieces of research have used the published Labour Force Survey definition of 'disabled'. This means that the range of disabilities covered by 'disabled' is very wide as it includes all people who have said that they have a condition that (a) substantially limits (or will limit due to progressive illness) their ability to carry out day-to-day activities and (b) affects either the amount or the type of paid work they might do.

14. There will be situations when it will be appropriate to use the factors as set out in the Section B tables to calculate a claimant's residual earning capacity on a multiplier/multiplicand basis. However, in many cases it will be appropriate to increase or reduce the discount in the tables to take account of the nature of a particular claimant's disabilities. There will also be some cases when the *Smith v. Manchester Corporation* or *Blamire* approach remains applicable. There may be still cases where a precise mathematical approach is inapplicable.

15. My view is that the findings of this research provide a very useful starting point for lawyers grappling with loss of earnings calculations and provide a basis for a more scientific approach than that which has been taken to date. There are fully worked examples in the Explanatory Notes but, clearly, they cannot cover every factual situation.

16. It also provides yet another justification for the importance of education, if such was ever needed, when faced with the unexpected hazards and problems of life visited on those who are the subject of these tables.

Variable future losses or expenses

17. The tables do not provide an immediate answer when the annual future loss or expense is likely to change at given points in time in the future, for example where a claimant's lost earnings would have increased on a sliding scale or changed due to promotion; or the claimant's future care needs are likely to change, perhaps because it is anticipated that a family carer will not be able to continue to provide help. In such situations it is usually necessary to split the overall multiplier, whether for working life or whole of life, into segments, and then to apply those smaller segmented multipliers to the multiplicand appropriate for each period. The Explanatory Notes now include some guidance on how to use the multipliers in such cases (see paragraphs 22 to 24).

Final remarks

18. We are conscious with each Edition of the Tables that we produce that we are being prescriptive about the way in which calculations are made.

19. When we make suggestions for the method of calculations, each change which is put forward is the result of long and careful debate by the whole Working Party, assisted by others from outside the Working Party, who put forward proposals which we consider.

20. The figures for the Tables themselves are produced by the Government Actuary's Department according to long established principles.

21. All other matters are the subject of careful and detailed analysis by all the members of the Working Party.

22. However, if anyone wishes to put forward further improvements, they are invited to do so. We travel like that Pilgrim on the Golden Journey to Samarkand, conscious of our failures and hoping for enlightenment. If you consider that you can assist us in that process, do not hesitate to write to the Government Actuary or myself.

23. I am grateful to those members of the Working Party (listed inside the front cover) who give up their time and mental energy to attend the meetings.

Robin de Wilde QC | 1 March 2007

EXPLANATORY NOTES

SECTION A: GENERAL

Purpose of tables

1. The tables have been prepared by the Government Actuary's Department. They provide an aid for those assessing the lump sum appropriate as compensation for a continuing future pecuniary loss or consequential expense or cost of care in personal injury and fatal accident cases.

Application of tables

2. The tables set out multipliers. These multipliers enable the user to assess the present capital value of future annual loss (net of tax) or annual expense calculated on the basis of various assumptions which are explained below. Accordingly, to find the present capital value of a given annual loss or expense, it is necessary to select the appropriate table, find the appropriate multiplier and then multiply the amount of the annual loss or expense by that figure.

3. Tables 1 to 26 deal with annual loss or annual expense extending over three different periods of time. In each case there are separate tables for men and women.

- In Tables 1 and 2 the loss or expense is assumed to begin immediately and to continue for the whole of the rest of the claimant's life, allowing for different potential lifespans, including the possibility of early death or prolonged life. The tables apply to both the deceased and the dependants' lives in fatal accident cases.

- In Tables 3 to 14 the loss or expense is assumed to begin immediately but to continue only until the claimant's retirement or earlier death. The age of retirement is assumed to be 50 in Tables 3 and 4, 55 in Tables 5 and 6, 60 in Tables 7 and 8, 65 in Tables 9 and 10, 70 in Tables 11 and 12, and 75 in Tables 13 and 14.

- In Tables 15 to 26 it is assumed that the annual loss or annual expense will not begin until the claimant reaches retirement but will then continue for the whole of the rest of his or her life. In Table 19 (males) and Table 20 (females) the age of retirement is assumed to be 60. In Table 21 (males) and Table 22 (females) the age of retirement is assumed to be 65 (and similarly for retirement ages 50, 55, 70 and 75). These tables all make due allowance for the chance that the claimant may not live to reach the age of retirement.

Mortality assumptions

4. For the previous edition of the Tables the Working Party agreed that the tables to be published should be based on a reasonable estimate of the future mortality likely to be experienced by average members of the population alive today. The mortality assumptions used in the 5th Edition were taken from the then latest available population projections (the 2002-based population projections) for England and Wales. The Tables are routinely used in Scotland and Northern Ireland. Although it would be possible to produce separate tables of multipliers for Scotland and Northern Ireland using mortality rates from population projections for Scotland and for Northern Ireland the Working Party agreed that rather than have three separate sets of Tables there should be one set calculated using mortality rates from the population projections for the United Kingdom as a whole.

5. On the basis of some reported cases, it appears that tables for pecuniary loss for life, e.g. cost of care, may have been misunderstood. The tables do not assume that the claimant dies after a period equating to the expectation of life, but take account of the possibilities that the claimant will live for different periods, e.g. die soon or live to be very old. The mortality assumptions relate to the general population of the United Kingdom. Unless there is clear evidence in an individual case to support the view that the individual is atypical and will enjoy longer or shorter expectation of life, no further increase or reduction is required for mortality alone.

6. For the purposes of preparing the official national population projections, the Government Actuary makes an estimate of the extent of future improvements in mortality. Tables 1 to 26 in this edition show the multipliers which result from the application of these projected mortality rates (derived from the 2004-based population projections for the United Kingdom, which were published in October 2005 on the GAD website www.gad.gov.uk. Details can also be found in the publication *National Population Projections 2004-based. PP2 No.25* from the Office for National Statistics). The actuaries on the Working Party consider that these alternative tables provide a more appropriate estimate of the value of future income streams than tables based on historic mortality which, given the rate at which mortality experience has improved, and continues to improve, are likely to underestimate future longevity to a significant extent. The Working Party therefore recommends the Courts use Tables 1 to 26 contained in this latest edition of the tables.

Use of tables

7. To find the appropriate figure for the present value of a particular loss or expense, the user must first choose that table which relates to the period of loss or expense for which the individual claimant is to be compensated and to the sex of the claimant, or, where appropriate, the claimant's dependants.

8. If, for some reason, the facts in a particular case do not correspond with the assumptions on which one of the tables is based (e.g. it is known that the claimant will have a different retiring age from that assumed in the tables), then the tables can only be used if an appropriate allowance is made for this difference; for this purpose the assistance of an actuary should be sought, except for situations where specific guidance is given in these explanatory notes.

Rate of return

9. The basis of the multipliers set out in the tables is that the lump sum will be invested and yield income (but that over the period in question the claimant will gradually reduce the capital sum, so that at the end of the period it is exhausted). Accordingly, an essential factor in arriving at the right figure is the choice of the appropriate rate of return.

10. The annual rate of return currently to be applied is 2½% (net of tax), as fixed by the Lord Chancellor on 25 June 2001, and reassessed on 27 July 2001, under the provisions of the Damages Act 1996 Section 1. An annual rate of return of 2½% was also set for Scotland by the Scottish Ministers on 8 February 2002. The Lord Chancellor may make a fresh determination of this rate, after receiving advice from the Government Actuary and the Treasury (and, in Scotland, the Scottish Ministers after consultation with the Government Actuary). In order to allow the Tables to continue to be used should a new discount rate be specified, the tables are accordingly shown for a range of possible annual rates of return ranging from ½% to 5%, as in the previous edition. In addition, a 0% column has been included to show the multiplier without any discount for interest (i.e. expectations of life, or the equivalent for different periods). These are supplied to assist in the calculation of multipliers in Fatal Accidents Act cases (see Section D).

11. Section 1(2) of the Damages Act 1996 makes provision for the Courts to make variations to the discount rate if any party to the proceedings shows that it is more appropriate in the case in question. Variations to the discount rate under this provision have, however, been rejected by the Court of Appeal in the cases of **Warriner v. Warriner [2002] 1 WLR 1703** and **Cooke & Others v. United Bristol Health Care & Others [2004] 1 WLR 251.**

12. Previous editions of these tables explained how the current yields on index-linked government bonds could be used as an indicator of the appropriate real rate of return for valuing future income streams. Such considerations were endorsed by the House of Lords in **Wells v. Wells** and the same argumentation was adopted by the Lord Chancellor when he set the rate on commencement of Section 1 of the Damages Act 1996. In cases outwith the scope of these tables, the advice of an actuary should be sought.

Different retirement ages

13. In paragraph 8 above, reference was made to the problem that will arise when the claimant's retiring age is different from that assumed in the tables. Such a problem may arise in valuing a loss or expense beginning immediately but ending at retirement; or in valuing a loss or expense which will not begin until the claimant reaches retirement but will then continue until death. Tables are provided for retirement ages of 50, 55, 60, 65, 70 and 75. Where the claimant's actual retiring age would have been between two of these retirement ages for which tables are provided, the correct multiplier can be obtained by consideration of the tables for retirement age immediately above and below the actual retirement age, keeping the period to retirement age the same. Thus a woman of 42 who would have retired at 58 can be considered as being in between the cases of a woman of 39 with a retirement age of 55 and a woman of 44 with a retirement age of 60. The steps to take are as follows:

(1) Determine between which retirement ages, for which tables are provided, the claimant's actual retirement age R lies. Let the lower of these ages be A and the higher be B.

(2) Determine how many years must be subtracted from the claimant's actual retirement age to get to A and subtract that period from the claimant's age. If the claimant's age is x, the result of this calculation is $(x+A-R)$.

(3) Look up this new reduced age in the Table corresponding to retirement age A at the appropriate rate of return. Let the resulting multiplier be M.

(4) Determine how many years must be added to the claimant's actual retirement age to get to B and add that period to the claimant's age. The result of this calculation is $(x+B-R)$.

(5) Look up this new increased age in the Table corresponding to retirement age B at the appropriate rate of return. Let the resulting multiplier be N.

(6) Interpolate between *M* and *N*. In other words, calculate:

(*B-R*) x *M* + (*R-A*) x *N*

and divide the result by *[(B-R) + (R-A)]*, (or equivalently *[B-A]*).

14. In the example given in paragraph 13, the steps would be as follows:

(1) *R* is 58, *A* is 55 and *B* is 60.

(2) Subtracting 3 years from the claimant's age gives 39.

(3) Looking up age 39 in Table 6 (for retirement age 55) gives 13.08 at a rate of return of 2½%.

(4) Adding 2 years to the claimant's age gives 44.

(5) Looking up age 44 in Table 8 (for retirement age 60) gives 13.00 at a rate of return of 2½%.

(6) Calculating 2 x 13.08 + 3 x 13.00 and dividing by (60-58) + (58–55) [equals 5] gives 13.03 as the multiplier.

15. When the loss or expense to be valued is that from the date of retirement to death, and the claimant's date of retirement differs from that assumed in the tables, a different approach is necessary, involving the following three steps.

(1) Assume that there is a present loss which will continue for the rest of the claimant's life and from Table 1 or 2 establish the value of that loss or expense over the whole period from the date of assessment until the claimant's death.

(2) Establish the value of such loss or expense over the period from the date of assessment until the claimant's expected date of retirement following the procedure explained in paragraphs 13 and 14 above.

(3) Subtract the second figure from the first. The balance remaining represents the present value of the claimant's loss or expense between retirement and death.

16. If the claimant's actual retirement age would have been earlier than 50, or later than 75, the advice of an actuary should be sought.

Younger ages

17. Tables 1 and 2, which concern pecuniary loss for life, and Tables 15 to 26, which concern loss of pension from retirement age, have been extended down to age 0. In some circumstances the multiplier at age 0 is slightly lower than that at age 1; this arises because of the relatively high incidence of deaths immediately after birth.

18. Tables for multipliers for loss of earnings (Tables 3 to 14) have not been extended below age 16. In order to determine the multiplier for loss of earnings for someone who has not yet started work, it is first necessary to determine an assumed age at which the claimant would have commenced work and to find the appropriate multiplier for that age from Tables 3 to 14, according to the assumed retirement age. This multiplier should then be multiplied by the deferment factor from Table 27 which corresponds to the appropriate rate of return and the period from the date of the trial to the date on which it is assumed that the claimant would have started work. A similar approach can be used for determining a multiplier for pecuniary loss for life where the loss is assumed to commence a fixed period of years from the date of the trial. For simplicity the factors in Table 27 relate purely to the impact of compound interest and ignore mortality. At ages below 30 this is a reasonable approximation but at higher ages it would normally be appropriate to allow explicitly for mortality and the advice of an actuary should be sought.

Contingencies

19. Tables 1 to 26 make reasonable provision for the levels of mortality which members of the population of the United Kingdom alive today may expect to experience in future. The tables do not take account of the other risks and vicissitudes of life, such as the possibility that the claimant would for periods have ceased to earn due to ill-health or loss of employment. Nor do they take account of the fact that many people cease work for substantial periods to care for children or other dependants. Section B suggests ways in which allowance may be made to the multipliers for loss of earnings, to allow for certain risks other than mortality.

Impaired lives

20. In some cases, medical evidence may be available which asserts that a claimant's health impairments are equivalent to adding a certain number of years to their current age, or to treating the individual as having a specific age different

from their actual age. In such cases, Tables 1 and 2 can be used with respect to the deemed higher age. For the other tables the adjustment is not so straightforward, as adjusting the age will also affect the assumed retirement age, but the procedures described in paragraphs 13 to 15 may be followed, or the advice of an actuary should be sought. In other cases, the medical evidence may state that the claimant is likely to live for a stated number of years. This is often then treated as requiring payment to be made for a fixed period equal to the stated life expectancy and using Table 28 to ascertain the value of the multiplier. In general, this is likely to give a multiplier which is too high since this approach does not allow for the distribution of deaths around the expected length of life. For a group of similarly impaired lives of the same age, some will die before the average life expectancy and some after; allowing for this spread of deaths results in a lower multiplier than assuming payment for a term certain equal to the life expectancy. In such cases, it is preferable to look up the age in the 0% column in Table 1 or 2 for which the value of the multiplier at 0% is equal to the stated life expectancy. The relevant multipliers are then obtained from the relevant tables using this age. Take, for example, an impaired male life which is stated to have a life expectancy of 20 years. By interpolation, the age for which the multiplier in the 0% column in Table 1 is 20 is:

$$(20 - 19.66)/(20.50 - 19.66) \times 64 + (20.50 - 20)/(20.50 - 19.66) \times 65$$

which equals 64.6 years.

The value of the whole of life multiplier is then obtained from the 2.5% column of Table 1 for age 64.6 years:

$$(65 - 64.6) \times 15.37 + (64.6 - 64) \times 14.88$$

which equals 15.08 (compared to 15.78 for the value for a term certain of 20 years using the 2.5% column of Table 28).

Fixed periods

21. In cases where pecuniary loss is to be valued for a fixed period, the multipliers in Table 28 may be used. These make no allowance for mortality or any other contingency but assume that regular frequent payments (e.g. weekly or monthly) will continue throughout the period. These figures should in principle be adjusted if the periodicity of payment is less frequent, especially if the payments in question are annually in advance or in arrears.

Variable future losses or expenses

22. The tables do not provide an immediate answer when the annual future loss or expense is likely to change at given points in time in the future. The most common examples will be where:

(a) the claimant's lost earnings would have increased on a sliding scale or changed due to promotion; or

(b) the claimant's future care needs are likely to change in the future, perhaps because it is anticipated that a family carer will not be able to continue to provide help.

In such situations it is usually necessary to split the overall multiplier, whether for working life or whole of life, into segments, and then to apply those smaller segmented multipliers to the multiplicand appropriate for each period.

There are a variety of methods which could be used for splitting a multiplier, especially where the age at which a payment is increased or decreased, or stops or begins, is one which is tabulated in Tables 1 to 26. The following examples serve to illustrate how multipliers might be split using the "apportionment method". This method can be extended for use in cases where none of the ages at which payments change are tabulated.

Example 1 – Variable future earnings

23. The claimant is female, a graduate with a degree, aged 25 at date of settlement/trial. Her probable career progression, in the absence of injury, would have provided her with salary increases at ages 30, 35 and 40; thereafter she would have continued at the same level to age 60, when she would have stepped down from full-time work to work part-time until 70. Post accident she is now incapable of working.

The multiplicands for lost future earnings are:

Age 25 to 30:	£16,000 a year
Age 30 to 35:	£25,000 a year
Age 35 to 40:	£35,000 a year
Age 40 to 60:	£40,000 a year
Age 60 to 70:	£20,000 a year

The multipliers for each stage of her career are calculated as follows:

(1) The working life will be 45 years and the multiplier from Table 12 for that period taking into account mortality risks but without any discounts for any other contingencies will be 26.66.

(2) The multiplier for a term certain of 45 years (ignoring mortality risks) from Table 28 is 27.17.

(3) The multiplier from Table 28 should be split so that each individual segment of the whole working life period (45 years) is represented by a figure. So, the first 5 years is represented by a multiplier for a term certain of 5 years, namely 4.70; the next 5 years is represented by a multiplier of 4.16 (being the difference between the figure for a term certain of 10 years, namely 8.86 and the figure for a term certain of 5 years, namely 4.70); the next 5 years by 3.68 (i.e. the 15 year figure of 12.54 less the 10 year figure of 8.86); the next 20 years by 10.89 (i.e. the difference between the 35 year figure which is 23.43 and the 15 year figure of 12.54); then, the final 10 years by the balance of 3.74 (the residual figure being 27.17 less 23.43).

(4) Each of those smaller segmented multipliers can be shown as a percentage or fraction of the whole: so, for the first 5 years the segmented multiplier of 4.70 is 17.30% of the whole figure of 27.17, and so on for each segment of the 45 year period.

(5) The working life multiplier from Table 12 can now be split up in identical proportions to the way in which the Table 28 multiplier has been treated above: thus the first 5 year period is now represented by a multiplier of 4.61, which is calculated by taking 17.30% of 26.66. Each segmented multiplier is calculated in the same way.

(6) Having now obtained multipliers for each segment of working life, taking into account mortality risks, it is then necessary to discount those figures for "contingencies other than mortality". The discount factor from Table C (using the column for a female, not disabled, with degree level education) is 0.89. So, the figure of 4.61 for the first 5 year period now becomes 4.10 (i.e. 4.61 x 0.89). Again, treat each segmented multiplier in the same way.

(7) The multiplicand for each segment of working life is now multiplied by the appropriate segmented multiplier to calculate the loss for that period. The sum total of those losses represents the full sum for loss of future earnings (ignoring any mitigation).

(8) The figures are set out in tabular form below and give a total lump sum award of £714,500:

Ages	Period (years)	Table 28	% Split	Table 12	Discounted Multipliers (Table C) (x 0.89)	Net Annual Earnings £	£ Loss
25 – 30	5	4.70	17.30	4.61	4.10	16,000	65,600
30 – 35	5	4.16	15.31	4.08	3.63	25,000	90,750
35 – 40	5	3.68	13.54	3.61	3.21	35,000	112,350
40 – 60	20	10.89	40.08	10.69	9.51	40,000	380,400
60 – 70	10	3.74	13.77	3.67	3.27	20,000	65,400
Totals:	45 years	27.17	100.00	26.66	23.72		**714,500**

N.B. the figures in the above table have been rounded at each step of the calculation.

Example 2 – Variable future care costs

24. A male aged 20 years at the date of settlement/trial requires personal care support for life. He has a normal life expectation for his age. Significant changes in his care regime are anticipated at age 30 and again at age 50.

The multiplicands for care costs are:

Age 20 to 30:	£30,000 a year
Age 30 to 50:	£60,000 a year
Age 50 for rest of life:	£80,000 a year

The multipliers for each stage of the care regime are calculated as follows:

(1) The life expectation will be 64.87 years (from the 0% column of Table 1) and the multiplier for that period taking into account mortality risks (from Table 1) will be 31.63.

(2) The multiplier for a term certain of 64.87 years (ignoring mortality risks) from Table 28 lies between 32.16 (for 64 years) and 32.36 (for 65 years) and is calculated thus:

$$(65 - 64.87) \times 32.16 + (64.87 - 64) \times 32.36 = 32.33$$

(3) The multiplier from Table 28 should be split so that each individual segment of the whole period of life expectation is represented by a figure. So, the first 10 years (20-30) are represented by a multiplier of 8.86; the next 20 years (30-50) are represented by a multiplier of 12.33 (being the difference between the 30 year figure of 21.19 and the 10 year figure of 8.86); then, the final years (50 to death) are represented by the balance of 11.14 (being the difference between the term certain multiplier of 32.33 and the 30 year figure of 21.19).

(4) Each of those smaller segmented multipliers can be shown as a percentage or fraction of the whole: so, for the first 10 years the segmented multiplier of 8.86 is 27.40% of the whole figure of 32.33, and so on for each segment of the life period.

(5) The life multiplier from Table 1 can now be split up in the way in which the Table 28 multiplier was treated above and in identical proportions: thus the first 10 year period is now represented by a multiplier of 8.67 which is calculated by taking 27.40% of 31.63.

(6) The figures are set out in tabular form below and give a total lump sum award of £1,855,700:

Age (years)	Table 28 (64.87 years) Split multipliers	% Split (of Table 28 figure)	Table 1 (multiplier allowing for mortality)	Care costs £ a year	Total £
20 - 30	8.86	27.40	8.67	30,000	260,100
30 - 50	12.33	38.14	12.06	60,000	723,600
50 till death	11.14	34.46	10.90	80,000	872,000
Totals	32.33 (no mortality discount)	100.00%	31.63 life multiplier		**1,855,700**

N.B. the figures in the above table have been rounded at each step of the calculation.

Spouses' pensions

25. If doubt exists whether the tables are appropriate to a particular case which appears to present significant difficulties of substance, it would be prudent to take actuarial advice. This might be appropriate in relation to the level of spouses' benefits, if these are to be assessed, since these are not readily valued using Tables 1 to 26. As a rough rule of thumb, if spouses' benefits are to be included when valuing pension loss from normal pension age, the multipliers in tables 15 to 26 should be increased by 5% for a female claimant (i.e. benefits to the male spouse) and by 14% for a male claimant if the spouse's pension would be half of the pension that the member was receiving at death. If the spouse's pension would be payable at a rate of two-thirds the member's pension at death the multipliers should be increased by 7% for a female claimant and by 19% for a male claimant.

SECTION B: CONTINGENCIES OTHER THAN MORTALITY

26. As stated in paragraph 19, the tables for loss of earnings (Tables 3 to 14) take no account of risks other than mortality. This section shows how the multipliers in these tables may be reduced to take account of these risks.

27. Tables of factors to be applied to the existing multipliers were first introduced in the Second Edition of the Ogden Tables. These factors were based on work commissioned by the Institute of Actuaries and carried out by Professor S Haberman and Mrs D S F Bloomfield (*Work time lost to sickness, unemployment and stoppages: measurement and application* (1990), Journal of the Institute of Actuaries 117, 533-595). Although there was some debate within the actuarial profession about the details of the work, and in particular about the scope for developing it further, the findings were broadly accepted and were adopted by the Government Actuary and the other actuaries who were members of the Working Party when the Second Edition of the Tables was published and have remained unchanged in later editions.

28. Some related work has more recently been published by Lewis, McNabb and Wass (*Methods of calculating damages for loss of future earnings*, Journal of Personal Injury Law, 2002 Number 2). Since the publication of the Fifth Edition of the Ogden Tables, the Ogden Working Party has been involved in further research into the impact of contingencies other than mortality carried out by Professor Richard Verrall, Professor Steven Haberman and Mr Zoltan Butt of City University, London and, in a separate exercise, by Dr Victoria Wass of Cardiff University. Their findings have been combined to produce the tables of factors given in this section.

29. The Haberman and Bloomfield paper relied on data from the Labour Force Surveys for 1973, 1977, 1981 and 1985 and English Life Tables No. 14 (1980-82). The Labour Force Survey (LFS) was originally designed to produce a periodic cross-sectional snapshot of the working age population and collects information on an extensive range of socio-economic and labour force characteristics. Since the winter of 1992/3, the LFS has been carried out on a quarterly basis, with respondents being included in the survey over 5 successive quarters. The research of Professor Verrall *et al* and Dr Wass has used data from the Labour Force Surveys conducted from 1998 to 2003 to estimate the probabilities of movement of males and females between different states of economic activity, dependent on age, sex, employment activity and level of disability. These probabilities permit the calculation of the expected periods in employment until retirement age, dependent on the initial starting state of economic activity, disability and educational attainment. These can then be discounted at the same discount rate that is used for obtaining the relevant multiplier from Tables 3 to 14, in order to give a multiplier which takes into account only those periods the claimant would be expected, on average, to be in work. These discounted working life expectancy multipliers can be compared to those obtained assuming the person remained in work throughout, to obtain reduction factors which give the expected proportion of time to retirement age which will be spent in employment.

30. The factors described in subsequent paragraphs are for use in calculating loss of earnings up to retirement age. The research work did not investigate the impact of contingencies other than mortality on the value of future pension rights. Some reduction to the multiplier for loss of pension would often be appropriate when a reduction is being applied for loss of earnings. This may be a smaller reduction than in the case of loss of earnings because the ill-health contingency (as opposed to the unemployment contingency) may give rise to significant ill-health retirement pension rights. A bigger reduction may be necessary in cases where there is significant doubt whether pension rights would have continued to accrue (to the extent not already allowed for in the post-retirement multiplier) or in cases where there may be doubt over the ability of the pension fund to pay promised benefits. In the case of a defined contribution pension scheme, loss of pension rights may be allowed for simply by increasing the future earnings loss (adjusted for contingencies other than mortality) by the percentage of earnings which the employer contributions to the scheme represent.

31. The methodology proposed in paragraphs 33 to 42 describes one method for dealing with contingencies other than mortality, which replaces that set out in earlier editions of the Ogden Tables. If this methodology is followed, in many cases it will be appropriate to increase or reduce the discount in the tables to take account of the nature of a particular claimant's disabilities. It should be noted that the methodology does not take into account the pre-accident employment history. The methodology also provides for the possibility of valuing more appropriately the possible mitigation of loss of earnings in cases where the claimant is employed after the accident or is considered capable of being employed. This will in many cases enable a more accurate assessment to be made of the mitigation of loss. However, there may be some cases when the *Smith v. Manchester Corporation* or *Blamire* approach remains applicable or otherwise where a precise mathematical approach is inapplicable.

32. The suggestions which follow are intended as a 'ready reckoner' which provides an initial adjustment to the multipliers according to the employment status, disability status and educational attainment of the claimant when calculating awards for loss of earnings and for any mitigation of this loss in respect of potential future post-injury earnings. Such a ready reckoner cannot take into account all circumstances and it may be appropriate to argue for higher or lower adjustments in particular cases. In particular, it can be difficult to place a value on the possible mitigating income when considering the potential range of disabilities and their effect on post-injury work capability, even within the interpretation of disability set out in paragraph 35. However, the methodology does offer a framework for consideration of a range of possible figures with the maximum being effectively provided by the post-injury multiplier assuming the

claimant was not disabled and the minimum being the case where there is no realistic prospect of post-injury employment.

The deduction for contingencies other than mortality

33. Under the proposed new method, multipliers for loss of earnings obtained from Tables 3 to 14 are multiplied by factors to allow for the risk of periods of non-employment and absence from the workforce because of sickness.

34. The new research by Professor Verrall *et al* and Dr Wass referred to in paragraphs 28 and 29 demonstrated that the key issues affecting a person's future working life are employment status, disability status and educational attainment.

35. The definitions of employed/not employed, disabled/not disabled and educational attainment used in this analysis and which should be used for determining which factors to apply to the multipliers to allow for contingencies other than mortality are as follows:

Employed	Those who at the time of the accident are employed, self-employed or on a government training scheme.
Not employed	All others (including those temporarily out of work, full-time students and unpaid family workers).
Disabled	A person is classified as being disabled if all three of the following conditions in relation to the ill-health or disability are met: (i) has either a progressive illness or an illness which has lasted or is expected to last for over a year, (ii) satisfies the Disability Discrimination Act definition that the impact of the disability substantially limits the person's ability to carry out normal day-to-day activities **and** their condition affects either the kind **or** the amount of paid work they can do.
Not disabled	All others.

Normal day-to-day activities are those which are carried out by most people on a daily basis, and we are interested in disabilities/health problems which have a substantial adverse effect on the respondent's ability to carry out these activities.

There are several ways in which a disability or health problem may affect the respondent's day-to-day activities:

Mobility - for example, unable to travel short journeys as a passenger in a car, unable to walk other than at a slow pace or with jerky movements, difficulty in negotiating stairs, unable to use one or more forms of public transport, unable to go out of doors unaccompanied.

Manual dexterity - for example, loss of functioning in one or both hands, inability to use a knife or fork at the same time, or difficulty in pressing buttons on a keyboard.

Physical co-ordination - for example, the inability to feed or dress oneself, or to pour liquid from one vessel to another except with unusual slowness or concentration.

Problems with bowel/bladder control - for example, frequent or regular loss of control of the bladder or bowel. Occasional bedwetting is not considered a disability.

Ability to lift, carry or otherwise move everyday objects (for example, books, kettles, light furniture) - for example, inability to pick up a weight with one hand but not the other, or to carry a tray steadily.

Speech - for example, unable to communicate (clearly) orally with others, taking significantly longer to say things. A minor stutter, difficulty in speaking in front of an audience, or inability to speak a foreign language would not be considered impairments.

Hearing - for example, not being able to hear without the use of a hearing aid, the inability to understand speech under normal conditions or over the telephone.

Eyesight - for example, while wearing spectacles or contact lenses - being unable to pass the standard driving eyesight test, total inability to distinguish colours (excluding ordinary red/green colour blindness), or inability to read newsprint.

Memory or ability to concentrate, learn or understand - for example, intermittent loss of consciousness or confused behaviour, inability to remember names of family or friends, unable to write a cheque without assistance, or an inability to follow a recipe.

Perception of risk of physical danger - for example, reckless behaviour putting oneself or others at risk, mobility to cross the road safely. This excludes (significant) fear of heights or underestimating risk of dangerous hobbies.

Three levels of educational attainment are defined for the purposes of the tables as follows:

D Degree or equivalent or higher.

GE-A GCSE grades A to C up to A levels or equivalents.

O Below GCSE grade C or CSE grade 1 or equivalent or no qualifications.

The following table gives a more detailed breakdown of the allocation of various types of educational qualification to each of the three categories above and are based on the allocations used in the research by Professor Verrall *et al* and Dr Wass.

Categories of highest educational attainment

D **Degree or equivalent or higher**	**GE-A** **GCSE grades A to C up to A levels or equivalent**	**O** **Below GCSE grade C or CSE grade 1 or equivalent or no qualifications**
Any degree (first or higher) Other higher education qualification below degree level Diploma in higher education	A or AS level or equivalent O level, GCSE grade A-C or equivalent	CSE below grade 1 GCSE below grade C
NVQ level 4 or 5	NVQ level 2 or 3	NVQ level 1 or equivalent
HNC/HND, BTEC higher, etc	BTEC/SCOTVEC first or general diploma OND/ONC, BTEC/SCOTVEC national	BTEC first or general certificate SCOTVEC modules or equivalent
RSA higher diploma	RSA diploma, advanced diploma or certificate	RSA other
Teaching Nursing, etc	GNVQ intermediate or advanced	GNVQ/GVSQ foundation level
	City and Guilds craft or advanced craft	City and Guilds other
	SCE higher or equivalent Trade apprenticeship Scottish 6th year certificate (CSYS)	YT/ YTP certificate Other qualifications No qualification Don't know

Note: "educational attainment" is used here as a proxy for skill level, so that those in professional occupations such as law, accountancy, nursing, etc who do not have a degree ought to be treated as if they do have one.

36. The research also considered the extent to which a person's future working life expectancy is affected by individual circumstances such as occupation and industrial sector, geographical region and education. The researchers concluded that the most significant consideration was the highest level of education achieved by the claimant and that, if this was allowed for, the effect of the other factors was relatively small. As a result, the Working Party decided to propose adjustment factors which allow for employment status, disability status and educational attainment only. This is a change

from previous editions of the Ogden Tables where adjustments were made for types of occupation and for geographical region.

37. A separate assessment is made for (a) the value of earnings the claimant would have received if the injury had not been suffered and (b) the value of the claimant's earnings (if any) taking account of the injuries sustained. The risk of non-employment is significantly higher post-injury due to the impairment. The loss is arrived at by deducting (b) from (a).

38. In order to calculate the value of the earnings the claimant would have received if the injury had not been suffered, the claimant's employment status and the disability status need to be determined as at the date of the accident (or the onset of the medical condition) giving rise to the claim, so that the correct table can be applied. For the calculation of future loss of earnings (based on actual pre-accident earnings and also future employment prospects), Tables A and C should be used for claimants who were not disabled at the time of the accident, and Tables B and D should be used for those with a pre-existing disability. In all of these tables the three left-hand columns are for those who were employed at the time of the accident and the three right-hand columns are for those who were not.

39. In order to calculate the value of the actual earnings that a claimant is likely to receive in the future (i.e. after settlement or trial), the employment status and the disability status need to be determined as at the date of settlement or trial. For claimants with a work-affecting disability at that point in time, Tables B and D should be used. The three left-hand columns will apply in respect of claimants actually in employment at date of settlement or trial and the three right-hand columns will apply in respect of those who remain non-employed at that point in time.

40. The factors in Tables A to D allow for the interruption of employment for bringing up children and caring for other dependants.

41. In the case of those aged under 16 at the date of the accident, the relevant factor from the tables would be chosen on the basis of the level of education the child would have been expected to have attained, had the injury not occurred, together with an assessment as to whether the child would have become employed or not. The relevant factor for age 16 would be chosen using the assessed employment status and educational status likely to be ultimately attained, discounted by the appropriate factor from Table 27 for the number of years from the age at the date of trial to age 16.

42. Tables A to D include factors up to age 54 only. For older ages the reduction factors increase towards 1 at retirement age for those who are employed and fall towards 0 for those who are not employed. However, where the claimant is older than 54, it is anticipated that the likely future course of employment status will be particularly dependent on individual circumstances, so that the use of factors based on averages would not be appropriate. Hence reduction factors are not provided for these older ages.

Table A
Loss of Earnings to Pension Age 65 (Males – Not disabled)

Age at date of trial	Employed D	Employed GE-A	Employed O	Not employed D	Not employed GE-A	Not employed O
16-19	0.90	0.90	0.85	0.85	0.85	0.82
20-24	0.92	0.92	0.87	0.89	0.88	0.83
25-29	0.93	0.92	0.89	0.89	0.88	0.82
30-34	0.92	0.91	0.89	0.87	0.86	0.81
35-39	0.90	0.90	0.89	0.85	0.84	0.80
40-44	0.88	0.88	0.88	0.82	0.81	0.78
45-49	0.86	0.86	0.86	0.77	0.77	0.74
50	0.83	0.83	0.83	0.72	0.72	0.70
51	0.82	0.82	0.82	0.70	0.70	0.68
52	0.81	0.81	0.81	0.67	0.67	0.66
53	0.80	0.80	0.80	0.63	0.63	0.63
54	0.79	0.79	0.79	0.59	0.59	0.59

Table B
Loss of Earnings to Pension Age 65 (Males – Disabled)

Age at date of trial	Employed			Not employed		
	D	GE-A	O	D	GE-A	O
16-19	0.61	0.55	0.32	0.61	0.49	0.25
20-24	0.61	0.55	0.38	0.53	0.46	0.24
25-29	0.60	0.54	0.42	0.48	0.41	0.24
30-34	0.59	0.52	0.40	0.43	0.34	0.23
35-39	0.58	0.48	0.39	0.38	0.28	0.20
40-44	0.57	0.48	0.39	0.33	0.23	0.15
45-49	0.55	0.48	0.39	0.26	0.20	0.11
50	0.53	0.49	0.40	0.24	0.18	0.10
51	0.53	0.49	0.41	0.23	0.17	0.09
52	0.54	0.49	0.41	0.22	0.16	0.08
53	0.54	0.49	0.42	0.21	0.15	0.07
54	0.54	0.50	0.43	0.20	0.14	0.06

Table C
Loss of Earnings to Pension Age 60 (Females – Not disabled)

Age at date of trial	Employed			Not employed		
	D	GE-A	O	D	GE-A	O
16-19	0.87	0.81	0.64	0.84	0.77	0.59
20-24	0.89	0.82	0.68	0.84	0.76	0.60
25-29	0.89	0.84	0.72	0.83	0.75	0.61
30-34	0.89	0.85	0.75	0.81	0.75	0.63
35-39	0.89	0.86	0.78	0.80	0.74	0.63
40-44	0.89	0.86	0.80	0.78	0.72	0.60
45-49	0.87	0.85	0.81	0.72	0.64	0.52
50	0.86	0.84	0.81	0.64	0.55	0.43
51	0.85	0.84	0.81	0.60	0.51	0.40
52	0.84	0.84	0.81	0.56	0.46	0.36
53	0.83	0.83	0.81	0.50	0.41	0.32
54	0.83	0.83	0.82	0.44	0.35	0.27

Table D
Loss of Earnings to Pension Age 60 (Females – Disabled)

Age at date of trial	Employed D	Employed GE-A	Employed O	Not employed D	Not employed GE-A	Not employed O
16-19	0.65	0.43	0.25	0.58	0.35	0.19
20-24	0.64	0.44	0.25	0.58	0.33	0.17
25-29	0.63	0.45	0.25	0.50	0.32	0.16
30-34	0.62	0.46	0.30	0.44	0.31	0.15
35-39	0.61	0.48	0.34	0.42	0.28	0.14
40-44	0.60	0.51	0.38	0.38	0.23	0.13
45-49	0.60	0.54	0.42	0.28	0.18	0.11
50	0.60	0.56	0.47	0.23	0.15	0.10
51	0.61	0.58	0.49	0.21	0.14	0.09
52	0.61	0.60	0.51	0.20	0.13	0.08
53	0.62	0.62	0.54	0.18	0.11	0.07
54	0.63	0.66	0.57	0.16	0.09	0.06

Different pension ages

43. The factors in the preceding tables assume retirement at age 65 for males and age 60 for females. It is not possible to calculate expected working life times assuming alternative retirement ages from the LFS data, since the employment data in the LFS are collected only for the working population, assumed aged between 16 and 64 for males and between 16 and 59 for females. Where the retirement age is different from age 65 for males or age 60 for females, it is suggested that this should be ignored and the reduction factor and the adjustments thereto be taken from the above tables for the age of the claimant as at the date of trial with no adjustment, i.e. assume that the retirement age is age 65 for males and age 60 for females. However, if the retirement age is close to the age at the date of trial, then it may be more appropriate to take into account the circumstances of the individual case.

44. It should be noted that the reduction factors in Tables A, B, C and D are based on data for the period 1998 to 2003. Whilst the reduction factors and adjustments allow for the age-specific probabilities of moving into, or out of, employment over future working life time, based on data for the period 1998-2003, the methodology assumes that these probabilities remain constant over time; there is no allowance for changes in these age-specific probabilities beyond this period. It is also assumed that there will be no change in disability status or educational achievement after the date of the accident. Future changes in the probabilities of moving into, and out of, employment are especially difficult to predict with any certainty. It is the intention that the factors should be reassessed from time to time as new data become available.

SECTION C: SUMMARY OF PERSONAL INJURY APPLICATIONS

45. To use the tables the guidance below should be followed:

(1) Choose the table relating to the appropriate sex of the claimant and period of loss or expense (e.g. loss for life, or loss of earnings to a set retirement age). Where loss of earnings is concerned, and none of the tables is relevant because the claimant's expected age of retirement differs from that assumed in the tables, the procedure in paragraphs 13 to 16 of the Explanatory Notes should be followed.

(2) Choose the appropriate discount column (currently 2½%).

(3) In that column find the appropriate figure for the claimant's age at trial ("the basic multiplier").

Loss of earnings

(4) When calculating **loss of earnings**, the tables should be used when a multiplier/multiplicand approach is appropriate. If it is, the basic multiplier should be adjusted to take account of contingencies other than mortality. These contingencies include the claimant's employment and disability status and educational

qualifications. The basic multiplier should be multiplied by the appropriate figure taken from Tables A to D. It may be necessary at this stage to modify the resulting figure further to allow for circumstances specific to the claimant.

This process gives "the adjusted table multiplier".

(5) Multiply the net annual loss (the multiplicand) by the adjusted table multiplier to arrive at a figure which represents the capitalised value of the future loss of earnings.

(6) If the claimant has a residual earning capacity, allowance should be made for any post-accident vulnerability on the labour market: the following paragraphs show one way of doing this, although there may still be cases where a conventional *Smith v. Manchester Corporation* award is appropriate.

Where it is appropriate to do so, repeat steps 1 to 5 above, replacing the pre-accident employment and disability status with the post-accident employment and disability status in step 4 and replacing the net annual loss by the assumed new level of net earnings at step 5. It will only be necessary to reconsider the claimant's educational attainments if these have changed between the accident and the date of trial or settlement.

The result will represent the capitalised value of the claimant's likely post-accident earnings. It is important to note that, when carrying out this exercise, the *degree* of residual disability may have a different effect on residual earnings depending on its relevance to the claimant's likely field of work. For example, the loss of a leg may have less effect on a sedentary worker's earnings than on a manual worker's.

(7) Deduct the sum yielded by step 6 from that yielded by step 5 to obtain the net amount of loss of earnings allowing for residual earning capacity. Where the above methodology is used there will usually be no need for a separate *Smith v. Manchester Corporation* award.

Lifetime losses

(8) Where a **loss** will continue **for life**, follow steps 1 to 3 above to find the appropriate multiplier in the table.

Where the normal life expectancy given by the table is inapplicable the approach set out in paragraph 20, using the lifetime tables rather than Table 28, is the correct approach.

(9) This figure may need adjustment to allow for the particular circumstances of the claimant.

(10) Multiply the annual loss or expense by the multiplier as adjusted.

Variable annual losses

(11) In cases where there will be different losses at different periods it may be necessary to split the multiplier. The approach set out at paragraphs 22 to 24 should be followed.

Fixed period and Deferred losses

(12) Where a loss will continue over a fixed period, the appropriate multiplier can be found in Table 28.

(13) Where a loss will not commence until some future date, multiply the appropriate multiplier by a discount figure taken from Table 27 (the use of which is explained in paragraph 18). This paragraph does not apply to loss of pensions, which have their own tables.

46. The following are examples of the use of the tables in illustrative personal injury cases with simplified assumptions.

Example 3

47. The claimant is female, aged 35 at the date of the trial. She has three A levels, but not a degree, and was in employment at the date of the accident at a salary of £25,000 a year net of tax. She was not disabled before the accident. As a result of her injuries, she is now disabled and has lost her job but has found part-time employment at a salary of £5,000 a year net of tax. Her loss of earnings to retirement age of 60 is assessed as follows:

(1) Look up Table 8 for loss of earnings to pension age 60 for females.

(2) The appropriate rate of return is determined to be 2½% (the rate currently set under Section 1 of the Damages Act 1996).

(3) Table 8 shows that, on the basis of a 2½% rate of return, the multiplier for a female aged 35 is 18.39.

(4) Now take account of risks other than mortality. Allowing for the claimant being employed, not disabled and having achieved A levels at the date of trial, Table C would require 18.39 to be multiplied by 0.86, resulting in a revised multiplier of 15.82.

(5) The damages for loss of earnings are assessed as £395,500 (15.82 x £25,000).

(6) Allow for mitigation of loss of earnings in respect of post-injury earnings. As before, Table 8 shows that, on the basis of a 2½% rate of return, the multiplier for a female aged 35 is 18.39.

(7) Now take account of risks other than mortality. Allowing for the claimant being employed, disabled and having achieved A levels at the date of trial, Table D would require 18.39 to be multiplied by 0.48, resulting in a revised multiplier of 8.83.

(8) The amount of mitigation for post-injury earnings is assessed as £44,150 (8.83 x £5,000).

(9) Hence award for loss of earnings after allowing for mitigation is
£395,500 – £44,150 = £351,350.

Example 4

48 The claimant is male, aged 48 at the date of the trial. He has no educational qualifications. His retirement age was 65, he was employed at the time of the accident and his pre-retirement multiplicand has been determined as £20,000 a year net of tax. He was not disabled before the accident. As a result of his injuries, he is now disabled and has lost his job. The multiplicand for costs of care is deemed to be £50,000 a year. He is unemployed at the date of trial but has been assessed as capable of finding work with possible future earnings of £5,000 a year net of tax. His loss of earnings to retirement age of 65 is assessed as follows:

(1) Look up Table 9 for loss of earnings to pension age 65 for males.

(2) The appropriate rate of return is determined to be 2½% (the rate currently set under Section 1 of the Damages Act 1996).

(3) Table 9 shows that, on the basis of a 2½% rate of return, the multiplier for a male aged 48 is 13.35.

(4) Now take account of risks other than mortality. Allowing for the claimant being employed, not disabled and having no educational qualifications at the date of trial, Table A would require 13.35 to be multiplied by 0.86, resulting in a revised multiplier of 11.48.

(5) The damages for loss of earnings are assessed as £229,600 (11.48 x £20,000).

(6) Allow for mitigation of loss of earnings in respect of post-injury earnings. As before, Table 9 shows that, on the basis of a 2½% rate of return, the multiplier for a male aged 48 is 13.35.

(7) Now take account of risks other than mortality. Allowing for the claimant being unemployed and disabled with no educational qualifications at the date of trial, Table B would require 13.35 to be multiplied by 0.11, resulting in a revised multiplier of 1.47.

(8) The amount of mitigation for post-injury earnings is assessed as £7,350 (1.47 x £5,000).

(9) Hence award for loss of earnings after allowing for mitigation is
£229,600 – £7,350 = £222,250.

49. The damages for cost of care are assessed as follows:

(1) Look up Table 1 for the multiplier at age 48.

(2) The appropriate rate of return is 2½%.

(3) Table 1 shows that, on the basis of a 2½% rate of return, the multiplier at age 48 is 22.68.

(4) No adjustment is made for risks other than mortality.

(5) The damages for cost of care are assessed at £1,134,000 (22.68 x £50,000).

Example 5

50. The claimant is female, aged 14 at the date of the trial. She is expected to achieve a degree and to be in employment thereafter on a salary, in current terms, of £30,000 a year net of tax. She was not disabled before the accident. As a result of her injuries, she is now disabled – she is still expected to achieve a degree and to be in employment, but with an average salary in current terms of £20,000 net of tax. Her loss of earnings to retirement age of 60 is assessed as follows:

(1) Look up Table 8 for loss of earnings to pension age 60 for females.

(2) The appropriate rate of return is determined to be 2½% (the rate currently set under Section 1 of the Damages Act 1996).

(3) Table 8 shows that, on the basis of a 2½% rate of return, the multiplier for a female aged 16 is 26.60. This needs to be discounted back to age 14. The factor at 2½% for a period for deferment for 2 years is 0.9518 from Table 27, giving a total multiplier of 26.60 x 0.9518 = 25.32.

(4) Now take account of risks other than mortality. Allowing for the claimant assessed as achieving a degree, being employed and not disabled, Table C would require 25.32 to be multiplied by 0.87, resulting in a revised multiplier of 22.03.

(5) The damages for loss of earnings are assessed as £660,900 (22.03 x £30,000).

(6) Allow for mitigation of loss of earnings in respect of post-injury earnings. As before, Table 8 shows that, on the basis of a 2½% rate of return, the multiplier for a female aged 16 is 26.60. As before, after discounting for two years to age 14 the multiplier is reduced to 26.60 x 0.9518 = 25.32.

(7) Now take account of risks other than mortality. Allowing for the claimant assessed as achieving a degree, being employed and disabled, Table D would require 25.32 to be multiplied by 0.65, resulting in a revised multiplier of 16.46.

(8) The amount of mitigation for post-injury earnings is assessed as £329,200 (16.46 x £20,000).

(9) Hence award for loss of earnings after allowing for mitigation is £660,900 – £329,200 = £331,700.

Example 6

51. The claimant is male, aged 40 at the date of the trial. He has achieved O levels. He was unemployed at the time of the accident. His potential pre-retirement multiplicand has been determined as £15,000 a year net of tax. He was disabled before the accident. As a result of his injuries, he has been assessed as having no future prospect of employment. His loss of earnings to retirement age of 65 is assessed as follows:

(1) Look up Table 9 for loss of earnings to pension age 65 for males.

(2) The appropriate rate of return is determined to be 2½% (the rate currently set under Section 1 of the Damages Act 1996).

(3) Table 9 shows that, on the basis of a 2½% rate of return, the multiplier for a male aged 40 is 18.01.

(4) Now take account of risks other than mortality. Allowing for the claimant being unemployed, disabled and having achieved O levels at the date of trial, Table B would require 18.01 to be multiplied by 0.23, resulting in a revised multiplier of 4.14.

(5) The damages for loss of earnings are assessed as £62,100 (4.14 x £15,000).

(6) As the claimant has been assessed as having no future prospect of employment following the accident, there is no mitigation of loss of earnings in respect of post-injury earnings.

(7) Hence award for loss of earnings after allowing for mitigation is £62,100.

SECTION D: APPLICATION OF TABLES TO FATAL ACCIDENT CASES

52. The approach of the courts is to assess the multiplier as at the date of death (**Cookson v. Knowles (1979) AC 556**).

53. That approach was criticised by the Law Commission in their Report 263 (*Claims for Wrongful Death*). The Law Commission recommended that multipliers should be assessed as at the date of trial and that the multipliers derived from the Ogden Tables should only take effect from the date of trial.

54. The Working Party, then under the Chairmanship of the late Sir Michael Ogden QC, considered that the Law Commission's criticism was valid. In the Fourth Edition of the Tables published in August 2000, the Working Party set out guidance in Section D of the Explanatory Notes on how damages should be calculated in such cases. That guidance was repeated in Section D of the Explanatory Notes to the Fifth Edition published in November 2004.

55. However the courts have considered themselves bound by **Cookson v. Knowles** and hence have not followed the guidance offered (**White v. Esab (2002) PIQR Q6** and **H v. S (2003) QB 965**).

56. The current approach also incorporates some actuarial flaws; in particular, it incorporates a discount for early receipt in the period prior to trial or assessment. Accordingly in these Notes, firstly we set out the current approach of the courts and secondly we repeat the suggestions for change already contained in the Fourth and Fifth Editions. An example is then provided which has been calculated using the current approach and also the two approaches set out in the Fifth Edition of the Ogden Tables.

Current law

57. Under the Fatal Accidents Act the loss is that of the dependants, i.e. those who relied upon the deceased for support. They may claim that part of the deceased's income (whether earnings, pension, unearned income or state benefits) that the deceased would have spent on them. They may also claim the loss of the services such as DIY, domestic/household or childcare which the deceased would have undertaken and from which they would have benefited. The position of each dependant must be considered separately.

58. Each head of dependency must be considered separately. For each head of claim for each dependant the court calculates a multiplicand. This is calculated on the basis of what is known at the date of trial. For pre-trial losses, the actual loss to date of trial is calculated. Interest is added. For post-trial losses the multiplicand is calculated as at the date of trial.

59. A multiplier for the period of dependency is applied to the multiplicand to arrive at an overall lump sum for each head of dependency.

Approach currently usually adopted by the courts

60. Under the approach currently usually followed by the courts, the multiplier is calculated as at the date of death. However, when making that calculation the court is entitled to take into account matters that have arisen between death and trial. For example, **Williamson v. Thorneycroft (1940) 2 KB 658** in which the deceased's widow died after her husband but before trial. Her dependency terminated at her death. See also **Corbett v. Barking, Havering & Brentwood HA (1991) 2 QB 408**.

61. There are two periods to be determined:

(i) The expected period from date of death in which the deceased would have been capable of providing the dependency;

(ii) The expected period from the date of the death in which the dependant would have been able to receive the dependency.

The shorter of those two periods provides the basis for the multiplier.

62. In respect of each of those periods consideration must be given as to what discount should be made for contingencies other than mortality. The most obvious contingencies other than mortality fall into the following three categories:

(i) Factors relating to the deceased. For example, the deceased's health may have been such as to seriously affect his ability to provide services or work until retirement age. In relation to earnings the starting point for the adjustment factor should be the figures contained in Tables A to D.

(ii) Factors relating to the dependant. For example, at trial it may be proved that a dependant has a significantly reduced life expectancy.

(iii) Factors relating to the relationship of the deceased and the dependant. For example, an unmarried couple who were on the point of separation before the deceased died. See also section 3(4) of the Act and **Drew v. Abassi**, Court of Appeal 24 May 1995.

63. The assessment of the multiplier involves the following steps:

(1) Determine the expected period from the date of death for which the deceased would have been capable of providing the dependency.

(2) Discount that period for early receipt using the appropriate table as at the date of death and a discount rate of 2.5%.

(3) Apply any adjustment to the above figure to reflect contingencies other than mortality.

(4) Determine the expected period from date of death for which the dependant would have been able to receive the dependency.

(5) Discount that period for early receipt using the appropriate table as at the date of death at a discount rate of 2.5%.

(6) Apply any adjustment to the figure in (5) to reflect contingencies other than mortality.

(7) Take the lower of the figures in (3) and (6) above. That is the overall multiplier from date of death.

(8) Subtract the period elapsed from date of death to date of trial. Losses in this period will be treated as in effect special damages and will attract an award of interest.

(9) The balance of the multiplier will be the multiplier for the post-trial multiplicand.

Approach based on calculations as at date of trial

64. Whereas in personal injury cases the problem to be solved is that of setting a value on an income stream during the potential life of one person (the claimant), the situation is generally more complicated in fatal accident cases. Here the compensation is intended to reflect the value of an income stream during the lifetime of one or more dependants of the deceased (or the expected period for which the dependants would have expected to receive the dependency, if shorter) but limited according to the expectation of how long the deceased would have been able to provide the financial support, had he or she not been involved in the fatal accident.

65. In principle, therefore, the compensation for post-trial dependency should be based on the present value at the date of the trial of the dependency during the expected future joint lifetime of the deceased and the dependant or claimant (had the deceased survived naturally to the date of the trial), subject to any limitations on the period of dependency and any expected future changes in the level of dependency, for example, on attaining retirement age. In addition there should be compensation for the period between the date of accident and the date of trial.

66. A set of actuarial tables to make such calculations accurately would require tables similar to Tables 1 to 26 but for each combination of ages as at the date of the trial of the deceased and the dependant to whom compensation is to be paid. The Working Party concluded that this would not meet the criterion of simplicity of application which was a central objective of these tables and recommends that, in complex cases, or cases where the accuracy of the multiplier is thought by the parties to be of critical importance and material to the resulting amount of compensation (for example in cases potentially involving very large claims where the level of the multiplicand is unambiguously established), the advice of a professionally qualified actuary should be sought. However, for the majority of cases, a certain amount of approximation will be appropriate, bearing in mind the need for a simple and streamlined process, and taking into consideration the other uncertainties in the determination of an appropriate level of compensation. The following paragraphs describe a methodology using Tables 1 to 26 which can be expected to yield satisfactory answers.

Damages for the period from the fatal accident to the date of trial

67. The period of pre-trial dependency will normally be equal to the period between the date of the fatal accident and the date of the trial, substituting where appropriate the lower figure of the expected period for which the deceased would have provided the dependency, had he or she not been killed in the accident, or if the period of dependency would have been limited in some way, for example if the dependant is a child.

68. A deduction may be made for the risk that the deceased might have died anyway, in the period between the date of the fatal accident and the date at which the trial takes place. In many cases this deduction will be small and could usually be regarded as *de minimis*. The need for a deduction becomes more necessary the longer the period from the date of accident to the date of trial and the older the deceased at the date of death. As an illustration of the order of magnitude of the deduction, Table E shows some examples of factors by which the multiplier should be multiplied for different ages of the deceased and for different periods from the date of accident to the date of the trial.

Table E
Factor by which pre-trial damages should be multiplied to allow for the likelihood that the deceased would not in any case have survived to provide the dependency for the full period to the date of trial

Age of deceased at date of accident	Period from date of accident to date of trial or date of cessation of dependency, if earlier (years)					
	Male deceased			Female deceased		
	3	6	9	3	6	9
10	1.00	1.00	1.00	1.00	1.00	1.00
20	1.00	1.00	1.00	1.00	1.00	1.00
30	1.00	1.00	0.99	1.00	1.00	1.00
40	1.00	0.99	0.99	1.00	1.00	0.99
50	0.99	0.99	0.98	1.00	0.99	0.99
60	0.98	0.96	0.94	0.99	0.98	0.96
65	0.98	0.94	0.90	0.99	0.96	0.94
70	0.96	0.91	0.84	0.98	0.94	0.89
75	0.93	0.85	0.75	0.95	0.90	0.83
80	0.89	0.77	0.64	0.92	0.83	0.73

N.B. The factor for a period of zero years is clearly 1.00. Factors for other ages and periods not shown in the table may be obtained approximately by interpolation.

69. The resultant multiplier, after application of any discount for the possibility of early death of the deceased before the date of trial, even had the accident not taken place, is to be applied to the multiplicand, which is determined in the usual way. Interest will then be added up to the date of trial on the basis of special damages.

Damages from the date of trial to retirement age

70. The assessment of the multiplier involves the following steps:

(1) Determine the expected period from the date of the trial for which the deceased would have been able to provide the dependency (see paragraph 71).

(2) Determine the expected period for which the dependant would have been able to receive the dependency (see paragraph 71).

(3) Take the lesser of the two periods.

(4) Treat the resulting period as a term certain for which the multiplier is to be determined and look up the figure in Table 28 for this period at the appropriate rate of interest.

(5) Apply any adjustment for contingencies other than mortality in accordance with Section B.

(6) If necessary, make an allowance for the risk that the deceased might have died anyway before the date of the trial (see paragraph 68).

71. The expected periods at (1) and (2) of paragraph 70 may be obtained from the 0% column of the appropriate table at the back of this booklet. For (1), Tables 3 to 14 will be relevant, according to the sex of the deceased and the expected age of retirement. The age at which the table should be entered is the age which the deceased would have been at the date

of the trial. For (2) Tables 1 and 2 can be used, according to the sex of the dependant and looking up the table at the age of the dependant at the date of the trial.

72. If the period for which the dependency would have continued is a short fixed period, as in the case of a child, the figure at (2) would be the outstanding period at the date of the trial.

73. A deduction may be made for the risk that the deceased might have died anyway before the date of trial. The need for such a deduction becomes more necessary the longer the period from the date of accident to the date of trial and the older the deceased at the date of death. As an illustration of the order of magnitude of the deduction, Table F shows some examples of the factor by which the multiplier, determined as above, should be multiplied for different ages of the deceased and for different periods from the date of accident to the date of the trial.

Table F

Factor by which post-trial damages should be multiplied to allow for the likelihood that the deceased would not in any case have survived to the date of trial in order to provide any post-trial dependency

Age of deceased at date of accident	Period from date of accident to date of trial (years)					
	Male deceased			Female deceased		
	3	6	9	3	6	9
10	1.00	1.00	1.00	1.00	1.00	1.00
20	1.00	1.00	0.99	1.00	1.00	1.00
30	1.00	0.99	0.99	1.00	1.00	0.99
40	0.99	0.99	0.98	1.00	0.99	0.99
50	0.99	0.97	0.95	0.99	0.98	0.97
60	0.97	0.93	0.87	0.98	0.95	0.92
65	0.95	0.88	0.79	0.97	0.93	0.87
70	0.92	0.81	0.66	0.95	0.87	0.77
75	0.86	0.69	0.51	0.91	0.78	0.64
80	0.78	0.54	0.33	0.84	0.65	0.45

N.B. The factor for a period of zero years is clearly 1.00. Factors for other ages and periods not shown in the table may be obtained approximately by interpolation.

74. The resulting multiplier, after application of any discount for the possibility of early death of the deceased before the date of trial, even had the accident not taken place, is to be applied to the appropriate multiplicand, determined in relation to dependency as assessed for the period up to retirement age.

75. If there are several dependants, to whom damages are to be paid in respect of their own particular lifetime (or for a fixed period of dependency), separate multipliers should be determined for each and multiplied by the appropriate multiplicand using the procedure in paragraphs 70 to 74. The total amount of damages is then obtained by adding the separate components. If a single multiplicand is determined, but the damages are to be shared among two or more dependants so long as they are each alive, or during a period of common dependency, then the multiplier will be calculated using the procedure in paragraphs 70 to 74. However, at step (2) of paragraph 70 the expected period will be the longest of the expected periods for which the dependency might last.

Damages for the period of dependency after retirement age

76. The method described in paragraphs 70 to 75 for pre-retirement age dependency cannot satisfactorily be applied directly to post-retirement age dependency with a sufficient degree of accuracy. We therefore propose a method which involves determining the multiplier by looking at dependency for the rest of life from the date of trial and then subtracting the multiplier for dependency up to retirement age.

77. The assessment of the multiplier for whole of life dependency involves the following steps:

(1) Determine the expectation of life which the deceased would have had as at the date of trial, or such lesser period for which the deceased would have been able to provide the dependency (see paragraph 78).

(2) Determine the expected period for which the dependant would have been able to receive the dependency (see paragraph 78).

(3) Take the lesser of the two periods.

(4) Treat the resulting period as a term certain for which the multiplier is to be determined and look up the figure in Table 28 for this period at the appropriate rate of interest.

78. The expected periods at (1) and (2) of paragraph 77 may be obtained from the 0% column of the appropriate table at the back of this booklet. For (1) Tables 1 or 2 will be relevant, according to the sex of the deceased. The age at which the table should be entered is the age which the deceased would have attained at the date of the trial. For (2) Tables 1 and 2 can be used, according to the sex of the dependant and looking up the table at the age of the dependant at the date of the trial.

79. Deduct the corresponding multiplier for post-trial pre-retirement dependency, as determined in paragraphs 70 to 75, but without any adjustment for contingencies other than mortality, or that the deceased may have died anyway before the date of trial. The result is the multiplier for post-retirement dependency, which must then be applied to the appropriate multiplicand, assessed in relation to dependency after retirement age. The adjustment for contingencies other than mortality in respect of the damages for the period of dependency after retirement age will often be less than that required for pre-retirement age damages (see paragraph 30).

80. A deduction may finally be made for the risk that the deceased might have died anyway before the date of trial. The need for such a deduction becomes more necessary the longer the period from the date of accident to the date of trial and the older the deceased at the date of death. As an illustration of the order of magnitude of the deduction, Table F shows some examples of the factor by which the multiplier, determined as above, should be multiplied for different ages of the deceased and for different periods from the date of accident to the date of the trial. The factors for this purpose are exactly the same deductions as used in the calculation at paragraphs 70 to 75.

Cases where dependency is not related to employment

81. The layout of paragraphs 70 to 80 is based on the assumption that the dependency provided by the deceased would have changed at retirement age. This may not be appropriate in some cases, particularly in the important case of the deceased wife and mother whose contribution has been solely in the home or in the case of an adult child caring for an elderly parent or parents. In cases like this, where the deceased might have provided the dependency throughout their lifetime, paragraphs 76 to 80 should be ignored and paragraphs 70 to 75 used, with the difference that the expected period required at step (1) of paragraph 70 should be a whole of life expectancy, taken from Tables 1 and 2. This is also the approach to use when the deceased was already a pensioner.

82. The following paragraphs give calculations of damages awards for the same example, but calculated on three different methodologies – the current approach adopted by the courts, the approach advocated in the Fifth Edition of the Ogden Tables and the alternative approach in the Fifth Edition of the Ogden Tables amended to use multipliers as at the date of death. In each case, the different methodology is applied to the following example:

Example 7

The dependant is female, aged 38 at the date of the trial, which is taking place 3 years after the date of the fatal accident which killed her husband, at that time aged 37, on whom she was financially dependent. The deceased had A levels, was in employment and in good health with no disability at the time of the fatal accident. The dependant was, at the date of death, and is at the date of trial, in good health. Their relationship was stable. The Court has determined a multiplicand of £30,000 up to the deceased's normal retirement age of 65 with no financial dependency post age 65, nor any services dependency. The damages are to be calculated as follows:

Current approach

83. (1) The deceased would have been capable of providing the financial dependency to the dependant for the period of 28 years from the date of his death aged 37 to his 65th birthday.

(2) The appropriate Table is 9. Using the 2.5% column the multiplier = 19.56.

(3) Adjustment factor for contingencies other than mortality (in accordance with Section B) for an employed male aged 37 with A levels and who is not disabled = 0.90 to give a multiplier of 19.56 x 0.90 = 17.60.

(4) The expected period for which the dependant would have been able to receive the dependency was between the ages of 35 and 63.

(5) The appropriate Tables are 8 and 10, and using the 2.5% column the multiplier = 19.86.

(6) The parties were married so section 3(4) does not apply. The relationship was stable. The dependant was and is in good health. The court is unlikely to make much of an adjustment to the figure in (5) above to reflect contingencies other than mortality.

(7) The lower of the two figures is that in (3) above, namely 17.60.

(8) The period that has elapsed between date of death and date of trial is 3 years. The pre-trial loss is therefore £30,000 x 3 = £90,000.

(9) Interest at half rate from date of death to date of trial: 3 years at 3% a year = 9%.
£90,000 x 9% = £8,100.

(10) The post-trial multiplier is 14.60 (17.60 – 3).

(11) The post-trial loss is therefore 14.60 x £30,000 = £438,000.

(12) Total financial dependency therefore £90,000 + £8,100 + £438,000 = £536,100.

Fifth edition approach

84. *Pre-trial damages:*

(1) Period between fatal accident and trial: 3 years.

(2) Factor for possible early death (Table E for male aged 37 and 3 years) = 1.00.

(3) Pre-trial damages = 3 x 1.00 x £30,000 = £90,000 (plus interest as special damages).

(4) Interest at half rate from date of death to date of trial: 3 years at 3% a year = 9%.
£90,000 x 9% = £8,100.

Post-trial damages:

(1) Expected period for which the deceased would have provided the dependency (Table 9 at 0% for male aged 40, the age as at the date of trial): 24.00.

(2) Expected period for which the dependant would have been able to receive the dependency (Table 2 at 0% for female aged 38): 49.14.

(3) Lesser of two periods at (1) and (2) = 24.00.

(4) Multiplier for term certain of 24.00 years at 2½% rate of return = 18.11.

(5) Adjustment factor for contingencies other than mortality (in accordance with Section B) for an employed male aged 40 with A levels and who was not disabled = 0.88 to give a multiplier of 18.11 x 0.88 = 15.94.

(6) Adjustment factor for the risk that the deceased might have died anyway before the date of trial (Table F for male aged 37 and 3 years): 0.99 to give a multiplier of 15.94 x 0.99 = 15.78.

(7) Post-trial damages = 15.78 x £30,000 = £473,400.

(8) Total financial dependency therefore £90,000 + £8,100 + £473,400 = £571,500.

Alternative Fifth edition approach amended to use multipliers as at the date of death

85. If the court wishes to select multipliers from the date of death instead of following the guidance given above, it is essential to ensure that the period before the trial does not include a discount for early receipt. This could be achieved by selecting multipliers from the 0% columns of the appropriate tables and then applying the discount for early receipt to the period after the trial (using the discount rate set under Section 1 of the Damages Act 1996). Thus, the calculations for example 7 above would then be:

(1) Expected period for which the deceased would have provided the dependency (Table 9 at 0% for male aged 37, the age as at the date of death): 26.93.

(2) Deduct period between accidental death and date of trial of 3 years to give post-trial period: 23.93.

(3) Expected post-trial period for which the dependant would have been able to receive the dependency (Table 2 at 0% for female aged 38): 49.14.

(4) Lesser of two periods at (2) and (3) = 23.93.

(5) Multiplier for term certain of 23.93 years at 2.5% rate of return (Table 28) = 18.07.

(6) Adjustment factor for contingencies other than mortality (in accordance with Section B) for an employed male aged 37 with A levels and who was not disabled = 0.90 to give a multiplier of 18.07 x 0.90 = 16.26.

(7) Pre-trial damages = 3 x £30,000 = £90,000 (plus interest as special damages of £8,100).

(8) Post-trial damages = 16.26 x £30,000 = £487,800.

(9) Total financial dependency therefore £90,000 + £8,100 + £487,800 = £585,900.

86. As can be seen the three methodologies give three different amounts of damages, namely £536,100 for the current approach used by the courts, £571,500 using the methodology set out in the Fifth Edition and £585,900 using the alternative methodology set out in the Fifth Edition with multipliers as at the date of death. The size of the disparities between the three methods depends on the length of the period between the date of death and the date of trial; if the example had assumed a period of 6 years the differences would have been greater.

87. The following paragraphs show extensions of the methodology set out in the Fifth Edition to more complex examples. The other methodologies detailed earlier can be extended similarly.

Example 8

88. The dependant is female, aged 50 at the date of the trial, which is taking place 4 years after the date of the fatal accident which killed the man, at that time aged 47, on whom she was financially dependent. The deceased was in employment at the time of the fatal accident, was not disabled and had achieved A levels. The Court has determined a multiplicand, up to the deceased's normal retirement age of 60, of £50,000 and has decided that post-retirement damages should be payable based on a multiplicand of £30,000. The damages are to be calculated as follows:

Pre-trial damages:

(1) Period between fatal accident and trial: 4 years.

(2) Factor for possible early death (Table E for male aged 47 and 4 years): 0.99.

(3) Pre-trial damages = 4 x 0.99 x £50,000 = £198,000 (plus interest as special damages).

Post-trial pre-retirement damages:

(1) Expected period for which the deceased would have provided the dependency (Table 7 at 0% for male aged 51, the age as at the date of trial): 8.80.

(2) Expected period for which the dependant would have been able to receive the dependency (Table 2 at 0% for female aged 50): 36.69.

(3) Lesser of two periods at (1) and (2) = 8.80.

(4) Multiplier for term certain of 8.80 years at 2½% rate of return (interpolating between the values for 8 and 9 in Table 28) = (9 – 8.80) x 7.26 + (8.80 – 8) x 8.07 = 7.91.

(5) Adjustment factor for contingencies other than mortality (in accordance with Section B) for an employed male aged 51 with A levels and who was not disabled = 0.82 to give a multiplier of 7.91 x 0.82 = 6.49.

(6) Adjustment factor for the risk that the deceased might have died anyway before the date of trial (Table F for male aged 47 and 4 years): 0.99 to give a multiplier of 6.49 x 0.99 = 6.43.

(7) Post-trial pre-retirement damages = 6.43 x £50,000 = £321,500.

Post-retirement damages:

(1) Expectation of life of deceased at date of trial (Table 1 at 0% for male aged 51): 32.44.

(2) Expected period for which the dependant would have been able to receive the dependency (Table 2 at 0% for female aged 50): 36.69.

(3) Lesser of two periods at (1) and (2) = 32.44.

(4) Multiplier for time certain of 32.44 years at 2½% rate of return (interpolating between the values for 32 and 33 in Table 28) = (33 – 32.44) x 22.12 + (32.44 – 32) x 22.57 = 22.32.

(5) Deduct multiplier for post-trial pre-retirement damages before application of adjustment factors for contingencies other than mortality and for the risk that the deceased might have died anyway before the date of trial: 22.32 – 7.91 = 14.41.

(6) Adjustment factor for the risk that the deceased might have died anyway before the date of trial (Table F for male aged 47 and 4 years): 0.99 to give a multiplier of 14.41 x 0.99 = 14.27.

(7) Post-retirement damages = 14.27 x £30,000 = £428,100.

Example 9

89. There are two dependants, respectively a child aged 10 and a male aged 41 at the date of the trial, which is taking place 3 years after the date of the fatal accident which killed the woman, at that time aged 35, on whom both were financially dependent. She had a degree and worked in London for a computer company. The Court has determined a multiplicand, up to the deceased's normal retirement age of 62, of £50,000 for the male dependant and £10,000 for the child, up to the age of 21, and has decided that post-retirement damages should be payable based on a multiplicand of £20,000. The damages are to be calculated as follows:

Pre-trial damages:

(1) Period between fatal accident and trial: 3 years.

(2) Factor for possible early death (Table E for female aged 35 and 3 years): 1.00.

(3) Pre-trial damages = 3 x 1.00 x (£50,000 + £10,000) = £180,000 (plus interest as special damages).

Post-trial pre-retirement damages:

(1) Expected period for which the deceased would have provided the dependency should be based on female aged 38 at the date of trial with retirement age of 62. First calculate as though deceased were aged 36 and had retirement age of 60 (Table 8 at 0% for female aged 36): 23.61.

Then calculate as though deceased were aged 41 and had retirement age of 65 (Table 10 at 0% for female aged 41): 23.37.

Interpolate for age 38 with retirement age of 62 = (3 x 23.61 + 2 x 23.37)/5 = 23.51.

(2) Expected period for which the male dependant would have been able to receive the dependency (Table 1 at 0% for male aged 41): 42.48.

Expected period for which child would have been able to receive the dependency = 11.00.

(3) Lesser of two periods at (1) and (2) = 11.00 (in case of child)
= 23.51 (in case of man).

(4) Multiplier for term certain of 11 years at 2½% (Table 28): 9.63.

Multiplier for term certain of 23.51 years at 2½% rate of return (interpolating between the values for 23 and 24 in Table 28)

= (24 – 23.51) x 17.55 + (23.51 – 23) x 18.11 = 17.84.

(5) Adjustment factor for contingencies other than mortality (in accordance with Section B) for an employed female aged 38 with a degree and who was not disabled = 0.89 (does not apply to child) to give a multiplier of 17.84 x 0.89 = 15.88.

(6) Adjustment factor for the risk that the deceased might have died anyway before the date of trial (Table F for female aged 35 and 3 years): 1.00, so multipliers are 9.63 and 15.88 respectively.

(7) Pre-retirement damages = 9.63 x £10,000 + 15.88 x £50,000
= £96,300 + £794,000 = £890,300.

Post-retirement damages:

(1) Expectation of life of deceased at date of trial (Table 2 at 0% for female aged 38): 49.14.

(2) Expected period for which the dependant would have been able to receive the dependency (Table 1 at 0% for male aged 41): 42.48 (no post-retirement dependency for child).

(3) Lesser of two periods at (1) and (2) = 42.48.

(4) Multiplier for time certain of 42.48 years at 2½% rate of return (interpolating between the values for 42 and 43 in Table 28)

= (43 – 42.48) x 26.14 + (42.48 – 42) x 26.49 = 26.31.

(5) Deduct multiplier for post-trial pre-retirement damages before application of adjustment factors for contingencies other than mortality and for the risk that the deceased might have died anyway before the date of trial: 26.31 – 17.84 = 8.47.

(6) Adjustment factor for the risk that the deceased might have died anyway before the date of trial (Table F for female aged 35 and 3 years) = 1.00, so multiplier is 8.47 x 1.00 = 8.47.

(7) Post-retirement damages = 8.47 x £20,000 = £169,400.

SECTION E: CONCLUDING REMARKS

90. These tables are designed to assist the courts to arrive at suitable multipliers in a range of possible situations. However, they do not cover all possibilities and in more complex situations, such as where there are significant pension rights, advice should be sought from a Fellow of the Institute of Actuaries or a Fellow of the Faculty of Actuaries.

CHRISTOPHER DAYKIN CB, MA, FIA
Government Actuary
London
March 2007

Table 1 Multipliers for pecuniary loss for life (males)

Age at date of trial	Multiplier calculated with allowance for projected mortality from the 2004-based population projections and rate of return of											Age at date of trial
	0.0%	0.5%	1.0%	1.5%	2.0%	2.5%	3.0%	3.5%	4.0%	4.5%	5.0%	
0	86.63	69.86	57.39	47.98	40.76	35.15	30.72	27.17	24.28	21.91	19.94	0
1	85.96	69.49	57.21	47.91	40.76	35.19	30.77	27.24	24.36	21.99	20.01	1
2	84.86	68.78	56.74	47.60	40.55	35.05	30.68	27.17	24.32	21.96	19.99	2
3	83.76	68.05	56.26	47.28	40.34	34.90	30.58	27.10	24.27	21.93	19.97	3
4	82.65	67.32	55.77	46.95	40.12	34.75	30.48	27.03	24.22	21.89	19.94	4
5	81.53	66.58	55.27	46.61	39.89	34.59	30.37	26.95	24.16	21.85	19.91	5
6	80.42	65.83	54.77	46.27	39.65	34.43	30.25	26.87	24.10	21.81	19.88	6
7	79.30	65.08	54.26	45.92	39.41	34.26	30.13	26.79	24.04	21.76	19.85	7
8	78.18	64.32	53.74	45.56	39.16	34.08	30.01	26.70	23.98	21.71	19.81	8
9	77.06	63.56	53.22	45.20	38.91	33.91	29.88	26.61	23.91	21.66	19.78	9
10	75.95	62.79	52.69	44.83	38.65	33.72	29.75	26.51	23.84	21.61	19.74	10
11	74.83	62.02	52.16	44.46	38.39	33.53	29.61	26.41	23.77	21.56	19.70	11
12	73.71	61.25	51.62	44.08	38.11	33.34	29.47	26.31	23.69	21.50	19.65	12
13	72.59	60.47	51.07	43.69	37.84	33.14	29.33	26.20	23.61	21.44	19.61	13
14	71.48	59.69	50.52	43.30	37.56	32.93	29.18	26.09	23.52	21.38	19.56	14
15	70.36	58.90	49.96	42.90	37.27	32.72	29.02	25.97	23.44	21.31	19.51	15
16	69.25	58.12	49.40	42.50	36.97	32.51	28.86	25.85	23.35	21.24	19.45	16
17	68.14	57.33	48.83	42.09	36.68	32.29	28.70	25.73	23.26	21.17	19.40	17
18	67.04	56.55	48.27	41.68	36.38	32.07	28.54	25.61	23.16	21.10	19.34	18
19	65.95	55.77	47.71	41.27	36.08	31.85	28.37	25.49	23.07	21.03	19.29	19
20	64.87	54.99	47.14	40.86	35.78	31.63	28.21	25.36	22.98	20.96	19.23	20
21	63.79	54.21	46.58	40.44	35.47	31.40	28.04	25.23	22.88	20.88	19.17	21
22	62.71	53.42	46.00	40.02	35.16	31.16	27.86	25.10	22.77	20.80	19.11	22
23	61.63	52.63	45.42	39.59	34.83	30.92	27.68	24.96	22.67	20.72	19.05	23
24	60.55	51.84	44.83	39.15	34.51	30.67	27.49	24.81	22.55	20.63	18.98	24
25	59.47	51.03	44.23	38.70	34.17	30.42	27.29	24.66	22.44	20.54	18.90	25
26	58.38	50.23	43.63	38.25	33.82	30.15	27.09	24.50	22.31	20.44	18.83	26
27	57.31	49.42	43.03	37.79	33.47	29.89	26.88	24.34	22.19	20.34	18.75	27
28	56.24	48.62	42.42	37.33	33.12	29.61	26.67	24.18	22.06	20.24	18.67	28
29	55.17	47.82	41.81	36.86	32.76	29.33	26.45	24.01	21.92	20.13	18.58	29
30	54.10	47.00	41.19	36.39	32.39	29.05	26.23	23.83	21.78	20.02	18.49	30
31	53.03	46.19	40.56	35.90	32.02	28.75	26.00	23.65	21.64	19.90	18.40	31
32	51.97	45.37	39.93	35.41	31.64	28.46	25.76	23.46	21.48	19.78	18.30	32
33	50.91	44.55	39.30	34.92	31.25	28.15	25.52	23.26	21.33	19.65	18.19	33
34	49.85	43.73	38.66	34.42	30.85	27.83	25.27	23.06	21.17	19.52	18.08	34
35	48.78	42.90	38.01	33.91	30.45	27.51	25.01	22.86	21.00	19.38	17.97	35
36	47.73	42.08	37.36	33.39	30.04	27.18	24.74	22.64	20.82	19.24	17.85	36
37	46.67	41.24	36.70	32.87	29.62	26.85	24.47	22.42	20.64	19.09	17.73	37
38	45.62	40.41	36.04	32.34	29.19	26.50	24.19	22.19	20.45	18.93	17.60	38
39	44.56	39.57	35.37	31.80	28.76	26.15	23.90	21.95	20.26	18.77	17.46	39
40	43.52	38.74	34.70	31.26	28.32	25.79	23.61	21.71	20.05	18.60	17.32	40
41	42.48	37.90	34.02	30.71	27.87	25.42	23.30	21.46	19.84	18.43	17.17	41
42	41.44	37.06	33.34	30.15	27.41	25.05	22.99	21.20	19.63	18.24	17.02	42
43	40.40	36.22	32.65	29.59	26.95	24.67	22.68	20.93	19.41	18.06	16.86	43
44	39.37	35.38	31.97	29.03	26.49	24.28	22.35	20.66	19.18	17.86	16.69	44
45	38.35	34.55	31.28	28.46	26.01	23.88	22.02	20.38	18.94	17.66	16.52	45
46	37.34	33.71	30.59	27.89	25.54	23.49	21.69	20.10	18.70	17.46	16.35	46
47	36.34	32.89	29.90	27.32	25.06	23.08	21.35	19.81	18.45	17.25	16.17	47
48	35.34	32.06	29.22	26.74	24.58	22.68	21.00	19.52	18.20	17.03	15.98	48
49	34.37	31.25	28.54	26.17	24.09	22.27	20.65	19.22	17.95	16.81	15.79	49
50	33.40	30.44	27.86	25.60	23.61	21.86	20.30	18.92	17.69	16.59	15.60	50
51	32.44	29.63	27.18	25.02	23.12	21.44	19.95	18.62	17.43	16.36	15.40	51
52	31.49	28.84	26.50	24.45	22.63	21.02	19.58	18.30	17.16	16.12	15.19	52
53	30.55	28.04	25.82	23.87	22.13	20.59	19.21	17.98	16.88	15.88	14.98	53
54	29.61	27.23	25.13	23.28	21.62	20.15	18.83	17.65	16.59	15.63	14.76	54
55	28.66	26.42	24.44	22.67	21.10	19.70	18.44	17.31	16.29	15.36	14.52	55
56	27.71	25.60	23.73	22.06	20.57	19.23	18.03	16.95	15.97	15.08	14.28	56
57	26.76	24.78	23.02	21.44	20.03	18.76	17.62	16.58	15.65	14.79	14.02	57
58	25.82	23.96	22.31	20.82	19.48	18.28	17.19	16.21	15.31	14.50	13.75	58
59	24.89	23.15	21.59	20.19	18.93	17.79	16.76	15.82	14.97	14.19	13.48	59
60	23.97	22.35	20.89	19.57	18.38	17.30	16.33	15.44	14.62	13.88	13.20	60
61	23.08	21.56	20.19	18.96	17.84	16.82	15.90	15.05	14.28	13.57	12.92	61
62	22.20	20.79	19.51	18.35	17.30	16.34	15.47	14.67	13.93	13.26	12.64	62
63	21.34	20.03	18.83	17.75	16.76	15.86	15.03	14.28	13.58	12.94	12.36	63
64	20.50	19.27	18.16	17.15	16.22	15.37	14.60	13.88	13.23	12.62	12.06	64
65	19.66	18.52	17.49	16.54	15.68	14.88	14.16	13.48	12.86	12.29	11.76	65
66	18.82	17.77	16.81	15.94	15.13	14.39	13.70	13.07	12.49	11.95	11.45	66
67	17.99	17.02	16.14	15.32	14.57	13.88	13.24	12.65	12.11	11.60	11.13	67
68	17.16	16.27	15.45	14.70	14.01	13.36	12.77	12.22	11.71	11.23	10.79	68
69	16.33	15.51	14.76	14.07	13.43	12.84	12.29	11.77	11.30	10.85	10.44	69

continued

Table 1 Multipliers for pecuniary loss for life (males) *continued*

Age at date of trial	Multiplier calculated with allowance for projected mortality from the 2004-based population projections and rate of return of											Age at date of trial
	0.0%	0.5%	1.0%	1.5%	2.0%	2.5%	3.0%	3.5%	4.0%	4.5%	5.0%	
70	15.50	14.75	14.07	13.43	12.85	12.30	11.79	11.32	10.87	10.46	10.08	70
71	14.67	14.00	13.38	12.80	12.26	11.76	11.29	10.85	10.44	10.06	9.70	71
72	13.86	13.25	12.69	12.16	11.67	11.21	10.78	10.38	10.00	9.65	9.32	72
73	13.07	12.52	12.01	11.53	11.09	10.67	10.28	9.91	9.56	9.24	8.94	73
74	12.31	11.81	11.35	10.92	10.51	10.13	9.78	9.44	9.13	8.83	8.55	74
75	11.57	11.13	10.71	10.32	9.95	9.61	9.29	8.98	8.70	8.42	8.17	75
76	10.86	10.47	10.09	9.74	9.41	9.10	8.81	8.53	8.27	8.03	7.79	76
77	10.19	9.84	9.50	9.19	8.89	8.61	8.35	8.10	7.86	7.64	7.42	77
78	9.55	9.24	8.94	8.66	8.39	8.14	7.90	7.68	7.46	7.26	7.06	78
79	8.95	8.67	8.40	8.15	7.91	7.69	7.47	7.27	7.08	6.89	6.71	79
80	8.38	8.13	7.89	7.67	7.45	7.25	7.06	6.88	6.70	6.53	6.38	80
81	7.83	7.61	7.40	7.20	7.01	6.83	6.66	6.49	6.34	6.19	6.04	81
82	7.31	7.12	6.93	6.75	6.58	6.42	6.27	6.12	5.98	5.85	5.72	82
83	6.81	6.64	6.47	6.32	6.17	6.02	5.89	5.75	5.63	5.51	5.39	83
84	6.32	6.17	6.03	5.89	5.76	5.63	5.51	5.39	5.28	5.17	5.07	84
85	5.87	5.73	5.61	5.49	5.37	5.26	5.15	5.05	4.95	4.85	4.76	85
86	5.44	5.33	5.22	5.11	5.01	4.91	4.81	4.72	4.64	4.55	4.47	86
87	5.05	4.95	4.85	4.76	4.67	4.58	4.50	4.42	4.34	4.27	4.19	87
88	4.68	4.60	4.51	4.43	4.35	4.27	4.20	4.13	4.06	4.00	3.93	88
89	4.35	4.28	4.20	4.13	4.06	4.00	3.93	3.87	3.81	3.75	3.69	89
90	4.05	3.99	3.92	3.86	3.80	3.74	3.68	3.63	3.57	3.52	3.47	90
91	3.76	3.71	3.65	3.59	3.54	3.49	3.44	3.39	3.34	3.30	3.25	91
92	3.49	3.44	3.39	3.34	3.30	3.25	3.21	3.16	3.12	3.08	3.04	92
93	3.26	3.21	3.17	3.12	3.08	3.04	3.00	2.96	2.93	2.89	2.86	93
94	3.06	3.02	2.98	2.94	2.91	2.87	2.83	2.80	2.77	2.73	2.70	94
95	2.88	2.85	2.81	2.78	2.75	2.71	2.68	2.65	2.62	2.59	2.56	95
96	2.71	2.68	2.65	2.62	2.59	2.56	2.53	2.51	2.48	2.45	2.43	96
97	2.55	2.52	2.49	2.46	2.44	2.41	2.39	2.36	2.34	2.32	2.29	97
98	2.38	2.36	2.33	2.31	2.29	2.26	2.24	2.22	2.20	2.18	2.16	98
99	2.22	2.20	2.18	2.15	2.13	2.12	2.10	2.08	2.06	2.04	2.02	99
100	2.06	2.04	2.02	2.01	1.99	1.97	1.95	1.94	1.92	1.90	1.89	100

Table 2 Multipliers for pecuniary loss for life (females)

Age at date of trial	Multiplier calculated with allowance for projected mortality from the 2004-based population projections and rate of return of											Age at date of trial
	0.0%	0.5%	1.0%	1.5%	2.0%	2.5%	3.0%	3.5%	4.0%	4.5%	5.0%	
0	90.15	72.21	58.98	49.06	41.51	35.67	31.09	27.43	24.48	22.06	20.05	0
1	89.44	71.83	58.79	48.99	41.50	35.70	31.14	27.50	24.55	22.13	20.11	1
2	88.36	71.13	58.34	48.70	41.32	35.58	31.06	27.44	24.51	22.10	20.10	2
3	87.27	70.43	57.88	48.40	41.12	35.45	30.97	27.38	24.47	22.08	20.08	3
4	86.17	69.72	57.42	48.09	40.92	35.32	30.88	27.32	24.43	22.05	20.06	4
5	85.07	69.00	56.95	47.78	40.71	35.18	30.79	27.26	24.38	22.01	20.04	5
6	83.97	68.28	56.47	47.46	40.49	35.03	30.69	27.19	24.34	21.98	20.01	6
7	82.87	67.55	55.99	47.14	40.28	34.88	30.59	27.12	24.29	21.95	19.99	7
8	81.77	66.82	55.50	46.81	40.05	34.73	30.48	27.04	24.23	21.91	19.96	8
9	80.67	66.08	55.00	46.47	39.82	34.57	30.37	26.97	24.18	21.87	19.93	9
10	79.57	65.34	54.50	46.13	39.59	34.41	30.26	26.89	24.12	21.83	19.90	10
11	78.47	64.60	53.99	45.78	39.35	34.24	30.14	26.80	24.06	21.79	19.87	11
12	77.36	63.85	53.48	45.43	39.10	34.07	30.02	26.72	24.00	21.74	19.84	12
13	76.26	63.10	52.96	45.07	38.85	33.89	29.89	26.63	23.94	21.69	19.80	13
14	75.16	62.34	52.44	44.71	38.60	33.71	29.76	26.53	23.87	21.64	19.77	14
15	74.06	61.58	51.91	44.34	38.34	33.53	29.63	26.44	23.80	21.59	19.73	15
16	72.97	60.82	51.38	43.97	38.07	33.34	29.49	26.34	23.73	21.54	19.69	16
17	71.88	60.06	50.85	43.59	37.80	33.15	29.36	26.24	23.65	21.48	19.65	17
18	70.79	59.30	50.31	43.21	37.53	32.95	29.21	26.14	23.57	21.43	19.60	18
19	69.70	58.53	49.77	42.82	37.25	32.75	29.07	26.03	23.50	21.37	19.56	19
20	68.61	57.76	49.22	42.42	36.97	32.54	28.91	25.92	23.41	21.30	19.51	20
21	67.52	56.98	48.66	42.02	36.68	32.33	28.76	25.80	23.33	21.24	19.46	21
22	66.43	56.20	48.10	41.62	36.38	32.11	28.60	25.68	23.23	21.17	19.41	22
23	65.34	55.42	47.53	41.20	36.08	31.89	28.43	25.55	23.14	21.10	19.36	23
24	64.25	54.63	46.96	40.78	35.77	31.66	28.26	25.42	23.04	21.02	19.30	24
25	63.16	53.84	46.38	40.36	35.45	31.42	28.08	25.29	22.94	20.94	19.24	25
26	62.08	53.05	45.79	39.92	35.13	31.18	27.90	25.15	22.83	20.86	19.17	26
27	60.99	52.25	45.20	39.48	34.80	30.93	27.71	25.01	22.72	20.78	19.10	27
28	59.91	51.45	44.61	39.04	34.46	30.67	27.51	24.86	22.61	20.69	19.03	28
29	58.83	50.64	44.01	38.58	34.12	30.41	27.31	24.70	22.49	20.59	18.96	29
30	57.74	49.83	43.40	38.12	33.77	30.15	27.11	24.54	22.36	20.49	18.88	30
31	56.66	49.02	42.78	37.66	33.41	29.87	26.89	24.38	22.23	20.39	18.80	31
32	55.58	48.20	42.16	37.18	33.05	29.59	26.68	24.21	22.10	20.28	18.71	32
33	54.50	47.38	41.54	36.70	32.68	29.30	26.45	24.03	21.96	20.17	18.63	33
34	53.43	46.56	40.91	36.22	32.30	29.01	26.22	23.85	21.81	20.06	18.53	34
35	52.35	45.74	40.27	35.73	31.92	28.71	25.98	23.66	21.66	19.93	18.43	35
36	51.28	44.91	39.63	35.22	31.52	28.40	25.74	23.46	21.50	19.81	18.33	36
37	50.21	44.08	38.98	34.72	31.13	28.08	25.49	23.26	21.34	19.67	18.22	37
38	49.14	43.25	38.33	34.20	30.72	27.76	25.23	23.05	21.17	19.54	18.11	38
39	48.07	42.41	37.67	33.68	30.30	27.43	24.96	22.84	21.00	19.39	17.99	39
40	47.01	41.58	37.01	33.16	29.89	27.09	24.69	22.61	20.82	19.25	17.87	40
41	45.95	40.74	36.35	32.63	29.46	26.74	24.41	22.39	20.63	19.09	17.74	41
42	44.90	39.90	35.68	32.09	29.02	26.39	24.12	22.15	20.44	18.93	17.61	42
43	43.85	39.06	35.00	31.55	28.59	26.04	23.83	21.91	20.24	18.77	17.47	43
44	42.80	38.22	34.33	31.00	28.14	25.67	23.53	21.66	20.03	18.59	17.33	44
45	41.77	37.39	33.65	30.45	27.69	25.30	23.23	21.41	19.82	18.42	17.18	45
46	40.74	36.55	32.97	29.90	27.24	24.93	22.92	21.15	19.61	18.24	17.03	46
47	39.71	35.72	32.29	29.34	26.77	24.55	22.60	20.89	19.38	18.05	16.87	47
48	38.70	34.89	31.61	28.77	26.31	24.16	22.28	20.62	19.16	17.86	16.70	48
49	37.69	34.06	30.93	28.21	25.84	23.77	21.95	20.34	18.92	17.66	16.53	49
50	36.69	33.23	30.24	27.64	25.36	23.37	21.61	20.06	18.68	17.46	16.36	50
51	35.69	32.41	29.56	27.07	24.88	22.96	21.27	19.77	18.44	17.25	16.18	51
52	34.70	31.59	28.87	26.49	24.40	22.55	20.92	19.47	18.18	17.03	15.99	52
53	33.71	30.76	28.17	25.90	23.90	22.13	20.56	19.17	17.92	16.80	15.80	53
54	32.73	29.93	27.47	25.31	23.39	21.70	20.19	18.85	17.64	16.56	15.59	54
55	31.74	29.09	26.76	24.70	22.88	21.26	19.81	18.52	17.36	16.32	15.38	55
56	30.75	28.25	26.05	24.09	22.36	20.81	19.42	18.18	17.07	16.06	15.15	56
57	29.77	27.42	25.33	23.48	21.82	20.35	19.03	17.84	16.77	15.80	14.92	57
58	28.80	26.58	24.61	22.86	21.29	19.88	18.62	17.48	16.46	15.52	14.68	58
59	27.83	25.75	23.89	22.23	20.75	19.41	18.21	17.12	16.14	15.24	14.43	59
60	26.88	24.93	23.18	21.61	20.20	18.94	17.79	16.76	15.81	14.96	14.18	60
61	25.94	24.11	22.47	20.99	19.66	18.46	17.37	16.38	15.49	14.67	13.92	61
62	25.02	23.30	21.76	20.37	19.11	17.98	16.95	16.01	15.15	14.37	13.65	62
63	24.10	22.49	21.05	19.75	18.56	17.49	16.51	15.62	14.81	14.06	13.38	63
64	23.18	21.69	20.34	19.12	18.01	17.00	16.07	15.23	14.46	13.75	13.10	64
65	22.28	20.89	19.63	18.49	17.45	16.50	15.63	14.83	14.10	13.42	12.80	65
66	21.38	20.09	18.92	17.85	16.88	15.99	15.17	14.42	13.73	13.09	12.50	66
67	20.48	19.29	18.20	17.21	16.30	15.47	14.70	13.99	13.34	12.74	12.18	67
68	19.58	18.48	17.47	16.55	15.71	14.93	14.22	13.55	12.94	12.38	11.85	68
69	18.66	17.66	16.73	15.88	15.10	14.38	13.71	13.10	12.52	11.99	11.50	69

continued

Table 2 Multipliers for pecuniary loss for life (females) *continued*

Age at date of trial	Multiplier calculated with allowance for projected mortality from the 2004-based population projections and rate of return of											Age at date of trial
	0.0%	0.5%	1.0%	1.5%	2.0%	2.5%	3.0%	3.5%	4.0%	4.5%	5.0%	
70	17.74	16.82	15.97	15.19	14.47	13.81	13.19	12.62	12.09	11.59	11.13	70
71	16.82	15.98	15.21	14.50	13.84	13.22	12.65	12.13	11.63	11.17	10.74	71
72	15.90	15.14	14.44	13.79	13.19	12.63	12.11	11.62	11.17	10.74	10.34	72
73	14.99	14.31	13.67	13.09	12.54	12.03	11.55	11.11	10.69	10.30	9.93	73
74	14.10	13.49	12.92	12.39	11.89	11.43	11.00	10.59	10.21	9.85	9.51	74
75	13.24	12.69	12.18	11.71	11.26	10.84	10.45	10.08	9.73	9.40	9.10	75
76	12.42	11.93	11.47	11.05	10.64	10.27	9.91	9.58	9.26	8.96	8.68	76
77	11.64	11.20	10.79	10.41	10.05	9.71	9.39	9.09	8.80	8.53	8.28	77
78	10.89	10.51	10.14	9.80	9.48	9.17	8.88	8.61	8.35	8.11	7.88	78
79	10.19	9.84	9.52	9.21	8.93	8.65	8.39	8.15	7.92	7.70	7.48	79
80	9.51	9.21	8.92	8.65	8.39	8.15	7.92	7.70	7.49	7.29	7.10	80
81	8.87	8.60	8.35	8.11	7.88	7.66	7.46	7.26	7.07	6.89	6.72	81
82	8.26	8.02	7.80	7.58	7.38	7.19	7.01	6.83	6.66	6.50	6.35	82
83	7.67	7.46	7.27	7.08	6.90	6.73	6.57	6.41	6.26	6.12	5.98	83
84	7.10	6.92	6.75	6.59	6.43	6.28	6.14	6.00	5.87	5.74	5.62	84
85	6.57	6.41	6.26	6.12	5.98	5.85	5.73	5.60	5.49	5.38	5.27	85
86	6.07	5.93	5.80	5.68	5.56	5.44	5.33	5.23	5.12	5.02	4.93	86
87	5.60	5.48	5.37	5.26	5.16	5.06	4.96	4.86	4.77	4.69	4.60	87
88	5.17	5.06	4.97	4.87	4.78	4.69	4.61	4.53	4.45	4.37	4.30	88
89	4.77	4.68	4.60	4.51	4.43	4.36	4.28	4.21	4.14	4.08	4.01	89
90	4.41	4.33	4.26	4.19	4.12	4.05	3.99	3.92	3.86	3.80	3.75	90
91	4.08	4.01	3.95	3.89	3.83	3.77	3.71	3.66	3.60	3.55	3.50	91
92	3.79	3.73	3.67	3.61	3.56	3.51	3.46	3.41	3.36	3.32	3.27	92
93	3.53	3.47	3.42	3.38	3.33	3.28	3.24	3.20	3.15	3.11	3.07	93
94	3.30	3.25	3.21	3.17	3.12	3.08	3.04	3.00	2.97	2.93	2.90	94
95	3.08	3.04	3.01	2.97	2.93	2.89	2.86	2.82	2.79	2.76	2.73	95
96	2.89	2.85	2.82	2.78	2.75	2.72	2.69	2.66	2.63	2.60	2.57	96
97	2.70	2.67	2.64	2.61	2.58	2.55	2.53	2.50	2.47	2.45	2.42	97
98	2.53	2.50	2.48	2.45	2.42	2.40	2.37	2.35	2.33	2.30	2.28	98
99	2.37	2.34	2.32	2.30	2.27	2.25	2.23	2.21	2.19	2.17	2.15	99
100	2.21	2.19	2.17	2.15	2.13	2.11	2.09	2.07	2.05	2.03	2.02	100

Table 3 Multipliers for loss of earnings to pension age 50 (males)

Age at date of trial	Multiplier calculated with allowance for projected mortality from the 2004-based population projections and rate of return of											Age at date of trial
	0.0%	0.5%	1.0%	1.5%	2.0%	2.5%	3.0%	3.5%	4.0%	4.5%	5.0%	
16	33.58	30.90	28.52	26.39	24.48	22.77	21.24	19.86	18.61	17.48	16.46	16
17	32.59	30.06	27.80	25.78	23.96	22.33	20.86	19.54	18.34	17.25	16.26	17
18	31.59	29.21	27.08	25.16	23.44	21.88	20.48	19.21	18.05	17.00	16.05	18
19	30.60	28.37	26.36	24.54	22.91	21.43	20.09	18.87	17.76	16.76	15.83	19
20	29.62	27.52	25.63	23.92	22.37	20.96	19.68	18.52	17.46	16.50	15.61	20
21	28.63	26.67	24.89	23.28	21.81	20.48	19.27	18.16	17.15	16.22	15.37	21
22	27.65	25.81	24.15	22.63	21.25	19.99	18.84	17.79	16.83	15.94	15.13	22
23	26.66	24.95	23.39	21.98	20.68	19.49	18.40	17.41	16.49	15.64	14.87	23
24	25.67	24.09	22.64	21.31	20.09	18.98	17.95	17.01	16.14	15.33	14.59	24
25	24.68	23.21	21.87	20.63	19.49	18.45	17.48	16.59	15.77	15.01	14.30	25
26	23.70	22.34	21.09	19.94	18.88	17.91	17.00	16.17	15.39	14.67	14.00	26
27	22.71	21.46	20.31	19.25	18.26	17.35	16.51	15.72	14.99	14.32	13.69	27
28	21.72	20.58	19.52	18.54	17.63	16.78	16.00	15.27	14.58	13.95	13.36	28
29	20.74	19.69	18.72	17.82	16.98	16.20	15.47	14.79	14.16	13.56	13.01	29
30	19.75	18.80	17.92	17.10	16.33	15.61	14.93	14.31	13.72	13.16	12.64	30
31	18.77	17.91	17.11	16.36	15.66	15.00	14.38	13.80	13.25	12.74	12.26	31
32	17.78	17.01	16.29	15.61	14.97	14.37	13.81	13.28	12.78	12.30	11.86	32
33	16.80	16.11	15.46	14.85	14.27	13.73	13.22	12.74	12.28	11.85	11.44	33
34	15.81	15.20	14.62	14.08	13.56	13.08	12.61	12.18	11.76	11.37	11.00	34
35	14.83	14.29	13.78	13.30	12.84	12.40	11.99	11.60	11.22	10.87	10.53	35
36	13.84	13.37	12.93	12.50	12.10	11.71	11.35	11.00	10.67	10.35	10.05	36
37	12.86	12.45	12.07	11.70	11.34	11.01	10.69	10.38	10.08	9.80	9.53	37
38	11.87	11.53	11.19	10.88	10.57	10.28	10.00	9.74	9.48	9.23	9.00	38
39	10.89	10.60	10.32	10.05	9.79	9.54	9.30	9.07	8.85	8.64	8.43	39
40	9.90	9.66	9.43	9.20	8.99	8.78	8.58	8.38	8.20	8.02	7.84	40
41	8.92	8.72	8.53	8.35	8.17	8.00	7.83	7.67	7.52	7.37	7.22	41
42	7.93	7.77	7.62	7.48	7.33	7.20	7.06	6.93	6.81	6.69	6.57	42
43	6.94	6.82	6.71	6.59	6.48	6.38	6.27	6.17	6.07	5.98	5.88	43
44	5.95	5.87	5.78	5.70	5.61	5.53	5.46	5.38	5.31	5.23	5.16	44
45	4.97	4.90	4.84	4.79	4.73	4.67	4.62	4.56	4.51	4.46	4.41	45
46	3.98	3.94	3.90	3.86	3.82	3.79	3.75	3.72	3.68	3.65	3.61	46
47	2.99	2.96	2.94	2.92	2.90	2.88	2.86	2.84	2.82	2.80	2.78	47
48	1.99	1.98	1.97	1.96	1.95	1.94	1.94	1.93	1.92	1.91	1.90	48
49	1.00	1.00	0.99	0.99	0.99	0.99	0.98	0.98	0.98	0.98	0.97	49

Table 4 Multipliers for loss of earnings to pension age 50 (females)

Age at date of trial	Multiplier calculated with allowance for projected mortality from the 2004-based population projections and rate of return of											Age at date of trial
	0.0%	0.5%	1.0%	1.5%	2.0%	2.5%	3.0%	3.5%	4.0%	4.5%	5.0%	
16	33.79	31.09	28.68	26.54	24.61	22.89	21.34	19.95	18.69	17.56	16.53	16
17	32.80	30.25	27.97	25.93	24.10	22.45	20.97	19.64	18.43	17.33	16.33	17
18	31.80	29.40	27.25	25.32	23.58	22.01	20.59	19.31	18.15	17.09	16.13	18
19	30.81	28.55	26.52	24.69	23.04	21.55	20.20	18.97	17.86	16.84	15.91	19
20	29.81	27.70	25.79	24.06	22.50	21.08	19.79	18.62	17.55	16.58	15.69	20
21	28.82	26.84	25.04	23.42	21.94	20.60	19.38	18.26	17.24	16.30	15.45	21
22	27.82	25.97	24.29	22.77	21.37	20.11	18.95	17.88	16.91	16.02	15.20	22
23	26.83	25.11	23.54	22.10	20.80	19.60	18.50	17.50	16.57	15.72	14.94	23
24	25.83	24.23	22.77	21.43	20.21	19.08	18.05	17.10	16.22	15.41	14.66	24
25	24.84	23.36	22.00	20.75	19.60	18.55	17.58	16.68	15.85	15.08	14.37	25
26	23.84	22.48	21.22	20.06	18.99	18.00	17.09	16.25	15.47	14.74	14.07	26
27	22.85	21.59	20.43	19.36	18.37	17.45	16.60	15.81	15.07	14.39	13.75	27
28	21.85	20.70	19.63	18.65	17.73	16.88	16.08	15.35	14.66	14.02	13.42	28
29	20.86	19.81	18.83	17.92	17.08	16.29	15.55	14.87	14.23	13.63	13.07	29
30	19.87	18.91	18.02	17.19	16.41	15.69	15.01	14.38	13.78	13.23	12.70	30
31	18.87	18.01	17.20	16.44	15.74	15.07	14.45	13.87	13.32	12.80	12.32	31
32	17.88	17.10	16.37	15.69	15.05	14.44	13.88	13.34	12.84	12.36	11.91	32
33	16.89	16.19	15.54	14.92	14.34	13.80	13.28	12.80	12.34	11.90	11.49	33
34	15.89	15.28	14.70	14.15	13.63	13.14	12.67	12.23	11.82	11.42	11.04	34
35	14.90	14.36	13.85	13.36	12.90	12.46	12.04	11.65	11.27	10.92	10.58	35
36	13.91	13.44	12.99	12.56	12.15	11.76	11.40	11.04	10.71	10.39	10.09	36
37	12.92	12.51	12.12	11.75	11.39	11.05	10.73	10.42	10.12	9.84	9.57	37
38	11.92	11.57	11.24	10.92	10.62	10.32	10.04	9.77	9.52	9.27	9.03	38
39	10.93	10.64	10.36	10.08	9.82	9.58	9.34	9.10	8.88	8.67	8.46	39
40	9.94	9.70	9.46	9.24	9.02	8.81	8.61	8.41	8.23	8.04	7.87	40
41	8.95	8.75	8.56	8.37	8.20	8.02	7.86	7.70	7.54	7.39	7.24	41
42	7.95	7.80	7.65	7.50	7.36	7.22	7.09	6.96	6.83	6.71	6.59	42
43	6.96	6.84	6.73	6.61	6.50	6.39	6.29	6.19	6.09	5.99	5.90	43
44	5.97	5.88	5.80	5.71	5.63	5.55	5.47	5.40	5.32	5.25	5.18	44
45	4.98	4.92	4.86	4.80	4.74	4.68	4.63	4.57	4.52	4.47	4.42	45
46	3.98	3.95	3.91	3.87	3.83	3.79	3.76	3.72	3.69	3.65	3.62	46
47	2.99	2.97	2.95	2.93	2.90	2.88	2.86	2.84	2.82	2.80	2.78	47
48	2.00	1.99	1.98	1.97	1.96	1.95	1.94	1.93	1.92	1.91	1.90	48
49	1.00	1.00	0.99	0.99	0.99	0.99	0.98	0.98	0.98	0.98	0.97	49

Table 5 Multipliers for loss of earnings to pension age 55 (males)

Age at date of trial	Multiplier calculated with allowance for projected mortality from the 2004-based population projections and rate of return of											Age at date of trial
	0.0%	0.5%	1.0%	1.5%	2.0%	2.5%	3.0%	3.5%	4.0%	4.5%	5.0%	
16	38.37	34.90	31.85	29.17	26.81	24.72	22.87	21.22	19.75	18.44	17.27	16
17	37.37	34.07	31.16	28.60	26.34	24.33	22.54	20.95	19.53	18.25	17.11	17
18	36.38	33.24	30.48	28.03	25.86	23.93	22.21	20.67	19.29	18.06	16.94	18
19	35.39	32.42	29.79	27.45	25.37	23.52	21.87	20.38	19.05	17.85	16.77	19
20	34.41	31.59	29.09	26.87	24.88	23.11	21.52	20.09	18.80	17.64	16.59	20
21	33.42	30.76	28.39	26.27	24.38	22.68	21.16	19.79	18.54	17.42	16.41	21
22	32.43	29.92	27.68	25.67	23.87	22.25	20.79	19.47	18.28	17.19	16.21	22
23	31.45	29.08	26.97	25.06	23.35	21.80	20.41	19.14	18.00	16.95	16.00	23
24	30.46	28.24	26.24	24.44	22.82	21.35	20.02	18.81	17.71	16.70	15.79	24
25	29.47	27.39	25.51	23.81	22.27	20.88	19.61	18.46	17.40	16.44	15.56	25
26	28.49	26.54	24.77	23.17	21.72	20.40	19.19	18.09	17.09	16.17	15.32	26
27	27.50	25.68	24.03	22.53	21.16	19.91	18.76	17.72	16.76	15.88	15.07	27
28	26.52	24.82	23.28	21.87	20.58	19.40	18.32	17.33	16.42	15.58	14.81	28
29	25.53	23.96	22.52	21.20	20.00	18.89	17.87	16.93	16.07	15.27	14.54	29
30	24.55	23.09	21.76	20.53	19.40	18.36	17.40	16.52	15.70	14.95	14.25	30
31	23.57	22.22	20.98	19.84	18.79	17.82	16.92	16.09	15.32	14.61	13.95	31
32	22.59	21.35	20.21	19.15	18.17	17.27	16.43	15.65	14.93	14.26	13.63	32
33	21.60	20.47	19.42	18.45	17.54	16.70	15.92	15.20	14.52	13.89	13.30	33
34	20.62	19.59	18.63	17.73	16.90	16.12	15.40	14.72	14.09	13.50	12.95	34
35	19.64	18.70	17.82	17.01	16.24	15.53	14.86	14.24	13.65	13.10	12.59	35
36	18.66	17.81	17.01	16.27	15.57	14.92	14.31	13.73	13.19	12.68	12.21	36
37	17.68	16.91	16.20	15.52	14.89	14.30	13.74	13.21	12.71	12.25	11.80	37
38	16.70	16.02	15.37	14.77	14.20	13.66	13.15	12.67	12.22	11.79	11.38	38
39	15.72	15.11	14.54	14.00	13.49	13.00	12.55	12.11	11.70	11.31	10.94	39
40	14.74	14.20	13.70	13.22	12.76	12.33	11.92	11.53	11.16	10.81	10.48	40
41	13.76	13.29	12.85	12.43	12.03	11.64	11.28	10.94	10.61	10.29	9.99	41
42	12.78	12.37	11.99	11.62	11.27	10.94	10.62	10.32	10.03	9.75	9.48	42
43	11.80	11.45	11.12	10.81	10.51	10.22	9.94	9.68	9.42	9.18	8.95	43
44	10.82	10.53	10.25	9.98	9.73	9.48	9.24	9.02	8.80	8.59	8.39	44
45	9.84	9.60	9.37	9.15	8.93	8.73	8.53	8.33	8.15	7.97	7.80	45
46	8.86	8.67	8.48	8.30	8.12	7.95	7.79	7.63	7.47	7.32	7.18	46
47	7.88	7.73	7.58	7.43	7.29	7.16	7.03	6.90	6.77	6.65	6.53	47
48	6.91	6.79	6.67	6.56	6.45	6.34	6.24	6.14	6.04	5.95	5.85	48
49	5.93	5.84	5.75	5.67	5.59	5.51	5.43	5.36	5.28	5.21	5.14	49
50	4.95	4.89	4.83	4.77	4.71	4.65	4.60	4.55	4.49	4.44	4.39	50
51	3.96	3.93	3.89	3.85	3.81	3.78	3.74	3.70	3.67	3.64	3.60	51
52	2.98	2.96	2.94	2.91	2.89	2.87	2.85	2.83	2.81	2.79	2.77	52
53	1.99	1.98	1.97	1.96	1.95	1.94	1.93	1.92	1.91	1.91	1.90	53
54	1.00	0.99	0.99	0.99	0.99	0.99	0.98	0.98	0.98	0.98	0.97	54

Table 6 Multipliers for loss of earnings to pension age 55 (females)

Age at date of trial	Multiplier calculated with allowance for projected mortality from the 2004-based population projections and rate of return of											Age at date of trial
	0.0%	0.5%	1.0%	1.5%	2.0%	2.5%	3.0%	3.5%	4.0%	4.5%	5.0%	
16	38.67	35.16	32.08	29.37	26.98	24.87	23.00	21.34	19.86	18.54	17.35	16
17	37.68	34.33	31.40	28.81	26.52	24.49	22.68	21.08	19.64	18.35	17.20	17
18	36.68	33.51	30.71	28.23	26.04	24.09	22.35	20.80	19.41	18.16	17.04	18
19	35.69	32.68	30.02	27.66	25.56	23.68	22.01	20.51	19.17	17.96	16.87	19
20	34.69	31.84	29.32	27.07	25.06	23.27	21.66	20.22	18.92	17.75	16.69	20
21	33.70	31.01	28.61	26.47	24.56	22.84	21.30	19.91	18.66	17.53	16.50	21
22	32.70	30.16	27.90	25.86	24.04	22.40	20.93	19.60	18.39	17.30	16.30	22
23	31.71	29.32	27.17	25.25	23.52	21.96	20.54	19.27	18.11	17.06	16.10	23
24	30.71	28.47	26.44	24.62	22.98	21.50	20.15	18.93	17.82	16.80	15.88	24
25	29.72	27.61	25.71	23.99	22.44	21.02	19.74	18.58	17.51	16.54	15.65	25
26	28.72	26.75	24.97	23.35	21.88	20.54	19.32	18.21	17.20	16.27	15.41	26
27	27.73	25.89	24.22	22.70	21.31	20.05	18.89	17.84	16.87	15.98	15.16	27
28	26.73	25.02	23.46	22.03	20.73	19.54	18.45	17.45	16.53	15.68	14.90	28
29	25.74	24.15	22.69	21.36	20.14	19.02	17.99	17.05	16.17	15.37	14.62	29
30	24.75	23.27	21.92	20.68	19.54	18.49	17.52	16.63	15.81	15.04	14.34	30
31	23.75	22.39	21.14	19.99	18.93	17.95	17.04	16.20	15.42	14.70	14.03	31
32	22.76	21.51	20.35	19.29	18.30	17.39	16.54	15.76	15.03	14.35	13.71	32
33	21.77	20.62	19.56	18.58	17.66	16.82	16.03	15.30	14.61	13.98	13.38	33
34	20.78	19.73	18.76	17.86	17.02	16.23	15.50	14.82	14.18	13.59	13.03	34
35	19.79	18.84	17.95	17.12	16.35	15.63	14.96	14.33	13.74	13.18	12.66	35
36	18.79	17.94	17.13	16.38	15.68	15.02	14.40	13.82	13.27	12.76	12.28	36
37	17.80	17.03	16.31	15.63	14.99	14.39	13.82	13.29	12.79	12.32	11.87	37
38	16.81	16.12	15.47	14.86	14.29	13.74	13.23	12.75	12.29	11.86	11.45	38
39	15.82	15.21	14.63	14.09	13.57	13.08	12.62	12.18	11.77	11.38	11.00	39
40	14.83	14.30	13.78	13.30	12.84	12.41	11.99	11.60	11.23	10.87	10.54	40
41	13.85	13.38	12.93	12.50	12.10	11.71	11.35	11.00	10.67	10.35	10.05	41
42	12.86	12.45	12.06	11.69	11.34	11.01	10.68	10.38	10.08	9.80	9.53	42
43	11.87	11.52	11.19	10.87	10.57	10.28	10.00	9.73	9.48	9.23	9.00	43
44	10.88	10.59	10.31	10.04	9.78	9.54	9.30	9.07	8.85	8.64	8.43	44
45	9.90	9.66	9.42	9.20	8.98	8.77	8.57	8.38	8.19	8.01	7.84	45
46	8.91	8.72	8.53	8.34	8.17	7.99	7.83	7.67	7.51	7.36	7.22	46
47	7.93	7.77	7.62	7.47	7.33	7.19	7.06	6.93	6.81	6.68	6.57	47
48	6.94	6.82	6.70	6.59	6.48	6.37	6.27	6.17	6.07	5.98	5.88	48
49	5.95	5.87	5.78	5.70	5.61	5.53	5.46	5.38	5.31	5.23	5.16	49
50	4.97	4.90	4.84	4.79	4.73	4.67	4.62	4.56	4.51	4.46	4.41	50
51	3.98	3.94	3.90	3.86	3.82	3.79	3.75	3.72	3.68	3.65	3.61	51
52	2.99	2.96	2.94	2.92	2.90	2.88	2.86	2.84	2.82	2.80	2.78	52
53	1.99	1.98	1.97	1.96	1.95	1.95	1.94	1.93	1.92	1.91	1.90	53
54	1.00	1.00	0.99	0.99	0.99	0.99	0.98	0.98	0.98	0.98	0.97	54

Table 7 Multipliers for loss of earnings to pension age 60 (males)

Age at date of trial	Multiplier calculated with allowance for projected mortality from the 2004-based population projections and rate of return of											Age at date of trial
	0.0%	0.5%	1.0%	1.5%	2.0%	2.5%	3.0%	3.5%	4.0%	4.5%	5.0%	
16	43.07	38.71	34.96	31.70	28.87	26.41	24.25	22.35	20.68	19.20	17.89	16
17	42.07	37.90	34.30	31.17	28.44	26.05	23.96	22.12	20.49	19.04	17.76	17
18	41.07	37.10	33.64	30.63	28.00	25.70	23.67	21.88	20.29	18.88	17.63	18
19	40.08	36.29	32.98	30.10	27.56	25.34	23.37	21.63	20.09	18.72	17.49	19
20	39.10	35.48	32.32	29.55	27.12	24.97	23.07	21.38	19.88	18.55	17.35	20
21	38.11	34.67	31.65	29.00	26.66	24.59	22.76	21.12	19.67	18.37	17.20	21
22	37.12	33.85	30.98	28.44	26.19	24.20	22.43	20.85	19.44	18.18	17.04	22
23	36.14	33.03	30.29	27.87	25.72	23.81	22.10	20.58	19.21	17.98	16.88	23
24	35.15	32.21	29.60	27.29	25.23	23.40	21.76	20.29	18.97	17.78	16.71	24
25	34.16	31.38	28.91	26.70	24.74	22.98	21.41	19.99	18.72	17.56	16.52	25
26	33.18	30.55	28.20	26.11	24.23	22.55	21.04	19.68	18.45	17.34	16.33	26
27	32.19	29.71	27.49	25.50	23.72	22.12	20.67	19.36	18.18	17.11	16.13	27
28	31.21	28.87	26.78	24.89	23.20	21.67	20.29	19.04	17.90	16.87	15.93	28
29	30.23	28.03	26.05	24.27	22.67	21.21	19.89	18.70	17.61	16.61	15.71	29
30	29.24	27.18	25.33	23.65	22.12	20.74	19.49	18.35	17.30	16.35	15.48	30
31	28.26	26.33	24.59	23.01	21.57	20.26	19.07	17.98	16.99	16.08	15.24	31
32	27.28	25.48	23.85	22.36	21.01	19.77	18.64	17.61	16.66	15.79	14.99	32
33	26.30	24.63	23.10	21.71	20.43	19.27	18.20	17.22	16.32	15.49	14.72	33
34	25.32	23.77	22.34	21.04	19.85	18.76	17.75	16.82	15.97	15.18	14.45	34
35	24.34	22.90	21.58	20.37	19.26	18.23	17.28	16.41	15.60	14.85	14.16	35
36	23.36	22.03	20.81	19.69	18.65	17.69	16.80	15.98	15.22	14.51	13.86	36
37	22.39	21.16	20.04	18.99	18.03	17.14	16.31	15.54	14.82	14.16	13.54	37
38	21.41	20.29	19.25	18.29	17.40	16.57	15.80	15.08	14.41	13.79	13.21	38
39	20.43	19.41	18.46	17.58	16.76	15.99	15.28	14.61	13.99	13.40	12.86	39
40	19.45	18.53	17.66	16.85	16.10	15.40	14.74	14.12	13.54	13.00	12.49	40
41	18.48	17.64	16.86	16.12	15.43	14.79	14.18	13.62	13.08	12.58	12.11	41
42	17.50	16.75	16.04	15.38	14.75	14.17	13.62	13.10	12.61	12.14	11.71	42
43	16.53	15.86	15.22	14.63	14.06	13.53	13.03	12.56	12.11	11.69	11.29	43
44	15.56	14.96	14.40	13.86	13.36	12.88	12.43	12.00	11.60	11.21	10.85	44
45	14.59	14.06	13.56	13.09	12.64	12.22	11.81	11.43	11.06	10.72	10.39	45
46	13.62	13.16	12.72	12.31	11.91	11.54	11.18	10.84	10.51	10.20	9.90	46
47	12.65	12.26	11.88	11.52	11.17	10.84	10.53	10.23	9.94	9.66	9.40	47
48	11.69	11.35	11.02	10.71	10.42	10.13	9.86	9.60	9.34	9.10	8.87	48
49	10.72	10.44	10.16	9.90	9.65	9.40	9.17	8.95	8.73	8.52	8.32	49
50	9.76	9.52	9.30	9.08	8.86	8.66	8.46	8.27	8.09	7.91	7.74	50
51	8.80	8.61	8.42	8.24	8.07	7.90	7.73	7.58	7.42	7.28	7.13	51
52	7.83	7.68	7.53	7.39	7.25	7.11	6.98	6.86	6.73	6.61	6.50	52
53	6.87	6.75	6.63	6.52	6.41	6.31	6.21	6.11	6.01	5.92	5.82	53
54	5.90	5.81	5.72	5.64	5.56	5.48	5.41	5.33	5.26	5.19	5.12	54
55	4.92	4.86	4.80	4.75	4.69	4.63	4.58	4.53	4.47	4.42	4.37	55
56	3.95	3.91	3.87	3.83	3.80	3.76	3.72	3.69	3.65	3.62	3.59	56
57	2.97	2.95	2.92	2.90	2.88	2.86	2.84	2.82	2.80	2.78	2.76	57
58	1.98	1.97	1.96	1.96	1.95	1.94	1.93	1.92	1.91	1.90	1.89	58
59	1.00	0.99	0.99	0.99	0.99	0.98	0.98	0.98	0.98	0.97	0.97	59

Table 8 Multipliers for loss of earnings to pension age 60 (females)

Age at date of trial	Multiplier calculated with allowance for projected mortality from the 2004-based population projections and rate of return of											Age at date of trial
	0.0%	0.5%	1.0%	1.5%	2.0%	2.5%	3.0%	3.5%	4.0%	4.5%	5.0%	
16	43.49	39.07	35.26	31.97	29.10	26.60	24.42	22.50	20.81	19.32	17.99	16
17	42.49	38.27	34.62	31.44	28.68	26.26	24.14	22.27	20.63	19.16	17.87	17
18	41.50	37.46	33.96	30.91	28.24	25.91	23.85	22.04	20.43	19.01	17.74	18
19	40.50	36.65	33.30	30.37	27.80	25.55	23.56	21.80	20.23	18.84	17.60	19
20	39.51	35.84	32.63	29.82	27.35	25.18	23.25	21.55	20.03	18.67	17.46	20
21	38.51	35.02	31.96	29.27	26.89	24.80	22.94	21.29	19.81	18.49	17.31	21
22	37.51	34.20	31.28	28.70	26.43	24.41	22.62	21.02	19.59	18.31	17.16	22
23	36.52	33.37	30.59	28.13	25.95	24.01	22.28	20.74	19.35	18.11	16.99	23
24	35.52	32.54	29.89	27.55	25.46	23.60	21.94	20.45	19.11	17.91	16.82	24
25	34.53	31.70	29.19	26.96	24.96	23.18	21.59	20.15	18.86	17.69	16.64	25
26	33.53	30.86	28.48	26.36	24.46	22.75	21.22	19.84	18.60	17.47	16.45	26
27	32.54	30.02	27.77	25.75	23.94	22.31	20.85	19.52	18.33	17.24	16.25	27
28	31.54	29.17	27.04	25.13	23.42	21.86	20.46	19.19	18.04	17.00	16.04	28
29	30.55	28.32	26.32	24.51	22.88	21.40	20.07	18.85	17.75	16.74	15.83	29
30	29.56	27.47	25.58	23.87	22.33	20.93	19.66	18.50	17.44	16.48	15.60	30
31	28.56	26.61	24.84	23.23	21.77	20.45	19.24	18.14	17.13	16.20	15.36	31
32	27.57	25.74	24.09	22.58	21.21	19.95	18.81	17.76	16.80	15.92	15.10	32
33	26.58	24.88	23.33	21.92	20.63	19.45	18.36	17.37	16.46	15.61	14.84	33
34	25.59	24.01	22.57	21.25	20.04	18.93	17.91	16.97	16.10	15.30	14.56	34
35	24.60	23.14	21.80	20.57	19.44	18.39	17.44	16.55	15.73	14.97	14.27	35
36	23.61	22.26	21.02	19.88	18.82	17.85	16.95	16.12	15.35	14.63	13.97	36
37	22.62	21.38	20.23	19.18	18.20	17.29	16.45	15.67	14.95	14.28	13.65	37
38	21.63	20.49	19.44	18.47	17.56	16.72	15.94	15.21	14.53	13.90	13.31	38
39	20.64	19.60	18.64	17.75	16.91	16.14	15.41	14.74	14.11	13.51	12.96	39
40	19.65	18.71	17.83	17.02	16.25	15.54	14.87	14.24	13.66	13.11	12.59	40
41	18.67	17.81	17.02	16.27	15.58	14.92	14.31	13.74	13.20	12.69	12.21	41
42	17.68	16.92	16.20	15.52	14.89	14.30	13.74	13.21	12.71	12.25	11.80	42
43	16.70	16.01	15.37	14.77	14.19	13.66	13.15	12.67	12.22	11.79	11.38	43
44	15.71	15.11	14.54	14.00	13.48	13.00	12.54	12.11	11.70	11.31	10.94	44
45	14.73	14.20	13.69	13.22	12.76	12.33	11.92	11.53	11.16	10.81	10.48	45
46	13.76	13.29	12.85	12.43	12.02	11.64	11.28	10.93	10.60	10.29	9.99	46
47	12.78	12.37	11.99	11.62	11.27	10.94	10.62	10.32	10.03	9.75	9.48	47
48	11.80	11.46	11.13	10.81	10.51	10.22	9.94	9.68	9.43	9.18	8.95	48
49	10.82	10.53	10.25	9.99	9.73	9.48	9.25	9.02	8.80	8.59	8.39	49
50	9.85	9.61	9.37	9.15	8.94	8.73	8.53	8.34	8.15	7.97	7.80	50
51	8.87	8.67	8.49	8.30	8.13	7.96	7.79	7.63	7.48	7.33	7.19	51
52	7.89	7.74	7.59	7.44	7.30	7.16	7.03	6.90	6.78	6.66	6.54	52
53	6.91	6.79	6.68	6.56	6.46	6.35	6.25	6.15	6.05	5.95	5.86	53
54	5.93	5.84	5.76	5.67	5.59	5.51	5.44	5.36	5.29	5.22	5.14	54
55	4.95	4.89	4.83	4.77	4.71	4.66	4.60	4.55	4.50	4.44	4.39	55
56	3.96	3.93	3.89	3.85	3.81	3.78	3.74	3.70	3.67	3.64	3.60	56
57	2.98	2.96	2.93	2.91	2.89	2.87	2.85	2.83	2.81	2.79	2.77	57
58	1.99	1.98	1.97	1.96	1.95	1.94	1.93	1.92	1.91	1.90	1.90	58
59	1.00	0.99	0.99	0.99	0.99	0.99	0.98	0.98	0.98	0.98	0.97	59

Table 9 Multipliers for loss of earnings to pension age 65 (males)

Age at date of trial	Multiplier calculated with allowance for projected mortality from the 2004-based population projections and rate of return of											Age at date of trial
	0.0%	0.5%	1.0%	1.5%	2.0%	2.5%	3.0%	3.5%	4.0%	4.5%	5.0%	
16	47.63	42.33	37.83	33.99	30.69	27.86	25.40	23.27	21.42	19.79	18.36	16
17	46.62	41.54	37.20	33.49	30.29	27.54	25.15	23.07	21.25	19.66	18.26	17
18	45.63	40.75	36.57	32.98	29.89	27.22	24.89	22.86	21.09	19.53	18.15	18
19	44.64	39.96	35.94	32.48	29.49	26.89	24.63	22.66	20.92	19.39	18.04	19
20	43.65	39.16	35.31	31.97	29.08	26.56	24.37	22.44	20.74	19.25	17.92	20
21	42.66	38.37	34.66	31.45	28.66	26.23	24.09	22.22	20.56	19.10	17.80	21
22	41.67	37.57	34.02	30.93	28.24	25.88	23.81	21.99	20.37	18.95	17.67	22
23	40.69	36.77	33.36	30.40	27.80	25.52	23.52	21.75	20.18	18.78	17.54	23
24	39.70	35.96	32.70	29.86	27.36	25.16	23.22	21.50	19.97	18.62	17.40	24
25	38.71	35.15	32.04	29.31	26.90	24.78	22.91	21.24	19.76	18.44	17.25	25
26	37.72	34.33	31.36	28.75	26.44	24.40	22.59	20.98	19.54	18.25	17.10	26
27	36.73	33.51	30.68	28.18	25.97	24.01	22.26	20.71	19.31	18.06	16.94	27
28	35.75	32.69	30.00	27.61	25.49	23.61	21.93	20.42	19.08	17.86	16.77	28
29	34.76	31.87	29.31	27.03	25.01	23.20	21.58	20.13	18.83	17.66	16.60	29
30	33.78	31.04	28.61	26.45	24.51	22.78	21.23	19.83	18.57	17.44	16.41	30
31	32.80	30.21	27.91	25.85	24.01	22.35	20.86	19.52	18.31	17.21	16.22	31
32	31.82	29.38	27.20	25.25	23.49	21.91	20.49	19.20	18.04	16.98	16.02	32
33	30.84	28.54	26.49	24.63	22.97	21.46	20.10	18.87	17.75	16.73	15.80	33
34	29.86	27.70	25.76	24.01	22.43	21.00	19.71	18.53	17.45	16.48	15.58	34
35	28.88	26.86	25.04	23.39	21.89	20.53	19.30	18.17	17.15	16.21	15.35	35
36	27.90	26.01	24.30	22.75	21.34	20.05	18.88	17.81	16.83	15.93	15.11	36
37	26.93	25.16	23.56	22.10	20.77	19.56	18.45	17.43	16.50	15.64	14.85	37
38	25.95	24.31	22.81	21.45	20.20	19.05	18.00	17.04	16.16	15.34	14.59	38
39	24.98	23.45	22.06	20.78	19.61	18.54	17.55	16.64	15.80	15.02	14.31	39
40	24.00	22.59	21.30	20.11	19.02	18.01	17.08	16.22	15.43	14.70	14.01	40
41	23.03	21.73	20.53	19.43	18.41	17.47	16.60	15.79	15.05	14.35	13.71	41
42	22.06	20.86	19.76	18.74	17.79	16.92	16.10	15.35	14.65	14.00	13.39	42
43	21.09	19.99	18.98	18.04	17.16	16.35	15.60	14.89	14.24	13.62	13.05	43
44	20.12	19.12	18.19	17.33	16.52	15.77	15.07	14.42	13.81	13.24	12.70	44
45	19.16	18.25	17.40	16.61	15.88	15.19	14.54	13.94	13.37	12.84	12.34	45
46	18.20	17.38	16.61	15.89	15.22	14.58	13.99	13.44	12.91	12.42	11.96	46
47	17.24	16.50	15.81	15.16	14.55	13.97	13.43	12.92	12.44	11.99	11.56	47
48	16.29	15.63	15.00	14.42	13.87	13.35	12.86	12.39	11.95	11.54	11.15	48
49	15.33	14.75	14.20	13.67	13.18	12.71	12.27	11.85	11.45	11.07	10.71	49
50	14.39	13.87	13.38	12.92	12.48	12.06	11.66	11.29	10.93	10.59	10.26	50
51	13.44	12.99	12.56	12.15	11.76	11.40	11.04	10.71	10.39	10.08	9.79	51
52	12.49	12.10	11.73	11.38	11.04	10.71	10.41	10.11	9.83	9.56	9.30	52
53	11.55	11.21	10.89	10.59	10.30	10.02	9.75	9.49	9.24	9.01	8.78	53
54	10.60	10.32	10.05	9.79	9.54	9.30	9.07	8.85	8.63	8.43	8.23	54
55	9.65	9.41	9.19	8.97	8.76	8.56	8.37	8.18	8.00	7.83	7.66	55
56	8.69	8.50	8.32	8.14	7.97	7.81	7.65	7.49	7.34	7.20	7.06	56
57	7.74	7.59	7.44	7.30	7.16	7.03	6.90	6.78	6.66	6.54	6.42	57
58	6.78	6.67	6.56	6.45	6.34	6.24	6.14	6.04	5.94	5.85	5.76	58
59	5.83	5.74	5.66	5.58	5.50	5.42	5.35	5.27	5.20	5.13	5.06	59
60	4.87	4.81	4.75	4.70	4.64	4.59	4.53	4.48	4.43	4.38	4.33	60
61	3.91	3.87	3.84	3.80	3.76	3.73	3.69	3.66	3.62	3.59	3.56	61
62	2.95	2.93	2.90	2.88	2.86	2.84	2.82	2.80	2.78	2.76	2.74	62
63	1.98	1.97	1.96	1.95	1.94	1.93	1.92	1.91	1.90	1.89	1.88	63
64	0.99	0.99	0.99	0.99	0.98	0.98	0.98	0.98	0.97	0.97	0.97	64

Table 10 Multipliers for loss of earnings to pension age 65 (females)

Age at date of trial	Multiplier calculated with allowance for projected mortality from the 2004-based population projections and rate of return of											Age at date of trial
	0.0%	0.5%	1.0%	1.5%	2.0%	2.5%	3.0%	3.5%	4.0%	4.5%	5.0%	
16	48.22	42.83	38.24	34.34	30.99	28.11	25.62	23.46	21.58	19.93	18.48	16
17	47.22	42.04	37.62	33.84	30.60	27.80	25.37	23.26	21.42	19.80	18.38	17
18	46.22	41.25	37.00	33.35	30.20	27.48	25.12	23.06	21.26	19.68	18.28	18
19	45.23	40.46	36.37	32.84	29.80	27.16	24.86	22.86	21.09	19.54	18.17	19
20	44.23	39.66	35.73	32.33	29.39	26.83	24.60	22.64	20.92	19.40	18.06	20
21	43.23	38.86	35.08	31.81	28.97	26.49	24.32	22.42	20.74	19.26	17.94	21
22	42.23	38.05	34.43	31.29	28.54	26.15	24.04	22.19	20.55	19.10	17.81	22
23	41.24	37.24	33.77	30.75	28.11	25.79	23.75	21.95	20.36	18.94	17.68	23
24	40.24	36.43	33.11	30.21	27.66	25.43	23.45	21.71	20.16	18.78	17.54	24
25	39.24	35.61	32.44	29.66	27.21	25.05	23.14	21.45	19.95	18.60	17.40	25
26	38.25	34.79	31.76	29.10	26.75	24.67	22.83	21.19	19.73	18.42	17.25	26
27	37.25	33.97	31.08	28.53	26.28	24.28	22.50	20.92	19.50	18.23	17.09	27
28	36.25	33.14	30.39	27.95	25.80	23.88	22.16	20.63	19.26	18.03	16.92	28
29	35.26	32.31	29.69	27.37	25.31	23.46	21.82	20.34	19.02	17.82	16.75	29
30	34.26	31.47	28.99	26.78	24.81	23.04	21.46	20.04	18.76	17.61	16.56	30
31	33.27	30.63	28.28	26.18	24.30	22.61	21.10	19.73	18.50	17.38	16.37	31
32	32.28	29.79	27.56	25.57	23.78	22.17	20.72	19.41	18.22	17.15	16.17	32
33	31.28	28.94	26.84	24.95	23.25	21.72	20.33	19.08	17.94	16.90	15.96	33
34	30.29	28.09	26.11	24.33	22.71	21.26	19.93	18.73	17.64	16.65	15.74	34
35	29.30	27.24	25.38	23.69	22.17	20.78	19.52	18.38	17.33	16.38	15.51	35
36	28.31	26.38	24.63	23.05	21.61	20.30	19.10	18.01	17.01	16.10	15.26	36
37	27.32	25.52	23.88	22.39	21.04	19.80	18.67	17.63	16.68	15.81	15.01	37
38	26.33	24.66	23.13	21.73	20.46	19.29	18.22	17.24	16.34	15.51	14.74	38
39	25.34	23.79	22.36	21.06	19.87	18.77	17.76	16.84	15.98	15.19	14.46	39
40	24.36	22.92	21.60	20.38	19.27	18.24	17.29	16.42	15.61	14.86	14.17	40
41	23.37	22.04	20.82	19.69	18.66	17.70	16.81	15.99	15.23	14.52	13.86	41
42	22.39	21.17	20.04	19.00	18.03	17.14	16.31	15.54	14.83	14.16	13.54	42
43	21.41	20.29	19.25	18.29	17.40	16.57	15.80	15.08	14.41	13.79	13.21	43
44	20.43	19.41	18.46	17.58	16.76	15.99	15.28	14.61	13.99	13.40	12.86	44
45	19.45	18.53	17.66	16.85	16.10	15.40	14.74	14.12	13.54	13.00	12.49	45
46	18.48	17.64	16.86	16.12	15.43	14.79	14.19	13.62	13.08	12.58	12.11	46
47	17.51	16.75	16.05	15.38	14.76	14.17	13.62	13.10	12.61	12.15	11.71	47
48	16.54	15.86	15.23	14.63	14.07	13.54	13.04	12.56	12.11	11.69	11.29	48
49	15.57	14.97	14.41	13.87	13.37	12.89	12.44	12.01	11.60	11.22	10.85	49
50	14.60	14.07	13.57	13.10	12.65	12.23	11.82	11.44	11.07	10.73	10.39	50
51	13.64	13.17	12.74	12.32	11.93	11.55	11.19	10.85	10.52	10.21	9.91	51
52	12.67	12.27	11.89	11.53	11.18	10.85	10.54	10.24	9.95	9.67	9.41	52
53	11.70	11.36	11.04	10.73	10.43	10.14	9.87	9.61	9.35	9.11	8.88	53
54	10.73	10.45	10.17	9.91	9.66	9.41	9.18	8.95	8.74	8.53	8.33	54
55	9.77	9.53	9.30	9.08	8.87	8.66	8.47	8.28	8.09	7.92	7.74	55
56	8.80	8.61	8.42	8.24	8.06	7.90	7.73	7.58	7.42	7.28	7.13	56
57	7.83	7.68	7.53	7.38	7.25	7.11	6.98	6.85	6.73	6.61	6.49	57
58	6.86	6.74	6.63	6.52	6.41	6.30	6.20	6.10	6.01	5.91	5.82	58
59	5.89	5.80	5.72	5.64	5.56	5.48	5.40	5.33	5.25	5.18	5.11	59
60	4.92	4.86	4.80	4.74	4.68	4.63	4.57	4.52	4.47	4.42	4.37	60
61	3.94	3.91	3.87	3.83	3.79	3.76	3.72	3.69	3.65	3.62	3.59	61
62	2.97	2.94	2.92	2.90	2.88	2.86	2.84	2.82	2.80	2.78	2.76	62
63	1.98	1.97	1.96	1.96	1.95	1.94	1.93	1.92	1.91	1.90	1.89	63
64	1.00	0.99	0.99	0.99	0.99	0.98	0.98	0.98	0.98	0.97	0.97	64

Table 11 Multipliers for loss of earnings to pension age 70 (males)

Age at date of trial	Multiplier calculated with allowance for projected mortality from the 2004-based population projections and rate of return of											Age at date of trial
	0.0%	0.5%	1.0%	1.5%	2.0%	2.5%	3.0%	3.5%	4.0%	4.5%	5.0%	
16	52.01	45.72	40.46	36.02	32.27	29.09	26.36	24.02	22.00	20.25	18.72	16
17	51.00	44.94	39.85	35.55	31.91	28.80	26.14	23.84	21.86	20.14	18.63	17
18	50.00	44.16	39.24	35.08	31.54	28.51	25.91	23.66	21.72	20.02	18.54	18
19	49.01	43.39	38.64	34.60	31.16	28.22	25.68	23.48	21.57	19.91	18.45	19
20	48.01	42.61	38.03	34.13	30.79	27.92	25.44	23.29	21.42	19.79	18.35	20
21	47.02	41.83	37.41	33.64	30.40	27.61	25.20	23.10	21.27	19.67	18.25	21
22	46.03	41.05	36.79	33.14	30.01	27.30	24.95	22.90	21.11	19.54	18.15	22
23	45.04	40.26	36.16	32.64	29.61	26.98	24.69	22.69	20.94	19.40	18.04	23
24	44.05	39.47	35.53	32.13	29.20	26.65	24.42	22.48	20.77	19.26	17.93	24
25	43.06	38.67	34.89	31.62	28.78	26.31	24.15	22.25	20.59	19.11	17.80	25
26	42.06	37.87	34.24	31.09	28.35	25.96	23.87	22.02	20.40	18.96	17.68	26
27	41.07	37.06	33.59	30.56	27.92	25.61	23.58	21.79	20.20	18.80	17.54	27
28	40.09	36.26	32.93	30.02	27.48	25.25	23.28	21.54	20.00	18.63	17.41	28
29	39.10	35.45	32.27	29.48	27.03	24.88	22.97	21.29	19.79	18.46	17.26	29
30	38.12	34.64	31.60	28.93	26.58	24.50	22.66	21.03	19.57	18.27	17.11	30
31	37.13	33.83	30.92	28.37	26.11	24.11	22.34	20.76	19.35	18.08	16.95	31
32	36.15	33.01	30.24	27.80	25.64	23.72	22.01	20.48	19.11	17.89	16.78	32
33	35.17	32.19	29.56	27.23	25.16	23.31	21.67	20.19	18.87	17.68	16.61	33
34	34.19	31.37	28.87	26.64	24.66	22.90	21.32	19.90	18.62	17.47	16.43	34
35	33.21	30.54	28.17	26.05	24.16	22.47	20.96	19.59	18.36	17.25	16.24	35
36	32.23	29.71	27.46	25.46	23.66	22.04	20.59	19.27	18.09	17.02	16.04	36
37	31.25	28.88	26.75	24.85	23.14	21.60	20.21	18.95	17.81	16.77	15.83	37
38	30.27	28.04	26.04	24.23	22.61	21.14	19.81	18.61	17.52	16.52	15.62	38
39	29.30	27.20	25.31	23.61	22.07	20.68	19.41	18.26	17.22	16.26	15.39	39
40	28.32	26.36	24.59	22.98	21.52	20.20	19.00	17.90	16.90	15.99	15.15	40
41	27.35	25.51	23.85	22.34	20.97	19.72	18.58	17.53	16.58	15.70	14.90	41
42	26.38	24.67	23.11	21.70	20.40	19.22	18.14	17.15	16.24	15.41	14.64	42
43	25.41	23.82	22.37	21.04	19.83	18.72	17.70	16.76	15.90	15.10	14.37	43
44	24.45	22.97	21.62	20.38	19.24	18.20	17.24	16.35	15.54	14.78	14.08	44
45	23.49	22.12	20.87	19.71	18.65	17.67	16.77	15.94	15.17	14.45	13.79	45
46	22.53	21.27	20.11	19.04	18.05	17.14	16.29	15.51	14.78	14.11	13.48	46
47	21.58	20.42	19.35	18.36	17.44	16.59	15.80	15.07	14.39	13.75	13.16	47
48	20.63	19.57	18.59	17.67	16.83	16.04	15.30	14.62	13.98	13.39	12.83	48
49	19.69	18.72	17.82	16.98	16.20	15.47	14.79	14.16	13.57	13.01	12.49	49
50	18.76	17.88	17.06	16.29	15.57	14.90	14.27	13.69	13.14	12.62	12.13	50
51	17.83	17.03	16.28	15.59	14.93	14.32	13.74	13.20	12.69	12.21	11.76	51
52	16.90	16.18	15.51	14.87	14.28	13.72	13.19	12.70	12.23	11.79	11.37	52
53	15.97	15.32	14.72	14.15	13.62	13.11	12.63	12.18	11.75	11.35	10.96	53
54	15.03	14.46	13.93	13.42	12.94	12.48	12.05	11.64	11.25	10.89	10.54	54
55	14.10	13.60	13.12	12.67	12.24	11.84	11.45	11.09	10.74	10.40	10.09	55
56	13.17	12.73	12.31	11.91	11.54	11.18	10.84	10.51	10.20	9.90	9.62	56
57	12.23	11.85	11.49	11.15	10.82	10.50	10.20	9.91	9.64	9.38	9.12	57
58	11.30	10.97	10.66	10.37	10.08	9.81	9.55	9.30	9.06	8.83	8.61	58
59	10.37	10.09	9.83	9.58	9.34	9.11	8.88	8.67	8.46	8.26	8.07	59
60	9.44	9.21	9.00	8.79	8.58	8.39	8.20	8.02	7.84	7.67	7.51	60
61	8.52	8.33	8.15	7.98	7.82	7.65	7.50	7.35	7.20	7.06	6.92	61
62	7.60	7.45	7.31	7.17	7.03	6.91	6.78	6.66	6.54	6.42	6.31	62
63	6.67	6.56	6.45	6.34	6.24	6.14	6.04	5.94	5.85	5.76	5.67	63
64	5.75	5.66	5.58	5.50	5.42	5.35	5.27	5.20	5.13	5.06	4.99	64
65	4.81	4.75	4.70	4.64	4.58	4.53	4.48	4.43	4.38	4.33	4.28	65
66	3.87	3.83	3.80	3.76	3.72	3.69	3.65	3.62	3.59	3.55	3.52	66
67	2.92	2.90	2.88	2.86	2.84	2.82	2.80	2.78	2.76	2.74	2.72	67
68	1.96	1.95	1.94	1.93	1.92	1.92	1.91	1.90	1.89	1.88	1.87	68
69	0.99	0.99	0.98	0.98	0.98	0.98	0.98	0.97	0.97	0.97	0.97	69

Table 12 Multipliers for loss of earnings to pension age 70 (females)

Age at date of trial	Multiplier calculated with allowance for projected mortality from the 2004-based population projections and rate of return of 0.0%	0.5%	1.0%	1.5%	2.0%	2.5%	3.0%	3.5%	4.0%	4.5%	5.0%	Age at date of trial
16	52.83	46.39	41.01	36.48	32.65	29.40	26.62	24.24	22.19	20.41	18.85	16
17	51.83	45.62	40.41	36.02	32.29	29.12	26.41	24.08	22.06	20.30	18.77	17
18	50.83	44.85	39.81	35.55	31.93	28.84	26.19	23.90	21.92	20.20	18.69	18
19	49.83	44.07	39.21	35.08	31.56	28.55	25.96	23.72	21.78	20.09	18.60	19
20	48.83	43.29	38.59	34.60	31.19	28.26	25.73	23.54	21.64	19.97	18.51	20
21	47.83	42.50	37.98	34.11	30.80	27.95	25.49	23.35	21.48	19.85	18.42	21
22	46.83	41.71	37.35	33.62	30.41	27.64	25.24	23.15	21.33	19.72	18.31	22
23	45.83	40.92	36.72	33.12	30.01	27.32	24.99	22.95	21.16	19.59	18.21	23
24	44.83	40.12	36.09	32.61	29.60	26.99	24.72	22.74	20.99	19.45	18.10	24
25	43.83	39.32	35.44	32.09	29.19	26.66	24.45	22.52	20.81	19.31	17.98	25
26	42.83	38.52	34.79	31.57	28.76	26.32	24.17	22.29	20.63	19.16	17.85	26
27	41.83	37.71	34.14	31.04	28.33	25.96	23.89	22.05	20.44	19.00	17.73	27
28	40.83	36.90	33.48	30.50	27.89	25.60	23.59	21.81	20.24	18.84	17.59	28
29	39.83	36.08	32.81	29.95	27.44	25.23	23.29	21.56	20.03	18.67	17.45	29
30	38.83	35.26	32.14	29.39	26.98	24.86	22.97	21.30	19.82	18.49	17.30	30
31	37.84	34.44	31.46	28.83	26.52	24.47	22.65	21.03	19.59	18.30	17.14	31
32	36.84	33.61	30.77	28.26	26.04	24.07	22.32	20.76	19.36	18.11	16.98	32
33	35.85	32.78	30.08	27.68	25.56	23.67	21.98	20.47	19.12	17.90	16.81	33
34	34.85	31.95	29.38	27.10	25.07	23.25	21.63	20.18	18.87	17.69	16.63	34
35	33.86	31.12	28.68	26.50	24.56	22.83	21.27	19.87	18.61	17.47	16.44	35
36	32.87	30.28	27.97	25.90	24.05	22.39	20.90	19.56	18.34	17.24	16.25	36
37	31.88	29.43	27.25	25.29	23.53	21.95	20.52	19.23	18.06	17.00	16.04	37
38	30.89	28.59	26.52	24.67	23.00	21.49	20.13	18.89	17.77	16.75	15.82	38
39	29.90	27.74	25.80	24.04	22.46	21.03	19.73	18.55	17.47	16.49	15.60	39
40	28.91	26.89	25.06	23.41	21.91	20.55	19.32	18.19	17.16	16.22	15.36	40
41	27.93	26.03	24.32	22.76	21.35	20.06	18.89	17.82	16.84	15.94	15.12	41
42	26.94	25.18	23.57	22.11	20.78	19.57	18.46	17.44	16.51	15.65	14.86	42
43	25.96	24.32	22.82	21.46	20.21	19.06	18.01	17.05	16.16	15.34	14.59	43
44	24.99	23.46	22.07	20.79	19.62	18.54	17.55	16.64	15.80	15.03	14.31	44
45	24.01	22.60	21.31	20.12	19.02	18.01	17.09	16.23	15.43	14.70	14.02	45
46	23.04	21.74	20.54	19.44	18.42	17.48	16.61	15.80	15.05	14.36	13.71	46
47	22.07	20.88	19.77	18.75	17.80	16.93	16.11	15.36	14.66	14.00	13.39	47
48	21.11	20.01	19.00	18.05	17.18	16.36	15.61	14.90	14.25	13.63	13.06	48
49	20.15	19.15	18.22	17.35	16.54	15.79	15.09	14.44	13.82	13.25	12.72	49
50	19.19	18.28	17.43	16.64	15.90	15.21	14.56	13.95	13.39	12.85	12.35	50
51	18.23	17.41	16.64	15.92	15.24	14.61	14.02	13.46	12.93	12.44	11.98	51
52	17.27	16.53	15.84	15.19	14.57	14.00	13.46	12.94	12.46	12.01	11.58	52
53	16.32	15.66	15.03	14.45	13.89	13.37	12.88	12.41	11.97	11.56	11.16	53
54	15.36	14.77	14.22	13.69	13.20	12.73	12.29	11.87	11.47	11.09	10.73	54
55	14.40	13.89	13.40	12.93	12.49	12.07	11.68	11.30	10.94	10.60	10.27	55
56	13.45	13.00	12.57	12.16	11.77	11.40	11.05	10.71	10.39	10.09	9.80	56
57	12.49	12.10	11.73	11.38	11.04	10.71	10.40	10.11	9.83	9.56	9.30	57
58	11.54	11.21	10.89	10.58	10.29	10.01	9.74	9.48	9.24	9.00	8.77	58
59	10.59	10.31	10.04	9.78	9.53	9.29	9.06	8.84	8.63	8.42	8.23	59
60	9.64	9.41	9.18	8.97	8.76	8.56	8.36	8.18	7.99	7.82	7.65	60
61	8.69	8.50	8.32	8.14	7.97	7.80	7.64	7.49	7.34	7.19	7.05	61
62	7.74	7.59	7.44	7.30	7.17	7.03	6.90	6.78	6.66	6.54	6.42	62
63	6.79	6.67	6.56	6.45	6.35	6.24	6.14	6.04	5.95	5.85	5.76	63
64	5.84	5.75	5.67	5.59	5.51	5.43	5.35	5.28	5.21	5.14	5.07	64
65	4.88	4.82	4.76	4.70	4.65	4.59	4.54	4.49	4.43	4.38	4.33	65
66	3.92	3.88	3.84	3.80	3.77	3.73	3.70	3.66	3.63	3.59	3.56	66
67	2.95	2.93	2.91	2.89	2.87	2.84	2.82	2.80	2.78	2.77	2.75	67
68	1.98	1.97	1.96	1.95	1.94	1.93	1.92	1.91	1.90	1.89	1.88	68
69	0.99	0.99	0.99	0.99	0.98	0.98	0.98	0.98	0.97	0.97	0.97	69

Table 13 Multipliers for loss of earnings to pension age 75 (males)

Age at date of trial	Multiplier calculated with allowance for projected mortality from the 2004-based population projections and rate of return of											Age at date of trial
	0.0%	0.5%	1.0%	1.5%	2.0%	2.5%	3.0%	3.5%	4.0%	4.5%	5.0%	
16	56.16	48.85	42.82	37.81	33.63	30.11	27.14	24.61	22.45	20.59	18.98	16
17	55.14	48.08	42.23	37.36	33.29	29.85	26.94	24.46	22.33	20.50	18.91	17
18	54.13	47.31	41.65	36.91	32.94	29.58	26.73	24.30	22.21	20.40	18.83	18
19	53.13	46.54	41.06	36.46	32.59	29.32	26.53	24.14	22.08	20.30	18.75	19
20	52.13	45.78	40.47	36.01	32.24	29.04	26.31	23.97	21.95	20.20	18.67	20
21	51.13	45.01	39.88	35.55	31.88	28.77	26.10	23.80	21.82	20.09	18.59	21
22	50.14	44.24	39.28	35.08	31.52	28.48	25.87	23.62	21.68	19.98	18.50	22
23	49.14	43.46	38.67	34.61	31.15	28.19	25.64	23.44	21.53	19.87	18.41	23
24	48.14	42.68	38.06	34.12	30.77	27.89	25.40	23.25	21.38	19.75	18.31	24
25	47.14	41.89	37.44	33.63	30.38	27.58	25.15	23.05	21.22	19.62	18.21	25
26	46.15	41.10	36.81	33.14	29.98	27.26	24.90	22.85	21.06	19.49	18.10	26
27	45.15	40.31	36.18	32.63	29.58	26.94	24.64	22.64	20.89	19.35	17.99	27
28	44.16	39.52	35.54	32.12	29.17	26.61	24.37	22.42	20.71	19.20	17.87	28
29	43.17	38.73	34.91	31.61	28.75	26.27	24.10	22.20	20.53	19.06	17.75	29
30	42.18	37.93	34.26	31.09	28.33	25.92	23.82	21.97	20.34	18.90	17.62	30
31	41.19	37.12	33.61	30.56	27.90	25.57	23.53	21.73	20.15	18.74	17.49	31
32	40.20	36.32	32.95	30.02	27.46	25.21	23.23	21.49	19.94	18.57	17.35	32
33	39.21	35.51	32.29	29.48	27.01	24.84	22.93	21.24	19.73	18.40	17.20	33
34	38.23	34.70	31.62	28.92	26.55	24.46	22.61	20.97	19.52	18.22	17.05	34
35	37.24	33.89	30.95	28.37	26.09	24.08	22.29	20.71	19.29	18.03	16.89	35
36	36.26	33.07	30.27	27.80	25.62	23.68	21.96	20.43	19.06	17.83	16.72	36
37	35.28	32.25	29.58	27.23	25.13	23.28	21.62	20.14	18.81	17.62	16.55	37
38	34.30	31.43	28.89	26.64	24.64	22.86	21.27	19.84	18.56	17.41	16.37	38
39	33.32	30.61	28.20	26.06	24.15	22.44	20.91	19.54	18.30	17.18	16.17	39
40	32.34	29.78	27.50	25.46	23.64	22.01	20.54	19.22	18.03	16.95	15.97	40
41	31.37	28.95	26.79	24.86	23.12	21.57	20.16	18.90	17.75	16.71	15.77	41
42	30.40	28.12	26.08	24.25	22.60	21.12	19.77	18.56	17.46	16.46	15.55	42
43	29.43	27.29	25.36	23.63	22.07	20.66	19.38	18.22	17.16	16.20	15.32	43
44	28.46	26.45	24.64	23.01	21.53	20.19	18.97	17.86	16.85	15.93	15.09	44
45	27.50	25.62	23.92	22.38	20.98	19.71	18.55	17.50	16.53	15.65	14.84	45
46	26.55	24.79	23.19	21.75	20.43	19.23	18.13	17.13	16.21	15.36	14.59	46
47	25.60	23.96	22.47	21.11	19.87	18.74	17.70	16.75	15.87	15.07	14.33	47
48	24.66	23.13	21.74	20.47	19.31	18.24	17.26	16.36	15.53	14.76	14.05	48
49	23.72	22.31	21.01	19.82	18.73	17.73	16.81	15.96	15.17	14.45	13.77	49
50	22.79	21.48	20.28	19.18	18.16	17.22	16.35	15.55	14.81	14.12	13.48	50
51	21.87	20.66	19.55	18.52	17.58	16.70	15.89	15.13	14.44	13.79	13.18	51
52	20.95	19.84	18.82	17.87	16.99	16.17	15.41	14.71	14.05	13.44	12.87	52
53	20.04	19.02	18.07	17.20	16.38	15.63	14.92	14.27	13.65	13.08	12.54	53
54	19.12	18.19	17.32	16.52	15.77	15.07	14.42	13.81	13.24	12.70	12.20	54
55	18.20	17.35	16.57	15.83	15.14	14.50	13.90	13.33	12.81	12.31	11.84	55
56	17.27	16.51	15.80	15.13	14.50	13.92	13.36	12.84	12.36	11.90	11.46	56
57	16.35	15.67	15.03	14.42	13.85	13.32	12.81	12.34	11.89	11.47	11.07	57
58	15.44	14.82	14.25	13.70	13.19	12.71	12.25	11.82	11.41	11.02	10.66	58
59	14.52	13.98	13.47	12.98	12.52	12.09	11.68	11.29	10.92	10.56	10.23	59
60	13.62	13.14	12.69	12.26	11.85	11.46	11.09	10.74	10.41	10.09	9.79	60
61	12.72	12.30	11.91	11.53	11.17	10.82	10.50	10.19	9.89	9.60	9.33	61
62	11.83	11.47	11.12	10.79	10.48	10.18	9.89	9.62	9.35	9.10	8.86	62
63	10.95	10.64	10.34	10.06	9.78	9.52	9.27	9.03	8.80	8.58	8.37	63
64	10.06	9.80	9.55	9.31	9.08	8.85	8.64	8.43	8.23	8.04	7.86	64
65	9.18	8.96	8.75	8.55	8.35	8.16	7.98	7.81	7.64	7.48	7.32	65
66	8.29	8.11	7.94	7.77	7.61	7.46	7.31	7.16	7.02	6.89	6.75	66
67	7.40	7.26	7.12	6.99	6.86	6.73	6.61	6.49	6.38	6.27	6.16	67
68	6.50	6.40	6.29	6.19	6.09	5.99	5.89	5.80	5.71	5.62	5.54	68
69	5.61	5.52	5.45	5.37	5.29	5.22	5.15	5.08	5.01	4.94	4.88	69
70	4.70	4.64	4.59	4.53	4.48	4.43	4.38	4.33	4.28	4.23	4.18	70
71	3.79	3.75	3.72	3.68	3.65	3.61	3.58	3.55	3.51	3.48	3.45	71
72	2.87	2.85	2.83	2.81	2.79	2.77	2.75	2.73	2.71	2.69	2.67	72
73	1.94	1.93	1.92	1.91	1.90	1.89	1.88	1.87	1.86	1.85	1.85	73
74	0.98	0.98	0.98	0.97	0.97	0.97	0.97	0.97	0.96	0.96	0.96	74

Table 14 Multipliers for loss of earnings to pension age 75 (females)

Age at date of trial	Multiplier calculated with allowance for projected mortality from the 2004-based population projections and rate of return of											Age at date of trial
	0.0%	0.5%	1.0%	1.5%	2.0%	2.5%	3.0%	3.5%	4.0%	4.5%	5.0%	
16	57.27	49.74	43.54	38.39	34.10	30.50	27.46	24.88	22.67	20.78	19.14	16
17	56.27	48.99	42.97	37.96	33.77	30.25	27.27	24.73	22.56	20.69	19.07	17
18	55.26	48.22	42.39	37.52	33.44	30.00	27.08	24.58	22.45	20.60	19.00	18
19	54.26	47.46	41.81	37.08	33.10	29.74	26.88	24.43	22.33	20.51	18.93	19
20	53.25	46.69	41.22	36.63	32.75	29.47	26.67	24.27	22.20	20.41	18.85	20
21	52.25	45.92	40.62	36.17	32.40	29.19	26.45	24.10	22.07	20.31	18.77	21
22	51.24	45.15	40.02	35.70	32.04	28.91	26.23	23.93	21.94	20.20	18.69	22
23	50.24	44.37	39.42	35.23	31.67	28.62	26.01	23.73	21.80	20.09	18.60	23
24	49.23	43.58	38.81	34.75	31.29	28.33	25.77	23.57	21.65	19.98	18.51	24
25	48.23	42.79	38.19	34.26	30.91	28.02	25.53	23.38	21.50	19.86	18.41	25
26	47.22	42.00	37.56	33.77	30.52	27.71	25.29	23.18	21.34	19.73	18.31	26
27	46.22	41.21	36.93	33.27	30.12	27.39	25.03	22.97	21.18	19.60	18.20	27
28	45.22	40.41	36.30	32.76	29.71	27.07	24.77	22.76	21.01	19.46	18.09	28
29	44.22	39.61	35.65	32.25	29.30	26.73	24.50	22.55	20.83	19.31	17.97	29
30	43.21	38.80	35.01	31.72	28.87	26.39	24.22	22.32	20.64	19.16	17.85	30
31	42.21	38.00	34.35	31.19	28.44	26.04	23.94	22.09	20.45	19.01	17.72	31
32	41.21	37.18	33.69	30.65	28.00	25.68	23.64	21.85	20.26	18.84	17.59	32
33	40.21	36.37	33.03	30.11	27.56	25.32	23.34	21.60	20.05	18.67	17.45	33
34	39.22	35.55	32.36	29.56	27.10	24.94	23.03	21.34	19.84	18.50	17.30	34
35	38.22	34.73	31.68	29.00	26.64	24.56	22.71	21.07	19.62	18.31	17.14	35
36	37.22	33.91	31.00	28.43	26.17	24.16	22.38	20.80	19.39	18.12	16.98	36
37	36.23	33.08	30.31	27.86	25.69	23.76	22.05	20.52	19.15	17.92	16.81	37
38	35.24	32.25	29.61	27.27	25.20	23.35	21.70	20.22	18.90	17.71	16.64	38
39	34.24	31.42	28.91	26.68	24.70	22.93	21.35	19.92	18.64	17.49	16.45	39
40	33.26	30.58	28.21	26.09	24.19	22.50	20.98	19.61	18.38	17.27	16.26	40
41	32.27	29.75	27.49	25.48	23.68	22.06	20.61	19.29	18.10	17.03	16.05	41
42	31.28	28.91	26.78	24.87	23.16	21.61	20.22	18.96	17.82	16.78	15.84	42
43	30.30	28.07	26.06	24.25	22.63	21.16	19.83	18.62	17.53	16.53	15.62	43
44	29.33	27.23	25.34	23.63	22.09	20.69	19.42	18.27	17.22	16.27	15.39	44
45	28.35	26.38	24.61	23.00	21.54	20.22	19.01	17.91	16.91	16.00	15.16	45
46	27.38	25.54	23.88	22.36	20.99	19.73	18.59	17.55	16.59	15.71	14.91	46
47	26.42	24.70	23.14	21.72	20.43	19.24	18.16	17.17	16.26	15.42	14.65	47
48	25.45	23.86	22.40	21.07	19.85	18.74	17.72	16.78	15.91	15.12	14.38	48
49	24.50	23.01	21.66	20.42	19.28	18.23	17.27	16.38	15.56	14.80	14.10	49
50	23.54	22.17	20.91	19.75	18.69	17.71	16.80	15.97	15.19	14.48	13.81	50
51	22.59	21.33	20.16	19.09	18.09	17.18	16.33	15.54	14.81	14.14	13.51	51
52	21.64	20.48	19.40	18.41	17.49	16.63	15.84	15.11	14.42	13.79	13.19	52
53	20.69	19.63	18.64	17.72	16.87	16.08	15.34	14.66	14.02	13.42	12.86	53
54	19.74	18.77	17.87	17.02	16.24	15.51	14.83	14.19	13.59	13.04	12.51	54
55	18.79	17.91	17.09	16.32	15.60	14.93	14.30	13.71	13.16	12.64	12.15	55
56	17.85	17.05	16.30	15.60	14.95	14.33	13.75	13.21	12.70	12.22	11.77	56
57	16.90	16.18	15.51	14.88	14.28	13.72	13.20	12.70	12.23	11.79	11.37	57
58	15.96	15.32	14.72	14.15	13.61	13.10	12.63	12.17	11.75	11.34	10.96	58
59	15.02	14.45	13.92	13.41	12.93	12.47	12.04	11.63	11.25	10.88	10.53	59
60	14.09	13.59	13.11	12.66	12.23	11.83	11.44	11.08	10.73	10.40	10.08	60
61	13.16	12.72	12.31	11.91	11.53	11.17	10.83	10.51	10.19	9.90	9.61	61
62	12.23	11.86	11.49	11.15	10.82	10.50	10.20	9.92	9.64	9.38	9.13	62
63	11.31	10.99	10.68	10.38	10.09	9.82	9.56	9.31	9.07	8.84	8.62	63
64	10.39	10.11	9.85	9.60	9.35	9.12	8.90	8.68	8.48	8.28	8.08	64
65	9.46	9.23	9.02	8.80	8.60	8.41	8.22	8.03	7.86	7.69	7.53	65
66	8.54	8.35	8.17	8.00	7.83	7.67	7.51	7.36	7.22	7.08	6.94	66
67	7.61	7.46	7.32	7.18	7.05	6.92	6.79	6.67	6.55	6.43	6.32	67
68	6.68	6.56	6.45	6.35	6.24	6.14	6.04	5.95	5.85	5.76	5.67	68
69	5.74	5.66	5.58	5.50	5.42	5.34	5.27	5.20	5.13	5.06	4.99	69
70	4.81	4.75	4.69	4.63	4.58	4.52	4.47	4.42	4.37	4.32	4.27	70
71	3.86	3.83	3.79	3.75	3.72	3.68	3.65	3.61	3.58	3.55	3.51	71
72	2.91	2.89	2.87	2.85	2.83	2.81	2.79	2.77	2.75	2.73	2.71	72
73	1.96	1.95	1.94	1.93	1.92	1.91	1.90	1.89	1.88	1.87	1.87	73
74	0.99	0.99	0.98	0.98	0.98	0.98	0.97	0.97	0.97	0.97	0.96	74

Table 15 Multipliers for loss of pension commencing age 50 (males)

Age at date of trial	Multiplier calculated with allowance for projected mortality from the 2004-based population projections and rate of return of											Age at date of trial
	0.0%	0.5%	1.0%	1.5%	2.0%	2.5%	3.0%	3.5%	4.0%	4.5%	5.0%	
0	37.30	26.17	18.48	13.13	9.38	6.75	4.87	3.54	2.58	1.90	1.40	0
1	37.37	26.36	18.71	13.36	9.60	6.94	5.04	3.68	2.70	1.99	1.47	1
2	37.27	26.42	18.85	13.54	9.77	7.10	5.18	3.80	2.80	2.08	1.54	2
3	37.16	26.49	19.00	13.71	9.95	7.26	5.33	3.93	2.91	2.17	1.62	3
4	37.04	26.54	19.14	13.88	10.13	7.43	5.48	4.06	3.02	2.26	1.70	4
5	36.93	26.60	19.28	14.05	10.30	7.60	5.63	4.19	3.14	2.36	1.78	5
6	36.81	26.66	19.42	14.23	10.49	7.77	5.79	4.33	3.26	2.46	1.87	6
7	36.70	26.71	19.56	14.41	10.67	7.95	5.95	4.47	3.38	2.57	1.96	7
8	36.58	26.77	19.70	14.59	10.86	8.13	6.12	4.62	3.51	2.68	2.05	8
9	36.47	26.82	19.85	14.77	11.05	8.31	6.29	4.78	3.65	2.79	2.15	9
10	36.35	26.88	19.99	14.95	11.25	8.50	6.46	4.93	3.78	2.92	2.26	10
11	36.24	26.93	20.14	15.14	11.45	8.70	6.64	5.10	3.93	3.04	2.36	11
12	36.12	26.99	20.28	15.33	11.65	8.90	6.83	5.27	4.08	3.17	2.48	12
13	36.01	27.04	20.43	15.52	11.85	9.10	7.02	5.44	4.24	3.31	2.60	13
14	35.89	27.10	20.58	15.71	12.06	9.31	7.22	5.62	4.40	3.45	2.72	14
15	35.78	27.15	20.73	15.91	12.27	9.52	7.42	5.81	4.56	3.60	2.86	15
16	35.66	27.21	20.88	16.11	12.49	9.74	7.62	6.00	4.74	3.76	3.00	16
17	35.55	27.27	21.03	16.31	12.71	9.96	7.84	6.20	4.92	3.92	3.14	17
18	35.45	27.33	21.19	16.52	12.94	10.19	8.06	6.40	5.11	4.09	3.29	18
19	35.35	27.40	21.35	16.73	13.17	10.42	8.29	6.62	5.31	4.27	3.45	19
20	35.25	27.47	21.52	16.95	13.41	10.67	8.52	6.84	5.51	4.46	3.62	20
21	35.16	27.54	21.68	17.17	13.66	10.92	8.77	7.07	5.73	4.66	3.80	21
22	35.07	27.61	21.85	17.39	13.90	11.17	9.02	7.31	5.95	4.86	3.99	22
23	34.98	27.68	22.02	17.61	14.16	11.43	9.27	7.55	6.18	5.07	4.18	23
24	34.88	27.75	22.20	17.84	14.41	11.70	9.54	7.81	6.42	5.30	4.39	24
25	34.78	27.82	22.36	18.07	14.67	11.97	9.81	8.07	6.67	5.53	4.60	25
26	34.69	27.89	22.54	18.30	14.94	12.25	10.09	8.34	6.92	5.77	4.83	26
27	34.60	27.96	22.71	18.54	15.21	12.53	10.37	8.62	7.19	6.02	5.06	27
28	34.51	28.04	22.90	18.79	15.49	12.83	10.67	8.91	7.47	6.29	5.31	28
29	34.43	28.12	23.08	19.04	15.78	13.13	10.98	9.21	7.76	6.57	5.57	29
30	34.35	28.20	23.27	19.29	16.07	13.44	11.29	9.53	8.07	6.86	5.85	30
31	34.27	28.28	23.45	19.54	16.36	13.76	11.62	9.85	8.38	7.16	6.13	31
32	34.19	28.36	23.64	19.80	16.66	14.08	11.95	10.18	8.71	7.47	6.44	32
33	34.11	28.44	23.84	20.07	16.97	14.42	12.30	10.53	9.05	7.81	6.75	33
34	34.03	28.53	24.03	20.34	17.29	14.76	12.65	10.89	9.40	8.15	7.09	34
35	33.96	28.61	24.23	20.61	17.61	15.11	13.02	11.26	9.77	8.51	7.44	35
36	33.88	28.70	24.43	20.89	17.94	15.47	13.39	11.64	10.16	8.89	7.81	36
37	33.81	28.79	24.63	21.17	18.27	15.84	13.78	12.04	10.56	9.28	8.19	37
38	33.74	28.88	24.84	21.46	18.62	16.22	14.19	12.45	10.97	9.70	8.60	38
39	33.68	28.98	25.05	21.75	18.97	16.61	14.60	12.88	11.40	10.13	9.03	39
40	33.62	29.08	25.27	22.05	19.33	17.01	15.03	13.33	11.86	10.58	9.48	40
41	33.56	29.18	25.49	22.36	19.70	17.43	15.47	13.79	12.33	11.06	9.95	41
42	33.51	29.29	25.72	22.68	20.08	17.85	15.93	14.27	12.82	11.56	10.45	42
43	33.46	29.40	25.95	23.00	20.47	18.29	16.40	14.76	13.33	12.08	10.98	43
44	33.42	29.52	26.19	23.33	20.87	18.74	16.89	15.28	13.87	12.63	11.53	44
45	33.38	29.64	26.43	23.67	21.29	19.21	17.40	15.82	14.43	13.20	12.12	45
46	33.36	29.78	26.69	24.03	21.72	19.70	17.94	16.39	15.02	13.81	12.73	46
47	33.35	29.92	26.96	24.40	22.16	20.21	18.49	16.98	15.64	14.45	13.39	47
48	33.35	30.08	27.25	24.78	22.62	20.73	19.07	17.59	16.29	15.12	14.08	48
49	33.37	30.25	27.54	25.18	23.11	21.28	19.67	18.24	16.97	15.83	14.82	49
50	33.40	30.44	27.86	25.60	23.61	21.86	20.30	18.92	17.69	16.59	15.60	50

Table 16 Multipliers for loss of pension commencing age 50 (females)

Age at date of trial	Multiplier calculated with allowance for projected mortality from the 2004-based population projections and rate of return of											Age at date of trial
	0.0%	0.5%	1.0%	1.5%	2.0%	2.5%	3.0%	3.5%	4.0%	4.5%	5.0%	
0	40.61	28.35	19.93	14.10	10.03	7.18	5.17	3.75	2.73	1.99	1.47	0
1	40.68	28.55	20.17	14.34	10.26	7.39	5.34	3.89	2.84	2.09	1.54	1
2	40.59	28.64	20.34	14.54	10.45	7.56	5.50	4.02	2.96	2.18	1.62	2
3	40.49	28.72	20.50	14.73	10.64	7.74	5.66	4.16	3.07	2.28	1.70	3
4	40.39	28.80	20.66	14.92	10.84	7.92	5.82	4.30	3.19	2.38	1.78	4
5	40.29	28.87	20.83	15.12	11.04	8.10	5.98	4.44	3.31	2.48	1.87	5
6	40.19	28.95	20.99	15.31	11.24	8.29	6.15	4.59	3.44	2.59	1.96	6
7	40.09	29.03	21.16	15.51	11.44	8.49	6.33	4.74	3.57	2.71	2.06	7
8	39.98	29.11	21.32	15.72	11.65	8.69	6.51	4.90	3.71	2.82	2.16	8
9	39.88	29.18	21.49	15.92	11.86	8.89	6.70	5.07	3.86	2.95	2.26	9
10	39.78	29.26	21.66	16.13	12.08	9.10	6.89	5.24	4.01	3.08	2.37	10
11	39.68	29.34	21.83	16.34	12.30	9.31	7.08	5.42	4.16	3.21	2.49	11
12	39.58	29.42	22.00	16.55	12.52	9.52	7.28	5.60	4.32	3.35	2.61	12
13	39.47	29.49	22.17	16.77	12.75	9.75	7.49	5.79	4.49	3.50	2.74	13
14	39.37	29.57	22.35	16.98	12.98	9.97	7.70	5.98	4.66	3.65	2.87	14
15	39.27	29.65	22.52	17.20	13.22	10.21	7.92	6.18	4.84	3.81	3.01	15
16	39.17	29.73	22.70	17.43	13.46	10.45	8.15	6.39	5.03	3.98	3.16	16
17	39.08	29.81	22.88	17.66	13.70	10.69	8.38	6.60	5.23	4.15	3.32	17
18	38.98	29.90	23.06	17.89	13.96	10.94	8.62	6.83	5.43	4.34	3.48	18
19	38.89	29.98	23.25	18.13	14.21	11.20	8.87	7.06	5.64	4.53	3.65	19
20	38.79	30.06	23.43	18.37	14.47	11.46	9.12	7.29	5.86	4.73	3.83	20
21	38.70	30.15	23.62	18.61	14.74	11.73	9.38	7.54	6.09	4.93	4.02	21
22	38.61	30.23	23.81	18.85	15.01	12.01	9.65	7.79	6.32	5.15	4.21	22
23	38.51	30.32	24.00	19.10	15.28	12.29	9.93	8.06	6.57	5.38	4.42	23
24	38.42	30.40	24.19	19.35	15.56	12.58	10.21	8.33	6.82	5.61	4.64	24
25	38.33	30.48	24.38	19.60	15.85	12.87	10.50	8.61	7.09	5.86	4.86	25
26	38.23	30.57	24.58	19.86	16.14	13.17	10.80	8.90	7.36	6.12	5.10	26
27	38.14	30.66	24.77	20.13	16.43	13.48	11.11	9.20	7.65	6.39	5.35	27
28	38.05	30.74	24.97	20.39	16.73	13.80	11.43	9.51	7.95	6.67	5.61	28
29	37.97	30.83	25.17	20.66	17.04	14.12	11.76	9.83	8.26	6.96	5.89	29
30	37.88	30.92	25.38	20.93	17.36	14.46	12.10	10.17	8.58	7.27	6.18	30
31	37.79	31.01	25.58	21.21	17.67	14.80	12.44	10.51	8.91	7.59	6.48	31
32	37.70	31.10	25.79	21.49	18.00	15.15	12.80	10.86	9.26	7.92	6.80	32
33	37.62	31.19	26.00	21.78	18.33	15.50	13.17	11.23	9.62	8.27	7.14	33
34	37.53	31.29	26.21	22.07	18.67	15.87	13.55	11.61	10.00	8.64	7.49	34
35	37.45	31.38	26.43	22.37	19.02	16.25	13.94	12.01	10.39	9.02	7.86	35
36	37.37	31.47	26.64	22.67	19.37	16.63	14.34	12.42	10.79	9.42	8.24	36
37	37.29	31.57	26.87	22.97	19.73	17.03	14.76	12.84	11.22	9.83	8.65	37
38	37.21	31.67	27.09	23.28	20.10	17.43	15.18	13.28	11.66	10.27	9.08	38
39	37.14	31.77	27.32	23.60	20.48	17.85	15.63	13.73	12.11	10.72	9.53	39
40	37.07	31.88	27.55	23.92	20.87	18.28	16.08	14.20	12.59	11.20	10.00	40
41	37.01	31.99	27.79	24.25	21.26	18.72	16.55	14.69	13.09	11.70	10.50	41
42	36.94	32.10	28.03	24.59	21.67	19.17	17.04	15.20	13.61	12.22	11.02	42
43	36.89	32.22	28.28	24.93	22.08	19.64	17.54	15.72	14.15	12.77	11.57	43
44	36.83	32.34	28.53	25.29	22.51	20.12	18.06	16.27	14.71	13.35	12.15	44
45	36.79	32.47	28.80	25.65	22.95	20.62	18.60	16.84	15.30	13.95	12.76	45
46	36.75	32.61	29.07	26.03	23.40	21.13	19.16	17.43	15.92	14.58	13.40	46
47	36.72	32.75	29.35	26.41	23.87	21.66	19.74	18.05	16.56	15.25	14.08	47
48	36.70	32.90	29.63	26.81	24.35	22.21	20.34	18.69	17.24	15.95	14.80	48
49	36.69	33.06	29.93	27.22	24.85	22.78	20.96	19.36	17.94	16.68	15.56	49
50	36.69	33.23	30.24	27.64	25.36	23.37	21.61	20.06	18.68	17.46	16.36	50

Table 17 Multipliers for loss of pension commencing age 55 (males)

Age at date of trial	Multiplier calculated with allowance for projected mortality from the 2004-based population projections and rate of return of											Age at date of trial
	0.0%	0.5%	1.0%	1.5%	2.0%	2.5%	3.0%	3.5%	4.0%	4.5%	5.0%	
0	32.51	22.49	15.64	10.94	7.69	5.43	3.86	2.75	1.97	1.42	1.03	0
1	32.56	22.64	15.83	11.13	7.86	5.59	3.99	2.86	2.06	1.49	1.08	1
2	32.45	22.68	15.94	11.27	8.00	5.71	4.10	2.95	2.14	1.55	1.13	2
3	32.35	22.73	16.06	11.40	8.14	5.84	4.21	3.05	2.22	1.62	1.19	3
4	32.23	22.77	16.17	11.54	8.28	5.97	4.33	3.15	2.30	1.69	1.25	4
5	32.12	22.81	16.28	11.68	8.43	6.11	4.45	3.25	2.39	1.76	1.31	5
6	32.01	22.84	16.39	11.82	8.57	6.24	4.57	3.36	2.48	1.84	1.37	6
7	31.89	22.88	16.51	11.97	8.72	6.38	4.70	3.47	2.57	1.92	1.43	7
8	31.78	22.92	16.62	12.11	8.87	6.53	4.83	3.58	2.67	2.00	1.50	8
9	31.67	22.96	16.73	12.26	9.02	6.67	4.96	3.70	2.77	2.09	1.57	9
10	31.55	23.00	16.85	12.41	9.18	6.82	5.09	3.82	2.88	2.17	1.65	10
11	31.44	23.03	16.96	12.55	9.34	6.98	5.23	3.95	2.99	2.27	1.73	11
12	31.33	23.07	17.08	12.71	9.50	7.13	5.38	4.07	3.10	2.37	1.81	12
13	31.21	23.11	17.19	12.86	9.66	7.29	5.53	4.21	3.22	2.47	1.90	13
14	31.10	23.14	17.31	13.01	9.83	7.45	5.68	4.34	3.34	2.57	1.99	14
15	30.99	23.18	17.43	13.17	9.99	7.62	5.83	4.49	3.46	2.68	2.09	15
16	30.88	23.22	17.55	13.33	10.17	7.79	6.00	4.63	3.59	2.80	2.19	16
17	30.77	23.26	17.67	13.49	10.34	7.97	6.16	4.78	3.73	2.92	2.29	17
18	30.66	23.30	17.80	13.65	10.52	8.15	6.33	4.94	3.87	3.04	2.40	18
19	30.56	23.35	17.92	13.82	10.71	8.33	6.51	5.10	4.02	3.18	2.52	19
20	30.47	23.40	18.05	13.99	10.90	8.52	6.69	5.27	4.17	3.31	2.64	20
21	30.37	23.45	18.18	14.17	11.09	8.71	6.88	5.45	4.33	3.46	2.77	21
22	30.28	23.50	18.32	14.35	11.29	8.91	7.07	5.63	4.50	3.61	2.90	22
23	30.19	23.55	18.45	14.53	11.49	9.12	7.27	5.82	4.67	3.76	3.04	23
24	30.09	23.60	18.59	14.71	11.69	9.33	7.47	6.01	4.85	3.93	3.19	24
25	29.99	23.64	18.72	14.89	11.89	9.54	7.68	6.21	5.03	4.10	3.34	25
26	29.90	23.69	18.86	15.07	12.10	9.75	7.89	6.41	5.23	4.27	3.51	26
27	29.81	23.74	19.00	15.26	12.32	9.98	8.12	6.62	5.43	4.46	3.68	27
28	29.72	23.80	19.14	15.46	12.54	10.21	8.34	6.85	5.63	4.65	3.86	28
29	29.64	23.85	19.29	15.66	12.76	10.45	8.58	7.07	5.85	4.86	4.04	29
30	29.55	23.91	19.43	15.86	12.99	10.69	8.82	7.31	6.08	5.07	4.24	30
31	29.47	23.97	19.58	16.06	13.22	10.93	9.07	7.55	6.31	5.29	4.45	31
32	29.38	24.02	19.73	16.26	13.46	11.19	9.33	7.81	6.55	5.52	4.67	32
33	29.30	24.08	19.88	16.47	13.71	11.45	9.59	8.07	6.81	5.76	4.89	33
34	29.22	24.14	20.03	16.69	13.95	11.71	9.87	8.34	7.07	6.02	5.13	34
35	29.14	24.20	20.18	16.90	14.21	11.98	10.15	8.62	7.34	6.28	5.38	35
36	29.07	24.27	20.34	17.12	14.46	12.26	10.43	8.91	7.63	6.55	5.65	36
37	28.99	24.33	20.50	17.34	14.73	12.55	10.73	9.21	7.93	6.84	5.92	37
38	28.92	24.40	20.66	17.57	15.00	12.84	11.04	9.52	8.23	7.14	6.22	38
39	28.85	24.46	20.83	17.80	15.27	13.15	11.36	9.84	8.55	7.46	6.52	39
40	28.78	24.54	21.00	18.04	15.55	13.46	11.68	10.18	8.89	7.79	6.84	40
41	28.72	24.61	21.17	18.28	15.84	13.78	12.02	10.52	9.24	8.13	7.18	41
42	28.66	24.69	21.35	18.53	16.14	14.11	12.37	10.88	9.60	8.50	7.54	42
43	28.60	24.77	21.53	18.78	16.44	14.45	12.73	11.26	9.98	8.87	7.91	43
44	28.55	24.85	21.72	19.04	16.76	14.80	13.11	11.65	10.38	9.27	8.31	44
45	28.51	24.95	21.91	19.31	17.08	15.16	13.50	12.05	10.79	9.69	8.73	45
46	28.48	25.05	22.11	19.59	17.42	15.54	13.90	12.47	11.23	10.13	9.17	46
47	28.45	25.16	22.33	19.88	17.77	15.93	14.32	12.92	11.68	10.59	9.63	47
48	28.44	25.28	22.55	20.18	18.13	16.33	14.76	13.38	12.16	11.08	10.13	48
49	28.44	25.41	22.78	20.50	18.50	16.76	15.22	13.87	12.67	11.60	10.65	49
50	28.45	25.55	23.03	20.83	18.90	17.20	15.70	14.37	13.20	12.15	11.21	50
51	28.48	25.71	23.29	21.17	19.31	17.66	16.21	14.91	13.76	12.72	11.80	51
52	28.51	25.88	23.57	21.53	19.74	18.15	16.73	15.47	14.34	13.33	12.42	52
53	28.56	26.06	23.85	21.90	20.18	18.65	17.28	16.06	14.96	13.98	13.08	53
54	28.61	26.24	24.14	22.29	20.64	19.17	17.85	16.67	15.61	14.65	13.78	54
55	28.66	26.42	24.44	22.67	21.10	19.70	18.44	17.31	16.29	15.36	14.52	55

Table 18 Multipliers for loss of pension commencing age 55 (females)

Age at date of trial	Multiplier calculated with allowance for projected mortality from the 2004-based population projections and rate of return of											Age at date of trial
	0.0%	0.5%	1.0%	1.5%	2.0%	2.5%	3.0%	3.5%	4.0%	4.5%	5.0%	
0	35.74	24.61	17.04	11.87	8.31	5.85	4.14	2.94	2.10	1.51	1.09	0
1	35.79	24.77	17.25	12.07	8.50	6.01	4.28	3.06	2.19	1.58	1.15	1
2	35.70	24.84	17.38	12.23	8.65	6.15	4.40	3.16	2.28	1.65	1.20	2
3	35.60	24.90	17.51	12.39	8.81	6.30	4.52	3.26	2.37	1.72	1.26	3
4	35.50	24.96	17.65	12.54	8.97	6.44	4.65	3.37	2.46	1.80	1.32	4
5	35.40	25.02	17.78	12.70	9.13	6.59	4.78	3.49	2.55	1.88	1.39	5
6	35.30	25.08	17.91	12.87	9.29	6.74	4.92	3.60	2.65	1.96	1.45	6
7	35.20	25.14	18.05	13.03	9.46	6.90	5.06	3.72	2.75	2.04	1.52	7
8	35.10	25.19	18.19	13.20	9.63	7.06	5.20	3.85	2.86	2.13	1.60	8
9	35.00	25.25	18.32	13.36	9.80	7.22	5.34	3.97	2.97	2.23	1.68	9
10	34.90	25.31	18.46	13.53	9.97	7.38	5.49	4.11	3.08	2.32	1.76	10
11	34.80	25.37	18.60	13.70	10.15	7.55	5.65	4.24	3.20	2.42	1.84	11
12	34.69	25.43	18.74	13.88	10.33	7.73	5.81	4.38	3.32	2.53	1.93	12
13	34.59	25.49	18.88	14.05	10.52	7.91	5.97	4.53	3.45	2.64	2.03	13
14	34.49	25.54	19.02	14.23	10.70	8.09	6.14	4.68	3.58	2.75	2.13	14
15	34.39	25.60	19.16	14.41	10.89	8.27	6.31	4.84	3.72	2.87	2.23	15
16	34.30	25.66	19.31	14.60	11.09	8.46	6.49	5.00	3.86	3.00	2.34	16
17	34.20	25.73	19.45	14.78	11.29	8.66	6.67	5.16	4.01	3.13	2.45	17
18	34.11	25.79	19.60	14.97	11.49	8.86	6.86	5.34	4.17	3.27	2.57	18
19	34.01	25.85	19.75	15.16	11.70	9.06	7.05	5.51	4.33	3.41	2.69	19
20	33.92	25.91	19.90	15.36	11.91	9.27	7.25	5.70	4.49	3.56	2.83	20
21	33.82	25.98	20.05	15.55	12.12	9.49	7.46	5.89	4.67	3.71	2.96	21
22	33.73	26.04	20.21	15.75	12.34	9.71	7.67	6.08	4.85	3.87	3.11	22
23	33.64	26.11	20.36	15.95	12.56	9.93	7.89	6.29	5.03	4.04	3.26	23
24	33.54	26.17	20.51	16.16	12.79	10.16	8.11	6.50	5.23	4.22	3.42	24
25	33.45	26.23	20.67	16.36	13.01	10.39	8.34	6.71	5.43	4.40	3.58	25
26	33.36	26.30	20.83	16.57	13.25	10.63	8.57	6.94	5.64	4.59	3.76	26
27	33.27	26.36	20.99	16.79	13.49	10.88	8.81	7.17	5.85	4.79	3.94	27
28	33.18	26.43	21.15	17.00	13.73	11.13	9.06	7.41	6.08	5.00	4.13	28
29	33.09	26.49	21.31	17.22	13.98	11.39	9.32	7.66	6.31	5.22	4.34	29
30	33.00	26.56	21.48	17.44	14.23	11.65	9.58	7.91	6.56	5.45	4.55	30
31	32.91	26.62	21.64	17.67	14.48	11.92	9.86	8.18	6.81	5.69	4.77	31
32	32.82	26.69	21.81	17.90	14.75	12.20	10.14	8.45	7.07	5.94	5.00	32
33	32.73	26.76	21.98	18.13	15.01	12.49	10.42	8.73	7.34	6.20	5.25	33
34	32.65	26.83	22.15	18.36	15.29	12.78	10.72	9.03	7.63	6.47	5.50	34
35	32.57	26.90	22.32	18.60	15.56	13.07	11.02	9.33	7.92	6.75	5.77	35
36	32.48	26.97	22.50	18.84	15.85	13.38	11.34	9.64	8.23	7.05	6.05	36
37	32.40	27.05	22.68	19.09	16.14	13.69	11.66	9.97	8.55	7.36	6.35	37
38	32.32	27.12	22.86	19.34	16.43	14.01	12.00	10.30	8.88	7.68	6.66	38
39	32.25	27.20	23.04	19.60	16.73	14.34	12.34	10.65	9.23	8.02	6.99	39
40	32.18	27.28	23.23	19.86	17.04	14.68	12.69	11.01	9.59	8.37	7.33	40
41	32.11	27.36	23.42	20.12	17.36	15.03	13.06	11.39	9.96	8.74	7.69	41
42	32.04	27.45	23.61	20.39	17.68	15.39	13.44	11.78	10.35	9.13	8.07	42
43	31.98	27.54	23.81	20.67	18.01	15.76	13.83	12.18	10.76	9.53	8.47	43
44	31.92	27.63	24.02	20.96	18.36	16.14	14.23	12.60	11.18	9.96	8.89	44
45	31.87	27.73	24.23	21.25	18.71	16.53	14.65	13.03	11.63	10.41	9.34	45
46	31.83	27.84	24.45	21.55	19.07	16.93	15.09	13.49	12.09	10.87	9.81	46
47	31.79	27.95	24.67	21.86	19.44	17.35	15.54	13.96	12.58	11.37	10.30	47
48	31.76	28.07	24.90	22.18	19.83	17.78	16.00	14.45	13.08	11.88	10.82	48
49	31.73	28.19	25.15	22.51	20.22	18.23	16.49	14.96	13.61	12.43	11.37	49
50	31.72	28.33	25.40	22.85	20.63	18.70	16.99	15.50	14.17	13.00	11.95	50
51	31.72	28.47	25.66	23.20	21.06	19.18	17.52	16.05	14.75	13.60	12.57	51
52	31.72	28.62	25.92	23.57	21.50	19.67	18.06	16.63	15.36	14.23	13.21	52
53	31.72	28.77	26.20	23.94	21.95	20.19	18.63	17.24	16.00	14.89	13.90	53
54	31.73	28.93	26.48	24.31	22.41	20.71	19.21	17.87	16.67	15.59	14.62	54
55	31.74	29.09	26.76	24.70	22.88	21.26	19.81	18.52	17.36	16.32	15.38	55

Table 19 Multipliers for loss of pension commencing age 60 (males)

Age at date of trial	Multiplier calculated with allowance for projected mortality from the 2004-based population projections and rate of return of											Age at date of trial
	0.0%	0.5%	1.0%	1.5%	2.0%	2.5%	3.0%	3.5%	4.0%	4.5%	5.0%	
0	27.80	18.95	12.98	8.94	6.18	4.29	3.00	2.10	1.48	1.04	0.74	0
1	27.83	19.07	13.13	9.09	6.32	4.41	3.09	2.18	1.54	1.09	0.78	1
2	27.72	19.10	13.22	9.19	6.42	4.51	3.18	2.25	1.60	1.14	0.82	2
3	27.62	19.12	13.31	9.30	6.53	4.61	3.27	2.32	1.66	1.19	0.86	3
4	27.51	19.15	13.39	9.41	6.64	4.71	3.35	2.40	1.72	1.24	0.90	4
5	27.40	19.17	13.48	9.52	6.76	4.81	3.45	2.48	1.79	1.29	0.94	5
6	27.28	19.19	13.56	9.63	6.87	4.92	3.54	2.55	1.85	1.35	0.98	6
7	27.17	19.21	13.65	9.74	6.98	5.03	3.63	2.64	1.92	1.40	1.03	7
8	27.06	19.24	13.74	9.85	7.10	5.14	3.73	2.72	1.99	1.46	1.08	8
9	26.95	19.26	13.82	9.97	7.22	5.25	3.83	2.81	2.07	1.53	1.13	9
10	26.84	19.28	13.91	10.08	7.34	5.36	3.94	2.90	2.14	1.59	1.18	10
11	26.73	19.30	14.00	10.20	7.46	5.48	4.04	2.99	2.22	1.66	1.24	11
12	26.62	19.32	14.09	10.31	7.58	5.60	4.15	3.09	2.31	1.73	1.30	12
13	26.51	19.34	14.17	10.43	7.71	5.72	4.26	3.19	2.39	1.80	1.36	13
14	26.40	19.36	14.26	10.55	7.84	5.85	4.38	3.29	2.48	1.88	1.43	14
15	26.29	19.38	14.35	10.67	7.97	5.97	4.50	3.40	2.57	1.96	1.49	15
16	26.18	19.40	14.44	10.79	8.10	6.10	4.62	3.50	2.67	2.04	1.56	16
17	26.08	19.43	14.53	10.92	8.24	6.24	4.74	3.62	2.77	2.13	1.64	17
18	25.97	19.45	14.63	11.05	8.38	6.37	4.87	3.73	2.87	2.22	1.72	18
19	25.87	19.48	14.72	11.18	8.52	6.52	5.00	3.85	2.98	2.31	1.80	19
20	25.78	19.51	14.82	11.31	8.66	6.66	5.14	3.98	3.09	2.41	1.89	20
21	25.68	19.54	14.92	11.44	8.81	6.81	5.28	4.11	3.21	2.51	1.98	21
22	25.59	19.57	15.02	11.58	8.96	6.96	5.43	4.24	3.33	2.62	2.07	22
23	25.50	19.60	15.13	11.72	9.12	7.12	5.57	4.38	3.46	2.73	2.17	23
24	25.40	19.63	15.23	11.86	9.27	7.27	5.73	4.52	3.59	2.85	2.27	24
25	25.30	19.65	15.33	12.00	9.43	7.43	5.88	4.67	3.72	2.97	2.38	25
26	25.21	19.68	15.43	12.14	9.59	7.60	6.04	4.82	3.86	3.10	2.50	26
27	25.12	19.71	15.53	12.29	9.75	7.77	6.21	4.98	4.01	3.23	2.62	27
28	25.03	19.75	15.64	12.43	9.92	7.94	6.38	5.14	4.16	3.37	2.74	28
29	24.95	19.79	15.75	12.59	10.09	8.12	6.56	5.31	4.32	3.52	2.87	29
30	24.86	19.82	15.86	12.74	10.27	8.31	6.74	5.49	4.48	3.67	3.01	30
31	24.77	19.85	15.97	12.89	10.45	8.49	6.92	5.66	4.65	3.82	3.16	31
32	24.69	19.89	16.08	13.05	10.63	8.68	7.12	5.85	4.82	3.99	3.31	32
33	24.61	19.93	16.20	13.21	10.81	8.88	7.31	6.04	5.01	4.16	3.47	33
34	24.52	19.96	16.31	13.37	11.00	9.08	7.52	6.24	5.20	4.34	3.64	34
35	24.44	20.00	16.43	13.54	11.19	9.28	7.73	6.45	5.40	4.53	3.81	35
36	24.36	20.04	16.54	13.70	11.39	9.49	7.94	6.66	5.60	4.72	3.99	36
37	24.28	20.08	16.66	13.87	11.59	9.71	8.16	6.88	5.82	4.93	4.19	37
38	24.21	20.12	16.78	14.05	11.79	9.93	8.39	7.11	6.04	5.14	4.39	38
39	24.13	20.17	16.91	14.22	12.00	10.16	8.62	7.34	6.27	5.37	4.60	39
40	24.06	20.21	17.03	14.40	12.22	10.39	8.87	7.59	6.51	5.60	4.83	40
41	24.00	20.26	17.16	14.59	12.44	10.63	9.12	7.84	6.76	5.84	5.06	41
42	23.93	20.31	17.30	14.77	12.66	10.88	9.38	8.10	7.02	6.10	5.31	42
43	23.87	20.36	17.43	14.97	12.89	11.13	9.64	8.38	7.29	6.37	5.57	43
44	23.81	20.42	17.57	15.17	13.13	11.40	9.92	8.66	7.58	6.65	5.85	44
45	23.76	20.48	17.72	15.37	13.37	11.67	10.21	8.96	7.88	6.94	6.14	45
46	23.72	20.55	17.87	15.58	13.63	11.95	10.51	9.26	8.19	7.25	6.44	46
47	23.68	20.63	18.03	15.80	13.89	12.24	10.82	9.59	8.52	7.58	6.77	47
48	23.66	20.72	18.20	16.03	14.16	12.55	11.14	9.92	8.86	7.93	7.11	48
49	23.64	20.81	18.37	16.27	14.45	12.86	11.48	10.28	9.22	8.29	7.47	49
50	23.64	20.91	18.56	16.52	14.74	13.20	11.84	10.65	9.60	8.67	7.86	50
51	23.64	21.03	18.76	16.78	15.06	13.54	12.21	11.04	10.00	9.08	8.26	51
52	23.66	21.15	18.97	17.06	15.38	13.90	12.60	11.45	10.42	9.51	8.70	52
53	23.68	21.29	19.19	17.34	15.72	14.28	13.01	11.88	10.87	9.96	9.16	53
54	23.71	21.42	19.41	17.63	16.06	14.67	13.43	12.32	11.33	10.44	9.64	54
55	23.74	21.56	19.63	17.93	16.41	15.07	13.86	12.78	11.81	10.94	10.15	55
56	23.77	21.70	19.86	18.23	16.78	15.48	14.31	13.26	12.32	11.46	10.69	56
57	23.80	21.84	20.09	18.54	17.15	15.90	14.78	13.76	12.84	12.01	11.26	57
58	23.84	21.99	20.34	18.86	17.54	16.34	15.26	14.29	13.40	12.60	11.86	58
59	23.89	22.16	20.60	19.20	17.95	16.81	15.78	14.84	13.99	13.22	12.51	59
60	23.97	22.35	20.89	19.57	18.38	17.30	16.33	15.44	14.62	13.88	13.20	60

Table 20 Multipliers for loss of pension commencing age 60 (females)

Age at date of trial	Multiplier calculated with allowance for projected mortality from the 2004-based population projections and rate of return of											Age at date of trial
	0.0%	0.5%	1.0%	1.5%	2.0%	2.5%	3.0%	3.5%	4.0%	4.5%	5.0%	
0	30.93	20.99	14.32	9.82	6.77	4.69	3.26	2.28	1.60	1.13	0.80	0
1	30.96	21.12	14.49	9.99	6.92	4.81	3.37	2.36	1.67	1.18	0.84	1
2	30.86	21.17	14.59	10.11	7.04	4.92	3.46	2.44	1.73	1.23	0.88	2
3	30.77	21.21	14.70	10.24	7.16	5.04	3.56	2.52	1.80	1.28	0.92	3
4	30.67	21.25	14.81	10.36	7.29	5.15	3.66	2.60	1.86	1.34	0.97	4
5	30.57	21.30	14.91	10.49	7.42	5.27	3.76	2.69	1.94	1.40	1.01	5
6	30.47	21.34	15.02	10.62	7.55	5.39	3.86	2.78	2.01	1.46	1.06	6
7	30.37	21.38	15.13	10.75	7.68	5.51	3.97	2.87	2.08	1.52	1.11	7
8	30.27	21.42	15.23	10.88	7.81	5.63	4.08	2.96	2.16	1.59	1.17	8
9	30.17	21.46	15.34	11.02	7.95	5.76	4.19	3.06	2.25	1.65	1.22	9
10	30.07	21.50	15.45	11.15	8.09	5.89	4.31	3.16	2.33	1.73	1.28	10
11	29.97	21.54	15.56	11.29	8.23	6.02	4.43	3.27	2.42	1.80	1.34	11
12	29.87	21.58	15.67	11.43	8.37	6.16	4.55	3.37	2.51	1.88	1.41	12
13	29.77	21.62	15.78	11.57	8.52	6.30	4.67	3.48	2.61	1.96	1.48	13
14	29.67	21.66	15.89	11.71	8.66	6.44	4.80	3.60	2.71	2.04	1.55	14
15	29.57	21.70	16.00	11.85	8.82	6.58	4.94	3.72	2.81	2.13	1.62	15
16	29.48	21.75	16.12	12.00	8.97	6.73	5.07	3.84	2.92	2.22	1.70	16
17	29.38	21.79	16.23	12.15	9.13	6.89	5.22	3.97	3.03	2.32	1.78	17
18	29.29	21.84	16.35	12.30	9.29	7.04	5.36	4.10	3.14	2.42	1.87	18
19	29.20	21.88	16.47	12.45	9.45	7.20	5.51	4.23	3.26	2.52	1.96	19
20	29.10	21.92	16.59	12.60	9.61	7.36	5.66	4.37	3.38	2.63	2.05	20
21	29.01	21.96	16.70	12.76	9.78	7.53	5.82	4.51	3.51	2.74	2.15	21
22	28.92	22.01	16.82	12.91	9.95	7.70	5.98	4.66	3.65	2.86	2.25	22
23	28.82	22.05	16.95	13.07	10.13	7.88	6.15	4.82	3.79	2.99	2.36	23
24	28.73	22.10	17.07	13.24	10.31	8.05	6.32	4.97	3.93	3.11	2.48	24
25	28.64	22.14	17.19	13.40	10.49	8.24	6.49	5.14	4.08	3.25	2.60	25
26	28.55	22.18	17.31	13.56	10.67	8.42	6.67	5.31	4.23	3.39	2.72	26
27	28.46	22.23	17.44	13.73	10.86	8.61	6.86	5.48	4.40	3.54	2.85	27
28	28.37	22.28	17.56	13.90	11.05	8.81	7.05	5.66	4.56	3.69	2.99	28
29	28.28	22.32	17.69	14.07	11.24	9.01	7.25	5.85	4.74	3.85	3.13	29
30	28.19	22.37	17.82	14.25	11.44	9.21	7.45	6.04	4.92	4.01	3.29	30
31	28.10	22.41	17.95	14.42	11.64	9.42	7.66	6.24	5.10	4.19	3.44	31
32	28.01	22.46	18.08	14.60	11.84	9.64	7.87	6.45	5.30	4.37	3.61	32
33	27.93	22.51	18.21	14.79	12.05	9.86	8.09	6.66	5.50	4.56	3.79	33
34	27.84	22.55	18.34	14.97	12.26	10.08	8.32	6.88	5.71	4.75	3.97	34
35	27.76	22.60	18.48	15.16	12.48	10.31	8.55	7.11	5.93	4.96	4.16	35
36	27.67	22.65	18.61	15.35	12.70	10.55	8.79	7.34	6.16	5.17	4.36	36
37	27.59	22.70	18.75	15.54	12.93	10.79	9.03	7.59	6.39	5.40	4.57	37
38	27.51	22.75	18.89	15.74	13.16	11.04	9.29	7.84	6.64	5.63	4.80	38
39	27.43	22.81	19.03	15.94	13.39	11.29	9.55	8.10	6.89	5.88	5.03	39
40	27.36	22.87	19.18	16.14	13.63	11.55	9.82	8.37	7.16	6.14	5.27	40
41	27.29	22.92	19.33	16.35	13.88	11.82	10.10	8.65	7.43	6.40	5.53	41
42	27.22	22.98	19.48	16.56	14.13	12.10	10.38	8.94	7.72	6.68	5.80	42
43	27.15	23.05	19.63	16.78	14.39	12.38	10.68	9.24	8.02	6.98	6.09	43
44	27.09	23.12	19.79	17.00	14.66	12.67	10.99	9.56	8.33	7.29	6.39	44
45	27.03	23.19	19.96	17.23	14.93	12.97	11.31	9.88	8.66	7.61	6.70	45
46	26.98	23.27	20.13	17.47	15.21	13.28	11.64	10.22	9.00	7.95	7.04	46
47	26.94	23.35	20.30	17.71	15.50	13.61	11.98	10.57	9.36	8.30	7.39	47
48	26.90	23.43	20.48	17.96	15.80	13.94	12.33	10.94	9.73	8.68	7.76	48
49	26.86	23.53	20.67	18.22	16.11	14.28	12.70	11.32	10.12	9.07	8.15	49
50	26.84	23.63	20.87	18.49	16.43	14.64	13.08	11.72	10.53	9.48	8.56	50
51	26.82	23.74	21.07	18.76	16.76	15.01	13.48	12.14	10.96	9.91	8.99	51
52	26.81	23.85	21.28	19.05	17.10	15.39	13.89	12.57	11.40	10.37	9.45	52
53	26.80	23.96	21.49	19.34	17.44	15.78	14.32	13.02	11.87	10.85	9.94	53
54	26.80	24.08	21.71	19.63	17.80	16.19	14.76	13.49	12.36	11.35	10.45	54
55	26.79	24.20	21.93	19.93	18.17	16.60	15.21	13.97	12.87	11.87	10.98	55
56	26.79	24.33	22.16	20.24	18.54	17.03	15.68	14.48	13.40	12.43	11.55	56
57	26.79	24.46	22.39	20.56	18.93	17.48	16.17	15.01	13.95	13.01	12.15	57
58	26.81	24.60	22.64	20.89	19.34	17.94	16.69	15.56	14.54	13.62	12.78	58
59	26.84	24.75	22.90	21.24	19.76	18.43	17.23	16.14	15.16	14.27	13.46	59
60	26.88	24.93	23.18	21.61	20.20	18.94	17.79	16.76	15.81	14.96	14.18	60

Table 21 Multipliers for loss of pension commencing age 65 (males)

Age at date of trial	Multiplier calculated with allowance for projected mortality from the 2004-based population projections and rate of return of											Age at date of trial
	0.0%	0.5%	1.0%	1.5%	2.0%	2.5%	3.0%	3.5%	4.0%	4.5%	5.0%	
0	23.20	15.58	10.51	7.12	4.85	3.31	2.27	1.56	1.08	0.75	0.52	0
1	23.21	15.67	10.63	7.24	4.95	3.40	2.34	1.62	1.13	0.79	0.55	1
2	23.11	15.68	10.69	7.32	5.03	3.47	2.41	1.67	1.17	0.82	0.58	2
3	23.00	15.69	10.75	7.40	5.11	3.55	2.47	1.73	1.21	0.85	0.60	3
4	22.90	15.70	10.82	7.48	5.20	3.62	2.54	1.78	1.26	0.89	0.63	4
5	22.79	15.71	10.88	7.56	5.28	3.70	2.60	1.84	1.30	0.93	0.66	5
6	22.68	15.72	10.94	7.65	5.36	3.78	2.67	1.89	1.35	0.96	0.69	6
7	22.58	15.73	11.00	7.73	5.45	3.86	2.74	1.95	1.40	1.00	0.72	7
8	22.47	15.73	11.06	7.81	5.54	3.94	2.81	2.02	1.45	1.05	0.76	8
9	22.36	15.74	11.13	7.90	5.63	4.02	2.89	2.08	1.50	1.09	0.79	9
10	22.25	15.75	11.19	7.98	5.72	4.11	2.96	2.14	1.56	1.13	0.83	10
11	22.15	15.75	11.25	8.07	5.81	4.19	3.04	2.21	1.61	1.18	0.87	11
12	22.04	15.76	11.31	8.15	5.90	4.28	3.12	2.28	1.67	1.23	0.91	12
13	21.93	15.77	11.38	8.24	5.99	4.37	3.20	2.35	1.73	1.28	0.95	13
14	21.83	15.77	11.44	8.33	6.09	4.46	3.29	2.43	1.80	1.34	1.00	14
15	21.72	15.78	11.50	8.42	6.18	4.56	3.37	2.50	1.86	1.39	1.04	15
16	21.62	15.78	11.57	8.51	6.28	4.66	3.46	2.58	1.93	1.45	1.09	16
17	21.52	15.79	11.63	8.60	6.38	4.75	3.55	2.66	2.00	1.51	1.14	17
18	21.42	15.80	11.70	8.70	6.49	4.85	3.65	2.75	2.08	1.57	1.20	18
19	21.32	15.81	11.77	8.79	6.59	4.96	3.74	2.83	2.15	1.64	1.25	19
20	21.22	15.82	11.84	8.89	6.70	5.06	3.84	2.92	2.23	1.71	1.31	20
21	21.13	15.84	11.91	8.99	6.81	5.17	3.94	3.02	2.31	1.78	1.37	21
22	21.04	15.85	11.98	9.09	6.92	5.29	4.05	3.11	2.40	1.85	1.44	22
23	20.95	15.86	12.06	9.19	7.03	5.40	4.16	3.21	2.49	1.93	1.51	23
24	20.85	15.87	12.13	9.30	7.15	5.51	4.27	3.31	2.58	2.01	1.58	24
25	20.76	15.88	12.20	9.40	7.26	5.63	4.38	3.42	2.67	2.10	1.65	25
26	20.67	15.90	12.27	9.50	7.38	5.75	4.50	3.53	2.77	2.19	1.73	26
27	20.58	15.91	12.34	9.61	7.50	5.88	4.62	3.64	2.87	2.28	1.81	27
28	20.49	15.93	12.42	9.72	7.63	6.00	4.74	3.75	2.98	2.37	1.89	28
29	20.41	15.94	12.50	9.83	7.75	6.14	4.87	3.87	3.09	2.47	1.98	29
30	20.32	15.96	12.58	9.94	7.88	6.27	5.00	4.00	3.21	2.58	2.08	30
31	20.23	15.97	12.65	10.05	8.01	6.40	5.13	4.13	3.33	2.69	2.18	31
32	20.15	15.99	12.73	10.17	8.14	6.54	5.27	4.26	3.45	2.80	2.28	32
33	20.07	16.01	12.81	10.28	8.28	6.69	5.41	4.40	3.58	2.92	2.39	33
34	19.99	16.03	12.89	10.40	8.42	6.83	5.56	4.54	3.71	3.04	2.50	34
35	19.90	16.04	12.97	10.52	8.56	6.98	5.71	4.68	3.85	3.17	2.62	35
36	19.82	16.06	13.05	10.64	8.70	7.13	5.86	4.83	3.99	3.31	2.74	36
37	19.74	16.08	13.14	10.76	8.85	7.29	6.02	4.99	4.14	3.45	2.88	37
38	19.67	16.10	13.22	10.89	8.99	7.45	6.18	5.15	4.30	3.59	3.01	38
39	19.59	16.12	13.31	11.02	9.15	7.61	6.35	5.31	4.46	3.75	3.16	39
40	19.52	16.15	13.40	11.15	9.30	7.78	6.53	5.49	4.62	3.91	3.31	40
41	19.45	16.17	13.49	11.28	9.46	7.95	6.71	5.67	4.80	4.07	3.47	41
42	19.38	16.20	13.58	11.42	9.62	8.13	6.89	5.85	4.98	4.25	3.63	42
43	19.31	16.23	13.68	11.56	9.79	8.32	7.08	6.04	5.17	4.43	3.81	43
44	19.25	16.26	13.77	11.70	9.96	8.50	7.28	6.24	5.37	4.62	3.99	44
45	19.19	16.30	13.88	11.85	10.14	8.70	7.48	6.45	5.57	4.82	4.18	45
46	19.14	16.34	13.98	12.00	10.32	8.90	7.69	6.67	5.79	5.03	4.39	46
47	19.10	16.39	14.10	12.16	10.51	9.11	7.91	6.89	6.01	5.26	4.61	47
48	19.06	16.44	14.22	12.32	10.71	9.33	8.15	7.13	6.25	5.49	4.83	48
49	19.03	16.50	14.34	12.50	10.92	9.56	8.39	7.37	6.50	5.74	5.08	49
50	19.01	16.57	14.48	12.68	11.13	9.80	8.64	7.63	6.76	6.00	5.33	50
51	19.00	16.65	14.62	12.87	11.36	10.04	8.90	7.91	7.04	6.28	5.61	51
52	19.00	16.73	14.77	13.07	11.59	10.30	9.18	8.19	7.33	6.57	5.90	52
53	19.00	16.82	14.93	13.28	11.84	10.57	9.47	8.49	7.63	6.87	6.20	53
54	19.01	16.92	15.09	13.49	12.09	10.85	9.76	8.80	7.95	7.20	6.53	54
55	19.02	17.01	15.25	13.70	12.34	11.14	10.07	9.13	8.28	7.53	6.86	55
56	19.02	17.10	15.41	13.92	12.60	11.43	10.39	9.46	8.63	7.89	7.22	56
57	19.02	17.19	15.58	14.14	12.87	11.73	10.71	9.80	8.99	8.26	7.60	57
58	19.04	17.30	15.75	14.37	13.14	12.04	11.05	10.17	9.37	8.65	8.00	58
59	19.06	17.41	15.93	14.61	13.43	12.37	11.41	10.55	9.77	9.06	8.42	59
60	19.10	17.54	16.13	14.87	13.74	12.72	11.79	10.96	10.20	9.51	8.88	60
61	19.17	17.69	16.36	15.16	14.08	13.09	12.20	11.39	10.66	9.98	9.37	61
62	19.26	17.86	16.61	15.47	14.44	13.50	12.64	11.86	11.15	10.50	9.90	62
63	19.37	18.06	16.88	15.80	14.82	13.93	13.12	12.37	11.68	11.05	10.47	63
64	19.50	18.28	17.17	16.16	15.24	14.39	13.62	12.91	12.25	11.65	11.09	64
65	19.66	18.52	17.49	16.54	15.68	14.88	14.16	13.48	12.86	12.29	11.76	65

Table 22 Multipliers for loss of pension commencing age 65 (females)

Age at date of trial	Multiplier calculated with allowance for projected mortality from the 2004-based population projections and rate of return of											Age at date of trial
	0.0%	0.5%	1.0%	1.5%	2.0%	2.5%	3.0%	3.5%	4.0%	4.5%	5.0%	
0	26.18	17.52	11.78	7.95	5.39	3.67	2.51	1.72	1.19	0.82	0.57	0
1	26.20	17.62	11.91	8.08	5.51	3.77	2.59	1.79	1.24	0.86	0.60	1
2	26.10	17.65	11.99	8.18	5.60	3.85	2.66	1.85	1.29	0.90	0.63	2
3	26.01	17.68	12.07	8.28	5.70	3.94	2.74	1.91	1.33	0.94	0.66	3
4	25.91	17.70	12.15	8.37	5.80	4.03	2.81	1.97	1.38	0.98	0.69	4
5	25.81	17.73	12.23	8.47	5.89	4.12	2.89	2.03	1.44	1.02	0.72	5
6	25.72	17.75	12.31	8.57	5.99	4.21	2.97	2.10	1.49	1.06	0.76	6
7	25.62	17.78	12.39	8.67	6.10	4.30	3.05	2.17	1.55	1.11	0.79	7
8	25.52	17.80	12.47	8.77	6.20	4.40	3.13	2.24	1.60	1.15	0.83	8
9	25.42	17.83	12.55	8.88	6.30	4.49	3.21	2.31	1.66	1.20	0.87	9
10	25.33	17.85	12.64	8.98	6.41	4.59	3.30	2.38	1.73	1.25	0.91	10
11	25.23	17.88	12.72	9.09	6.52	4.69	3.39	2.46	1.79	1.31	0.96	11
12	25.13	17.90	12.80	9.19	6.63	4.80	3.48	2.54	1.86	1.36	1.00	12
13	25.03	17.92	12.88	9.30	6.74	4.90	3.58	2.62	1.93	1.42	1.05	13
14	24.94	17.95	12.97	9.41	6.85	5.01	3.67	2.70	2.00	1.48	1.10	14
15	24.84	17.97	13.05	9.52	6.97	5.12	3.77	2.79	2.07	1.54	1.15	15
16	24.75	18.00	13.14	9.63	7.09	5.23	3.88	2.88	2.15	1.61	1.21	16
17	24.66	18.02	13.23	9.74	7.21	5.35	3.98	2.98	2.23	1.68	1.27	17
18	24.56	18.05	13.31	9.86	7.33	5.47	4.09	3.07	2.31	1.75	1.33	18
19	24.47	18.07	13.40	9.98	7.45	5.59	4.20	3.17	2.40	1.82	1.39	19
20	24.38	18.10	13.49	10.09	7.58	5.71	4.32	3.27	2.49	1.90	1.46	20
21	24.29	18.13	13.58	10.21	7.71	5.84	4.43	3.38	2.58	1.98	1.52	21
22	24.20	18.15	13.67	10.33	7.84	5.96	4.55	3.49	2.68	2.07	1.60	22
23	24.11	18.18	13.76	10.45	7.97	6.10	4.68	3.60	2.78	2.15	1.67	23
24	24.01	18.20	13.85	10.58	8.10	6.23	4.81	3.72	2.89	2.25	1.75	24
25	23.92	18.23	13.94	10.70	8.24	6.37	4.94	3.84	2.99	2.34	1.84	25
26	23.83	18.25	14.03	10.83	8.38	6.51	5.07	3.96	3.11	2.44	1.92	26
27	23.74	18.28	14.13	10.95	8.52	6.65	5.21	4.09	3.22	2.55	2.02	27
28	23.66	18.31	14.22	11.08	8.67	6.80	5.35	4.22	3.34	2.65	2.11	28
29	23.57	18.34	14.31	11.21	8.81	6.95	5.50	4.36	3.47	2.77	2.21	29
30	23.48	18.36	14.41	11.35	8.96	7.10	5.65	4.50	3.60	2.88	2.32	30
31	23.39	18.39	14.50	11.48	9.11	7.26	5.80	4.65	3.73	3.01	2.43	31
32	23.30	18.41	14.60	11.61	9.27	7.42	5.96	4.80	3.87	3.14	2.55	32
33	23.22	18.44	14.70	11.75	9.43	7.58	6.12	4.95	4.02	3.27	2.67	33
34	23.14	18.47	14.80	11.89	9.59	7.75	6.29	5.11	4.17	3.41	2.79	34
35	23.05	18.50	14.90	12.03	9.75	7.92	6.46	5.28	4.33	3.55	2.93	35
36	22.97	18.53	15.00	12.18	9.92	8.10	6.64	5.45	4.49	3.71	3.07	36
37	22.89	18.56	15.10	12.32	10.09	8.28	6.82	5.63	4.66	3.86	3.21	37
38	22.81	18.59	15.20	12.47	10.26	8.47	7.00	5.81	4.83	4.03	3.37	38
39	22.73	18.62	15.31	12.62	10.44	8.65	7.20	6.00	5.02	4.20	3.53	39
40	22.65	18.66	15.42	12.78	10.62	8.85	7.40	6.20	5.21	4.38	3.70	40
41	22.58	18.70	15.53	12.93	10.80	9.05	7.60	6.40	5.40	4.57	3.88	41
42	22.51	18.73	15.64	13.09	10.99	9.25	7.81	6.61	5.61	4.77	4.07	42
43	22.44	18.77	15.75	13.26	11.19	9.46	8.03	6.83	5.82	4.98	4.26	43
44	22.37	18.82	15.87	13.42	11.39	9.68	8.26	7.06	6.05	5.19	4.47	44
45	22.31	18.86	15.99	13.60	11.59	9.91	8.49	7.29	6.28	5.42	4.69	45
46	22.26	18.91	16.12	13.77	11.80	10.14	8.73	7.54	6.52	5.66	4.92	46
47	22.21	18.97	16.25	13.95	12.02	10.38	8.98	7.79	6.78	5.91	5.16	47
48	22.16	19.03	16.38	14.14	12.24	10.62	9.24	8.06	7.04	6.17	5.41	48
49	22.12	19.09	16.52	14.34	12.47	10.88	9.51	8.33	7.32	6.44	5.68	49
50	22.08	19.16	16.67	14.54	12.71	11.14	9.79	8.62	7.61	6.73	5.97	50
51	22.06	19.23	16.82	14.74	12.96	11.42	10.08	8.92	7.91	7.03	6.26	51
52	22.03	19.31	16.98	14.96	13.21	11.70	10.38	9.23	8.23	7.35	6.58	52
53	22.01	19.40	17.13	15.18	13.47	11.99	10.69	9.56	8.56	7.69	6.91	53
54	21.99	19.48	17.30	15.40	13.74	12.29	11.02	9.90	8.91	8.04	7.26	54
55	21.97	19.56	17.46	15.62	14.01	12.60	11.35	10.24	9.27	8.40	7.63	55
56	21.96	19.65	17.63	15.85	14.29	12.91	11.69	10.61	9.64	8.79	8.02	56
57	21.94	19.74	17.80	16.09	14.58	13.24	12.05	10.99	10.04	9.19	8.43	57
58	21.94	19.84	17.98	16.34	14.88	13.58	12.42	11.38	10.45	9.61	8.86	58
59	21.94	19.95	18.17	16.60	15.19	13.93	12.81	11.80	10.89	10.06	9.32	59
60	21.96	20.07	18.38	16.87	15.52	14.31	13.22	12.23	11.35	10.54	9.81	60
61	22.00	20.20	18.60	17.16	15.87	14.70	13.65	12.70	11.83	11.05	10.33	61
62	22.05	20.36	18.84	17.47	16.23	15.12	14.11	13.19	12.35	11.59	10.89	62
63	22.11	20.52	19.09	17.79	16.62	15.55	14.59	13.71	12.90	12.16	11.49	63
64	22.19	20.70	19.35	18.13	17.02	16.01	15.09	14.25	13.48	12.77	12.12	64
65	22.28	20.89	19.63	18.49	17.45	16.50	15.63	14.83	14.10	13.42	12.80	65

Table 23 Multipliers for loss of pension commencing age 70 (males)

Age at date of trial	Multiplier calculated with allowance for projected mortality from the 2004-based population projections and rate of return of											Age at date of trial
	0.0%	0.5%	1.0%	1.5%	2.0%	2.5%	3.0%	3.5%	4.0%	4.5%	5.0%	
0	18.76	12.41	8.24	5.50	3.68	2.47	1.67	1.13	0.77	0.52	0.36	0
1	18.75	12.47	8.32	5.58	3.75	2.53	1.72	1.17	0.80	0.55	0.37	1
2	18.65	12.47	8.37	5.64	3.81	2.59	1.76	1.20	0.83	0.57	0.39	2
3	18.55	12.47	8.41	5.69	3.87	2.64	1.81	1.24	0.86	0.59	0.41	3
4	18.45	12.46	8.45	5.75	3.93	2.69	1.85	1.28	0.89	0.62	0.43	4
5	18.35	12.46	8.49	5.81	3.99	2.75	1.90	1.32	0.92	0.64	0.45	5
6	18.24	12.45	8.53	5.87	4.05	2.80	1.95	1.36	0.95	0.67	0.47	6
7	18.14	12.45	8.57	5.93	4.11	2.86	2.00	1.40	0.98	0.69	0.49	7
8	18.04	12.44	8.61	5.98	4.17	2.92	2.05	1.44	1.02	0.72	0.51	8
9	17.94	12.44	8.65	6.04	4.24	2.98	2.10	1.49	1.06	0.75	0.54	9
10	17.84	12.43	8.70	6.10	4.30	3.04	2.15	1.53	1.09	0.78	0.56	10
11	17.74	12.43	8.74	6.16	4.36	3.10	2.21	1.58	1.13	0.81	0.59	11
12	17.64	12.42	8.78	6.23	4.43	3.16	2.26	1.63	1.17	0.85	0.61	12
13	17.53	12.41	8.82	6.29	4.50	3.23	2.32	1.68	1.21	0.88	0.64	13
14	17.43	12.41	8.86	6.35	4.56	3.29	2.38	1.73	1.26	0.92	0.67	14
15	17.33	12.40	8.90	6.41	4.63	3.36	2.44	1.78	1.30	0.95	0.70	15
16	17.23	12.39	8.94	6.47	4.70	3.42	2.50	1.83	1.35	0.99	0.73	16
17	17.14	12.39	8.98	6.54	4.77	3.49	2.57	1.89	1.40	1.03	0.77	17
18	17.04	12.38	9.03	6.60	4.84	3.56	2.63	1.95	1.45	1.08	0.80	18
19	16.95	12.38	9.07	6.67	4.92	3.64	2.70	2.01	1.50	1.12	0.84	19
20	16.86	12.38	9.12	6.74	4.99	3.71	2.77	2.07	1.55	1.17	0.88	20
21	16.77	12.38	9.16	6.81	5.07	3.79	2.84	2.13	1.61	1.21	0.92	21
22	16.68	12.37	9.21	6.88	5.15	3.87	2.91	2.20	1.67	1.26	0.96	22
23	16.59	12.37	9.26	6.95	5.23	3.95	2.99	2.27	1.72	1.32	1.01	23
24	16.50	12.37	9.30	7.02	5.31	4.03	3.06	2.34	1.79	1.37	1.05	24
25	16.41	12.37	9.35	7.09	5.39	4.11	3.14	2.41	1.85	1.43	1.10	25
26	16.32	12.36	9.39	7.16	5.47	4.19	3.22	2.48	1.92	1.48	1.15	26
27	16.23	12.36	9.44	7.23	5.55	4.28	3.30	2.56	1.99	1.54	1.21	27
28	16.15	12.36	9.49	7.31	5.64	4.37	3.39	2.64	2.06	1.61	1.26	28
29	16.07	12.36	9.54	7.38	5.73	4.46	3.48	2.72	2.13	1.68	1.32	29
30	15.99	12.36	9.59	7.46	5.82	4.55	3.57	2.80	2.21	1.74	1.38	30
31	15.90	12.36	9.64	7.54	5.91	4.64	3.66	2.89	2.29	1.82	1.44	31
32	15.82	12.36	9.69	7.61	6.00	4.74	3.75	2.98	2.37	1.89	1.51	32
33	15.74	12.36	9.74	7.69	6.09	4.84	3.85	3.07	2.46	1.97	1.58	33
34	15.66	12.36	9.79	7.77	6.19	4.94	3.95	3.17	2.54	2.05	1.65	34
35	15.58	12.37	9.84	7.85	6.28	5.04	4.05	3.26	2.64	2.13	1.73	35
36	15.50	12.37	9.89	7.93	6.38	5.14	4.16	3.37	2.73	2.22	1.81	36
37	15.42	12.37	9.95	8.02	6.48	5.25	4.26	3.47	2.83	2.31	1.90	37
38	15.34	12.37	10.00	8.10	6.58	5.36	4.37	3.58	2.93	2.41	1.98	38
39	15.27	12.37	10.05	8.19	6.69	5.47	4.49	3.69	3.04	2.51	2.08	39
40	15.20	12.38	10.11	8.28	6.79	5.59	4.61	3.81	3.15	2.61	2.17	40
41	15.13	12.39	10.17	8.37	6.90	5.71	4.73	3.93	3.27	2.72	2.27	41
42	15.06	12.39	10.23	8.46	7.01	5.83	4.85	4.05	3.39	2.84	2.38	42
43	14.99	12.40	10.29	8.55	7.13	5.95	4.98	4.18	3.51	2.96	2.49	43
44	14.92	12.41	10.35	8.65	7.24	6.08	5.11	4.31	3.64	3.08	2.61	44
45	14.86	12.43	10.41	8.75	7.36	6.21	5.25	4.45	3.77	3.21	2.73	45
46	14.81	12.44	10.48	8.85	7.49	6.35	5.39	4.59	3.92	3.35	2.86	46
47	14.76	12.47	10.55	8.96	7.62	6.49	5.54	4.74	4.06	3.49	3.00	47
48	14.71	12.49	10.63	9.07	7.75	6.64	5.70	4.90	4.22	3.64	3.15	48
49	14.67	12.52	10.71	9.19	7.89	6.79	5.86	5.06	4.38	3.80	3.30	49
50	14.64	12.56	10.80	9.31	8.04	6.95	6.03	5.24	4.55	3.97	3.47	50
51	14.61	12.61	10.90	9.44	8.19	7.12	6.20	5.42	4.74	4.15	3.64	51
52	14.60	12.66	11.00	9.57	8.35	7.30	6.39	5.61	4.93	4.34	3.82	52
53	14.59	12.71	11.10	9.71	8.52	7.48	6.58	5.80	5.12	4.53	4.02	53
54	14.57	12.77	11.21	9.86	8.69	7.67	6.78	6.01	5.33	4.74	4.22	54
55	14.56	12.82	11.31	10.00	8.86	7.86	6.99	6.22	5.55	4.96	4.43	55
56	14.55	12.88	11.42	10.15	9.03	8.06	7.20	6.44	5.77	5.18	4.66	56
57	14.53	12.93	11.53	10.30	9.21	8.26	7.41	6.67	6.01	5.42	4.89	57
58	14.52	12.99	11.64	10.45	9.40	8.47	7.64	6.90	6.25	5.67	5.14	58
59	14.52	13.06	11.76	10.61	9.59	8.69	7.88	7.15	6.51	5.93	5.41	59
60	14.53	13.13	11.89	10.79	9.80	8.92	8.13	7.42	6.78	6.21	5.69	60
61	14.56	13.23	12.04	10.97	10.02	9.17	8.40	7.70	7.08	6.51	6.00	61
62	14.61	13.34	12.20	11.18	10.26	9.43	8.69	8.01	7.40	6.84	6.33	62
63	14.67	13.47	12.38	11.41	10.52	9.72	9.00	8.34	7.74	7.19	6.69	63
64	14.75	13.61	12.58	11.65	10.80	10.03	9.33	8.69	8.10	7.56	7.07	64
65	14.85	13.77	12.79	11.90	11.09	10.35	9.68	9.06	8.49	7.97	7.49	65
66	14.95	13.94	13.02	12.18	11.41	10.70	10.05	9.45	8.90	8.40	7.93	66
67	15.07	14.12	13.26	12.46	11.73	11.06	10.45	9.88	9.35	8.86	8.41	67
68	15.20	14.32	13.51	12.77	12.08	11.45	10.86	10.32	9.82	9.35	8.92	68
69	15.34	14.53	13.78	13.09	12.45	11.86	11.31	10.80	10.33	9.89	9.47	69
70	15.50	14.75	14.07	13.43	12.85	12.30	11.79	11.32	10.87	10.46	10.08	70

Table 24 Multipliers for loss of pension commencing age 70 (females)

Age at date of trial	Multiplier calculated with allowance for projected mortality from the 2004-based population projections and rate of return of											Age at date of trial
	0.0%	0.5%	1.0%	1.5%	2.0%	2.5%	3.0%	3.5%	4.0%	4.5%	5.0%	
0	21.54	14.21	9.41	6.25	4.17	2.80	1.88	1.27	0.86	0.58	0.40	0
1	21.54	14.28	9.50	6.35	4.26	2.87	1.94	1.31	0.89	0.61	0.42	1
2	21.45	14.29	9.56	6.42	4.33	2.93	1.99	1.36	0.93	0.64	0.44	2
3	21.35	14.30	9.62	6.49	4.40	2.99	2.04	1.40	0.96	0.66	0.46	3
4	21.26	14.31	9.68	6.57	4.47	3.06	2.10	1.44	1.00	0.69	0.48	4
5	21.17	14.32	9.73	6.64	4.54	3.12	2.15	1.49	1.03	0.72	0.50	5
6	21.07	14.34	9.79	6.71	4.62	3.19	2.21	1.54	1.07	0.75	0.53	6
7	20.98	14.35	9.85	6.79	4.69	3.26	2.27	1.59	1.11	0.78	0.55	7
8	20.88	14.36	9.91	6.86	4.77	3.33	2.33	1.64	1.15	0.81	0.58	8
9	20.79	14.37	9.96	6.94	4.85	3.40	2.39	1.69	1.19	0.85	0.60	9
10	20.70	14.38	10.02	7.01	4.93	3.47	2.45	1.74	1.24	0.88	0.63	10
11	20.60	14.39	10.08	7.09	5.00	3.54	2.52	1.80	1.28	0.92	0.66	11
12	20.51	14.39	10.14	7.17	5.09	3.62	2.59	1.85	1.33	0.96	0.69	12
13	20.41	14.40	10.20	7.25	5.17	3.70	2.65	1.91	1.38	1.00	0.73	13
14	20.32	14.41	10.26	7.33	5.25	3.78	2.72	1.97	1.43	1.04	0.76	14
15	20.23	14.42	10.32	7.41	5.33	3.86	2.80	2.03	1.48	1.08	0.80	15
16	20.14	14.43	10.38	7.49	5.42	3.94	2.87	2.10	1.54	1.13	0.83	16
17	20.05	14.44	10.44	7.57	5.51	4.02	2.95	2.16	1.59	1.18	0.87	17
18	19.96	14.45	10.50	7.66	5.60	4.11	3.02	2.23	1.65	1.23	0.91	18
19	19.87	14.46	10.56	7.74	5.69	4.20	3.10	2.30	1.71	1.28	0.96	19
20	19.78	14.47	10.62	7.82	5.78	4.28	3.19	2.37	1.78	1.33	1.00	20
21	19.69	14.48	10.69	7.91	5.87	4.38	3.27	2.45	1.84	1.39	1.05	21
22	19.60	14.49	10.75	8.00	5.97	4.47	3.36	2.53	1.91	1.45	1.10	22
23	19.52	14.50	10.81	8.09	6.07	4.56	3.44	2.61	1.98	1.51	1.15	23
24	19.43	14.51	10.87	8.17	6.16	4.66	3.54	2.69	2.05	1.57	1.20	24
25	19.34	14.52	10.94	8.26	6.26	4.76	3.63	2.77	2.13	1.63	1.26	25
26	19.25	14.53	11.00	8.35	6.36	4.86	3.72	2.86	2.20	1.70	1.32	26
27	19.17	14.54	11.07	8.45	6.47	4.97	3.82	2.95	2.29	1.77	1.38	27
28	19.08	14.55	11.13	8.54	6.57	5.07	3.92	3.05	2.37	1.85	1.44	28
29	18.99	14.56	11.20	8.63	6.68	5.18	4.03	3.14	2.46	1.92	1.51	29
30	18.91	14.57	11.26	8.73	6.79	5.29	4.13	3.24	2.55	2.01	1.58	30
31	18.82	14.58	11.33	8.82	6.89	5.40	4.24	3.34	2.64	2.09	1.66	31
32	18.74	14.59	11.39	8.92	7.01	5.52	4.36	3.45	2.74	2.18	1.73	32
33	18.66	14.60	11.46	9.02	7.12	5.64	4.47	3.56	2.84	2.27	1.82	33
34	18.57	14.61	11.53	9.12	7.24	5.76	4.59	3.67	2.94	2.36	1.90	34
35	18.49	14.62	11.60	9.22	7.35	5.88	4.71	3.79	3.05	2.46	1.99	35
36	18.41	14.63	11.67	9.32	7.47	6.00	4.84	3.90	3.16	2.56	2.08	36
37	18.33	14.65	11.74	9.43	7.59	6.13	4.96	4.03	3.28	2.67	2.18	37
38	18.25	14.66	11.81	9.53	7.72	6.26	5.10	4.16	3.40	2.78	2.29	38
39	18.17	14.67	11.88	9.64	7.84	6.40	5.23	4.29	3.52	2.90	2.39	39
40	18.10	14.69	11.95	9.75	7.97	6.54	5.37	4.43	3.65	3.02	2.51	40
41	18.03	14.70	12.03	9.86	8.11	6.68	5.52	4.57	3.79	3.15	2.62	41
42	17.95	14.72	12.10	9.98	8.24	6.83	5.67	4.71	3.93	3.28	2.75	42
43	17.88	14.74	12.18	10.09	8.38	6.97	5.82	4.86	4.08	3.42	2.88	43
44	17.82	14.76	12.26	10.21	8.52	7.13	5.98	5.02	4.23	3.57	3.02	44
45	17.75	14.79	12.35	10.33	8.67	7.29	6.14	5.19	4.39	3.72	3.16	45
46	17.70	14.81	12.43	10.46	8.82	7.45	6.31	5.36	4.55	3.88	3.31	46
47	17.64	14.84	12.52	10.59	8.97	7.62	6.49	5.53	4.73	4.05	3.47	47
48	17.59	14.88	12.61	10.72	9.13	7.79	6.67	5.71	4.91	4.22	3.64	48
49	17.54	14.91	12.71	10.86	9.29	7.97	6.86	5.91	5.10	4.41	3.82	49
50	17.50	14.96	12.81	11.00	9.46	8.16	7.05	6.10	5.29	4.60	4.01	50
51	17.46	15.00	12.92	11.15	9.64	8.35	7.25	6.31	5.50	4.80	4.20	51
52	17.43	15.05	13.03	11.30	9.82	8.55	7.47	6.53	5.72	5.02	4.41	52
53	17.40	15.10	13.14	11.45	10.01	8.76	7.68	6.75	5.94	5.24	4.63	53
54	17.37	15.15	13.25	11.61	10.20	8.97	7.91	6.98	6.18	5.47	4.86	54
55	17.33	15.20	13.36	11.77	10.39	9.19	8.14	7.22	6.42	5.72	5.10	55
56	17.30	15.26	13.48	11.93	10.58	9.41	8.38	7.47	6.67	5.97	5.36	56
57	17.28	15.31	13.60	12.10	10.79	9.63	8.62	7.73	6.94	6.24	5.62	57
58	17.26	15.37	13.72	12.27	11.00	9.87	8.88	8.00	7.22	6.52	5.91	58
59	17.24	15.44	13.85	12.45	11.22	10.12	9.15	8.28	7.51	6.82	6.21	59
60	17.24	15.52	14.00	12.65	11.45	10.38	9.43	8.58	7.82	7.14	6.52	60
61	17.25	15.61	14.15	12.85	11.69	10.66	9.73	8.90	8.15	7.47	6.87	61
62	17.27	15.71	14.31	13.07	11.95	10.95	10.04	9.23	8.49	7.83	7.23	62
63	17.31	15.82	14.49	13.29	12.22	11.25	10.37	9.58	8.86	8.21	7.62	63
64	17.35	15.94	14.68	13.53	12.50	11.57	10.72	9.95	9.25	8.61	8.03	64
65	17.40	16.07	14.87	13.79	12.80	11.90	11.09	10.34	9.66	9.04	8.47	65
66	17.46	16.21	15.08	14.05	13.11	12.26	11.47	10.76	10.10	9.49	8.94	66
67	17.53	16.36	15.30	14.32	13.44	12.62	11.88	11.19	10.56	9.98	9.44	67
68	17.60	16.51	15.52	14.61	13.77	13.00	12.30	11.64	11.04	10.48	9.97	68
69	17.67	16.66	15.74	14.90	14.12	13.40	12.73	12.12	11.55	11.02	10.53	69
70	17.74	16.82	15.97	15.19	14.47	13.81	13.19	12.62	12.09	11.59	11.13	70

Table 25 Multipliers for loss of pension commencing age 75 (males)

Age at date of trial	Multiplier calculated with allowance for projected mortality from the 2004-based population projections and rate of return of											Age at date of trial
	0.0%	0.5%	1.0%	1.5%	2.0%	2.5%	3.0%	3.5%	4.0%	4.5%	5.0%	
0	14.52	9.46	6.18	4.06	2.67	1.76	1.17	0.78	0.52	0.35	0.23	0
1	14.50	9.49	6.24	4.11	2.72	1.81	1.20	0.80	0.54	0.36	0.24	1
2	14.41	9.48	6.26	4.15	2.76	1.84	1.23	0.83	0.56	0.38	0.26	2
3	14.31	9.47	6.29	4.19	2.80	1.88	1.26	0.85	0.58	0.39	0.27	3
4	14.22	9.46	6.31	4.23	2.84	1.91	1.29	0.88	0.60	0.41	0.28	4
5	14.12	9.44	6.33	4.26	2.88	1.95	1.33	0.90	0.62	0.42	0.29	5
6	14.03	9.43	6.36	4.30	2.92	1.99	1.36	0.93	0.64	0.44	0.30	6
7	13.93	9.41	6.38	4.34	2.96	2.03	1.39	0.96	0.66	0.46	0.32	7
8	13.84	9.40	6.40	4.38	3.00	2.06	1.42	0.99	0.68	0.48	0.33	8
9	13.74	9.38	6.42	4.41	3.04	2.10	1.46	1.01	0.71	0.49	0.35	9
10	13.65	9.36	6.45	4.45	3.08	2.14	1.49	1.04	0.73	0.51	0.36	10
11	13.56	9.35	6.47	4.49	3.13	2.18	1.53	1.07	0.76	0.53	0.38	11
12	13.46	9.33	6.49	4.53	3.17	2.22	1.57	1.11	0.78	0.56	0.40	12
13	13.37	9.32	6.51	4.57	3.21	2.27	1.60	1.14	0.81	0.58	0.41	13
14	13.27	9.30	6.53	4.61	3.26	2.31	1.64	1.17	0.84	0.60	0.43	14
15	13.18	9.28	6.56	4.65	3.30	2.35	1.68	1.20	0.87	0.62	0.45	15
16	13.09	9.27	6.58	4.69	3.35	2.40	1.72	1.24	0.90	0.65	0.47	16
17	13.00	9.25	6.60	4.73	3.39	2.44	1.76	1.28	0.93	0.67	0.49	17
18	12.91	9.24	6.63	4.77	3.44	2.49	1.81	1.31	0.96	0.70	0.51	18
19	12.83	9.22	6.65	4.81	3.49	2.54	1.85	1.35	0.99	0.73	0.54	19
20	12.74	9.21	6.67	4.85	3.54	2.58	1.89	1.39	1.02	0.76	0.56	20
21	12.66	9.19	6.70	4.89	3.59	2.63	1.94	1.43	1.06	0.79	0.59	21
22	12.57	9.18	6.72	4.94	3.64	2.68	1.99	1.47	1.10	0.82	0.61	22
23	12.49	9.17	6.75	4.98	3.69	2.74	2.04	1.52	1.13	0.85	0.64	23
24	12.41	9.16	6.77	5.03	3.74	2.79	2.08	1.56	1.17	0.88	0.67	24
25	12.32	9.14	6.80	5.07	3.79	2.84	2.13	1.61	1.21	0.92	0.70	25
26	12.24	9.12	6.82	5.11	3.84	2.89	2.19	1.66	1.26	0.96	0.73	26
27	12.16	9.11	6.85	5.16	3.90	2.95	2.24	1.70	1.30	0.99	0.76	27
28	12.08	9.10	6.87	5.21	3.95	3.01	2.29	1.75	1.34	1.03	0.79	28
29	12.00	9.09	6.90	5.25	4.01	3.07	2.35	1.81	1.39	1.07	0.83	29
30	11.92	9.08	6.93	5.30	4.06	3.12	2.41	1.86	1.44	1.12	0.87	30
31	11.85	9.06	6.95	5.35	4.12	3.18	2.47	1.91	1.49	1.16	0.91	31
32	11.77	9.05	6.98	5.39	4.18	3.25	2.53	1.97	1.54	1.21	0.95	32
33	11.69	9.04	7.01	5.44	4.24	3.31	2.59	2.03	1.59	1.25	0.99	33
34	11.62	9.03	7.03	5.49	4.30	3.37	2.65	2.09	1.65	1.30	1.03	34
35	11.54	9.02	7.06	5.54	4.36	3.44	2.72	2.15	1.71	1.36	1.08	35
36	11.46	9.00	7.09	5.59	4.42	3.50	2.78	2.21	1.76	1.41	1.13	36
37	11.39	8.99	7.11	5.64	4.48	3.57	2.85	2.28	1.83	1.47	1.18	37
38	11.32	8.98	7.14	5.69	4.55	3.64	2.92	2.35	1.89	1.52	1.23	38
39	11.25	8.97	7.17	5.74	4.61	3.71	2.99	2.42	1.96	1.59	1.29	39
40	11.18	8.96	7.20	5.80	4.68	3.78	3.06	2.49	2.02	1.65	1.35	40
41	11.11	8.95	7.23	5.85	4.75	3.86	3.14	2.56	2.09	1.72	1.41	41
42	11.04	8.94	7.26	5.91	4.81	3.93	3.22	2.64	2.17	1.78	1.47	42
43	10.97	8.94	7.29	5.96	4.89	4.01	3.30	2.72	2.24	1.86	1.54	43
44	10.91	8.93	7.33	6.02	4.96	4.09	3.38	2.80	2.32	1.93	1.61	44
45	10.85	8.93	7.36	6.08	5.03	4.17	3.47	2.89	2.41	2.01	1.68	45
46	10.79	8.93	7.40	6.14	5.11	4.26	3.56	2.97	2.49	2.09	1.76	46
47	10.74	8.93	7.44	6.21	5.19	4.35	3.65	3.07	2.58	2.18	1.84	47
48	10.69	8.93	7.48	6.27	5.27	4.44	3.74	3.16	2.68	2.27	1.93	48
49	10.64	8.94	7.53	6.35	5.36	4.54	3.84	3.26	2.78	2.36	2.02	49
50	10.60	8.95	7.57	6.42	5.45	4.64	3.95	3.37	2.88	2.47	2.11	50
51	10.57	8.97	7.63	6.50	5.54	4.74	4.06	3.48	2.99	2.57	2.22	51
52	10.54	8.99	7.69	6.58	5.64	4.85	4.17	3.60	3.10	2.68	2.32	52
53	10.52	9.02	7.75	6.67	5.75	4.96	4.29	3.72	3.22	2.80	2.44	53
54	10.49	9.04	7.81	6.75	5.85	5.08	4.41	3.84	3.35	2.92	2.56	54
55	10.47	9.07	7.87	6.84	5.96	5.20	4.54	3.97	3.48	3.05	2.68	55
56	10.44	9.09	7.93	6.93	6.07	5.32	4.67	4.10	3.61	3.19	2.81	56
57	10.41	9.11	7.99	7.02	6.18	5.44	4.80	4.24	3.75	3.33	2.95	57
58	10.39	9.14	8.06	7.11	6.29	5.57	4.94	4.39	3.90	3.47	3.10	58
59	10.37	9.17	8.13	7.21	6.41	5.70	5.08	4.54	4.05	3.63	3.25	59
60	10.36	9.21	8.20	7.32	6.53	5.84	5.23	4.70	4.22	3.79	3.41	60
61	10.36	9.26	8.29	7.43	6.67	6.00	5.40	4.87	4.39	3.97	3.59	61
62	10.37	9.32	8.39	7.56	6.82	6.16	5.57	5.05	4.58	4.16	3.78	62
63	10.40	9.39	8.49	7.69	6.98	6.34	5.76	5.24	4.78	4.36	3.99	63
64	10.43	9.47	8.61	7.84	7.15	6.52	5.96	5.45	5.00	4.58	4.21	64
65	10.48	9.56	8.74	8.00	7.33	6.72	6.17	5.68	5.23	4.82	4.44	65
66	10.53	9.66	8.87	8.16	7.52	6.93	6.40	5.91	5.47	5.07	4.70	66
67	10.59	9.77	9.02	8.33	7.71	7.15	6.63	6.16	5.73	5.33	4.97	67
68	10.65	9.87	9.16	8.51	7.92	7.38	6.88	6.42	6.00	5.61	5.25	68
69	10.72	9.99	9.32	8.70	8.14	7.62	7.14	6.70	6.29	5.91	5.56	69

continued

Table 25 Multipliers for loss of pension commencing age 75 (males) ***continued***

Age at date of trial	Multiplier calculated with allowance for projected mortality from the 2004-based population projections and rate of return of											Age at date of trial
	0.0%	0.5%	1.0%	1.5%	2.0%	2.5%	3.0%	3.5%	4.0%	4.5%	5.0%	
70	10.80	10.11	9.48	8.90	8.36	7.87	7.41	6.99	6.60	6.23	5.89	70
71	10.88	10.25	9.66	9.11	8.61	8.14	7.71	7.30	6.93	6.58	6.25	71
72	10.99	10.41	9.86	9.35	8.88	8.44	8.03	7.65	7.29	6.96	6.65	72
73	11.14	10.60	10.09	9.63	9.19	8.78	8.40	8.04	7.70	7.39	7.09	73
74	11.33	10.83	10.37	9.94	9.54	9.16	8.81	8.48	8.16	7.87	7.59	74
75	11.57	11.13	10.71	10.32	9.95	9.61	9.29	8.98	8.70	8.42	8.17	75

Table 26 Multipliers for loss of pension commencing age 75 (females)

Age at date of trial	Multiplier calculated with allowance for projected mortality from the 2004-based population projections and rate of return of											Age at date of trial
	0.0%	0.5%	1.0%	1.5%	2.0%	2.5%	3.0%	3.5%	4.0%	4.5%	5.0%	
0	17.05	11.07	7.22	4.72	3.10	2.04	1.35	0.90	0.60	0.40	0.27	0
1	17.03	11.12	7.29	4.79	3.16	2.10	1.39	0.93	0.62	0.42	0.28	1
2	16.94	11.12	7.33	4.84	3.21	2.14	1.43	0.96	0.64	0.43	0.29	2
3	16.85	11.12	7.36	4.89	3.26	2.18	1.47	0.99	0.67	0.45	0.31	3
4	16.76	11.12	7.40	4.94	3.31	2.23	1.50	1.02	0.69	0.47	0.32	4
5	16.67	11.11	7.44	4.99	3.36	2.27	1.54	1.05	0.72	0.49	0.34	5
6	16.58	11.11	7.47	5.04	3.41	2.32	1.58	1.08	0.74	0.51	0.35	6
7	16.49	11.11	7.51	5.09	3.47	2.37	1.62	1.11	0.77	0.53	0.37	7
8	16.40	11.11	7.55	5.15	3.52	2.42	1.66	1.15	0.79	0.55	0.38	8
9	16.31	11.10	7.58	5.20	3.57	2.46	1.70	1.18	0.82	0.57	0.40	9
10	16.22	11.10	7.62	5.25	3.63	2.51	1.75	1.22	0.85	0.60	0.42	10
11	16.14	11.10	7.66	5.30	3.68	2.57	1.79	1.26	0.88	0.62	0.44	11
12	16.05	11.09	7.70	5.35	3.74	2.62	1.84	1.29	0.91	0.65	0.46	12
13	15.96	11.09	7.73	5.41	3.79	2.67	1.88	1.33	0.95	0.67	0.48	13
14	15.87	11.09	7.77	5.46	3.85	2.72	1.93	1.37	0.98	0.70	0.50	14
15	15.78	11.08	7.81	5.52	3.91	2.78	1.98	1.42	1.02	0.73	0.53	15
16	15.70	11.08	7.84	5.57	3.97	2.84	2.03	1.46	1.05	0.76	0.55	16
17	15.61	11.08	7.88	5.63	4.03	2.89	2.08	1.50	1.09	0.79	0.58	17
18	15.53	11.07	7.92	5.68	4.09	2.95	2.14	1.55	1.13	0.82	0.60	18
19	15.44	11.07	7.96	5.74	4.15	3.01	2.19	1.60	1.17	0.86	0.63	19
20	15.36	11.07	8.00	5.80	4.22	3.07	2.25	1.65	1.21	0.89	0.66	20
21	15.27	11.06	8.04	5.86	4.28	3.14	2.30	1.70	1.25	0.93	0.69	21
22	15.19	11.06	8.08	5.91	4.34	3.20	2.36	1.75	1.30	0.97	0.72	22
23	15.10	11.06	8.12	5.97	4.41	3.26	2.42	1.80	1.34	1.00	0.75	23
24	15.02	11.05	8.15	6.03	4.48	3.33	2.48	1.86	1.39	1.05	0.79	24
25	14.94	11.05	8.19	6.09	4.54	3.40	2.55	1.91	1.44	1.09	0.82	25
26	14.85	11.04	8.23	6.15	4.61	3.47	2.61	1.97	1.49	1.13	0.86	26
27	14.77	11.04	8.27	6.21	4.68	3.54	2.68	2.03	1.55	1.18	0.90	27
28	14.69	11.04	8.31	6.28	4.75	3.61	2.74	2.09	1.60	1.23	0.94	28
29	14.61	11.03	8.35	6.34	4.82	3.68	2.81	2.16	1.66	1.28	0.99	29
30	14.53	11.03	8.39	6.40	4.90	3.75	2.89	2.22	1.72	1.33	1.03	30
31	14.45	11.02	8.43	6.46	4.97	3.83	2.96	2.29	1.78	1.38	1.08	31
32	14.37	11.02	8.47	6.53	5.04	3.91	3.03	2.36	1.84	1.44	1.13	32
33	14.29	11.01	8.51	6.59	5.12	3.99	3.11	2.43	1.91	1.50	1.18	33
34	14.21	11.01	8.55	6.66	5.20	4.07	3.19	2.51	1.97	1.56	1.23	34
35	14.13	11.01	8.59	6.73	5.28	4.15	3.27	2.58	2.04	1.62	1.29	35
36	14.05	11.00	8.63	6.79	5.36	4.23	3.35	2.66	2.12	1.69	1.35	36
37	13.98	11.00	8.68	6.86	5.44	4.32	3.44	2.74	2.19	1.76	1.41	37
38	13.90	11.00	8.72	6.93	5.52	4.41	3.53	2.83	2.27	1.83	1.47	38
39	13.83	10.99	8.76	7.00	5.60	4.50	3.62	2.91	2.35	1.90	1.54	39
40	13.75	10.99	8.81	7.07	5.69	4.59	3.71	3.00	2.44	1.98	1.61	40
41	13.68	10.99	8.85	7.14	5.78	4.68	3.80	3.10	2.52	2.06	1.69	41
42	13.61	10.99	8.90	7.22	5.87	4.78	3.90	3.19	2.61	2.15	1.77	42
43	13.54	11.00	8.95	7.29	5.96	4.88	4.00	3.29	2.71	2.23	1.85	43
44	13.48	11.00	8.99	7.37	6.05	4.98	4.11	3.39	2.81	2.33	1.93	44
45	13.42	11.00	9.04	7.45	6.15	5.09	4.21	3.50	2.91	2.42	2.02	45
46	13.36	11.01	9.10	7.53	6.25	5.19	4.32	3.61	3.02	2.52	2.12	46
47	13.30	11.02	9.15	7.62	6.35	5.30	4.44	3.72	3.13	2.63	2.22	47
48	13.24	11.03	9.21	7.70	6.45	5.42	4.56	3.84	3.24	2.74	2.32	48
49	13.19	11.05	9.27	7.79	6.56	5.54	4.68	3.96	3.36	2.86	2.43	49
50	13.14	11.06	9.33	7.88	6.67	5.66	4.81	4.09	3.49	2.98	2.55	50
51	13.10	11.08	9.40	7.98	6.79	5.79	4.94	4.23	3.62	3.11	2.67	51
52	13.06	11.11	9.46	8.08	6.91	5.92	5.08	4.37	3.76	3.24	2.80	52
53	13.02	11.13	9.53	8.18	7.03	6.05	5.22	4.51	3.90	3.38	2.93	53
54	12.98	11.16	9.60	8.28	7.15	6.19	5.37	4.66	4.05	3.53	3.08	54
55	12.94	11.18	9.67	8.38	7.28	6.33	5.52	4.81	4.21	3.68	3.23	55
56	12.91	11.20	9.74	8.49	7.41	6.48	5.67	4.97	4.37	3.84	3.38	56
57	12.87	11.23	9.82	8.60	7.54	6.62	5.83	5.14	4.53	4.01	3.55	57
58	12.84	11.26	9.89	8.71	7.68	6.78	5.99	5.31	4.71	4.18	3.72	58
59	12.81	11.30	9.98	8.83	7.82	6.94	6.17	5.49	4.89	4.37	3.90	59
60	12.79	11.34	10.06	8.95	7.97	7.11	6.35	5.68	5.09	4.56	4.10	60
61	12.78	11.39	10.16	9.08	8.13	7.29	6.54	5.88	5.29	4.77	4.30	61
62	12.78	11.44	10.26	9.22	8.29	7.47	6.74	6.09	5.51	4.99	4.53	62
63	12.79	11.51	10.38	9.37	8.47	7.67	6.95	6.31	5.74	5.22	4.76	63
64	12.80	11.58	10.49	9.52	8.65	7.88	7.18	6.55	5.98	5.47	5.01	64
65	12.82	11.66	10.62	9.69	8.85	8.09	7.41	6.80	6.24	5.74	5.28	65
66	12.84	11.74	10.75	9.86	9.05	8.32	7.66	7.06	6.51	6.01	5.56	66
67	12.87	11.83	10.89	10.03	9.26	8.55	7.91	7.33	6.79	6.31	5.86	67
68	12.90	11.91	11.02	10.21	9.47	8.79	8.17	7.61	7.09	6.61	6.18	68
69	12.92	12.00	11.15	10.38	9.68	9.03	8.44	7.90	7.40	6.94	6.51	69

continued

Table 26 Multipliers for loss of pension commencing age 75 (females) ***continued***

Age at date of trial	Multiplier calculated with allowance for projected mortality from the 2004-based population projections and rate of return of											Age at date of trial
	0.0%	0.5%	1.0%	1.5%	2.0%	2.5%	3.0%	3.5%	4.0%	4.5%	5.0%	
70	12.94	12.07	11.29	10.56	9.90	9.28	8.72	8.20	7.72	7.27	6.86	70
71	12.95	12.16	11.42	10.74	10.12	9.54	9.01	8.51	8.05	7.63	7.23	71
72	12.98	12.25	11.57	10.94	10.36	9.82	9.32	8.85	8.41	8.01	7.63	72
73	13.03	12.36	11.74	11.16	10.62	10.12	9.65	9.21	8.81	8.42	8.07	73
74	13.11	12.50	11.94	11.41	10.91	10.45	10.02	9.62	9.24	8.88	8.55	74
75	13.24	12.69	12.18	11.71	11.26	10.84	10.45	10.08	9.73	9.40	9.10	75

Table 27 Discounting factors for term certain

Factor to discount value of multiplier for a period of deferment

Term	0.5%	1.0%	1.5%	2.0%	2.5%	3.0%	3.5%	4.0%	4.5%	5.0%	Term
1	0.9950	0.9901	0.9852	0.9804	0.9756	0.9709	0.9662	0.9615	0.9569	0.9524	1
2	0.9901	0.9803	0.9707	0.9612	0.9518	0.9426	0.9335	0.9246	0.9157	0.9070	2
3	0.9851	0.9706	0.9563	0.9423	0.9286	0.9151	0.9019	0.8890	0.8763	0.8638	3
4	0.9802	0.9610	0.9422	0.9238	0.9060	0.8885	0.8714	0.8548	0.8386	0.8227	4
5	0.9754	0.9515	0.9283	0.9057	0.8839	0.8626	0.8420	0.8219	0.8025	0.7835	5
6	0.9705	0.9420	0.9145	0.8880	0.8623	0.8375	0.8135	0.7903	0.7679	0.7462	6
7	0.9657	0.9327	0.9010	0.8706	0.8413	0.8131	0.7860	0.7599	0.7348	0.7107	7
8	0.9609	0.9235	0.8877	0.8535	0.8207	0.7894	0.7594	0.7307	0.7032	0.6768	8
9	0.9561	0.9143	0.8746	0.8368	0.8007	0.7664	0.7337	0.7026	0.6729	0.6446	9
10	0.9513	0.9053	0.8617	0.8203	0.7812	0.7441	0.7089	0.6756	0.6439	0.6139	10
11	0.9466	0.8963	0.8489	0.8043	0.7621	0.7224	0.6849	0.6496	0.6162	0.5847	11
12	0.9419	0.8874	0.8364	0.7885	0.7436	0.7014	0.6618	0.6246	0.5897	0.5568	12
13	0.9372	0.8787	0.8240	0.7730	0.7254	0.6810	0.6394	0.6006	0.5643	0.5303	13
14	0.9326	0.8700	0.8118	0.7579	0.7077	0.6611	0.6178	0.5775	0.5400	0.5051	14
15	0.9279	0.8613	0.7999	0.7430	0.6905	0.6419	0.5969	0.5553	0.5167	0.4810	15
16	0.9233	0.8528	0.7880	0.7284	0.6736	0.6232	0.5767	0.5339	0.4945	0.4581	16
17	0.9187	0.8444	0.7764	0.7142	0.6572	0.6050	0.5572	0.5134	0.4732	0.4363	17
18	0.9141	0.8360	0.7649	0.7002	0.6412	0.5874	0.5384	0.4936	0.4528	0.4155	18
19	0.9096	0.8277	0.7536	0.6864	0.6255	0.5703	0.5202	0.4746	0.4333	0.3957	19
20	0.9051	0.8195	0.7425	0.6730	0.6103	0.5537	0.5026	0.4564	0.4146	0.3769	20
21	0.9006	0.8114	0.7315	0.6598	0.5954	0.5375	0.4856	0.4388	0.3968	0.3589	21
22	0.8961	0.8034	0.7207	0.6468	0.5809	0.5219	0.4692	0.4220	0.3797	0.3418	22
23	0.8916	0.7954	0.7100	0.6342	0.5667	0.5067	0.4533	0.4057	0.3634	0.3256	23
24	0.8872	0.7876	0.6995	0.6217	0.5529	0.4919	0.4380	0.3901	0.3477	0.3101	24
25	0.8828	0.7798	0.6892	0.6095	0.5394	0.4776	0.4231	0.3751	0.3327	0.2953	25
26	0.8784	0.7720	0.6790	0.5976	0.5262	0.4637	0.4088	0.3607	0.3184	0.2812	26
27	0.8740	0.7644	0.6690	0.5859	0.5134	0.4502	0.3950	0.3468	0.3047	0.2678	27
28	0.8697	0.7568	0.6591	0.5744	0.5009	0.4371	0.3817	0.3335	0.2916	0.2551	28
29	0.8653	0.7493	0.6494	0.5631	0.4887	0.4243	0.3687	0.3207	0.2790	0.2429	29
30	0.8610	0.7419	0.6398	0.5521	0.4767	0.4120	0.3563	0.3083	0.2670	0.2314	30
31	0.8567	0.7346	0.6303	0.5412	0.4651	0.4000	0.3442	0.2965	0.2555	0.2204	31
32	0.8525	0.7273	0.6210	0.5306	0.4538	0.3883	0.3326	0.2851	0.2445	0.2099	32
33	0.8482	0.7201	0.6118	0.5202	0.4427	0.3770	0.3213	0.2741	0.2340	0.1999	33
34	0.8440	0.7130	0.6028	0.5100	0.4319	0.3660	0.3105	0.2636	0.2239	0.1904	34
35	0.8398	0.7059	0.5939	0.5000	0.4214	0.3554	0.3000	0.2534	0.2143	0.1813	35
36	0.8356	0.6989	0.5851	0.4902	0.4111	0.3450	0.2898	0.2437	0.2050	0.1727	36
37	0.8315	0.6920	0.5764	0.4806	0.4011	0.3350	0.2800	0.2343	0.1962	0.1644	37
38	0.8274	0.6852	0.5679	0.4712	0.3913	0.3252	0.2706	0.2253	0.1878	0.1566	38
39	0.8232	0.6784	0.5595	0.4619	0.3817	0.3158	0.2614	0.2166	0.1797	0.1491	39
40	0.8191	0.6717	0.5513	0.4529	0.3724	0.3066	0.2526	0.2083	0.1719	0.1420	40
41	0.8151	0.6650	0.5431	0.4440	0.3633	0.2976	0.2440	0.2003	0.1645	0.1353	41
42	0.8110	0.6584	0.5351	0.4353	0.3545	0.2890	0.2358	0.1926	0.1574	0.1288	42
43	0.8070	0.6519	0.5272	0.4268	0.3458	0.2805	0.2278	0.1852	0.1507	0.1227	43
44	0.8030	0.6454	0.5194	0.4184	0.3374	0.2724	0.2201	0.1780	0.1442	0.1169	44
45	0.7990	0.6391	0.5117	0.4102	0.3292	0.2644	0.2127	0.1712	0.1380	0.1113	45
46	0.7950	0.6327	0.5042	0.4022	0.3211	0.2567	0.2055	0.1646	0.1320	0.1060	46
47	0.7910	0.6265	0.4967	0.3943	0.3133	0.2493	0.1985	0.1583	0.1263	0.1009	47
48	0.7871	0.6203	0.4894	0.3865	0.3057	0.2420	0.1918	0.1522	0.1209	0.0961	48
49	0.7832	0.6141	0.4821	0.3790	0.2982	0.2350	0.1853	0.1463	0.1157	0.0916	49
50	0.7793	0.6080	0.4750	0.3715	0.2909	0.2281	0.1791	0.1407	0.1107	0.0872	50
51	0.7754	0.6020	0.4680	0.3642	0.2838	0.2215	0.1730	0.1353	0.1059	0.0831	51
52	0.7716	0.5961	0.4611	0.3571	0.2769	0.2150	0.1671	0.1301	0.1014	0.0791	52
53	0.7677	0.5902	0.4543	0.3501	0.2702	0.2088	0.1615	0.1251	0.0970	0.0753	53
54	0.7639	0.5843	0.4475	0.3432	0.2636	0.2027	0.1560	0.1203	0.0928	0.0717	54
55	0.7601	0.5785	0.4409	0.3365	0.2572	0.1968	0.1508	0.1157	0.0888	0.0683	55
56	0.7563	0.5728	0.4344	0.3299	0.2509	0.1910	0.1457	0.1112	0.0850	0.0651	56
57	0.7525	0.5671	0.4280	0.3234	0.2448	0.1855	0.1407	0.1069	0.0814	0.0620	57
58	0.7488	0.5615	0.4217	0.3171	0.2388	0.1801	0.1360	0.1028	0.0778	0.0590	58
59	0.7451	0.5560	0.4154	0.3109	0.2330	0.1748	0.1314	0.0989	0.0745	0.0562	59
60	0.7414	0.5504	0.4093	0.3048	0.2273	0.1697	0.1269	0.0951	0.0713	0.0535	60
61	0.7377	0.5450	0.4032	0.2988	0.2217	0.1648	0.1226	0.0914	0.0682	0.0510	61
62	0.7340	0.5396	0.3973	0.2929	0.2163	0.1600	0.1185	0.0879	0.0653	0.0486	62
63	0.7304	0.5343	0.3914	0.2872	0.2111	0.1553	0.1145	0.0845	0.0625	0.0462	63
64	0.7267	0.5290	0.3856	0.2816	0.2059	0.1508	0.1106	0.0813	0.0598	0.0440	64
65	0.7231	0.5237	0.3799	0.2761	0.2009	0.1464	0.1069	0.0781	0.0572	0.0419	65
66	0.7195	0.5185	0.3743	0.2706	0.1960	0.1421	0.1033	0.0751	0.0547	0.0399	66
67	0.7159	0.5134	0.3688	0.2653	0.1912	0.1380	0.0998	0.0722	0.0524	0.0380	67
68	0.7124	0.5083	0.3633	0.2601	0.1865	0.1340	0.0964	0.0695	0.0501	0.0362	68
69	0.7088	0.5033	0.3580	0.2550	0.1820	0.1301	0.0931	0.0668	0.0480	0.0345	69
70	0.7053	0.4983	0.3527	0.2500	0.1776	0.1263	0.0900	0.0642	0.0459	0.0329	70

continued

Table 27 Discounting factors for term certain *continued*

Factor to discount value of multiplier for a period of deferment

Term	0.5%	1.0%	1.5%	2.0%	2.5%	3.0%	3.5%	4.0%	4.5%	5.0%	Term
71	0.7018	0.4934	0.3475	0.2451	0.1732	0.1226	0.0869	0.0617	0.0439	0.0313	71
72	0.6983	0.4885	0.3423	0.2403	0.1690	0.1190	0.0840	0.0594	0.0420	0.0298	72
73	0.6948	0.4837	0.3373	0.2356	0.1649	0.1156	0.0812	0.0571	0.0402	0.0284	73
74	0.6914	0.4789	0.3323	0.2310	0.1609	0.1122	0.0784	0.0549	0.0385	0.0270	74
75	0.6879	0.4741	0.3274	0.2265	0.1569	0.1089	0.0758	0.0528	0.0368	0.0258	75
76	0.6845	0.4694	0.3225	0.2220	0.1531	0.1058	0.0732	0.0508	0.0353	0.0245	76
77	0.6811	0.4648	0.3178	0.2177	0.1494	0.1027	0.0707	0.0488	0.0337	0.0234	77
78	0.6777	0.4602	0.3131	0.2134	0.1457	0.0997	0.0683	0.0469	0.0323	0.0222	78
79	0.6743	0.4556	0.3084	0.2092	0.1422	0.0968	0.0660	0.0451	0.0309	0.0212	79
80	0.6710	0.4511	0.3039	0.2051	0.1387	0.0940	0.0638	0.0434	0.0296	0.0202	80

Table 28 Multipliers for pecuniary loss for term certain

Multiplier for regular frequent payments for a term certain at rate of return of

Term	0.5%	1.0%	1.5%	2.0%	2.5%	3.0%	3.5%	4.0%	4.5%	5.0%	Term
1	1.00	1.00	0.99	0.99	0.99	0.99	0.98	0.98	0.98	0.98	1
2	1.99	1.98	1.97	1.96	1.95	1.94	1.93	1.92	1.91	1.91	2
3	2.98	2.96	2.93	2.91	2.89	2.87	2.85	2.83	2.81	2.79	3
4	3.96	3.92	3.88	3.85	3.81	3.77	3.74	3.70	3.67	3.63	4
5	4.94	4.88	4.82	4.76	4.70	4.65	4.59	4.54	4.49	4.44	5
6	5.91	5.82	5.74	5.66	5.58	5.50	5.42	5.35	5.27	5.20	6
7	6.88	6.76	6.65	6.54	6.43	6.32	6.22	6.12	6.02	5.93	7
8	7.84	7.69	7.54	7.40	7.26	7.12	6.99	6.87	6.74	6.62	8
9	8.80	8.61	8.42	8.24	8.07	7.90	7.74	7.58	7.43	7.28	9
10	9.75	9.52	9.29	9.07	8.86	8.66	8.46	8.27	8.09	7.91	10
11	10.70	10.42	10.15	9.88	9.63	9.39	9.16	8.93	8.72	8.51	11
12	11.65	11.31	10.99	10.68	10.39	10.10	9.83	9.57	9.32	9.08	12
13	12.59	12.19	11.82	11.46	11.12	10.79	10.48	10.18	9.90	9.63	13
14	13.52	13.07	12.64	12.23	11.84	11.46	11.11	10.77	10.45	10.14	14
15	14.45	13.93	13.44	12.98	12.54	12.12	11.72	11.34	10.98	10.64	15
16	15.38	14.79	14.24	13.71	13.22	12.75	12.30	11.88	11.48	11.11	16
17	16.30	15.64	15.02	14.43	13.88	13.36	12.87	12.41	11.97	11.55	17
18	17.22	16.48	15.79	15.14	14.53	13.96	13.42	12.91	12.43	11.98	18
19	18.13	17.31	16.55	15.83	15.17	14.54	13.95	13.39	12.87	12.38	19
20	19.03	18.14	17.30	16.51	15.78	15.10	14.46	13.86	13.30	12.77	20
21	19.94	18.95	18.03	17.18	16.39	15.65	14.95	14.31	13.70	13.14	21
22	20.84	19.76	18.76	17.83	16.97	16.17	15.43	14.74	14.09	13.49	22
23	21.73	20.56	19.48	18.47	17.55	16.69	15.89	15.15	14.46	13.82	23
24	22.62	21.35	20.18	19.10	18.11	17.19	16.34	15.55	14.82	14.14	24
25	23.50	22.13	20.87	19.72	18.65	17.67	16.77	15.93	15.16	14.44	25
26	24.38	22.91	21.56	20.32	19.19	18.14	17.18	16.30	15.48	14.73	26
27	25.26	23.68	22.23	20.91	19.71	18.60	17.59	16.65	15.80	15.01	27
28	26.13	24.44	22.90	21.49	20.21	19.04	17.97	16.99	16.09	15.27	28
29	27.00	25.19	23.55	22.06	20.71	19.47	18.35	17.32	16.38	15.52	29
30	27.86	25.94	24.20	22.62	21.19	19.89	18.71	17.64	16.65	15.75	30
31	28.72	26.67	24.83	23.17	21.66	20.30	19.06	17.94	16.91	15.98	31
32	29.58	27.41	25.46	23.70	22.12	20.69	19.40	18.23	17.16	16.19	32
33	30.43	28.13	26.07	24.23	22.57	21.08	19.73	18.51	17.40	16.40	33
34	31.27	28.85	26.68	24.74	23.01	21.45	20.04	18.78	17.63	16.59	34
35	32.12	29.56	27.28	25.25	23.43	21.81	20.35	19.04	17.85	16.78	35
36	32.95	30.26	27.87	25.74	23.85	22.16	20.64	19.28	18.06	16.96	36
37	33.79	30.95	28.45	26.23	24.26	22.50	20.93	19.52	18.26	17.13	37
38	34.62	31.64	29.02	26.70	24.65	22.83	21.20	19.75	18.45	17.29	38
39	35.44	32.32	29.58	27.17	25.04	23.15	21.47	19.97	18.64	17.44	39
40	36.26	33.00	30.14	27.63	25.42	23.46	21.73	20.19	18.81	17.58	40
41	37.08	33.67	30.69	28.08	25.78	23.76	21.97	20.39	18.98	17.72	41
42	37.89	34.33	31.23	28.52	26.14	24.06	22.21	20.59	19.14	17.86	42
43	38.70	34.98	31.76	28.95	26.49	24.34	22.45	20.78	19.30	17.98	43
44	39.51	35.63	32.28	29.37	26.83	24.62	22.67	20.96	19.44	18.10	44
45	40.31	36.27	32.80	29.78	27.17	24.88	22.89	21.13	19.58	18.21	45
46	41.10	36.91	33.30	30.19	27.49	25.15	23.10	21.30	19.72	18.32	46
47	41.90	37.54	33.80	30.59	27.81	25.40	23.30	21.46	19.85	18.43	47
48	42.69	38.16	34.30	30.98	28.12	25.64	23.49	21.62	19.97	18.53	48
49	43.47	38.78	34.78	31.36	28.42	25.88	23.68	21.77	20.09	18.62	49
50	44.25	39.39	35.26	31.74	28.72	26.11	23.86	21.91	20.20	18.71	50
51	45.03	40.00	35.73	32.10	29.00	26.34	24.04	22.05	20.31	18.79	51
52	45.80	40.60	36.20	32.47	29.28	26.56	24.21	22.18	20.42	18.87	52
53	46.57	41.19	36.66	32.82	29.56	26.77	24.37	22.31	20.51	18.95	53
54	47.34	41.78	37.11	33.17	29.82	26.97	24.53	22.43	20.61	19.03	54
55	48.10	42.36	37.55	33.51	30.08	27.17	24.69	22.55	20.70	19.10	55
56	48.86	42.93	37.99	33.84	30.34	27.37	24.83	22.66	20.79	19.16	56
57	49.61	43.50	38.42	34.17	30.59	27.56	24.98	22.77	20.87	19.23	57
58	50.36	44.07	38.84	34.49	30.83	27.74	25.12	22.88	20.95	19.29	58
59	51.11	44.63	39.26	34.80	31.06	27.92	25.25	22.98	21.03	19.34	59
60	51.85	45.18	39.67	35.11	31.29	28.09	25.38	23.07	21.10	19.40	60
61	52.59	45.73	40.08	35.41	31.52	28.26	25.50	23.17	21.17	19.45	61
62	53.33	46.27	40.48	35.70	31.74	28.42	25.62	23.26	21.24	19.50	62
63	54.06	46.81	40.88	36.00	31.95	28.58	25.74	23.34	21.30	19.55	63
64	54.79	47.34	41.26	36.28	32.16	28.73	25.85	23.42	21.36	19.59	64
65	55.52	47.86	41.65	36.56	32.36	28.88	25.96	23.50	21.42	19.64	65
66	56.24	48.39	42.02	36.83	32.56	29.02	26.07	23.58	21.47	19.68	66
67	56.95	48.90	42.40	37.10	32.75	29.16	26.17	23.65	21.53	19.72	67
68	57.67	49.41	42.76	37.36	32.94	29.30	26.27	23.73	21.58	19.75	68
69	58.38	49.92	43.12	37.62	33.13	29.43	26.36	23.79	21.63	19.79	69
70	59.09	50.42	43.48	37.87	33.31	29.56	26.45	23.86	21.68	19.82	70

continued

Table 28 Multipliers for pecuniary loss for term certain *continued*

Multiplier for regular frequent payments for a term certain at rate of return of

Term	0.5%	1.0%	1.5%	2.0%	2.5%	3.0%	3.5%	4.0%	4.5%	5.0%	Term
71	59.79	50.91	43.83	38.12	33.48	29.68	26.54	23.92	21.72	19.85	71
72	60.49	51.41	44.17	38.36	33.65	29.80	26.63	23.98	21.76	19.88	72
73	61.19	51.89	44.51	38.60	33.82	29.92	26.71	24.04	21.80	19.91	73
74	61.88	52.37	44.85	38.83	33.98	30.03	26.79	24.10	21.84	19.94	74
75	62.57	52.85	45.18	39.06	34.14	30.15	26.87	24.15	21.88	19.97	75
76	63.26	53.32	45.50	39.29	34.30	30.25	26.94	24.20	21.92	19.99	76
77	63.94	53.79	45.82	39.51	34.45	30.36	27.01	24.25	21.95	20.02	77
78	64.62	54.25	46.14	39.72	34.60	30.46	27.08	24.30	21.99	20.04	78
79	65.29	54.71	46.45	39.93	34.74	30.56	27.15	24.35	22.02	20.06	79
80	65.97	55.16	46.75	40.14	34.88	30.65	27.21	24.39	22.05	20.08	80

14 THE COMPENSATION RECOVERY UNIT

14 THE COMPENSATION RECOVERY UNIT

Contents

14.1 Introduction

The Compensation Recovery Unit (The CRU) is a part of the Department for Work and Pensions (The DWP).

Individuals who are injured or disabled are entitled, in certain circumstances, to receive government benefits. Such benefits may run for the rest of an individual's life (if permanently disabled) or simply whilst that person recovers from his or her injuries.

If such benefits are as a result of an injury caused by another's wrong doing, then those benefits must be repaid to the CRU.

Such benefits must be repaid to the CRU by the compensator, who is usually an insurance company.

The idea behind the repayment is to prevent the Claimant being compensated twice.

For example, the Claimant may have claimed compensation for lost earnings and for care provided by his family. At the same time, he may have been in receipt of Government Benefits. Those benefits may have been paid to replace loss of income and to provide for care.

The Government has reasoned that it is only just in those circumstances, that the benefits are repaid; and are repaid by the compensator.

The compensator is, in certain circumstances, entitled to withhold from the Claimant's compensation a sum equivalent to the benefits that have to be repaid to the CRU.

No sum equivalent to the recoverable benefits can be withheld from compensation for General Damages. Compensation for general damages as such, is said to be "ring fenced".

Sums equivalent to other recoverable benefits can be withheld from the compensation that is to be paid to the Claimant, but only on a "like for like" basis. *(See table below.)*

14.2 Heads of Compensation and their Corresponding Recoverable Benefits

Head of compensation	*Benefit (which can be withheld from the associated head of compensation)*
1. Compensation for earnings lost during the relevant period	• Disability Working Allowance • Industrial Injuries Disablement Benefit • Incapacity Benefit • Income Support • Invalidity Pension • Invalidity Allowance

	• Jobseeker's Allowance • Reduced Earnings Allowance • Severe Disablement Allowance • Sickness Benefit • Statutory Sick Pay (paid before 6th April 1994) • Unemployability Supplement • Unemployment Benefit
2. Compensation for Costs of Care incurred during the relevant period	• Attendance Allowance • Care Component of Disability Living Allowance (DLA care) • Disablement Pension increase for constant Attendance Allowance • Exceptionally Severe Disablement Allowance
3. Compensation for Loss of Mobility during the relevant period	• Mobility Allowance • Mobility Component of Disability Living Allowance (DLA mobility)

14.3 Registering the Matter with the Compensation Recovery Unit

It is the responsibility of each compensator to register each claim with the Compensation Recovery Unit.

If a claim is settled and money is paid to a Claimant without the claim being registered with the Compensation Recovery Unit, the compensator will find that it has lost the chance to deduct a sum equivalent to the recoverable benefits and still have to repay the full amount of benefits to the DSS.

It is therefore crucial at the time that a claim is notified, that the compensator takes steps to register the matter with the DSS.

The following information will be required from the Claimant:

1. The Claimant's full name and title
2. The Claimant's date of birth
3. The Claimant's address
4. The Claimant's National Insurance Number.

5. Details of any hospitals attended for in-patient or outpatient treatment arising out of the accident (required for the payment of NHS charges) (see below).

14.4 Like for Like Recoupment

It must be remembered that benefits can only be withheld from their associated compensation claim. (See paragraph 14.2 for details of heads of compensation and their associated benefits.)

It is easier to understand this position by accepting that subject to a Review or Appeal, the compensator must repay all benefits to the CRU as at the date of settlement (subject to the rules below).

The compensator can withhold a sum equal to the benefits to be repaid from the Claimant's claim on a "like for like" basis only.

Take for example, a Claimant who has received incapacity benefit of £10,000.00 and seeks compensation for lost earnings of £7,000.00. A sum equivalent to the Incapacity Benefit to be repaid to the CRU by the compensator can be withheld from the Claimant's claim for loss of earnings.

If the compensator, after due investigations, accepts the loss of earnings claim of £7,000.00 and that is agreed with the Claimant's solicitors, the Claimant will not receive a penny of compensation for the lost earnings claim.

The compensator will have to pay all of the Incapacity Benefit (£10,000.00) back to the CRU. As the benefits exceed the total sum claimed by way of loss of earnings, the Claimant receives nothing for that head of claim.

Similarly, if Incapacity Benefit of £4,000.00 has been paid by the DWP to a Claimant and lost earnings of £6,000.00 have been claimed, the compensator must pay all of the benefits to the CRU. The compensator will then pay the balance of the claim of £2,000.00 to the Claimant. The compensator has withheld a sum equivalent to the benefits to be repaid to the CRU from the Claimant's compensation for lost earnings on a "like for like basis".

14.5 Five Year Limit

The compensator is only obliged to pay those benefits that are attributable to a particular accident and which accrue up to the date of settlement or up to the 5th anniversary of the date of the accident, whichever is earlier.

Although benefits that are attributable to the accident may run for the rest of the Claimant's life, those that are paid to the Claimant beyond the 5th anniversary of the injury will not have to be repaid by the compensator. (See also section below)

14.6 Benefits to be Repaid

These stop on the date of settlement.

Compensators are actively encouraged by the current legislation to settle claims as quickly as possible. If the claim is settled before the 5th anniversary of the accident date the compensator need only repay the benefits due at the date of settlement.

Therefore, if a claim is settled 12 months after the date of injury, only those benefits that are attributable to the injury and which have been paid to the Claimant by the DWP before those 12 months will have to be repaid to the CRU.

Therefore, claims handlers should take all reasonable steps (subject to proper investigations) to settle claims without delay.

14.7 Working CRU Example

The following example assumes that the Claimant and Defendant have been able to agree quantum as follows:

a) General Damages:	£5,000.00
b) Loss of earnings:	£3,000.00
c) Pre-accident vehicle value:	£3,500.00
d) Cost of care:	£4,000.00
Total:	£15,500.00

The benefits in this case to the date of settlement are as follows:

i) incapacity benefit:	£2,000.00

ii) disability working allowance:	£1,500.00
iii) attendance allowance:	£2,000.00
Total benefits:	£5,500.00

It can therefore been seen that the total worth of the claim is £15,500.00. Benefits paid by the DWP to the Claimant as a result of the accident total £5,500.00.

Please refer back to the table at paragraph 14.2 of "Heads of Compensation and their corresponding benefits".

The Claimant will receive the following:

a) General Damages (ring fenced):	£5,000.00
b) Loss of earnings: *(£3,000.00 as agreed less £2,000.00 incapacity benefit less £1,500.00 disability working allowance)*	nil
c) Pre-accident vehicle value:	£3,500.00
a) Cost of care: *(£4,000.00 as agreed less £2,000.00 attendance allowance)*	£2,000.00

The Claimant receives a total of £10,500.00

Compensator will pay

a) General Damages:	£5,000.00
b) Loss of earnings:	nil
i) incapacity benefit:	£2,000.00
ii) disability working allowance:	£1,500.00
c) Pre-accident vehicle value:	£3,500.00
d) Cost of care:	£2,000.00
iii) attendance allowance:	£2,000.00

The compensator will pay a total of £16,000.00.

As can be seen from the above example, although the total worth of the claim is £15,500.00 that is not the maximum that the compensator is obliged to pay.

In the example given above, the loss of earnings figure of £3,000.00 will be cancelled out by Incapacity Benefits of £2,000.00 and Disability Working Allowance of £1,500.00 (a total of £3,500.00).

Both of those benefits relate to the claim for lost income.

The surplus £500.00 cannot be deducted from any other aspect of the Claimant's claim. That excess of £500.00 therefore must be borne by the compensator and paid back to the CRU.

14.8 The Payment of NHS Charges

Health and Social Care (Community Health & Standards) Act 2003

Parts of this Act allows the NHS to recover some of the cost of treating an Accident victim from the party who pays compensation to that victim. Prior to 29 January 2007, only NHS charges incurred following a Road Traffic Accident were repayable. Afer this date, NHS charges incurred following RTA's and Employers' liability and Public liability accidents are repayable.

The NHS has a tariff that it applies to compensators. This alters year-by-year and so Claims Handlers are advised to check the DWP/CRU website after the 1st April 2008 for changes to the tariff.

The tariff is currently as follows:

Where compensation is paid following an accident which occurred on or after 1 April 2008 the following charges apply:

- where the casualty receiving NHS treatment at a hospital in respect of his injury, but was not admitted to hospital, the without admission treatment is a flat rate, one-off charge of **£547**; or
- where the casualty received NHS treatment at a hospital in respect of his injury and was admitted to hospital, the sum of **£672** is charged for each day or part day of admission;
- where the casualty received NHS ambulance services as a result of his injury (unless the person was dead on arrival at the hospital) the sum of **£165** is charged per person, per journey.
- the maximum amount which may be charged is **£40,179**.

Where compensation is paid following an accident which occurred on or after 29 January 2007 the following charges apply:

- where the casualty receiving NHS treatment at a hospital in respect of his injury, but was not admitted to hospital, the without admission treatment is a flat rate, one-off charge of **£505**; or

- where the casualty received NHS treatment at a hospital in respect of his injury and was admitted to hospital, the sum of **£620** is charged for each day or part day of admission;
- where the casualty received NHS ambulance services as a result of his injury (unless the person was dead on arrival at the hospital) the sum of **£159** is charged per person, per journey.
- the maximum amount which may be charged is **£37,100**.

Where compensation is paid following an accident which occurred on or after 1 April 2006 the following charges apply:

- where the casualty receiving NHS treatment at a hospital in respect of his injury, but was not admitted to hospital, the without admission treatment is a flat rate, one-off charge of **£505**; or
- where the casualty received NHS treatment at a hospital in respect of his injury and was admitted to hospital, the sum of **£620** is charged for each day or part day of admission;
- the maximum amount which may be charged is **£37,100**.
- the fee that is to be repaid applies to all road traffic accidents that have occurred after 1 April 2006 and to all other accidents only where those accidents have occurred after 29 January 2007.

Where compensation is paid following an accident which occurred on or after 1 April 2005 the following charges apply:

- where the RTA casualty received NHS treatment at a hospital in respect of his injury, but was not admitted to hospital, the "without admission treatment" is a flat rate, one-off charge of **£483**; or
- where the traffic casualty received NHS treatment at a hospital in respect of his injury and was admitted to hospital, the sum of **£593** is charged for each day or part day of admission;
- the maximum amount which may be charged is **£35,500**.

Where compensation is paid following an accident which occurred on or after 1 April 2004 the following charges apply:

- where the traffic casualty received NHS treatment at a hospital in respect of his injury, but was not admitted to hospital, the "without admission treatment" is a flat rate, one-off charge of **£473**;
- or where the traffic casualty received NHS treatment at a hospital in respect of his injury and was admitted to hospital, the sum of **£582** is charged for each day or part day of admission;
- the maximum amount which may be charged is **£34,800**.

Where compensation is paid following an accident which occurred on or after 1 April 2003 the following charges apply:

- where the RTA casualty received NHS treatment at a hospital in respect of his injury, but was not admitted to hospital, the "without admission treatment" is a flat rate, one-off charge of **£452**; or
- where the RTA casualty received NHS treatment at a hospital in respect of his injury and was admitted to hospital, the sum of **£556** is charged for each day or part day of admission;
- the maximum amount which may be charged is **£33,000.**

Where compensation is paid following an accident which occurred on or after 1 January 2003 the following charges apply:

- where the RTA casualty received NHS treatment at a hospital in respect of his injury, but was not admitted to hospital, the "without admission treatment" is a flat rate, one-off charge of **£440**; or
- where the RTA casualty received NHS treatment at a hospital in respect of his injury and was admitted to hospital, the sum of **£541** is charged for each day or part day of admission;
- the maximum amount which may be charged is **£30,000.**

Where compensation is paid following an accident, which occurred on or after 2 July 1997 the following charges apply:

- where the RTA casualty received NHS treatment at a hospital in respect of his injury, but was not admitted to hospital, the "without admission treatment" is a flat rate, one-off charge of **£354**; or

- where the RTA casualty received NHS treatment at a hospital in respect of his injury and was admitted to hospital, the sum of **£435** is charged for each day or part day of admission;
- the maximum amount which may be charged is **£10,000.**

The CRU will dispatch a form CRU1 that the compensator is obliged to complete and return to the DWP. The form asks for details of any hospitals that the Claimant has attended as an out or as an in-patient.

It is important that claims handlers return this form and remember to factor the possible NHS charges into any reserve placed on a file.

As can be seen from the figures above, the NHS can demand more than £40,000 in certain cases.

When reserving a file, claims handlers must therefore allow an appropriate sum in relation to NHS charges.

14.9 NHS Charges – Contributory Negligence

This paragraph applies only to incidents or injuries sustained after the 29 January 2007.

As has been indicated above, NHS charges were only repayable with regards to incidents or injuries prior to 29 January 2007 if those injuries had been sustained in road traffic accidents.

If injuries had been sustained in employers' liability, public liability or indeed road traffic accidents on or after 29 January 2007 as has been seen above, NHS charges must now be repaid.

If an accident or injury has occurred on or after 29 January 2007 the 2003 Act makes provision for the compensator to take into account contributory negligence in all cases where it is a factor in the primary compensation claim. It is therefore possible for the compensator to reduce the NHS charges by the same proportion as the finding or agreement on contributory negligence.

In order to reduce the NHS charges the compensator must provide to the CRU the following evidence:

a) A statement of the proportion by which the damage is payable in respect of the claim to be reduced, to reflect the injured person's share in the responsibility of the injury in question, and

b) A copy of the order, judgment, minute or document, which provides for that reduction.

It is recommended that claims handlers refer to the DWP website as to the precise information that is going to be required **prior to** any final settlement as to contributory negligence in order to ensure that the appropriate documentation and information can then be provided.

14.10 Compensation Recovery Unit and Defendant's Part 36 Offers/Benefits

14.10.1 Before Issue of Proceedings

It is open to one party to make an offer to another under Part 36 of the Civil Procedure Rules 1998.

This subject is dealt with in more detail in the chapter dealing with the Civil Procedure Rules in chapter 15.

14.10.2 After Issue of Proceedings

However, in a case involving a claim for damages for personal injuries, if an up to date Certificate of Total Benefits/Certificate of Recoverable Benefits is awaited from the CRU then the Defendant in those circumstances can put forward a written offer under Part 36.15(7) of the CPR 1998. The offer must make it clear that a benefit certificate is awaited.

Within seven days of the benefit certificate being received, clarification of the Part 36 must be provided. The clarification must:

a) Set out the total amount represented by the Part 36 Payment (the gross compensation).

b) State the name and amount of any deductible benefit by which that gross amount is reduced; and

c) Set out the net amount being paid after the deduction of the appropriate amount of benefit.

14.11 Reviews and Appeals – Benefits

The Compensation Recovery Unit will provide the compensator with Certificates of Total or Recoverable Benefits. Those certificates will set out the benefits that the Compensation Recovery Unit believe are attributable to the injuries in question and which have to be repaid by the compensator at the date of settlement.

However, there are cases in which the Benefits Agency are incorrect and not all of the benefits listed on the Certificate will be repayable by a compensator. Such cases will include the following circumstances:

a) The Claimant who had a pre-existing medical condition and was receiving benefits for that condition before the accident occurred. If the type or the amount of the benefit has not materially altered, it may not be appropriate for the compensator to repay all benefits paid to the Claimant, after the injury date, back to the CRU. Some or all of the benefits may relate to the Claimant's pre-existing condition.

b) If the Claimant is exaggerating or malingering and as a result of the exaggeration or malingering the DWP have been fooled into paying additional benefits, it would not be reasonable to expect the compensator to repay benefits to the DWP.

c) The Claimant may have had a pre-existing condition which has been made worse by the accident in question but which has then settled down or has been accelerated by the accident in question by a finite period (less than 5 years). In those circumstances, the length of the exacerbation or the period of acceleration would contain those benefits that are directly attributable to the accident. Benefits that fall outside of those periods would not be attributable to the accident and it would not be reasonable for the compensator to have to repay them to the DWP.

The DWP may be unaware of relevant facts and if that is the case those facts should be brought to the CRU's attention.

This can be done in one of two ways.

14.11.1 A Review of the CRU Certificate.

In the first instance claims handlers should seek a review of the CRU Certificate. This should be done in writing and full evidence should be submitted to the CRU with an explanation as to why it is felt that the compensator should not have to pay those benefits set out.

Claims Handlers should not be afraid to seek more than one review.

Certainly, if the first review is rejected, a second review should be sought if an inadequate explanation for the rejection is provided by the CRU.

At the date of publication it is apparent that the CRU is becoming more reluctant to grant reviews. It now argues that if the injury is one of several causes of the Claimant's need for benefits, then all of those benefits need to be repaid to the CRU by the compensator.

Take for example, a Claimant who has a pre-existing orthopaedic condition. That condition is then accelerated by two years by an accident, that results in benefits being paid by the DWP to the Claimant for the rest of the Claimant's life.

The CRU may well try to argue that it is the accident that has caused the benefits to be triggered and that therefore the compensator should repay all benefits that have arisen following the accident and for the following five years in full.

That, it is submitted, is plainly wrong. It is submitted that at most compensators should only have to pay those benefits that have been paid during the period of acceleration.

A review can be sought after settlement, but before benefits are repaid to the CRU. If reviews are unsuccessful then an Appeal may have to be made.

14.11.2 Appeals

The DWP publish a document entitled " Recovery of Benefits Appeal Guide" This can be found on their website.

This sets out the procedure for an Appeal which can be summarised as follows:

1. An Appeal can generally only be pursued once the compensation claim has been concluded and;

2. The compensator has repaid the recoverable benefits to the CRU.
3. The Appeal must be made within 1 month after the date that the compensator makes full payment to the CRU.
4. The Appeal must be made on the form contained within the leaflet referred to above.

The CRU will then return further forms for completion upon which the compensator will have to state whether they wish the matter to proceed to an oral hearing at which their case can be argued, or whether they would wish matters to be dealt with on paper.

It is strongly recommended that an oral hearing is sought whenever it is commercially viable to do so.

It is therefore suggested that if the benefits position is to be challenged the following procedure is adopted:

1. Seek a review of Certificate before settlement if possible. If unsuccessful then;
2. Settle the claim
3. Seek a review (thereby not having to refund monies to the CRU)
4. If unsuccessful, then repay the benefits to the CRU and simultaneously seek to appeal within one month.

14.12 Review and Appeals – NHS Charges

The compensator may ask the CRU to review any aspect of a certificate of NHS charges at any time. For a road traffic accident which occurred prior to 29 January 2007, there is no time limit to make a request for a review of NHS charges.

For incidents or injuries after 29 January 2007, there is a time limit of three months from the date on the certificate, or if later, no more than three months from the date the compensation payment was made. The CRU requires that the request must be made in writing, clearly stating the grounds on which a review is being sought.

A compensator also has the right of appeal against the certificate of NHS charges if it is thought that the previous review decision is incorrect.

The CRU requires that the form NHS 30 is used to lodge the appeal.

As for benefits, an appeal can only be made after final settlement of the compensation claim and full payment of recoverable NHS charges have been repaid to the CRU.

An appeal against NHS charges following a road traffic accident that occurred prior to 29 January 2007 must be made within three months of the date on which the compensator makes the full payment of NHS charges to the DWP.

For incidents on or after the 29 January 2007, the time limit is no later than three months from the date on the certificate, or if later, no more than three months from the date the compensation payment was made.

Again, claims handlers are directed to the DWP website for further details.

15 THE CIVIL PROCEDURE RULES 1998

15 THE CIVIL PROCEDURE RULES 1998

Contents

15.1 Introduction

Lord Woolf in his report "Access To Justice" concluded that Civil Litigation was too protracted, too expensive and was not managed sufficiently by the Courts.

A wholesale reform of the Civil Justice system was therefore undertaken and the Civil Procedure Rules 1998 came into force on the 26th April 1999.

The aim of the rules is:

1. To provide alternative dispute resolution methods to potential litigants in order to avoid litigation in the first place. Alternative dispute resolution may take the form of mediation or conciliation, which are less formal and confrontational than litigation.

2. If litigation is unavoidable, to put in place protocols for both parties to comply with before proceedings are issued. The aim here is to encourage the parties to give greater disclosure of their case in evidence in an effort to avoid litigation commencing.

3. To shorten where appropriate, the litigation process by allocating cases to an appropriate "track".

4. To place the management of cases in the hands of the Court in an effort to speed up the litigation process.

5. To put in place a new costs regime, the main stay of which is "proportionality".

The Civil Procedure Rules are to a great extent the domain of lawyers.

They will need to be interpreted by the parties' lawyers after proceedings have been issued.

However, every aspect of the Civil Procedure Rules and every decision made by a Judge under them is subject to "an overriding objective". That overriding objective is that:

> **"These rules are a new procedural code with the overriding objective of enabling the Court to deal with cases justly".**

Rule 1.12(2) of the CPR 1998 defines what is meant by dealing with cases justly as follows:

a) Ensuring that the parties are on an equal footing;

b) Saving expense.

c) Dealing with the case in ways which are proportionate:

   (i) to the amount of money involved;
   (ii) to the importance of the case,
   (iii) to the complexities of the issues,
   (iv) to the financial position of each party,
   (v) ensuring that it is dealt with expeditiously and fairly,
   (vi) allotting it to an appropriate share of the Court's resouces whilst taking into account the need to allot resources to other cases.

Although, as stated above, the CPR 1998 will usually be the territory of the parties' legal representatives, there are two particularly important areas under The Rules that Claims Handlers must be aware of.

Part 36 Offers to Settle

Part 36 of the Civil Procedure Rules 1998 allows either party, to put forward a written offer of settlement of the claim.

Claims Handlers will now be used to seeing Claimant's Part 36 Offers to settle. A suggested draft for a Part 36 Offer to settle letter can be found below. Defendants should also consider making Part 36.15(7) offers whilst an up-to-date certificate of total, or certificate of recoverable benefits is awaited from the DWP (see chapter on CRU).

It should also be remembered that offers can be made for all or for particular parts , such a general damages, of a Claimant's claim.

Part 36 Offer to Settle Letter

Dear Sirs,

Re: Claimant v Defendant

Take notice that the Defendant hereby offers to settle the Claimant's claim for the sum of £.......... in full and final satisfaction of all causes of action in respect of which the Claimant claims inclusive of interest. In addition the Defendant will pay the Claimant's reasonable costs to be assessed if not agreed [or subject to any predictive costs regime].

[or in the case of liability you may wish to state:

Take notice that the Defendant hereby offers to settle the Claimant's claim accepting X% of the liability for the matters complained of. In addition the Defendant will pay the Claimant's reasonable costs of and occasioned by the liability aspect of these proceedings, subject to any limits imposed by any predictive costs regime]

This offer remains open for 21 days from the date of this letter.

After the 21 day period, the Claimant may only accept this offer if:

i) the parties agree the liability for costs. The Defendant will expect its costs to be paid from the time after which the Claimant could have accepted this offer, or

ii) the Court gives permission.

In making this offer the Defendant agrees to pay any damages due within 14 days of the date of service of notice of acceptance of this offer.

Yours faithfully

Either party can accept the other party's offer within 21 days of it being made.

Claims handlers must ensure that the relevant benefits position is stated with any Part 36 offer.

Defendant accepts Claimant's offer

If the Defendant accepts the Claimant's offer within 21 days then subject to the appropriate costs rules, the Claimant's costs will also become payable on a standard basis. The Defendant must pay the damages within 14 days of acceptance of the Claimant's offer.

If a Claimant makes an offer that that Claimant then subsequently fails to match, there do not appear to be any costs consequences to be borne by the Claimant as long as he recovers some compensation. That of course assumes that the Defendant has not made an offer that has not been beaten.

Claimant accepts Defendant's offer

If a Claimant accepts the Defendant's offer within 21 days then again, subject to the appropriate costs rules, the Defendant will pay the Claimant's costs on a standard basis from the date of acceptance. The Defendant must pay the Claimant the damages due within 14 days of the Claimant's acceptance.

Claimant fails to beat the Defendant's offer

If the Defendant makes a Part 36 offer that is not beaten by the Claimant, then the Claimant will recover costs up to 21 days after the offer was made (the time that the Claimant has to accept the offer). Thereafter the Claimant will have to pay the Defendant's costs. This assumes that the Claimant recovers some compensation.

Defendant fails to do better than Claimant's offer

If the Claimant makes an offer which is not accepted by the Defendant and which the Claimant subsequently matches or beats, the Claimant can ask the Court to make one or more of the following Orders:

1. An Order that the Defendant pay the Claimant's costs of the action
2. An Order for interest on the whole of the Judgment awarded to the Claimant at a rate of up to 10% above the bank base rate starting with the latest date on which the Defendant could have accepted the offer without needing the permission of the Court.
3. An Order that costs be paid on an indemnity basis from the latest date on which the Defendant could have accepted the offer without needing the permission of the Court.
4. Interest on those costs at a rate of up to 10% above the base rate.

It is important therefore that Claims Handlers consider the terms of any offer made by the Claimant closely.

However, it must also be noted that truly speculative offers made by Claimant's solicitors, as soon as a claim is intimated, can for the most part be ignored.

In deciding whether to make the above punitive Orders against the Defendant, the Court will look at what information was available to the Defendant at the time that the offer was made, and whether or not the Defendant could have assessed the worth of the claim at the time that the offer was made with the information that was to hand.

Ford v GKR Construction & Others (November 1999 – Court of Appeal)

Lord Woolf made it clear that the process of making Part 36 Offers before the commencement of litigation was to ensure that the rules worked as intended and that the parties had to be provided with the information that they required in order to assess whether to make or accept an offer.

If it was found that a party had not enabled another party to assess properly whether to make or accept an offer because of non-disclosure of material matters, or if a party had come to a decision which was different from that which would have been reached if there had been proper disclosure, that was a material matter for a Court to take into account when considering what subsequent costs order to make.

Therefore if a Claimant (or Defendant) makes a speculative Part 36 Offer that is unsupported by the evidence that has been disclosed, it is submitted that the Court would be slow to penalise a party who did not accept the offer. The Court may penalise the party making the offer if evidence which is available and which is subsequently relied on, is not disclosed by the offering party at the time the offer is made.

15.2 The Personal Injury Pre-action Protocol

The Personal Injury Pre-action Protocol (PIPAP) is one of nine pre-action protocols that are now in force. As well as Personal Injury, the other protocols cover Construction Disputes, Judicial Review, Rent/Possession Cases, Housing Disrepair Cases, Defamation, Clinical Negligence, Disease and Illness Claims and Professional Negligence.

For the purposes of this chapter we will focus on the personal injury protocol.

The PIPAP has now been in place for some time and was published before the Civil Procedure Rules came into force. It is amended regularly and Claims Handlers should periodically check the website of the Ministry of Justice to ensure that they keep abreast of recent developments.

It is a set of rules by which the Claimant and Defendant (and their representatives) must abide by prior to the issue of proceedings. The aim is to avoid proceedings if at all possible.

If proceedings are inevitable, the Protocol's aim is to allow the parties to identify, prior to the issue of proceedings, those issues that will need to be concentrated upon in litigation. It has been said that the aim of the protocols is to encourage a "cards on the table" approach as opposed to the old system that was often approached by parties, insurers and lawyers like a game of poker.

The Protocol and it's annexes are reproduced in full at the end of this chapter and it is strongly recommended that Claims handlers thoroughly familiarise themselves with the original text. For ease of reference we set out below the main parts of the protocol.

The protocol is as follows:

Step 1

A Claimant must send to the proposed Defendant two copies of the letter of claim that contains a clear summary of the facts, the nature of the injuries and details of any financial loss incurred. That letter must provide sufficient information to enable a Defendant's Insurance Company to commence full investigations and to assess a reserve figure. The letter does not have to be set out as a Pleading. The Protocol provides an example of the pre-action letter (see example at the end of the chapter).

Step 2

The Defendant (or his insurer) should reply within 21 days of the date of the posting of the letter of claim, identifying the Insurer if there is one. The party replying should at this stage identify any significant omissions from the letter of claim. It is suggested in such circumstances that the Defendant's time to investigate the claim (see step 3 below) should not be triggered until the Claimant has provided that information. If there is no response to the letter of claim within the 21-day period the Claimant is entitled to issue proceedings.

Step 3

The Defendant or his Insurers then have a maximum of 3 months (from the date of their letter of acknowledgement) to investigate matters. At the end of that period the Defendant must reply stating whether liability is denied and if so, giving reasons for the denial of liability. **Full reasons and details must be given.** It is no longer sufficient to simply say, for example, "having investigated the matter, we do not feel that our Insured is responsible and therefore have no offers to make".

If the Insurer admits liability, the presumption now is that the Defendant will be bound by that admission. If the Defendant subsequently becomes aware of fresh facts that cause it to change it's mind as to liability, those new facts and the new repudiation of liability should be communicated to the Claimant's advisors immediately. It is unlikely that a Defendant will be able to resile from any earlier admission and so it is crucial that liability is only admitted when propr investigations have been carried out and completed.

Step 4

If the Defendant denies liability then, with his letter of reply, he should provide documents in his possession which are material to the issues between the parties, and which are likely to be ordered to be disclosed by the Court either on an application for pre-action disclosure or on disclosure during proceedings. Again, the Protocol gives examples of lists of such documents (see below). If incomplete disclosure is given a Claimant is likely to issue an application for Pre action disclosure (see below).

Step 5

A Schedule of Special Damages with supporting documentation should be prepared and served by the Claimant upon the Defendant's Insurers.

Step 6

Experts

Before either party instructs an expert the other party must be shown a list of the names of one or more experts to whom it is intended instructions are to be sent.

Within 14 days the other party may indicate an objection to one or more of those experts. The first party should then instruct a mutually acceptable expert.

If the other party objects to all of the experts on the list then the parties can instruct experts of their own choice.

However, the Court may impose costs sanctions if the instruction of 2 experts is, in the Court's opinion, unnecessary.

If the second party does not object to an expert nominated then he will not be entitled to rely upon his own expert evidence unless:

a) The first party agrees;

b) The Court so directs or;

c) The first party's expert report has been amended and the first party is not prepared to disclose the original report.

It should be understood that of course the Claimant has an advantage here. If experts are not agreed under the protocol it is very likely that the Claimant will press on to obtain a unilateral report whilst refusing to consent to being examined or interviewed by the Defendant's proposed expert. There is nothing that the Defendant can do in such circumstances other than to place a request for a medical examination of the Claimant in writing.

The Defendant in such circumstances must then wait for the Claimant's expert's report to be served. Of course, the report may be acceptable in which case settlement should be possible. There are occasions however when the report will not be acceptable. Examples for that unacceptability are often as follows:

1. The Claimant's expert has not had access to the Claimant's pre and post accident medical or other records

2. The expert is not properly qualified or experienced to provide the opinion in question.

3. The expert has failed to set out a range of possible alternative opinions that other experts may reasonably hold.

4. The expert has unreasonably failed to reach any firm conclusions.

In such circumstances the Defendant may be able to move matters forward pragmatically by putting questions to the expert in order to solve the problems that are perceived with the report. Questions in such circumstances should certainly be put. The replies may be acceptable and, again, make a settlement possible. If they are not we suggest that a Defendant then repeats the request to have the Claimant examined by an alternative expert. If the Claimant again refuses the Defendant, if settlement can still not be achieved, will have to wait for the Claimant to issue proceedings. At that point the Defendant's solicitors should apply to the Court for permission to rely upon fresh medical evidence.

If the Defendant has good reason for being dissatisfied with the Claimant's expert's report after questions have been put and answered, and has asked for an earlier examination which has been refused; a

Court will tend to have sympathy and allow the Defendant to obtain it's own evidence. If the Court considers that the Claimant has acted unreasonably in refusing the Defendant's request to obtain it's own report, costs may be awarded against the Claimant and a stay of the proceedings imposed until such time as the Defendant's report has been obtained.

Step 7

When a medical expert is to be instructed, the Claimant will organise access to relevant medical records. Again, there is a specimen letter in the Protocol (see example at end of chapter).

Under **Rule 35.9** the Court has power to direct a party to provide information about documentation to the other party. The Rule reads:

> **"Where a party has access to information which is not reasonably available to the other party, the Court may direct the party who has access to the information to**:
>
> **a) Prepare and file a document recalling the information and;**
>
> **b) Serve a copy of that document on the other party.**

This Rule can be used to obtain the Claimant's medical records for transmission to the Defendant's own expert in appropriate circumstances.

Step 8

Either party may then send the expert written questions on the report, relevant to the issues, via the instructing party's Solicitors.

The expert should send answers to the questions separately and directly to each party.

If liability has been admitted, the Claimant should wait 21 days before issuing proceedings in order to allow the parties to attempt to settle the case.

Step 9

A relatively new requirement under the PIPAP relates to rehabilitation. Traditionally, insurers have tended to focus on rehabilitation in the most serious injury cases.

The PIPAP now requires both parties to consider "as early as possible whether the Claimant has reasonable needs that could be met by rehabilitation treatment or other measures"

The parties are required to consider moving matters forward under the Rehabilitation Protocol (reproduced below).

Any report obtained in order to consider rehabilitation can only be used within the litigation by the consent of both parties.

General

A failure to comply with the Protocols may lead the Court to refuse to extend any period for the serving of a Statement of Case and penalise any one party in costs at any stage of the proceedings. Indeed, there is a specific provision within the Costs Rules that the Court will take into account whether or not the Protocols have been followed when deciding on the awarding of costs and their level.

The Court will also take into account an unreasonable refusal by either party to attempt to settle a case before litigation as a factor in relation to the awarding of costs.

As can be seen, disclosure needs to be provided prior to the issue of proceedings by the Defendant. The Lord Chancellor's Department has prepared disclosure lists. These are primarily for fast track cases but have been adopted as a useful guide for pre-action disclosure under the PIPAP.

15.2.1 Claims Handlers' Investigations under the Personal Injury Pre-action Protocol

In accordance with the PIPAP and Disclosure Lists it is important that claims handlers seek from their clients the following:

1. A fully completed incident report form, if possible, hand written by the driver (in motor claim) or the appropriate officer (if EL/PL).
2. Full documentation in accordance with the PIPAP Disclosure Lists. (see below).

3. Where appropriate, witness statements – properly set out with a statement of truth.

4. Where appropriate, plans of the scene of the incident together with photographs.

If the first letter received from the Claimant does not contain sufficient information to allow you to investigate the claim fully, ask for the additional information that you need.

15.2.2 Pre-action Disclosure

Part 31.16 of the CPR 1998 allows a party to seek disclosure of relevant documents before proceedings are started.

The Court will make such an Order where:

a) The respondent is likely to be a party to subsequent proceedings;

b) The applicant is also likely to be party to those proceedings;

c) If proceedings have started, the respondent's duty by way of standard disclosure will extend to the documents of which the applicant seeks disclosure;

d) Before proceedings have started it is desirable in order to:

   i) dispose fairly of the anticipated proceedings,
   ii) assist the dispute to be resolved without proceedings or,
   iii) save costs.

Therefore, if a Defendant under the PIPAP gives incomplete disclosure, a Court may not only impose sanctions at a later stage, but the Claimant may seek an Order under Part 31.16 of the CPR 1998.

15.2.3 PROTOCOLS

Pre-Action Protocol for Personal Injury Claims

Contents

1 Introduction

1.1 Lord Woolf in his final Access to Justice Report of July 1996 recommended the development of pre-action protocols:
To build on and increase the benefits of early but well informed settlement which genuinely satisfy both parties to dispute.

1.2 The aims of pre-action protocols are:

- more pre-action contact between the parties
- better and earlier exchange of information
- better pre-action investigation by both sides
- to put the parties in a position where they may be able to settle cases fairly and early without litigation
- to enable proceedings to run to the court's timetable and efficiently, if litigation does become necessary
- to promote the provision of medical or rehabilitation treatment (not just in high value cases) to address the needs of the claimant

1.3 The concept of protocols is relevant to a range of initiatives for good litigation and pre-litigation practice, especially:

- predictability in the time needed for steps pre-proceedings
- standardisation of relevant information, including documents to be disclosed.

1.4 The Courts will be able to treat the standards set in protocols as the normal reasonable approach to pre-action conduct. If proceedings are issued, it will be for the court to decide whether non-compliance with a protocol should merit adverse consequences. Guidance on the court's likely approach will be given from time to time in practice directions.

1.5 If the court has to consider the question of compliance after proceedings have begun, it will not be concerned with minor infringements, e.g. failure by a short period to provide relevant information. One minor breach will not exempt the 'innocent' party from following the protocol. The court will look at the effect of non-compliance on the other party when deciding whether to impose sanctions.

2 Notes of guidance

2.1 The protocol has been kept deliberately simple to promote ease of use and general acceptability. The notes of guidance which follows relate particularly to issues which arose during the piloting of the protocol.

Scope of the Protocol

2.2 This protocol is intended to apply to all claims which include a claim for personal injury (except those claims covered by the Clinical Disputes and Disease and Illness Protocols) and to the entirety of those claims: not only to the personal injury element of a claim which also includes, for instance, property damage.

2.3 This protocol is primarily designed for those road traffic, tripping and slipping and accident at work cases which include an element of personal injury with a value of less than £15,000 which are likely to be allocated to the fast track. This is because time will be of the essence, after proceedings are issued, especially for the defendant, if a case is to be ready for trial within 30 weeks of allocation. Also, proportionality of work and costs to the value of what is in dispute is particularly important in lower value claims. For some claims within the value 'scope' of the fast track some flexibility in the timescale of the protocol may be necessary, see also paragraph 3.8.

2.4 However, the 'cards on the table' approach advocated by the protocol is equally appropriate to higher value claims. The spirit, if not the letter of the protocol, should still be followed for multi-track type claims. In accordance with the sense of the civil justice reforms, the court will expect to see the spirit of reasonable pre-action behaviour applied in all cases, regardless of the existence of a specific protocol. In particular with regard to personal injury cases worth more than £15,000, with a view to avoiding the necessity of proceedings parties are expected to comply with the protocol as far as possible e.g. in respect of letters before action, exchanging information and documents and agreeing experts.

2.5 The timetable and the arrangements for disclosing documents and obtaining expert evidence may need to be varied to suit the circumstances of the case. Where one or both parties consider the detail of the protocol is not appropriate to the case, and proceedings are subsequently issued, the court will expect an explanation as to why the protocol has not been followed, or has been varied.

Early Notification

2.6 The claimant's legal representative may wish to notify the defendant and/or his insurer as soon as they know a claim is likely to be made, but before they are able to send a detailed letter of claim, particularly for instance, when the defendant has no or limited knowledge of the incident giving rise to the claim or where the claimant is incurring significant expenditure as a result of the accident which he hopes the defendant might pay for, in whole or in part. If the claimant's representative chooses to do this, it will not start the timetable for responding.

The Letter of Claim

2.7 The specimen letter of claim at Annex A will usually be sent to the individual defendant. In practice, he/she may have no personal financial interest in the financial outcome of the claim/dispute because he/she is insured. Court imposed sanctions for non-compliance with the protocol may be ineffective against an insured. This is why the protocol emphasises the importance of passing the letter of claim to the insurer and the possibility that the insurance cover might be affected. If an insurer receives the letter of claim only after some delay by the insured, it would not be unreasonable for the insurer to ask the claimant for additional time to respond.

2.8 In road traffic cases, the letter of claim should always contain the name and address of the hospital where the claimant was treated and, where available, the claimant's hospital reference number.

2.9 The priority at letter of claim stage is for the claimant to provide sufficient information for the defendant to assess liability. Sufficient information should also be provided to enable the defendant to estimate the likely size of the claim.

2.10 Once the claimant has sent the letter of claim no further investigation on liability should normally be carried out until a response is received from the defendant indicating whether liability is disputed.

Reasons for Early Issue

2.11 The protocol recommends that a defendant be given three months to investigate and respond to a claim before proceedings are issued. This may not always be possible, particularly where a claimant only consults a solicitor close to the end of any relevant limitation period. In these circumstances, the claimant's solicitor should give as much notice of the intention to issue proceedings as is practicable and the parties should consider whether the court might be invited to extend time for service of the claimant's supporting documents and for service of any defence, or alternatively, to stay the proceedings while the recommended steps in the protocol are followed.

Status of Letters of Claim and Response

2.12 Letters of claim and response are not intended to have the same status as a statement of case in proceedings. Matters may come to light as a result of investigation after the letter of claim has been sent, or after the defendant has responded, particularly if disclosure of documents takes place outside the recommended three-month period. These circumstances could mean that the 'pleaded' case of one or both parties is presented slightly differently than in the letter of claim and response. It would not be consistent with the spirit of the protocol for a party to 'take a point' on this in the proceedings, provided that there was no obvious intention by the party who changed their position to mislead the other party.

Disclosure of Documents

2.13 The aim of the early disclosure of documents by the defendant is not to encourage 'fishing expeditions' by the claimant, but to promote an early exchange of relevant information to help in clarifying or resolving issues in dispute. The claimant's solicitor can assist by identifying in the letter of claim or in a subsequent letter the particular categories of documents which they consider are relevant.

Experts

2.14 The protocol encourages joint selection of, and access to, experts. The report produced is not a joint report for the purposes of CPR Part 35. Most frequently this will apply to the medical expert, but on occasions also to liability experts, e.g. engineers. The protocol promotes the practice of the claimant obtaining a medical report, disclosing it to the defendant who then asks questions and/or agrees it and does not obtain his own report. The Protocol provides for nomination of the expert by the claimant in personal injury claims because of the early stage of the proceedings and the particular nature of such claims. If proceedings have to be issued, a medical report must be attached to these proceedings. However, if necessary after proceedings have commenced and with the permission of the court, the parties may obtain further expert reports. It would be for the court to decide whether the costs of more than one expert's report should be recoverable.

2.15 Some solicitors choose to obtain medical reports through medical agencies, rather than directly from a specific doctor or hospital. The defendant's prior consent to the action should be sought and, if the defendant so requests, the agency should be asked to provide in advance the names of the doctor(s) whom they are considering instructing.

Alternative Dispute Resolution

2.16 The parties should consider whether some form of alternative dispute resolution procedure would be more suitable than litigation, and if so, endeavour to agree which form to adopt. Both the Claimant and Defendant may be required by the Court to provide evidence that alternative means of resolving their dispute were considered. The Courts take the view that litigation should be a last resort, and that claims should not be issued prematurely when a settlement is still actively being explored. Parties are warned that if the protocol is not followed (including this paragraph) then the Court must have regard to such conduct when determining costs.

2.17 It is not practicable in this protocol to address in detail how the parties might decide which method to adopt to resolve their particular dispute. However, summarised below are some of the options for resolving disputes without litigation:

- Discussion and negotiation.
- Early neutral evaluation by an independent third party (for example, a lawyer experienced in the field of personal injury or an individual experienced in the subject matter of the claim).
- Mediation – a form of facilitated negotiation assisted by an independent neutral party.

2.18 The Legal Services Commission has published a booklet on 'Alternatives to Court', CLS Direct Information Leaflet 23 (www.clsdirect.org.uk/legalhelp/leaflet23.jsp), which lists a number of organisations that provide alternative dispute resolution services.

2.19 *It is expressly recognised that no party can or should be forced to mediate or enter into any form of ADR.*

Stocktake

2.20 Where a claim is not resolved when the protocol has been followed, the parties might wish to carry out a 'stocktake' of the issues in dispute, and the evidence that the court is likely to need to decide those issues, before proceedings are started. Where the defendant is insured and the pre-action steps have been conducted by the insurer, the insurer would normally be expected to nominate solicitors to act in the proceedings and the claimant's solicitor is recommended to invite the insurer to nominate solicitors to act in the proceedings and do so 7–14 days before the intended issue date.

3 The protocol

Letter of claim

3.1 The claimant shall send to the proposed defendant two copies of a letter of claim, immediately sufficient information is available to substantiate a realistic claim and before issues of quantum are addressed in detail. One copy of the letter is for the defendant, the second for passing on to his insurers.

3.2 The letter shall contain **a clear summary of the facts** on which the claim is based together with an indication of the **nature of any injuries** suffered and of **any financial loss incurred**. In cases of road traffic accidents, the letter should provide the name and address of the hospital where treatment has been obtained and the claimant's hospital reference number. Where the case is funded by a conditional fee agreement (or collective conditional fee agreement), notification should be given of the existence of the agreement and where appropriate, that there is a success fee and/or insurance premium, although not the level of the success fee or premium.

3.3 Solicitors are recommended to use a **standard format** for such a letter – an example is at Annex A: this can be amended to suit the particular case.

3.4 The letter should ask for **details of the insurer** and that a copy should be sent by the proposed defendant to the insurer where appropriate. If the insurer is known, a copy shall be sent directly to the insurer. Details of the claimant's National Insurance number and date of birth should be supplied to the defendant's insurer once the defendant has responded to the letter of claim and confirmed the identity of the insurer. This information should not be supplied in the letter of claim.

3.5 **Sufficient information** should be given in order to enable the defendant's insurer/solicitor to commence investigations and at least put a broad valuation on the 'risk'.

3.6 The **defendant should reply within 21 calendar days** of the date of posting of the letter identifying the insurer (if any) and, if necessary, identifying specifically any significant omissions from the letter of claim. If there has been no reply by the defendant or insurer within 21 days, the claimant will be entitled to issue proceedings.

3.7 The **defendant** ('s insurers) will have a **maximum of three months** from the date of acknowledgment of the claim **to investigate**. No later than the end of that period the defendant (insurer) shall reply, stating whether liability is denied and, if so, giving reasons for their denial of liability including any alternative version of events relied upon.

3.8 Where the accident occurred outside England and Wales and/or where the defendant is outside the jurisdiction, the time periods of 21 days and three months should normally be extended up to 42 days and six months.

3.9 Where the claimant's investigation indicates that the value of the claim has increased to more than £15,000 since the letter of claim, the claimant should notify the defendant as soon as possible.

Documents

3.10 If the **defendant denies liability**, he should enclose with the letter of reply, **documents** in his possession which are **material to the issues** between the parties, and which would be likely to be ordered to be disclosed by the court, either on an application for pre-action disclosure, or on disclosure during proceedings.

3.11 Attached at Annex B are **specimen**, but non-exhaustive, **lists** of documents likely to be material in different types of claim. Where the claimant's investigation of the case is well advanced, the letter of claim could indicate which classes of documents are considered relevant for early disclosure. Alternatively these could be identified at a later stage.

3.12 Where the defendant admits primary liability, but alleges contributory negligence by the claimant, the defendant should give reasons supporting those allegations and disclose those documents from Annex B which are relevant to the issues in dispute. The claimant should respond to the allegations of contributory negligence before proceedings are issued.

3.13 No charge will be made for providing copy documents under the Protocol.

Special damages

3.14 The claimant will send to the defendant as soon as practicable a Schedule of Special Damages with supporting documents, particularly where the defendant has admitted liability.

Experts

3.15 Before any party instructs an expert he should give the other party a list of the **name** (s) of **one or more experts** in the relevant speciality whom he considers are suitable to instruct.

3.16 Where a medical expert is to be instructed the claimant's solicitor will organise access to relevant medical records – see specimen letter of instruction at Annex C.

3.17 **Within 14 days** the other party may indicate **an objection** to one or more of the named experts. The first party should then instruct a mutually acceptable expert (which is not the same as a joint expert). It must be emphasised that if the Claimant nominates an expert in the original letter of claim, the defendant has 14 days to object to one or more of the named experts after expiration of the period of 21 days within which he has to reply to the letter of claim, as set out in paragraph 3.6.

3.18 If the second party objects to all the listed experts, the parties may then instruct **experts of their own choice**. It would be for the court to decide subsequently, if proceedings are issued, whether either party had acted unreasonably.

3.19 If the **second party does not object to an expert nominated**, he shall not be entitled to rely on his own expert evidence within that particular speciality unless:
(a) the first party agrees,
(b) the court so directs, or
(c) the first party's expert report has been amended and the first party is not prepared to disclose the original report.

3.20 **Either party may send to an agreed expert written questions** on the report, relevant to the issues, via the first party's solicitors. The expert should send answers to the questions separately and directly to each party.

3.21 The cost of a report from an agreed expert will usually be paid by the instructing first party: the costs of the expert replying to questions will usually be borne by the party which asks the questions.

4 Rehabilitation

4.1 The claimant or the defendant or both shall consider as early as possible whether the claimant has reasonable needs that could be met by rehabilitation treatment or other measures.

4.2 The parties shall consider, in such cases, how those needs might be addressed. The Rehabilitation Code (which is attached at Annex D) may be helpful in considering how to identify the claimant's needs and how to address the cost of providing for those needs.

4.3 The time limit set out in paragraph 3.7 of this Protocol shall not be shortened, except by consent to allow these issues to be addressed.

4.4 The provision of any report obtained for the purposes of assessment of provision of a party's rehabilitation needs shall not be used in any litigation arising out of the accident, the subject of the claim, save by consent and shall in any event be exempt from the provisions of paragraphs 3.15 to 3.21 inclusive of this protocol.

5 Resolution of issues

5.1 Where the defendant admits liability in whole or in part, before proceedings are issued, any medical reports obtained under this protocol on which a party relies should be disclosed to the other party. The claimant should delay issuing proceedings for 21 days from disclosure of the report (unless such delay would cause his claim to become time-barred), to enable the parties to consider whether the claim is capable of settlement.

5.2 The Civil Procedure Rules Part 36 permit claimants and defendants to make offers to settle pre-proceedings. Parties should always consider before issuing if it is appropriate to make Part 36 Offer. If such an offer is made, the party making the offer must always supply sufficient evidence and/or information to enable the offer to be properly considered.

5.3 Where the defendant has admitted liability, the claimant should send to the defendant schedules of special damages and loss at least 21 days before proceedings are issued (unless that would cause the claimant's claim to become time-barred).

A Letter of claim

To

Defendant

Dear Sirs

Re: Claimant's full name

Claimant's full address

Claimant's Clock or Works Number

Claimant's Employer (name and address)

We are instructed by the above named to claim damages in connection with an ***accident at work/road traffic accident/tripping accident***

on day of ***(year)*** at ***(place of accident which must be sufficiently detailed to establish location)***

Please confirm the identity of your insurers. Please note that the insurers will need to see this letter as soon as possible and it may affect your insurance cover and/or the conduct of any subsequent legal proceedings if you do not send this letter to them.

The circumstances of the accident are:-

(brief outline)

The reason why we are alleging fault is:

(simple explanation e.g. defective machine, broken ground)

A description of our clients' injuries is as follows:-

(brief outline)

(In cases of road traffic accidents)

Our client (state hospital reference number) received treatment for the injuries at name and address of hospital).

Our client is still suffering from the effects of his/her injury. We invite you to participate with us in addressing his/her immediate needs by use of rehabilitation.

He is employed as ***(occupation)*** and has had the following time off work ***(dates of absence).***

His approximate weekly income is (insert if known).

If you are our client's employers, please provide us with the usual earnings details which will enable us to calculate his financial loss.

We are obtaining a police report and will let you have a copy of the same upon your undertaking to meet half the fee.

We have also sent a letter of claim to ***(name and address)*** and a copy of that letter is attached.

We understand their insurers are ***(name, address and claims number if known).***

At this stage of our enquiries we would expect the documents contained in parts ***(insert appropriate parts of standard disclosure list)*** to be relevant to this action.

Please note that we have entered into a conditional fee agreement with our client dated in relation to this claim which provides for a success fee within the meaning of section 58(2) of the Courts and Legal Services Act 1990. Our client has taken out an insurance policy with [name of insurance company] of [address of insurance company] to which section 29 of the Access Justice Act 1999 applies. The policy number is and the policy is dated . Where the funding arrangement is an insurance policy, the party must state the name and address of the insurer, the policy number and the date of the policy, and must identify the claim or claims to which it relates (including Part 20 claims if any).

A copy of this letter is attached for you to send to your insurers. Finally we expect an acknowledgment of this letter within 21 days by yourselves or your insurers.

Yours faithfully

B Pre-action personal injury protocol standard disclosure lists

FAST TRACK DISCLOSURE

RTA CASES

SECTION A

In all cases where liability is at issue –
(i) Documents identifying nature, extent and location of damage to defendant's vehicle where there is any dispute about point of impact.
(ii) MOT certificate where relevant.
(iii) Maintenance records where vehicle defect is alleged or it is alleged by defendant that there was an unforeseen defect which caused or contributed to the accident.

SECTION B

Accident involving commercial vehicle as defendant –
(i) Tachograph charts or entry from individual control book.
(ii) Maintenance and repair records required for operators' licence where vehicle defect is alleged or it is alleged by defendant that there was an unforeseen defect which caused or contributed to the accident.

SECTION C

Cases against local authorities where highway design defect is alleged.
(i) Documents produced to comply with Section 39 of the Road Traffic Act 1988 in respect of the duty designed to promote road safety to include studies into road accidents in the relevant area and documents relating to measures recommended to prevent accidents in the relevant area.

HIGHWAY TRIPPING CLAIMS

Documents from Highway Authority for a period of 12 months prior to the accident –
(i) Records of inspection for the relevant stretch of highway.
(ii) Maintenance records including records of independent contractors working in relevant area.
(iii) Records of the minutes of Highway Authority meetings where maintenance or repair policy has been discussed or decided.
(iv) Records of complaints about the state of highways.
(v) Records of other accidents which have occurred on the relevant stretch of highway.

WORKPLACE CLAIMS

(i) Accident book entry.
(ii) First aider report.
(iii) Surgery record.
(iv) Foreman/supervisor accident report.

(v) Safety representatives accident report.
(vi) RIDDOR (Reporting of Injuries, Diseases and Dangerous Occurrences Regulations) report to HSE.
(vii) Other communications between defendants and HSE.
(viii) Minutes of Health and Safety Committee meeting(s) where accident/matter considered.
(ix) Report to DSS.
(x) Documents listed above relative to any previous accident/matter identified by the claimant and relied upon as proof of negligence.
(xi) Earnings information where defendant is employer.

Documents produced to comply with requirements of the Management of Health and Safety at Work Regulations 1992 –

(i) Pre-accident Risk Assessment required by Regulation 3.
(ii) Post-accident Re-Assessment required by Regulation 3.
(iii) Accident Investigation Report prepared in implementing the requirements of Regulations 4, 6 and 9.
(iv) Health Surveillance Records in appropriate cases required by Regulation 5.
(v) Information provided to employees under Regulation 8.
(vi) Documents relating to the employees health and safety training required by Regulation 11.

WORKPLACE CLAIMS – DISCLOSURE WHERE SPECIFIC REGULATIONS APPLY

SECTION A – Workplace (Health Safety and Welfare) Regulations 1992

(i) Repair and maintenance records required by Regulation 5.
(ii) Housekeeping records to comply with the requirements of Regulation 9.
(iii) Hazard warning signs or notices to comply with Regulation 17 (Traffic Routes).

SECTION B – Provision and Use of Work Equipment Regulations 1998

(i) Manufacturers' specifications and instructions in respect of relevant work equipment establishing its suitability to comply with Regulation 5.
(ii) Maintenance log/maintenance records required to comply with Regulation 6.
(iii) Documents providing information and instructions to employees to comply with Regulation 8.
(iv) Documents provided to the employee in respect of training for use to comply with Regulation 9.
(v) Any notice, sign or document relied upon as a defence to alleged breaches of Regulations 14 to 18 dealing with controls and control systems.
(vi) Instruction/training documents issued to comply with the requirements of regulation 22 insofar as it deals with maintenance operations where the machinery is not shut down.
(vii) Copies of markings required to comply with Regulation 23.
(viii) Copies of warnings required to comply with Regulation 24.

SECTION C – Personal Protective Equipment at Work Regulations 1992

(i) Documents relating to the assessment of the Personal Protective Equipment to comply with Regulation 6.
(ii) Documents relating to the maintenance and replacement of Personal Protective Equipment to comply with Regulation 7.

(iii) Record of maintenance procedures for Personal Protective Equipment to comply with Regulation 7.
(iv) Records of tests and examinations of Personal Protective Equipment to comply with Regulation 7.
(v) Documents providing information, instruction and training in relation to the Personal Protective Equipment to comply with Regulation 9.
(vi) Instructions for use of Personal Protective Equipment to include the manufacturers' instructions to comply with Regulation 10.

SECTION D – Manual Handling Operations Regulations 1992

(i) Manual Handling Risk Assessment carried out to comply with the requirements of Regulation 4(1)(b)(i).
(ii) Re-assessment carried out post-accident to comply with requirements of Regulation 4(1)(b)(i).
(iii) Documents showing the information provided to the employee to give general indications related to the load and precise indications on the weight of the load and the heaviest side of the load if the centre of gravity was not positioned centrally to comply with Regulation 4(1)(b)(iii).
(iv) Documents relating to training in respect of manual handling operations and training records.

SECTION E – Health and Safety (Display Screen Equipment) Regulations 1992

(i) Analysis of work stations to assess and reduce risks carried out to comply with the requirements of Regulation 2.
(ii) Re-assessment of analysis of work stations to assess and reduce risks following development of symptoms by the claimant.
(iii) Documents detailing the provision of training including training records to comply with the requirements of Regulation 6.
(iv) Documents providing information to employees to comply with the requirements of Regulation 7.

SECTION F – Control of Substances Hazardous to Health Regulations 1999

(i) Risk assessment carried out to comply with the requirements of Regulation 6.
(ii) Reviewed risk assessment carried out to comply with the requirements of Regulation 6.
(iii) Copy labels from containers used for storage handling and disposal of carcinogenics to comply with the requirements of Regulation 7(2A)(h).
(iv) Warning signs identifying designation of areas and installations which may be contaminated by carcinogenics to comply with the requirements of Regulation 7(2A)(h).
(v) Documents relating to the assessment of the Personal Protective Equipment to comply with Regulation 7(3A).
(vi) Documents relating to the maintenance and replacement of Personal Protective Equipment to comply with Regulation 7(3A).
(vii) Record of maintenance procedures for Personal Protective Equipment to comply with Regulation 7(3A).
(viii) Records of tests and examinations of Personal Protective Equipment to comply with Regulation 7(3A).

(ix) Documents providing information, instruction and training in relation to the Personal Protective Equipment to comply with Regulation 7(3A).
(x) Instructions for use of Personal Protective Equipment to include the manufacturers' instructions to comply with Regulation 7(3A).
(xi) Air monitoring records for substances assigned a maximum exposure limit or occupational exposure standard to comply with the requirements of Regulation 7.
(xii) Maintenance examination and test of control measures records to comply with Regulation 9.
(xiii) Monitoring records to comply with the requirements of Regulation 10.
(xiv) Health surveillance records to comply with the requirements of Regulation 11.
(xv) Documents detailing information, instruction and training including training records for employees to comply with the requirements of Regulation 12.
(xvi) Labels and Health and Safety data sheets supplied to the employers to comply with the CHIP Regulations.

SECTION G – Construction (Design and Management) (Amendment) Regulations 2000

(i) Notification of a project form (HSE F10) to comply with the requirements of Regulation 7.
(ii) Health and Safety Plan to comply with requirements of Regulation 15.
(iii) Health and Safety file to comply with the requirements of Regulations 12 and 14.
(iv) Information and training records provided to comply with the requirements of Regulation 17.
(v) Records of advice from and views of persons at work to comply with the requirements of Regulation 18.

SECTION H – Pressure Systems and Transportable Gas Containers Regulations 1989

(i) Information and specimen markings provided to comply with the requirements of Regulation 5.
(ii) Written statements specifying the safe operating limits of a system to comply with the requirements of Regulation 7.
(iii) Copy of the written scheme of examination required to comply with the requirements of Regulation 8.
(iv) Examination records required to comply with the requirements of Regulation 9.
(v) Instructions provided for the use of operator to comply with Regulation 11.
(vi) Records kept to comply with the requirements of Regulation 13.
(vii) Records kept to comply with the requirements of Regulation 22.

SECTION I Lifting Operations and Lifting Equipment Regulations 1998

(i) Record kept to comply with the requirements of Regulation 6.

SECTION J – The Noise at Work Regulations 1989

(i) Any risk assessment records required to comply with the requirements of Regulations 4 and 5.
(ii) Manufacturers' literature in respect of all ear protection made available to claimant to comply with the requirements of Regulation 8.

(iii) All documents provided to the employee for the provision of information to comply with Regulation 11.

SECTION K – Construction (Head Protection) Regulations 1989

(i) Pre-accident assessment of head protection required to comply with Regulation 3(4).
(ii) Post-accident re-assessment required to comply with Regulation 3(5).

SECTION L – The Construction (General Provisions) Regulations 1961

(i) Report prepared following inspections and examinations of excavations etc. to comply with the requirements of Regulation 9.

SECTION M – Gas Containers Regulations 1989

(i) Information and specimen markings provided to comply with the requirements of Regulation 5.
(ii) Written statements specifying the safe operating limits of a system to comply with the requirements of Regulation 7.
(iii) Copy of the written scheme of examination required to comply with the requirements of Regulation 8.
(iv) Examination records required to comply with the requirements of Regulation 9.
(v) Instructions provided for the use of operator to comply with Regulation 11.

C Letter of instruction to medical expert

Dear Sir,
Re: ***(Name and Address)***
D.O.B. –
Telephone No. –
Date of Accident –

We are acting for the above named in connection with injuries received in an accident which occurred on the above date. The main injuries appear to have been **(main injuries)**.

We should be obliged if you would examine our Client and let us have a full and detailed report dealing with any relevant pre-accident medical history, the injuries sustained, treatment received and present condition, dealing in particular with the capacity for work and giving a prognosis.

It is central to our assessment of the extent of our Client's injuries to establish the extent and duration of any continuing disability. Accordingly, in the prognosis section we would ask you to specifically comment on any areas of continuing complaint or disability or impact on daily living. If there is such continuing disability you should comment upon the level of suffering or inconvenience caused and, if you are able, give your view as to when or if the complaint or disability is likely to resolve.

Please send our Client an appointment direct for this purpose. Should you be able to offer a cancellation appointment please contact our Client direct. We confirm we will be responsible for your reasonable fees.

We are obtaining the notes and records from our Client's GP and Hospitals attended and will forward them to you when they are to hand/or please request the GP and Hospital records direct and advise that any invoice for the provision of these records should be forwarded to us.

In order to comply with Court Rules we would be grateful if you would insert above your signature a statement that the contents are true to the best of your knowledge and belief.

In order to avoid further correspondence we can confirm that on the evidence we have there is no reason to suspect we may be pursuing a claim against the hospital or its staff.

We look forward to receiving your report within _______ weeks. If you will not be able to prepare your report within this period please telephone us upon receipt of these instructions.

When acknowledging these instructions it would assist if you could give an estimate as to the likely time scale for the provision of your report and also an indication as to your fee.

Yours faithfully

D The rehabilitation code

4.11 The revised Rehabilitation Code

THE REHABILITATION CODE
(Code of Best Practice on Rehabilitation, Early Intervention and Medical Treatment in Personal Injury Claims)

The main aim of this Code, first introduced in 1999, is to promote the use of rehabilitation and early intervention in the claims process so that the injured person makes the best and quickest possible medical, social and psychological recovery. This objective applies whatever the severity of the injury sustained by the claimant. The Code provides a framework supported by all the main associations for insurers and personal injury lawyers in the UK, but is neither compulsory nor the only way to approach rehabilitation. The objectives of the Rehabilitation Code will be met whenever the parties co-operate to assess and then provide for the claimant's rehabilitation needs.

1. INTRODUCTION

1.1 It is recognised that, in many claims for damages for personal injuries, the claimant's current medical situation, and/or the long-term prognosis, may be improved by appropriate medical treatment, including surgery, being given at the earliest practicable opportunity, rather than waiting until the claim has been settled. Similarly, claims may involve a need for non-medical treatment, such as physiotherapy, counselling, occupational therapy, speech therapy and so forth ("rehabilitation"): again, there is a benefit in these services being provided as early as practicable.

1.2 It is also recognised that (predominantly in cases of serious injury) the claimant's quality of life can be immediately improved by undertaking some basic home adaptations and/or by the provision of aids and equipment and/or appropriate medical treatment as soon as these are needed ("early intervention"), rather than when the claim is finally settled.

1.3 It is further recognised that, where these medical or other issues have been dealt with, there may be employment issues that can be addressed for the benefit of the claimant, to enable the claimant to keep his/her existing job, to obtain alternative suitable employment with the same employer or to retrain for new employment. Again, if these needs are addressed at the proper time, the claimant's quality of life and long-term prospects may be greatly improved.

1.4 Solicitors acting for claimants understand that, taking all these matters into account, they can achieve more for the claimant - by making rehabilitation available - than just the payment of compensation. The insurance industry realises that great benefit may be had in considering making funds available for these purposes.

1.5 The aim of this Rehabilitation Code is therefore to ensure that the claimant's solicitor and the insurer (and the insurer's solicitor or handling agent) both actively consider the use of rehabilitation services and the benefits of an early assessment of the claimant's needs. The further aim is that both should treat the possibility of improving the claimant's quality of life and their present and long-term physical and mental well-being as issues equally as important as the payment of just, full and proper compensation.

1.6 The report mentioned in section 6 of the Code focuses on the early assessment of the claimant's needs in terms of treatment and/or rehabilitation. The assessment report is not intended to determine the claimant's long-term needs for care or medical treatment, other than by way of general indication and comment.

2. THE CLAIMANT'S SOLICITOR'S DUTY

2.1 It shall be the duty of every claimant's solicitor to consider, from the earliest practicable stage, and in consultation with the claimant and/or the claimant's family, whether it is likely or possible that early intervention, rehabilitation or medical treatment would improve their present and/or long-term physical or mental well-being. This duty is ongoing throughout the life of the case but is of most importance in the early stages.

2.2 It shall be the duty of a claimant's solicitor to consider, with the claimant and/or the claimant's family, whether there is an immediate need for aids, adaptations or other matters that would seek to alleviate problems caused by disability, and then to communicate with the insurer as soon as practicable about any rehabilitation needs, with a view to putting this Code into effect.

2.3 It shall not be the responsibility of the solicitor to decide on the need for treatment or rehabilitation or to arrange such matters without appropriate medical consultation. Such medical consultation should involve the claimant and/or the claimant's family, the claimant's primary care physician and, where appropriate, any other medical practitioner currently treating the claimant.

2.4 Nothing in this Code shall in any way affect the obligations placed on a claimant's solicitor by the Pre-Action Protocol for Personal Injury Claims ("the Protocol"). However, it must be appreciated that very early communication with the insurer will enable the matters dealt with here to be addressed more effectively.

2.5 It must be recognised that the insurer will need to receive from the claimant's solicitor sufficient information for the insurer to make a proper decision about the need for intervention, rehabilitation or treatment. To this extent, the claimant's solicitor must comply with the requirements of the Protocol to provide the insurer with full and adequate details of the injuries sustained by the claimant, the nature and extent of any, or any likely, continuing disability and any suggestions that may already have been made concerning rehabilitation and/or early intervention. There is no requirement under the Protocol, or this Code, for the claimant's solicitor to have obtained a full medical report. It is recognised that many cases will be identified for consideration under this Code before medical evidence has actually been commissioned.

3. THE INSURER

3.1 It shall be the duty of the insurer to consider, from the earliest practicable stage in any appropriate case, whether it is likely that the claimant will benefit in the immediate, medium or longer term from further medical treatment, rehabilitation or early intervention. This duty is ongoing throughout the life of the case but is of most importance in the early stages.

3.2 If the insurer considers that a particular claim might be suitable for intervention, rehabilitation or treatment, the insurer will communicate this to the claimant's solicitor as soon as practicable.

3.3 On receipt of such communication, the claimant's solicitor will immediately discuss these issues with the claimant and/or the claimant's family pursuant to his duty as set out above and, where appropriate, will seek advice from the claimant's treating physicians/surgeons.

3.4 Nothing in this or any other Code of Practice shall in any way modify the obligations of the insurer under the Protocol to investigate claims rapidly and in any event within three months (except where time is extended by the claimant's solicitor) from the date of the formal claim letter. It is recognised that, although the rehabilitation assessment can be done even where liability investigations are outstanding, it is essential that such investigations proceed with the appropriate speed.

4. ASSESSMENT

4.1 Unless the need for intervention, rehabilitation or treatment has already been identified by medical reports obtained and disclosed by either side, the need for and extent of such intervention, rehabilitation or treatment will be considered by means of an independent assessment.

4.2 "Independent assessment" in this context means that the assessment will be carried out by either:

a. One or more of the treating physicians/surgeons, or

b. By an agency suitably qualified and/or experienced in such matters, which is financially and managerially independent of the claimant's solicitor's firm and the insurers dealing with the claim.

4.3 It is essential that the process of assessment and recommendation be carried out by those who have an appropriate qualification (to include physiotherapists, occupational therapists, psychologists, psychotherapists and so forth). It would be inappropriate for assessments to be done by someone who does not have a medical or other appropriate qualification. Those doing the assessments should not only have an appropriate qualification but should have experience in treating the type of disability from which the individual claimant suffers.

5. THE ASSESSMENT PROCESS

5.1 Where possible, the agency to be instructed to provide the assessment should be agreed between the claimant's solicitor and the insurer. The instruction letter will be sent by the claimant's solicitor to the medical agency and a copy of the instruction letter will be sent to the insurer.

5.2 The medical agency will be asked to interview the claimant at home (or in hospital, if the claimant is still in hospital, with a subsequent visit to the claimant's home) and will be asked to produce a report, which covers the following headings:

1. The injuries sustained by the claimant

2. The claimant's present medical condition (medical conditions that do not arise from the accident should also be noted where relevant to the overall picture of the claimant's needs)

3. The claimant's domestic circumstances (including mobility, accommodation and employment), where relevant

4. The injuries/disability in respect of which early intervention or early rehabilitation is suggested

5. The type of intervention or treatment envisaged

6. The likely cost

7. The likely short/medium-term benefit to the claimant

5.3 The report will not deal with diagnostic criteria, causation issues or long-term care requirements.

6. THE ASSESSMENT REPORT

6.1 The reporting agency will, on completion of the report, send copies to both the instructing solicitor and the insurer simultaneously. Both parties will have the right to raise queries on the report, disclosing such correspondence to the other party.

6.2 It is recognised that for this independent assessment report to be of benefit to the parties, it should be prepared and used wholly outside the litigation process. Neither side can therefore rely on its contents in any subsequent litigation. With that strict proviso, to be confirmed in writing by the individual solicitor and insurer if required, the report shall be disclosed to both parties.

6.3 The report, any correspondence relating to it and any notes created by the assessing agency will be covered by legal privilege and will not under any circumstances be disclosed in any legal proceedings. Any notes or documents created in connection with the assessment process will not be disclosed in any litigation, and any person involved in the preparation of the report or involved in the assessment process shall not be a compellable witness at court.

6.4 The provision in paragraph 6.3 above as to treating the report, etc. as outside the litigation process is limited to the assessment report and any notes relating to it. Once the parties have agreed, following an assessment report, that a particular regime of rehabilitation or treatment should be put in place, the case management of that regime falls outside this Code and paragraph 6.3 does not therefore apply. Any notes and reports created during the subsequent case management will be governed by the usual principles relating to disclosure of documents and medical records relating to the claimant.

6.5 The insurer will pay for the report within 28 days of receipt.

6.6 The need for any further or subsequent assessment shall be agreed between the claimant's solicitor and the insurer. The provisions of this Code shall apply to such assessments.

7. **RECOMMENDATIONS**

7.1 When the assessment report is disclosed to the insurer, the insurer will be under a duty to consider the recommendations made and the extent to which funds will be made available to implement all or some of the recommendations. The insurer will not be required to pay for intervention or treatment that is unreasonable in nature, content or cost. The claimant will be under no obligation to undergo intervention, medical investigation or treatment that is unreasonable in all the circumstances of the case.

7.2 Any funds made available shall be treated as an interim payment on account of damages. However, if the funds are provided to enable specific intervention, rehabilitation or treatment to occur, the insurers warrant that they will not, in any legal proceedings connected with the claim, dispute the reasonableness of that treatment nor the agreed cost, provided of course that the claimant has had the recommended treatment.

15.3 MOJ Proposals

At the date of this edition the Ministry of Justice have published proposals aimed at streamlining the claims process. Current proposals include the increase of the Fast Track limit to £25,000 and accelerated investigation periods for Defendants alongside admissions, when made, that are binding.

It is the intention of the authors to provide a supplement in due course which deals with any new rules brought into force.

15.4 Suggested Further Reading

The Civil Court Practice 2000

Buchan, Kennedy and Woolf: Personal Injury Practice .

16 SUBSIDENCE

16 SUBSIDENCE

Contents

16.1 Introduction

The Concise Oxford Dictionary defines Subsidence as;

> **"The caving in or sinking of ground or the settling down or lowering in the ground of a building"**.

The crucial element of subsidence is a downward movement.

Before the early 1970s, subsidence as a risk was not included on domestic household insurance policies.

Prior to the inclusion in domestic household policies of subsidence cover, a great number of those homeowners who now claim that their houses have subsided, would have simply filled cracks and redecorated their homes themselves. Minor and some moderate cracking would have been accepted.

Insurers now need to be able to identify subsidence and, through the use of their engineers, to be able to repair any damage that has been caused as a result of subsidence in a proportionate way.

Underpinning is by no means always necessary. Indeed, some engineers believe that the partial underpinning of a building can simply create problems for the future.

Insurers should always be alive to the alternative possibilities of vegetation management and simple repair as being the most cost effective way of dealing with subsidence claims.

Of course, such alternatives will not always be possible and in serious cases underpinning will be required.

Claims Handlers must firstly ascertain whether the damage claimed for is of a type covered by the insurance policy.

16.2 Subsidence v General Movement

Matters other than the weight of the building simply compressing the ground on which it stands cause subsidence. Any downward movement caused by the weight of the building is known as settlement.

Subsidence can be caused, for example, by moisture being extracted from the soil beneath the building by vegetation, or the drying out of the soil beneath the building during a particularly dry spell.

In either case, moisture is extracted which reduces the volume of the soil below a building, causing the whole, or a particular part, of the building to drop lower into the soil.

If the whole building drops slowly and at the same rate, then no damage is likely to arise. If however the building drops rapidly, if different parts drop at different rates, or if only part of the building subsides, cracks will appear.

Are all cracks caused by subsidence?

The simple answer to this is 'no'. New buildings for example, often settle and cracks will appear in plaster because the plaster is drying out over a period of time.

Similarly, in the same way that subsidence can be caused by the extraction of moisture from the soil, a sudden addition of moisture to soil can cause the soil to swell and the building standing on such soil to be pushed up.

That is known as heave.

16.3 Causes of Subsidence

There are a number of causes of subsidence. The movement of soil below the depth to which the foundations of a particular property reach causes most if not all of them.

Any soil movement that occurs only between ground level and the bottom of the foundations will not affect the property.

Therefore, it is the condition of the soil below the depth of foundations that causes subsidence in buildings.

16.3.1 Subsidence due to soil drying/shrinkage

This is currently the most common cause of subsidence.

This will affect clay or clay based soils. The Thames Valley and the South-East of Britain generally have clay soils and therefore suffer particularly from this type of subsidence.

As the clay soil dries, it's volume decreases and it therefore "shrinks".

In the winter, soil dries through normal evaporation. However, winter rainfall tends to replace the moisture lost through such evaporation.

The volume of the soil in such circumstances will therefore remain constant and buildings standing on it will stay level.

However, in the summer months, particularly in droughts, there will not be sufficient rainfall to counteract the effects of evaporation and drying. The volume of the soil will decrease, and buildings will subside if the soil below the foundations is affected.

Drying will also be caused by vegetation. Vegetation will extend its roots out and will continuously extract moisture from the soil. That will reduce the volume of the soil as the moisture is extracted. If the roots extend under part of the foundation of a property the soil there may shrink and subsidence can occur.

16.3.2 Burst drains, pipes etc

The escape of water from pipes, drains or water mains etc. will, over a period of time, cause subsidence. Heave may appear to be the natural consequence of water being discharged into the soil and this may well occur. However the discharge of water into the soil over a period of time can wash away small particles of soil from between the larger particles. That reduces the volume of the soil, causing it to be further compacted. Buildings standing on such an area of soil will therefore drop in level. Again subsidence will occur.

There are other causes of subsidence that need not be dealt with in this guide. The above are the main causes that a Claims Handler will encounter.

16.4 Investigating the Subsidence Claim

The Insurance policy in question may cover subsidence, but may not cover settlement or a situation where the building is sinking because of disintegrating foundations.

A proper diagnosis of subsidence is therefore necessary.

Further, proper investigations are vital if insurers have any intention at all of seeking to recover the cost of remedial works from the owners of a neighbouring property or County Council. Insurers may be able to do so if an effective cause of the subsidence is vegetation found other than on the insured within the boundaries of the insured's own property.

It is suggested that claim handlers use the attached Tree Subsidence Claims – Documentary Guidance "Wish List" that is attached (kindly provided by Wardell Armstrong).

16.4.1 The Appointment of a Loss Adjuster

The loss adjuster's job is to co-ordinate the investigations into the cause of the damage. They will instruct an engineer to investigate the problem and to provide a diagnosis.

Having received the engineer's report, the adjuster can arrange for tenders to be submitted to contractors for remedial works and thereafter to co-ordinate those works.

16.4.2 The Engineer

The engineer is arguably the most important member of a Claims Handler's team during the investigation stage.

The engineer may be required to carry out the following tasks:

i) to prepare a plan and photographs of the building. This will highlight vegetation on the insured property and on neighbouring land that may be affecting the building. Photographs will provide evidence of the damage that exists before any remedial works are carried out.

ii) to have trial pits dug to a depth below the property's foundation. These will identify the type of soil upon which the property is standing. The trial pits will also assist in identifying whether any roots are present from vegetation underneath or near to the foundations. Soil can also be analysed to determine whether it is drier than it should be (i.e. it has been desiccated) in order to establish if moisture is being lost to any roots that are found.

iii) if a recovery against a third party is possible, any roots found should be kept safely and in a state which will prevent them from deteriorating. They should be analysed immediately so that the species of plant from which they came can be identified accurately at an early stage. This will allow appropriate remedial action to be placed in hand.

iv) the property should be surveyed. The engineer/surveyor will check drains and water mains etc. to see whether any are leaking or damaged.

v) crack and level monitoring results – cracks should be monitored over a period of time. For example if cracks widen during the summer and close during the winter the damage is most likely to be caused by seasonal variations in the water content of the soil. Usually it is the case that these variations are caused by vegetation near to the property. Results over at least one complete cycle are necessary to analyse a pattern consistent with moisture extraction from vegetation.

The engineer having diagnosed the problems may recommend a number of solutions.

These may include:

a) Simple vegetation management and repair of the property
If the engineer concludes that the damage being caused to the property is due to effects of vegetation, the vegetation can be removed or cut back. The insured property can then be repaired and the damage should not occur again as long as the vegetation is kept in check. Repairs should be carried out after the moisture content of the soil has stabilised. Vegetation management on the insured property should not present a problem. The position may be difficult if the vegetation to be managed is on a neighbouring property *(see "other action against a Third Party" below).*

b) Underpinning
If solely carrying out vegetation management is not an option, and if the reason for the subsidence is not one that can be readily reversed, underpinning may be recommended. Underpinning involves the excavation of the soil from below the foundations of a property in order to under pin the property. It effectively increases the depth of the foundations. This allows damage to the property to be repaired and prevent the problems from reoccurring.

c) Partial Underpinning
If only part of the property has subsided an engineer may recommend partial underpinning. For example if an old

scullery in an Edwardian house has subsided it may be decided that only that part of the building should be underpinned. However, some engineers are very wary of partially underpinning a property.

Generally, a property will rise and fall with the seasons, steadily and at the same rate. The whole property will move and when it does that minimises stresses on the structure and prevents major damage from occurring.

If only part of the property is made more stable through partial underpinning, and the rest of the building moves more readily because of seasonal variations in the moisture content of the soil beneath the foundations, additional damage can be caused. This is because the part that had been underpinned would move much less than the part of the building that has not.

d) Vegetation Management
This is dealt with in (a).

This may involve pollarding trees, cutting back vegetation or indeed removing trees and vegetation completely.

Tree root barriers can be installed in an attempt to prevent roots reaching the foundations of the affected building. Some engineers question the effectiveness of using root barriers. They are also expensive.

16.5 Recovery from a Third Party

Insurers are often confronted with damage caused to an insured property that has subsided because of roots that have encroached from a neighbouring property's vegetation.

In order to seek a recovery from the neighbour/their insurers it is often said that an action will be founded in "tree root trespass". It is certainly true that the roots may have trespassed upon the insured property. The action however will be founded in the torts of negligence or nuisance (see chapters on "Negligence" and "Nuisance").

16.5.1 Forseeability

If roots encroach onto property and cause damage, the owner of the damaged property (and their insurers) may seek compensation for that damage. If the owner of the land upon which the roots are encroaching knew or should have known of the encroachment and the damage caused by it, and if it was foreseeable that the encroachment would have caused the damage; such a claim for compensation is likely to succeed.

It may be difficult to show that a private homeowner should or ought to have known that their vegetation had roots that were encroaching on a neighbouring property **and** that such roots were likely to cause damage to that property.

However, it would be relatively easy to satisfy that test against a local authrority, ***Paterson v Humberside County Council***, The Times April 19th 1995/CLY1995 3661.

In this case the Claimant sought damages against the local council for subsidence damage to his home. He claimed in nuisance and negligence.

He alleged that the local council's tree was drying out the soil under his property and that the soil was of a type that was likely to "shrink".

The Court allowed the claim. It was found that the County Council's knowledge about the soil type meant that it was foreseeable to the Council that there was a risk of damage being caused by their tree's roots. Therefore, the Council that was responsible for the trees was held to be liable in nuisance and negligence.

Consider also the case of ***Solloway v Hampshire County Council (1981) 79L.G.R. 449, C.A.***

In this case, the Claimant was a homeowner who sued the local County Council. It was shown that the tree in the highway that was owned by the Council was causing damage to the Claimant's home. It's roots were extracting moisture from beneath the foundations of the Claimant's home causing it to subside.

It was shown in Court that the tree would not normally have caused damage but did so on this occasion because of a small pocket of clay soil on which the Claimant's home was standing and which could not have been seen on a geological survey.

The Council argued successfully that the damage was not foreseeable because they did not know that the Claimant's home was standing on a particularly susceptible type of soil (i.e. clay soil which is highly shrinkable).

The Court agreed and dismissed the Claimant's action.

Local authorities are now deemed to have knowledge of appropriate soil conditions within their boundaries. Other than in circumstances such as those arising in the case of ***Solloway***, a local authority will be held to be responsible if it can be shown that they should have known that a tree or vegetation which is under their control would be likely to cause damage to properties in their locality.

16.5.2 Causation

It will also be necessary for the Claimant to prove that the roots that are trespassing on to his or her land are causing the damage.

This matter was dealt with in the case of ***Patterson v Humberside County Council*** referred to above.

The ***Patterson*** case concerned lime trees that were approximately ten meters from the Claimant's house. The house was built in 1882 on a clay soil site. The trees were over 100 years old at the date of the trial in 1996.

The question for the Court was whether the lime trees were the cause of subsidence to the house.

The Judge held that:

1. It was enough to show that the tree roots were an effective and substantial cause of the damage to the house although not the sole cause, and
2. Although the house had shallow foundations that made the damage more likely, the Defendants remained liable because "the roots took their victim as they found it".

The issue of causation in subsidence cases came before the House of Lords in 2001 in the matter of ***Delaware Mansions Ltd v Westminster City Council***.

In this case the House of Lords had to determine whether the cost of repairing damage to the Claimants' property, that had apparently occurred before the Claimants acquired ownership of that property could be recovered from the local authority responsible for the offending tree.

In the leading judgment of the Court Lord Cooke stated,

> *"It matters not that further cracking of the superstructure may not have occurred after [the date that the Claimant acquired ownership]. The encroachment of the roots was causing continuing damage to the land by dehydrating the soil and inhibiting rehydration. Damage consisting of impairment of the load-bearing qualities of residential land is, in my view, itself a nuisance"*

He went on to say,

> *"Having regard to the proximity of the plane tree to Delaware mansions, a real risk of damage to the land and the foundations was foreseeable on the part of Westminster.*

He further stated,

> *"...I see* ***Solloway v Hampshire County Council*** *... as important as a salutary warning against imposing unreasonable and unacceptable burdens on local authorities or other tree owners. If reasonableness between neighbours is the key to the solution of problems in this field, it cannot be right to visit the [local] authority or owner responsible for the tree with a large bill for underpinning without giving them notice of the damage and the opportunity of avoiding further damage by removal of the tree. Should they elect to preserve the tree for environmental reasons, they may fairly be expected to bear the cost of underpinning or other reasonably necessary remedial works; and the party on whom the cost has fallen may recover it, even though there may be elements of hitherto unsatisfied pre-proprietorship or protection for the future. But, as a general proposition, I think that the Defendant is entitled to notice and a reasonable opportunity of abatement before liability for remedial expenditure can arise.*

He concluded,

> *"In the end, in my opinion, the law can be summed up in the proposition that, where there is a continuing nuisance of which the Defendant knew or ought to have known, reasonable remedial expenditure may be recovered by the owner who has to incur it."*

Following Delaware it can be said that the House of Lords has laid down the following principles:

a) The cost of repairs for damage arising over a period of time as a consequence of a continuing nuisance can be recovered. This can be so even if damage has arisen before a Claimant owned the damaged property.

b) The owner of the vegetation causing the damage must be given a reasonable opportunity to remedy the situation and properly avoid further damage being caused.

c) That if the owner of the vegetation, having been given such an opportunity, does nothing or does not do enough, the Claimant can recover damages for reasonable remedial expenditure.

The Court of Appeal was asked to consider the issue of subsidence again in 2003 in the case of ***Loftus-Brigham v Ealing LBC***.

The Court in this case considered whether the Claimant had to show that the Defendant's trees were a dominant cause of the damage to the Claimant's property in order to succeed.

Chadwick LJ held that,

> *"The question that [the trial Judge] should have asked himself was.... whether desiccation from the tree roots materially contributed to the damage."*

The Court was also asked to consider the issue of apportionment between the parties on the basis that the Claimant's own vegetation was also contributing to the damage in question. On this issue Chadwick LJ stated,

> *"A recurrent suggestion...was that this Court might ...simply apportion the loss amongst the parties, on the basis that since both had caused the damage both should bear some part of the cost of that damage. The Court has no power to take that step. Apportionment in law has to be based on liability, not simply on causation. Since the Judge found that the Claimants were not contributorily negligent ...they were not liable in law for any part of the damage whether caused by them or not. [The Defendant] has to take its victim as it finds it"*

Following Loftus-Brigham it can be said that the Court of Appeal has laid down the following principles:

(i) that the Claimant has to show only that the Defendant's vegetation is materially contributing to the damage; and not that it is a dominant cause.

(ii) the amount that the Claimant can recover will be reduced if the Claimant has acted in a contributorily negligent manner and if that contributory negligence has also resulted in damage to the Claimant's property.

It cannot be stated too often that the mere presence of tree roots does not prove a claim, nor does the proximity of trees to a building. Different trees act in different ways. Oak trees are a persistent culprit (their roots grow unusually deep) but it should not be simply assumed that a particular tree is responsible. Many oak trees exist near buildings without causing problems. About 90% of damage from oak trees occur at distances up to 18 metres from buuildings. In 50% of cases the distance is les than 9.5 metres. However the maximum distance recorded is 30 metres. Nevertheless, even at less than 9.5 metres it is thought that less than 1% of oak trees founded in clay soils cause damage. 'Trees, Roots & Buildings', Cutler v Richardson, Longman, 1989.

Examples of successfully defended cases include ***Siddiqui v Hillingdon London Borough Council (2003)*** **EWHC 726.** On expert evidence the council proved that subsidence was not caused by roots of trees in a neighbouring wood but by heave resulting from re-hydration of the ground after removal of trees and root systems from the site. In particular, the Judge was persuaded by evidence that the level of the house had risen, indicating a continual process of re-hydration in the sub-soil. Another recent case was the decision in ***Lumb v United Utilities water Limited*** (Lands Tribunal 7 June 2001, unreported) in which damage was attributed to blasting in the course of nearby sewer construction. While following the decision of Loftus Brigham it is hard for Defendants to make headway with arguments about competing causes of damage. However, they should not be ruled out. The Courts have not overruled older authorities such as ***Murray v Hutchinson*** (1995) 116EG467, in which it was held that a Defendant tree owner was 25% responsible for damage which could be attributed to faulty construction, general settlement in the area, dry summers and war damage.

16.5.3 A Claimant's contributory negligence

The contributory negligence point is an important one. The Courts have now held that it matters not whether the Claimant's own vegetation is a dominant cause of the damage if the Defendant's vegetation is materially contributing to that damage. If the Claimant has not been contributorily negligent the Defendant will, subject to the test for forseeability, have to pay for the full cost of remedial works.

In what circumstances, then, will a Claimant act in a contributorily negligent way?

Take for example a Claimant whose house is subsiding. His own insurers instruct an engineer to report. That engineer then advises that the subsidence is caused by a combination of the Claimant's vegetation and the Defendant local authority's tree. If the Claimant, having been made aware that his vegetation is causing damage, then takes no steps to avoid future damage he may well be found to have acted in a contributory manner.

It is suggested however that the Claimant would need first, to be reasonably aware that he should take steps to prevent his own vegetation causing further damage to his property. Only then we suggest, would such a failure to carry out such steps be likely to constitute contributory negligence.

16.6 Quantum

Most claims for damages will centre around the cost of repairs, both the superstructure and structural repairs generally should underpinning be required. Claims will also be made in respect of the costs of involving experts, project management and investigation fees. Care needs to be taken to ensure that claims handling fees are not tied up as part of the claim for expert fees. Often claims will include ground works to drains and CCTV investigation. However, most engineers (not only those that are instructed by the Defendant) accept that tree roots will only enter drainage systems if they are already damaged, and as such these claims should be resisted.

Expert engineering evidence should be obtained to comment on the value of the structural repairs claims.

(a)Diminution in value

A classic measure for damage to land is the diminution in the value of the land caused by the damage. However, it is conventional in tree root cases to award the cost of the repair works as being equivalent to the diminution in value. This approach hs been recognised by the House of Lords in **Delaware Mansions**. A Defendant should be alert to any arguments that the cost of the reinstatement exceeds the diminution in value. Furthermore, where Defendants have not removed the cause of the damage and only superstructural repairs have been carried out, diminution in value claims have still been brought. Valuation evidence will be required if the claim is to be made out;

(b) Unforseeable extent

Even in cases where expensive underpining works are required, the Defendant can argue that the full extent was not forseeable. The normal rule is that if damage of a particular type was forseeable, damages are recoverable for its full extent if that extent exceeded what could have been forseen. However, some doubt may be cast on the operation of this principle in treee root cases by reference to ***Holbeck Hotel limited v Scarborough Borough Council*** **(2000) QBD 836.** In this case there was a landslip caused by negligent removal of support on adjacent land. The Court of appeal distinguished the early principle on the basis that the damage had been caused by nonfeasance, as in a tree root case the council had done nothing to cause the damage, but it had failed to prevent it. The Court of appeal held that the duty in such cases is much more limited and Stewart Smith LJ stated, *"I do not think that a Defendant should be held liable for damage which, albeit at the same time, was vastly more extensive than that which was foreseen or could have been foreseen without extensive further geological investigations, and this is particularly so where the defect existed just as much on the plaintiff's land as on their own. Considering the scope of the measured duty of care, the Courts are still in relatively uncharted waters."*

It was held on the facts that the Defendant's duty went no further than to warn the Claimant of such risk of landslip. Since the Claimant could not prove what would they would have done if they had this information their claim failed.

(c) Unnecessary works

The most important question will turn on whether the works, in particular underpinning, are necessary. Often landowners will make arrangements for major works because they are advised that they are required urgently, and then seek to recover the costs from the Defendant. This raises two questions. First, whether the Defendant had been given an opportunity to abate the nuisance as required and stated in the **Delaware Mansions** case, and second whether the works were actually necessary. The Defendant may be able to prove with expert evidence from engineers/arboriculturals that tree management, ie pruning, felling, etc, would have been sufficient to curtail the problem.

It should be borne in mind that the Defendants will have to convince the Court that had they been given the opportunity to manage the tree that would have done so. For example, in the **Delaware Mansions** case, the council had the opportunity to fell the tree and failed to do so. in the case of ***Le Jones (Insurance Brokers) Limited v Portsmouth City Council (2002)*** the Defendant argued that the Claimant had failed to mitigate his loss by failing to ask them to manage the tree. The Court rejected this argument even though it was agreed that tree managent would have been a satisfactory solution. n the absence of any assurance from the Defendant that the tree would be managed, the Claimant was entitled to proceed with underpinning.

It would therefore be advisable for Defendants at an early stage to set out in writing the options which may be available to abate the nuisance, and their wish to investigate the problem so as to decide which (if any) solution is necessary and its willingness to implement whichever solution is found to be reasonable, at least if the matter can be shown to be the Council's responsibility.

16.7 ABI Domestic Subsidence Tree Roots Claims Agreement

The ABI Agreement is a contract between those insurers who subscribe to it. It relates to disputes between neighbouring domestic property owners.

If damage has been caused to a domestic property because of the effect of vegetation from a neighbouring domestic property, generally domestic insurers will not seek to recover losses arising from each other. This is because of the operation of the ABI Domestic Subsidence Tree Roots Claims Agreement.

Insurers who have subscribed to this agreement have contracted not to pursue insurers of domestic owners of neighbouring trees that have caused damage to the insured property.

This agreement operates as follows:

1. It takes effect from the 1st October 1997.
2. It applies to domestic property only.
3. The Defendant must be insured.

The agreement will not apply, **"if, having been given adequate warning that a nuisance existed and that it was necessary to remove vegetation, the neighbour took no action to abate the nuisance"**.

This is an inter-insurance agreement very much like the "knock for knock" agreement that motor insurers operated.

It therefore does not prevent policyholders from pursuing one another for uninsured losses such as their policy excess, which is usually £1,000.00.

16.8 Joint Mitigation Protocol

A copy of this is attached. It applies mainly to London Local Authorities and was the result of much hard work by the London Tree Officer's Association working in conjunction with arboriculturists, engineers, domestic insurers and Local Authorities' insurance departments. The aim is to try and agree minimum evidential standards that will be provided by usual domestic insurers seeking to reclaim monies from Local Authorities. Hostorically the London Tree Officers have been dissatisfied with the lack of evidence provided to argue for the removal of vegetation and compensation from Local Authorities. The parties to the 'JMP' have agreed to a formula (CAVAT system) for valuing the alleged offending vegetation. The Claimant's insurers notify the Local Authority of the implicated tree, the Local Authority supplies a valuation (low, medium or high) and depending on the valuation the Claimant agrees to supply differing levels of evidence. Historically, household insurers have only been prepared to accept removal of vegetation as an acceptable solution. However, under the protocol there is an acceptance that in certain circumstances pruning may be considered an alternative management option.

While the protocol does not form part of the Court sanction pre-action protocols it provides enough incentive to both sides to sign up to the protocol and adopt its principles. The advantage to insurers includes a much speedier resolution of claims. The investigations and actions under the protocol are carried out under a 'without prejudice' basis, although evidence gathered will more likley than not be used in subsequent recovery claims.

On a practical point, it is worth checking whether the Defendant is a signatory to the protocol.

16.9 'Non-Domestic' Recoveries

The most common type of recovery action for "tree roots trespass" is brought against local authorities for damage to properties caused by trees in the highway.

In such cases, properties have been damaged because moisture has been extracted from the soil beneath their foundations by trees that are in the street. The London Plane Tree is particularly vigorous and has caused problems for London Boroughs and other local authorities over recent years.

Claims Handlers will need to satisfy the following criteria to pursue a successful recovery against any third party:

i) the cause of the subsidence will need to be shown.

   Therefore a detailed engineer's report carefully backed by a survey, soil samples, photographs, trial pits and root samples, if appropriate, will be needed. Bear in mind the decision of ***Patterson v Humberside County Council*** above.

   Bear in mind possible arguments of contributory negligence and causation and the principles laid down in the cases of ***Delaware Mansions* and *Loftus-Brigham*** (see above) must be considered.

ii) the insurer seeking to recover will need to show that the repairs carried out were reasonable, proportionate and commercial.

   The principles laid down by the House of Lords in the case of *Delaware Mansions* must be considered here.

   Again, an engineer's report will be required.

An insurer who has been presented with a claim for damage caused by subsidence to an insured property , caused by seasonal variations in the moisture content of the soil beneath the insured's property and which is exacerbated by the effects of vegetation; would normally remedy the situation by carrying out vegetation management and by repairing the damage. That, it is submitted, would be reasonable, proportionate and commercial.

An insurer in the same situation who decided to totally underpin the insured property without giving the other party an opportunity to take remedial steps would be very unlikely indeed to recover the full cost of those works. The cost of such works could run into tens of thousands of pounds.

The engineer's report is crucial therefore in providing evidence to any third party that the actions of the repairing insurers were reasonable and proportionate.

iii) the actual costs of the works must themselves be reasonable.

Here an adjuster's assistance is required.

The insurer will need to show that a number of estimates were obtained from contractors. These will normally be provided in the form of tender documents. Usually the lowest quote will have been accepted or if it has not, the adjusters must be able to advise why that is the case. Estimates, tenders, and final invoices all need to tally and need to provide evidence of the sums paid by the insurer.

iv) the above evidence will need to be provided to the third party or their representatives. The engineer's report, tender documents, estimates and invoices will all need to be sent together with a letter of claim covering the above categories.

16.10 Other Action Against a Third Party.

A situation often arises that the cause of the subsidence is situated on land over which the policyholder has no control.

The insurer can carry out remedial works.

However, if the cause of the damage is not removed, damage may well occur again causing further expense to the insurer and further inconvenience to the policyholder.

In those circumstances is it open to the insurer, in its policyholder's name, to pursue additional remedies as well as seeking repayment of outlays incurred for remedial works.

These are as follows:

a) Abatement – *please see Chapter 3 on nuisance.*

b) Injunction – *please see Chapter 3 on nuisance.*

16.11 The Party Wall Act 1996

As the name of this Act suggests, this affects neighbours on either side of a party wall.

If a party wall is subsiding, this Act obliges parties on either side of the wall to bear a proportion of the cost to remedy the situation, relative to their use of that wall.

If there are only two parties involved, for example in a semi-detached house, they (their insurers) will therefore each bear one half of the cost of the works.

16.12 The Latent Damage Act 1986

The **Latent Damage Act 1986** (LDA 1986 modified the limitation period for negligence (but not nuisance) in non-injury cases.

The 1986 Act retains the six year limitation period from the date on which the damage occurred but in the alternative allows a Claimant three years to issue proceedings from the date on which he knew he had an action.

Therefore, a Claimant now has three years from the date that they became aware of damage, even if the damage had been caused by a negligent act or omission of a neighbour many years before.

However, the LDA 1986 imposes a maximum limitation period of 15 years. A Claimant therefore has a maximum of 15 years from the date that the damage occurred within which to issue proceedings, subject to the above rules.

For example, the negligence of a neighbour (failing to prune, cut back vegetation etc.) may have first caused damage to the Claimant's home in 2000. Such damage may then first become visible in 2006. That is outside of the six year limitation period imposed by Section 2 of the **Limitation Act 1980.**

However, The LDA 1986 permits the Claimant, until 2021 to issue Court proceedings because the Claimant only became aware of the damage in 2006.

16.13 Previous Subsidence Damage – The "Change of Insurer" Claims Agreement

An insurance policy is a contract between an insurer and policyholder that generally lasts for a year. It can of course be renewed.

The contract of insurance will generally only cover damage arising within the life of the policy.

Consider therefore the position of a homeowner who has owned his property for 20 years. In that period, he may have changed his insurers five times and most recently only one year ago.

Having changed his insurer a year ago, he has discovered subsidence damage in his home.

Engineers instructed by his current insurers may determine that the damage has arisen over a number of years. His insurers may therefore argue that they should not be responsible for the total cost of repairs under the policy, some of the damage having arisen outside of the life of that policy.

As a result of this difficulty, insurers have agreed between themselves as to how they will share the expenses of the claim in these circumstances between them.

Most insurers have now subscribed to the **Association of British Insurers' Subsidence/Heave/Landslip "Change of Insurer" Claims Agreement**.

The agreement however will not normally bridge a change of ownership and therefore if subsidence is present when a policyholder buys a property, they may not be covered for the full cost of repairs under that policy. That is the reason for the importance of a structural survey when a property is purchased.

16.14 Subsidence Check-list

1. Is it subsidence? What diagnosis does the engineer make?
2. Is it covered by the policy?
3. What is the cause?
4. Can the cause be removed permanently? If so how?
5. Is the Claimant seeking an injunction for the removal of the vegetation?
6. If the cause is removed will simple repairs be sufficient?
7. If the cause cannot or will not be removed – consider injunction or abatement.
8. If the cause can be removed and simple repairs are not likely to be sufficient, what is the most proportionate way of rectifying the problem?
9. Is there a possible Third Party recovery? – Collate evidence and make claim.

   a) – Engineer's report with opinion as to cause of damage.
   – Tender documents, quotations, estimates and invoices.
   – Evidence of payments made.

   b) – Who is the recovery against?
   – Will "foreseeability" be a problem?
   – ABI Domestic Subsidence Tree Roots Claims Agreement?
   – ABI Subsidence/Heave/Landslip Change of Insurer
   – Claims Agreement?

10. Contributory Negligence?
11. Consider the Tree Subsidence Claims – Documentary Evidence "Wish List" attached.

16.15 Use of Appropriate Experts

Experts play a crucial role in these cases and their evidence is frequently decisive on any of the main issues. These issues include:

(a) The species of the trees and their propensity to cause damage;

(b) The presence and species of tree roots in the soil;

(c) The type of soil and its vulnerability to root damage;

(d) The extent of damage caused, and the probable causes of that damage;

(e) Foreseeability of damage and what precautions might have been taken;

(f) The choice of remedial measures and associated risks

(g) The cost of remedial measures.

1. Arboriculturist

The arboriculturists will tell you about the tree or trees. Frequently more than one tree is potentially implicated in the damage. The arboriculturist is best qualified to comment on what the roots of a particular tree are likely to do and how thirsty the trees are. the arboriculturist will be able to advise on whether pruning is sufficient or the trees need to be removed. The arboriculturist will also comment on the argument on the health and viability of the trees.

2. Engineering evidence

The engineer will consider the matters such as the foundation depths, the soil studies, level monitoring and crack monitoring results and issues of dessication. A structural engineer will also be able to consider proposed remedial works and the reasonableness of the tenders submitted. Overall the engineer is the most frequently turned to expert in considering whether subsidence is occuring to the property. The structural engineer's evidence will form the basis of any case put forward by the Defendant of the damage arising from causes other than the trees.

3. Soil consultants

The role of the soil scientist is to interpret and evaluate the soil and soil related information with the aim of understanding how soil resources contribute to the effects of tree roots founded in different types of soil. The soil consultant can provide specialist evidence of what is underneath a house having examined the results of the trial pits and bore hole samples. Usually their evidence forms part of the overall report completed by the engineer.

16.16 Tree Subsidence Claims – Documentary Evidence 'Wish List'

1. All relevant historical data including any information related to:

   - date of construction of property;
   - date of purchase by Claimant;
   - any known previous alterations to the structure;
   - date and circumstances of discovery of damage;
   - processing of insurance claim (inspections, reports thereon, etc);
   - notification to LA/tree owner;
   - implementation of repairs;
   - any post-repair damage.

2. Any descriptions of property - usually in loss adjusters' or engineers' reports.

3. Descriptions and/or photographs of damage – usually in engineers' or loss adjusters' reports.

4. Details of any relevant damage to nearby properties (ie damage of a similar nature and/or occurring around the same time).

5. All relevant site investigation information, including:

   - trial pit and borehole locations;
   - trial pit and borehole logs;
   - in situ test results;
   - laboratory soil test results;
   - root identification results.

6. Any information relating to type, location, size, age, etc of trees in the area – usually in (Claimants') arboriculturalist's report.

7. Crack, level or other monitoring results, including positions of monitoring points (which seem often to be missing).

8. Details of any drainage surveys or drainage repairs undertaken.

9. Any evidence of leaking services or damp within property

10. Repair/underpinning details – drawings, specifications, contract documents, (priced) schedules, etc.

11. Any details relating to implementation of repairs, especially evidence of roots encountered, any difficulties, etc. (NB Many repair contracts contain provision for record photographs to be taken as the repairs progress but, for reasons which are never quite clear, these rarely seem to be available).

JOINT MITIGATION PROTOCOL

May 2008

Version	Comment	Author
Version 1 - 8 May 2008	Initial version of combined document	JAP
Version 2 -12 May 2008	Summary evidence amended to include comment on further engineering information. Engineer report deleted	JAP

Contents

Preamble

The Protocol is intended to reflect the spirit of the Civil Procedure Rules and aims to ensure that before the commencement of any proceedings:

- Pre action contact and exchange of information are encouraged
- Improved quality evidence and information is presented in support of the claim
- Both parties have provided sufficient clear evidence and information regarding their position on the matter
- Each party has had the opportunity to consider the evidence and information
- Each party can accept or reject the claim or each other's position at the earliest possible stage
- Each party can modify its own position at the earliest possible stage
- The time period between notification and completion of co-operation or rejection of the claim is reduced
- The issue of tree removal / reduction / replanting is completed on a non-adversarial and ecologically friendly basis
- There is an opportunity for both parties to meet informally without prejudice to liability and resolve disputed cases

Protocol

First Notification

When the Insurer first becomes aware of a potential claim for subsidence damage resulting from tree root encroachment, they will, within 7 days of identifying the tree controller, notify the tree controller of the situation by letter providing detail of the address of the damaged property and general identification of the subject tree(s).

The letter requests the following information from the tree controller within 14 days:

a) Contact details of the individual / department responsible for the control of the tree, along with any reference, to assist communication regarding tree management and liability.
b) Contact details of their liability Insurer if appropriate.
c) The value of the tree (low, medium or high) as determined by the CAVAT System.

Evidence

Within 60 days of giving notice to the tree controller the insurer (or their adjusters on their behalf) will submit either:

a) A letter confirming withdrawal of the case and that the file should be closed.
b) A "Submission of Evidence" per Appendix A.

The "Submission of Evidence" should normally present full "Summary Evidence" and thus be conclusive with regard to causation, damage, and mitigation requested. It is appreciated that occasionally specific evidence such as tree root identification or soil analysis may be delayed and in such cases the submission should clearly identify its "Interim Evidence" status and the date of expected submission of the "Summary Evidence" report.

The levels of evidence will relate to the value of the tree as calculated by the CAVAT system and are detailed on the flow chart Appendix B Any subsequent "Summary Evidence" submission will be fully inclusive, not supplementary, per Appendix A.
(Submissions of Evidence to be copied to Property Insurer)

Consideration

If the tree controller does not accept the full scope of the mitigation request set out in the "Summary Evidence" then the protocol encourages immediate 'without prejudice discussion' between the tree controller and the insurer (or their appointed handler/advisor) with the aim to achieve agreement to the scope of mitigation works.

Rejection

If agreement to the full scope of the mitigation request set out in the "Summary Evidence" or any revised scope as may have been proposed under 'Consideration' above is not achieved within 28 days of submission of the "Summary Evidence" then the case then falls outside this protocol.
(It is expected that Insurers will set SLAs for their adjusters to achieve % recovery cases managed within the Protocol)

Mitigation

Having been provided with the “Summary Evidence” under the terms of the protocol, mitigation should be carried out and completed within 13 weeks of the date of submission of the “Summary Evidence”.

The mitigation will be undertaken on a “without prejudice” basis to avoid any delay created by debate over liability.

Liability and Quantum

Following completion of mitigation on the agreed basis, liability and quantum may be reviewed:

- Any claim will be based on the principles of law and indemnity applicable to England & Wales acknowledging insurer’s rights and duties of contribution and subrogation.
- Without prejudice to subrogation rights the tree controller should be given notice of the start date scope and estimated costs, before works start. All substantial variations in repair costs compared to the initial estimate must be explained by the Insurer / Adjuster.
- Without prejudice to rights at law Insurers may waive rights of recovery if the tree is removed within the protocol period. This will be negotiated on a claim by claim basis.
- Failure to complete the requested or agreed mitigation works within the protocol period will result in appropriate remedial works including stabilization being carried out to the property without further delay.
- Building Insurers will proceed in the spirit of the Civil Procedure Rules and Part 36 offers may be made in an effort to settle.
- Agreement as to the scope of mitigation does not affect responsibility at law regarding liability for ongoing Nuisance. Any future claim in respect of further damage due to continuing or repeated Nuisance will not be reduced by any suggestion of contributory negligence in having agreed a scheme of mitigation. The duty of abatement remains with the tree controller.
- Neither party will recover costs regarding the appointment of solicitors with regard to progressing mitigation on cases conducted under this protocol
- For the purposes of trialing this protocol this protocol will only apply to Local Authority owned trees

Submission of Evidence Appendix A

Date of Submission	31-03-2008	Interim	Summary	☐
Statutory Authority	Any Town Council			
Property Owner	A.N.Other			
Damage Address	Address: 2 The Avenue Any Town SX1 5PH			
Area of Damage	Stepped cracking to front lounge, entrance hall stairs, plus front two bedrooms.		**Category per BRE 251**	3
Site Plan To include all relevant vegetation and significant drain layout. Plan to indicate position of rooms	Attached. Drainage to rear not detailed as remote beyond any potential significance.			
Photographs These are indicative and are not a complete record of the full extent of the damage	Attached – showing general situation, policyholder's hedge and Local Authority street tree			
Arboricultural report	Not obtained			
Details of Statutory Authority Third Party Vegetation	One - Street tree within pavement to front right of house			
Details of Policyholder Vegetation	Beech hedge 2m high 3m from corner of house			
Details of Other Third Party Vegetation	None			
Root Analysis	Plane (confirms subject tree) 1.5m below fdn			
Foundation depth	750mm below ground level			
Subsoil	Clay - see attached analysis			
Factors indicating clay shrinkage	Pattern of damage shows rotation towards the street tree Timing of damage - started late summer, not now progressive Attached site investigation data indicates desiccation to 3.00M as shown by the soil suction profile, compares with root profile to 2.70M			
Date damage discovered	September 2007			
Monitoring	Not obtained. All evidence obtained clearly demonstrates influence of the street tree			
Drains	None to front of property			
Estimated cost of repairs	**Protocol Mitigation**	**Delayed / Rejected Mitigation**		
Investigation	£ 800	£ 1,400		
Substructure	Not anticipated	£ 8,300		
Superstructure	£ 6,800	£ 7,400		
Alt Accn	Not anticipated	Not anticipated		
Fees & Expenses	£ 1,900	£ 2,100		
Total	£ 9,500	£19,200		
Mitigation Request	Immediate removal of street tree			
Comments (use this box to add further engineering comments if required or advise if engineering report attached)	Customer's beech hedge not considered relevant and all roots sampled were Plane			

Appendix B: Joint Mitigation Protocol Evidential Requirements for Council Owned Trees

Maximum Timeline in	Building Insurer (or their representative) visits the property & assesses if cause of damage is subsidence and if council tree or other factors are likely to be implicated. If the tree, then the Tree Controller/Risk Manager is identified.
7 days	Building Insurer (or their rep.) writes to Tree Controller within 7 calendar days of identifying Tree Controller seeking: 1. Contact details of the individual/department responsible for control of the tree, along with any reference, to assist communication regarding tree management and liability. 2. Contact details of their liability Insurer if appropriate. 3. The value of the tree (low, medium or high) as determined by the Tree Officer.
21 days	Within 14 calendar days of receiving the correspondence referred to above, the Tree Controller/Tree Officer will respond to the Building Insurer (or their rep.) giving responses to questions 1, 2 & 3 above.
81 days	Within 60 calendar days of receiving the value of the council tree, the Building Insurer (or their rep.) will submit either: a) A letter confirming withdrawal of the case, on the basis that the site investigation has not implicated the council tree in the damage, and that the file should bo closed. b) A **"Submission of Evidence"** based on the tree's CAVAT value with the requested mitigation (pruning/felling). Low Value Trees - may be removed & replaced. Medium Value Trees - make an important contribution to the area. High Value Trees - make an extremely important contribution to the area. **Low Value Trees:** 1. Report on damage to building. 2. Plan & profile of foundations. 3. Plan of site showing location of building in relation to all trees and significant vegetation in vicinity of site. 4. Trial pit cross section to underside of foundation depth plus borehole through base of trial pit to a minimum depth of 3m (explanation to be provided if borehole unable to reach 3m depth). Borehole log to be provided. 5. Root ID from beneath underside of foundation. **Medium Value Trees:** All of the above plus: 6. Soil moisture content readings at 0.5m centres, starting at the underside of the foundation, down to 3m depth of B/H. 7. Liquid limit test results at underside of foundation and approx 2m depth 8. Plastic limit test results at underside of foundation and approx 2m depth. 9. Soil plasticity calculated from LL – PL. 10. Control borehole to 3m depth with log, with same tests as above, if it is possible to locate such a borehole on the site and remote from the influence of any vegetation. If impossible then explanation needed 11. Oedometer or suction test results at underside of foundation & 1.0m centres down depth of 3m borehole **ONLY** when there is **NO** control borehole. If there is a control borehole then other tests listed are sufficient. 12. Shear vane test results at 0.5m centres, starting at the underside of the foundation, down to 3m depth of borehole(s). 13. CCTV & hydraulic testing to drains (excluding Water Board owned) located within 3m distance of area of subsidence damage. If unable to water test due to no access/blind entries/etc then give reason. 14. Crack monitoring is required on a maximum of 2 month frequency and is to be set up ideally at time of first visit by building insurer representative or within 7 days of 1st visit. Send all available readings with Submission of Evidence. **High Value Trees:** All of the above **EXCEPT crack width monitoring**, plus: 15. Control borehole (if possible) & point of subsidence borehole, each to 5m depth (not 3m as for medium value). 16. Level monitoring commencing at outset of claim for a relevant period (max. 12 months) using a deep datum (if possible) to 8m depth, otherwise use deep manhole. 17. Particle Size Distribution Analysis to BS 1377 Part 2 test 9.0 on a single soil sample taken from a 1m zone below the underside of foundation (Only if drains are present within 3m of the site of damage).

	Joint Mitigation Protocol Evidential Requirements For Council Owned Trees (Continued)
109 days **172 days** **1 year**	A. Unless mutually agreed to the contrary, if the requested mitigation scope is not accepted within 28 calendar days of submission of the "Evidence" then the case falls outside this Joint Mitigation Protocol. B. Mitigation is to be completed within a maximum of 13 weeks of the date of the Submission of Evidence. If tree removal cannot be agreed without longer term, crack or level monitoring evidence, then the Tree Controller will arrange for pruning to be completed as soon as is practicable but no later than 13 weeks from date of Submission of Evidence. C. In cases other than single trees owned by the local authority, e.g. where there are multiple trees/vegetation and/or multiple ownerships an arboricultural report may be required at the discretion and expense of the building insurer. This report should identify & detail the physical attributes of ALL trees & significant woody vegetation in the area of damage. It should also state proposed mitigation which should include the option of pruning/on going maintenance if thought to stand a reasonable chance of bringing about stability. D. The Building Insurer will want to proceed with repairs within 1 year from outset of claim. E. By mutual agreement all the above timescales may be varied. F. Protocol to be reviewed after 12 months in operation.

Appendix C

Contact details and subscribers to the protocol

To be completed

17 HIGHWAYS CLAIMS

17 HIGHWAYS CLAIMS

Contents

17.1 Introduction

Highways – essential elements

A highway is not simply a road or street or footpath. It is a way over which there exists a public right of passage. The essential elements of this are that:

1. It must be a regular way and not simply a piece of open land over which the public can go where they like.
2. All members of the public have the right to use it and its use is not restricted to certain sections of the public, for instance visitors to properties located along the way.
3. The public may use the highway at any season of the year.
4. The public may use it freely and at their will to pass and re-pass without let or hindrance.

Limitations and types

Whilst there can be no limitation as to who may use a highway or when it may be used, there may be limitations as to what class of traffic may use the highway. For example a footpath may be a highway but it is only for pedestrians.

There are essentially three kinds of highway:

1. Carriageway
2. Bridleway
3. Footpath.

Over a carriageway the public have rights of passage with vehicles, on and with beasts of burden, and by foot. A bridleway excludes the use of vehicles and sometimes the right to drive cattle, but retains the other rights of passage and includes the use of a bicycle.

A footpath is restricted to passage by foot.

Dedication

At common law the fact that a way is a highway is established by proving dedication of the way and the public's acceptance of it as a highway. The dedication can be presumed from the action of the owner of the land in permitting the public to pass over the way and the acceptance by the public can be presumed from the simple fact that the public use that way.

Since the passing of The Rights of Way Act 1932, public use for a period of twenty years may give rise to presumption that a way is a highway unless there is sufficient evidence that there was no intention to dedicate the way as highway.

17.2 Highways Maintainable at Public Expense

Historical overview

Until 1835 all highways were maintainable by the inhabitants at large, that is the inhabitants of a parish were bound to repair the highways within their area. That responsibility continued for highways which were in existence in 1835 but any new highways brought into existence after 1835 were not maintainable by the inhabitants at large unless they were specially adopted.

In 1960, with the coming into force of the Highways Act 1959, the concept of repair by the inhabitants at large was replaced by the concept of highways maintainable at public expense by which Highway Authorities had a duty to maintain the highways in their area. All the highways maintainable at that time by the inhabitants at large became highways maintainable at public expense.

Highways which were footpaths or bridle-ways in 1949 became repairable by the inhabitants at large with the passing of The National Parks and Access to the Countryside Act 1949 and subsequently became in consequence highways maintainable at public expense.

Other ways of becoming maintainable

Other highways created between 1835 and present day have become highways maintainable at public expense in a number of ways:

a) They have been adopted by the Highway Authority.

b) They have been constructed by the Highway Authority.

c) They have been constructed by a council within its own area under The Housing Act 1985.

d) They are a highway which is a footpath or bridleway created in consequence of a public path creation or a public path diversion order, or under an order under the Town & Planning Legislation or dedicated in pursuance to a public planning agreement.

e) They are a footpath or bridleway created under a rail crossing diversion order or under an order made under certain powers relating to transport.

It can be seen from this however that there are inevitably a number of highways which have come into being since 1835 which are not maintainable at public expense and which it may well be that no one has a duty to maintain.

Maintainable or not?

The simple way of establishing whether a highway is maintainable at public expense is to refer to the list which each County, Metropolitan District, and London Borough Council must maintain of streets within its area which are highways maintainable at public expense.

Such lists are not however absolutely definitive and if there is doubt as to whether a highway is truly maintainable at public expense, and if so to what level, then a search into the history and user of the highway will have to be carried out.

Usually the best source of the documents necessary for the search will be the Council responsible for maintaining the list.

17.3 Highway Authorities

The main legislation relating to highways is currently The Highways Act 1980. The Act sets out which bodies are highway authorities.

Essentially the Secretary of State for Transport is the Highway Authority in respect of motorways and trunk roads.

Outside London, the Highway Authority in respect of all other highways maintainable at public expense is the County Council or Metropolitan District Council. Within London the Highway Authority is the relevant Borough Council.

The position has been modified by the setting up in April 1998 of a number of unitary authorities who since that date have replaced the

County Council as the Highway Authority within their area, and by the setting up in 2000 of Transport for London which is the Highway Authority for 580 km of main roads in London.

District Councils

District Council's are not highway authorities under the Act. It is possible under Section 42 of The Highways Act 1980 for District Councils to assume responsibility for maintenance of certain roads within their area. These roads must not be classified and they must have a speed limit of 30 mph or less.

It has not been uncommon for District Councils to act as agents for the Highway Authority in respect of the maintenance of other highways within the District Council's area.

The role of the District Council can cause confusion. Under no circumstances, unless it has become a unitary authority, will the District Council be the Highway Authority for a particular highway. If a claim goes into litigation then it would be sensible for the Claimant to sue the Highway Authority as the duty to maintain the highway is laid upon it.

However in the pre-litigation stage there will be a difference in respect of roads claimed by the District Council under Section 42 and the remainder of highways. In the former case the District Council will almost certainly have provided an indemnity to the County Council in respect of any claims arising from these roads and the Claimant will be dealing with the District Council, its claims handlers and insurers. In the case of other highways whilst the Claimant may well find himself initially in contact with the District Council ultimately he should be dealing with the Highway Authority itself or its Claims Handlers or its insurers. It is important at an early stage to establish in what capacity a District Council is acting so that time is not wasted by prolonged correspondence with the District Council only to find that the matter is then referred to the County Council as Highway Authority.

Powers

The Highways Act 1980 gives a large number of powers to Highway Authorities mainly to do with the improvement of the highway.

It is important to remember that these are powers and not duties and that failure to exercise these powers will not render the Highway Authority liable to a person who has sustained an accident, which would have probably been averted if those powers had been used.

The position in this respect was very much clarified by the decision of the House of Lords in the case of ***Stovin v Wise (Norfolk County Council Third Party)*** (1996). In that case the Claimant was injured when his motorcycle collided with a car driven by the Defendant at a junction where the view from the Claimant's direction of the side road from which the Defendant emerged was obscured by an earth bank on railway land adjacent to the road. Norfolk County Council, the Highway Authority were aware that the presence of the bank made the junction dangerous and had approached the railway authority with an offer to remove the bank and pay the cost. At the time of the accident no further action had been taken. At the original trial the Judge found that the Highway Authority was in breach of its common law duty of care though not in breach of its statutory duty. The Judge found them 30% to blame for the accident. The Court of Appeal dismissed an Appeal by the Highway Authority. However the House of Lords allowed the appeal.

Lord Hoffman first disposed of the argument that the Council could be held responsible as occupier referring with approval to the Judgment in ***McGeown v Northern Ireland Housing Executive*** (1994) and said in his speech:

> *"it therefore seems clear that if Station Road and Cemetery Road had been highways over private land which happened to be owned and occupied by the Norfolk County Council instead of being repairable at the public expense, there would have been no liability. The analogy of an occupier is therefore insufficient for the purpose of imposing liability."*

Lord Hoffman went on to deal with the distinction between policy and operations. Following the speech of Lord Wilberforce in ***Anns v Merton London Borough*** (1977) the Courts took the view that an authority's statutory powers could be divided into policy or "discretion", and an operational area which was concerned with the practical execution of policy decisions. Lord Wilberforce said;

> *"It can safely be said that the more "operational" a power or duty may be the easier it is to superimpose upon it a common law duty of care."*

Following that doctrine the Judge at first instance and the Court of Appeal held that the decision to move the bank having been taken they were simply dealing with the operational question of when the work should be done. Lord Hoffman felt that this distinction between policy and operation was an inadequate tool and that the decision when the work should be done was as much a part of the Council's discretion as to whether it should be done at all.

Lord Hoffman went on to find that even if the Council should have in the past removed the bank there was no legislative intent that the Council should pay compensation for damage arising because of that failure. He also found that it was not in the public interest that there should be such a duty as it would distort the priorities of local authorities spending more on road improvements to the disadvantage of other areas.

In summary, Lord Hoffman's view was as follows;

> *"I think that the minimum pre-conditions for basing a duty of care upon the existence of a statutory power, if it can be done at all, are first that it would in the circumstances have been irrational not to have exercised the power so that there was in effect a public law duty to act and secondly that there are exceptional grounds for holding that the policy of the statute requires compensation to be paid to persons who have suffered a loss because the power was not exercised."*

In ***Gorringe v Calderdale MBC*** (2002) Lord Hoffmann seemed to go even further,

> *"I find it difficult to imagine a case in which a common law duty can be founded simply upon the failure (however irrational) to provide some benefit which a public authority has power (or a public law duty) to provide."*

In the light of this it would seem impossible to found a claim against a Highway Authority on the basis of a failure to carry out a power.

Duties

The principal duty with which we are concerned in accident claims is the duty of the Highway Authority to maintain the highway which duty is currently established under Section 41.1 of The Highways Act 1980 which states quite simply that:

> *"the authority who are for the time being the Highway Authority for a highway maintainable at public expense are under a duty to maintain the highway".*

No standard of maintenance is set by the Act. The standard adopted by the Court has been that the highway must not be dangerous.

Until the decision of the House of Lords in ***Goodes v East Sussex County Council*** (June 2000) one would have said that the duty to maintain the highway goes beyond simply repairing the surface. It would include removing snow, ice, mud, obstructions and draining the highway. However it would now seem that "maintenance" is to be interpreted as being restricted to keeping the structure in good repair, and that extraneous substances on the surface of the highway would not render the Highway Authority in breach of it's duty under s 41 nor would repainting of a worn out sign on the surface of the highway constitute maintenance of the structure of the highway ***Gorringe v. Calderdale Metropolitan Borough Council*** (2002).

17.4 Is the Highway Dangerous?

The concept of dangerousness

It cannot be emphasised too strongly that there is no mechanistic approach to determining what constitutes a danger on the highway. Probably the most famous section of any Judgment on a highway claim is in the Judgment of Cumming-Bruce J in ***Littler v Liverpool Corporation*** (1968).

> *"Uneven surfaces and differences in level between flagstones of about an inch may cause a pedestrian temporarily off balance to trip and stumble, but such characteristics have to be accepted. A highway is not to be criticised by the standards of a bowling green".*

Many people have made the assumption that a one inch trip was the standard by which dangerousness is judged. If a trip of an inch is dangerous, less than an inch is not. That is to misconstrue the Judgment. Earlier Cumming-Bruce J had said;

> *"it is a mistake to isolate and emphasise a particular difference in levels between flagstones unless that difference is such that a*

reasonable person who noticed it and considered it would regard it as a real source of danger".

There is a widely held belief that trips of less than ¾ of an inch to one inch are not dangerous and trips in excess of that level are. This is not the approach of the Courts.

Test applied by the Courts

The test applied by the Court is whether a reasonable man would consider that a particular defect had rendered the road dangerous and of course the reasonable man is inevitably the Judge himself.

18.31 In ***Rider v Rider*** (1973) Lawton LJ said:

> *"whether a part of the highway is a danger for traffic is a question of fact and the answer to the question would be in the evaluation of evidence by the Judge .... in a common sense way".*

In the case of ***Mills v Barnsley Metropolitan Borough Council*** (1992) Steyn LJ said:

> *"for my part I find that it is a sterile exercise to make a comparison between the facts and reported decisions in tripping cases and the facts of the present case".*

Character of road and traffic

Clearly each case has to be judged on its own facts, upon the size of the defect, its position in the highway, the volume and type of traffic that might be expected to encounter it.

The character of the road and the character of the traffic using it are important considerations. Again in ***Rider v Rider*** Lawton LJ said:

> *"a stretch of uneven pavement outside a factory probably would not be a danger to traffic but a similar stretch outside an old people's home and much used by the inmates to the knowledge of the highway authority might be".*

18.35 In ***Mills v Barnsley,*** Steyn LJ gave a warning that the Court should not impose an unreasonably high burden on Highway Authorities. Allowing the appeal he said;

> *"In this case the Judge set a standard which, if generally used, would impose an unreasonable burden on the Highway Authority in respect*

of minor depressions and holes in the street which, in a less than perfect world the public must simply regard as a fact of life".

Danger created by Highway Authority

You should note however that if the danger was actually created by the Highway Authority the Court may well apply higher standards.

In the case of ***Pitman v Southern Electricity Board*** (1978) the Court found that a metal plate, an eighth of an inch thick, placed on the highway nonetheless constituted a danger because it was unexpected.

17.5 Special Defence

If a highway is dangerous and damage ensues then the Highway Authority may still be able to avoid liability on the basis of the special defence provided under **The Highways Act 1980, s 58(1)**

Defence in relation to s 41

It is essential to note however that s 58 only comes into play if it is shown that the Highway Authority is in breach of s 41 of the Act. This was stressed again by Steyn LJ in ***Mills v Barnsley MBC***. He said:

> *"the Claimant must prove that:*
>
> *a) the highway was in such a condition that it was dangerous,*
>
> *b) the dangerous condition was caused by the failure to maintain,*
>
> *c) the injury or damage resulted from such failure.*
>
> *Only if the Claimant does prove these facta probanda does it become necessary to turn to the Highway Authority's reliance on the special Defence".*

Court's considerations under s 58(2)

In practice it is often difficult to disentangle the two sections. Section 58 (2) sets requirements of what the Court has to take into consideration in respect of the Section 58 Defence as follows:

> '58(2) For the purposes of a defence under subsection (1) above, the Court shall in particular have regard to the following matters:

a) The character of the highway and the traffic which was reasonably expected to use it;

b) The standard of maintenance appropriate for a highway of that character and used by such traffic;

c) The state of repair in which a reasonable person would expect to find the highway'.

These are all matters which the Court will have to consider in deciding whether there has been a breach of s 41. It is important that the Court and the parties realise that before going on to consider any other parts of s 58 it must be first of all be established that there has been a breach of s 41.

Question of causation

Section 58.1 of the **Highways Act 1980** states that;

> *"In an action against a highway authority in respect of damages resulting from their failure to maintain a highway maintainable at public expense, it is a defence to prove that the authority had taken such care as in all the circumstances was reasonably required to secure the part of the highway to which the action relates not dangerous to traffic".*

On the face of it, the requirements seem to be no more than a statement that the Highway Authority should not be negligent. There is in fact an important difference and it relates to the question of causation. This is perhaps best explained by example.

Let us assume that a deep pothole has formed over which the Claimant has tripped. If we consider the matter in negligence, putting aside the defence of non-feasence, it would be necessary for the Claimant to show that a lack of care on the part of the Highway Authority had caused the pothole to form or perhaps more likely, to be failed to be seen and repaired quickly enough. If the Authority could show that although it had no regular system or maintenance of that road, that nonetheless it had perhaps by chance looked at that road only a week before and that the road appeared to be in perfectly good condition, then the Claimant might well have a struggle to make up his case.

Under the Act however, the position is different. The Authority are already on the back foot as they are clearly in breach of s 41 of the Act.

They must therefore make up their Defence under s 58. In those circumstances it is not sufficient for them to say that they had looked at the highway a week before and it seemed in good condition then. They must show that they have a proper system of inspection and maintenance and that they have properly carried out that system of inspection and maintenance. If they had for example missed three inspections in a row and then carried out the inspection immediately before the accident, although those missed inspections may well have not been causative of the accident, they probably would lead the Court to find that the Authority had not fulfilled its duties and therefore could not make up the s 58 Defence.

Section 58(2) of the Highways Act 1980 sets out those matters which the Court has to take into consideration when deciding whether or not the Highway Authority has taken the care required of it by s 58(1). We have already quoted subsections a, b and c. The remainder of s 58(2) requires the Court to consider:

> "(d) whether the Highway Authority knew, or reasonably could have been expected to know, that the condition of the part of the highway to which the action relates was likely to cause danger to the users of the highway;
>
> (e) where the Highway Authority could not have been reasonably expected to repair that part of the highway before the cause of the action arose, what warning notices of the condition had been displayed".

Section 58 goes on to say:

> *"for the purposes of such a defence it is not relevant to prove that the Highway Authority had arranged for a competent person to carry out or supervise the maintenance of the part of the highway to which the action relates unless it is also proved that the authority had given him proper instructions with regard to the maintenance of the highway and that he had carried out the instructions".*

In determining whether or not the Highway Authority has taken such care as in all the circumstances is reasonably required we look to the assistance of s 58(2) and to what the general standards are and what has been found to be reasonable in the past.

17.6 The Section 58 Defence in Practice

Establishing a defence

In order to make up a s 58 Defence, a Highway Authority has to establish two things:

1. That it has a reasonable maintenance policy; and
2. That the policy has been properly carried out.

Reasonable maintenance policy

The main elements of a reasonable maintenance policy are:

a) A reasonable inspection policy; and

b) Reasonable timescales for repair.

Inspection policy

The main elements of an inspection policy are:

c) Road Hierarchy – that is the roads and footways within a Highway Authority area are categorised according to the importance of the road and the amount of traffic that each carries (compare this with s 58(2)(a);

d) The frequency of inspection set for each category of road;

e) The way in which the inspection is to be carried out; and

f) The intervention levels set, that is how bad does a defect have to be before it warrants repair.

Repair policy

As regards to the repair policy, the important elements are:

g) A reasonable timescale for repair should be set according to the severity of the defect;

h) Where a repair cannot be effected immediately, proper steps are taken to render the highway safe by signing or other appropriate means *(compare this with s 58(2)(e)*.

17.7 Code of Good Practice

The Local Authorities Association (LAA) for some years produced a Code of Good Practice for Highway Maintenance, setting out a basic road hierarchy and suggesting inspection intervals both for safety inspections and service inspections. It also set out guidelines for intervention levels. This was superseded by *"Delivering Best Value in Highway Maintenance"* published in July 2001 by The Institution of Highways and Transportation. This in turn was superseded in July 2005 by *"Well Maintained Highways"* published by The Stationery Office.

In so far as the Highway Authority's policy coincides with the practice proposed by the Code it would be hard for a Court to find that the Highway Authority's policy was unreasonable.

Set out below at Table1 is the Code's suggestion for road hierarchy and how each type of road should be slotted into the hierarchy. This in the past was based on traffic volumes but is now based on a number of criteria, no doubt as a result of the constantly increasing volume of traffic. Table 2 sets out the hierarchy for footways. Table 3 sets out their suggestion for inspection intervals for each category of road and footway.

Table 1 – Carriageway Hierarchy

Category	Hierarchy Description	Type of Road General Description	Description
1	Motorway	Limited access motorway regulations apply	Routes for fast moving long distance traffic. Fully grade separated and restrictions on use.
2	Strategic Route	Trunk and some Principal 'A' roads between Primary Destinations	Routes for fast moving long distance traffic with little frontage access or pedestrian traffic. Speed limits are usually in excess of 40 mph and there are few junctions. Pedestrian crossings are either segregated or controlled and parked vehicles are generally prohibited.
3a	Main Distributor	Major Urban Network and Inter-Primary Links. Short-medium distance traffic	Routes between Strategic Routes and linking urban centres to the strategic network with limited frontage access. In urban areas speed limits and very high levels of pedestrian acticity with some crossing facilities including zebra crossings. On-street parking is generally unrestricted except for safety reasons.
3b	Secondary Distributor	Classified Road (B and C class) and unclassified urban bus routes carrying local traffic with frontage access and frequent junctions	In rural areas these roads link the smaller villages to the distributor roads. They are of varying width and not always capable of carrying two way traffic. In urban areas they are residential or industrial inter-connecting roads with 30 mph speed limits random pedestrian movements and uncontrolled parking.
4a	Link Road	Roads linking between the Main and Secondary Distributor Network with frontage access and frequent junctions	In rural areas these roads link the smaller villages to the distributor roads. They are of varying width and not always capable of carrying two way traffic. In urban areas they are residential or industrial inter-connecting roads with 30 mph speed limits random pedestrian movements and uncontrolled parking.
4b	Local Access Road	Roads serving limited numbers of properties carrying only access traffic	In rural areas these roads seerve small settlements and provide access to individual properties and land. They are often only single lane width and unsuitable for HGVs. In urban areas they are often residential loop roads or cul-de-sacs.

Table 2 – Footway Hierarchy

Category	Category Name	Description
1a	Prestige Walking Zones	Very busy areas of towns and cities with high public space and streetscene contribution.
1	Primary Walking Routes	Busy urban shopping and business areas and main pedestrian routes.
2	Secondary Walking Routes	Medium usage routes through local areas feeding into primary routes, local shopping centres etc.
3	Link Footways	Linking local access footways through urban areas and busy rural footways.
4	Local Access Footways	Footways associated with low usage, short estate roads to the main routes and cul-de-sacs.

Table 3 – Safety Inspection Frequency

Feature	Description	Category	Frequency
Roads	Strategic Route Main Distributor Secondary Distributor Link Road Local Access	2 3(a) 3(b) 4(a) 4(b)	1 month 1 month 1 month 3 months 1 year
Footways	Prestige Area Primary Walking Route Secondary Walking Route Link Footway Local Access Footway	1(a) 1 2 3 4	1 month 1 month 3 months 6 months 1 year
Cycle Route	Part of Carriageway Remote from Carriageway Cycle Trails	A B C	As for Roads 6 months 1 year

Inspections

Safety inspections will look for defects, which are dangerous or are likely to become dangerous in the very near future. Service inspections are more detailed inspections tailored to the requirements of particular highway elements.

When looking at the adequacy of inspection frequencies it is important not only to compare the Highways Authority's frequency of inspection with that proposed by the Code, but also to consider whether or not the road in question has been correctly slotted into the right category within the hierarchy. Inspection frequencies in line with the Code will also not avail a Highway Authority if they know that there is a special problem on the road which will cause more rapid deterioration and therefore warrants more frequent inspection: ***Jacobs v Hants County Council*** (1984).

Intervention levels

An intervention level is the degree to which a section of highway must be out of maintenance in order to trigger some form of remedial action by the Highway Authority.

Given the wide variety of defects that can occur, the question of intervention levels is really far too wide a subject to go into in detail in this chapter. The important thing with an intervention level is that it should be set lower than the level at which the Highway Authority believes that the highway or footway is rendered dangerous, the aim being to prevent the highway becoming dangerous. The Code refers to category 1 and Category 2 Defects. Traditionally Category, 1 Defects are those that require prompt attention because they represent an immediate or imminent hazard or because there is a risk of short-term deterioration. Category 2 encompasses all other defects.

Well maintained Highways has introduced a Risk Matrix sbown below:

Table 4 – Risk Matrix

Probability →Impact↓	**Very low (1)**	**Low (2)**	**Medium (3)**	**High (4)**
Neglible (1)	1	2	3	4
Low (2)	2	4	6	8
Noticeable (3)	3	6	9	12
High (4)	4	8	12	16

Response Category	Category 2(L) response	Category 2(M) response	Category 2(H) response	Category 1 response

This balances the probability of an accident happening against its likely impact if it does. This means that Category 1 defects are those with a high probability of an accident and a high impact if an accident occurs. Category 2 defects are divided into Low, Medium, High.

If we take a trip on the footway as being the most common form of highway accident, the Code is rather unspecific as to what the intervention level should be. Many authorities have however settled on 20 millimetres as being the level at which they will order an urgent repair. One has to bear in mind a Court's reluctance to set minimum standards and to treat each case on its own merits. To that end a sensible highway authority will not set rigid guidelines for its highways inspectors but give them authority to deal urgently with any defect they find that they believe to be dangerous or believe to be on the verge of becoming dangerous.

Time scale for Repairs and/or making safe

The Code recommends four response times to match the four categories of risk:

Category 1	make safe or repair within 24 hours
Category 2 (high)	make safe or repair within 5 working days
Category 2 (medium)	repair within four weeks
Category 2 (low)	repair during next available programme, or schedule more detailed inspection, or review at next inspection

It goes on to say that if a defect with potentially serious consequences for network safety is made safe by means of temporary signing or repair arrangements then there should be special inspections to check the integrity of the signing or temporary repair until the permanent repair is carried out.

17.8 Carrying Out the Policy

Assuming that it is established that the Highway Authority's maintenance policy is reasonable, the next question is whether they have carried out that policy correctly. Important points to consider are:

1. Have there been any missed inspections? One missed inspection may not condemn the Highway Authority providing it is not the one immediately before the accident. Several missed inspections may cause the Section 58 Defence to fail even though it can be shown that those missed inspections were not causative of the accident.

2. Were the inspections carried out appropriately? We would suggest that the Court would not be convinced that a footway in a busy pedestrian area could be adequately inspected from a slow moving motor vehicle.

3. Was the Highway Inspector who carried out the inspections sufficiently well trained and competent to carry them out? It is all very well if the Highway Authority has an excellent maintenance policy but no use at all if it does not communicate it to its Highways Inspectors.

4. Could it be that the Highways Inspector whilst carrying out an inspection simply missed a defect which already existed? It may be that there will be witnesses who will say that they were aware of the defect prior to the last safety inspection before the accident. You should bear in mind however that such witnesses will be open to the attack that they did not consider the defect dangerous otherwise they would have reported it.

A common feature of these claims however is that you will find that the Highways Inspector did not notice the defect until it was brought to his attention by the Claimant. It is important therefore to see the inspection report for the routine inspection post-accident as well as for the one before the accident. If the defect is not spotted in a post-accident inspection then the implication is that the Highways Inspector may have equally missed it in the pre-accident inspection.

17.9 Common Law Liability – Highway Authority

It is common for claims against the Highway Authority to be pleaded not only in breach of their duty under Section 41 of the Highways Act but also in negligence and nuisance.

It is also occasionally pleaded that they are in breach of their common duty of care under the **Occupiers' Liability Act**. Again we would argue that none of these extend the duty of the Highway Authority beyond that stated in the **Highways Act 1980.**

Negligence

With regard to negligence the position remains that the Highway Authority is only liable in negligence where the actions of the Highway Authority itself have brought about a dangerous state of affairs on the road (misfeasance). It is not liable for non-feasence; that is where the road has become dangerous because of its failure to act.

With regards to its potential liability as occupier of the highway we would suggest that members of the public cannot acquire rights as visitors to the highway as they are not visitors. They are on the highway by right, they do not have to be invited or permitted to go onto the highway ***Whiting v Hilliingdon London Borough Council*** (1970) and ***Holden v White*** (1982)

It has to be borne in mind that if the definition of the highway is restricted to its structure then ancillary items such as street furniture, which are occupied by or are the responsibility of the Highway Authority will not enjoy the same privileged position as regards non-feasance. So that if a Highway Authority fails to maintain a bollard, which becomes defective and causes injury, whilst the highway authority cannot be in breach of Section 41 of the Highways Act, it can be found to be negligent. ***Shine v Tower Hamlets London Borough Council (CA 2006).***

Nuisance

With regard to nuisance, clearly if the Highway Authority itself created the danger it would be liable in negligence in any event for misfeasance. If, however, someone else created the danger and the Highway Authority had not dealt with it then it would be nonsense if they were deprived of the special Defence enacted by statute simply because the case was pleaded in nuisance.

We do not believe that the Courts would be prepared to look at a highways claim in that way, nor are we aware of any cases in which they have. Clearly the Highway Authority can be guilty of nuisance and one respect would be in regard to trespass from a highways tree causing damage to a neighbouring property. That is clearly a different matter from dangers on the highway with which we are concerned in this chapter.

We will now deal briefly with three other areas; lighting, winter maintenance and accident prevention.

17.10 Lighting

There is no duty on the Highways Authority to light a highway. Section 97 of the Highways Act 1980 gives the Highway Authority a power to light the highway. It was established in ***Sheppard v Glossop Corporation*** (1921) that there was no common law duty to light the highway even if the highway was dangerous when unlit.

Interestingly the power under s 97 of the Highways Act 1980 is to construct and *maintain*. We would say, therefore, having lit a highway, a Highway Authority has no duty to maintain that lighting merely a power. Following *Stovin v Wise* they would not be liable if that power was not exercised.

There is, however, a contradictory Judgment in ***Farrell v Northern Ireland Electricity Service*** (1977) where the Judgment stated:

> *"where an authority to do so provides street lights to a certain standard it receives an obligation to exercise reasonable care in maintaining those lights to a reasonable standard"*

We would suggest, however, bearing in mind this is a Northern Ireland decision and bearing in mind that it precedes the House of Lords decision in *Stovin v Wise* that a Court is likely to find that there is no duty to maintain the street lighting. The exception to that is where a Highway Authority creates a danger on the highway and makes it safe by lighting, in which case there is a duty to maintain that lighting: ***Polkinghorn v Lambeth Borough Council*** (1938).

17.11 Winter Maintenance

The Approach Prior to 2000

The duty of the Highway Authority to maintain the highway under the Highways Act was interpreted from 1978 to 2000 to include the duty to remove ice and snow from the surface of the highway: ***Haydon v Kent County Council*** (1978).

The Courts had, during this period, taken the attitude that as ice and snow was likely to occur over a large section, if not the whole of a Highway Authority's network at the same time it would be unrealistic to expect them to clear the entire network instantly. The Highway Authority's Defence therefore was essentially similar to a Defence under s 58 in that it had a reasonable policy in force and that it carried out that policy correctly. An important element of the policy was the priority which it attributed to each of the roads within its area.

Highway Authorities reasonably took the view that both in terms of economic damage and health and safety it was important to keep open the most strategically important and most heavily trafficked roads. That meant that minor roads and footways were not dealt with for some considerable time and indeed it was not uncommon for them not to be dealt with at all, but simply to await the thaw.

Provided that these priorities were applied reasonably and sensibly the Court was likely to approve this conduct ***Cross v Kirklees Metropolitan Borough Council (1997); Wilcox v East Riding of Yorkshire District Council (1998)***.

The Approach 2000-2003

The position changed radically in June 2000 with the House of Lords decision in ***Goodes v East Sussex County Council***. There the House of Lords decided that Lord Denning who had been in the minority in the case of ***Haydon v Kent County Council*** in finding that maintenance of the highway did not include the removal of snow and ice was, in fact, correct.

The House of Lords found that the **Highways Act 1959** and its successor in 1980 had not extended the duty to maintain beyond what was imposed by the Common Law prior to the passing of those Acts and found that the duty to maintain prior to 1959 had clearly not included the duty to remove ice and snow and still less to prevent them falling upon the road.

That also led to a view that, given that s 41 imposed an absolute duty to maintain the highway, it was illogical to include within that duty a duty to keep the highway free of snow and ice because no highway authority could avoid, from time to time, being in breach of that duty. They took the view that the Court of Appeal in it's decision in ***Haydon v Kent County Council*** had got itself into difficulty because by including the removal of ice and snow from the road within the duty to maintain it had been forced to water down the absolute nature of that duty.

Whilst Lord Hoffman in the leading speech in this case largely restricts himself to the question of whether or not the removal of ice and snow is included within the definition of maintenance, Lord Clyde's speech also finding for the appellants makes it clear that there are wider ramifications. Firstly, he is firm in his view that the duty of maintenance does not extend beyond matters of repair. Secondly, that if the highway was made unsafe by the presence of extraneous material upon it that likewise did not constitute a failure to maintain:

The Current Approach

There was within Lord Hoffman's speech an open invitation to the government to consider legislation in order to make a failure by a highway authority to take reasonable steps to keep the highway clear of snow and ice actionable. The Government responded by amending Section 41 of the **Highways Act 1980** to include Paragraph 1A.

> (1A) In particular, a Highway Authority are under a duty to ensure, so far as is reasonably practicable, that safe passage along a highway is not endangered by snow or ice.

This came into force on 31.10.2003

The Highway Authority will have to satisfy the Court that it took reasonable steps to obtain warnings of snow and ice and that it had a reasonable plan for dealing with them – in terms of gritting and ploughing. The key constituent of which will be the gritting of routes. The timing of gritting, the density of grit used, and the system used for receiving, recording and dealing with isolated reports of ice will be important. Finally, it will have to show that it carried out that policy efficiently, for example that the gritters were working efficiently and covering the whole road.

At the time of writing there has only been one reported case in which the duty under 41.1A has been considered. That is ***Rhiannon Pace v City and County of Swansea (2007)*** heard in the Swansea County Court in July 2007 and following an accident on 17th January 2004.

In that case it was found that there was ice on the road and that this caused the Claimant to lose control. The road had been gritted but patches of ice had still formed. The Council's winter maintenance plan was in line with the Code of Practice for Maintenance Management and was found to be adequate.

The Claimant's main lines of attack were on implementation of the plan, that the spread rate of grit was too low and that the gritter driver in fact did not cover the relevant section of the route. The Judge rejected both these contentions as matters of fact.

The Judge found that the Council had an adequate and proper policy for salting and that the policy was implemented. The claim was dismissed. The Judge found that if he had found against the Council he would have found that there was 60% contributory negligence on the part of the Claimant.

It needs to be remembered that only a duty in respect of snow and ice has been reintroduced by this legislation. There remains no duty on the Highway Authority to remove other extraneous materials such as mud or leaves from the Highway.

Water and Other Substances on the Highway

Lord Clyde in ***Goodes v East Sussex County Council*** expressed the view that maintenance did not go beyond repair and that the duty to maintain did not extend to the removal of extraneous matter from the surface of the Highway. Consequently mud, or leaves or oil on the road would not found a case for breach of Section 41.

Flooding of the road however was found to be a different matter in ***DTER v Mott McDonald Ltd Amey Mouchel Ltd and Cornwall County Council (CA 2006)***. Here the Court of Appeal found that maintenance of the highway included maintenance of the highway drains and extended to the unblocking of drains as well as the repair of their structure. If therefore the highway became dangerous by reason of a failure to maintain the Highway drains then the highway authority would be liable under Section 41 for ensuing injury loss and damage.

17.12 Accident Prevention

Section 39 of the **Road Traffic Act 1988** imposes a duty to carry out studies into road traffic accidents. The authority shall:

> "in the light of those studies take such measures as appear to the authority to be appropriate to prevent such accidents

> including the construction, improvement, maintenance or repair of roads and other measures taken in the exercise of their powers for controlling, protecting or assisting in the movement of traffic on roads".

Although this is expressed as a duty it should be noted that the authority only has to take measures "which seem to it appropriate".

The extent of the highways authorities duty under s 39 of the Road Traffic Act 1988 has been considered by the Court of Appeal in ***Larner v. Solihull Metropolitan Borough Council*** (2000). The Court decided the duty under the Section could properly be described as a "target" duty, which required the Council to do no more than exercise its powers in the manner that it considered appropriate. The Court went on to express the view that although a common law duty of care might in exceptional circumstances be imposed upon the statutory duty of s 39 of the Act it would have to be shown that the default of the relevant authority fell outside the ambit of the discretion given to the authority by that section for example whether the authority had acted wholly unreasonably, that finding was followed by the Court of Appeal in ***Gorringe v. Calderdale Metropolitan Borough Council*** (2002).

In the case of Larner the Claimant was alleging that greater advance warning of a road junction should have been provided, in the case of Gorringe a slow sign which had disappeared should have been repainted to give warning of a section of road where there was a sharp left hand bend and adverse camber which was hidden from motorists on its approach by a crest. The essential points that emerge from these Judgments are that: -

i) an action will have to be founded upon a common law duty arising out of the duty under the Act rather than directly upon breach of duty under the Act itself.

ii) the Court will have to find that the highway authority has acted wholly unreasonably in not taking steps under the Act.

iii) that it will only be in very exceptional circumstances that a Court will so find.

17.13 Statutory Undertakers

Many bodies have the need to place equipment in or under the highway. For example, Water Companies, Gas Companies, Telephone

Companies and Electricity Companies. Their powers and duties in respect of this are dealt with under the **New Road and Street Works Act 1991.**

Section 65 deals with the safety measurers that they must take, s 70 deals with their duty to reinstate and s 71 deals with the standard of reinstatement and the maintenance period.

Reinstatement

Unlike s 41 of the **Highways Act**, which makes no definition of the standard of highway maintenance, standards of reinstatement have been set in a Code of Practice 2nd Edition published in 2002 and approved by the Secretaries of State for Transport for Wales and Scotland under their powers under the New Road and Street Works Act. We certainly do not have the space here to go into the technical details of the standard of reinstatement and would refer you to the Code of Practice. However we would draw your attention particularly to Section S1.2.1 which states:

> "the Undertakers shall ensure that the interim reinstatement conforms to the prescribed standard until the permanent reinstatement is completed and that the permanent reinstatement conforms to the prescribed standard throughout the guarantee".

The Code goes on to say that the permanent guarantee will begin on completion of the permanent reinstatement and will run for two years or three years in the case of "deep openings" and a "deep opening" is 1.5 metres or more.

If a highway defect was the result of the failure of a statutory undertakers reinstatement then the Highway Authority would be entitled to refer any claim to the statutory undertaker if the accident occurred within the guarantee period.

Equipment

Where a statutory undertaker's equipment is actually located in the surface of the highway, the undertaker is responsible for maintaining the apparatus. The undertaker does not have the common law defence of non-feasance which is available to the Highway Authority.

A statutory undertaker is entitled to rely upon the highways inspections carried out by the Highway Authority but is deemed to have the same knowledge as the Highway Authority as to the state of his highways equipment. It is not a defence therefore for an undertaker to say that the Highway Authority had not informed him of a defect in his equipment.

The duty to maintain the Highway remains with the Highway Authority and if the highway is dangerous because of the defective equipment of a statutory undertaker both the undertaker and the Highway authority can be jointly and severally liable in which case it is highly likely that liability will be apportioned 50/50 between them as in ***Nolan v Merseyside County Council*** (CA1982)

17.14 Contractors

Much of work that is carried out by Highway Authorities is now contracted out. It is important to appreciate that the Highway Authority cannot rely upon the Defence that it has discharged its duty by employing a competent contractor. The duty of the Highway Authority is non-delegable. If the highway is dangerous because of the fault or failure of the contractor, the Highway Authority will remain liable. The Highway Authority may well have a right to indemnity or contribution from the contractor but the injured party's cause of action will lie against the Highway Authority.

17.15 Evidence

The essential evidence that needs to be gathered in the majority of cases is as follows.

Under s 41

1. Photographs and dimension of the defect
2. Evidence of the type of traffic which uses that particular highway and it may be important (for example) to consider whether a high proportion of old people use that particular footway. It may, for certain types of defects, be important to establish whether the section of road in question is used by cyclists and motorcyclist who can be endangered by ridges and ruts running along the length of the carriageway rather than

across it in a way which would not inconvenience a pedestrian or a motorist.

Under s 58

There is guidance in the standard disclosure list attached to the Pre-Action Personal Injury Protocol that stipulates disclosure of documents for a period of 12 months prior to the accident. The documents being:

1. Records of inspection of the relevant stretch of highway.
2. Maintenance records including records of independent contractors working in the relevant area.
3. Records of the minutes of Highway Authority meetings where maintenance or repair policy has been discussed or decided.
4. Records of complaints about the state of the highways.
5. Records of other accidents that have occurred on the relevant stretch of the highway.

We would suggest that in addition the following documents need to be seen:

a) Records of inspection for the period immediately post-accident to see whether the defect was picked up at the next routine highways inspections after the accident took place. If it was not and the defect had not already been repaired then the chances are that it was overlooked at the pre-accident routine inspection; also,

b) any repair documents relating to repairs ordered as a result of the inspections in the 12 months preceding the accident. It is important to establish whether these repairs were carried out. It may be that the accident occurred because of a long-standing defect, which had been identified but not yet repaired. Secondly to ensure that the Highway Authority is repairing defects in line with reasonable time scales; and

c) the document that sets out the Highway Authority's policy regarding highway maintenance. This may not have been discussed at Highway Authority meetings within the last 12 months prior to the accident.

17.16 Highways Claims Check-list

1. Is the highway maintainable at public expense?
2. Is the condition of the highway dangerous? You must when considering this point bear in mind the amount and type of traffic using that particular highway.
3. If the highway is in a dangerous condition, nonetheless can the Highway Authority make up the Defence under s 58 of the Highways Act 1980? Points to consider in this regard are:
   (a) Is their policy for highway maintenance adequate? How does it compare with Well-Maintained Highways?
   (b) Has the policy been fully carried out? Is there for example evidence that a defect has been missed at an inspection or that it has not been repaired in the time scale set by the Highway Authority's own policy.
   (c) Were there any special factors known to the Highway Authority, which made their maintenance policy inadequate in these circumstances? An example would be the frequent subsidence of the road surface due to the washing away of the sub-surface.

17.17 Suggested Further Reading

Bingham and Berryman's *Personal Injury and Motor Claims Cases* (12th Edition 2006 Butterworths)

Well-Maintained Highways (The Stationery Office 2005)

18 CHILD ABUSE CLAIMS

18 CHILD ABUSE CLAIMS

Contents

Background

Whilst the physical and sexual abuse of children has been perpetrated by those in positions of trust for many decades, abusers and their employers have historically denied the existence and extent of such abuse.

An important factor that has led to greater public awareness in these cases has been the number of high profile public enquiries, in particular the report into child abuse in Cleveland in 1987.

Claims for compensation arising out of child abuse only became significant in the 1990's.

18.1 Causes of Action

Cases against Public Authorities for failure to remove the child

One of the earlier and most important cases setting out the various causes of action against Local Authorities in relation to failure to remove a child from an abusive home environment is the case of ***X (Minors) v Bedfordshire County Council (1994)*** *2 AC 633.*

In this case Lord Browne-Wilkinson separated these types of claims into three categories:

i) Breach of statutory duty (irrespective of carelessness);

ii) Carer's performance of statutory duty;

iii) Common law duty of care owing from statutory duty.

It was held by Lord Browne-Wilkinson that in order to succeed in an abuse related claim against a Local Authority, it would be necessary for a Claimant to first establish that a duty of care existed in common law. The three stages for establishing a common law duty of care had previously been laid down in the case of ***Caparo v Dickman (1988)***:

i) Was the damage reasonably foreseeable;

ii) Was the relationship to the Claimant and the Defendant sufficiently proximate;

iii) It is just and reasonable to impose a duty of care.

In reaching his judgment in ***X (Minors) v Bedfordshire County Council (1994),*** it was necessary for Lord Browne-Wilkinson to distinguish between allegations of direct liability on the part of the Local Authority and allegations of possible vicarious liability in relation to the acts of its employees.

Direct liability claims involve cases where the Local Authority makes a decision in relation to the placement of a child or children or obtains Court Orders in relation thereto. Some such allegations are sustainable, and some decisions by the Local Authority might be seen to be unreasonable and outside the remit of the Local Authority's discretion.

In ***X v Bedfordshire County Council (1994),*** the Local Authority accepted that a relationship of proximity existed between it and the Claimants. It was further accepted that it was foreseeable that the children would suffer if the Local Authority carried out its duty negligently.

However, Lord Browne-Wilkinson concluded that there were such potent considerations that to impose a common law duty of care on the Local Authority in relation to the performance of its statutory duties would be unfair and unreasonable. As such, Lord Browne-Wilkinson found that the Local Authority did not owe the Claimants a common law duty of care.

In addition, Lord Browne-Wilkinson concluded that the Local Authority could not be vicariously liable for the actions of the social workers and psychiatrists whom it employed to advise in relation to the Claimants. This was due to the fact that such professionals were retained by the Local Authority, as opposed to the Claimants and, therefore, owed a duty of care to the Local Authority but did not assume any professional duty of care to the Claimants.

It should be noted, however, that the decision in ***X*** did not involve a claim by children suffering ill treatment or abuse whilst in the care of a Local Authority or other institution. Rather, ***X*** involved children who suffered abuse at home and alleged that the Local Authority should have taken action to remove them from their homes and place them into care.

Claims against Public Authorities for abuse suffered whilst in care

Claims arising out of child abuse suffered by children in the care of a Local Authority may have a number of potential causes of action at common law:

a) A claim against the Local Authority for breach of direct duty in respect of the running of the home and the choice and supervision of staff.

b) A claim against the carer/social worker for failure to monitor progress or uncover the abuse.

c) A claim for vicarious liability for the behaviour of the abuser.

Vicarious liability for trespass

Abuse cases will often arise as a result of abuse perpetrated by an employee of a care home or other similar institution. In these cases the Claimant's case will be based on the assertion that the employer (i.e. the Local Authority) is vicariously liable for the acts of its employees.

The leading case of ***Lister v Hesley Hall Ltd (2001)*** involved a claim for damages arising from sexual abuse perpetrated by the warden of a boarding school for children with emotional and behavioural difficulties. The school was privately run but children were sent there by the Local Authority.

So far as the warden's abuse was concerned Lord Clyde stated that:

> *"His position as warden and the close contact with the boys which his work involved created a sufficient connection between acts of abuse which he committed and the work that he had been employed to do. His general duty was to look after and care for the children, and the fact that he performed the function in a way which was an abuse of his position did not sever the connection with his employment.*
>
> *Given that he had general authority in the management of the house and in the care and supervision of the boys in it, the employers should be liable for the way in which he behaved towards them."*

Liability of the employer

Vicarious liability is imposed on a Local Authority on the basis that there is a specific assumption of responsibility by it towards the child. The Local Authority's duty and responsibilities are then entrusted to its employee, and the Local Authority is in breach of that duty of care if the employee abuses that position.

18.2 Causation

Establishing that the abuse suffered at a particular institution at the hands of an individual led to the damage sustained will often be a difficult issue for the Claimant. These types of claims by their nature often involve children who have been in and out of care and have been the victims of abuse in more than one place, for example they may have suffered abuse in their own home, only to be removed from the home and later suffer abuse in care.

Whilst an act of physical abuse may be easy to ascribe to one abuser, it will not be so easy to ascribe the psychological illnesses resulting from such an act. The Claimant will have to establish that he or she is suffering from an identifiable medical condition (***Page v Smith***). The Claimant must also demonstrate sufficient evidence that the actions of the Local Authority or its employee made a material contribution to the Claimant's psychiatric injury (***McGhee v National Coal Board (1972)***).

Abuse claims will often be commenced many years after the abuse took place, and the Court will have to establish whether the problems in adult life were caused by the period of abuse or by other factors. These complex issues of causation will be matters for the medical experts instructed to unravel. The Court will then have to do its best in each individual case after weighing up all the evidence.

18.3 Damages

There have been three main multi-party actions detailing the assessment of the level of damages in child abuse cases. The JSB Guidelines also set out the damages for psychiatric injury.

Various claims against Leicestershire CC

i) Claimant X was subjected to forced regression including confinement to her room for up to six weeks at a time leading to self-mutilation and attempted suicide. At the date of the trial the Claimant suffered from self-mutilation and a number of other serious psychiatric ailments.

General damages were assessed at **£15,000.00**.

ii) Claimant Y was raped and buggered and subjected to a number of indecent assaults and brutal physical attacks including torture. The Claimant suffered PTSD flashbacks, sexual disfunction and attempted suicide.

General damages were assessed at **£80,000.00**.

Various claims against Brentshire CC July 2000

i) Claimant A was physically assaulted by a care worker, indecently assaulted, and unlawfully incarcerated. The Claimant suffered psychiatric effects later in life.

General damages were assessed at **£35,000.00.**

ii) Claimant B was abused over a period of 12 months by the officer in charge of the care home including grabbing his penis on two or three occasions. Minor effect on adult life no PTSD established.

General damages were assessed at **£9,500.00**.

iii) Claimant C was abused by Defendant's employees including oral sex, sexual acts with a dog, masturbation and indecent assault. The abuse was accepted as being severe and persistent.

The Claimant suffered PTSD a major depressive disorder, sexual problems and personality disorder.

General damages were assessed at **£30,000.00.**

iv) Claimant D was subject to repeated acts of sexual abuse including touching the genital area, and oral sex. Abuse included killing the Claimant's pet squirrels and the forcing the Claimant to take part in boxing matches with older children, resulting in physical injury. As a result of this abuse the Claimant suffered psychological damage (not PTSD) and experienced difficulty with relationships.

General damages were assessed at **£25,000.00.**

v) Claimant E's allegation of a breakdown was not sustained but damages were awarded for physical assault, including forcing the Claimant to have her hair cut and to eat toast with unpleasant substances on. The Defendants were found not to be responsible for her considerable problems later in life.

General damages were assessed at **£2,500.00.**

vi) Claimant F was subjected to sexual intercourse instigated by a female member of staff whilst the Claimant was aged 15½ and oral sex which caused confusion and upset to the Claimant and difficulty in relationships.

General damages were assessed at **£5,000.00.**

vii) Claimant G was subjected to three incidents of sexual assault including masturbation.

General damages were assessed at **£2,000.00.**

Various claims against the Bryn Alyn Community Homes Limited June 2003

i) Claimant A was the victim of attempted buggery and a number of other physical assaults and was later diagnosed with PTSD and adjustment disorder, affecting relationships with others and employment.

General damages were assessed at **£35,000.00.**

ii) Claimant B was subjected to a regime of persistent assaults by various members of staff, as a result of which the Claimant suffered from a personality disorder and psychiatric illness.

General damages were assessed at **£35,000.00**.

iii) Claimant C suffered physical and sexual abuse including allegations of buggery. Physical abuse included cold showers, being forced to scrub floors, slapping, punching and beatings. The Claimant was found to be suffering from PTSD, although this was not severe.

General damages were assessed at **£25,000.00**.

iv) Claimant D was subjected to a violent regime, forced to scrub floors, punched, hair pulled and kicked. The Claimant's placement at the home was her 26th placement and she was found to be significantly damaged in any event.

General damages were assessed at **£5,000.00**.

v) Claimant E was subjected to inappropriate violence. The Claimant suffered significant problems in adulthood due to her experience elsewhere, although her time at the home was found to have caused some additional material damage.

General damages were assessed at **£5,000.00**.

vi) Claimant F was subjected to sexual abuse on 6 occasions. However, the claim was statute barred and the Court of Appeal held that deliberate abuse was subject to a 6 year non-extendable limitation period, in accordance with section 2 of the Limitation Act 1980. The Claimant did not develop an identifiable psychiatric disorder and the abuse did not have a major impact on his personality.

Had general damages been awarded they would have been under **£7,000.00**.

vii) Claimant G had suffered considerable abuse previously and upon arrival at the care home already had a history of petty crime and violence. He was subjected to sexual abuse, was buggered and offered to friends as a sexual plaything in return for presents and money. He was also physically abused, being slapped, punched, kicked, hit with a stick, forced to take cold showers and scrub floors. The Claimant had a criminal record and delayed chronic PTSD.

General damages were assessed at **£50,000.00**. In addition **£2,520.00** was awarded for the cost of therapy.

viii) Claimant H was indecently assaulted on a number of occasions. The Judge was prepared to attribute what might be called PTSD to the recollection of the abuse suffered.

General damages were assessed at **£12,000.00**. **£5,000.00** was awarded for the cost of therapy.

ix) Claimant I was sexually abused with a suggestion of buggery. She lost a child in 1990, which the Judge found had made a significant contribution to the symptoms of depression and to the borderline personality disorder from which she was considered to be suffering.

General damages were assessed at **£28,000.00**.

x) Claimant J was indecently assaulted, buggered and forced to masturbate in return for money and presents on approximately 30 occasions. He was also subjected to physical abuse through slapping and being forced to scrub floors. The Claimant suffered from a personality disorder, opiate dependence syndrome and PTSD with flashbacks, intrusive memories, nightmares and a poor sleep pattern.

General damages were assessed at **£45,000.00**. An award for future loss of employment was **£10,000.00** and for counselling was **£13,800.00**.

xi) Claimant K suffered indecent assaults over a significant period of time including mutual masturbation, oral sex and attempted buggery. He was rewarded with sweets and gifts. He also suffered physical abuse, being clipped around the ear, punched and kicked. The Claimant had delayed onset PTSD, Alcohol Dependence Syndrome and poor anger control.

General damages were assessed at **£50,000.00** with **£10,000.00** awarded for loss of earnings.

xii) Claimant L was subjected to violence. The Claimant suffered from chronic PTSD.

General damages were assessed at **£30,000.00** with **£4,000.00** awarded for the cost of therapy.

xiii Claimant M was physically and sexually abused, including oral sex, buggery and mutual masturbation. He attempted suicide on a couple of occasions and ran away several times. The Claimant suffered from PTSD.

General damages were assessed at **£35,000.00** with **£8,100.00** awarded for therapy.

xiv) Claimant N was kicked, bullied, indecently assaulted and buggered. The Claimant suffered from PTSD.

General damages were assessed at **£37,500.00**.

18.4 Limitation

Limitation is often one of the main issues in child abuse claims. Historically the period of limitation depended upon the cause of action giving rise to the claim. However, the House of Lords decision in ***A v Hoare & Others (2008)*** has radically changed the law of limitation, overruling the House of Lords earlier decision in ***Stubbings v Webb (1992)*** and reviewing the interaction of Sections 14 and 33 of the Limitation Act 1980. As a result of this decision the Courts are now entitled to treat Sections 11 to 14 as applying to tortious acts of abuse as well as negligent acts or omissions.

Trespass to the person

The general rule is that the period of limitation for an action in tort is 6 years from the date of which the cause of action accrues (Section 2 of the Limitation Act 1980). However, section 11 contains provisions that create a different regime for actions for "damages for negligence, nuisance or breach of duty where the damages are in respect of personal injuries". In such cases the limitation period is 3 years from either the date the course of action accrued or "the date of knowledge", as defined by section 14, whichever is the latest, although this period is extendable at the Court's discretion under section 33.

The relevant statutory provisions are set out below.

Prior to the recent House of Lords decision in ***A v Hoare & Others (2008)*** the Courts had no power to disapply the limitation period of 6 years where this applied in accordance with section 2 of the Act.

In the case of ***Stubbings v Webb*** the Claimant had been sexually abused by her stepfather and stepbrother during childhood. She was over 30 when she began proceedings and the abuse had ceased 15 years before issue of proceedings.

The issue in this matter was whether section 2 or section 11 of the Limitation Act applied to the claim. If section 2 applied the limitation period was six years from the date the cause of action arose (i.e. when the Claimant turned 18) and, therefore, the claim was statute barred. However, if section 11 applied the limitation period was three years from the date the Claimant realised that significant injury resulted from the abuse she suffered. The Claimant alleged she did not have knowledge of significant injury until 3 years prior to the date of issue of proceedings and, therefore, sought to rely upon section 11 of the **Limitation Act 1980.**

The House of Lords held that actions of intentional trespass to a person cannot be said to arise from negligence and common nuisance or breach of duty within section 11 and, therefore, section 2 must apply. The Claimant was therefore outside the limitation period and the claim was statute barred.

The case historically allowed the perpetrator of the abuse immunity after the expiry of the limitation period under section 2. However, a person who had allowed the abuse, usually in the context of a claim for vicarious liability, is vulnerable to a claim in negligence as this falls within the remit of section 11 and is, therefore, subject to the Courts discretion to extend the limitation period in accordance with section 33.

Limitation Period – key provisions

Section 11 – Special time limit for actions in respect of personal injuries

(1) This section applies to any action for damages for negligence, nuisance or breach of duty (whether the duty exists by virtue of a contract or of provision made by or under a statute or independently of any contract or any such provision) where the damages

claimed by the plaintiff for the negligence, nuisance or breach of duty consist of or include damages in respect of personal injuries to the plaintiff or any other person.

The period applicable is three years from:

(a) the date on which the cause of action accrued; or

(b) the date of knowledge (if later) of the person injured.

(2) If the person injured dies before the expiration of the period mentioned in the subsection above, the period applicable as respects the cause of action surviving for the benefit of his estate by virtue of section 1 of the Law Reform (Miscellaneous Provisions) Act 1934 shall be three years from:

(a) the date of death;

(b) the date of the personal representative's knowledge,

whichever is the later.

Section 14 – Definition of date of knowledge for purposes of sections 11 and 12

(1) [Subject to subsection (1A) below,] In sections 11 and 12 of this Act references to a person's date of knowledge are references to the date on which he first had knowledge of the following facts:

(a) that the injury in question was significant; and

(b) that the injury was attributable in whole or in part to the act or omission which is alleged to constitute negligence, nuisance or breach of duty; and

(c) the identity of the Defendant; and knowledge that any acts or omissions did or did not, as a matter of law, involve negligence, nuisance or breach of duty is irrelevant.

(d) if it is alleged that the act or omission was that of a person other than the Defendant, the identity of that person and the additional facts supporting the bringing of an action against the Defendant;

(2) For the purposes of this section an injury is significant if the person whose date of knowledge is in question would reasonably have considered it sufficiently serious to justify his instituting proceedings for damages against a Defendant who did not dispute liability and was able to satisfy a judgment.

(3) For the purposes of this section a person's knowledge includes knowledge which he might reasonably have been expected to acquire:-

(a) from facts observable or ascertainable by him; or

(b) from facts ascertainable by him with the help of medical or other appropriate expert advice which it is reasonable for him to seek; but a person shall not be fixed under this subsection with knowledge of a fact ascertainable only with the help of expert advice so long as he has taken all reasonable steps to obtain (and, where appropriate, to act on) that advice.

A v Hoare & Others (2008)

This case overruled the House of Lords earlier decision in ***Stubbings v Webb***.

The case concerned a retired teacher who had brought a claim against her attacker 19 years after the attack occurred. The Defendant, Mr Hoare, won 7 million pounds in the lottery in 2004 whilst serving a custodial sentence for his attack on the Claimant. Prior to this win the Defendant had not been worth suing, however, upon hearing of the Defendant's change in circumstances Mrs A brought a claim which was unsuccessful in the first instance due to the House of Lords earlier decision in ***Stubbings v Webb,*** which restricted the limitation period to a non-extendable period of 6 years.

Lord Hoffman identified that before the law recognised potential vicarious liability on the employers for acts of assault there had been little effect of the earlier decision on the perpetrator of assaults who was seldom worth suing. He commented that in ***Stubbings*** the

Claimant seemed to be motivated with something other than the recovery of compensation.

The historical anominally of the different treatment of limitation cases was put starkly in the case of ***S v W (Child Abuse Damages 1995)***, in which the Plaintiff sued her father and mother for sexual abuse she had suffered at the hands of her father. The action was commenced nearly 10 years after the last act of abuse.

The cause of action against the father was intentional assault, and the claim was therefore struck out as statute barred under section 2. The cause of action against the mother, however, was negligent failure to protect the Plaintiff against the father. As such, this fell under section 11 of the 1980 Act and was subject to a discretionary extension under section 33, which the Judge granted, and the Court of Appeal later affirmed. The action against the mother was therefore allowed to proceed. The result of this case was commented on as being *"illogical and a surprise"* and deserving of the attention of the Law Commission.

As such, in abuse cases where the claim against the perpetrator of abuse (or his or her employer by way of vicarious liability) has become statute barred in accordance with section 2 of the Act, it had to be established that the abuse suffered was the result of systemic negligence on the part of the abuser's employer in order that the limitation period under section 11 can be applied and the Claimant can be awarded damages against the employer on the grounds of negligence. This has been the case notwithstanding the fact that in such cases the real cause of complaint is clearly the abuse for which the employer was vicariously liable.

It was for this reason that the House of Lords departed from the decision in ***Stubbings v Webb***.

The House of Lords went on to consider a number of other appeals along with ***A v Hoare***.

In the case of ***C v Middlesbrough Council (2004)*** the appellant claimed to have been sexually abused at various times between 1982 and 1988. At the trial in the first instance the Judge found the appellant had been subjected to sexual abuse and the Council were vicariously liable and, had the action come within section 11 of the 1980 Act, he would have exercised his discretion to allow it to proceed. However, in accordance with the earlier decision in ***Stubbings*** he held the action was barred by section 2 and dismissed allegations vicarious liability against the Council. However, the House of Lords judgment in relation to ***A v Hoare*** applied equally to this case and, therefore, the matter came within section 11 of the Limitation Act and the Court exercised its discretion under section 33 to extend the limitation period for bringing the claim.

In ***A v Suffolk County Council (2006)*** the Claimant claimed that while residing in a school for difficult children managed by the Council during 1989 and 1990, he was sexually abused by a member of staff. The question of limitation was tried as a preliminary point by the Judge in the first instance and in accordance with ***Stubbings*** it was held that the claim against the Council on the grounds of vicarious liability for the actions of the member of staff was statute barred by section 2. The Judge also tried and dismissed a claim based on allegations of negligence against the Council.

However, once it had overturned the ruling in ***Stubbings***, the House of Lords was able to allow the appeal against the ruling on limitation only and the case reverted back to the Judge in the first instance to decide whether he should exercise his discretion under section 33 and allow the claim to proceed.

The House of Lords dealt with the case of ***X & Y v Wandsworth London Borough Council*** in a similar way.

Consideration of Section 14 (2) of the Limitation Act 1980

In ***A v Hoare*** the House of Lords also considered whether the test regarding the Claimant's knowledge that she or he had sustained a sufficiently serious injury was an objective or subjective one pursuant to section 14(2). The House of Lords held that section 14 must run from the date that the Claimant had knowledge of certain facts, rather than from the date when he or she could have been expected to take certain steps. The House of Lords referred to Lord Griffiths' comments in ***Stubbings v Webb*** and he stated that he had *"the greatest difficulty in accepting the woman who knew that she had been raped did not know that she had suffered a serious injury"*.

This did not mean that the law regards as irrelevant the question of whether the actual Claimant, taking into account her psychological state in consequence of the injury, could reasonably have been expected to institute proceedings, but it deals with that question under section 33 which specifically provides that one of the matters to be taken into account is the "reason for delay on the part of the Plaintiff".

Exercise of Section 33 discretion

When considering the exercise of section 33 discretion in ***A v Hoare***, Lord Hoffman rejected the Court of Appeal's approach in ***Bryn v Alyn (2006)*** that delay in bringing a claim was a product of the abuse and, therefore, a matter best dealt with under section 14, stating *"I am of precisely the opposite view, if the Lords agree the approach to the discretion will have to change"*. Lord Hoffman's views were accepted and Lord Brown added the following guidance in relation to the discretion under Section 33:

i) In so far as future claims may be expected to be brought against employers on the basis of vicarious liability rather than for systemic negligence in failing to prevent them, they would probably involve altogether narrower factual disputes than before. This is likely to bear significantly upon the possibility of having a fair trial.

ii) Through the combined effects of ***Lister*** and ***Stubbings*** a substantially greater number of allegations are now likely to be made many years after the abuse complained of. Whether the Defendant can investigate (and therefore lead to a fair trial) depends on a number of factors, not least when the complaint was first made and to what effect the complaint was resolved. For example, was there a prosecution against the abuser, or did the allegations come out of the blue with no apparent support for them? A fair trial, which must include a fair opportunity for the Defendant to investigate the allegations, is in many cases likely to be found quite simply impossible after such a long delay.

The misconstruction of Section 14 (2) has given an absolute right to proceed to anyone able to say that he would not reasonably turn his mind to litigation (more than 3 years earlier). Section 33 will not invariably replicate that position.

Section 33 – Discretionary exclusion of time limit for actions in respect of personal injuries or death

(1) If it appears to the court that it would be equitable to allow an action to proceed having regard to the degree to which:-

(a) the provisions of section 11 [or 11A] or 12 of this Act prejudice the plaintiff or any person whom he represents; and

(b) any decision of the court under this subsection would prejudice the Defendant or any person whom he represents; the court may direct that those provisions shall not apply to the action, or shall not apply to any specified cause of action to which the action relates.

[(1A) The court shall not under this section disapply;-

(a) subsection (3) of section 11A; or

(b) where the damages claimed by the plaintiff are confined to damages for loss of or damage to any property, any other provision in its application to an action by virtue of Part I of the Consumer Protection Act 1987.]

(2) The court shall not under this section disapply section 12(1) except where the reason why the person injured could no longer maintain an action was because of the time limit in section 11 [or subsection (4) of section 11A].

If, for example, the person injured could at his death no longer maintain an action under the Fatal Accidents Act 1976 because of the time limit in Article 29.

(3) In acting under this section the court shall have regard to all the circumstances of the case and in particular to

(a) the length of, and the reasons for, the delay on the part of the plaintiff;

(b) the extent to which, having regard to the delay, the evidence adduced or likely to be adduced by the plaintiff or the Defendant is or is likely to be less cogent than if the action had been brought within the time allowed by section 11 [, by section 11A] or (as the case may be) by section 12;

(c) the conduct of the Defendant after the cause of action arose, including the extent (if any) to which he responded to requests reasonably made by the plaintiff for information or inspection for the purpose of ascertaining facts which were or might be relevant to the plaintiff's cause of action against the Defendant;

(d) the accrual of the cause of action;

(e) the extent to which the plaintiff acted promptly and reasonably once he knew whether or not the act or omission of the Defendant, to which the injury was attributable, might be capable at that time of giving rise to an action for damages;

(f) the steps, if any, taken by the plaintiff to obtain medical, legal or other expert advice and the nature of any such advice he may have received.

(4) In a case where the person injured died when, because of section 11 [or subsection (4) of section 11A], he could no longer maintain an action and recover damages in respect of the injury, the court shall have regard in particular to the length of, and the reasons for, the delay on the part of the deceased.

(5) In a case under subsection (4) above, or any other case where the time limit, or one of the time limits, depends on the date of knowledge of a person other than the plaintiff, subsection (3) above shall have effect with appropriate modifications, and shall have effect in particular as if references to the plaintiff included references to any person whose date of knowledge is or was relevant in determining a time limit.

(6) A direction by the court disapplying the provisions of section 12(1) shall operate to disapply the provisions to the same effect in section 1(1) of the **Fatal Accidents Act 1976.**

(7) In this section "the court" means the court in which the action has been brought.

(8) References in this section to section 11 [or 11A] include references to that section as extended by any of the preceding provisions of this Part of this Act or by any provision of Part III of this Act.

In ***Lister v Hesley Hall Limited (2001)*** the House of Lords found the Defendants vicariously liable for the action of the warden. In this case the Court was entitled to apply the criteria in relation to the date of knowledge. The Claimant's date of knowledge are references to the date upon which the Claimant had knowledge of the following facts:

i) The injury was significant – ***Dobbie v Medway Health Authority (1994) 1WLR*** established that time does not run against a Claimant even if he is aware of the injury if he reasonably accepted it as a fact of life and not worth bothering about, and in accordance with Section 14 (1) (b) that the injury was attributable in whole or in part to the act or omission which is alleged to constitute negligence, nuisance or breach of statutory duty.

   For example a claim where the Claimant was unlikely to know what checks the Defendant (the Care Home) carried out and the wardens to reveal any history or sexual offences. A failure might be the only basis upon which fault could be alleged. In this case the result was that the Claimant's relevant date of knowledge was the date that the Claimant discovered that the Defendant knew or ought to have known of the warden's conviction.

ii) Actual constructive knowledge can be decided with reference to all of the sections listed above. The knowledge of facts will include those facts which the Claimant could have been expected to acquire directly or with the help of an expert (e.g. medical or legal). The test to apply is one of objectivity.

The most important decision in relation to the interpretation of section 33, prior to ***A v Hoare,*** was the Court of Appeal decision in ***KR v Bryn Alyn Community (Holdings) Limited (February 2003)*** which provided useful guidance.

In all cases of abuse in ***Bryn Alyn*** the Court exercised its discretion under section 33 and extended the limitation period for claims to be issued against the Defendants.

Section 33 provides the Court with an opportunity to waive limitation and provides a non-exhaustive list of circumstances to which the Court should have regard. The burden of showing that it would be equitable to disapply the limitation period rests on the Claimant and it is a heavy burden. The longer the delay in issuing proceedings, the greater the prejudice to the Defendant and, therefore, the less likely the Court will be to exercise its discretion.

The Court of Appeal held that the Judge at first instance in Bryn Alyn was flawed in exercising discretion under section 33 in a number of cases. The outcome of the application of section 33 depends on firstly whether the Judge correctly found the Claimant to be barred under section 14 so as to engage his discretion under section 33, and secondly if the case should have found a later date which would still have barred the claim, it would have been equitable to exercise his discretion.

However following the decision in ***A v Hoare*** in particular Lord Hoffman and Lord Brown comments the section 14 discretion exercised in this case should have been dealt with pursuant to section 33. Please see earlier comments on the case of ***A v Hoare*** for further guidance.

Cases of Vicarious Liability and Limitation

Prior to the decision in ***A v Hoare*** unless the Claimant could demonstrate systemic abuse on the part of the employee rather than relying on the acts of the abuser themselves, cases were susceptible to the non-extendable 6 year limitation period for tortious acts under section 2 of the Act. However, since the decision in ***A v Hoare*** no such distinction is necessary. The Courts no longer have to carry out an exercise in intellectual gymnastics to find physical acts of abuse caused by systemic negligence on the part of employees, they are now able to apply sections 11 to 14 to all types of causes of action, and where applicable review whether a it is appropriate to extend the limitation period under section 33.

The correct approach, therefore, is to identify the wrongful act, deliberate or otherwise, in respect of which vicarious liability is claimed and to assess the closeness of its connection to the employment in question.

Conclusion

The application of the limitation issue had led to a situation where if the Claimant brought a claim against the abuser directly for trespass then the claim would be statute barred pursuant to section 2 with no exercise of discretion. However, in cases where the Defendants have been arguably less culpable for breach of duty (such as managers in care homes), the Claimant could ask the Court to exercise discretion pursuant to Section 33 of the Limitation Act. This anomaly has now been overturned with the decision in ***A v Hoare.***

19 HOUSING DISREPAIR CLAIMS

19 HOUSING DISREPAIR CLAIMS

Contents

19.1 Introduction

This chapter deals with claims brought by tenants against their Landlords for breach of covenants either expressly stated in the tenancy agreement or implied by statute. Claims have recently been subject to a new pre-action protocol which came into force in December 2003. The protocol governs the pre-action behaviour between the parties. As with other protocols the overriding objective is to resolve claims without recourse to litigation. There are a variety of remedies open to tenants including an application for an injunction to remedy continuing breaches of the Landlords' repairing obligations. The most common remedies will be for damages and orders for repairs to be carried out.

19.2 Causes of Action

The most important section under which most claims for disrepair are brought is Section 11 of the **Landlord and Tenant Act 1985**.

Section 11 (1)

Under Section 11 the two aspects of the Landlord's responsibility are to keep in repair the structure and exterior of the property and keeping in repair and working order the installations of the house.

Do the complaints give rise to a liability?

- ***Cresswell v Sandwell Metropolitan Borough Council (2000)*** – outbuildings consisting of a garden shed, a coal store and WC were not 'structure and exterior' for the purposes of s11 Landlord and Tenant Act 1985.
- ***O'Connor and Ors v Old Etonian Housing Association Ltd (2002)*** – the court offered guidance as to the meaning of the s11 phrase 'keep in ...proper working order' in relation to water pipes. The issue was whether the local authority was liable for the failure in water supply due to a fall in pressure of the supply coupled with the pipes fitted by the local authority being too small.
- ***Sam-Yorke v Jawad (2002)*** – failure to service a gas fire was a breach of duty under s11(1)(c) Landlord and Tenant Act 1985. However with no evidence of any inconvenience caused by the breach no damages were awarded.
- ***Southwark London Borough Council v McIntosh (2001)*** – The landlord was not under an obligation to warn the tenant not to dry clothes in the heated cupboard.
- ***Liliana Montoya v Hackney London Borough Council (2004)*** – An expert assessed the defects as commensurate with the age and type of property and were therefore not disrepair under s11 Landlord and Tenant Act. The judge departed from this opinion. On appeal it was held that there was no evidence to support this course of action and the appeal was allowed.
- ***Ruth Lee v Leeds County Council (2002): Ratcliffe and Ors v Sandwell Metropolitan Borough Council (2002)*** - Defects in design do not fall under s11 Landlord and Tenant Act 1985.
- ***Welsh v Greenwich London Borough Council (2000)*** – condensation and mould were conceded to not be disrepair. However a term in the tenancy agreement increased the

landlord's obligation beyond that normally understood by repair to render him liable.

Brown v The Liverpool Corporation (1969) & Hopwood v Cannock Chase District Council (1974)

The ***Brown*** case involved a Claimant who had fallen on steps which were in a state of disrepair leading to a path which gave access to the property. The question for the Court of Appeal was whether the steps and pathway were an integral part of the building. In this instance the Court found that they were so attached to the manner of the house in order to gain access that they were.

In the case of ***Hopwood*** again in the Court of Appeal the facts were slightly different, normal access was from the front of the house, although egress of the property was also possible from the rear of the property from the back door through a yard. The Claimant's accident was in the yard. On this occasion the Court of Appeal chose to distinguish ***Brown*** on the basis that it was not the primary route of access.

This seems an artificial distinction, and it is noteworthy that the Court were influenced by the fact that in the ***Brown*** case the Council knew about the defective step, had known about it for sometime and had promised to mend it.

19.3 Dampness and Condensation

- ***Sally Ann Ball and Mark Anthony Ball v Plymouth County Council (2004)*** – the Claimants failed to prove causation in relation to the dampness. The dampness must be caused by an actionable defect.
- ***Hassib v Hackney London Borough Council (2002)*** – damages of £3,600 were awarded for 3 years of disrepair caused by dampness.
- ***Southwark London Borough Council v Denisia McIntosh (2001)*** – damp in itself did not evidence a breach of s11 Landlord and Tenant Act 1985. It was up to the tenant to establish that the damp arose from either damage to the structure or exterior, or that damp had caused damage to the structure or exterior, which had then caused the damp.

- ***Ruth Lee v Leeds County Council (2002): Ratcliffe and Ors v Sandwell Metropolitan Borough Council (2002)*** – damp caused by a defect in design did not fall under s11 Landlord and Tenant Act 1985.
- ***Welsh v Greenwich London Borough Council (2000)*** – condensation and mould were conceded to not be disrepair.

A large majority of disrepair claims arise from some form of damp in the property. Where the dampness has been caused by condensation there is often a dispute as to whether the dampness is caused by a defect to the structure of the property, or poor usage/design. In the ***Quick v Taff-Ely Borough Council (1985)*** the Claimant was a Council tenant whose property suffered from severe condensation caused by a combination of window lintels, metal frame windows, and inadequate heating and ventilation. The Court of Appeal rejected the argument that anything defective or inherently inefficient for living in or ineffective to provide the conditions of ordinary habitation is to be considered an aspect of disrepair. In other words just because there was a problem affecting the habitation of the property or the design, it did not automatically follow that there was a failure to repair.

However, in the case of ***Leach City Council*** the Defendant alleged the dampness in the property was caused by condensation. Three years after the complaints the Council cured the condensation problem. The Council were not helped by a letter referring to the plaster being so saturated it required replacement. The test so far as the Court were concerned was does the repair relate to the psychical condition of whatever has to be repaired? A stay was considered in the case of ***Irvine's Estate v Moran (1990)***. The question for the Court on considering dampness was set out, the structure of the dwelling house consists of those elements of the overall dwelling house which gives its essential appearance, stability and shape. "Plaster is more a decorative finish". The view that the plaster made up part of the psychical structure of the property was questioned as only a decorative finish.

Notice

- ***Jeffers v West Lancashire District Council (2002)*** – it is reasonable for the local authority to expect the tenants to report any disrepair. (Occupiers Liability Act 1984)

- ***Sykes v Harry (2001)*** – under s11 Landlord and Tenant Act 1985 the Landlord must have notice of a defect to be in breach. This is in contrast to s4 Defective Premises Act 1972 under which the landlord was found liable for the defective gas fire.

The Landlord must be put on notice of the defective premises. The tenant must demonstrate unreasonable delay. In cases where the Landlord has the right of entry to the property the Landlord still has to be put on notice of the defect. In the case of ***Morris v Liverpool City Council (1987)*** the Fire Brigade had to force entry to the property as a result of which the front door had to be replaced. However, before the Council had an opportunity to replace the front door the property was burgled. The Court of Appeal held that the duty of the Court was to explore the reasonableness of the delay. In this case the factors included difficulty in obtaining and fitting the door, including the Council's workload and steps taken to secure the property.

19.4 Damages Remedies

- ***English Churches Housing Group v Avrom Shine (2004)*** – when making an award of damages under s11 Landlord and Tenant Act 1985 the guidance in ***Wallace v Manchester City Council (1998)*** should be applied or clear reasons given for departing from that guidance.
- ***Mitchell v Barnsley Metropolitan Borough Council (2003)*** – general damages of £300 per year for 2 years were awarded
- ***Welsh v Greenwich London Borough Council (2000)*** - £9,000 damages were awarded for disrepair during the 4 years residence in the council flat.

The usual remedies for disrepair will be:

1. Damages for inconvenience and discomfort
2. Special damages
3. Interim Injunction
4. Personal injury
5. Diminution in value
6. Specific performance

19.5 Damages for Inconvenience and Discomfort.

- ***Peirce v City of Westminster (2001)*** – the property was affected by subsidence. The court held that although the interference with enjoyment of the property was low there had been real disruption to the Claimant's life. Damages of £5,450 were awarded.
- ***Mulligan v Halton Borough Council (1999)*** – damages were awarded in relation to inconvenience and discomfort of £1,750 per year.
- ***English Churches Housing Group v Avrom Shine (2004)*** – any award for stress and inconvenience should be related to the fact that the tenant is not getting value for the rent being paid. The award is for breach of contract not tort.

The limitation period for claims under this heading is 6 years prior to issue.

i) ***Wallace v Manchester City Council (1998)***

In ***Wallace*** the Court of Appeal recognised an unofficial tariff of between £1,000 and £2,700 per year for each year the property was considered to be in a state of disrepair;

ii) ***Elmcroft Developments Ltd v Tankersley – Sawyer (1984)***

In ***Elmcroft*** the award was £2,600 per annum for a 2 year period where the property was affected by severe rising damp. The Court also took into account that the flat was in an expensive and fashionable part of town.

iii) ***Chiodi v De Marney (1988)***

In ***Chiodi*** the award was £2,600 for severe water penetration. There had been no hot water and there were electrical problems, and damaged windows.

iv) ***Brent LBC v Carmel (1995)***

In ***Brent*** the award was for £3,000 for water penetration throughout the whole flat, there was no central heating and two out of three bedrooms were uninhabitable.

v) ***Calabar Properties Limited v Sticher (1983)***

The disrepair had been over a 5 year period during which there had been substantial water penetration affecting the tenants health. An award of £1,200 per year was made.

19.6 Special Damages

- ***Mitchell v Barnsley Metropolitan Borough Council (2003)*** - £70 was awarded in relation to repairs.

These usually include the following types of items:

i) re-decoration costs;

ii) extra heating costs;

iii) replacement furniture;

iv) other personal belongings.

Receipts should be produced for all items claimed. There may be an issue of betterment to be considered.

Interim Injunction

In cases where the tenant alleges continuing breach of the Landlord's repairing obligations the tenant may apply to the Court for an interim injunction compelling the Landlord to carry out repairs to stop a continuing breach. The Courts recognise that by their very nature the granting of an injunction is an onerous obligation and will usually involve the Council in outlay. The Courts are therefore reluctant to grant this remedy. The leading authority is the decision in ***Parker v Camden LBC (1985)***. The Court held:

i) that the work required must be agreed between the parties, or it must be clear what needs to be done i.e. there should not be substantial dispute between the surveyors

ii) the circumstances must be exceptional, e.g. there is an immediate risk to health and safety.

Personal injury

- ***Mulligan v Halton Borough Council (1999)*** – aggravation of pre existing asthma led to an award of £1,000.

- ***L (A Child) v Empire Estates (2002)*** – a 6-year-old girl's asthma was exacerbated by the damp conditions. General damages of £1,750 were awarded.
- ***C (A Child) v Empire Estates (2002)*** – a baby boy developed asthma while living in a damp property. Although it was felt he would have been likely to develop it anyway later in life due to the family history, general damages of £8,500 were awarded.
- ***Conroy v Hire Token Ltd (2001)*** – claim brought under s4 Defective Premises Act 1972 for 2 children's chest conditions. No treatment was ever sought nor any diagnosis of asthma obtained, but general damages of £650 for each child were awarded.

Damages will usually be on the low side although claims for minors will be higher. Claims will need to be substantiated with medical evidence, and it is worth checking the medical records as the Claimant may have suffered from the condition irrespective of the accident, or the claim might be limited to an exacerbation of the existing condition. The types of personal injury include pneumonia, depression, asthma, and bronchitis.

Diminution in value – *Wallace v Manchester City Council (1998)*

- ***Hassib v Hackney London Borough Council (2002)*** – the guidelines in ***Wallace v Manchester City Council*** were held to be more useful in assessing damages than diminution in value.

In ***Wallace*** the Court of Appeal stated that there is no requirement to calculate this loss separately for damages for inconvenience and discomfort. If the claim is pleaded separately expert evidence from the surveyor will be necessary to formulate the difference in the value of the property in the state of disrepair against the usual rental value. For example a three-roomed flat where only two rooms are habitable the formulation would be a value of a two-roomed as opposed to a three-roomed flat.

19.7 Specific performance

Specific performance would be to force the Landlord to carry out the terms of the tenancy agreement. The order must be clear, and in normal circumstances you would expect the surveyor or experts to draw up a schedule of works to be agreed between the parties if possible together with a realistic time scale.

Failure to comply with an injunction can lead to committal proceedings for contempt of Court. The Court Order can be served on a suitable officer of the Local Authority who may be committed for that breach.

Human Rights Act 1998

- ***Ruth Lee v Leeds County Council (2002): Ratcliffe and Ors v Sandwell Metropolitan Borough Council (2002)*** – discussed the effect of the Act on Landlords' obligations under s11 Landlord and Tenant Act 1985. The Landlord was under no obligation to rectify design faults as a result of the HRA 1998.

19.8 The Housing Disrepair Protocol

The protocol came into force in December 2003. As with other protocols the Housing Disrepair protocol governs the behaviour of the parties pre-litigation. The specific aims of the protocol are:

i) to avoid unnecessary litigation;

ii) appropriate carrying out of any repairs which are the Landlord's responsibility,

iii) to ensure that tenants receive any compensation to which they are entitled to as speedily as possible;

iv) to promote good pre-litigation practice including the early exchange of information, and to give guidance about the instruction of experts, and to keep the costs of resolving disputes down.

Areas covered by the protocol

Please note that there are civil claims arising from the condition of residential properties that may include a related personal injury claim;

- Section 11.9 of the Tenant Act 1983;
- Section 4 of the Defective Premises Act 1974;
- Common law claims touches negligence and nuisance;

- Claims brought by tenants and tenants include lessees and members of the tenant's family.

Key components of the protocol

The protocol will be triggered by either writing:

i) an early notification letter by the Claimant or the Claimant's solicitors or;

ii) a letter of claim by the Claimant or the Claimant's solicitors.

The protocol envisages writing an early notification letter but either type of letter may be received.

The parties' responsibilities:

The Tenant	The Landlord
As early as possible notification letter sent to Landlord. May not be necessary if repair is urgent.	Respond to early notification letter within 20 days of receipt.
Letter should give basic details, should request disclosure from the Landlord, and should have authorisation signed by tenant, should propose an expert.	Disclosure of all relevant documents including tenancy agreement, documents, and all records relating to notice of disrepair and inspection reports.
Letter of instruction to expert	Whether or not the letter of instruction is agreed. If the appointment of a single expert is not agreed whether the Landlord agrees to a joint inspection

Experts

It will not always be necessary for a tenant to instruct an expert if for example only damages are in issue.

The expert should be instructed to report on all items of disrepair which the Landlord will reasonably need to know about. The expert should provide a schedule of works, an estimate of costs of repair, and a separate list if any urgent works are required.

The tenant would have proposed an early expert in either the early notification letter or the Letter of Claim. The Landlord within 20 days of receipt of the proposal can object to the expert, but if he fails to do so the tenant will instruct the proposed expert as a single joint expert. If no agreement is reached on the proposed experts the parties should try and agree an alternative expert.

Time limits

The property should be inspected within 20 working days. Where there is a joint inspection the experts should produce an agreed schedule of works detailing:

i) the defects of the required works which are agreed and the time table for the agreed works;

ii) the areas of disagreement and the reasons for disagreement;

The agreed schedule should be sent to both the Landlord and the tenant within 10 working days of the joint inspection.

If there is a single joint expert, a copy of the report should be sent to both the Landlord and the tenant within 10 working days of the inspection. Either party can ask questions of the expert.

Other options

Other options should be considered before application of the protocol. The Claimant should be encouraged to pursue other avenues. For Council tenants these include:

i) Local Authorities repairs and complaints procedure;

ii) The Right to Repair Scheme;

iii) The Local Government Ombudsman.

With private Landlords the tenants should consider:

i) The Independent Housing Ombudsman;

ii) The Local Authority Environmental Health Officers.

A copy of the full protocol is reproduced below.

There is implied a covenant by the Lessor:

a) To keep in repair the structure and exterior of the dwelling house (including drains, gutters and external pipes);

b) To keep in repair and working order installations in the dwelling house for the supply of water, gas and electricity and for sanitation (basins, sinks, baths and sanitary conveniences, but not other fixtures, fittings and appliances for the use of the supply of water, gas or electricity), and;

c) To keep in repair and proper working order the installations in the dwelling house for the space heating and heating water.

Notice

In order for a Landlord to be liable a tenant must demonstrate that the Landlord has been given notice of the defect and given an opportunity to effect repairs.

20 THE ROAD TRAFFIC ACT 1988 – THIRD PARTY LIABILITIES

20 THE ROAD TRAFFIC ACT 1988 – THIRD PARTY LIABILITIES

Contents

20.1 INTRODUCTION

The main requirements regarding compulsory insurance or security against third party risks are contained in sections 143-159 of the Road Traffic Act 1988 and are summarised in the following table:

Section of the Road Traffic Act 1988	Ground covered
S 143	Establishes the requirement to insure against third party risks.
S 144	Provides the alternative of depositing a sum with the Accountant General of the Supreme Court and provides exemptions from the need to insure to local government, the police, the armed forces and the National Health Service, although in practice most of these bodies will in fact carry insurance.
S 145	Specifies who may issue a policy of insurance and what the policy must cover.
S 146	Makes similar provision in respect of the provision of securities.
S 147	Deals with the issue and surrender of Certificates of Insurance and of Security.
S 148	Greatly restricts the ability of an insurer to avoid liability to third parties by reason of breach of policy condition.
S 149	Prohibits the avoidance of liability to passengers by agreement.
S 150	Aimed at preventing restrictions in the use of the vehicle under the insurance policy from preventing the vehicle from being used in a car-sharing scheme.
S 151	Deals with the duty of insurers to satisfy Judgments against persons insured under their policy.
S 152	Sets out the circumstances in which insurers would not have to meet such Judgments.
S 153	Preserves the rights of third parties to claim against insured parties who have become bankrupt.
S 154	Establishes the duty of a person against whom a claim is made to provide details of his insurance.

S 155	Deals with deposits.
S 156	Deals with the duty to provide details of insurance when applying for a vehicle excise licence.
S 157-159	Deals with medical treatment following an accident.

20.2 Who must Insure?

Subject to the exceptions set out in S 144 and summarised above, any person who uses or causes or permits any other person to use a motor vehicle on a road or other public place must have insurance. Use does not simply mean driving but can include having a car laid-up on a road. The duty to insure lies not simply on the owner but also on the user.

If the owner of a vehicle permits another person to drive the vehicle whilst there is no insurance in force, both would be guilty of an offence.

Definitions

A motor vehicle is a mechanically propelled vehicle intended or adapted for use on roads.

A road does not simply mean a highway but includes any other road to which the public has access.

"Other public place", is a place to which the public at large have access and is not a place where people are permitted to be because of some special characteristic or reason personal to themselves.

You should note that until 3 April 2000 this Section of the Act referred only to road and not to other public places. The change was brought into effect by the Motor Vehicles (Compulsory Insurance) Regulations 2000 (SI200/726).

20.3 Who can Issue an Insurance Policy?

An insurance policy can only be issued by an authorised insurer. That is any person or body of persons carrying on motor vehicle insurance business in Great Britain, that is within the Insurance Companies Act 1982. The authorised insurer must also be a member of the Motor Insurers' Bureau.

20.4 What Risks Must the Insurance Cover?

Insurance must cover:

i) liability for death of or bodily injury to any person;

ii) liability for damage to property limited to £1,000,000;

iii) liability incurred in respect of emergency treatment,

caused by or arising out of the use of the vehicle on a road or other public place in Great Britain.

The policy must also provide insurance cover in respect of any liability which may be incurred in respect of the use of the vehicle and of any trailer whether or not coupled, within the territory of each of the other member states of the European Community, up to the standards set by the law on compulsory insurance within the state in which the vehicle is being used, or up to the standard set by the **Road Traffic Act 1988** (RTA 1988), whichever is higher.

The requirement to cover liability for damage is restricted to £1,000,000 and that is the sum of all liabilities arising out of one accident. There is no requirement to cover liability in respect of damage to the vehicle itself, to cover liability in respect of damage to goods carried for hire or reward within the vehicle, or to cover liability in respect of goods which are within the custody or the control of the insured person or to cover any contractual liability.

In respect of personal injury, exceptions that relate to employees are complex and will be dealt with separately.

20.5 Certificates of Insurance

The Certificate of Insurance is a vitally important document. The policy of insurance is of no effect unless and until the Certificate is delivered by the insurer to the person by whom the policy is effected.

A "Cover Note" will contain a Certificate of Insurance otherwise the provisions of the RTA 1988 will not apply. It is the delivery of the Certificate that establishes an insurer's obligations under the Act. If the policy is cancelled, it is only with the return of the Certificate, subject to exceptions, which we shall deal with under s 152 of the RTA 1988, that an insurer's liability ceases under the Act.

For that reason there is an obligation on the insured person to surrender the Certificate of Insurance within seven days of cancellation (s 147(4)(a)) or if the Certificate has been lost or destroyed make a statutory declaration to that effect (s 147(4)(b)).

It is a criminal offence not to return the Certificate or make a statutory declaration in those circumstances (s 147(5)).

There is no reason why an insurer should not lay an information in the Magistrates' Court if a Certificate is not returned although in practice it is cheaper and quicker to bring an action in the County Court for the delivery of the Certificate.

20.6 Avoidance of Certain Exceptions in Policies

It is quite likely that an insurer will have conditions in his policy regarding the user of the vehicle, the condition of the vehicle and the use of the vehicle. It is quite reasonable that an insurer should do so. An insurer may not want to cover an 18 year old driving a powerful car. They will certainly not want a car driven in an un-roadworthy condition.

An insurer will also no doubt have conditions in his policy as to what must be done in the event of an accident. There will no doubt be a requirement for the reporting of the accident and again it is quite reasonable that this should be so.

Nonetheless, Section 148 prevents an insurer from avoiding his liability to a third party who has suffered injury or damage by reason of the insured person's breach of certain conditions. The conditions in question are as follows:

- the age or physical or mental condition of the persons driving the vehicle;
- the condition of the vehicle;
- the number of persons that the vehicle carries;
- the weight or physical characteristics of the goods that the vehicle carries;
- the time at which or the areas in which the vehicle is used;
- the horse power or cylinder capacity of the vehicle;

- the carrying on the vehicle of any particular apparatus;
- the carrying on the vehicle of any particular means of identification other than any means of identification required to be carried by or under the **Vehicles Excise Act 1971;**
- conditions relating to requirements of some specified thing being done or being omitted to be done after the happening of the event giving rise to the claim under the policy.

Where the insurer has had to meet claims only by reason of the provisions of this section of the Act, he is entitled to recover the money from his insured. In respect of the first 8 types of condition referred to above, the right to recover lies directly in this section of the Act (s 148(4)).

Where it relates to the doing of or the failing to do something following the occurrence of the incident which leads to the claim, then this section of the Act permits the insurer to have a policy condition which requires the repayment of the monies (s 148(6)).

20.7 Duty of Insurers to Satisfy Judgments

Section 151(5) requires an insurer to meet Judgments under the following conditions where:

- a Certificate of Insurance has been delivered under Section 147 of the Act to the person effecting the insurance;
- a Judgment has actually been obtained;
- the Judgment is in respect of a liability which is required to be covered by a policy of insurance under Section 145 of the Act (see above);
- it is a liability covered by the terms of the policy;
- the vehicle is being used in a way which is not excluded under the terms of the policy or if it is excluded the exclusion falls into one of the categories deemed to be of no effect by Section 148 of the Act.

Despite the fact that the insurer may be entitled to avoid or cancel the policy and indeed may already have avoided or cancelled the policy, if all the other conditions are met, nonetheless the insurer must meet the Judgment.

These conditions if they stood alone would still permit the insurer to avoid liability if the vehicle was being used by someone who was not permitted to use the vehicle under the policy or did not hold a driving licence.

However s 151(3) prevents the insurer from avoiding payment if the user of the vehicle does not hold a driving licence and s 151(2)(b) provides that as long as the liability is not an excluded liability the policy will be treated as covering all persons. Therefore the insurer will have to satisfy a Judgment obtained against any person using the vehicle whether or not his liability is covered under the policy.

20.7.1 Excluded Liability

In this context an excluded liability means a liability in respect of the death of or bodily injury to, or damage to the property of, any person who at the time of the use which gave rise to the liability was allowing himself to be carried in or upon the vehicle and knew or had reason to believe that the vehicle had been stolen or unlawfully taken. If, however, the person concerned only became aware that the vehicle had been unlawfully taken after the commencement of his journey and could not then have reasonably been expected to alight from the vehicle, it will not be an excluded liability.

20.7.2 Calculations of Sums Payable under Judgment

The sums payable under the Judgment are damages, interest and costs.

In respect of death and personal injury, the sum payable is the total amount of damages, interest and costs. In respect of damage there is a more complex calculation because the insurer is entitled to restrict his liability to pay claims for property damage to £1,000,000 for all claims for property damage arising out of the same incident. Where the total of claims arising out of the one incident for property damage is less that £1,000,000 then the insurer clearly has to pay the full amount of the Judgment.

Formulae for calculation

Where the total of claims exceeds £1,000,000, there are two means of calculation. The first formula is as follows:

Amount payable = Judgment + interest x 1,000,000 / total amounts payable in respect of one incident

The second formula applies to the situation where all of the other claims have already been paid, then the sum payable is £1,000,000 less the total of any amounts already paid. Interest on that sum is calculated on the following formula:

Interest awarded on Judgment x amount payable of damages by insurer / damages awarded in Judgement

The insurer is entitled to make payment in these circumstances on which ever of the two bases produces the lower figure.

20.7.3 The Effect of Sections 148 and 151

The combined effect of sections 148 and 151 means that in most circumstances, if a person is injured or his property damaged as a result of an incident involving a vehicle which is insured, and in respect of which a Certificate of Insurance has been delivered by the insurer to the person effecting the insurance, the insurer will be obliged to meet a Judgment.

Even if the policy has been avoided or cancelled, subject to what we will have to say about s 152, the insurer will have to meet a Judgment. Even if the person driving the vehicle is a person not permitted to drive under the terms of the insurance or did not have a driving licence, the insurer will still have to meet a Judgment. Even if the vehicle is not roadworthy, is carrying more people than it can safely do so, has been fitted with a more powerful engine than the insurers believed to be the case, the insurer will still have to meet the Judgments.

One area however where the ability of the insurer to exclude his liability is not affected is that in respect of the use of the vehicle. If the insurer restricts his cover to social, domestic and pleasure use he would still be able to avoid liability if the vehicle is used for business use, for example as a taxi. Likewise if he excludes racing he can exclude his liability if the incident which gives rise to the Judgment happens in the course of a race.

20.7.4 Avoiding the Duty to meet Judgment by Reason of s 152

Section 152 provides four other important ways in which the insurer can avoid the duty to meet Judgments imposed on him by s 151.

One of these is simply that an insurer does not have to meet any Judgments so long as execution on the Judgment is stayed pending an appeal. That is really a postponement rather than an avoidance of the liability. The other three are more important.

Duty to give Notice of Proceedings

The first is that a Judgment is only enforceable against an insurer if before or within seven days after the commencement of the proceedings in which the Judgment was given the insurer has been given notice of the bringing of the proceedings.

Courts have become rather liberal as to what constitutes notice but the fact remains that if the Claimant does not comply with this provision he will not be able to require the insurer to meet the Judgment. The provision is of course only of use to the insurer if he is not indemnifying his insured. If he is indemnifying his insured and his insured has a Judgment against him then he will have to meet that Judgment in order to fulfil his contractual obligation to his insured.

Cancellation of the Policy

The second important provision relates to the cancellation of the policy within its normal term, either by the insured himself or by the insurer or by mutual consent. Even though the policy has been cancelled, as we have already said in relation to s 151, the insurer still remains liable to meet Judgments unless and until one of the following three things happen:

1. Either the Certificate of Insurance is returned to the insurer or if it has been lost or destroyed, a statutory declaration is made by the insured to that effect, *before* the incident giving rise to the Judgment takes place.
2. Within 14 days of the cancellation of the policy the Certificate of Insurance is surrendered to the insurer or the insured makes a statutory declaration that the Certificate has been lost or destroyed. This provision is effective even if the Certificate is surrendered after the incident giving rise to the Judgment.
3. Within 14 days of the cancellation of the policy the insurer has commenced proceedings under the Act in respect of the failure to surrender the Certificate. This may be either before or after

the happening of the incident giving rise to the Judgment provided it happens within 14 days of the cancellation of the policy.

What is meant by the insurer commencing proceedings under the Act in respect of the failure to surrender the Certificate is not entirely clear.

An obvious interpretation would be that the insurer should lay an information against his insured for failing to surrender the Certificate, which is of course a criminal offence under s 147(5) of the RTA 1988.

This is however a clumsy and expensive way of proceeding and a more efficient way of dealing with this is to bring County Court action under the Part 8 Procedure of the CPR for an Order from the Court ordering the insured to deliver up the Certificate or to make a statutory declaration.

It is important however that those proceedings be brought in respect of a failure to comply with the Act rather than in respect of a failure to comply with a policy condition.

Avoidance by Reason of Misrepresentation or Non-disclosure

The final provision which enables an insurer to avoid his liability to meet Judgments under s 151 RTA 1988 relates to a situation in which the insurance has been obtained on the basis of non-disclosure of a material fact or by misrepresentation and the insurer is therefore entitled to avoid the policy from the outset. The situation may be that the insurer has already purported to avoid the policy or it may be that he has not yet done so having only just discovered the non-disclosure or misrepresentation and wishes to do so.

In either case the insurer must bring proceedings against his insured for a declaration from the Court that he is or was so entitled to avoid the policy. To successfully avoid liability to meet Judgment the insurer must:

- state that the avoidance of the policy is on the basis of non-disclosure or mis representation and not on the basis of any policy condition;
- begin proceedings for the declaration before or within 3 months of the commencement of the proceedings in which the Judgment which he is seeking to avoid was given;

- must give notice to the Claimant of the proceedings within 7 days of the commencement of his proceedings for a declaration specifying in that notice the non-disclosure or false representation upon which he proposes to rely. The 3 month and the 7 day time limits referred to above are vital and the declaration from the Court will not avail the insurer if he does not comply with them.

20.8 Entitlement of Insurer to Recover Sums Paid Under Section 151

As we have already seen, s 148 entitles the insurer to recover from his insured such sums he has had to pay the Claimant where there has been a breach of his policy condition or where he would be entitled to rely upon an exception under the policy but for s 148.

Section 151 has added to insurers' problems by preventing them from avoiding liability even when the person driving the vehicle is not one permitted under the policy or where the person driving the vehicle did not hold a driving licence.

Section 151 gives the insurer the right to recover his outlay from a person insured under the policy but who does not hold a driving licence and whose liability would not have had to be met but for the provisions of this section of the Act.

Likewise where the insurer has had to meet the liability of a person who would not be permitted to drive under the policy, he may recover his outlay either from that person himself or from a person insured under the policy if that person caused or permitted the use of the vehicle which gave rise to the liability.

20.9 Further Restrictions Upon Insurers' Ability to Rely Upon Exceptions in the Policy

Sections 149 and 150 make provisions which also have bearing on the restrictions upon the insurer's ability to rely upon exceptions in the policy. Section 149 means that any agreements made with passengers that they will not be able to hold the user of the vehicle liable for injury or damage or that they will only be able to do so on the fulfilment of certain conditions are of no effect. Section 150 seeks to prevent car sharing schemes falling foul of any exclusion of business use under the policy.

20.10 Duty to Give Information as to Insurance or Security where Claim is Made

The person against whom a claim is made in respect of death or bodily injury or damage arising out of the use of a vehicle on the road must provide the following information listed below:

1. Whether or not he was insured.
2. Whether or not he would have been insured but for the fact that his insurer has avoided or cancelled the policy.
3. If he was insured, such particulars as are specified in a Certificate of Insurance that he held.
4. Where no Certificate was delivered give the following particulars, the registration mark, the number of the policy, the name of the insurer and the period of the insurance cover.

Failure to provide that information is an offence and there is no reason why a Claimant or a Claimant's insurer should not lay an information against a person who failed to provide this information.

20.11 POINTS OF SPECIAL DIFFICULTY

20.11.1 Employees

There is under s 145 RTA 1988 provision that a motor policy does not have to cover an employer's liability for the death of or a personal injury to an employee arising out of and in the course of his employment. Such liability was required to be covered under an Employers' Liability Insurance.

However, as a consequence of the EEC Directive 90/232, the Motor Vehicle (Compulsory Insurance) Regulation 1992 (SI1992/3064) were brought into force and a new subsection 4A was added to s 145 of the RTA on the 31st December 1992. This stated that the exception in respect of employees did not apply unless that liability was in fact insured under an Employers' Liability Insurance.

The situation was altered further by the Employers' Liability (Compulsory Insurance) Exemption (Amendment) Regulations 1992

(S1 1992/3172) which came into effect on 1st July 1994 and no longer required the employer to cover his liability to an employee, who was being carried on or upon a vehicle or was entering or getting onto or alighting from a vehicle, under his Employers' Liability Insurance.

The new Subsection 4A of S 145 of the **Road Traffic Act** left some dubiety regarding the position of drivers injured in the course of their employment because it referred to "a person (a) carried in or upon a vehicle or (b) entering or getting on to or alighting from a vehicle" which a layman would certainly interpret as including drivers. The position was clarified by Popplewell J in ***Regina v. Secretary of State for the Department of Transport (ex-parte The National Insurance Guarantee Corporation Plc)*** 8 May 1996. He concluded that the Section did not apply to drivers.

The case of ***AXA Insurance UK PLC v Norwich Union Insurance Ltd (2007)*** has further refined the meaning of a person "carried in or upon a vehicle". It was held that "carried" connoted transportation or movement from one place to another. So an employee, working in an elevated bucket affixed to the bed of a stationary vehicle, was not deemed to be carried in or upon the vehicle. His claim was accordingly outside S145 4A and fell to be dealt with by the employers' liability insurer.

It is important to note that the transfer of responsibility from the Employers Liability Insurer to the Road Traffic Act Insurer is only in respect of "passengers". There has been no such transfer in respect of employees killed or injured as pedestrians and that risk still remains with the Employer's Liability Insurer as does the risk in respect of employees killed or injured as drivers.

20.11.2 Definition of a Road

Section 145 of the Act makes insurance obligatory in respect of the use of a vehicle on a road in Great Britain. The difficulty is to decide what actually constitutes a road. A road is not synonymous with a highway so a road to which the public have access even though it is not highway or highway maintainable at public expense would still be a road for the purposes of the Act although a road within a factory *for* example to which the public did not have access would not: ***O'Brien v Trafalgar Insurance (1945).***

The law has tended to push the definition of a road ever wider. For example a forecourt, which was, clearly in private ownership but which was nevertheless used by the public as a shortcut, has been found to be a road ***Bugge v Taylor*** (1941). On the other hand in the cases of ***Clarke v General Accident Fire and Life Assurance Corporation Plc (1998)*** and ***Cutter v Eagle Star Insurance Company Limited (1998)*** the decision that a car park was a road was reversed by the Court of Appeal.

Other Public Place

On the 3 April 2000 the Motor Vehicles Compulsory Insurance Regulations 2000 came into effect and added the term "or other public place" after "road" in S 143 and 145 of the Road Traffic Act. This amendment brought these Sections into line with those Sections dealing with dangerous driving and driving under the influence of drugs and alcohol.

Clearly the term other public place is wider than road. An accident in a public car park would now certainly fall under the terms of the Act. The test is whether the public have access not simply by right but also by permission or even acquiescence of the owner so in the case of ***Rodger v Normand (1994)*** where the Defendant was charged with dangerous driving in the grounds of a secondary school it was held that this was a public place even though the public had no official right of access because the public did regularly use it as a leisure park outside school hours and this was tolerated or acquiesced in by the Education Authority.

That permission or toleration or acquiescence however must be extended to the public at large for an area to constitute a public place. In ***DPP v. Coulman (1992)***, Man LJ stated "it would appear from the analysis of a case called ***DPP v. Vickers*** that the enquiry is as to whether those who are permitted to use the road are so permitted because of some special characteristic or reason personal to themselves, which is not possessed by the public at large."

Guests or visitors using a private road or a private car park are persons with special characteristics or reasons personal to themselves and they do not render such private roads or private car parks a public place ***(R v. DPP ex-part Taussik 2000 and Young v. Carmichael 1991)***.

20.12 Conclusion

Sections 148 and 151 of the Road Traffic Act 1988 make it difficult for an insurer to avoid having to meet Judgments, even when there has been clear breach of his policy conditions or even where he has cancelled the policy. However, before deciding that he must definitely meet a Judgment, an insurer who has refused indemnity to his insured for whatever reason should consider the following points.

1. Is this a liability that is required to be covered under Section 145? If it concerns death, bodily injury or damage it almost certainly is, but consider the following:
    a) Did the incident take place on a road or other public place?
    b) Is the Claimant an employee not being carried as a passenger, or working on a stationary vehicle?
    c) If the vehicle was stolen, is the Claimant a passenger who knew or had reason to believe it was stolen?
2. Is the breach of condition that he is concerned with one, which under Section 148 he is not allowed to take into account or does it, for example, relate to the use of the vehicle which is not an excluded exception?
3. Was notice given either before the commencement of proceedings or within 7 days of the commencement of proceedings as required by Section 151 of the Act?
4. Once he cancelled the policy did he obtain the return of the Certificate or a statutory declaration, either:
    a) Before the accident occurred?
    b) Within 14 days of cancellation of the policy? Or,
    c) Did he bring proceedings against his insured within 14 days of cancellation of the policy?

If he did any of these he does not have a statutory duty to meet the Judgment.

5. Has there been non-disclosure or misrepresentation involved in the obtaining of the policy of insurance? If so can he bring proceedings for a declaration within 3 months of the commencement of the Claimant's own proceedings. If so he

must remember to give the Claimant notice of the commencement of the proceedings within 7 days of their commencement, and also to provide him with details of the non-disclosure or misrepresentation as alleged.

Article 75

Lying between the insurers obligations under the Road Traffic Act and the MIB's obligations dealt with in the Agreements set out below are the obligations of what used to be termed the "Insurer concerned" under the MIB's Article 75. The current Article 75 came into force in July 2006.

The obligations upon the Claimant as regards notice are more onerous than under the Road Traffic Act and the Insurer does not have to deal with subrogated claims from Insurers.

The purpose of this section is to highlight those circumstances in which an Insurer, whilst having no obligation under the Road Traffic Act, would have a liability under Article 75.

Article 75 2 (a)

Defines the Article 75 Insurer as the Member who for the time of the accident which gave rise to the Road traffic act liability was providing any insurance in respect of the vehicle from the use of which the liability of the judgement debtor arose.

Article 75 2 (d)

Defines insurance as the issue of any document or promise by or on behalf of a Member whether legally or otherwise purporting to cover against RTA liability, whether or not a certificate has been prepared, issued or delivered.

Article 75 2 (a) the insurer is Article 75 Insurer notwithstanding that

1. The insurance has been obtained by fraud, misrepresentation, non-disclosure of material facts or mistake.

2. Cover has been backdated.

3. Use of the vehicle is other than that permitted.

Article 75 2 (a) 2 i-iii

The insurer ceases to be Article 75 insurer on the "natural" expiry of the policy.

Article 75 2 (a) iv

If the policy is cancelled mid-term the Insurer only ceases to be Article 75 Insurer upon the recovery of the Certificate.

Article 75 2 (a) v

The insurer is not Article 75 Insurer if he obtains a court declaration that the policy is void or unenforceable before the happening of the accident.

Article 75 2 (a) vi

The insurer is not Article 75 Insurer when the insurance has ceased to operate by reason of a transfer of interest in the vehicle involved in the accident, which transfer is proved by evidence.

Article 75 2 (a) vii

The insurer is not Article 75 Insurer if the Certificate has been stolen and its theft reported to the Police within 30 days of discovery of the theft.

Article 75 2 (a) viii

The insurer is not Article 75 Insurer if the Certificate has been forged by someone other than the member or his intermediary or an officer, employee or agent of either.

You will have noted the following differences between Article 75 liability and RTA liability:

i) Before RTA liability starts an Insurance Certificate must be issued, that is not the case under Article 75.

ii) Under the RTA it is possible to apply to the Court for a declaration that a policy is void by reason of non-disclosure or misrepresentation. Proceedings for such a declaration can be brought up to 3 months after proceedings are commenced by the injured party (S 152 of the RTA) however the Insurer would remain liable as the Article 75 Insurer unless he had obtained that declaration before the accident which is the subject matter of the claim had taken place.

iii) As we have already stated showing that the use of the vehicle is other than permitted by the policy does permit the Insurer to avoid liability under the Road Traffic Act but it does not allow him to avoid his liability under Article 75.

iv) Where a policy has been issued for less than 12 months, to avoid liability as Insurer after the insurance period has terminated, the Insurer must show that he had no intention to renew and no renewal documents have been issued, and that no new insurance for the same policyholder had been incepted within a period of 15 days of the date of expiry. Clearly if renewal documents have been issued but not taken up by the policyholder the insurer could find himself still the Article 75 Insurer even though the insurance has expired.

v) Under the Road Traffic Act S 152 if an Insurer cancels a policy he can protect himself against continued Road Traffic Act liability by bringing proceedings for the return of the Certificate of Insurance within 14 days of the cancellation. Even if he does not obtain the Certificate those proceedings will provide him with protection. That is not the situation under Article 75, the Insurer must actually recover the Certificate of Insurance before the accident takes place.

It can be seen from this that where a policy is cancelled midterm or avoidance is sought because of misrepresentation or non-disclosure that there are in each case three possibilities for who should deal with the matter and how.

If a policy has been cancelled mid-term but the Certificate not recovered and no proceedings brought for the recovery of the Certificate within 14 days then the liability remains with the insurer as Road Traffic Act Insurer.

If a policy has been cancelled mid-term but the Insurer has not been successful in recovering the Certificate but has brought proceedings for its return within the 14 days period then he is the Article 75 Insurer.

If the Insurer has successfully recovered the Certificate before the accident then the matter falls to be dealt with by the MIB.

If the Insurer seeks to avoid the policy on the basis of misrepresentation or non-disclosure but does not do so within 3 months of the Claimant commencing proceedings and does not give 7 days notice of his proceedings for the declaration to the Claimant then the Insurer remains the RTA Insurer. If the Insurer brings proceedings for a declaration within 3 months of the Claimant's own proceedings but after the accident then he is the Article 75 Insurer.

If the Insurer obtains his declaration that he is entitled to avoid the policy on the basis of misrepresentation or non-disclosure prior to the accident then the claim falls to be dealt with by the MIB.

You will note that the insurer is relieved of liability even though the policy has not been cancelled and the Certificate of Insurance returned if he can prove there has been a transfer of interest in the vehicle prior to the accident.

There are two changes to the previous version of Article 75, which also appear to limit the liability of the Insurer.

Formerly when an Insurer had issued a certificate covering "Any Vehicle" he was deemed to be Article 75 Insurer in respect of each and every vehicle owned, leased or in the custody or control of the policyholder in the same taxation class as that insured. This provision has gone.

It is replaced by 75 2 (d) "Where after 1.1.2002 a record is held on the MID the existence of such a record covering the date of an accident shall unless there is documentary evidence to the contrary be sufficient to establish the existence of insurance for the purpose of this Article.

If, therefore an Insurer issues a policy on a specified vehicle basis but issues a certificate on any vehicle basis for administrative convenience, and the policyholder obtains a vehicle of which he does not inform the insurer so that it is not entered on the MID, then it would appear that the Insurer would not be Article 75 Insurer under the present Article 75 though he would have been under the previous form of the Article.

The second change is that under the previous agreement clause 3 stated "For the purposes of this Article where an insurance includes cover for driving other vehicles then unless that cover has been specifically withdrawn and the Certificate returned notwithstanding that the original subject matter of the policy may have cease to exist or have been subject to of a transfer of interest the Insurer will be Article 75 Insurer unless another Member is found to be Article 75 Insurer relative to any cover other than driving other cars cover."

This has now gone. This suggests that whilst an Insurer can still be Article 75 Insurer where the only insurance on a vehicle is under the Driving Other Cars extension, if the subject matter of the policy has ceased to exist or there has been a transfer of interest in it then the Insurer would not be Article 75 insurer.

You should note that the application of the July 2006 Article is retrospective, applying to any accident not settled by July 2006.

Direct Right of Action against Insurer

On 19th January 2003 the European Communities (Rights Against Insurers) Regulations 2002 came into force. These form part of the UK Government's implementation of the 4th EC Motor Insurance Directive. The Directive required EC nationals living outside the home country of the Defendant motorist to have the right to sue the Motor Insurer directly. The Regulations went beyond this by permitting UK resident Claimants also to bring proceedings directly against the UK based Motor Insurer of the party he holds responsible for the accident. If he is successful the Insurer will be directly liable to him.

The advantage for the Claimant is that whilst it may be difficult to find and serve proceedings on the driver, the Insurer is easy to find and serve upon. Also the Insurer will immediately be liable to pay any judgement, there is no need for further proceedings if the Insurer does not pay. The Claimant can simply enforce the Judgement against the Insurer.

What the Regulations do not do is enable the Claimant to sue the Insurer where he cannot identify the driver. For the Regulations to apply there has to be an "insured person". An insured person has been issued with a policy of insurance, which is in force, which covers his use of the vehicle on a road or other public place and fulfils the requirements of Section 145 of the Road Traffic Act 1988.

They do not enable the Claimant to successfully sue the Insurer when the Insurer is not obliged to indemnify the driver. The Insurer is only liable to the Claimant to the extent that he is liable to the insured person.

It would seem to be unwise for a Claimant to sue the Insurer where the Insurer is entitled to refuse indemnity to its insured. That would give the Insurer a Defence which the insured himself would not have and might well defeat the claim.

It would equally be unwise for an Insurer to settle a claim where the insurer was sued directly but was entitled to refuse an indemnity. That is because the judgement would not be one to which Section 148 or 151 of the Road Traffic Act applied and there would consequently be no right of recovery against the insured.

The Motor Insurers Bureau Agreements

The application of the Uninsured Driver's Agreement (13th August 1999)and Compensation of victims of Untraced Drivers Agreement (7th February 2003) lies outside the day-to-day experience of most Claims Handlers as generally they will be dealt with by the MIB or their instructed agents. It is important to be aware of them however in that they do impact on the handling of claims against insured drivers. Of particular importance is the requirement that where there is a meaningful degree of negligence on the part of an insured driver involved in an accident his insurer will deal with the claims arising in full without contribution from the MIB.

The Agreements are set out below.

13th August 1999

Motor Insurers' Bureau
(COMPENSATION OF VICTIMS OF UNINSURED DRIVERS)
Text of an Agreement dated the 13th August 1999 between the Secretary of State for the Environment, Transport and the Regions and Motor Insurers' Bureau together with some notes on its scope and purpose

THIS AGREEMENT is made the thirteenth day of August 1999 between the SECRETARY OF STATE FOR THE SECRETARY OF STATE FOR THE ENVIRONMENT, TRANSPORT AND THE REGIONS (hereinafter referred to as "the Secretary of State") and the MOTOR INSURERS' BUREAU, whose registered office is at 152 Silbury Boulevard, Milton Keynes MK9 1NB (hereinafter referred to as "MIB") and is SUPPLEMENTAL to an Agreement (hereinafter called "the Principal Agreement") made the 31st Day of December 1945 between the Minister of War Transport and the insurers transacting compulsory motor insurance business in Great Britain by or on behalf of whom the said Agreement was signed and in pursuance of paragraph 1 of which MIB was incorporated.

IT IS HEREBY AGREED AS FOLLOWS:

INTERPRETATION
General definitions
1. In this Agreement, unless the context otherwise requires, the following expressions have the following meanings -

"1988 Act" means the Road Traffic Act 1988;

"1988 Agreement" means the Agreement made on 21 December 1988 between the Secretary of State for Transport and MIB;

"bank holiday" means a day which is, or is to be observed as, a bank holiday under the Banking and Financial Dealings Act 1971;

"claimant" means a person who has commenced or who proposes to commence relevant proceedings and has made an application under this Agreement in respect thereof;

"contract of insurance" means a policy of insurance or a security covering a relevant liability;

"insurer" includes the giver of a security;

"MIB's obligation" means the obligation contained in clause 5;

"property" means any property whether real, heritable or personal;

"relevant liability" means a liability in respect of which a contract of insurance must be in force to comply with Part VI of the 1988 Act;

"relevant proceedings" means proceedings in respect of a relevant liability (and "commencement", in relation to such proceedings means, in England and Wales, the date on which a Claim Form or other originating process is issued by a Court or, in Scotland, the date on which the originating process is served on the Defender);

"relevant sum" means a sum payable or remaining payable under an unsatisfied judgment, including -

(a) an amount payable or remaining payable in respect of interest on that sum, and

(b) either the whole of the costs (whether taxed or not) awarded by the Court as part of that judgment or, where the judgment includes an award in respect of a liability which is not a relevant liability, such proportion of those costs as the relevant liability bears to the total sum awarded under the judgment;

"specified excess" means £300 or such other sum as may from time to time be agreed in writing between the Secretary of State and MIB;

"unsatisfied judgment" means a judgment or order (by whatever name called) in respect of a relevant liability which has not been satisfied in full within seven days from the date upon which the claimant became entitled to enforce it.

Meaning of references

2.1 Save as otherwise herein provided, the Interpretation Act 1978 shall apply for the interpretation of this Agreement as it applies for the interpretation of an Act of Parliament.

2.2 Where, under this Agreement, something is required to be done -

(a) within a specified period after or from the happening of a particular event, the period begins on the day after the happening of that event;

(b) within or not less than a specified period before a particular event, the period ends on the day immediately before the happening of that event.

2.3 Where, apart from this paragraph, the period in question, being a period of seven days or less, would include a Saturday, Sunday or bank holiday or Christmas Day or Good Friday, that day shall be excluded.

2.4 Save where expressly otherwise provided, a reference in this Agreement to a numbered clause is a reference to the clause bearing that number in this Agreement and a reference to a numbered paragraph is a reference to a paragraph bearing that number in the clause in which the reference occurs.

2.5 In this Agreement

(a) a reference (however framed) to the doing of any act or thing by or the happening of any event in relation to the claimant includes a reference to the doing of that act or thing by or the happening of that event In relation to a Solicitor or other person acting on his behalf, and

(b) a requirement to give notice to, or to serve documents upon, MIB or an insurer mentioned in clause 9(1)(a) shall be satisfied by the giving of the notice to, or the service of the documents upon, a Solicitor acting on its behalf in the manner provided for.

Claimants not of full age or capacity

3.1 Where, under and in accordance with this Agreement -

(a) any act or thing is done to or by a Solicitor or other person acting on behalf of a claimant,

(b) any decision is made by or in respect of a Solicitor or other person acting on behalf of a claimant, or

(c) any sum is paid to a Solicitor or other person acting on behalf of a claimant, then, whatever may be the age or other circumstances affecting the capacity of the claimant, that act, thing, decision or sum shall be treated as if it had been done to or by, or made in respect of or paid to a claimant of full age and capacity.

PRINCIPAL TERMS

Duration of Agreement

4.1 This Agreement shall come into force on 1st October 1999 in relation to accidents occurring on or after that date and, save as provided by clause 23, the 1988 Agreement shall cease and determine immediately before that date.

4.2 This Agreement may be determined by the Secretary of State or by MIB giving to the other not less than twelve months' notice in writing but without prejudice to its continued operation in respect of accidents occurring before the date of termination.

MIB's obligation to satisfy compensation claims

5.1 Subject to clauses 6 to 17, if a claimant has obtained against any person in a Court in Great Britain a judgment which is an unsatisfied judgment then MIB will pay the relevant sum to, or to the satisfaction of, the claimant or will cause the same to be so paid.

5.2 Paragraph (1) applies whether or not the person liable to satisfy the judgment is in fact covered by a contract of insurance and whatever may be the cause of his failure to satisfy the judgment.

EXCEPTIONS TO AGREEMENT

6.1 Clause 5 does not apply in the case of an application made in respect of a claim of any of the following descriptions (and, where part only of a claim satisfies such a description, clause S does not apply to that part)

(a) a claim arising out of a relevant liability incurred by the user of a vehicle owned by or in the possession of the Crown, unless -

(i) responsibility for the existence of a contract of insurance under Part VI of the 1988 Act in relation to that vehicle had been undertaken by some other person (whether or not the person liable was in fact covered by a contract of insurance), or

(ii) the relevant liability was in fact covered by a contract of insurance;

(b) a claim arising out of the use of a vehicle which is not required to be covered by a contract of insurance by virtue of section 144 of the 1988 Act, unless the use is in fact covered by such a contract;

(c) a claim by, or for the benefit of, a person ("the beneficiary") other than the person suffering death, injury or other damage which is made either -

(i) in respect of a cause of action or a judgment which has been assigned to the beneficiary, or

(ii) pursuant to a right of subrogation or contractual or other right belonging to the beneficiary;

(d) a claim in respect of damage to a motor vehicle or losses arising there from where, at the time when the damage to it was sustained -

(i) there was not in force in relation to the use of that vehicle such a contract of insurance as is required by Part VI of the 1988 Act, and

(ii) the claimant either knew or ought to have known that that was the case;

(e) a claim which is made in respect of a relevant liability described in paragraph (2) by a claimant who, at the time of the use giving rise to the relevant liability was voluntarily allowing himself to be carried in the vehicle and, either before the commencement of his journey in the vehicle or after such commencement if he could reasonably be expected to have alighted from it, knew or ought to have known that -

(i) the vehicle had been stolen or unlawfully taken,

(ii) the vehicle was being used without there being in force in relation to its use such a contract of insurance as would comply with Part VI of the 1988 Act,

(iii) the vehicle was being used in the course or furtherance of a crime, or

(iv) the vehicle was being used as a means of escape from, or avoidance of, lawful apprehension.

6.2 The relevant liability referred to in paragraph (1)(e) is a liability incurred by the owner or registered keeper or a person using the vehicle in which the claimant was being carried.

6.3 The burden of proving that the claimant knew or ought to have known of any matter set out in paragraph (1)(e) shall be on MIB but, in the absence of evidence to the contrary, proof by MIB of any of the following matters shall be taken as proof of the claimant's knowledge of the matter set out in paragraph (1)(e)(ii) -

(a) that the claimant was the owner or registered keeper of the vehicle or had caused or permitted its use;

(b) that the claimant knew the vehicle was being used by a person who was below the minimum age at which he could be granted a licence authorising the driving of a vehicle of that class;

(c) that the claimant knew that the person driving the vehicle was disqualified for holding or obtaining a driving licence;

(d) that the claimant knew that the user of the vehicle was neither its owner nor registered keeper nor an employee of the owner or registered keeper nor the owner or registered keeper of any other vehicle.

6.4 Knowledge which the claimant has or ought to have for the purposes of paragraph (1)(e) includes knowledge of matters which he could reasonably be expected to have been aware of had he not been under the self-induced influence of drink or drugs.

6.5 For the purposes of this clause -

(a) a vehicle which has been unlawfully removed from the possession of the Crown shall be taken to continue in that possession whilst it is kept so removed,

(b) references to a person being carried in a vehicle include references to his being carried upon, entering, getting on to and alighting from the vehicle, and

(c) "owner", in relation to a vehicle which is the subject of a hiring agreement or a hire-purchase agreement, means the person in possession of the vehicle under that agreement.

CONDITIONS PRECEDENT TO MIB'S OBLIGATION

Form of application

7.1 MIB shall incur no liability under MIB's obligation unless an application is made to the person specified in clause 9(1) -

(a) in such form,
(b) giving such information about the relevant proceedings and other matters relevant to this Agreement, and
(c) accompanied by such documents as MIB may reasonably require.

7.2 Where an application is signed by a person who is neither the claimant nor a Solicitor acting on his behalf MIB may refuse to accept the application (and shall incur no liability under MIB's obligation) until it is reasonably satisfied that, having regard to the status of the signatory and his relationship to the claimant, the claimant is fully aware of the contents and effect of the application but subject thereto MIB shall not refuse to accept such an application by reason only that it is signed by a person other than the claimant or his Solicitor.

Service of notices etc.

8.1 Any notice required to be given or documents to be supplied to MIB pursuant to clauses 9 to 12 of this Agreement shall be sufficiently given or supplied only if sent by facsimile transmission or by Registered or Recorded Delivery post to MIB's registered office for the time being and delivery shall be proved by the production of a facsimile transmission report produced by the sender's facsimile machine or an appropriate postal receipt.

Notice of relevant proceedings

9.1 MIB shall incur no liability under MIB's obligation unless proper notice of the bringing of the relevant proceedings has been given by the claimant not later than fourteen days after the commencement of those proceedings -

> (a) in the case of proceedings in respect of a relevant liability which is covered by a contract of insurance with an insurer whose identity can be ascertained, to that insurer;
> (b) in any other case, to MIB.

9.2 In this clause "proper notice" means, except in so far as any part of such information or any copy document or other thing has already been supplied under clause 7 -

> (a) notice in writing that proceedings have been commenced by Claim Form, Writ, or other means,
>
> (b) a copy of the sealed Claim Form, Writ or other official document providing evidence of the commencement of the proceedings and, in Scotland, a statement of the means of service,
>
> (c) a copy or details of any insurance policy providing benefits in the case of the death, bodily injury or damage to property to which the proceedings relate where the claimant is the insured party and the benefits are available to him,
>
> (d) copies of all correspondence in the possession of the claimant or (as the case may be) his Solicitor or agent to or from

the Defendant or the Defender or (as the case may be) his Solicitor, insurers or agent which is relevant to -

(i) the death, bodily in jury or damage for which the Defendant or Defender is alleged to be responsible,
or
(ii) any contract of insurance which covers, or which may or has been alleged to cover, liability for such death, injury or damage the benefit of which is, or is claimed to be, available to Defendant or Defender,

(e) subject to paragraph (3), a copy of the Particulars of Claim whether or not indorsed on the Claim Form, Writ or other originating process, and whether or not served (in England and Wales) on any Defendant or (in Scotland) on any Defender, and

(f) a copy of all other documents which are required under the appropriate rules of procedure to be served on a Defendant or Defender with the Claim Form, Writ or other originating process or with the Particulars of Claim,

(g) such other information about the relevant proceedings as MIB may reasonably specify.

9.3 If, in the case of proceedings commenced in England or Wales, the Particulars of Claim (including any document required to be served therewith) has not yet been served with the Claim Form or other originating process paragraph (2)(e) shall be sufficiently complied with if a copy thereof is served on MIB not later than seven days after it is served on the Defendant.

Notice of service of proceedings

10.1 This clause applies where the relevant proceedings are commenced in England or Wales.

10.2 MIB shall incur no liability under MIB's obligation unless the claimant has, not later than the appropriate date, given notice in writing to the person specified in clause 9(1) of the date of service of the Claim Form or other originating process in the relevant proceedings.

10.3 In this clause, "the appropriate date" means the day falling -

(a) seven days after -

(I) the date when the claimant receives notification from the Court that service of the Claim Form or

other originating process has occurred,
(ii) the date when the claimant receives notification from the Defendant that service of the Claim Form or other originating process has occurred, or
(iii) the date of personal service, or

(b) fourteen days after the date when service is deemed to have occurred in accordance with the Civil Procedure Rules, whichever of those days occurs first.

Further information

11.1 MIB shall incur no liability under MIB's obligation unless the claimant has, not later than seven days after the occurrence of any of the following events, namely -

(a) the filing of a defence in the relevant proceedings,

(b) any amendment to the Particulars of Claim or any amendment of or addition to any schedule or other document required to be served therewith, and

(c) either -

(i) the setting down of the case for trial, or

(ii) where the court gives notice to the claimant of the trial date, the date when that notice is received, given notice in writing of the date of that event to the person specified in clause 9.1 and has, in the case of the filing of a defence or an amendment of the Particulars of Claim or any amendment of or addition to any schedule or other document required to be served therewith, supplied a copy thereof to that person.

11.2 MIB shall incur no liability under MIB's obligation unless the claimant furnishes to the person specified in clause 9.1 within a reasonable time after being required to do so such further information and documents in support of his claim as MIB may reasonably require notwithstanding that the claimant may have complied with clause 7.1.

Notice of intention to apply for judgment

12.1 MIB shall incur no liability under MIB's obligation unless the claimant has, after commencement of the relevant proceedings and not less than thirty-five days before the appropriate date, given notice in writing to the person specified in clause 9.1 of his intention to apply for or to sign judgment in the relevant proceedings.

12.2 In this clause, "the appropriate date" means the date when the application for judgment is made or, as the case may be, the signing of judgment occurs.

Section 154 of the 1988 Act

13.1 MIB shall incur no liability under MIB's obligation unless the claimant has as soon as reasonably practicable -

(a) demanded the information and, where appropriate, the particulars specified in section 154(1) of the 1988 Act, and

(b) if the person of whom the demand is made fails to comply with the provisions of that subsection -

(i) made a formal complaint to a police officer in respect of such failure, and

(ii) used all reasonable endeavours to obtain the name and address of the registered keeper of the vehicle or, if so required by MIB, has authorised MIB to take such steps on his behalf.

Prosecution of proceedings

14.1 MIB shall incur no liability under MIB's obligation -

(a) unless the claimant has, if so required by MIB and having been granted a full indemnity by MIB as to costs, taken all reasonable steps to obtain judgment against every person who may be liable (including any person who may be vicariously liable) in respect of the injury or death or damage to property, or
(b) if the claimant, upon being requested to do so by MIB, refuses to consent to MIB being joined as a party to the relevant proceedings.

Assignment of judgment and undertakings

15.1 MIB shall incur no liability under MIB's obligation unless the claimant has -

(a) assigned to MIB or its nominee the unsatisfied judgment, whether or not that judgment includes an amount in respect of a liability other than a relevant liability, and any order for costs made in the relevant proceedings, and

(b) undertaken to repay to MIB any sum paid to him -

(i) by MIB in discharge of MIB's obligation if the judgment is subsequently set aside either as a whole or in respect of the part of the relevant liability to which that sum relates;

(ii) by any other person by way of compensation or benefit for the death, bodily injury or other damage to which the relevant proceedings relate, including a sum which would have been deductible under the provisions of clause 17 if it had been received before MIB was obliged to satisfy MIB's obligation.

LIMITATIONS ON MIB's LIABILITY

Compensation for damage to property

16.1 Where a claim under this Agreement includes a claim in respect of damage to property, MIB's obligation in respect of that part of the relevant sum which is awarded for such damage and any losses arising therefrom (referred to in this clause as "the property damage compensation") is limited in accordance with the following paragraphs.

16.2 Where the property damage compensation does not exceed the specified excess, MIB shall incur no liability.

16.3 Where the property damage compensation in respect of any one accident exceeds the specified excess but does not exceed £250,000, MIB shall incur liability less the specified excess.

16.4 Where the property damage compensation in respect of any one accident exceeds £250,000, MIB shall incur liability only in respect of the sum of £250,000 less the specified excess.

Compensation received from other sources

17.1 Where a claimant has received compensation from -

(a) the Policyholders Protection Board under the Policyholders Protection Act 1975, or
(b) an insurer under an insurance agreement or arrangement, or
(c) any other source, in respect of the death, bodily injury or other damage to which the relevant proceedings relate and such compensation has not been taken into account in the calculation of the relevant sum MIB may deduct from the relevant sum, in addition to any sum deductible under clause 16, an amount equal to that compensation.

MISCELLANEOUS

Notifications of decisions by MIB

18.1 Where a claimant -

(a) has made an application in accordance with clause 7, and
(b) has given to the person specified in clause 9.1 proper notice of the relevant proceedings in accordance with clause 9.2,

MIB shall -

(i) give a reasoned reply to any request made by the claimant relating to the payment of compensation in pursuance of MIB's obligation, and
(ii) as soon as reasonably practicable notify the claimant in writing of its decision regarding the payment of the relevant sum, together with the reasons for that decision.

Reference of disputes to the Secretary of State

19.1 In the event of any dispute as to the reasonableness of a requirement made by MIB for the supply of information or documentation or for the taking of any step by the claimant, it may be referred by the claimant or MIB to the Secretary of State whose decision shall be final.

19.2 Where a dispute is referred to the Secretary of State -

(a) MIB shall supply the Secretary of State and, if it has not already done so, the claimant with notice in writing of the requirement from which the dispute arises, together with the reasons for that requirement and such further information as MIB considers relevant, and
(b) where the dispute is referred by the claimant, the claimant shall supply the Secretary of State and, if he has not already done so, MIB with notice in writing of the grounds on which he disputes the reasonableness of the requirement.

Recoveries

20.1 Nothing in this Agreement shall prevent an insurer from providing by conditions in a contract of insurance that all sums paid by the insurer or by MIB by virtue of the Principal Agreement or this Agreement in or towards the discharge of the liability of the insured shall be recoverable by them or by MIB from the insured or from any other person.

Apportionment of damages, etc.

21.1 Where an unsatisfied judgment which includes an amount in respect of a liability other than a relevant liability has been assigned to MIB or its nominee in pursuance of clause 15 MIB shall -

(a) apportion any sum it receives in satisfaction or partial satisfaction of the judgment according to the proportion which the damages awarded in respect of the relevant liability bear to the damages awarded in respect of the other liability, and
(b) account to the claimant in respect of the moneys received properly apportionable to the other liability.

21.2 Where the sum received includes an amount in respect of interest or an amount awarded under an order for costs, the interest or the amount received in pursuance of the order shall be dealt with in the manner provided in paragraph (1).

Agents

22.1 MIB may perform any of its obligations under this agreement by agents.

Transitional provisions

23.1 The 1988 Agreement shall continue in force in relation to c1aims arising out of accidents occurring before 1st October 1999 with the modifications contained in paragraph (2).

23.2 In relation to any claim made under the 1988 Agreement after this Agreement has come into force, the 1988 Agreement shall apply as if there were inserted after clause 6 thereof
"6A. Where any person in whose favour a judgment In respect of a relevant liability has been made has -

(a) made a claim under this Agreement, and
(b) satisfied the requirements specified in clause 5 hereof,

MIB shall, if requested to do so, give him a reasoned reply regarding the satisfaction of that claim".

IN WITNESS whereof the Secretary of State has caused his Corporate Seal to be hereunto affixed and the Motor Insurers' Bureau has caused its Common Seal to be hereunto affixed the day and year first above written.

THE CORPORATE SEAL of the
SECRETARY OF STATE FOR THE
ENVIRONMENT~ TRANSPORT AND
THE REGIONS hereunto affixed is
authenticated by: -

Authorised by the Secretary of State

THE COMMON SEAL of the MOTOR INSURERS'
Bureau was hereunto affixed in the presence of:

Directors of the Board of Management
Secretary

NOTES FOR THE GUIDANCE OF VICTIMS OF ROAD TRAFFIC ACCIDENTS

The following notes are for the guidance of anyone who may have a claim on the Motor Insurers' Bureau under this Agreement and their legal advisers. They are not part of the Agreement, their purpose being to deal in ordinary language with the situations which most readily occur. They are not in any way a substitute for reading and applying the terms of this or any other relevant Agreement.
At the request of the Secretary of State, these notes have been revised with effect from 15th April 2002 and in their revised form have been agreed and approved by MIB, the Law Society of England and Wales, the Law Society of Scotland, the Motor Accident Solicitors' Society and the Association of Personal Injury Lawyers. Any application made under the Agreement after this date (unless proceedings have already been issued) will be handled by MIB in accordance with these notes.
Where proceedings have been issued in Scotland, for the words "Claimant" and "Defendant" there shall be substituted in these Notes where appropriate the words "Pursuer" and "Defender" respectively.
Enquiries, requests for application forms and general correspondence In connection with the Agreement should be addressed to: -

Motor Insurers Bureau
Linford Wood House
6-12 Capital Drive
MILTON KEYNES
MK14 6XT

Tel: 01908 830001
Fax: 01908 671681
DX: 142620 Milton Keynes

1. Introduction - MIB's role and application of the Agreement

1.1 The role of MIB under this Agreement is to provide a safety net for innocent victims of drivers who have been identified but are uninsured. MIB's funds for this purpose are obtained from levies charged upon insurers and so come from the premiums which are charged by those insurers to members of the public.

1.2 MIB has entered into a series of Agreements with the Secretary of State and his predecessors in office. Under each Agreement MIB undertakes obligations to pay defined compensation in specific circumstances. There are two sets of Agreements, one relating to victims of uninsured drivers (the "Uninsured Drivers" Agreements) and the other concerned with victims of hit and run or otherwise untraceable drivers (the "Untraced Drivers"

Agreements). These Notes are addressed specifically to the procedures required to take advantage of the rights granted by the Uninsured Drivers Agreements. However, it is not always certain which of the Agreements applies. For guidance in such cases please see the note on Untraced Drivers at paragraph 11 below.

1.3 In order to determine which of the Uninsured Drivers Agreements is applicable to a particular victim's claim, regard must be had to the date of the relevant accident. This Agreement only applies in respect of claims arising on or after 1st October 1999. Claims arising earlier than that are covered by the following Agreements:-

1.3.1 Claims arising in respect of an incident occurring between 1st July 1946 and 28th February 1971 are governed by the Agreement between the Minister of Transport and the Bureau dated 17th June 1946.

1.3.2 Claims arising in respect of an incident occurring between 1st March 1971 and 30th November 1972 are governed by the Agreement between the Secretary of State for the Environment and the Bureau dated 1st February 1971.

1.3.3 Claims arising in respect of an incident occurring between 1st December 1972 and 30th December 1988 are governed by the Agreement between the Secretary of State and the Bureau dated 22nd November 1972.

1.3.4 Claims arising in respect of an incident occurring between 31st December 1988 and 30th September 1999 are governed by the Agreement between the Secretary of State and the Bureau dated 21st December 1988.

2. MIB's obligation

2.1 MIB's basic obligation (see clause 5) is to satisfy judgments which fall within the terms of this Agreement and which, because the Defendant to the proceedings is not insured, are not satisfied.

2.2 This obligation is, however, not absolute. It is subject to certain exceptions where MIB has no liability (see clause 6), there are a number of pre-conditions which the claimant must comply with (see clauses 7 to 15) and there are some limitations on MIB's liability (see clauses 16 and 17).

2.3 Nothing in the Agreement is intended to vary the limitation rules applying to claimants not of full age or capacity. Limitation for personal injury remains 3 years from the date of full age or capacity.

2.4 MIB does not have to wait for a judgment to be given; it can become party to the proceedings or negotiate and settle the claim if it wishes to do so.

3. Claims which MIB is not obliged to satisfy

MIB is not liable under the Agreement in the case of the following types of claim.

3.1 A claim made in respect of an unsatisfied judgment which does not concern a liability against which Part VI of the Road Traffic Act 1988 requires a vehicle user to insure (see section 145 of the Act). An example would be a case where the accident did not occur in a place specified in the Act. See the definitions of "unsatisfied judgment" and "relevant liability" in clause 1.

3.2 A claim in respect of loss or damage caused by the use of a vehicle owned by or in the possession of the Crown (that is the Civil Service, the armed forces and so on) to which Part VI does not apply. If the responsibility for motor insurance has been undertaken by someone else or the vehicle is in fact insured, this exception does not apply. See clause 6(1)(a).

3.3 A claim made against any person who is not required to insure by virtue of section 144 of the Road Traffic Act 1988. See clause 6(1)(b).

3.4 A claim (commonly called subrogated) made in the name of a person suffering damage or injury but which is in fact wholly or partly for the benefit of another who has indemnified, or is liable to indemnify that person. See clause 6(1)(c).

It is not the intention of this Clause to exclude claims for the gratuitous provision of care, travel expenses by family members or friends, or miscellaneous expenses incurred on behalf of the Claimant, where the claimant is entitled to include such claims in his claim for damages.

3.5 A claim in respect of damage to a motor vehicle or losses arising from such damage where the use of the damaged vehicle was itself not covered by a contract of insurance as required by law. See clause 6(1)(d).

3.6 A claim made by a passenger in a vehicle where the loss or damage has been caused by the user of that vehicle if:-

3.6.1 the use of the vehicle was not covered by a contract of insurance; and

3.6.2 the claimant knew or could be taken to have known that the vehicle was being used without insurance, had been stolen or unlawfully taken or was being used in connection with crime.

See clause 6(1)(e), (2), (3) and (4).

For an interpretation of "knew or ought to have known" refer to the House of Lords judgment in White v White of 1st March 2001.

3.7 A claim in respect of property damage amounting to £300 or less, £300 being the "specified excess". See clause 16(2).

3.8 Where the claim is for property damage, the first £300 of the loss and so much of it as exceeds £250,000. See clause 16(3) and (4).

4. Procedure after the accident and before proceedings

4.1 The claimant must take reasonable steps to establish whether there is in fact any insurance covering the use of the vehicle which caused the injury or damage. First, a claimant has statutory rights under section 154 of the Road Traffic Act 1988 to obtain relevant particulars which he must take steps to exercise even if that involves incurring expense and MIB will insist that he does so. See clause 13(a).

MIB accept that if the MIB application form is sufficiently completed and signed by the Claimant, the Claimant will have complied with this Clause of the Agreement.

4.2 Other steps will include the following:

4.2.1 The exchange of names, addresses and insurance particulars between those involved either at the scene of the accident or afterwards.

4.2.2 Corresponding with the owner or driver of the vehicle or his representatives. He will be obliged under the terms of his motor policy to inform his insurers and a letter of claim addressed to him will commonly be passed to the insurers who may reply on his behalf. See clause 9(2)(d).

4.2.3 Where only the vehicle's number is known, enquiry of the Driver and Vehicle Licensing Agency at Swansea SA99 1BP as to the registered keeper of the vehicle is desirable so that through him the identity of the owner or driver can be established or confirmed.

4.2.4 Enquiries of the police (see clause 13(b) and Note 4.1 above).

4.3 If enquiries show that there is an insurer who is obliged to accept and does accept the obligation to handle the claim against the user of the vehicle concerned, even though the relevant liability may not be covered by the policy in question, then the claim should be pursued with such insurer.

4.4 If, however, enquiries disclose that there is no insurance covering the use of the vehicle concerned or if the insurer cannot be identified or the insurer asserts that it is under no obligation to handle the claim or if for any other reason it is clear that the insurer will not satisfy any judgment, the claim should be directed to MIB itself.

5. When proceedings are commenced or contemplated

5.1 As explained above, MIB does not have to wait for a judgment to be obtained before intervening. Claimants may apply to MIB before the commencement of proceedings. MIB will respond to any claim which complies with clause 7 and must give a reasoned reply to any request for compensation in respect of the claim (see clause 18) although normally a request for compensation will not be met until MIB is satisfied that it is properly based. Interim compensation payments are dealt with at paragraph 8 below.

Application Forms are available from MIB's office or their website: www.mib.org.uk.

Where a claim is made by the Claimant in person, who has not received legal advice, then if the claim is first made within 14 days prior to expiry of the limitation period, MIB will require the completed application form within the 21 days after the issue of proceedings.

5.2 It is important that wherever possible claims should be made using MIB's application form, fully completed and accompanied by documents supporting the claim, as soon as possible to avoid unnecessary delays. See clause 7(1). Copies of the form can be obtained on request made by post, telephone, fax or the DX or on personal application to MIB's offices.

5.3 The claimant must give MIB notice in writing that he has commenced legal proceedings. The notice, the completed application form (if appropriate) and all necessary documents must be received by MIB no later than 14 days after the date of commencement of proceedings. See clause 9(1) and (2)(a). The date of commencement is determined in accordance with the definitions of "relevant proceedings" and "commencement" given in clause 1.

When it is decided to commence legal proceedings, MIB should be joined as a defendent (unless there is good reason not to do so). Once MIB is a defendant, the Court will advise the relevant events direct and clauses 9(3), 11 and 12 will no longer apply.

The form of words set out below should be used for the joinder of MIB as second defendant:

1. The Second Defendant is a Company limited by guarantee under the Companies Act. Pursuant to an Agreement with the Secretary of State for the Environment Transport and the Regions dated 13th August 1999, the Second Defendant provides compensation in certain circumstances to persons suffering injury or damage as a result of the negligence of uninsured motorists.
2. The Claimant has used all reasonable endeavours to ascertain the liability of an insurer for the First Defendant and at the time of the commencement of these proceedings verily believes that the First Defendant is not insured.
3. The Claimant accepts that only if a final judgment is obtained against the First Defendant (which judgment is not satisfied in full within seven days from the date uponwhich the Claimant became entitled to enforce it) can the Second Defendant be required to satisfy the judgement and then only if the

terms and conditions set out in the Agreement are satisfied. Until that time, any liability of the Second Defendant is only contingent .
4. To avoid the Second Defendant having later to apply to join itself to this action (which the Claimant must consent to in any event, pursuant to Clause 14(b) of the Agreement) the Claimant seeks to include the Second Defendant from the outset recognising fully the Second Defendant's position as reflected in 3 above and the rights of the Second Defendant fully to participate in the action to protect its position as a separate party to the action.
5. With the above in mind, the Claimant seeks a declaration of the Second Defendant's contingent liability to satisfy the claimant's judgment against the First Defendant.

5.4 This notice must have with it the following:

5.4.1 a copy of the document originating the proceedings, usually in England and Wales a Claim Form and in Scotland a Sheriff Court Writ or Court of Session Summons (see clause 9(2)(b));

5.4.2 normally the Particulars of Claim endorsed on or served with the Claim Form or Writ (see clause 9(2)(e), although this document may be served later in accordance with clause 9(3) if that applies);

5.4.3 in any case the documents required by the relevant rules of procedure (see clause 9(2)(f).

Provided that the documents referred to above are forwarded to MIB, it is not necessary to enclose the Response Pack or the Notice of Issue.

5.5 In addition, other items as mentioned in clause 9(2), e.g. correspondence with the Defendant (or Defender) or his representatives, need to be supplied where appropriate.

5.6 It is for the claimant to satisfy himself that the notice has in fact been received by MIB. However, where the Claimant proves that service by DX, First Class Post, Personal Service or any other form of service allowed by the Civil Procedure Rules, was effected, MIB will accept that such notice has been served in the same circumstances in which a party to litigation would be obliged to accept that he had been validly served by such means.

5.7 It should be noted that when MIB has been given notice of a claim, it may elect to require the claimant to bring proceedings and attempt to secure a judgment against the party whom MIB alleges to be wholly or partly responsible for the loss or damage or who may be contracted to indemnify the claimant. In such a case MIB must indemnify the claimant against the costs of such proceedings. Subject to that, however, MIB's obligation to satisfy the judgment in the action will only arise if the claimant commences the proceedings and takes all reasonable steps to obtain a judgment. See clause 14(a).

6. Service of proceedings

6.1 If proceedings are commenced in England or Wales the claimant must inform MIB of the date of service (see clause 10(1) and (2)).

6.2 If service of the Claim Form is effected by the Court, notice should be given within 7 days from the earliest of the dates listed in clause 10(3)(a)(i) or (ii) or within 14 days from the date mentioned in clause 10(3)(b) (the date of deemed service under the court's rules of procedure). Claimants are advised to take steps to ensure that the court or the defendant's legal representatives inform them of the date of service as soon as possible. Although a longer period is allowed than in other cases, service may be deemed to have occurred without a Claimant knowing of it until some time afterwards.

6.3 Where proceedings are served personally, notice should be given 7 days from the date of personal service (clause 10(3)(a)(iii)).

6.4 However, by concession MIB will accept the notice referred to in note 6.1 above if it is received by MIB within 14 days from the dates referred to in notes 6.2 and 6.3.

6.5 In Scotland, proceedings are commenced at the date of service (see clause 1) so notice should already have been given under clause 9 and clause 10 does not apply there.

7. After service and before judgment

See Note 5.3 above.

7.1 Notice of the filing of a defence, of an amendment to the Statement or Particulars of Claim, and the setting down of the case for trial should be given not later than 7 days after the occurrence of such events and a copy of the document must be supplied (clause 11(1)).

7.2 However, by concession MIB will accept the notice referred to in note 7.1 above if it is received by MIB within 14 days after the proven date on which it was received by the claimant

7.3 MIB may request further information and documents to support the claim where it is not satisfied that the documents supplied with the application form are sufficient to enable it to assess its liability under the Agreement (see clause 11(2)).

7.4 If the claimant intends to sign or apply for judgment he must give MIB notice of the fact before doing so. This notice must be given at least 35 days before the application is to be made or the date when judgment is to be signed (see clause 12).

The 35 days notice does not apply where the court enters judgment of its own motion.

7.5 At no time must the claimant oppose MIB if it wishes to be joined as a party to proceedings and he must if requested consent to any application by MIB to be joined. Conflicts may arise between a Defendant and MIB which require MIB to become a Defendant or, in Scotland, a party Minuter if a defence is to be filed on its behalf (see clause 14(b)).

8. Interim payments

In substantial cases, the claimant may wish to apply for an interim payment. MIB will consider such applications on a voluntary basis but otherwise the claimant has the right to apply to the court for an interim payment order which, if granted, will be met by MIB.

9. After judgment

9.1 MIB's basic obligation normally arises if a judgment is not satisfied within 7 days after the claimant has become entitled to enforce it (see clause 1). However, that judgment may in certain circumstances be set aside and with it MIB's obligation to satisfy it. Sometimes MIB wishes to apply to set aside a judgment either wholly or partially. If MIB decides not to satisfy a judgment it will notify the claimant as soon as possible. Where a judgment is subsequently set aside, MIB will require the claimant to repay any sum previously paid by MIB to discharge its obligation under the Agreement (see clause 15(b)).

9.2 MIB is not obliged to satisfy a judgment unless the claimant has in return assigned the benefit to MIB or its nominee (see clause 15(a)). If such assignment is effected and if the subject matter of the judgment includes claims in respect of which MIB is not obliged to meet any judgment and if MIB effects any recovery on the judgment, the sum recovered will be divided between MIB and the claimant in proportion to the liabilities which were and which were not covered by MIB's obligation (see clause 21).

10. Permissible deductions from payments by MIB

10.1 Claims for loss and damage for which the claimant has been compensated or indemnified, e.g. under a contract of insurance or under the Policyholders Protection Act 1975, and which has not been taken into account in the judgment, may be deducted from the sum paid in settlement of MIB's obligation (see clause 17).

10.2 If there is a likelihood that the claimant will receive payment from such a source after the judgment has been satisfied by MIB, MIB will require him to undertake to repay any sum which duplicates the compensation assessed by the court (see clause 15(b)).

11. Untraced drivers

11.1 Where the owner or driver of a vehicle cannot be identified application may be made to MIB under the relevant Untraced Drivers Agreement. This provides, subject to specified conditions, for the payment of compensation for personal injury. It does not provide for compensation in respect of damage to property.

11.2 In those cases where it is unclear whether the owner or driver of a vehicle has been correctly identified it is sensible for the claimant to register a claim under both this Agreement and the Untraced Drivers Agreement following which MIB will advise which Agreement will, in its view, apply In the circumstances of the particular case.

14th February 2003

THE UNTRACED DRIVERS' AGREEMENT
DEPARTMENT OF TRANSPORT
MOTOR INSURERS' BUREAU
(COMPENSATION OF VICTIMS OF UNTRACED DRIVERS)

THIS AGREEMENT is made the seventh day of February 2003 between the **SECRETARY OF STATE FOR TRANSPORT** (hereinafter referred to as "the Secretary of State") and the **MOTOR INSURERS' BUREAU**, whose registered office is at Linford Wood House 6-12 Capital Drive Linford Wood Milton Keynes MK14 6XT (hereinafter referred to as "MIB").

IT IS HEREBY AGREED AS FOLLOWS:-

INTERPRETATION

General interpretation

1. (1) In this Agreement, unless the context otherwise requires, the following expressions have the following meanings–

"1988 Act" means the Road Traffic Act 1988;

"1996 Agreement" means the Agreement made on 14 June 1996 between the Secretary of State for Transport and MIB providing for the compensation of victims of untraced drivers;

"1999 Agreement" means the Agreement dated 13th August 1999 made between the Secretary of State for the Environment, Transport and the Regions and MIB providing for the compensation of victims of uninsured drivers;

"applicant" means the person who has applied for compensation in respect of a death, bodily injury or damage to property (or the person on whose behalf such an application has been made) and "application" means an application made by or on behalf of an applicant;

"arbitrator", where the arbitration takes place under Scottish law, includes an arbiter;

"award" means the aggregate of the sums which MIB is obliged to pay under this Agreement;

"bank holiday" means a day which is, or is to be observed as, a bank holiday under the Banking and Financial Dealings Act 1971;

"judgement" means, in relation to a court in Scotland, a court decree;

"property" means any property whether (in England and Wales) real or personal, or (in Scotland) heritable or moveable;

"relevant proceedings" means civil proceedings brought by the applicant (whether or not pursuant to a requirement made under this Agreement) against a person other than the unidentified person in respect of an event described in clause 4(1);

"specified excess" means £300 or such other sum as may from time to time be agreed in writing between the Secretary of State and MIB;

"unidentified person" means a person who is, or appears to be, wholly or partly liable in respect of the death, injury or damage to property to which an application relates and who cannot be identified.

(2) Save as otherwise herein provided, the Interpretation Act 1978 shall apply for the interpretation of this Agreement as it applies for the interpretation of an Act of Parliament.

(3) Where, under this Agreement, something is required to be done within a specified period after a date or the happening of a particular event, the period begins on the day after the happening of that event.

(4) Where, apart from this paragraph, the period in question, being a period of 7 days or less, would include a Saturday, Sunday, bank holiday, Christmas Day or Good Friday, that day shall be excluded.

(5) Save where expressly otherwise provided, a reference in this Agreement to a numbered clause is a reference to the clause bearing that number in this Agreement and a reference to a numbered paragraph is a reference to a paragraph bearing that number in the clause or schedule in which the reference occurs.

(6) In this Agreement–

(a) a reference (however framed) to the doing of any act or thing by or the happening of any event in relation to the applicant includes a reference to the doing of that act or thing by or the happening of that event in relation to a Solicitor or other person acting on his behalf, and

(b) a requirement to give notice or send documents to MIB shall, where MIB has appointed a Solicitor to act on its behalf in relation to the application, be satisfied by the giving of the notice or the sending of the documents, in the manner herein provided for, to that Solicitor.

Applicants' representatives

2. Where, under and in accordance with this Agreement–

(a) any notice or other document is given to or by a Solicitor or other person acting on behalf of an applicant,

(b) any act or thing is done by or in respect of such Solicitor or other person,

(c) any decision is made by or in respect of such Solicitor or other person, or

(d) any payment is made to such Solicitor or other person,

then, whatever may be the age or other circumstances affecting the capacity of the applicant, that act, thing, decision or payment shall be treated as if it had been done to or by, or made to or in respect of an applicant of full age and capacity.

APPLICATION OF AGREEMENT

Duration of Agreement

3. (1) This Agreement shall come into force on 14 February 2003.

(2) This Agreement may be determined by the Secretary of State or by MIB giving to the other not less than twelve months notice in writing to that effect.

(3) Notwithstanding the giving of notice of determination under paragraph (2) this Agreement shall continue to operate in respect of any application made in respect of death, bodily injury or damage to property arising from an event occurring on or before the date of termination specified in the notice.

Scope of Agreement

4. (1) Save as provided in clause 5, this Agreement applies where–

(a) the death of, or bodily injury to, a person or damage to any property of a person has been caused by, or arisen out of, the use of a motor vehicle on a road or other public place in Great Britain, and

(b) the event giving rise to the death, bodily injury or damage to property occurred on or after fourteenth day February 2003, and

(c) the death, bodily injury or damage to property occurred in circumstances giving rise to liability of a kind which is required to be covered by a policy of insurance or a security under Part VI of the 1988 Act, and

(d) it is not possible for the applicant–

(i) to identify the person who is, or appears to be, liable in respect of the death, injury or damage, or

(ii) (where more than one person is or appears to be liable) to identify any one or more of those persons,

and

(e) the applicant has made an application in writing to MIB for the payment of an award in respect of such death, bodily injury or damage to property (and in a case where they are applicable the requirements of paragraph (2) are satisfied), and

(f) the conditions specified in paragraph (3), or such of those conditions as are relevant to the application, are satisfied.

(2) Where an application is signed by a person who is neither the applicant nor a Solicitor acting on behalf of the applicant MIB may refuse to accept the application (and shall incur no liability under this Agreement) until it is reasonably satisfied that, having regard to the status of the signatory and his relationship with the applicant, the applicant is fully aware of the content and effect of the application but subject thereto MIB shall not refuse to accept an application by reason only of the fact that it is signed by a person other than the applicant or his Solicitor.

(3) The conditions referred to in paragraph (1)(f) are that–

(a) except in a case to which sub-paragraph (b) applies, the application must have been made not later than –

(i) three years after the date of the event which is the subject of the application in the case of a claim for compensation for death or bodily injury (whether or not damage to property has also arisen from the same event), or

(ii) nine months after the date of that event in the case of a claim for compensation for damage to property (whether or not death or bodily injury has also arisen from the same event);

(b) in a case where the applicant could not reasonably have been expected to have become aware of the existence of bodily injury or damage to property, the application must have been made as soon as practicable after he did become (or ought reasonably to have become) aware of it and in any case not later than–

(i) fifteen years after the date of the event which is the subject of the application in the case of a claim for compensation for death or bodily injury (whether or not damage to property has also arisen from the same event), or

(ii) two years after the date of that event in the case of a claimfor compensation for damage to property (whether or not death or bodily injury has also arisen from the same event);

(c) the applicant, or a person acting on the applicant's behalf, must have reported that event to the police–

(i) in the case of an event from which there has arisen a death or bodily injury alone, not later than 14 days after its occurrence, and

(ii) in the case of an event from which there has arisen property damage (whether or not a death or bodily injury has also arisen from it), not later than 5 days after its occurrence,

but where that is not reasonably possible the event must have been reported as soon as reasonably possible;

(d) the applicant must produce satisfactory evidence of having made the report required under sub-paragraph (c) in the form of an acknowledgement from the relevant force showing the crime or incident number under which that force has recorded the matter;

(e) after making, or authorising the making of, a report to the police the applicant must have co-operated with the police in any investigation they have made into the event.

(4) Where both death or bodily injury and damage to property have arisen from a single event nothing contained in this clause shall require an applicant to make an application in respect of the death or bodily injury on the same occasion as an application in respect of the damage to property and where two applications are made in respect of one event the provisions of this Agreement shall apply separately to each of them.

Exclusions from Agreement

5. (1) This Agreement does not apply where an application is made in any of the following circumstances (so that where an application is made partly in such circumstances and partly in other circumstances, it applies only to the part made in those other circumstances)–

(a) where the applicant makes no claim for compensation in respect of death or bodily injury and the damage to property in respect of which compensation is claimed has been caused by, or has arisen out of, the use of an unidentified vehicle;

(b) where the death, bodily injury or damage to property in respect of which the application is made has been caused by or has arisen out of the use of a motor vehicle which at the time of the event giving rise to such death, injury or damage was owned by or in the possession of the Crown, unless at that time some other person had undertaken responsibility for bringing into existence a policy of insurance or security satisfying the requirements of the 1988 Act;

(c) where, at the time of the event in respect of which the application is made the person suffering death, injury or damage to property was voluntarily allowing himself to be carried in the responsible vehicle and before the commencement of his journey in the vehicle (or after such commencement if he could reasonably be expected to have alighted from the vehicle) he knew or ought to have known that the vehicle–

(i) had been stolen or unlawfully taken, or

(ii) was being used without there being in force in relation to its use a contract of insurance or security which complied with the 1988 Act; or

(iii) was being used in the course or furtherance of crime; or

(iv) was being used as a means of escape from or avoidance of lawful apprehension;

(d) where the death, bodily injury or damage to property was caused by, or in the course of, an act of terrorism;

(e) where property damaged as a result of the event giving rise to the application is insured against such damage and the applicant has recovered the full amount of his loss from the insurer on or before the date of the application (but without prejudice to the application of the Agreement in the case of any other claim for compensation made in respect of the same event);

(f) where a claim is made for compensation in respect of damage to a motor vehicle (or losses arising therefrom) and, at the time when the damage to it was sustained–

(i) there was not in force in relation to the use of that vehicle such a contract of insurance as is required by Part VI of the 1988 Act, and

ii) the person suffering damage to property either knew or ought to have known that was the case

(but without prejudice to the application of the Agreement in the case of any other claim for compensation made in respect of the same event);

(g) where the application is made neither by a person suffering injury or property damage nor by the personal representative of such a person nor by a dependant claiming in respect of the death of another person but is made in any of the following circumstances, namely–

(i) where a cause of action or a judgment has been assigned to the applicant, or

(ii) where the applicant is acting pursuant to a right of subrogation or a similar contractual or other right belonging to him.

(2) The burden of proving that the person suffering death, injury or damage to property knew or ought to have known of any matter set out in paragraph (1)(c) shall be on MIB but, in the absence of evidence to the contrary, proof by MIB of any of the following matters shall be taken as proof of his knowledge of the matter set out in paragraph (1)(c)(ii)–

(a) that he was the owner or registered keeper of the vehicle or had caused or permitted its use;

(b) that he knew the vehicle was being used by a person who was below the minimum age at which he could be granted a licence authorising the driving of a vehicle of that class;

(c) that he knew that the person driving the vehicle was disqualified for holding or obtaining a driving licence;

(d) that he knew that the user of the vehicle was neither its owner nor registered keeper nor an employee of the owner or registered keeper nor the owner or registered keeper of any other vehicle.

(3) Where–

(a) the application includes a claim for compensation both in respect of death or bodily injury and also in respect of damage to property, and

(b) the death or injury and the property damage has been caused by, or has arisen out of, the use of an unidentified vehicle,

the Agreement does not apply to the claim for compensation in respect of the damage to property.

(4) For the purposes of paragraphs (1) and (2)–

(a) references to a person being carried in a vehicle include references to his being carried in or upon, or entering or getting on to or alighting from the vehicle;

(b) knowledge which a person has or ought to have for the purposes of sub-paragraph (c) includes knowledge of matters which he could reasonably be expected to have been aware of had he not been under the self-induced influence of drink or drugs;

(c) "crime" does not include the commission of an offence under the Traffic Acts, except an offence under section 143 (use of a motor vehicle on a road without there being in force a policy of insurance), and "Traffic Acts" means the Road Traffic Regulation Act 1984, the Road Traffic Act 1988 and the Road Traffic Offenders Act 1988;

(d) "responsible vehicle" means the vehicle the use of which caused (or through the use of which there arose) the death, bodily injury or damage to property which is the subject of the application;

(e) "terrorism" has the meaning given in section 1 of the Terrorism Act 2000;

(f) "dependant" has the same meaning as in section 1(3) of the Fatal Accidents Act 1976.

Limitation on application of Agreement

6. (1) This clause applies where an applicant receives compensation or other payment in respect of the death, bodily injury or damage to property otherwise than in the circumstances described in clause 5(1)(e) from any of the following persons–

(a) an insurer or under an insurance policy (other than a life assurance policy) or arrangement between the applicant or his employer and the insurer, or

(b) a person who has given a security pursuant to the requirements of 1988 Act under an agreement between the applicant and the security giver, or

(c) any other source other than a person who is an identified person for the purposes of clauses 13 to 15 or an insurer of, or a person who has given a security on behalf of, such a person.

(2) Where the compensation or other payment received is equal to or greater than the amount which MIB would otherwise be liable to pay under the provisions of clauses 8 and 9 MIB shall have no liability under those provisions (to the intent that this Agreement shall immediately cease to apply except to the extent that the applicant is entitled to a contribution to his legal costs under clause 10).

(3) Where the compensation or other payment received is less than the amount which MIB would otherwise be liable to pay under the provisions of clauses 8 and 9 MIB's liability under those provisions shall be reduced by an amount equal to that compensation or payment.

PRINCIPAL TERMS AND CONDITIONS

MIB's obligation to investigate claims and determine amount of award

7. (1) MIB shall, at its own cost, take all reasonable steps to investigate the claim made in the application and–

(a) if it is satisfied after conducting a preliminary investigation that the case is not one to which this Agreement applies and the application should be rejected, it shall inform the applicant accordingly and (subject to the following provisions of this Agreement) need take no further action, or

(b) in any other case, it shall conduct a full investigation and shall as soon as reasonably practicable having regard to the availability of evidence make a report on the applicant's claim.

(2) Subject to the following paragraphs of this clause, MIB shall, on the basis of the report and, where applicable, any relevant proceedings–

(a) reach a decision as to whether it must make an award to the applicant in respect of the death, bodily injury or damage to property, and

(b) where it decides to make an award, determine the amount of that award.

(3) Where MIB reaches a decision that the Agreement applies and that it is able to calculate the whole amount of the award the report shall be treated as a full report and the award shall (subject to the following provisions of this Agreement) be treated as a full and final award.

(4) Where MIB reaches a decision that the Agreement applies and that it should make an award but further decides that it is not at that time able to calculate the final amount of the award (or a part thereof), it may designate the report as an interim report and where it does so–

(a) it may, as soon as reasonably practicable, make one or more further interim reports, but

(b) it must, as soon as reasonably practicable having regard to the availability of evidence, make a final report.

(5) Where it makes an interim or final report MIB shall, on the basis of that report and, where applicable, any relevant proceedings–

(a) in the case of an interim report, determine the amount of any interim award it wishes to make, and

(b) in the case of its final report, determine the whole amount of its award which shall (subject to the following provisions of this Agreement) be treated as a full and final award.

(6) MIB shall be under an obligation to make an award only if it is satisfied, on the balance of probabilities, that the death, bodily injury or damage to property was caused in such circumstances that the unidentified person would (had he been identified) have been held liable to pay damages to the applicant in respect of it.

(7) MIB shall determine the amount of its award in accordance with the provisions of clauses 8 to 10 and (in an appropriate case) clauses 12 to 14 but shall not thereby be under a duty to calculate the exact proportion of the award which represents compensation, interest or legal costs.

Compensation

8. (1) MIB shall include in its award to the applicant, by way of compensation for the death, bodily injury or damage to property, a sum equivalent to the amount which a court –

(a) applying the law of England and Wales, in a case where the event giving rise to the death, injury or damage occurred in England or Wales, or

(b) applying the law of Scotland, in a case where that event occurred in Scotland,

would have awarded to the applicant (where applying English law) as general and special damages or (where applying the law of Scotland) as solatium and patrimonial loss if the applicant had brought successful proceedings to enforce a claim for damages against the unidentified person.

(2) In calculating the sum payable under paragraph (1), MIB shall adopt the same method of calculation as the court would adopt in calculating damages but it shall be under no obligation to include in that calculation an amount in respect of loss of earnings suffered by the applicant to the extent that he has been paid wages or salary (or any sum in lieu of them) whether or not such payments were made subject to an agreement or undertaking on his part to repay the same in the event of his recovering damages for the loss of those earnings.

(3) Where an application includes a claim in respect of damage to property, MIB's liability in respect of that claim shall be limited in accordance with the following rules–

(a) if the loss incurred by an applicant in respect of any one event giving rise to a claim does not exceed the specified excess, MIB shall incur no liability to that applicant in respect of that event;

(b) if the aggregate of all losses incurred by both the applicant and other persons in respect of any one event giving rise to a claim ("the total loss") exceeds the specified excess but does not exceed £250,000–

(i) MIB's liability to an individual applicant shall be the amount of the claim less the specified excess, and

(ii) MIB's total liability to applicants in respect of claims arising from that event shall be the total loss less a sum equal to the specified excess multiplied by the number of applicants who have incurred loss through damage to property;

(c) if the total loss exceeds £250,000–

(i) MIB's liability to an individual applicant shall not exceed the amount of the claim less the specified excess, and

(ii) MIB's total liability to applicants in respect of claims arising from that event shall be £250,000 less a sum equal to the specified excess multiplied by the number of applicants who have incurred loss due to property damage.

(4) MIB shall not be liable to pay compensation to an appropriate authority in respect of any loss incurred by that authority as a result of its failure to recover a charge for the recovery, storage or disposal of an abandoned vehicle under a power contained in the Refuse Disposal (Amenity) Act 1978 or Part VIII of the Road Traffic Regulation Act 1984 (and in this paragraph "appropriate authority" has the meaning given in the Act under which the power to recover the charge was exercisable).

Interest

9. (1) MIB shall in an appropriate case also include in the award a sum representing interest on the compensation payable under clause 8 at a rate equal to that which a court–

(a) applying the law of England and Wales, in a case where the event giving rise to the death, bodily injury or damage to property occurred in England or Wales, or

(b) applying the law of Scotland, in a case where that event occurred in Scotland,

would have awarded to a successful applicant.

(2) MIB is not required by virtue of paragraph (1) to pay a sum representing interest in respect of the period before the date which is one month after the date on which MIB receives the police report (but, where MIB has failed to seek and obtain that report promptly after the date of the application, interest shall run from the date which falls one month after the date on which it would have received it had it acted promptly).

Contribution towards legal costs

10. (1) MIB shall, in a case where it has decided to make a compensation payment under clause 8, also include in the award a sum by way of contribution towards the cost of obtaining legal advice from a Solicitor, Barrister or Advocate in respect of–

(a) the making of an application under this Agreement;

(b) the correctness of a decision made by MIB under this Agreement; or

(c) the adequacy of an award (or a part thereof) offered by MIB under this Agreement that sum to be determined in accordance with the Schedule to this Agreement.

(2) MIB shall not be under a duty to make a payment under paragraph (1) unless it is satisfied that the applicant did obtain legal advice in respect of any one or more of the matters specified in that paragraph.

Conditions precedent to MIB's obligations

11. (1) The applicant must–

(a) make his application in such form,

(b) provide in support of the application such statements and other information (whether in writing or orally at interview), and

(c) give such further assistance,

as may reasonably be required by MIB or by any person acting on MIB's behalf to enable an investigation to be carried out under clause 7 of this Agreement.

(2) The applicant must provide MIB with written authority to take all such steps as may be reasonably necessary in order to carry out a proper investigation of the claim.

(3) The applicant must, if MIB reasonably requires him to do so before reaching a decision under clause 7, provide MIB with a statutory declaration, made by him, setting out to the best of his knowledge and belief all the facts and circumstances upon which his application is based or such facts and circumstances in relation to the application as MIB may reasonably specify.

(4) The applicant must, if MIB reasonably requires him to do so before it reaches a decision or determination under clause 7 and subject to the following provisions of this clause–

(a) at MIB's option (and subject to paragraph (5)) either–

(i) bring proceedings against any person or persons who may, in addition or alternatively to the unidentified person, be liable to the applicant in respect of the death, bodily injury or damage to property (by virtue of having caused or contributed to that death, injury or damage, by being vicariously liable in respect of it or having failed to effect third party liability insurance in respect of the vehicle in question) and co-operate with MIB in taking such steps as are reasonably necessary to obtain judgement in those proceedings, or

(ii) authorise MIB to bring such proceedings and take such steps in the applicant's name;

(b) at MIB's expense, provide MIB with a transcript of any official shorthand or recorded note taken in those proceedings of any evidence given or judgement delivered therein;

(c) assign to MIB or to its nominee the benefit of any judgement obtained by him (whether or not obtained in proceedings brought under sub-paragraph (a) above) in respect of the death, bodily injury or damage to property upon such terms as will secure that MIB or its nominee will be accountable to the applicant for any amount by which the aggregate of all sums recovered by MIB or its nominee under the judgement (after deducting all reasonable expenses incurred in effecting recovery) exceeds the award made by MIB under this Agreement in respect of that death, injury or damage;

(d) undertake to assign to MIB the right to any sum which is or may be due from an insurer, security giver or other person by way of compensation for, or benefit in respect of, the death, bodily injury or damage to property and which would (if payment had been made before the date of the award) have excluded or limited MIB's liability under the provisions of clause 6.

(5) If, pursuant to paragraph (4)(a), MIB requires the applicant to bring proceedings or take steps against any person or persons (or to authorise MIB to bring such proceedings or take such steps in his name) MIB shall indemnify the applicant against all costs and expenses reasonably incurred by him in complying with that requirement.

(6) Where the applicant, without having been required to do so by MIB, has commenced proceedings against any person described in paragraph (4)(a) –

(a) the applicant shall as soon as reasonably possible notify MIB of such proceedings and provide MIB with such further information about them as MIB may reasonably require, and

(b) the applicant's obligations in paragraph (4)(a) to (c) shall apply in respect of such proceedings as if they had been brought at MIB's request.

JOINT AND SEVERAL LIABILITY

Joint and several liability: interpretation

12. In clauses 13 to 15–

"identified person" includes an identified employer or principal of a person who is himself unidentified;

"original judgement" means a judgement obtained against an identified person at first instance in relevant proceedings;

"three month period" means the period of three months specified in clause 13(3); and

"unidentified person's liability" means–

(a) the amount of the contribution which (if not otherwise apparent) would, on the balance of probabilities, have been be recoverable from the unidentified person in an action brought –

(i) in England and Wales, under the Civil Liability (Contribution) Act 1978, or

(ii) in Scotland, under the Law Reform (Miscellaneous Provisions) (Scotland) Act 1940,

by an identified person who had been held liable in full in an earlier action brought by the applicant, and

(b) where a court has awarded the applicant interest or costs in addition to damages, an appropriate proportion of that interest or those costs.

MIB's liability where wrongdoer is identified

13. (1) This clause applies where the death, bodily injury or damage to property in respect of which the application is made is caused, or appears on the balance of probabilities to have been caused–

(a) partly by an unidentified person and partly by an identified person, or

(b) partly by an unidentified person and partly by another unidentified person whose employer or principal is identified,

in circumstances making (or appearing to make) the identified person liable, or vicariously liable, to the applicant in respect of the death, injury or damage.

(2) Where this clause applies, MIB's liability under this Agreement shall not exceed the unidentified person's liability and the following provisions shall apply to determine MIB's liability in specific cases.

(3) Where the applicant has obtained a judgement in relevant proceedings in respect of the death, injury or damage which has not been satisfied in full by or on behalf of the identified person within the period of three months after the date on which the applicant became entitled to enforce it–

(a) if that judgement is wholly unsatisfied within the three month period MIB shall make an award equal to the unidentified person's liability;

(b) if the judgement is satisfied in part only within the three month period, MIB shall make an award equal to–

(i) the unsatisfied part, if it does not exceed the unidentified person's liability; and

(ii) the unidentified person's liability, if the unsatisfied part exceeds the unidentified person's liability.

(4) A judgment given in any relevant proceedings against an identified person shall be conclusive as to any issue determined in those proceedings which is relevant to the determination of MIB's liability under this Agreement.

(5) Where the applicant has not obtained (or been required by MIB to obtain) a judgement in respect of the death, injury or damage against the identified person but has received an agreed payment from the identified person in respect of the death, bodily injury or damage to property, that payment shall be treated for the purposes of this Agreement as a full settlement of the applicant's claim and MIB shall be under no liability under this Agreement in respect thereof.

(6) Where the applicant has not obtained (or been required by MIB to obtain) a judgement in respect of the death, injury or damage against the identified person nor received any payment by way of compensation in respect thereof from the identified person MIB shall make an award equal to the unidentified person's liability.

Appeals by identified persons

14. (1) This clause applies where an appeal against, or other proceeding to set aside, the original judgement is commenced within the three month period.

(2) If, as a result of the appeal or other proceeding–

(a) the applicant ceases to be entitled to receive any payment in respect of the death, bodily injury or damage to property from any identified person, clause 13 shall apply as if he had neither obtained nor been required by MIB to obtain a judgement against that person;

(b) the applicant becomes entitled to recover an amount different from that which he was entitled to recover under the original judgement the provisions of clause 13(3) shall apply, but as if for each of the references therein to the original judgement there were substituted a reference to the judgement in that appeal or other proceeding;

(c) the applicant remains entitled to enforce the original judgement the provisions of clause 13(3) shall apply, but as if for each of the references therein to the three month period there were substituted a reference to the period of three months after the date on which the appeal or other proceeding was disposed of.

(3) Where the judgement in the appeal or other proceeding is itself the subject of a further appeal or similar proceeding the provisions of this clause shall apply in relation to that further appeal or proceeding in the same manner as they apply in relation to the first appeal or proceeding.

(4) Nothing in this clause shall oblige MIB to make a payment to the applicant until the appeal or other proceeding has been determined.

Compensation recovered under Uninsured Drivers Agreements

15. (1) Where, in a case to which clause 13 applies, judgement in the relevant proceedings is given against an identified person in circumstances which render MIB liable to satisfy that judgement under any of the Uninsured Drivers Agreements, MIB shall not be under any liability under this Agreement in respect of the event to which the relevant proceedings relate.

(2) In this clause "Uninsured Drivers Agreements" means–

(a) the Agreement dated 21st December 1988 made between the Secretary of State for Transport and MIB providing for the compensation of victims of uninsured drivers,

(b) the 1999 Agreement, and

(c) any agreement made between the Secretary of State and MIB (or their respective successors) which supersedes (whether immediately or otherwise) the 1999 Agreement.

NOTIFICATION OF DECISION AND PAYMENT OF AWARD

Notification of decision

16. MIB shall give the applicant notice of a decision or determination under clause 7 in writing and when so doing shall provide him–

(a) if the application is rejected because a preliminary investigation has disclosed that it is not one made in a case to which this Agreement applies, with a statement to that effect;

(b) if the application has been fully investigated, with a statement setting out–

(i) all the evidence obtained during the investigation, and

(ii) MIB's findings of fact from that evidence which are relevant to the decision;

(c) if it has decided to make an interim award on the basis of an interim report under clause 7(4), with a copy of the report and a statement of the amount of the interim award;

(d) if it has decided to make a full report under clause 7(3) or a final report under clause 7(4)(b), with a copy of the report and a statement of the amount of the full and final award;

(e) in a case to which clause 13 applies, with a statement setting out the way in which the amount of the award has been computed under the provisions of that clause; and

(f) in every case, with a statement of its reasons for making the decision or determination.

Acceptance of decision and payment of award

17. (1) Subject to the following paragraphs of this clause, if MIB gives notice to the applicant that it has decided to make an award to him, it shall pay him that award–

(a) in the case of an interim award made pursuant to clause 7(5)(a), as soon as reasonably practicable after the making of the interim report to which the award relates;

(b) in the case of a full and final award made pursuant to clause 7(3) or (5)(b)–

(i) where the applicant notifies MIB in writing that he accepts the offer of the award unconditionally, not later than 14 days after the date on which MIB receives that acceptance, or

(ii) where the applicant does not notify MIB of his acceptance in accordance with sub-paragraph (a) but the period during which he may give notice of an appeal under clause 19 has expired without such notice being given, not later than 14 days after the date of expiry of that period, and that payment shall discharge MIB from all liability under this Agreement in respect of the death, bodily injury or damage to property for which the award is made.

(2) MIB may, upon notifying an applicant of its decision to make an award, offer to pay the award in instalments in accordance with a structure described in the decision letter (the "structured settlement") and if the applicant notifies MIB in writing of his acceptance of the offer–

(a) the first instalment of the payment under the structured settlement shall be made not later than 14 days after the date on which MIB receives that acceptance, and

(b) subsequent payments shall be made in accordance with the agreed structure.

(3) Where an applicant has suffered bodily injury and believes either that there is a risk that he will develop a disease or condition other than that in respect of which he has made a claim or that a disease or condition in respect of which he has made a claim will deteriorate, he may–

(a) by notice given in his application, or

(b) by notice in writing received by MIB before the date on which MIB issues notification of its full or (as the case may be) final report under clause 16,

state that he wishes MIB to make a provisional award and if he does so paragraphs (4) and (5) shall apply.

(4) The applicant must specify in the notice given under paragraph (3)–

(a) each disease and each type of deterioration which he believes may occur, and

(b) the period during or within which he believes it may occur.

(5) Where MIB receives a notice under paragraph (3) it shall, not later than 14 days after the date of such receipt (or within such longer period as the applicant may agree)–

(a) accept the notice and confirm that any award it makes (other than an interim award made pursuant to clause 7(5)(a)) is to be treated as a provisional award, or

(b) reject the notice and inform the applicant that it is not willing to make a provisional award.

6) Where MIB has notified the applicant that it accepts the notice, an award which would otherwise be treated a full or final award under this Agreement

shall be treated as a provisional award only and the applicant may make a supplementary application under this Agreement but–

(a) only in respect of a disease or a type of deterioration of his condition specified in his notice, and

(b) not later than the expiration of the period specified in his notice.

(7) Where MIB has notified the applicant that it rejects the notice, subject to any decision to the contrary made by an arbitrator, no award which MIB makes shall be treated as a provisional award.

APPEALS AGAINST MIB's DECISION

Right of appeal

18. Where an applicant is not willing to accept–

(a) a decision or determination made by MIB under clause 7 or a part thereof, or

(b) a proposal for a structured settlement or a rejection of the applicant's request for a provisional award under clause 17,

he may give notice (a "notice of appeal") that he wishes to submit the matter to arbitration in accordance with the provisions of clauses 19 to 25.

Notice of appeal

19. (1) A notice of appeal shall be given in writing to MIB at any time before the expiration of a period of 6 weeks from–

(a) the date on which the applicant receives notice of MIB's decision under clause 16;

(b) where he disputes a notification given under clause 17(5)(b), the date when such notification is given;

(c) in any other case, the date on which he is given notification of the decision, determination or requirement.

(2) The notice of appeal–

(a) shall state the grounds on which the appeal is made,

(b) shall contain the applicant's observations on MIB's decision,

(c) may be accompanied by such further evidence in support of the appeal as the applicant thinks fit, and

(d) shall contain an undertaking that (subject, in the case of an arbitration to be conducted England and Wales, to his rights under sections 67 and 68 of the Arbitration Act 1996) the applicant will abide by the decision of the arbitrator made under this Agreement.

Procedure following notice of appeal

20. (1) Not later than 7 days after receiving the notice of appeal MIB shall–

(a) apply to the Secretary of State for the appointment of a single arbitrator, or

(b) having notified the applicant of its intention to do so, cause an investigation to be made into any further evidence supplied by the applicant and report to the applicant upon that investigation and of any change in its decision which may result from it.

(2) Where the only ground stated in the notice of appeal is that the award is insufficient (including a ground contesting the degree of contributory negligence attributed to the applicant or, as the case may be, the person in respect of whose death the application is made), MIB may give notice to the applicant of its intention, if the appeal proceeds to arbitration, to ask the arbitrator to decide whether its award exceeds what a court would have awarded or whether the case is one in which it would make an award at all and shall in that notice set out such observations on that matter as MIB considers relevant to the arbitrator's decision.

(3) Where MIB has made a report under paragraph (1)(b) or given to the applicant notice under paragraph (2), the applicant may, not later than 6 weeks after the date on which the report or (as the case may be) the notice was given to him–

(a) notify MIB that he wishes to withdraw the appeal, or

(b) notify MIB that he wishes to continue with the appeal and send with that notification–

(i) any observations on the report made under paragraph (1)(b) which he wishes to have drawn to the attention of the arbitrator,

(ii) any observations on the contents of the notice given under paragraph (2), including any further evidence not previously made available to MIB and relevant to the matter, which he wishes to have drawn to the attention of the arbitrator.

(4) Where the applicant notifies MIB under paragraph (3)(b) of his wish to continue the appeal, or if the applicant fails within the specified period of 6 weeks to give notification of his wish either to withdraw or to continue with the appeal, MIB shall, not later than 7 days after receiving the notification or 7 days after the expiry of the said period (as the case may be)–

(a) apply to the Secretary of State for the appointment of an arbitrator, or

(b) having notified the applicant of its intention to do so, cause a further investigation to be made into the further evidence sent under paragraph (3)(b)(ii).

(5) Where MIB has caused an investigation to be made into any further evidence supplied by the applicant under paragraph (3)(b)(ii), it shall report to the applicant upon that investigation and of any change in a decision or determination made under clause 7 which may result from it and the applicant may, not later than 6 weeks after the date on which he receives the report–

(a) notify MIB that he wishes to withdraw the appeal, or

(b) notify MIB that he wishes to continue with the appeal.

(6) Where the applicant notifies MIB under paragraph (5)(b) of his wish to continue the appeal, or if the applicant fails within the specified period of 6 weeks to give notification of his wish either to withdraw or to continue with the appeal, MIB shall not later than 7 days after receiving the notification or 7 days after the expiry of the said period (as the case may be) apply to the Secretary of State for the appointment of an arbitrator.

(7) When applying to the Secretary of State for the appointment of an arbitrator MIB may send with the application such written observations as it wishes to make upon the applicant's notice of appeal but must at the same time send a copy of those observations to the applicant.

Appointment of arbitrator

21. (1) In the event of MIB neither applying to the Secretary of State for the appointment of an arbitrator in accordance with the provisions of clause 20 nor taking such further steps as it may at its discretion take in accordance with that clause, the applicant may apply to the Secretary of State for the appointment of an arbitrator.

(2) For the purposes of the Arbitration Act 1996 (where the arbitration is to be conducted in England and Wales) the arbitral proceedings are to be regarded as commencing on the date of the making of the application by the Secretary of State or the applicant (as the case may be).

(3) The Secretary of State shall, upon the making of an application for the appointment of an arbitrator to hear the appeal, appoint the first available member, by rotation, of a panel of Queen's Counsel appointed for the purpose of determining appeals under this Agreement (where the event giving rise to the death, bodily injury or damage to property occurred in England and Wales) by the Lord Chancellor or (where the event giving rise to the death, bodily injury or damage to property occurred in Scotland) by the Lord Advocate and shall forthwith notify the applicant and MIB of the appointment.

Arbitration procedure

22. (1) Upon receiving notification from the Secretary of State of the appointment of an arbitrator, MIB shall send to the arbitrator–

(a) the notice of appeal,

(b) (if appropriate) its request for a decision as to whether its award exceeds what a court would have awarded or whether the case is one in which it would make an award at all,

(c) copies of–

(i) the applicant's application,

(ii) its decision; and

(iii) all statements, declarations, notices, reports, observations and transcripts of evidence made or given under this Agreement by the applicant or MIB.

(2) The arbitrator may, if it appears to him to be necessary or expedient for the purpose of resolving any issue, ask MIB to make a further investigation and to submit a written report of its findings to him for his consideration and in such a case–

(a) MIB shall undertake the investigation and send copies of the report to the arbitrator and the applicant,

(b) the applicant may, not later than 4 weeks after the date on which a copy of the report is received by him, submit written observations on it to the arbitrator and if he does so he shall send a copy of those observations to MIB.

(3) The arbitrator shall, after considering the written submissions referred to in paragraphs (1) and (2), send to the applicant and MIB a preliminary decision letter setting out the decision he proposes to make under clause 23 and his reasons for doing so.

(4) Not later than 28 days after the date of sending of the preliminary decision letter (or such later date as the applicant and MIB may agree) the applicant and MIB may, by written notification given to the arbitrator and copied to the other, either–

(a) accept the preliminary decision, or

(b) submit written observations upon the preliminary decision or the reasons or both, or

(c) request an oral hearing,

and if either of them should within that period fail to do any of those things (including a failure to provide the other person with a copy of his notification) he or it shall be treated as having accepted the decision.

(5) If the applicant submits new evidence with any written observations under paragraph (4)(b) MIB may at its discretion, but within 28 days or such longer period as the arbitrator may allow, do any of the following–

(a) make an investigation into that evidence,

(b) submit its own written observations on that evidence, and

(c) if it has not already done so, request an oral hearing,

and, except where an oral hearing has been requested, the arbitrator shall (in exercise of his powers under section 34 of the Arbitration Act 1996 if the arbitration is being conducted in England and Wales) determine whether, and if so how, such evidence shall be admitted and tested.

(6) If both the applicant and MIB accept the reasoned preliminary decision that decision shall be treated as his final decision for the purposes of clause 23 (so that clause 23(2) shall not then apply) but if either of them submits observations on that decision the arbitrator must take those observations into account before making a final decision.

(7) If the applicant or MIB requests an oral hearing, the arbitrator shall determine the appeal in that manner and in such a case–

(a) the hearing shall be held in public unless the applicant requests that it (or any part of it) be heard in private;

(b) the hearing shall take place at a location–

(i) in England or Wales, where the event giving rise to the death, bodily injury or damage to property occurred in England or Wales and the applicant is resident in England or Wales,

(ii) in Scotland, where the event giving rise to the death, bodily injury or damage to property occurred in Scotland and the applicant is resident in Scotland, or

(iii) in England, Wales or Scotland in any other case,

which in the opinion of the arbitrator (after consultation with each of them) is convenient for both MIB and the applicant as well as for himself;

(c) a party to the hearing may be represented by a lawyer or other person of that party's choosing;

(d) a party to the hearing shall be entitled to address the arbitrator, to call witnesses and to put questions to those witnesses and any other person called as a witness.

Arbitrator's decision

23. (1) The arbitrator, having regard to the subject matter of the proceedings, may in an appropriate case–

(a) determine whether or not the case is one to which this Agreement applies;

(b) remit the application to MIB for a full investigation and a decision in accordance with the provisions of this Agreement;

(c) determine whether MIB should make an award under this Agreement and if so what that award should be;

(d) determine such other questions as have been referred to him as he thinks fit;

(e) (subject to the provisions of paragraph (4) of this clause and clause 24) order that the costs of the proceedings shall be paid by one party or allocated between the parties in such proportions as he thinks fit;

and where the arbitrator makes a determination under sub-paragraph (a) that the case is one to which this Agreement applies, all the provisions of this Agreement shall apply as if the case were one to which clause 7(1)(b) applies.

(2) The arbitrator shall notify MIB and the applicant of his decision in writing.

(3) MIB shall pay to the applicant any amount which the arbitrator has decided shall be awarded to him, and that payment shall discharge MIB from

all liability under this Agreement in respect of the death, bodily injury or damage to property in respect of which that decision is given.

(4) Where an oral hearing has taken place at the request of the applicant and the arbitrator is satisfied that it was unnecessary and that the matter could have been decided on the basis of the written submissions referred to in clause 22(1) and (2) he shall take that into account when making an order under paragraph (1)(e).

Payment of arbitrator's fee and costs of legal representation

24. (1) Subject to paragraph (2), MIB shall upon being notified of the decision of the arbitrator pay the arbitrator a fee approved by the Lord Chancellor or the Lord Advocate, as the case may be, after consultation with MIB.

(2) In a case where it appears to the arbitrator that, having regard to all the surrounding circumstances of the case, there were no reasonable grounds for making the appeal or bringing the question before him, the arbitrator may, in his discretion, order–

(a) the applicant or,

(b) where he considers it appropriate to do so, any Solicitor or other person acting on behalf of the applicant,

to reimburse MIB the fee it has paid to the arbitrator or any part thereof.

(3) Where, pursuant to paragraph (2), the arbitrator orders–

(a) the applicant to reimburse MIB, MIB may deduct an amount equal to the fee from any amount which it pays to the applicant to discharge its liability under this Agreement;

(b) a Solicitor or other person to reimburse MIB, MIB may deduct an amount equal to the fee from any amount which it pays to that Solicitor or other person to discharge its liability to the applicant under this Agreement.

(4) Where there is an oral hearing and the applicant secures an award of compensation greater than that previously offered, then (unless the arbitrator orders otherwise) MIB shall make a contribution of £500 per half day towards the cost incurred by the applicant in respect of representation by a Solicitor, Barrister or Advocate.

Applicants under a disability

25. (1) If in any case it appears to MIB that, by reason of the applicant being a minor or of any other circumstance affecting his capacity to manage his affairs, it would be in the applicant's interest that all or some part of the award should be administered for him by an appropriate representative, MIB may establish for that purpose a trust of the whole or part of the award (such trust to take effect for such period and under such provisions as appears to MIB to be appropriate in the circumstances of the case) or, as the case may be, initiate or cause any other person in initiate the proceedings necessary to have the award administered by an appropriate representative and otherwise cause any amount payable under the award to be paid to and administered by the appropriate representative.

(2) In this clause "appropriate representative" means–

(a) in England and Wales–

(i) the Family Welfare Association, or a similar body or person, as trustee of the trust, or

(ii) the Court of Protection; and

(b) in Scotland–

(i) a Judicial Factor, or

(ii) a guardian under the Adults with Incapacity (Scotland) Act 2000, or

(iii) (where the applicant is a child) the tutor or curator of the child or a person having parental responsibilities under the Children (Scotland) Act 1995.

ACCELERATED PROCEDURE

Instigation of accelerated procedure

26. (1) In any case where, after making a preliminary investigation under clause 7, MIB has decided that–

(a) the case is one to which this Agreement applies, and

(b) it is not one to which clause 13, applies,

MIB may notify the applicant of that decision and, instead of causing a full investigation and report to be made under clause 7, may make to the applicant an offer to settle his claim by payment of an award specified in the offer representing compensation assessed in accordance with clause 8 together, in an appropriate case, with interest thereon assessed in accordance with clause 9 and a contribution towards the cost of obtaining legal advice in respect of the making of the application.

(2) Where an offer is made under paragraph (1), MIB shall send to the applicant a statement setting out–

(a) the relevant evidence it has collected disclosing the circumstances in which the death, bodily injury or damage to property occurred, and

(b) its reasons for the assessment of the award.

Settlement by accelerated procedure

27. (1) The applicant shall not later than 6 weeks after he receives an offer under clause 26 notify MIB of his acceptance or rejection thereof.

(2) Where the applicant notifies MIB of his acceptance of the offer–

(a) MIB shall not later than 14 days after receipt of the acceptance pay to the applicant the amount of the award, and

(b) MIB shall be discharged from all liability under this Agreement in respect of the death, bodily injury or damage to property for which that payment is made.

(3) In the event of the applicant failing to accept the offer within the specified period, the application shall be treated as one to which clause 7(1)(b) applies.

MISCELLANEOUS

Referral of disputes to arbitrator

28. (1) Any dispute between the applicant and MIB concerning a decision, determination or requirement made by MIB under the terms of this Agreement, other than a dispute relating to MIB's decision for which provision is made by clause 18, shall be referred to and determined by an arbitrator.

(2) Where an applicant wishes to refer such a dispute to arbitration, he shall not later than 4 weeks after the decision, determination or requirement is communicated to him, give notice to MIB that he wishes the matter to be so resolved.

(3) For the purposes of the Arbitration Act 1996 (where the arbitration is to be conducted in England and Wales) the arbitral proceedings are to be regarded as commencing on the date of such application.

(4) Upon receipt of the applicant's notice MIB shall apply immediately to the Secretary of State for the appointment of an arbitrator and in the event of MIB failing to do so the applicant may make the application.

(5) The Secretary of State shall, upon receiving the application for the appointment of an arbitrator to hear the appeal, appoint the first available

member, by rotation, of a panel of Queen's Counsel appointed for the purpose of determining appeals under this Agreement (where the event giving rise to the death, bodily injury or damage to property occurred in England and Wales) by the Lord Chancellor or (where the event giving rise to the death, bodily injury or damage to property occurred in Scotland) by the Lord Advocate and shall forthwith notify the applicant and MIB of the appointment.

(6) The applicant and MIB shall, not later than 4 weeks after receiving notification of the appointment of the arbitrator, submit to him a written statement of their respective cases with supporting documentary evidence where available.

(7) Subject to paragraphs (8) to (10), the arbitrator shall decide the appeal on the documents submitted to him under paragraph (6) and no further evidence shall be produced to him.

(8) The applicant may, by notice in writing given to the arbitrator and MIB not later than the date on which he submits the statement of his case, ask the arbitrator to determine the appeal by means of an oral hearing and shall submit to the arbitrator and MIB a written statement, with supporting documentary evidence where appropriate, in support of that request.

(9) The arbitrator shall in such a case seek the view of MIB on the need for an oral hearing and MIB may submit to the arbitrator and the applicant a written statement, with supporting documentary evidence where appropriate, in support of its view.

(10) If, after considering those written submissions, the arbitrator decides that an oral hearing is necessary to determine the dispute–

> (a) the hearing shall be held in public unless the applicant requests that it (or any part of it) be heard in private;
>
> (b) the hearing shall take place at a location–
>
> > (i) in England or Wales, where the event giving rise to the death, bodily injury or damage to property occurred in England or Wales and the applicant is resident in England or Wales,
> >
> > (ii) in Scotland, where the event giving rise to the death, bodily injury or damage to property occurred in Scotland and the applicant is resident in Scotland, or
> >
> > (iii) in England, Wales or Scotland in any other case,

which in the opinion of the arbitrator (after consultation with each of them) is convenient for both MIB and the applicant as well as for himself;

(c) a party to the hearing may be represented by a lawyer or other person of that party's choosing;

(d) a party to the hearing shall be entitled to address the arbitrator, to call witnesses and to put questions to those witnesses and any other person called as a witness.

(11) The arbitrator may, having regard to the subject matter of the proceedings and in an appropriate case, order that his fee or the costs of the proceedings (as determined according to clause 10(1)(b) of, and the Schedule to, this Agreement) or both his fee and those costs shall be paid by one party or allocated between the parties in such proportions as he thinks fit.

(12) Unless otherwise agreed, the decision, determination or requirement in respect of which notice is given under paragraph (2) shall stand unless reversed by the arbitrator.

Services of notices, etc, on MIB

29. Any notice required to be served on or any other notification or document required to be given or sent to MIB under the terms of this Agreement shall be sufficiently served or given sent by fax or by Registered or Recorded Delivery post to MIB's registered office and delivery shall be proved by the production of a fax report produced by the sender's fax machine or an appropriate postal receipt.

Agents

30. MIB may perform any of its obligations under this Agreement by agents.

Contracts (Rights of Third Parties) Act 1999

31. (1) For the purposes of the Contracts (Rights of Third Parties) Act 1999 the following provisions shall apply.

(2) This Agreement may be–

(a) varied or rescinded without the consent of any person other than the parties hereto, and

(b) determined under clause 3(2) without the consent of any such person.

(3) Save for the matters specified in paragraph (4), MIB shall not have available to it against an applicant any matter by way of counterclaim or set-

off which would have been available to it if the applicant rather than the Secretary of State had been a party to this Agreement.

(4) The matters referred to in paragraph (3) are any counterclaim or set-off arising by virtue of the provisions of–

(a) this Agreement;

(b) the 1996 Agreement;

(c) the 1999 Agreement;

(d) either of the agreements which were respectively superseded by the 1996 Agreement and the 1999 Agreement.

(5) This agreement, being made for the purposes of Article 1(4) of Council Directive 84/5/EEC of 30th December 1983–

(a) is intended to confer a benefit on an applicant but on no other person, and

(b) to confer such benefit subject to the terms and conditions set out herein.

Enforcement against MIB

32. If MIB fail to pay compensation in accordance with the provisions of this agreement the applicant is entitled to enforce payment through the courts.

Transitional provisions

33. The 1996 Agreement shall cease to have effect after the 13 February 2003 but shall continue in force in relation to any claim arising out of an event occurring on or before that date.

IN WITNESS whereof the Secretary of State has caused his Corporate Seal to be hereunto affixed and the Motor Insurer's Bureau has caused its Common Seal to be hereunto affixed the day and year first above written.

SCHEDULE

MIB's CONTRIBUTION TOWARDS APPLICANT'S LEGAL COSTS

1. Subject to paragraph 4, MIB shall pay a contribution towards the applicant's costs of obtaining legal advice determined in accordance with paragraph 2,

2. That amount shall be the aggregate of–

(a) the fee specified in column (2) of the table below in relation to the amount of the award specified in column (1) of that table,

(b) the amount of value added tax charged on that fee,

(c) where the applicant has opted for an oral hearing under clause and

(d) reasonable disbursements.

TABLE

Amount of the award (1)	Specified fee (2)
Not exceeding £150,000	15% of the amount of the award, subject to a minimum of £500 and a maximum of £3000
Exceeding £150,000	2% of the amount of the award

3. For the purposes of paragraph 2–

"amount of the award" means the aggregate of the sum awarded by way of compensation and interest under clauses 8 and 9, before deduction of any reimbursement due to be paid to the Secretary of State for Work and Pensions through the Compensation Recovery Unit (CRU) of his Department (or to any successor of that unit), but excluding the amount of any payment due in respect of benefits and hospital charges.

"reasonable disbursements" means reasonable expenditure incurred on the applicant's behalf and agreed between the applicant and MIB before it is incurred (MIB's agreement not having been unreasonably withheld) but includes Counsel's fees only where the applicant is a minor or under a legal disability.

4. The foregoing provisions of this Schedule are without prejudice to MIB's liability under the provisions of this Agreement to pay the costs of arbitration proceedings or an arbitrator's fee.

THE CORPORATE SEAL of the Secretary of State)

FOR TRANSPORT hereunto affixed is authenticated by:-)

Authorised by the Secretary of State

Richard Jones

THE COMMON SEAL of the Motor Insurers')

BUREAU was hereunto affixed in the presence of:-)

J A Read *R D Snook*

Directors of the Board of Management

B Louisy

Secretary

21 FUNDING METHODS

21 FUNDING METHODS

Contents

21.1 Introduction

There are various methods available to Claimants to fund personal injury claims. These various options have an impact on the potential costs for which a Defendant will be liable if the claim is successful and also means that there are tactical considerations as to how a claims handler should deal with the claim.

The starting point for understanding the various funding methods is to appreciate the indemnity principle. This is a concept in legal costs where the receiving party cannot recover from the paying party more than the receiving party is liable to pay his or her own solicitor.

21.2 Types of Funding

21.2.1 Ordinary Private Client Retainer

The traditional form of funding a claim is for a client to instruct solicitors on a private basis and agree to pay a certain sum per hour for the solicitor's time. The client is liable to pay his solicitor's costs whatever the outcome of the action. If successful, he will usually be able to recover most of these costs from the other side, and if unsuccessful, he will usually become liable for the other side's costs as well as his own.

21.2.2 Legal Aid

Previously, many personal injury claims were funded by way of the Legal Aid system. However, since 1st April 2000 most personal injury cases (except clinical negligence) have not had Legal Aid funding available.

21.2.3 Before-the-Event (BTE) Insurance

Many claims are now funded through pre-purchased legal expenses insurance. This is through an insurance policy which is purchased in advance of an accident occurring and is therefore referred to as Before-the-Event (BTE) insurance.

Many people have BTE insurance as part of their existing car insurance, home insurance or even through their credit cards. In the event that a policy holder has an accident the insurance company will normally refer the matter to one of their panel solicitors. The policy will usually indemnify the Claimant is respect of their own legal costs and those of the other side if the claim is lost.

The cost of these premiums is not recoverable from the other side if a claim is successful.

21.2.4 Conditional Fee Agreements

A Conditional Fee Agreement (CFA) is an agreement whereby a party's solicitor's fees are only payable in certain circumstances. Although there are a number of potential ways for these agreements to work, the most typical is that if the case is lost the solicitor makes no charge, but if he wins he charges his normal costs plus a percentage uplift (success fee) on those fees. They are therefore commonly referred to as 'no win, no fee agreements'.

21.2.5 'CFA Lite'

Amendments to the rules on 2nd June 2003 allowed for the creation of simplified CFAs where the solicitor agrees to charge the client no more than is recovered from the other side. This is an exception to the well established indemnity principle. These agreements have been termed 'CFA Lite' or 'CFA Simple' although they remain fairly uncommon.

21.2.6 After-the-Event (ATE) Insurance

The risk to an unsuccessful Claimant is not limited to failing to recover their own costs. They are also likely to have to pay the other side's legal fees, although this risk is only likely to occur in personal injury cases after proceedings have been issued because, until that stage, an insurance company is likely to deal with the matter in-house without incurring solicitors' fees. To protect the Claimant from these costs a number of insurance products have come into existence. These are known as 'After-the-Event' (ATE) insurance policies because they are entered into after the accident (event) has occurred and when legal proceedings are being contemplated. These are to be distinguished from BTE policies mentioned above. Where the ATE policy was entered into after 1st April 2000, the premium, subject to reasonableness and proportionality, in the event of a successful claim, is recoverable from the other side.

ATE policies usually insure the Claimant against the costs of the Defendant if the claim is lost. Many also cover the Claimant's own disbursements if the claim is unsuccessful.

It is normal for such policies to be entered into in conjunction with the Claimant's solicitor acting under a CFA. However, there is no obligation for this to happen and there may be a CFA without there being ATE in place, and vice versa.

21.2.7 Collective Conditional Fee Agreements

CFAs were introduced principally for individual Claimants in individual claims. Subsequently, new rules were introduced enabling the bulk purchase and provision of legal services through Collective Conditional Fee Agreements (CCFAs). These were designed for bodies such as trade unions. There had been a long tradition of trade unions funding personal injury claims brought by their members, usually against their employers. The trade union paid for their member's solicitor's fees and agreed to indemnify them for any adverse costs order made against them.

CCFAs enable such bodies to enter into a single agreement with solicitors to govern the way in which cases for its members will be run and paid for. These cases are treated in a similar fashion as those run under a CFA, and a success fee can be claimed, but individual CFAs do not have to be prepared and signed for each Claimant whose case is run under the agreement.

21.2.8 Notional Insurance Premiums

In addition to the need to allow for organisations such as trade unions to enter into CCFAs it was recognised that the normal rules concerning ATE insurance were not always appropriate for such bodies. It had always been common practice for them to indemnify their members against any adverse costs orders that were incurred in litigation. In effect, the body would be self-insuring their members.

To allow for this situation, the law was changed to allow these bodies to recover a notional amount to reflect this element in a similar way to how individual Claimants could recover ATE premiums. The relevant provision is contained within section 30 of the Access to Justice Act 1999, and these amounts are often referred to as 'section 30 premium equivalents' or 'notional insurance premiums'.

A party cannot recover a notional insurance premium in an amount greater than the likely cost of buying an ATE insurance policy on the open market. Notional insurance premiums became recoverable from the losing party from 1st April 2000.

21.3 Date of Conditional Fee Agreement

The rules relating to CFAs have undergone a number of changes and it is essential to consider the date of a CFA to understand which rules apply and what impact this has on recoverability of costs.

21.3.1 Pre-1st April 2000 CFAs

CFAs were lawful prior to 1st April 2000. However, at that stage the success fee was not recoverable from the other side and was the sole responsibility of the Claimant. The effect of the subsequent rule change was that the success fee remained irrecoverable from the other side where the CFA, or the first CFA in a case, was entered into pre-1st April 2000. This is regardless of when the claim was settled.

The same rule also applies to ATE premiums where the policy, or first policy, was entered into pre-1st April 2000. The other side is not liable for the cost.

21.3.2 CFAs Between 1st April 2000 and 30th October 2005

From 1st April 2000 success fees (plus ATE premiums and notional insurance premiums) became recoverable from the other side. However, section 27 of the Access to Justice Act 1999 required CFAs entered into after that date to comply with various requirements. The most significant of these were contained in the Conditional Fee Agreement Regulations 2000. If the CFA materially breaches the Regulations then it is invalid. The consequence of this is that the client has no liability to pay his solicitor's fees and therefore no costs can be recovered from the other side (as per the indemnity principle). The exception to this relates to certain disbursements and any ATE premium. The ATE premium will be recoverable in any event, as its recoverability rests on the wording of the Act rather than the terms of any retainer. Further, any disbursements which the Claimant has in fact paid 'up front', whether personally or by taking out a loan to do so, will also be recoverable as they will be costs of the Claimant and not their solicitor.

The Court of Appeal produced a test to determine whether a breach of the Regulations was material. The question to ask was whether the breach 'had a materially adverse effect either upon the protection afforded to the client or upon the proper administration of justice' (see ***Hollins v Russell [2003]*** EWCA Civ 718). It has been further held that the date for determining whether a breach is material is at the time the agreement is entered into. Whether there is actual detriment suffered by the client is irrelevant. It is the potential for detriment that creates the breach (see ***Garrett v Halton Borough Council [2006]*** EWCA Civ 1017).

21.3.3 The Conditional Fee Agreement Regulations 2000

The Regulations are fairly complex and lengthy and need to be carefully considered in conjunction with a CFA to determine whether it is valid. However, the following are examples of breaches that the Court of Appeal has held to be material resulting in the costs being disallowed:

- a failure to specify in the CFA how much of the success fee related to postponement – breach of Regulation 3(1)(b) (see ***Spencer v Wood [2004]*** EWCA Civ 352)
- a failure by the solicitor, before the CFA was entered into, to consider whether the client had BTE cover that would have insured the claim – breach of Regulation 4(2)(c) (see ***Myatt v National Coal Board [2006]*** EWCA Civ 1017)
- a failure to inform the client whether the solicitor had an interest in recommending a particular ATE policy – breach of Regulation 4(2)(e)(ii) (see ***Garrett v Halton Borough Council 2006***)
- a risk assessment setting the success fee at over 100% - breach of Conditional Fee Agreements Order 2000 (see ***Jones v Caradon Catnic Ltd [2005]*** Civ 1821)

21.3.4 CFAs Entered into on or after 1st November 2005

The complexities of the CFA Regulations led to numerous technical challenges to CFAs. The satellite litigation that this generated, and the problems solicitors experienced in properly complying with the rules, resulted in a decision to revoke the CFA Regulations 2000 entirely. Although the Regulations continue to apply to those CFAs entered into pre-1st November 2005, for those entered into on or after that date the only requirements for a CFA to be valid are that the agreement is in writing and the success fee does not exceed 100%.

21.3.5 CCFAs

CCFAs first came into existence with the coming into force of the Collective Conditional Fee Agreement Regulations 2000 on 30th November 2000. Where solicitors accepted a claim under a CCFA from this date, a claim for a success fee could be made. CCFAs initially had to comply with the CCFA Regulations to be valid. However, the Regulations were not onerous and it would be rare to find one that was defective. These Regulations were also revoked from 1st November 2005 in respect of new CCFAs. The only likely problem with a pre or post-1st November 2005 CCFA that would invalidate the agreement is where the success fee is set at above 100%.

21.4 Operation of CFAs/CCFAs

21.4.1 Basic Charges

The Claimant's solicitor's basic charges will be their base profit costs (without a success fee added) and disbursements. The Claimant will usually only become liable to pay his solicitor's base profit costs if the claim is successful. The Claimant may still be liable for the disbursements depending on the terms of the CFA.

A successful Claimant will then usually be able to seek recovery of these costs from the Defendant (the paying party). The paying party can challenge these at a detailed assessment. The hourly rate, time spent and disbursements must be reasonable and proportionate in accordance with the Civil Procedure Rules 1998.

21.4.2 Success Fees

The success fee is the percentage increase in the solicitor's base profit costs payable in the event that a win is achieved. The success fee is set at the time the CFA is entered into and should reflect the risks to the solicitor of losing the case and therefore recovering no costs. Therefore, in theory, the success fees that solicitors recover in successful cases compensates them for those cases where they lose and recover no costs. The paying party can challenge the success fee at the conclusion of the case but its reasonableness will be assessed based upon the facts and circumstances as they reasonably appeared to the solicitor at the time the agreement was entered into. Hindsight cannot be used.

The success fee is based on the following factors:

(a) the fact that if the Claimant wins the Claimant's solicitor will not be paid their basic charges until the end of the claim;

(b) whether the solicitor will be liable for the Claimant's disbursements if the case is lost;

(c) the risk to the solicitor that a win will not be achieved and they will therefore not be able to charge their costs

The first of these factors is not an element recoverable from the paying party. So, for example, if 10% of the success fee relates to the postponement of the payment of the fees the paying party is not liable for that 10%. The Claimant must bear this element themselves.

Further, the reasonableness of a success fee will depend on whether other methods of financing the costs were available to the receiving party. This means that if the receiving party had available suitable BTE insurance then the court may find that it was unreasonable to enter into a CFA and may therefore disallow the success fee in full.

Although most success fees are set at a single level to govern the whole case, a CFA can equally have different success fees applying to different stages. A success fee might, for example, be set at 20% if liability is admitted within 3 months but rise to 100% if it is not.

It is also possible for counsel to enter into CFAs. The same basic principles apply when considering any success fee claimed by counsel.

21.4.3 Fixed Success Fees

To reduce the number of disputes that arose in relation to the appropriate success fee to allow, fixed success fees were introduced for certain categories of case. Although the detailed rules are quite complicated, the basic principles for solicitors' success fees are as follows:

Type of ClaimCategory Name	Date from which Fixed Success Fees Apply
Road Traffic Accident	Accident on or after 6/10/03
Employers' Liability	Accident on or after 1/10/04
Employers' Liability Disease	Letter Before Action sent on or after 1/10/05

Where the case settles pre-trial the solicitor's success fee will be as follows:

Type of Case	Ordinary	Membership Organisation*
Road Traffic Accident	12.5%	12.5%
Employers' Liability	25.0%	27.5%
Asbestos related claims	27.5%	30.0%
Vibration White Finger	62.5%	70.0%
Noise induced hearing loss	62.5%	70.0%
Stress/RSI Claims	100.0%	100.0%
Any other type of disease claim	62.5%	70.0%

* These success fees will apply where a membership organisation has undertaken to meet the Claimant's liabilities for legal costs in accordance with section 30 of the **Access to Justice Act 1999** (ie where there is a notional insurance premium).

Where the case proceeds to trial in respect of any of the above cases the success fee will be 100%.

Different success fees apply to counsels' fees depending on the stage at which a case settles and the detailed rules should be referred to.

Where the success fee is fixed then, unlike with non-fixed success fee cases, the court has no discretion to disallow the success fee even though there was alternative funding, such as BTE insurance, available (see ***Kilby v Gawith*** [2008] EWCA Civ 812).

For cases which pre-date these rules, the appropriate success fee will depend on the individual facts of the case. The fixed success fees do not apply retrospectively.

21.5 After-the-Event Insurance Premiums

As previously mentioned, an ATE premium will only be recoverable to the extent that the amount is reasonable and proportionate.

Defendants have successfully challenged some ATE premiums on the basis that not all of the amount claimed as premium was actually premium. This issue particularly arose in relation to insurance premiums linked to claims management companies (see ***Claims Direct Test Cases*** [2003] EWCA Civ 136 and ***Accident Group Test Cases*** [2004] EWCA Civ 575).

More recently, as evidence has emerged that the ATE market may be in a fragile state, the courts have become reluctant to reduce premiums simply because the amount claimed appears high (see ***Rogers v Merthyr Tydfil CBC*** [2006] EWCA Civ 1134). Successful challenges to premiums are therefore likely to become harder in the absence of precise technical challenges.

21.6 The Costs Rules

The rules relating to the recoverability of additional liabilities are to be found in the Civil Procedure Rules (CPR) and the corresponding Costs Practice Direction (CPD).

Rule 44.3A(1)

The court will not assess any additional liability until the conclusion of the proceedings. Therefore the court will only assess base costs if there is a costs order relating to an interim application/hearing where the costs are summarily assessed. The success fee and any ATE/notional premium will be reserved until the conclusion of the matter.

Rule 44.3B(1)(a)

The Claimant cannot recover any proportion of the success fee relating to the cost to the legal representative of the postponement of the payment of his fees and expenses.

Rule 44.3B(1)(b)

The Claimant cannot recover any provision (notional premium) made by a membership organisation which exceeds the likely cost of purchasing an ATE premium to cover the same claim.

Rule 44.3B(1)(c)

The Claimant cannot recover any additional liability for any period in the proceedings during which he failed to provide information about a funding arrangement in accordance with the rules.

Therefore, if a Claimant fails to serve notice in accordance with the rules (see below) the paying party does not have to pay for any additional liability during the period of default. If a Notice of Funding is served late, the additional liability will run from the date that the service was affected.

Rule 44.3B(1)(d)

Where, during detailed assessment proceedings, a Claimant fails to disclose the reasons for setting the percentage increase at the level stated in the CFA, the success fee will not be recoverable.

Rule 44.15(1)

Rule 44.15(1) states:

> 'A party who seeks to recover an additional liability must provide information about the funding arrangement to the court and to other parties as required by a rule, practice direction or court order.' (see below)

Rule 44.15(2)

Where the funding arrangement has changed so that the information previously provided is no longer accurate, the Claimant must advise all parties and the court within 7 days.

CPD 10.1

Where a receiving party finds themselves in breach of Rule 44.3B(1)(c) or (d) they may make an application to the court for relief from the sanction. If such an application is successful, then the additional liability will be recoverable despite the earlier breach.

CPD 11.8

CPD 11.8 states:

'(1) In deciding whether a percentage increase is reasonable relevant factors to be taken into account may include:
- (a) the risk that the circumstances in which the costs, fees or expenses would be payable might or might not occur;
- (b) the legal representative's liability for any disbursements;
- (c) what other methods of financing the costs were available to the receiving party.'

'In deciding whether the cost of insurance cover is reasonable, relevant factors to be taken into account include:

(1) where the insurance cover is not purchased in support of a conditional fee agreement with a success fee, how its cost compares with the likely cost of funding the case with a conditional fee agreement with a success fee and supporting insurance cover;

(2) the level and extent of the cover provided;

(3) the availability of any pre-existing insurance cover;

(4) whether any part of the premium would be rebated in the event of early settlement;

(5) the amount of commission payable to the receiving party or his legal representatives or other agents.'

CPD 19

A party wishing to recover an additional liability must serve a Notice of Funding on the court and all the parties with the claim form when it is issued. If the funding agreement is entered into after proceedings are issued, the party has 7 days to give notice.

There is currently conflicting case law on whether there is a duty to give notification of a funding arrangement prior to proceedings being issued. This confusion stems from the fact that the Protocols Practice Direction, which relates to the Pre-Action Protocols, states that a Claimant 'should' disclose the existence of a funding arrangement. The conflicting decisions have hinged on whether 'should' in this context means 'must'.

Notice of Funding

The Notice of Funding must contain the following information:

(1) Where the funding arrangement is a CFA/CCFA the party must state the date of the agreement and identify the claim or claims to which it relates.

(2) Where the funding arrangement is an ATE insurance policy the party must state the name and address of the insurer, the policy number and the date of the policy, and must identify the claim or claims to which it relates.

(3) Where the funding arrangement is by way of an arrangement (a notional premium) with a membership organisation the party must state the name of the organisation and set out the date and terms of the undertaking it has given and must identify the claim or claims to which it relates.

(4) Where the funding arrangement is an ATE insurance policy incorporating two or more staged premiums ('a staged policy')

the party must state that it is a staged policy and must identify the points at which each of the stages are or will be reached.

There is no duty during a case to give details of the level of the success fee or the amount of any ATE premium. The reasoning behind this is that if these were disclosed it would enable the Defendant to assess whether or not the Claimant's solicitors assessed the claim as being a weak one.

A Notice of Funding is reproduced overleaf.

Notice of funding of case or claim

Notice of funding by means of a conditional fee agreement, insurance policy or undertaking given by a prescribed body should be given to the court and all other parties to the case:
- on commencement of proceedings
- on filing an acknowledgment of service, defence or other first document; and
- at any later time that such an arrangement is entered into, changed or terminated.

In the

The court office is open between 10 am and 4 pm Monday to Friday. When writing to the court, please address forms or letters to the Court Manager and quote the claim number.

Claim No.	
Claimant (include Ref.)	
Defendant (include Ref.)	

Take notice that in respect of

☐ all claims herein

☐ the following claims

☐ the case of *(specify name of party)*

[is now][was] being funded by:

(Please tick those boxes which apply)

☐ a conditional fee agreement
Dated
which provides for a success fee

☐ an insurance policy issued on
Date **Policy no.**
Name and address of insurer

☐ an undertaking given on
Date
by
Name of prescribed body
in the following terms

The funding of the case has now changed:

☐ the above funding has now ceased

☐ the conditional fee agreement has been terminated

☐ a conditional fee agreement
Dated
which provides for a success fee has been entered into;

☐ an insurance policy
Date
has been cancelled

☐ an insurance policy has been issued on
Date **Policy no.**
Name and address of insurer

☐ an undertaking given on
Date
has been terminated

☐ an undertaking has been given on
Date
Name of prescribed body
in the following terms

Signed
Solicitor for the (claimant) (defendant)
(Part 20 defendant) (respondent) (appellant)

Dated

N251 Notice of funding of case or claim (06.04)

The Court Service Publications Branch

Detailed Assessment

If, at the conclusion of a claim, costs cannot be agreed then it will be necessary for the receiving party to commence detailed assessment proceedings. Various documents must be served on the paying party at this stage although generally it will be equally appropriate for such documents to be served on a voluntary basis beforehand to try to facilitate agreement. The relevant documents include:

- A copy of the CFA/CCFA. Although the rules do not state that this document must be disclosed, the Court of Appeal has made it clear that they would expect this to be disclosed as a matter of routine (see ***Hollins v Russell***).
- A statement of the reasons for the percentage increase (success fee).
- If the additional liability is an ATE insurance premium: a copy of the insurance certificate showing whether the policy covers the receiving party's own costs; his opponents costs; or his own costs and his opponent's costs; and the maximum extent of that cover, and the amount of the premium paid or payable.
- If the receiving party claims an additional amount under section 30 of the **Access of Justice Act 1999** (a notional premium): a statement setting out the basis upon which the receiving party's liability for the additional amount is calculated.

21.7 Tactical Considerations

Where a Claimant's case is being funded by way of a funding arrangement this can have a dramatic effect of the level of costs potentially recovered. It is therefore essential to have this fact in mind throughout the course of a case. Equally, there may be ways to use this to a Defendant's advantage.

21.7.1 Disputing Liability/Quantum

A court, when assessing the reasonableness of a success fee, is not meant to use the benefit of hindsight. How the claim is therefore actually defended is not meant to be a relevant consideration. In reality, the fact that liability is subsequently disputed, or where there are complex disputes on causation or quantum, is something a court is likely to bear in mind as it would seem to justify the accuracy of a

success fee set at a high level. Equally, where these issues are dealt with very quickly that would seem to suggest that a high success fee had been set at an unrealistic level. Therefore, in cases which are not subject to fixed success fees there is much potentially to be gained by resolving these issues as quickly as possible. This will also assist in keeping base costs as low as possible. A decision to dispute aspects of a claim should only be taken once a consideration of the costs implications has been undertaken.

Conversely, if a claim is lost on liability at trial, the Claimant's solicitors will not recover any costs if the matter is funded by way of a CFA/CCFA. They therefore have an incentive, where liability is not clear cut, to advise their client to accept an offer, even if it is less than the full potential value of the claim, rather than encourage the Claimant to press on to trial. There may therefore be an advantage in a claims handler making an offer for less than the full value of a claim.

21.7.2 Fixed Success Fees

Where a case is being run under a CFA or CCFA and fixed success fees apply, this may have an important impact on how willing a Claimant's solicitor is to settle a claim shortly before trial. If the matter proceeds to trial, the solicitors will receive a 100% success fee. This 100% success fee will apply even where a Claimant fails to beat a Part 36 offer made by the Defendant (see ***Lamont v Burton*** [2007] EWCA Civ 429). The recoverable success fee will be significantly lower in EL, PL and some disease claims where the case settles even a day before trial. Where only quantum is in dispute this may be, at least subconsciously, an influencing factor on whether or not the Claimant will be advised to settle at the last moment or press on to trial. Therefore it is advisable for a Defendant to ensure that reasonable settlement proposals are made at an early stage to avoid this dilemma arising.

21.7.3 Notification

As noted above, a party cannot recover an additional liability for any period during the proceedings where notification was not given. Where a party has failed to give proper notification, they can apply to the court for relief from sanctions. One of the factors that the court will take into account when considering whether to grant relief is whether the other side will suffer prejudice if such relief is granted. This can be used to a Defendant's advantage. During the course of a case, if the

Claimant has not given notification that there is a funding arrangement in place, it is probably advisable not to ask whether one exists. That will simply remind the Claimant's solicitor of their duty. However, it will often be advisable for a claims handler to prepare a note of the fact that they have taken into account the fact that no Notice of Funding has been served, that it is therefore assumed that no funding arrangement in place and this is a factor that has been considered when deciding whether to settle the claim. This will therefore assist in resisting any subsequent application for relief if it later turns out that there is an additional liability being claimed.

21.7.4 Recovering Costs

In the past, legally aided Claimants could exploit the fact that the rules meant that any insured Defendant who succeed against them at trial would not be able to recover their costs from them or from the Legal Aid Board.

That situation, in the past, encouraged insurers to settle legally aided cases on a commercial basis notwithstanding the fact that they may have a good defence to the claim. It was often more expensive to fight the case to trial and win than to settle the claim before trial.

That a claim is being funded with a CFA/CCFA backed by ATE/notional premium should become apparent, at the latest, when proceedings are issued. A claims handler who feels that they have a good case on liability may now decide to fight on safe in the knowledge that they will be able to recover their costs from the Claimant's ATE insurer/membership organisation.

There should be a note of caution however. There appear to be a number of ATE insurers who are extremely reluctant to pay out on a lost case. Others will only pay out in limited circumstances, such as where the Claimant is entirely unsuccessful but not where they have a partial costs order. The level of indemnity can vary enormously, sometimes being as low as £10,000. This means that there may be insufficient cover in anything but the most straightforward of claims. These various factors can considerably reduce the advantage that should be gained when facing a Claimant who has ATE insurance. The ATE provider, and their previous track record, should therefore be taken into account when considering tactics.

Claimants can experience problems obtaining ATE cover especially where insurance was not obtained at an early stage in the case or where liability is not straightforward. Claims handlers therefore need to be conscious of cases where notification has been given that the claim is being run under a CFA but there is no mention of ATE insurance. Does the Claimant have the financial means to privately pay an adverse costs order?

21.7.5 Part 36 Payments/Offers

It is also possible for claims handlers to seek an advantage against Claimants who they know are being funded by BTE or ATE insurance. A number of ATE/BTE insurers will put pressure upon their policyholders/solicitors in the event that a Defendant makes a Part 36 offer to settle. It may be that the offer is below the sum that could reasonably be expected to be awarded to the Claimant if the matter proceeded to court.

However, several BTE/ATE insurers currently threaten to withdraw funding from their policyholders in the event that a Part 36 offer, which falls within a margin of 10% to 20% of the valuation of the claim made by the Claimant's solicitors, is not accepted by their policyholder. Those insurers argue in that situation that the offer falls within the 20% 'litigation risk' bracket and that as a result they do not consider it reasonable to continue to fund the claim.

In this situation, solicitors will find it difficult to advise their clients to proceed with the claim, where they will find themselves uninsured, and may therefore feel compelled to advise acceptance of the offer.

Claims handlers should be alive to the above difficulties that are often faced by Claimants whose cases are funded by BTE/ATE insurance. It may be that claims handlers will gain experience of those BTE/ATE insurers who behave in this way. Claims handlers should consider whether to adjust any offer that is to be put forward to a Claimant whose claim is being funded in this way.

GLOSSARY

Additional Liability

The success fee, insurance premium, or the notional premium, as the case may be.

ATE

After-the-Event Insurance – An insurance policy taken out to insure against the risk of incurring a costs liability in the proceedings, taken out after the event (hence ATE) that is the subject matter of the claim. The costs of such policies are potentially recoverable.

Base costs

Costs excluding the amount of any additional liability.

BTE

Before-the-Event insurance – An insurance policy entered into before an accident has occurred that provides insurance cover in respect of potential legal costs in the event of a future accident and legal claim. The costs of such policies are not recoverable between the parties.

Conditional Fee Agreement (CFA)

An agreement where the solicitor's fees are dependant, in whole or in part, on the outcome of the litigation. A CFA may allow for a success fee to also be charged in the event the claim is successful.

Collective Conditional Fee Agreement (CCFA)

An agreement where the solicitor's fees are dependant, in whole or in part, on the outcome of the litigation. Unlike a CFA, the agreement does not refer to a specific claim but covers a number of potential cases that may be run under the umbrella agreement. A CCFA may allow for a success fee to also be charged in the event the claim is successful.

Detailed Assessment

A court hearing where the reasonableness and proportionality of the costs claimed is assessed by the court. The paying party will attempt to persuade the court to reduce or disallow those items they consider to be unreasonably incurred or of an unreasonable amount. The receiving party will attempt to persuade the court that the items identified by the paying party were reasonably incurred or are of a reasonable amount.

Disbursements

Payments made by a solicitor on behalf of their client, such as court fees, experts' fees, etc.

Funding Arrangement –

An arrangement where a person has-

(i) entered into a conditional fee agreement or a collective conditional fee agreement which provides for a success fee;

(ii) taken out an insurance policy to which section 29 of the Access to Justice Act 1999 (recovery of insurance premiums by way of costs) applies; or

(iii) made an agreement with a membership organisation to meet his legal costs.

Hourly Rate

The amount charged per hour by a solicitor or other fee earner in respect of the work they perform.

Indemnity Principle

A concept in legal costs where the receiving party cannot recover from the paying party more than the receiving party is liable to pay his or her own solicitor.

Insurance Premium

A sum of money paid or payable for ATE insurance. The cost of such policies is potentially recoverable.

Membership Organisation

A body prescribed for the purposes of section 30 of the Access to Justice Act 1999 (recovery where body undertakes to meet costs liabilities).

Notional Premium

The amount potentially recoverable by a membership organisation for the purposes of section 30 of the Access to Justice Act 1999 (recovery where a body undertakes to meet costs liabilities). This amount is the sum that is treated as being the equivalent of an insurance premium even though no policy has been purchased (hence 'notional premium').

Notice of Funding

A notice (usually in Form N251) by which one party warns another of the existence of any additional liability which may later be recoverable.

Paying party

A party who has become liable to pay another party's costs.

Percentage increase

See *Success Fee*

Profit Costs

A solicitor's charges for the supply of legal services. Usually calculated based on the number of hours work performed by the solicitor. Excludes disbursements.

Receiving Party

A party who is having their costs, or part of their costs, paid by another party.

Retainer

The terms upon which a solicitor is engaged to carry out work on behalf of a client - usually set out in a client care letter or CFA/CCFA.

Success Fee

The additional fee, over and above the ordinary fees charged by a successful lawyer in a conditional fee case. The percentage by which the amount of a legal representative's profit costs can be increased in accordance with a conditional fee agreement which provides for a success fee.

Summary Assessment

The procedure by which the Court, when making an award of costs, immediately calculates and specifies the sum of costs it allows.

By Courtesy of

Simon T B Gibbs
Gibbs Wyatt Stone

22 FIXED RECOVERABLE COSTS IN RTAs

22 Fixed Recoverable Costs in RTAs

Contents

22.1 Introduction

To reduce the number of disputes concerning legal costs, and to introduce more certainty into the system, fixed recoverable costs have been introduced for most low value road traffic accident (RTA) cases that settle without proceedings being issued. This scheme is often referred to as Predictable Costs.

22.2 Which Cases are Covered by the Scheme?

The following conditions are necessary for a case to fall within the scheme:

- the dispute must arise from an RTA (Rule 45.7(2)(a));
- the substantive claim must settle prior to proceedings being issued (Rule 45.7(1)(a) or the only proceedings are for approval of a settlement or compromise of a child or patient under Rule 21.10(2) (Rule 45.7(1)(b));
- the agreed damages must include damages in respect of personal injury, damage to property, or both (Rule 45.7(2)(b));
- the total value of the agreed damages must not exceed £10,000 (Rule 45.7(2)(c));
- if a claim had been issued for the amount of the agreed damages, the small claims track would not have been the normal track for that claim (the small claims track would be the normal track if the total agreed damages does not exceed £5,000 and the personal injury element does not exceed £1,000) (Rule 45.7(2)(d)); and
- the accident which gave rise to the dispute occurred on or after 6 October 2003 (CPD 25A.1)

The scheme specifically applies to cases which fall within the scope of the Uninsured Drivers Agreement dated 13 August 1999 (CPD 25A.4).

The relevant terms are defined by Rule 45.7(4)

'(a) 'road traffic accident' means an accident resulting in bodily injury to any person or damage to property caused by, or arising out of, the use of a motor vehicle on a road or other public place in England and Wales;

(b) 'motor vehicle' means a mechanically propelled vehicle intended for use on roads; and

(c) 'road' means any highway and any other road to which the public has access and includes bridges over which a road passes.'

It can be seen that the scheme would therefore include such claims as:

- pedestrian knocked down by car;

- standing passenger on bus being injured by being thrown to ground by bus driver's negligent driving;
- bus passenger injuring hand in faulty mechanical doors on bus

22.3 Which Cases are not Covered?

The following cases are excluded from the scheme:

- where the Claimant is a litigant in person (Rule 45.7(3))
- cases which fall within the scope of the Untraced Drivers Agreement dated 14 February 2003 (CPD 25A.4)

22.4 Calculating Damages

CPD 25A.3 explains how damages are calculated to determine whether the overall amount agreed is such that the case falls within the scheme:

'Fixed recoverable costs are to be calculated by reference to the amount of agreed damages which are payable to the receiving party. In calculating the amount of these damages:

(a) account must be taken of both general and special damages and interest;

(b) any interim payments made must be included;

(c) where the parties have agreed an element of contributory negligence, the amount of damages attributed to that negligence must be deducted;

(d) any amount required by statute to be paid by the compensating party directly to a third party (such as sums paid by way of compensation recovery payments and National Health Service expenses) must not be included.'

Example 1

The full value of a claim, on a 100% basis, is £17,000. The claim settles on a 50/50 basis in respect of liability and the Claimant therefore recovers £8,500. The figure of £8,500 is the relevant figure for determining whether the fixed costs scheme applies. As the agreed figure does not exceed £10,000 fixed costs apply.

Example 2

The full value of a claim is £17,000. The Claimant receives £8,500 directly from the Defendant and the Defendant pays a further £8,500 by way of CRU (compensation recovery payment). The figure of £8,500 is the relevant figure for determining whether the fixed costs scheme applies. As the agreed figure does not exceed £10,000 fixed costs apply.

22.5 Amount of Fixed Recoverable Costs

The costs to which a solicitor is entitled where the fixed costs scheme applies are dealt with at Rule 45.9(1):

> 'Subject to paragraphs (2) and (3), the amount of fixed recoverable costs is the total of -
>
> (a) £800;
>
> (b) 20% of the damages agreed up to £5,000; and
>
> (c) 15% of the damages agreed between £5,000 and £10,000.'

The following example is given in CPD 25A.5:

> 'For example, agreed damages of £7,523 would result in recoverable costs of £2,178.45 i.e.
>
> £800 + (20 per cent of £5,000) + (15 per cent of £2,523).'

A further amount is payable where the Claimant lives or works in or around London **and** instructs a solicitor who practises in that area by virtue of Rule 45.9(2):

'Where the Claimant -

> (a) lives or works in an area set out in the relevant practice direction; and
>
> (b) instructs a solicitor or firm of solicitors who practise in that area,
>
> the fixed recoverable costs shall include, in addition to the costs specified in paragraph (1), an amount equal to 12.5% of the costs allowable under that paragraph.'

The relevant areas to qualify for this extra amount are defined by CPD 25A.6:

> 'The area referred to in rule 45.9(2) consists of (within London) the county court districts of Barnet, Bow, Brentford, Central London,

Clerkenwell, Edmonton, Ilford, Lambeth, Mayors and City of London, Romford, Shoreditch, Wandsworth, West London, Willesden and Woolwich and (outside London) the county court districts of Bromley, Croydon, Dartford, Gravesend and Uxbridge.'

Example

Sue's damages are agreed at £3,000. Sue works in London and her solicitors practise in London. Therefore 'London weighting' applies. The fixed recoverable costs are:

	£
Base fee	800
20% of £3,000	600
12.5% 'London weighting' on above figures	175
	1,575

22.6 All Damages?

As can be seen above, a Claimant's solicitor has a direct financial interest in maximising the damages agreed as, the higher the level, the higher the fixed cost they recover.

This has created a problem where disputes have arisen as to what should properly be included in the figure for calculating the 'agreed damages'. It is not uncommon for repair/car-hire charges to be agreed directly between the Defendant's insurer and the Claimant's insurer. Should those elements be included in the 'agreed damages' figure if the Claimant's solicitor had no involvement in the settlement of those elements? The court said 'no' in ***Swatton v Smithurst (2005)*** (Oxford County Court, 3/2/05). Only those damages recovered as a result of the solicitor's efforts should be included. A ruling from a higher court is required to give certainty to this issue.

22.7 Multiple Claimants

The fixed recoverable costs are recoverable in respect of each qualifying Claimant in any accident by virtue of CPD 25A.7:

'Where there is more than one potential Claimant in relation to a dispute and two or more Claimants instruct the same solicitor or firm of solicitors, the provisions of the section apply in respect of each Claimant.'

This also means that the relevant level of damages is that recovered by each Claimant, not the total value of all claims.

Example

Five Claimants are involved in the same RTA and instruct the same firm of solicitors. The damages that each recovers are as follows:

Jack	£750
John	£3,000
Janet	£4,000
Peter	£7,000
Wendy	£12,000

The solicitors are entitled to the following costs in respect of each Claimant:

Jack	small claims track costs only (fixed recoverable costs do not apply as agreed damages in respect of personal injury do not exceed £1,000)
John	fixed costs of £1,400 (ie £800 + (20% of £3,000))
Janet	fixed costs of £1,600 (ie £800 + (20% of £4,000))
Peter	fixed costs of £2,100 (ie £800 + (20% of £5,000) + (15% of £2,000))
Wendy	costs to be assessed in the normal way (fixed costs do not apply as agreed damages exceed £10,000)

22.8 Disbursements

In addition to the solicitors' costs and VAT, a claim for certain disbursements can be made under Rule 45.10:

'(1) The court:

(a) may allow a claim for a disbursement of a type mentioned in paragraph (2); but

(b) must not allow a claim for any other type of disbursement.

(2) The disbursements referred to in paragraph (1) are:

(a) the cost of obtaining:

(i) medical records;

(ii) a medical report [note the use of the singular];

(iii) a police report;

(iv) an engineer's report;

(v) a search of the records of the Driver Vehicle Licensing Authority;

(b) the amount of an insurance premium; where a membership organisation undertakes to meet liabilities incurred to pay the costs of other parties to proceedings, a sum not exceeding such additional amount of costs as would be allowed under section 30 in respect of provision made against the risk of having to meet such liabilities;

(c) where they are necessarily incurred by reason of one or more of the Claimants being a child or patient as defined in Part 21:

(i) fees payable for instructing counsel; or

(ii) court fees payable on an application to the court;

(d) any other disbursement that has arisen due to a particular feature of the dispute.'

One area of dispute that has arisen since the introduction of the scheme is whether, where a medical report is obtained through a medical agency, the recoverable costs are limited to the amount paid to the actual medical expert or whether the additional charges of the medical agency are also recoverable. Paying parties have argued that the recoverable amount should be limited to that paid to the expert. The work performed by the medical agency is of a fee earner nature that would traditionally be performed by the solicitor and should therefore be covered by the fixed costs. However, in ***Woollard v Fowler*** (SCCO, 24/5/06) the Senior Costs Judge, Master Hurst, sitting as a Recorder, rejected this argument and held that the medical agents' charges were also recoverable, subject to reasonableness and proportionality. A mediated agreement has now been reached between a number of insurers and medical agencies in relation to the quantum of medical reports in claims where the damages are not anticipated to exceed £15,000.

22.9 Children and Patients

As is clear from Rule 45.7(1)(b), the fixed costs scheme specifically applies to children and patients where the only proceedings that are issued are those seeking the court's approval of the settlement under Rule 21. Therefore the solicitor is not entitled to more than the fixed cost amount even where the matter proceeds to an infant approval hearing.

However, as noted above, a claim can be made for the appropriate court fee and the fees payable to counsel in relation to the application.

22.10 Claiming more than the Fixed Recoverable Costs

Solicitors can seek to escape the fixed costs scheme in limited circumstances under Rule 45.12:

> '(1) The court will entertain a claim for an amount of costs (excluding any success fee or disbursements) greater than the fixed recoverable costs but only if it considers that there are exceptional circumstances making it appropriate to do so.
>
> (2) If the court considers such a claim appropriate, it may:
>
> (a) assess the costs; or
>
> (b) make an order for the costs to be assessed.
>
> (3) If the court does not consider the claim appropriate, it must make an order for fixed recoverable costs only.'

It can therefore be seen that there have to be 'exceptional circumstances' to justify escaping the scheme. The mere fact that the solicitor has conduced more, even significantly more, work than the fixed costs covers would not be sufficient justification. The very nature of the scheme is that it operates on a 'swings and roundabouts' principle. Inevitably the solicitor will have done more work on some cases than the fixed costs adequately covers. 'Exceptional circumstances' would have to be facts that were exceptional in terms of RTA claims. It is not obvious what facts would fall within this definition and it is clearly envisaged that very few cases will qualify.

Even where the first hurdle is overcome, there are further difficulties a solicitor faces as dealt with by Rule 45.13 and 45.14:

> '45.13(1) This rule applies where:
>
> (a) costs are assessed in accordance with rule 45.12(2); and
>
> (b) the court assesses the costs (excluding any VAT) as being an amount which is less than 20% greater than the amount of the fixed recoverable costs.

(2) The court must order the Defendant to pay to the Claimant the lesser of:

(a) the fixed recoverable costs; and

(b) the assessed costs.

45.14 Where:

(a) the court makes an order for fixed recoverable costs in accordance with rule 45.12(3); or

(b) rule 45.13 applies,

the court must:

(i) make no award for the payment of the Claimant's costs in bringing the proceedings under rule 44.12A; and

(ii) order that the Claimant pay the Defendant's costs of defending those proceedings.'

22.11 Success Fees

Where the solicitor is acting under a CFA or CCFA which provides for a success fee (see the chapter on Funding Methods), a success fee can also be claimed on the fixed costs (Rule 45.11(1)). The amount of the success fee will be 12.5% of the fixed recoverable costs disregarding any additional 'London weighting' amount (Rule 45.11(2)). Therefore the success fee applies to the figure reached before the 'London weighting' enhancement is added.

Example 1

John's solicitors act for him under a CFA with a success fee. Damages are agreed at £4,000. John lives in London but his solicitors practise in Manchester. Therefore 'London weighting' does not apply. The fixed recoverable costs are:

	£
Base fee	800
20% of £4,000	800
12.5% success fee on above unenhanced figures	200
	1,800

Example 2

Jane's solicitors act for her under a CFA with a success fee. Damages are agreed at £4,000. Jane lives in London and her solicitors practise in London. Therefore 'London weighting' does apply. The fixed recoverable costs are:

	£
Base fee	800
20% of £4,000	800
12.5% 'London weighting' on above figures	200
12.5% success fee on above figures except for 'London weighting' enhancement element	200
	2,000

22.12 VAT

VAT, where appropriate, is payable in addition to the fixed costs (Rule 45.9(3)).

22.13 Validity of CFA/CCFA

The fixed recoverable costs scheme is an exception to the normal indemnity principle that applies to costs issues (see chapter on Funding Issues). This extension also applies to cases conducted under a CFA/CCFA. It was confirmed in the case of ***Nizami v Butt*** [2006] EWHC 159 (QB) that it was not necessary to show that a CFA was valid for the fixed costs to be recovered. However, this exception only applied to the solicitors' fixed costs and any success fee. The indemnity principle continues to apply in relation to disbursements. Therefore, disbursements will not be recoverable if the CFA/CCFA is found to be invalid unless they are disbursements that have been paid 'up front' by the Claimant.

22.14 Disputes

It should generally be possible for parties to agree the appropriate costs recoverable between themselves. The CPD deals with the procedure where this is not possible:

'Information to be included in the claim form

25A.8 Costs only proceedings are commenced using the procedure set out in rule 44.12A. A claim form should be issued in accordance with Part 8. Where the Claimant is claiming an amount of costs which exceed the amount of the fixed recoverable costs he must include on the claim form details of the exceptional circumstances which he considers justifies the additional costs.

25A.9 The Claimant must also include on the claim form details of any disbursements or success fee he wishes to claim. The disbursements that may be claimed are set out in rule 45.10(1). If the disbursement falls within 45.10(2)(d) (disbursements that have arisen due to a particular feature of the dispute) the Claimant must give details of the particular feature of the dispute and why he considers the disbursement to be necessary.

Disbursements and success fee

25A.10 If the parties agree the amount of the fixed recoverable costs and the only dispute is as to the payment of, or amount of, a disbursement or as to the amount of a success fee, then proceedings should be issued under rule 44.12A in the normal way and not by reference to Section II of Part 45.'

22.15 Fixed Recoverable Costs Flowchart

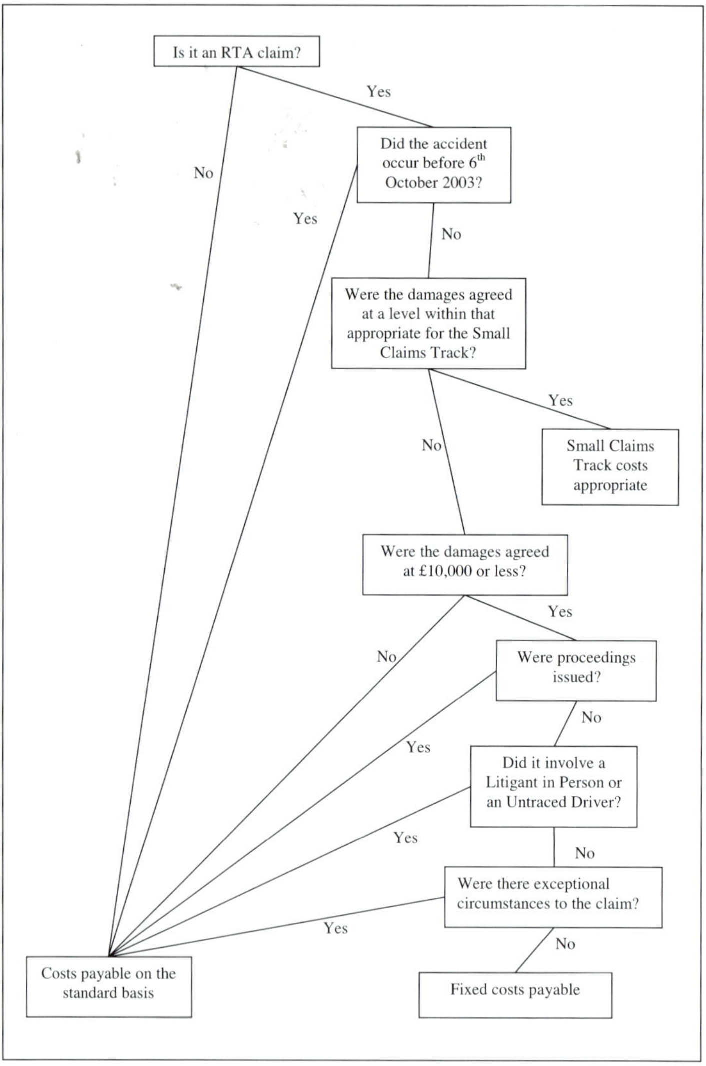

Simon T B Gibbs
Gibbs Wyatt Stone